A
POLITICAL
ECONOMY
OF THE
MIDDLE EAST

A POLITICAL ECONOMY OF THE MIDDLE EAST

FOURTH EDITION

Melani Cammett
HARVARD UNIVERSITY

Ishac Diwan
PARIS SCHOOL OF ECONOMICS

Alan Richards
UNIVERSITY OF CALIFORNIA, SANTA CRUZ

John Waterbury
PRINCETON UNIVERSITY

WESTVIEW
PRESS

A Member of the Perseus Books Group

Westview Press was founded in 1975 in Boulder, Colorado, by notable publisher and intellectual Fred Praeger. Westview Press continues to publish scholarly titles and high-quality undergraduate and graduate-level textbooks in core social science disciplines. With books developed, written, and edited with the needs of serious nonfiction readers, professors, and students in mind, Westview Press honors its long history of publishing books that matter.

Copyright © 2015 by Westview Press
Published by Westview Press,
A Member of the Perseus Books Group
2465 Central Avenue
Boulder, CO 80301
www.westviewpress.com

Westview Press books are available at special discounts for bulk purchases in the United States by corporations, institutions, and other organizations. For more information, please contact the Special Markets Department at the Perseus Books Group, 2300 Chestnut Street, Suite 200, Philadelphia, PA 19103, or call (800) 810-4145, ext. 5000, or e-mail special.markets@perseusbooks.com.

Library of Congress Cataloging-in-Publication Data
Cammett, Melani Claire, 1969–
  A political economy of the Middle East / Melani Cammett, Harvard University, Ishac Diwan, Paris School of Economics, Alan Richards, University of California, Santa Cruz, John Waterbury, Princeton University, NYU Abu Dhabi. — Fourth edition.
     pages cm
  Includes bibliographical references and index.
  ISBN 978-0-8133-4938-1 (paperback) — ISBN 978-0-8133-4939-8 (e-book) 1. Middle East—Economic conditions—1979– 2. Middle East—Economic policy. 3. Working class—Middle East. 4. Middle East—Politics and government—1979–
I. Diwan, Ishac. II. Richards, Alan, 1946– III. Richards, Alan, 1946– Political economy of the Middle East. IV. Title.
  HC415.15.C36 2015
  330.956—dc23
                              2015001543
10 9 8 7 6 5 4 3 2 1

CONTENTS

14 CONCLUSION 515

ILLUSTRATIONS

TABLES

FIGURES

BOXES

PREFACE TO THE
FOURTH EDITION

The last edition of this book was published six years ago. In the interim, much has changed. First and foremost, the whole region has witnessed massive upheavals with the resurgence of the street—first in the Green Movement in Iran in 2009 and later with the Arab uprisings that began in Tunisia in December 2010 and spread across the region at greater or lesser levels of intensity, making a variety of societal demands on rulers. The authors of this book, too, have changed. The founding authors of this classic text, Alan Richards and John Waterbury, wrote the first three editions, which laid out an important agenda for the study of the region. We are privileged to take over co-authorship of the book, building on the excellent work of our predecessors and updating it to address the momentous shifts occurring in the Middle East. As we undertook this formidable task, we were struck by the prescience of many of the observations that Alan and John made at least two years before uprisings erupted across the region in 2011.

Since the third edition appeared, not only the region itself, but also Americans' perceptions of and involvement in the region have undergone considerable change. Mass social mobilization in the Arab uprisings resulted in the ouster of some dictators (in Tunisia, Egypt, Libya, with the help of international intervention, and Yemen, although its deposed ruler retains significant influence in the country). Elsewhere, such as Bahrain, Jordan, and Morocco, large-scale social protests became the foundation of sustained opposition or pro-reform movements and have altered the nature of politics in enduring ways, even if incumbent rulers remain in place. In still other countries, demonstrations and similar forms of opposition did not occur on a mass scale, particularly in the oil-rich countries, which have small indigenous populations and rulers who can afford to respond to or preempt some citizen demands. Even in the OECD countries of the region, Israel and Turkey, large-scale social protests erupted, albeit in quite distinct political and economic contexts.

Meanwhile, some Middle Eastern countries are in the midst of protracted violent conflicts that are subjecting civilian populations to increasingly harsh living conditions and leading to sharp drops in human development achievements. In Iraq, state institutions continue to be weak while extremist Islamist groups are presently making territorial gains in the country and in neighboring Syria. Peaceful demonstrations against President Bashar al-Assad in Syria turned violent as the state cracked down harshly on protesters, and opposition forces have become increasingly dominated by extremist organizations. As in Iraq and elsewhere, the war in Syria has unraveled many impressive human development achievements and also spilled across borders, placing enormous pressures on neighboring countries such as Jordan and Lebanon. Libya is facing mounting unrest as government officials struggle to strengthen state institutions and control the national territory while nonstate actors exert virtually unchecked authority in many parts of the country. And in the summer of 2014, Palestine and Israel were engaged in yet another cycle of heavy violence that would leave more than 1,800 Gazans dead and thousands injured, with limited prospects for medical care in the overtaxed health care system, while more than 60 Israelis, mostly soldiers, were killed.

Other aspects of the region exhibit some continuity since the last edition of this book was published. The so-called War on Terror remains in full swing, even if US troops have been withdrawn from Iraq and Afghanistan, and the public debate about the appropriate role for the United States in the region persists, with much of it still ill informed. Public uneasiness with the largely military approaches of the United States to the region since 9/11 helps to explain the Obama administration's reluctance to fully engage in the crisis in Syria and other parts of the region. Heated debates among specialists and policymakers enumerate the pros and cons of more direct intervention in these conflicts. Despite these deep differences of opinion, most now agree that the problems of the bulk of the countries in the region are structural and deeply entrenched and therefore do not readily lend themselves to simple solutions, as Richards and Waterbury noted in these pages six years ago. Neither government officials, whether in the region or in the West, nor opposition groups, which at least until recently have been dominated by Islamists, have thus far identified and pursued viable strategies for leading the Middle East economies and societies down a path toward more inclusive and sustainable development.

In this edition of the book, as in previous editions, we aim to provide readers with an understanding of the complexity and depth of the region's challenges with respect to economic, social, and political development. In the introductory chapter, we present the framework of the book. We maintain that any attempt to understand the varied development trajectories within the region (or in any region) must start with politics—the struggles over resources that ultimately produce the formal and informal rules in a given society. Yet politics does not operate in a vacuum: the decisions and actions of political actors, especially those in the state, are shaped by the demands and behavior of societal actors as well as by economic opportunities and limitations. Indeed, the nature of state institutions, the choices of state actors, the actions of individuals and groups in society, and economic trends and circumstances evolve in an interactive, mutually constitutive fashion.

This tripartite framework focusing on the state, society, and the economy guides our analyses of events and trends in the region—whether in the decades since independence or, most recently, in the Arab uprisings. Indeed, many elements of the book provide, in our estimation, critical background for identifying the foundations of the social grievances that have been bubbling beneath the surface until recently in the diverse political economies of the region. Our framework for understanding social mobilization and political unrest across the region therefore connects patterns of economic development (especially a shift toward more market-based systems, the decline of public welfare functions, and the rise of crony capitalism), social change (the rise in popular aspirations and grievances), and political shifts (particularly the defection of the middle classes from the authoritarian coalition). This combination of changing economic circumstances and the attendant increase in inequality of opportunities fueled a spike in perceived inequality that helped to unravel the implicit bargain between authoritarian rulers and key constituents.

Chapters 2 and 3 trace patterns of economic and political change in the Middle East, both across time and across the distinct political economy subtypes within the region. In these chapters, as well as throughout the book, we emphasize the centrality of politics and differentiate between three country groupings—those with high populations and low natural resource endowments (the resource-poor, labor-abundant, or RPLA, countries); those with high populations and high oil wealth (the resource-rich, labor-abundant, or RRLA, countries); and those with sparse indigenous populations and high oil deposits (the resource-rich, labor-poor, or RRLP, countries). Although resource endowments hardly explain economic, social, and political trends—and in fact are partly influenced by them—they do present certain structural constraints and opportunities within which political and social actors operate. As a result, they are not inconsequential for understanding development, broadly defined, within the region.

The remaining chapters of the book zero in on specific aspects of the points we make in general terms in the opening section of the book. In Chapters 4, 5, and 6, we trace trends and patterns in social development and human capital formation across the diverse political economies of the region. Chapters 7 and 8 go into greater depth in analyzing the rise and decline of the state as the central actor in the economy and the subsequent emergence of crony capitalism with the turn toward markets in the context of limited competition. In Chapter 9, we focus on patterns of economic and societal development in the RRLP countries of the Gulf subregion, which in many ways has bucked the general trend of economic underperformance and belies aspects of the "resource curse" hypothesis. The next three chapters delve more deeply into politics and society in the Middle East. Chapter 10 highlights the important and often shifting role of the military and security apparatus in the state and economy. In Chapter 11, we trace the region's record of social mobilization—which is far more lively than many have presumed—and trace the evolution of social actors and groups before, during, and after the Arab uprisings, the Green Movement in Iran, and the protest movements in Israel and Turkey. Chapter 12 homes in on one type of societal actor that, in some countries, has held or continues to hold the reins of power—Islamists. In Chapter 13, we adopt a macro-regional approach by looking at the record of integration in labor markets, finance, and trade within and beyond the region.

In preparing this edition, we have incurred many debts. The greatest, of course, is to Alan and John, who wrote and rewrote the first three editions. Although we revised the book substantially for this edition, the book rightly also bears their names, since they developed the foundations of the analyses. We also thank colleagues who provided feedback on many of the chapters, including Lahcen Achy, Izak Atiyas, Dina Bishara, Laryssa Chomiak, Kristin Diwan, Roger Diwan, Kevan Harris, Steffen Hertog, Ellen Lust, Valentine Moghadam, Stacey Philbrick Yadav, Hugh Roberts, Djavad Salehi-Esfahani, Hoda Selim, and Ala'a Shehabi. Excellent research assistance enabled us to complete the manuscript in a timely fashion. We are especially grateful to Gomez Agou, Ali Abboud, Olivier Gaddah, Michael Galant, and Andrew Leber. Annika Lichtenbaum, Michael Marcusa, Lana Salman, Aytuğ Şaşmaz, Brian Tilley, and Marcus Walton also provided valuable research support. Finally, we would like to thank Westview Press, especially our editor Ada Fung, our project editor Cisca Schreefel, and our copyeditor Cindy Buck. Of course, none of these people is in any way responsible for what we have written.

Melani Cammett
Cambridge, MA

and

Ishac Diwan
Paris, France

JANUARY 5, 2015

ACRONYMS AND ABBREVIATIONS

AAAID	Arab Authority for Agricultural Investment and Development
AMIO	Arab Military Industrialization Organization
ANM	Arab National Movement
ASU	Arab Socialist Union
CBR	crude birth rate
CIA	Central Intelligence Agency
CNRA	National Council of the Algerian Revolution
CPA	Coalition Provisional Authority
DC	developed country
DISK	Confederation of Progressive Trade Unions
DOP	Declaration of Principles
FAO	Food and Agriculture Organization
FATAH	Palestine Liberation Movement
FDI	foreign direct investment
FIS	Islamic Salvation Front
FLN	National Liberation Front
GATT	General Agreement on Tariffs and Trade
GCC	Cooperative Council for the Arab States of the Gulf (aka Gulf Cooperation Council)
GDI	gross domestic investment
GDP	gross domestic product
GNP	gross national product
HAMAS	Islamic Resistance Movement
ICOR	incremental capital-to-output ratio
ICP	Iraqi Communist Party
IDPs	internally displaced persons
ILO	International Labor Organization
IMF	International Monetary Fund
IMR	infant mortality rate
ISI	import substitution industrialization
ISIL	Islamic State of Iraq and the Levant
LDC	less developed country
LEB	life expectancy at birth
MAPAI	Israel Labor Party

MENA	Middle East and North Africa
MNC	multinational corporation
MVA	market value added
NATO	North Atlantic Treaty Organization
NER	net enrollment ratio
NIC	newly industrializing country
NIF	National Islamic Front
NLF	National Liberation Front
OECD	Organization for Economic Cooperation and Development
OPEC	Organization of the Petroleum-Exporting Countries
ÖYAK	Armed Forces Mutual Assistance Fund
PA	Palestinian Authority
PDRY	People's Democratic Republic of Yemen
PKK	Kurdistan Workers' Party
PLO	Palestine Liberation Organization
PPP	purchasing power parity
PRC	People's Republic of China
RCC	Revolutionary Command Council (Iraq, Egypt)
RCD	Democratic Constitutional Rally
RPP	Republican People's Party
RPLA	resource-poor labor-abundant
RRLA	resource-rich labor-abundant
RRLP	resource-rich labor-poor
SAVAK	Iranian Security and Intelligence Organization
SNS	National Steel Corporation
SPLA	Sudan People's Liberation Army
SSU	Sudanese Socialist Union
TFR	total fertility rate
UAE	United Arab Emirates
UAR	United Arab Republic
UGTA	General Confederation of Algerian Workers
UGTT	General Confederation of Tunisian Workers
UNESCO	United Nations Economic, Scientific, and Cultural Organization
UNICEF	United Nations International Children's Emergency Fund
USAID	United States Agency for International Development
VAT	value-added tax
WHO	World Health Organization
WTO	World Trade Organization

A

POLITICAL
ECONOMY
OF THE
MIDDLE EAST

Map 0.1   The Middle East and North Africa

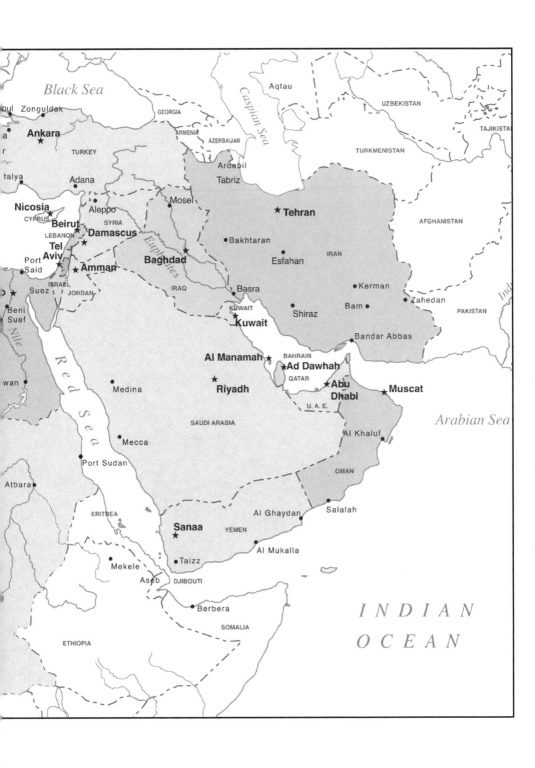

1

INTRODUCTION AND
FRAMEWORK OF THE STUDY

Since 2007, when the last edition of this book was published, revolutionary move-ments have swept across the Middle East, changing the region greatly. These revo-lutions, known collectively as the "Arab uprisings," began on December 17, 2010, in Tunisia, where Mohamed Bouazizi, a vegetable seller in the central Tunisian town of Sidi Bouzid, set himself on fire to protest mistreatment by local police and gov-ernment authorities. Beginning in rural areas and later spreading to urban coastal areas, the wave of protests incited by Bouazizi's act encompassed a diverse array of participants, ranging from informal-sector workers, like Bouazizi himself, to unem-ployed graduates, workers, lawyers, and cyber-connected youth. Ultimately, these mass protests led to the ouster of Zine El Abidine Ben Ali, who had ruled Tunisia in an increasingly repressive manner for over two decades. Protesters demanded justice and accountability from their government and refused to step down, even in the face of brutal repression and government promises to create new jobs and expand civil and political liberties.

The revolutionary movement then spread to Egypt, where Hosni Mubarak, who had held power for almost thirty years, was ousted after several weeks of protests in Cairo and other cities. In Egypt, too, protesters remained steadfast in the face of a harsh crackdown, calling for Mubarak and his key henchmen to step down. In February 2011, Mubarak resigned and later faced trial for complicity in the murder of protesters. From Tunisia and Egypt, protests spread across the region to Yemen, Libya, Morocco, Syria, Jordan, and Bahrain. More sporadic and, in some cases, short-lived protests took place in Algeria, Iraq, Lebanon, Palestine, and even Saudi Arabia. Now, three years after the uprisings, the region has undergone profound po-litical transformations. Much of the region seems to have entered a period of relative chaos, driven by the fierce competition between the new political forces that seek to have more influence on the way their countries are governed. But it is already clear that these societies have come of age and that they are unlikely to be dominated by autocrats in the future as they have been in the past.

Revolutions and rebellions are complex phenomena. Likewise, the motivations for the Arab uprisings have been multifaceted. Political concerns, such as outrage over dictatorial rule, repression, and restrictions on basic liberties, were undoubtedly important. For many people, however, economic issues were equally if not more salient. In 2005 a poll conducted by Zogby International found that expanding employment opportunities, improving health care and educational systems, and ending corruption were the most important priorities of citizens across the region. Democracy and civic and political rights were also cited but were ranked lower than socioeconomic concerns (Zogby International 2005). More recently, the 2010 Arab Youth Survey found that the greatest perceived challenge and concern of Arab youth was the cost of living, followed by unemployment and then human rights. The largest *change* relative to the 2009 Arab Youth Survey was the increased perception of income inequality (ASDA'A/Burson-Marsteller 2010).

Despite momentous political changes in the region, many insights from the third edition of this book, which was published more than two years before Bouazizi set himself on fire, remain relevant. Some of the core economic and political challenges described in the third edition were important factors that either directly or indirectly contributed to the uprisings, including insufficient job creation, labor market pressures exacerbated by the youth bulge, the mismatch between educational systems and labor market needs, the declining quantity of water and rising dependency on food imports, the continuing decay of the public sector, the mixed record of economic liberalization, a growing housing crisis in urban areas, and the rise of political Islam across the region.

The Arab uprisings highlight issues that require more in-depth analysis than they received in prior editions of this book. For example, the rise of crony capitalism underscores the ways in which politics and, more specifically, political connections shape economic opportunities in the region. As implied by the slogan "Bread, freedom, and social justice," which protesters chanted on Avenue Bourguiba, in Tahrir Square, and elsewhere in the region, both economic and political issues were central concerns. Thus, the perceived increase in inequalities, the discontent with public services, the political economy of cronyism, the narrowing composition of authoritarian coalitions, and succession issues in Arab republics have proven to be important developments across the Arab world.

This fourth edition of the book differs significantly from previous editions in that, to fully appreciate and understand the new developments brought on by the Arab uprisings, we have needed to develop new analytical tools. Ousted leaders and struggles over the construction of new political institutions in some countries have led us to revise the classification of regime types, and even in countries where incumbent rulers remain entrenched, the nature of the political game has changed. Across the region, "street politics" is an increasingly important form of political expression and citizens are presenting demands to their leaders more forcefully and frequently. At this juncture, the context of policymaking is altered: with the emergence of new political regimes and the rise of claim-making, rulers are compelled to respond more effectively to citizen demands. Evolving political systems as well as economic developments demand new perspectives on the political economies on the region.

What explains the origins and dynamics of the Arab uprisings? We believe that a political economy approach has much to offer in addressing this question. Neither purely political concerns, such as the desire for democracy, nor simple economic trends can explain protesters' calls for the downfall of autocratic rulers. Rather, the interaction of political factors and real and perceived economic developments brought about the uprisings. As we argue here, the narrowing of authoritarian coalitions in the context of crony capitalism, the rollback of the state, and the decline of welfare regimes alienated formal-sector workers and tenuous middle classes. In the context of unequal life chances and rising insecurity, growing portions of Arab societies perceived that the distribution of social services, justice, good education, good jobs, and, more generally, social mobility were increasingly unequal and unjust. Thus, growth rates or absolute levels of income inequality cannot account for these popular movements to overthrow incumbent dictators. Rather, it was the *perceptions* of socioeconomic trends in the context of evolving political economies and, as we contend throughout the book, the perceived rise in the *inequality of opportunities* (in the labor market and in access to services) that were at the root of the mass protests.

In this introduction to the new edition, we develop these claims in more detail. First, we sketch a picture of regional variation in the uprisings, pointing to a variety of factors that differentiate the countries of the region and help to explain their distinct trajectories thus far during this period of momentous change. Next, we set up the analytical framework used in the book. Then we describe a typology of Arab countries that we also employ throughout the book. Finally, we use the framework and the typology to provide a broad-brush description of the politico-economic developments that led to the uprisings.

THE ARAB UPRISINGS OF 2011: HOW DID WE GET THERE?

Many of the characteristics of the recent Arab uprisings are puzzling and do not fit easily within popular intellectual frames. Why did the uprisings occur at the end of 2010, when there were no apparent direct triggers such as declines in subsidies or shifts in foreign alliances, rather than in the 1990s, when welfare states in the region began to be rolled back? Why did the revolutions start in Tunisia and Egypt, the countries with some of the highest economic growth in the region in the preceding few years, rather than in countries such as Syria or Yemen, where economic conditions were more dire and political repression more severe? Why were the uprisings initiated by secularist middle-class youth, the supposed beneficiaries of the modernizing republics, rather than by the long-standing Islamist opposition? Why did some of the regimes fight back more fiercely than others? And following the uprisings, why did social polarization rise everywhere in the region, and why did this polarization center on issues of identity rather than on divisions over economic policies?

In the early days of the Arab uprisings, debates about the relative importance of economic versus political factors permeated journalistic and scholarly discussions about the motivations for the mass protests across the region. On the face of it, economic factors hold little explanatory value. In the preceding decade, economic growth in the "revolution" countries was at about 4 to 5 percent of gross domestic product (GDP) per year, which is not considered low. In 2010 growth stood at 3.1 percent in Tunisia, 5.1 percent in Egypt, 3.4 percent in Syria, 3.7 percent in Libya, 7.7 percent in Yemen, 3.7 percent in Morocco, and 2.3 percent in Jordan (World Development Indicators 2010). The macroeconomic situation was also relatively stable after the imbalances of the early 2000s had been absorbed: on the eve of the uprisings, budget and current account deficits were shrinking, debt levels were reasonable, and international reserves were at comfortable levels. The unemployment rate was high in most Arab countries—between 10 and 15 percent of the labor force, higher than in other developing regions—but stable. Inequality as measured by GINI coefficients was lower than in other regions, with values at around 0.3 to 0.4, and was not rising fast (Belhaj and Wissa 2011).

To be sure, the 2008 global recession, coupled with the oil and food crises, did affect the region. Growth slowed down after 2008, and while it had recovered somewhat by 2010, it remained below the levels reached in 2006 to 2008. Energy subsidies increased with international prices, further eroding the ability of the state to spend on public investment and wages, while inflation rose and real wages fell. Furthermore, the region's rising growth rates in the 2000s were unable to reach Asian double-digit levels, which would have been needed to absorb the youth wave and the unemployed in the labor market. In cross-regional comparative perspective, youth unemployment was high in the Arab world, at around 25 percent, but this was not a new development and therefore cannot explain the timing of the protests. Similarly, the decline of public welfare functions and the rise of parallel networks of social welfare provision were not recent phenomena. The rollback of the state originated in the fiscal crises that most countries in the region, particularly those with low per capita oil reserves, experienced in the 1980s. In short, by 2011, on the eve of the revolts, there was no singular economic shock to point to as the spark that ignited the uprisings. Subsidies were not being cut; unemployment, while high, was not rising; and growth rates and investment ratios were on the rise and at comfortable levels. Furthermore, as the literature on social movements argues, economic grievances at best provide incomplete explanations for mass mobilization (McAdam 1982).

Instead, as we argue in this book, *discontent on the economic front interacted with a broader sociopolitical context to ignite the uprisings.* In particular, economic stagnation mixed with the *perceived* rise in inequalities and lack of "social justice," which had been mounting as a result of the rollback of the state and economic liberalization characterized by cronyism. Access to economic opportunities was seen to be neither meritocratic nor governed by a level playing field but, rather, mediated by connections to political leaders and their narrowing circles of allies. In the context of redistributive commitments by rulers to their populations, which arguably increased citizen expectations of the state in both the "populist" republics and the more conservative monarchies, the inability of government to provide for citizens was particularly egregious and combined with a growing sense of economic insecurity. Countries that were unable to address these grievances through rising state support, as the richer Gulf countries could do, increasingly used state repression to maintain order, generating a sense of indignity among their populations. This combination of factors dammed up the accumulated grievances and rising aspirations, which were ready to burst.

We can illustrate our argument by briefly applying it to the case of Tunisia, where the revolts began. At first glance, Tunisia was the least likely country in the region to have ignited the Arab uprisings. Tunisia had experienced steady growth rates in the previous decade and exceeded the regional average on a variety of social indicators, such as literacy, school enrollment, and life expectancy. Among the non-oil economies in the region, Tunisia had the most developed welfare state institutions, which helped to create a more robust middle class than was found in other Arab countries. The state also ran a variety of social assistance programs, and poverty rates were lower than in neighboring countries. In addition, until the late 1990s, business-government relations were less corrupt and capital was less concentrated than in other countries with similar industrial profiles. Politically, Tunisia also appeared to be an improbable place to set off the uprisings. The Tunisian state was notoriously repressive, leaving its citizens with far less scope for civil society activism and public expression than was the case in many other countries in the region, and the ruling party's penetration of all aspects of civic and political life was further facilitated by the country's small size. Although many Tunisians did not like Ben Ali, their fear of unrest, as experienced in neighboring Algeria, which underwent a bloody civil war in the 1990s, seemed to reduce their appetite for regime change.

Paradoxically, Tunisia's socioeconomic achievements may be one important reason for the spread of mass mobilization against Ben Ali. Older generations of Tunisians had experienced genuine social mobility in their lifetimes, particularly during the first few decades after independence under Habib Bourguiba's rule, and they had developed high expectations of their state. Their children could no longer expect to advance socioeconomically, even with graduate degrees. Furthermore, the history of relatively minimal corruption in state-business relations made the concentration of economic opportunities in the hands of the Ben Ali and Trabelsi families all the more scandalous. In effect, under Ben Ali's rule, the authoritarian coalition gradually narrowed. By the time those who were marginalized in Tunisian society and those who lived in neglected regions rose up against Ben Ali, the state's traditional sources of support—the middle classes and business interests—joined in the revolt again the ruler and his cronies (Kaboub 2013).

Tunisia's story included all of the main components of the story that was emerging across the Arab world. In the mid-1980s, the rollback of the state began without a concomitant democratic opening, enabling an elite, capitalistic class to benefit from personal connections and acquire disproportionate access to lucrative opportunities. The elite allied with state security apparatuses, which enforced the elite's dominance through repression (sticks) and economic co-optation (carrots) to maintain the support of the middle class. Tight state-business relations within a supposedly "liberal" economic environment dependent on political repression did not translate into a successful industrial policy. Instead, the state and key constituents developed a system of gift exchange that performed moderately well but also inhibited growth and failed to create good jobs. Across the Arab world, countries that had initially adopted distinct economic strategies and political regimes ended up with variants of the same crony capitalist system. Increasingly, fragile coalitions governed through divide-and-rule strategies based on a combination of blanket subsidies, repression, and fearmongering about political Islam.

Supported by the West, this autocratic low equilibrium lasted for several decades. For a time, with the co-optation of the middle classes through subsidies and fear of a takeover by Islamists, and with the poor repressed and struggling to make ends meet, authoritarianism could endure. Mounting fiscal pressures, however, driven in large part by rising subsidies and lower tax revenues, led to deteriorating social services and lower public investment. As the pain increased among the poor and in peripheral regions, populations identified more and more with the poor rather than the middle classes. In this context, middle-class elements began to defect from authoritarian coalitions and evolve into champions of change, driven by the lack of opportunities for socioeconomic advancement and anger about what they perceived as rising inequality.

CROSS-REGIONAL VARIATION IN THE ARAB UPRISINGS

The outcomes of the uprisings thus far have varied across the Arab world. In some countries, such as Tunisia, Egypt, and Libya, rulers have been deposed and political actors are engaged in struggles over the creation of new institutional rules. In Yemen, regime change occurred through a more "pacted" transfer of power negotiated by elites, although mass mobilization initially precipitated the ouster of former president Ali Abdullah Saleh. In February 2012, voters endorsed a deal brokered by the Gulf Cooperation Council, approving a two-year transitional presidency for Saleh's vice president of eighteen years, Abd Rabbuh Mansur Hadi.

In other countries, regimes have pushed back decisively against protesters. In Syria, the regime's harsh crackdown on initial protests sparked a bloody conflict that continues unabated as of this writing. In Bahrain, too, the ruling al-Khalifa family harshly repressed protesters calling for regime change, although far less blood has been spilled than in Syria. The international community has responded in divergent ways to the crises in Syria and Bahrain. Direct intervention from neighboring Saudi Arabia and limited condemnation from the United States, which has a strategic alliance with Bahrain, have bolstered the ruling family's control. The United States and other countries have hesitated to intervene directly in Syria, in part because of Russian opposition to international involvement and in part because of their concerns about the fragmentation of the opposition and the role of Islamist extremists in the armed opposition to the Assad regime.

Not all uprisings in the Arab world have culminated in, or were even calling for, the dismissal of authoritarian rulers. In some countries, sustained protests were met with concessions by rulers. In Jordan, protesters by and large have not demanded an end to the monarchy but rather have issued demands for increased economic opportunities and greater freedoms under the current system. In response, King Abdullah II replaced the prime minister multiple times and called early elections, although these moves have failed to appease the opposition. In Morocco, King Mohammed VI pledged to introduce greater political freedoms and held a referendum on constitutional reforms that ostensibly reduced the power of the monarch but, in practice, brought about little substantive change in the system (Benchemsi 2012). At this juncture, protests have abated in Morocco, but if the king's alleged commitment to gradual reform does not bring about meaningful change, they could reignite. Protests of varying scales and duration have also erupted in Algeria, Iraq, and Lebanon, compelling rulers to make some real and rhetorical concessions. Fragmented political systems and citizens' exhaustion after prolonged conflicts in these countries, however, have hampered the ability of opposition movements to gain traction and bring about meaningful reform.

Opposition groups have even staged protests in the wealthy Arab Gulf monarchies. In Kuwait, which has a comparatively long history of political contestation, the parliament was dissolved and the prime minister replaced. In general, however, protests have been more limited and short-lived across the Gulf. In most cases, incumbent rulers have benefited enough from high oil prices to be able to quell protests through economic incentives.

Several basic economic and political factors differentiate the countries of the region, and these differences explain some of the variation in the trajectories of the Arab uprisings. Oil wealth is the most obvious distinction among Arab countries. In the oil-rich countries with low populations, high oil rents keep the autocratic bargain—or the exchange of material benefits for political quiescence—functioning. To be sure, oil is not determinative and cannot explain all politics in the Gulf, as the case of Kuwait demonstrates. At a minimum, high per capita oil wealth enables rulers to postpone serious challenges to their authority and may even prevent the emergence or spread of opposition groups in the first place.

In a second category of oil-exporting countries—those with medium levels of oil rents per capita, such as Syria, Libya, Yemen, Iraq, Algeria, and Sudan, which all have large populations—oil revenues were insufficient to develop a workable system of patronage and have been more intensively used to build a mighty repressive apparatus. These countries are the ones that have tended to react most violently to the uprisings, partly because their narrow governing coalitions stand to lose the most compared to other regimes in the region, and partly because their welfare is more dependent on sharing the oil spoils among their ruling elites than on the economic performance of their society.

The extent of ethno-religious diversity and, most important, politicized identity-based cleavages also accounts for some variation in the dynamics of the uprisings across the Arab countries. Particularly in the Levant—notably Syria, Iraq, Lebanon, and, to a lesser degree, Jordan—ethno-religious politics has shaped the demands of opposition groups and the course of the protests. Autocratic coalitions have historically favored some groups over others, a strategy of political control that dates back to the colonial period and that continued after independence. In some of these countries, rulers incorporated minorities who feared the tyranny of majorities. For example, in Syria the majority-Sunni population has been less privileged than Alawis and other minority groups, although Sunni elites have prospered under the

Assad family's rule as well. The Hashemite monarchy in Jordan has historically favored East Bank "Transjordanian" tribes and families, rewarding them with positions in the civil service and military that come with job security and benefits, while Jordanians of Palestinian origin tend to dominate the private sector and the informal economy.

The uprisings have undermined or destabilized core political settlements and have sometimes also resulted in violence. In Syria, the regime's harsh crackdown on the initial protests sparked a bloody conflict that is now increasingly described in sectarian terms: an overwhelmingly Sunni opposition is pitted against a minority-Alawi regime. The dynamics of protest in Bahrain are also depicted as sectarian: the ruling al-Khalifa family, a Sunni monarchy ruling over a majority-Shi'a population, has used harsh repression to put down the largely Shi'a opposition. The uprisings have even upset the balance in comparatively stable Jordan: with economic deterioration, the core Transjordanian constituency of the monarchy is increasingly disgruntled and more sympathetic to the opposition movement.

It is vital to emphasize, however, that an interpretation of political struggles based on sectarian grievances vastly oversimplifies the political and economic realities in Bahrain, Syria, and other countries in the region. Ethno-religious cleavages per se do not necessarily produce conflict (Brubaker 2006; Chandra 2012; Fearon and Laitin 1996; Lieberman and Singh 2012). Rather, identity-based differences only form the basis for political mobilization when they become politically salient. A surefire way to activate ethno-religious identity is to distribute resources along ostensibly identity-based lines. For example, in Iraq most people did not prioritize their identity as Shi'a or Sunni Muslims until well into the twentieth century (Jabar 2003). Saddam Hussein's policies and, more generally, the breakdown of the state during the sanctions period and following the US invasion in 2003 were instrumental in activating religious identities in Iraq. Saddam increasingly favored Sunnis, especially those from his native town of Tikrit, and repressed the Shi'a and the Kurds, whose networks posed a threat to his rule. As a result, the Shi'a and the Kurds felt marginalized in Saddam's Iraq, and their political leaders have taken advantage of his overthrow to consolidate their authority. But even in Iraq, where sectarianism appears to define political life, some of the most intense conflict occurs among coreligionists. Political competition is particularly intense among different Shi'a groups and has even erupted in violence.

Finally, regime type appears to explain some differences in the nature and intensity of uprisings across the Arab world, although upon closer inspection this may be a spurious correlation. The record suggests that the monarchies have been less vulnerable to demands for regime change and have even witnessed fewer sustained opposition movements. As noted earlier, high per capita oil wealth is one reason why uprisings in oil-rich monarchies have been more muted; however, per capita oil wealth cannot account for the situations in Jordan and Morocco. Monarchs in Jordan and Morocco emphasize their legitimacy in order to justify their longevity, an argument that is more convincing for Morocco, where the monarchy has been in place since the seventeenth century, than in Jordan, which was a colonial construction (Massad 2001). But even in Morocco, legitimacy is an unconvincing explanation, in part because it is vague and difficult to measure and in part because there was nothing inevitable about the monarchy's survival and perpetuation in the post-independence period. Rather, the structure of patronage helps to explain why monarchies have been less destabilized than republics in the Arab uprisings. In particular, monarchies have tended to establish multifaceted authoritarian coalitions, which broaden their support base in society and reduce the potential demand for their overthrow (Yom and Gause 2012). Thus, rather than regime type per se, the structure of authoritarian coalitions in monarchies versus republics provides a more convincing account of the varied trajectories of uprisings in the Arab world today.[1] This is why the rising grievances among Transjordanians, who are key members of the authoritarian coalition in Jordan, are particularly worrisome for the Hashemite monarchy.

Our emphasis on the composition of authoritarian coalitions in explaining the durability and breakdown of authoritarian rule points to the broader value of a political economy approach for understanding the emergence and progression of uprisings in the Arab countries. In the next section, we spell out the core elements of such an approach. Following that, we look at the key elements of our analytic framework for understanding the evolution of development paths, then applying it to develop a more systematic account of the Arab uprisings.

A POLITICAL ECONOMY FRAMEWORK

The intuitive framework that emerges from this rapid exploration of the Arab uprisings connects patterns of economic development (especially a shift toward a more market-based system, the decline of public welfare functions, and the rise of crony capitalism), social change (growing inequalities and the rise in popular aspirations and grievances), and political change (rising levels of repression, a narrowing of the governing coalition, and the defection of the middle classes from the authoritarian coalition). This combination of changing economic circumstances and the attendant increase in inequality of opportunities fueled a spike in perceived inequality, which helped to unravel the implicit bargain between authoritarian rulers and key constituents.

We believe that any framework for understanding development trajectories—that is, the patterns of economic change and structural transformation manifested in a society—must start with politics. This is as true for countries in the Middle East as it is for those in any other developing or industrialized region of the world. By politics we mean the struggle over resources and, more fundamentally, the often conflicting interactions that ultimately produce the formal and informal rules or institutions that determine who controls what types of resources and how they exercise this control (Lasswell 1936).

This definition of politics underscores the critical role of institutions in shaping development, a point supported by a growing consensus among social scientists.[2] Specific types of institutions are especially central to economic growth and development, most notably capable state institutions and, in many accounts, secure property rights. But different types of institutions may be more conducive to distinct patterns of economic growth. As Kunal Sen (2013, 78) argues, formal institutions such as property rights, checks on government power, and social policies that foster equality of opportunity are most critical for steady, sustained growth. Bursts of growth acceleration as well as early periods of development takeoff are likely to result from more informal institutional configurations such as patron-client relations, which can serve as credible commitments in the absence of formal institutions to elicit compliance from powerful social actors.[3]

Therefore, to understand why political leaders make policy choices—and ultimately why and how countries are launched on distinct developmental paths—we must start with the political struggles that result in specific institutional configurations. As we discuss in more detail in the next section, this analysis requires a three-pronged focus on the interactions between the state, economic forces, and societal actors. But before elaborating on each of these components of our framework, we first describe our general approach to development trajectories in the Middle East.

Our account of development trajectories in the Middle East builds on the notion of "political settlements" (Khan 2009), or the relative distribution of power among different groups and organizations contesting the distribution of resources. Political and economic elites are key actors in forging political settlements. Thomas Parks and William Cole (2010, 5) highlight the centrality of elites in creating political settlements, which they define as an "expression of a common understanding, usually forged between elites, about how power is organized and exercised." The elite bargains that result from "informal processes of conflict, negotiation, and compromise" in turn shape "governance, stability, and the quality and pace of development" (Parks and Cole 2010). Thus, a political settlement is the depiction of the institutional arrangements that emerges from conflicts over resources most proximately among elites. For the most part, these institutional equilibria are not codified but rather take the form of norms and social practices that guide social behavior and interactions. At the same time, as our empirical analyses underscore throughout the book and as Chapter 11 examines in more detail, we emphasize the importance of non-elites as collective actors in influencing the course of inter-elite bargains and as members of governing coalitions.

The coalition of rulers and societal actors at the core of political settlements ensures the security of the regime by using the threat of force and by extracting and distributing rents in order to maintain some popular support. Depending on the breadth of the coalition, these coalitions may result in policies and practices that are more or less "efficient" economically and that use varied levels of repression. Broader coalitions are more conducive to the rise of inclusive political institutions, or those that "feature secure private property, an unbiased system of law, and a provision of public services that provides a level playing field . . . and permit the entry of new businesses and allow people to choose their careers" (Acemoglu and Robinson 2012, 74–75). Inclusive institutions can promote innovation and investment when they are fiscally manageable, and they are critical for long-term, sustainable development to take root.[4] Extractive political institutions, in which a narrow elite wields relatively unchecked power and extracts resources for its own benefit, undercut incentives for investment and reduce time horizons, deterring development (Acemoglu and Robinson 2012, 81).

The concept of political settlements is also analytically useful for our purposes because it highlights the social foundations of the state and societal institutions that shape development trajectories and thus provides insight into where institutions come from, how they operate, and ultimately how they change or may change in the future. As we contend in the next chapter and throughout the book, a major reason for variation in development trajectories in the Middle East and North Africa (MENA) region arises from the fact that political settlements differ across the countries of the Middle East (and have differed over time in the same countries and territories, in part driven by changes in the price of oil). Ruling elites in diverse MENA countries exercise their power in varied ways, and these ruling coalitions have been established with different elite and non-elite elements of society to legitimize and maintain their rule. In subsequent chapters, we trace which individuals or political factions gained power at independence, the evolving social bases of ruling elites over time, and which social groups were privileged in distinct post-independence periods. This entails analyses of the shifting relationships between rulers and distinct factions of the business community; the role of the military in politics and the economy; the relationship between state institutions and labor as well as other social groups; and the treatment of citizens and noncitizen residents in the polity. The political settlements that encapsulate distinct patterns of state-society relations in turn generate varied trends in the rule of law, corruption, government effectiveness, and other institutional factors that potentially shape development trajectories. We explore these dimensions of governance in Middle Eastern countries in chapter 3.

Political settlements arise out of struggles among actors with varied levels of power. But these struggles, usually among economic and political elites, do not play out in a vacuum. To the contrary, economic trends and linkages to societal groups affect the resources of competing actors whose interactions ultimately crystallize in political settlements, and they also affect how these settlements evolve over time. Thus, to characterize development pathways, we also need to focus on the larger socioeconomic context within which power struggles occur by analyzing the linkages between the state, economic forces, and society. The next section describes each of these spheres and its relationship to development.

THE THREE PILLARS OF THE FRAMEWORK: THE STATE, THE ECONOMY, AND SOCIETY

Outcomes in the political economy of development can best be conceptualized as the political interactions between three domains: (1) the state, state policies, and state structures; (2) the economic agents operating, and how the economy behaves over time; and (3) social actors, whether groups or individuals. We start with fairly conventional definitions of each of these concepts and then discuss the major conceptual difficulties, disputes, and so forth, surrounding each.

By *the state, its policies, and state structures,* we mean the organization of the monopoly of coercive means within society, the interventions into the economy that such a monopoly makes possible, and the institutions through which these interventions are carried out. *Economic growth* is almost always quite uneven, with some groups' wealth and power increasing faster than those of other groups. It can also entail great social transformation involving sectoral change, rural migration, and urbanization. Finally, by *social actors,* we mean any and all interests, groups, and classes that interact with the state, seek to shape its policies, and are affected by the state's growth strategies. Each of these definitions can be questioned. Normative and empirical debates continue unabated on the role of the state in the development process—on its freedom of choice of policy with respect to powerful domestic classes and international actors. Economic growth may not be associated with increasing welfare for some groups, and inequality among social groups may increase. What drives groups—material interests, shared values, shared blood—is at the heart of debates in the social sciences. We believe that each of the major variables is vital for an understanding of the political economy of the Middle East, as we hope to show through our concrete analyses of specific development problems in subsequent chapters.

Before proceeding to a more detailed discussion of each of our three domains in the context of the Middle East, it is worth emphasizing that they are interdependent. Each domain influences and shapes the other two; each is therefore both cause and effect, both starting point and outcome. Our model is one of reciprocal causation (see Figure 1.1).

We do not imply any rank ordering of the arrows in Figure 1.1; this is a fully simultaneous model. The meaning of the interconnections may be illustrated as follows:

1. Political elites formulate and implement economic policies, and their interests as well as ideological orientations affect the general nature of these policies.
2. Although there is much debate on the precise effect of specific policies, few deny that state policies—such as fiscal, monetary, and trade policies, as well as the extent to which markets are allowed to operate and how they are regulated—affect the rate and form of economic growth.
3. The state shapes, even creates, social actors, including classes. When states choose to enforce property rights, private actors are strengthened. On the other hand, the state may choose to redistribute property through nationalizations, land reforms, and privatizations.

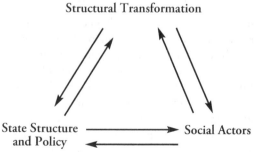

Structural Transformation

State Structure and Policy ⟶ **Social Actors**

FIGURE 1.1. The Three Main Axes of Middle Eastern Political Economy

4. Social actors mold state policy. Interest and pressure groups and, most broadly, proprietary classes seek to protect and promote their own interests through the state. In some cases, the influence of a particular social actor may be so strong that the state becomes its "instrument."

5. Economic growth and structural transformation have unintended outcomes to which state actors must respond. For example, if the pattern of industrialization is highly capital-intensive, the state may need to respond to a growing employment problem.

6. Economic growth and structural transformation shape social actors. Growth and a rise in incomes strengthen the middle class, and the presence of a strong middle class tends to generate demands for improved social services and more social emancipation. As the private sector grows, the demand for the rule of law increases. High rates of unemployment among educated youth, or rising income inequalities, lead to the rise of social discontent.

7. The global context also matters. International oil prices have profound effects throughout the Middle East. Labor migration produces a large flow of remittances to households, which reduces social tensions; foreign exchange to the economy, which reduces the incentives for exports; and brain drain, which influences both the economy and policy. Capital movement can support good policy but can also severely punish policy failures.

We now turn to a more detailed discussion of each vertex of our triangle and of the interactions among these variables.

The State and State Capacity

The most basic definition of the state comes from the German sociologist Max Weber, who defines it as the organization with a monopoly over the *legitimate* use of force over a given territory. Weber's definition emphasizes the security dimensions of "stateness," but over time the state has acquired multiple additional functions, and even people in poor countries with weak states have come to expect more from their political leaders. Domestically, states are the set of political institutions that generate and carry out policies and encompass multiple functions with organizational embodiments such as the army, police, tax and other administrative bureaucracies, courts, and welfare agencies. Externally, states are sovereign entities with control over their territories and the mandate to conduct international relations, such as by waging war or carrying out diplomatic initiatives.

States are often described as "strong" or "weak," although these blanket terms obscure more than they illuminate. Instead, it is more useful to analyze states in terms of their "autonomy" and "capacity" and to treat them not as unitary actors but rather as a collection of institutions with distinct functions, each of which may be more or less effective. *Autonomy* refers to the ability of the state to perform basic tasks with a minimum of interference from social groups, although connections between state officials and social actors, such as business groups, are important for the formulation and implementation of policies (Evans 1995). *Capacity*, which is increasingly invoked as a sine qua non for successful and sustainable economic development, refers to the ability of state representatives or rulers to design and execute their decisions and initiatives. Capacity taps into a variety of state activities, such as defending the national territory, making and enforcing rules and regulations, collecting taxes, and managing the economy.

Two caveats are in order with respect to state capacity. First, to reiterate, states have uneven capacities; they are not unitary actors. For example, many Middle Eastern countries have advanced coercive capabilities to control their populations and wage war (through police, army, and internal security forces) but are less adept at collecting direct taxes from households and corporations. Second, state intervention in the economy does not necessarily signify high levels of state capacity. To the contrary, state promotion of markets where private actors interact freely entails a well-developed regulatory infrastructure, including the construction of sophisticated administrative, regulatory, fiscal, and judicial institutions to enable the *indirect* supervision of the economy. This requires far more advanced capacities than outright state ownership (Chaudhry 1993; Rodrik 2013).

Typically, as countries develop, governance systems evolve, from direct personalized control by a ruler (in the form of deals), where decisions and enforcement depend to a large extent on the ruler's own initiative, to a system where institutions rule (Levy and Fukuyama 2010). In the former case, power is wielded in a context of patron-client deals in which the respective bargaining positions of the ruler and the client determine the outcome (Levy and Fukuyama 2013). In the latter, more advanced situation, often termed an "open order system," rules become more predictable and are ideally applied in a fairer way across the population (North et al. 2013). Although "development" is thought of as a process that moves from "deals" to "rules," Middle Eastern history reminds us that movement in the other direction is also possible; for example, in Saddam Hussein's Iraq and Bashar al-Assad's Syria, regimes became more repressive over time—or in the words of Clement Henry and Robert Springborg (2010), more "praetorian"—relying on a narrower elite coalition and on a more repressive system led by family and tribe (Bellin 2004).

However, since the 1980s, when scholars and policymakers first recognized the importance of the state in driving the high growth rates of East Asian economies, states are increasingly expected to promote economic transformation. This requires the development of precisely those advanced state administrative and regulatory capacities that are deficient in most developing countries. Owing in part to variable levels of state capacity, not all states pursue and achieve economic development goals with equal effectiveness. An idealized typology distinguishes between "predatory" and "developmental" states (Evans 1995). In the former, which are characterized by extractive political institutions, rulers pursue their own goals, with wealth maximization for themselves and their close associates taking precedence over the collective good, however defined. In this context, personal ties trump more formal linkages between state organizations and citizens and bureaucratic capacity is underdeveloped. On the other end of the spectrum, developmental states have effective government bureaucracies whose civil servants are recruited through selective and meritocratic means and rewarded for long-term careers. Inclusive political institutions, which require capable state institutions to guarantee property rights, provide impartial regulations, and supply public services, implicitly rest on effective, developmental states.

The way states are governed can be autocratic, competitive (as in democracies), or many shades in between. Most states in the Middle East have been of the autocratic type, with the partial exceptions of Israel, Turkey, and Lebanon, which score higher on democratic indices. Given that most countries of the world had become democratic after the "third wave of democratization" in the 1980s and 1990s, this has led to a belief that the Middle East is exceptional in this dimension, and much ink has been spilled by authors trying to identify the sources of the region's exceptionalism, whether in its culture, factor endowments, social structures, or history. There is also a large literature that focuses on the tools used by autocrats to stay in power, especially the roles of the repression of regime opponents and the co-optation of potential allies (Posusney and Angrist 2005; Schlumberger 2007).

Although there are heated debates on the role of the discovery and exploitation of natural resource endowments in the political and institutional development of the countries in the Middle East, it is undeniable that oil has exerted important influences on the growth of states and the persistence of autocracy. But the origins of capable state institutions also matter to the extent that state characteristics display persistence over time. The issue of origins is the subject of a thriving research agenda among social scientists. While some contend that geography or culture explains why some countries enjoy more effective state institutions (Diamond 1997; Sachs 2001), a growing chorus of scholars claim that colonialism is either the primary or a contributing factor to the emergence of capable states. Time horizons vary in this line of debate. For some, relatively recent colonial experiences are the source of current levels of institutional capacity. For example, Atul Kohli (2004) claims that Japanese colonialism transformed Korean state institutions, such as the bureaucracy and the police force, into strong institutions capable of spearheading a development drive.[5] Other explanations for the origins of variable state capacity in postcolonial states adopt a longer-term historical perspective (Acemoglu, Johnson, and Robinson 2001). Ultimately, the precise mechanisms by which colonial institutions have shaped postcolonial institutional development pose an empirical question and are likely to vary across global regions. In the Middle East, postcolonial institutions were greatly shaped first by the legacies of Ottoman rule and subsequently by the interventions of European colonial powers, notably Britain and France (discussed in more detail in Chapter 3).

The Economy

Economic performance is tightly tied to the type of political governance in place (and its impact on political stability), the quality of institutions (for example, those that protect property rights), and the state of public services. The development of the economy increases incomes and creates a middle class, and thus its influence on society, as well as on governance and the economy, is profound.

The most effective input for economic development over the long term is an educated and skilled labor force. There is a strong connection between economic development and the development of skills, or "human-capital formation." Indeed, education and other types of skill formation are the core of the development process (see, for example, Schultz 1981). In particular, technological change, which lies at the core of the process of economic growth, is impossible without an increasingly skilled population. But equally, education empowers the rise of a middle class, which tends to become, as incomes rise, more demanding with respect to governance and public services.

Economic growth invariably entails unevenness across sectors, or structural transformation. Despite wide variation in patterns of economic growth, in virtually all countries rising per capita income is accompanied by a decline in agriculture's share of output and employment and a corresponding increase in the share of industry and services. Since labor productivity and therefore incomes are much higher in industry than in agriculture, the transfer of population to industry and to urban areas raises national income. But a premature decline of the agricultural sector can be equally disastrous. The agricultural sector provides not only labor but also much-needed foreign exchange and a domestic market for local industry. As we shall see, Middle Eastern states, like many less developed countries (LDCs), have neglected agriculture, undermining long-term growth. An increase in the proportion of the population employed in "services," which includes activities as diverse as government service, finance, information technology, and street peddling, may be an indicator of economic weakness as much as an indicator of economic strength. Economic development may be strong in countries where government, telecommunications, and finance services, which are all complementary to other productive activities, are increasing and some services, such as tourism and trade, have become final goods in their own right. But a precipitous rise in services can also be a sign of weakness when large numbers of unskilled rural migrants arrive in the cities and engage in a host of small-scale, low-tech activities that generate paltry incomes.

The course of economic growth and structural change is far from smooth. Extensive state intervention, numerous bottlenecks, and serious macro- and microeconomic problems are the norm. Premature urban migration is an example of what can go wrong. Such migration has often been exacerbated by strong pull factors, such as the greater availability of social services in towns, as much as by push factors related to the state's inattention to agriculture and the scarcity of infrastructure in remote areas. Technically, the policy response should have been to reverse these biases, but as we shall see later, governments tend to put their resources where political gains are larger, and in the Middle East of the 1960s and 1970s this predilection typically led states to enlarge urban public employment and invest in industry rather than in rural areas and in agriculture.

A more recent example is the rise of informality, which has been related to small firms' inability to grow due to their poor access to the financial sector and the unfair competition from a formal private sector dominated by networks of privilege. The advocated policy response is to improve the access of small and medium enterprises (SMEs) to financial resources. But since the 1990s, when market liberalization became the norm, the incentives of autocratic governments have been to favor cronies that support their rule rather than small firms that may support the opposition. As a result, the shape of the business pyramid has increasingly become lopsided, with large and politically connected firms on top, a large but atomistic informal sector at the bottom, and a gnawingly missing middle. This lopsidedness has reduced the dynamism of the private sector, since typically it is the medium-size firms that are most driven to innovation and growth. In addition, this dualistic corporate structure with no middle and a lack of confidence between small and large firms has weakened the ability of the private sector to become an effective political actor and source of economic dynamism over time.

The distortions generated by state policy can be classified as being of micro origin, or related to the macro economy. The first type deals with distortions that bias individuals' incentives to use resources efficiently. One classical source of distortion, known as the Laffer curve (actually first identified, not in the twentieth century by Arthur Laffer, but in the fourteenth-century writings of the Arab scholar Ibn Khaldun), is connected with high levels of taxation, which reduce the incentives of producers to produce. For example, countries like Egypt in the 1950s needed to tax agriculture because there was no alternative source of investable funds, but the level of taxation was sometimes inefficiently high and thus wasteful. Another micro-origin distortion is connected with the inefficient use of capital. In particular, industry in Egypt (and in many other countries) tended to be capital-intensive because planners believed that this was necessary to support infant industries in order to create a modern industrial core. Growth and the modernization of production took precedence over employment generation and agricultural development, which were expected to be provided by growth itself. In the more recent period of neoliberal policy, politically connected firms in some countries have been able to obtain a large share of the credit going to the private sector, thus starving small firms of credit and giving small firms more incentives to hide from taxation in the informal sector.

There are also distortions of a macroeconomic nature. These are primarily concerned with the fiscal and balance-of-payment accounts, the so-called internal and external balances. These balances are intimately connected to two strategic choices that states make—the role of the state vis-à-vis that of the market, and the incentives it will provide, through trade policy and subsidies, to produce for the domestic versus the global market.

One central strategic decision that policymakers face is how much to intervene in the economy and how much to allow the private sector and market forces to determine economic outcomes. Development policy entails large expenditures by the state, whether in social services, such as in health and education, or in infrastructure. Indeed, in the Middle East, as we will see, states have also become directly involved in the process of production. How the expenditures related to this role are financed can influence the growth of the economy. Too often in the Middle East, the state itself has become a drain on resources. This is not to say that the state should not (still less, could not) intervene in the development process. In certain conjunctures, however, the state can inhibit the very process that, at least officially, it seeks to promote. Not only do its interventions often generate misleading price signals for private actors (for example, undervaluing foreign exchange and local capital), but its bloated bureaucracies and inefficient state-owned enterprises often devour resources. When the state borrows to finance its own activities, private investors may be crowded out of credit markets. Some of the burdens that the state itself creates for the growth process may be military spending and the cost of maintaining large, lethal arsenals and standing armies (see Chapter 10).

Rapid industrial development under state auspices was also held to be essential to national security in this region. State-led growth was designed to weaken or destroy internal and external enemies. States intervened to accelerate the process of economic growth and to forge powerful modern nations. Their leaders held certain visions of the future that explicitly included industrialization, but the reality often turned out to be different. Until the 1980s, most Middle Eastern states advocated some form of socialism, however vague the content of the label. Egypt and Tunisia, even as they moved in the 1970s toward greater reliance on the market, the private sector, and profits as incentives, still spoke of themselves as socialist states, as they relied on labor unions as an important actor in their governing coalitions. The dominant philosophy in Israel, until the advent of the Likud government under Menachem Begin in 1977, was a kind of Zionist hybrid of Fabian socialism. Sudan, the Yemen Arab Republic (YAR), Syria, Iraq, Libya, and Algeria have also laid claim to socialism. One has the impression, however, that their socialism has existed mainly in large and extensive public-sector welfare programs. Morocco vaunts its political and economic liberalism, like Turkey since the 2000s. Still, self-proclaimed liberals in these countries maintain large state sectors and interfere in all aspects of market transactions. Similarly, socialist regimes tolerate and sometimes aid and abet private-sector actors in trade, small-scale manufacturing, construction, and farming. By any measure, the largest and most dominant state sectors in the Middle East lie in the small oil-exporting countries, where petroleum deposits, the producing and refining companies, and all the proceeds of oil sales are under the control of the state.

But when the state withdraws from getting directly involved in national production, it needs to get involved in regulating markets so that they can function properly. Less involvement in production does not necessarily mean less influence, and the state can continue to play a preponderant role in shaping the growth process through the control of credit, foreign exchange, tax policy, and various investment incentives. Neither is it abdication when the state honors the market by stimulating the private sector. The prominent role of the state in the Korean "miracle" (and even more so in China) is instructive in this respect.

Another macroeconomic distortion to the process of economic growth is the problem of foreign exchange, which is largely connected to strategic choices regarding the production side of the economy, especially the extent to which local production is exported to the global market. For a variety of reasons, some Middle Eastern governments have found their growth process interrupted by the inadequacy of foreign exchange. Turkey's growth in the late 1970s was slowed by the steadily increasing demand for imports at the same time as export revenues lagged. Both external factors (falling terms of trade) and internal policies that encourage imports and discourage exports can create these problems. But equally, the sudden influx of large amounts of foreign exchange can cause problems, as discussed here in the section on oil.

Foreign exchange strategy is principally constrained by the relative gains and losses that will be incurred by domestic interests, classes, and ideological factions—this indeed is the primary focus of this book. The strategy can be further influenced by a country's regional and international allies, any of which may have their own vision of the future and some levers with which to promote it. And of course, foreign exchange strategy is shaped by international markets and financial flows. In the 1950s and 1960s, the strategy of choice in the region, and more generally among developing countries, was import substitution industrialization (ISI)—an attempt to industrialize on the back of internal demand and under protective trade barriers that insulated domestic markets from foreign competition. Although initially it was the favored strategy, ISI produced a host of unintended and undesirable consequences, at which point most countries attempted to shift to an export-led strategy. Turkey, Egypt, Israel, Morocco, and Tunisia have all proceeded in this fashion.

The temptation to focus on ISI was supported by many factors from the 1950s into the 1980s. First, newly independent states saw it as their responsibility to engineer a rapid transition away from what they saw as the exploitative insertion in the global division of labor of their economies coupled with the economies of their colonial masters and to find a more profitable strategy. Second, this temptation was encouraged by the leading economic fashions of the day, such as dependency theory, state-led development, and agricultural-led industrialization. Third, when these policies started to show their weaknesses, the first oil boom allowed the countries of the region to resist reform, either because of the large amount of remittances they were receiving (Egypt, Jordan) or because of the oil revenues themselves (Algeria, Syria).

Economic policies were also influenced by the increased globalization of the world economy after the 1980s. In the 1950s and 1960s, when global markets were relatively closed, there was little attraction to export-led growth. The first oil boom prevented the region from moving aggressively toward exports, as had happened successfully in some Asian countries. However, when the need to change course became irrefutable toward the late 1980s, global markets were already dominated by cheap Asian manufactured goods. Moreover, the development of global trading rules prevented Middle Eastern countries from benefiting from the kind of mixed strategies that were successfully implemented in an earlier period in Asia. Since the 1980s, under the rules developed by the World Trade Organization (WTO), it has become increasingly difficult to combine protected ISI sectors with policies designed to promote exports and open the economy to untaxed imports. Yet most countries in the region, as they gradually joined the WTO, have had to open their economies and reduce their protection of domestic markets.

The globalization of capital has also exerted profound influences on the region's ability to develop policies independently. Initially, Middle Eastern countries delayed their adjustment to globalized capital by resorting to international debt. With the sudden increase in interest rates in the 1980s (a global response to the first oil boom), the failure to service private external debt narrowed the range of choices available to countries in the region in the same way as elsewhere in the developing world. Once a financial crisis arises, the global market and the agencies of the core gain significant leverage over the policy and strategy choices of LDCs. New lines of credit, rescheduled debt, and new infusions of foreign direct investment are traded against structural reforms in the economy of the developing country. Since the mid-1970s, scores of developing countries have been driven toward far-reaching and painful structural adjustment programs designed in consultation with the International Monetary Fund (IMF), the World Bank, and Western aid agencies, and the countries in the Middle East are no exception. More recently, the movement of "portfolio" money through emerging markets is increasingly influenced by levels of domestic savings, current account balances, and constrained monetary policy, leading to higher interest rates and pressures to adjust exchange rates more rapidly. When domestic savings are low, investment is high, and the current account balance is in deficit, portfolio money heads elsewhere at literally the speed of light, as Turkey discovered in the early 2000s.

Social Actors

The final vertex of our theoretical triangle consists of social actors. There is nothing neat or tidy about this category. It includes a variety of class-based interests, economic groups, and other actors whose interests are both material and nonmaterial. What needs to be stressed, however, is that social actors are not inert or passive in the face of state initiatives. Societal interests and social actors penetrate the state and colonize parts of it. They form alliances with key state actors and enter into explicit or implicit coalitions with public officials, including the head of state. Well before the Arab uprisings, social actors defied or resisted the state through the sabotage of policies or through open resistance, a trend that has been accentuated in many countries in the region since the uprisings began.

The state and economic change can constitute and alter social actors in a variety of ways, and social actors can reciprocally affect state initiatives and economic policies. For example, structural transformation and the nearly universal shift toward the non-agrarian, urban sector produces new social actors and economic interests and undermines the old, irrespective of differing production systems, ideologies, or state formations. At a less macroeconomic level, a given development strategy may set in motion a process that virtually creates new social actors. The policy levers at the disposal of the Middle Eastern state to act in this manner are formidable. It may own and manage the major productive assets in the economy; own and derive revenue from mineral resources; act as the single largest employer in the economy; control, if not own, the major banking institutions; regulate and tax economic activities of all kinds; set basic education policy; control prices; and exercise, in Max Weber's terms, the legitimate monopoly of coercive force. The effects of state initiatives on the relative fortunes of distinct social actors do not necessarily provide conclusive evidence that the state acts in the interests of a class or economic pressure group that has yet to take shape, but it can be seen as an unintended by-product of this strategy. One case in point is the increasing strength of the Turkish private industrial bourgeoisie emerging out of decades of statist, ISI-oriented politics.

Different economic strategies generate clear winners and losers. It is generally the case that the rural sector does not benefit from ISI strategies because the state usually turns the domestic terms of trade against it. In an export-led strategy, it is likely that capitalist farmers, not the peasantry as a whole, will benefit from export incentives. Among the urban constituencies affected by ISI, organized labor in the new industries, the managerial strata charged with implementing state-financed projects, and middle- and upper-income consumers are generally the major beneficiaries. Large-scale industrialists in the private sector may suffer when state banking institutions and government investment programs favor public-sector enterprise. In contrast, small-scale industrialists may benefit from subcontracting on public-sector projects, especially in the construction sector. The move toward a strategy led by manufactured exports has an adverse effect on the real incomes of workers, since wages are usually allowed to lag behind inflation. Moreover, if the strategy is accompanied by devaluation, a shift in the domestic terms of trade in favor of agriculture, and some reduction in consumer subsidies, then all citizens in the non-farm sector, and especially those on fixed incomes, will experience a sharp rise in the cost of living.

In the Middle East, as in most LDCs, class alignments and interest group formation are fluid. Traditional class and economic interests had lost influence, until the recent uprisings. For instance, landowning groups were undermined by land reforms, and peasantries were unable to develop class cohesion. To the extent that capitalist bourgeoisies existed in the first half of this century, they were frequently made up of foreigners and preferred trade to manufacturing. Because industrialization came very late to the region and because regimes suppressed labor, the proletariat tended to be weak, although organized labor played an important role in independence movements and continues to be an important social actor in some countries. State employees constituted a powerful group of middle-class interests, but they tended to be manipulated by the state and could not emerge as an autonomous political actor in most countries. The interests of the poorer parts of populations are typically at odds with those of the richer parts of society—since the poor benefit from higher levels of taxation and redistribution (Acemoglu and Robinson 2012)—and in the Middle East the poor have been as controlled as the middle class, often through sheer repression. Control has also been supported by a populist political discourse that portrays the various parts of society as a large family (the *Umma*) that needs to live in harmony to foster national development. Today, with the partial exception of Islamist parties (see Chapter 12), formal political parties are generally weak throughout the region and, in some countries, are even banned. Until the recent uprisings overthrew authoritarian rulers, most leaders of political parties were either co-opted by the state, heavily repressed, or forced into exile. This goes a long way toward explaining why the recent uprisings were leaderless, although leaders have emerged in some countries, notably Tunisia, in the context of more pluralistic politics after the uprisings.

Until well into the 1980s, most Middle Eastern countries had a relatively pow-erful state apparatus, with its legions of civil servants and managers, a relatively powerful military establishment, a small formal private sector, and a numerically dominant but organizationally weak stratum of craftspeople, service workers, small-scale manufacturers, and myriad petty tradespeople who are the backbone of the large informal sector. For the most part, these social actors were not sufficiently cohesive or well defined enough to manipulate the state. Like any other collectivity, they must have found it difficult to act as a group in the face of serious "free-rider" problems.[6] The typical Middle Eastern state was best seen as the instrument of the upper echelons of its own personnel, who ensured that the state continued to control as much of the economic resources of the society as possible. Indeed, the postcolonial state in the Middle East has gone much further than either the Islamic or the colonial state in redrafting the class map of the region. Few postcolonial states initially had strong links to wealthy classes in their societies, and the few that did could not sustain these ties for long. Syria and Iraq up to 1958, Lebanon, and Morocco were the only major exceptions. The more autonomous states—Tur-key, Iran, Egypt, Algeria, Syria, and Iraq after 1958—engaged in far-reaching class engineering.

Since the liberal economic reforms of the 1980s, however, political settlements have started to change. The well-connected private-sector elite has gained increas-ing prominence alongside the "state bourgeoisie." But instead of giving rise to a dynamic form of capitalism, economic liberalization without a parallel political opening has produced a narrow and cronyistic form of market economy. Even if most business associations remain weak vehicles for the organization and represen-tation of private-sector interests, informal channels have enabled well-connected elites to transmit their preferences to rulers, gain preferential access to business op-portunities, and enhance their private holdings. The emergence of crony capitalism across the Middle East marks a major reconfiguration of core political settlements. In many countries, privileged business elites have become an important component of authoritarian coalitions. The other side of the coin has been the development of a large informal economy that has little access to state largesse or economic oppor-tunities and typically supports the (usually Islamic) opposition.

Since the mid-1980s, the array of social actors interacting with and confronting the Middle Eastern state has become far more complex than it was in earlier times. The middle classes—those owning "real" and intellectual capital (that is, special-ized educational training)—have grown prodigiously. Economic specialization has spawned new interests, and the creation of new wealth has slowly given those inter-ests the ability to further their objectives. Thirty years ago, most social actors were "policy-takers" in the face of autonomous states that they could not significantly in-fluence, much less hold accountable. But by the 1990s, bargaining between the state and social actors had become common. The state responded, not by opening up the political space, but instead by deploying instruments of selective co-optation—for example, providing subsidies for goods consumed more by the middle class, such as energy products. Nevertheless, there are signs in the dynamism of the civil rights movement that the middle class has become increasingly restive over time, and one of its main sources of grievance has been the rising unemployment among educated youth. As their transition to adulthood has been delayed by poor economic conditions, some analysts have described them as being in a state of "waithood" (Dhillon and Yousef 2009).

Our initial inclination is always to search for the material or economic incentives that shape group and individual action. Our generalizations apply best to the actions of economic interest groups (for example, the union of secondary school teachers) or of class actors (such as private industrialists or public-sector managers). In a fundamental sense, the state's allocation and protection of property rights is the starting point for understanding interest group and class formation. The property "regime" encapsulated in formal laws and informal bargains and often maintained by force will be defended by the beneficiaries and contested by those who feel excluded.

That said, we recognize that not all groups are defined by economic interests alone. The literature on Middle Eastern civil society (see Beinin and Vairel 2012; Kazemi and Norton 1995; Salamé 1994), sectarianism (Cammett 2014; Makdisi 2000; Weiss 2010), and Islamism (Cammett and Luong 2014; Masoud 2014; Schwedler 2007; Wickham 2002, 2013; Wiktorowicz 2004) grapple with the nature of group identity (see Chapters 11 and 12). Are Islamic political movements driven primarily by religious values and fervor or by less edifying struggles for power and resources? Are ethnic and sectarian groups and movements explained best by near-mystical notions of blood, ancestry, and historical injustice, or are they mainly seeking recognized claims to national resources? Are Islamists and ethno-religious movements crassly manipulated by politicians who see in religion or blood powerful implements for mobilizing a following? Are Islamist movements best seen as an attempt to forge a culturally authentic vision of modernity? Undoubtedly hunger for power, material betterment, group fear, creative political vision, and true piety all play their part. But we maintain that material explanations are often part of the picture.

RESOURCE ENDOWMENTS AND POLITICAL DEVELOPMENT

The Middle East has about two-thirds of the world's oil, nearly all of which is in the Persian Gulf (OPEC 2005). Over half (about 57 percent) of all oil reserves are in the Gulf, while Saudi Arabia alone has about one-quarter of all the oil on the planet; its reserves are more than twelve times those of the United States. The region is not particularly rich, however, in non-hydrocarbon mineral resources.[7] Oil revenues are a form of economic rent. Economic rent is the difference between the market price of a good or a factor of production and its opportunity cost—the price needed to produce the good or to keep the factor of production in its current use. So, oil rents are the difference between the market price (as of this writing, about US $57.00 per barrel) and the cost of producing oil there (about US$6.50).

The presence of abundant oil and gas reserves has shaped political and economic development trajectories in tangible ways in much of the MENA region. In particular, the "resource curse" thesis has been invoked to explain economic underperformance in the Middle East. This prominent line of research emphasizes the correlation between resource abundance and outcomes such as poor economic performance, unbalanced growth, and low levels of private-sector development. Another growing literature links resource wealth with a variety of political ills, including authoritarian rule, weak state institutions, and fragmented social development.

In its economic dimensions, the resource curse centers on the concept of the "Dutch Disease," or the theory that an increase in revenues from natural resources will lead to a decline in a country's industrial sector by raising the exchange rate, which makes the manufacturing sector less competitive.[8] The Dutch Disease can distort the economy and offset some of the benefits brought about by oil wealth.

The inflow of oil revenues can also have important direct political consequences. In the MENA region, oil rents are collected directly by governments, increasing their freedom of maneuver and their politically centralizing tendencies. Oil wealth enables rulers to distribute patronage more easily, shaping patterns of state-society relations and potentially "buying" political quiescence. They can also help finance large repressive institutions. The lack of taxation can weaken citizens' demand for representation, as well as the need to establish efficient tax institutions.

At the same time, a growing body of research has qualified the resource curse argument by suggesting that it is at best an insufficient and perhaps even an unnecessary explanation for underdevelopment. To the extent that it is valid, the resource curse argument applies only to a subset of MENA economies. Not all countries in the region enjoy large natural resource endowments. When viewed from a larger historical and comparative perspective, resource inflows per se do not necessarily hinder development. Other oil-rich countries, such as Norway, have managed to escape the alleged inevitability of the resource curse. In the developing world, resource-rich countries such as Indonesia, a major oil exporter (and Muslim-majority country), and Botswana, which has vast mineral deposits, have also managed to attain sustained records of economic growth.

Even if we accept the claim that oil has allowed autocratic regimes to remain entrenched in the region, this would not by itself explain underdevelopment. International and historical experiences do not support the view that autocratic states experience less economic growth than democratic states. The evidence is that, on average, both types of countries have grown at the same rate over the past fifty years, but that the growth rate of autocracies has a larger variance. That is, there is a higher probability that an autocratic state will be either far above or far below the average, as compared to democratic states, where growth is more predictable (Besley and Kudamatsu 2008).

It is important to discern whether natural resources reinforce or exacerbate pre-existing patterns of development or actually set countries on suboptimal development trajectories. We are not economic determinists. The development policy choices and ideological orientations of postcolonial leaders and the economic and political trajectories of Middle Eastern states have resulted from a combination of factors beyond resource endowments—including historical legacies of institution-building and the relative power of the distinct elements of ruling social coalitions as embodied in political settlements. Yet resource wealth alters the structural context within which political struggles unfold and policies are made. As a result, the development paths of oil-rich countries differ from those of their poorer neighbors. This is a topic to which we return later in the book.

The oil producers vary significantly among themselves. There are two possible angles from which to study these variations: a focus on oil per capita, and a focus on types of regimes.

As argued throughout this book, important differences, both political and economic, exist between oil-rich countries with large populations and those with a relatively small population. The first group has high levels of oil production per capita, while the second group has more modest (though still large) levels of oil production per capita. A striking difference between these groups is that the richer states, and especially those of the Gulf Cooperation Council (GCC), concentrate their efforts on distributing wealth to the population, often in the form of public-sector jobs as well as consumer subsidies, to buy social peace and preempt greater societal demands for accountability, while the group with more modest per capita oil production, such as Algeria, Iraq, and Iran, tend to allocate most of the oil rents among their elites and to use a large portion to finance a repressive apparatus that establishes their rule (Ali and Elbadawi 2012). These regimes also differ in the extent to which they rely on private-sector initiative, which tends to be more dynamic under those regimes with higher oil production per capita than those with lower oil production per capita, although all the oil-rich economies tend to be more dominated by their state given its sheer size (Beblawi 1990).

An emphasis on regime types and how they have evolved can be equally illuminating (see Chapter 3 for a more detailed discussion). The richer oil producers are all monarchies, while the countries with average levels of oil production per capita are republican and, at times, revolutionary states. It should be recognized that the republican oil exporters made strong attempts in their early phase of state-building (up until the 1980s) to spread public goods and rents widely: education and health services were rolled out quickly and comprehensively (even if at low quality), state employment was expansive, and subsidies for energy and consumer staples were at least as widespread as in the GCC. But with the failure of their development model, resources became spread so thin that the masses could not be pacified, hence necessitating repression. Moreover, these regimes were more brutal than the conservative monarchies at the outset, and they (at least initially) had a higher appetite for risk and for social engineering, and a sense that they were on the winning side of history. When resources dwindled, they naturally resorted to higher levels of repression and their bases narrowed.

Since two important differences in shaping development paths are how much a country relies on oil and its regime type, we use both angles as a way to classify countries in a typology that has some analytical teeth. We first divide our countries into three groups, depending on their level of oil production per capita (see Table 1.1), and in the next chapter we add in more fully the dimension of regime type.

1. *Resource-rich labor-poor (RRLP):* These are the countries with high per capita oil rent—we take the cutoff point somewhat arbitrarily at $10,000. The group includes the GCC countries, which are all monarchies, and Libya, which is a

republican state. Libya stands at the margin of this group—its oil production per capita, at about $11,000 in 2010, is lower than all the GCC countries. At $23,000 per capita, Saudi Arabia is the distant second-lowest in the group.

2. *Resource-rich labor-abundant (RRLA):* These are the countries where oil production per capita varies between $250 and $10,000. The group includes Algeria, Iran, Iraq, Sudan, Syria, and Yemen. We note that they are all republican states. Syria, Yemen, and Sudan are in this group, but not Egypt and Tunisia, although their oil production per capita figures are not largely different ($250–$430 per capita for Syria, Yemen, and Sudan versus about $170 per capita for Egypt and Tunisia). However, these countries are more clearly different in terms of the relative importance of oil in their economy, as reflected by the oil/GDP ratio—Syria, Yemen, and Sudan have ratios in the range of 20 percent, while for Egypt and Tunisia the ratio is well below 10 percent.

3. *Resource-poor labor-abundant (RPLA):* We group here the countries with no or small oil production (below $250 of oil rent per capita). Egypt, Jordan, Lebanon, Morocco, Palestine, and Tunisia belong to this group. In these countries, oil rents per capita range from about zero, as in Jordan, Lebanon, Morocco, and Palestine, to approximately $167 in Egypt and Tunisia, where oil rents as a percentage of GDP are also far lower than in the other two country groupings, as noted previously.

This taxonomy is meant only to be suggestive—its boundaries are porous. Libya could have been classified as an RRLA country if we had picked a larger cutoff point for oil production per capita in defining our three groups. Egypt and Tunisia used to derive larger rents from oil in the past (19 and 9 percent of their GDP, respectively, in the 1980s), but these have fallen in the most recent period (to 6.3 and 4.1 percent of their GDP, respectively, in the 2000s). Syria used to also derive sizable revenues from oil, and while these revenues have fallen, they remain relatively large. And unless important new discoveries are made soon, dwindling Algerian oil reserves will turn that country into an RPLA in a generation. The oil wealth of Sudan and Yemen is recent. Some countries also have other significant sources for their rents—Syria, Jordan, and Egypt collect rents on their strategic locations, and Morocco's exports are dominated by phosphates (30 percent).

PROLONGED DISCONTENT: TOWARD A POLITICAL ECONOMY OF THE ARAB UPRISINGS

Now that we are equipped with these analytical tools, let us go back to finding a broad answer to our initial question: how do the development paths of Arab countries explain why some of them experienced major revolts but not others, and how did the various regimes respond? A framework that not only explains the Arab uprisings but can be useful in thinking about the future should provide an empirically verifiable account of the socioeconomic and political evolution of the Arab republics that accounts for the persistence of autocracy until 2011 as well as for its eventual collapse. This new edition of the book focuses centrally on this challenge.

Different analysts would approach such ambitious questions in distinct ways. Some would stress contingency and agency, and undeniably, there are such elements

TABLE 1.1. Gross Domestic Product, Oil Rents, and Country Classification in the MENA Region, 2010

	GDP (in billions of 2010 dollars)	Population (in millions)	Oil Rent (in billions of 2010 dollars)	Oil Rent per Capita (in 2010 dollars)	Oil Rent (% of GDP)	GDP per Capita (in 2010 dollars)
Resource-rich labor-poor (RRLP)	**1,231.3**	**49.8**	**438.8**	**9,248.5**	**32.3**	**32,435.5**
Bahrain	22.9	1.26	4.4	3,489.5	19.2	18,174.6
Kuwait	124.0	2.74	59.9	21,858.4	48.3	45,255.5
Libya	74.8	6.36	31.6	4,974.9	42.3	11,761.0
Oman	57.8	2.78	20.9	7,505.7	36.1	20,791.4
Qatar	127.0	1.76	18.5	10,535.2	14.6	72,159.1
Saudi Arabia	526.8	27.40	248.6	9,074.8	47.2	19,226.3
United Arab Emirates	298.0	7.51	54.8	7,301.2	18.4	39,680.4
Resource-rich labor-abundant (RRLA)	**882.3**	**235.3**	**259.1**	**1,015.1**	**28.1**	**3,250.9**
Algeria	162.0	37.4	27.4	732.0	16.9	4,331.6
Iran	422.6	78.9	99.3	1,259.2	23.5	5,358.4
Iraq	142.8	33.7	105.1	3,118.7	73.6	4,237.4
Sudan	64.8	37.2	11.3	303.1	17.4	1,741.9
Syria	59.1	22.5	9.6	427.6	16.3	2,623.2
Yemen	31.0	25.6	6.4	249.8	20.6	1,212.8
Resource-poor labor-abundant (RPLA)	**425.1**	**140.3**	**15.6**	**55.8**	**2.1**	**4,032.8**
Egypt	219.0	82.3	13.8	167.7	6.3	2,661.6
Jordan	26.4	6.3	0.0	0.1	0.0	4,183.8
Lebanon	37.1	4.3		0.0	0.0	8,627.9
Morocco	90.8	32.6	0.0	0.1	0.0	2,785.3
Palestine	7.4	4.1	0.0	0.0		1,827.2
Tunisia	44.4	10.8	1.8	166.9	4.1	4,111.1
OECD economies						
Israel	217.0	7.9	0.0	0.2	0.0	27,468.4
Turkey	731.0	74.0	1.2	15.6	0.2	9,878.4
Overall MENA	**3,486.7**	**507.3**	**714.7**	**2,067.0**	**20.5**	**15,413.2**

Source: World Bank, World Bank Indicators (WBI), and International Monetary Fund (IMF), *World Economic Outlook* (*WEO*).

in the particular timing of the uprisings in Tunisia and Egypt. But we contend here that there must also have been structural factors that opened up a window of opportunity from which the main protagonists in the uprisings profited. In this section, we examine each of the key structural factors in more detail in order to illustrate the framework that we have developed to depict the historical transformations that have affected the countries of the region in the past half-century.

Our account begins with the phenomenal rise of the state, followed by its rollback and the decline of public services, which coincided with a period of economic liberalization that relied more on markets than the state as an engine for growth. Both phenomena palpably increased insecurity among non-elite populations. With the state's fiscal crisis and the adoption of market-oriented reforms, the social constituencies of authoritarian rulers gradually narrowed, allowing for the emergence of a class of privileged, well-connected elites who profited from special access to economic opportunities. The rise of crony capitalism and the growing de facto exclusion of the middle classes from opportunities for socioeconomic advancement across the region reflected shifts in economic structure. Perhaps most important, cronyism and rising economic insecurity fueled perceptions of both inequality and violations of norms of social justice. We also address the role of political Islam before, during, and after the revolts. Finally, we distinguish between the three types of countries defined earlier according to important differences between them with respect to the type of social demands made during the uprisings and the responses of regimes to these demands.

The Evolution of the Authoritarian Coalition, Social Change, and the Role of the Middle Classes

In the postcolonial period, the state played an unusually important role in economies across the Arab world. It is thus natural that the leading structural narratives on social discontent, even before the Arab uprisings, focused on the slow transition from quasi-socialism that began in the mid-1980s; the market liberalization and rollback of the state accompanying this transition, and ultimately the breakdown of the social contract underlying the autocratic bargain (Karshenas and Moghadam 2006; Yousef 2004). Such accounts cannot claim that state rollback was the proximate cause of the revolts, given the long time lag. Nonetheless, we cannot understand the ultimate collapse of the system without first understanding why and how reforms were delayed, which mechanisms were used by autocrats to remain in power even as market forces chipped away at their authority, and which contradictions emerged in this late autocratic "equilibrium" characterized by selective repression, co-optation, and cronyism.

In the post-independence period, rulers across the region, in both the "populist" republics and the "conservative" monarchies, expanded the public welfare infrastructure as part of state- and nation-building processes. In some countries, citizens had constitutional guarantees to basic health care and education. Thus, Arab citizens enjoyed important and tangible socioeconomic gains in the decades after independence, an experience that arguably raised their aspirations for themselves and their children. Access to basic services and stable employment provided a sense of economic security, while human development gains enabled earlier generations in post-independence Arab countries to enjoy some social mobility. Formal-sector workers have always received far more benefits and job security than the large portion of Arab populations who work in the informal sector. Formal-sector workers and especially civil servants and members of the security forces, then, were important foundations of authoritarian bargains across the region and therefore were more politically consequential for incumbent rulers. As a result, any breakdown in the public welfare infrastructure that affected employees in the public sector was bound to be politically risky.

The middle classes appear to be a central actor of change in the Arab republics. For decades, Arab autocrats had placed a premium on retaining the mainly secular, middle class–led parties and factions either within the authoritarian coalition or as part of the legal opposition. For the republics in particular, their Arab nationalist foundations were built on secular and liberal ideologies (Browers 2009). In the 1950s, leaders such as Habib Bourguiba and Gamal Abdel Nasser adopted an Ataturkian model of modernization (see Chapters 3 and 7), in which a strong secular state is a driving force for development and the middle classes play a legitimizing role. Thus, for Arab autocrats, losing their middle-class anchors was tantamount to becoming naked dictatorships with no operational narrative.

There are indications that the middle classes were hurt by the economic liberalization programs of the 1990s, and especially by their acceleration in the 2000s. Apart from the direct effects on the labor market, the interests of the middle classes have been threatened in many ways by the rollback of the state and the rise of neoliberalism. In addition, low public-sector wages fueled petty corruption in areas such as health and education, generating discontent from another major source. To be sure, governments retained important policies aiding the middle classes, such as subsidies on food and fuel. Given policy lock-in and the threat of political backlash from a key constituency in regime coalitions, it was difficult for governments to eliminate subsidies. As a result, the authoritarian bargain of the past decade evolved into an alliance between elite capital and elements of the middle classes that delivered economic benefits to coalition members, partly in the form of subsidies, but was less and less supportive of non-elite elements.

Beyond their relative size, the nature of the middle classes has changed over time. Until recently, experts did not seem to believe that the middle classes could play an active role in leading political change (Bellin 2002; Cammett 2007). As civil servants and employees of state-owned enterprises, the middle classes were effectively incorporated into the system, and thus their influence on policy formulation and ability to play the role of an "autonomous actor" were undercut. In response to economic liberalization, however, new market-oriented middle classes rose in the late 1990s that mostly comprised small merchants and industrialists, often in the informal sector, who benefited from the pro-market reforms as well as the small but expanding skilled component of the formal private-sector labor market. This group has been more politically active than older elements of the private sector (Nasr 2009). For example, the new pro-market middle classes of the region played an important role in the success of the Iranian revolution in 1979, they were instrumental in the rise of the Justice and Development Party (AKP) in Turkey, and they have become a more vocal and assertive element in the Moroccan business community (Cammett 2007; Catusse 2008; Demiralp 2009; Gumuscu and Sert 2009).

Deteriorating socioeconomic conditions combined with high aspirations increased discontent among the middle classes, resulting in their gradual withdrawal of support for authoritarian regimes. Dissatisfaction with the status quo, however, cannot simply be inferred from real economic conditions. Perceived conditions are more important in translating grievances into action than objective economic indicators. To understand the unraveling of authoritarian coalitions, we must comprehend how the middle classes interpreted changing socioeconomic conditions in their societies.

There is no evidence of a sharp spike in income inequality in the Arab countries—levels of inequality varied across the countries that witnessed mass protests, and the region as a whole does not exhibit particularly high levels of income inequality. Recent analyses indicate, however, that inequalities of opportunity were on the rise across the non-oil-exporting countries of the region. In the context of post-independence social bargains, in which citizens experienced and came to expect real social mobility as a result of state economic and welfare policies, the inability to advance socioeconomically may have been especially frustrating. In this respect, it may have been the inability of the new "liberalized" order to create sufficient numbers of good jobs to absorb the large cohorts of educated youth that generated much of the social frustration that ultimately led to the uprisings.

The Rise of Cronyism and the Job Deficit

By the mid-1990s, the ISI model was already bankrupt and reforms were under way to replace it with a more dynamic, private sector-led export model. But contrary to the "Washington Consensus" theory, which posits that market liberalization is the engine of significant economic growth, private-sector activity did not rise significantly over time. Instead of leading to a freer market, market liberalization saw instead the old regimes consolidating their shaky rule by forging new alliances with elements of the old elite capital and elements of the state bourgeoisie. In retrospect it can be seen that this new regime, dubbed "crony capitalism" by many, inflamed the passion of the Tahrir Square and Avenue Bourguiba demonstrators in three important ways. First, crony capitalism seems to explain the economic underperformance of the region. Second, it fueled perceptions of rising inequality, and in particular of inequality of opportunities. And finally, it signaled the narrowing of the authoritarian coalitions that were squeezing out the middle classes, a key constituency of post-independence Arab regimes.

Popular perceptions of business elites have become very negative in the region. Cronyism is now seen as the key characteristic of the economic opening that started in the 1990s and accelerated in the 2000s and as the source of many ills, including the job deficit, the rise in inequalities, and the perpetuation of authoritarian rule. The perceived "corruption" of the political and business elites was a key driving force of popular discontent. For example, a Pew survey reveals that in 2010 corruption was the top concern of Egyptians, with 46 percent listing it as their main concern even ahead of lack of democracy and poor economic conditions (Pew Research Center 2011). Changes in the corruption ratings of Arab countries in Transparency International's Corruption Perceptions Index (CPI) confirm popular perception: for example, in 2005, out of 158 countries, Egypt ranked 70th, Tunisia ranked 43rd, Libya ranked 117th, and Yemen ranked 103rd. Perceived corruption increased markedly in the following three years. In 2008 Egypt dropped to 115th, Tunisia to 62nd, Libya to 126th, and Yemen to 141st out of 180 rankings on the CPI.

The literature on contemporary Arab capitalism is rich in describing the links between economics and politics. Some work analyzes state-business relations in the period prior to the uprisings in Egypt (Kienle 2001; Roll 2010; Sfakianakis 2004), Morocco (Cammett 2007; Catusse 2008; Henry 1996), Syria (Haddad 2012; Kienle 2002), Tunisia (Bellin 2002; Cammett 2007; Hibou 2006), and the Gulf (Chaudhry 1997; Hertog 2010; Moore 2004; Vitalis 2006), as well as in the region as a whole (Heydemann 2004; Schlumberger 2007). The precise nature of state-business relations has varied from country to country, with important ramifications for the dynamics of authoritarian stability and breakdown. For example, in the aftermath of the uprising, the importance of the military in the Egyptian domestic economy is well known, albeit in imprecise terms. The important stakes of military institutions and high-ranking officers in protected industries help to explain why the Supreme Council of the Armed Forces (SCAF), a key backbone of the authoritarian regime, allowed Hosni Mubarak to fall but stymied substantive democratization in post-Mubarak Egypt (Marshall and Stacher 2012). Without an understanding of the military's role in the domestic political economy, it is impossible to make sense of political developments during and after the uprisings. In Tunisia, the fact that the military was far less central in the authoritarian coalition accounts in part for General Rachid Ammar's unwillingness to fire on protesters, a key juncture in the overthrow of Ben Ali. Furthermore, the elite coalition in Ben Ali's regime appeared to have narrowed much more than in Egypt, although this hypothesis deserves more systematic analysis. As a result, by the time mass protests erupted against the Ben Ali regime, many Tunisian capitalists, not being integrated into his networks of privilege, accepted his downfall. In Egypt, Gamal Mubarak and his allies had gained important footholds in the economy and profited from lucrative international deals, but this faction of the regime was counterbalanced by a strong and historically powerful protectionist bourgeoisie, which included, but was not limited to, the military.

THE ROLE OF POLITICAL ISLAM IN THE ARAB UPRISINGS

Before concluding, we need to bring in one additional and essential factor—the role of political Islam in the evolution of politics across the region both prior to and during the uprisings. In the aftermath of the Arab uprisings, Islamists became increasingly important if not, at least temporarily, dominant actors in Tunisia and Egypt and, to a lesser degree, in Libya and Yemen. It is widely accepted that the uprisings were not driven by Islamists or even by increased popular support for Islamists, who were the most vocal opponents of authoritarian rulers. Rather, Islamists were the main beneficiaries of the transitional political systems that emerged after dictators were ousted.

Although Islamists did not initiate or lead the revolts, they may have played an indirect role in driving the Arab uprisings.[9] In particular, two situations related to political Islam may have contributed to the defection of the middle classes from authoritarian bargains. First, Islamists across the region had become less threatening since the 1990s because they had increasingly moderated their ideology and tactics. For example, in 2004 the Muslim Brotherhood in Egypt committed publicly to abiding by a constitutional and democratic system that called for the recognition of "the people as the source of all authority," and it endorsed the principles of the transfer of power through free elections, the freedom of belief and expression, the freedom to form political parties, and the independence of the judiciary (Shahin 2005).[10] The moderation of Islamists may have altered the calculations of socially liberal groups, whose members feared a takeover by Islamic parties because of their divergent views on issues such as civil rights, the separation of mosque and state, the role of women in society, and foreign policy. Even in the context of declining economic benefits, the middle classes may have opted to support autocrats as long as Islamists championed a very different picture of civic and political life. However, as more moderate Islamic parties emerged, they may have garnered more support, or at least tolerance, among the middle classes.[11] At the same time, insurgent groups using violent tactics declined. If fear of Islamism had perpetuated authoritarian rule (Lust 2011), then declining fear of Islamism undercut support for dictators.

Second, some of the messages of Islamist parties, which emphasized corruption and the lack of social justice under authoritarian rulers, reflected and may even have amplified growing discontent among the middle classes. Indeed, the leaders and cadres of mainstream Islamist groups, such as the Muslim Brotherhood in Egypt and its branches and analogous organizations in other Arab countries, were composed of middle-class professionals who were shut out of employment and other opportunities under crony capitalist systems (Burgat 2003; Esposito 1997; Fuller 2004). Islamism does not offer a clear-cut and uniform ideology on the market, and Islamic thinkers and groups disagree on the extent to which the teachings of Islam call for redistributive measures. However, a dominant ideological strain associated with the rise of moderate Islamist parties, such as the AKP in Turkey, the Muslim Brotherhood in Egypt, and Al-Nahda in Tunisia, is congruent with middle-class redistributive goals and supportive of market-based systems. Islamists were not central actors in the uprisings that toppled authoritarian rulers, but their role in society and politics may have contributed to the defection of the middle classes from authoritarian coalitions, a key step in the breakdown of authoritarian rule.

While in opposition, the Islamist movements that initially came to power in Egypt and Tunisia had frequently criticized the economic policies of the previous regimes and promised to combat corruption, poverty, and inequality. However, in the face of the political turmoil generated by the rush to fill the power vacuum, write constitutions, and compete for elections, they were unable to move on any of

8

86

their big promises. Islamist commitments to promote social justice, reduce subsidies in order to provide more fiscal space in budgets, attack cronyism, and eliminate waste in bloated bureaucracies have not been realized during their short period at the helm of the economy.

CONCLUSIONS

Although the three variables that undergird our analysis—state institutions and policies, economic growth patterns, and social actors—will be treated sequentially in the following chapters, one should not lose sight of the fact that they interact simultaneously. We begin with a more detailed presentation of our understanding of economic growth and structural change in Chapter 2, followed by a fuller discussion of the types of political regimes in Chapter 3. Later in the book, we detail the range of social actors whose preferences and behavior shape and are shaped by state policies and the economic context (see especially Chapters 11 and 12). A full consideration of the development and evolution of state institutions and social actors requires a detailed investigation of trends in human capital and labor markets, the ecological environment, the rise and decline of the public sector, and macroeconomic trends in the Middle East. Subsequent chapters elaborate on the context in which the rapid social and economic change in the region over the past one hundred years has occurred.

NOTES

1. See Pepinsky (2009) and Slater (2010) on the importance of coalitions for authoritarian durability.

2. Douglass North (1990, 3) defines institutions as the "humanly devised constraints that shape human interaction."

3. Sen (2013, 76–78) associates these distinct approaches to institutions and economic development with the work of Daron Acemoglu and James Robinson (2012) and Mushtaq Khan (2010), respectively.

4. North et al. (2013) show how coalitions that become "too" large require large rent extractions that end up hurting the economy when they become unsustainable.

5. See Haggard, Kang, and Moon (1997) for a critique of Kohli's account of the Korean experience.

6. The free-rider problem arises when an actor cannot be excluded from the benefits of collective action. Consequently, he or she may shirk or fail to participate, but still reap the benefits; he or she thus gets a "free ride" on the efforts of others. See the classic treatment by Mancur Olson (1965) and the more nuanced analyses of Robert Axelrod (1984) and Elinor Ostrom (1990).

7. A wide variety of minerals are exploited, but with the exception of phosphates in Morocco and Jordan, no country's output amounts to even 5 percent of world production. Morocco and Western Sahara hold over two-thirds of the world's phosphate deposits, and Morocco is the third-largest world producer. Algeria and Turkey produce some iron ore, and only Turkey has significant coal deposits. All of this is in marked contrast to the region's hydrocarbon resources.

8. The term "Dutch Disease" derives from the experience of the Dutch economy with the large influx of North Sea gas revenues in the 1970s (see further details in Chapters 2 and 9).

9. During the sustained protests in Tahrir Square that led to Mubarak's resignation, the Muslim Brotherhood and other Islamist groups (along with other non-Islamist citizen groups) helped to solve the coordination problems that constrained social mobilization by opening up mosques as meeting points and medical treatment centers.

10. Similar moderation took place in Turkey and Tunisia. In Turkey, a combination of the lessons from repression, opportunism, and the growth of a friendly middle class compelled the AKP to moderate (Demiralp 2009; Mecham 2004). In Tunisia, the Al-Nahda leadership claimed in 1981 that "we have no right to interpose between the people and those whom the people choose and elect" (Tamimi 2001).

11. In Egypt, state repression increased after the electoral gains of the Muslim Brotherhood in the 2005 elections. When the party emerged as a credible alternative, the ruling regime cracked down on it more forcefully (Osman 2010).

2

ECONOMIC PERFORMANCE
AND SOCIAL OUTCOMES

In 2010 the total population of the countries in the MENA region was approximately 507 million, or roughly 8 percent of the population of all developing countries. Three countries in the region—Turkey, Iran, and Egypt—have populations exceeding 70 million, which is comparable to Italy, France, or the United Kingdom, but the region also contains eleven countries with populations less than 10 million and seven (Algeria, Morocco, Iraq, Saudi Arabia, Sudan, Syria, and Yemen) with populations between 20 million and 40 million.

There are now more than four times as many Middle Easterners and North Africans as there were in the late 1950s. The region's population is growing at about 2.2 percent per year, which means that it will double in about thirty-two years. Within just three generations, the region's population will have increased *twelvefold*. The current number of residents in the greater Cairo area, at more than 17 million, exceeds the total population of Egypt in 1919 (12–13 million). Of all major world regions, only the population of sub-Saharan Africa is growing more rapidly. Because of this rapid rate of population growth, most people in the region are young—about half the population is under twenty-four years old, and nearly two-thirds are younger than thirty. A large and growing percentage of these people live in cities. (Chapter 4 delves more deeply into the demographic characteristics of the region.) Although different countries use different criteria for defining a "city"—making cross-country comparisons notoriously unreliable—at least 58 percent of the inhabitants of the MENA region live in urban areas, with, again, wide variations among countries. Cities were always central to the pre-industrial and precolonial social formations in the region, and their importance has steadily increased: the region now has more than sixteen cities with more than 1 million inhabitants.

In 2010 the region's total gross domestic product (GDP) hovered around $3.5 trillion, which is a bit more than the GDP of Germany (see Table 2.1). The countries in the resource-rich labor-poor (RRLP) group had the largest GDP, at about

$1.2 trillion (about the size of Korea's or Mexico's GDP), followed by the resource-rich labor-abundant (RRLA) group at $882 billion (about the size of Malaysia and Thailand combined), and then by the resource-poor labor-abundant (RPLA) group at $425 billion (the size of Iran's economy). Turkey ($730 billion) has the highest GDP in the region, followed by Saudi Arabia ($527 billion).

The region displays a huge diversity in per capita income. More than any other major region. It includes extraordinarily wealthy city-states—incomes per national in Qatar and the United Arab Emirates (UAE) are the highest in the world—and high-income countries (Bahrain, Israel, Saudi Arabia, Oman, Kuwait) whose inhabitants enjoy a material standard of living like that in the developed countries. At the

---

BOX 2.1 Gross Domestic Product and Its Measurement

Economic growth is usually measured by gross domestic product (GDP) in a unit of common currency, usually dollars, in order to facilitate international comparisons. GDP is obtained by weighing all outputs by their prices and adding them up. Since output and income are closely related concepts, the measure also serves as a kind of summary statistic for the level of income in a country. When expressed in per capita terms, the GDP is often employed as a crude indicator of average social welfare. A more precise measure of average income is given by the gross national income (GNI), which essentially adds remittances to GDP.

Several criticisms have been made of this concept. First, measurement errors, particularly for natural capital, may be serious. This problem is particularly acute for those countries that sell oil. Some of the GDP in the Gulf is not "income" but "liquidation of capital." Second, measurement problems go beyond negative environmental externalities. For example, measured GDP usually excludes nonmarketed output and thus tends to neglect household production; much of women's contribution to production thus escapes notice. A variant of this problem is that the value of production and services in the "informal sector" is at best crudely estimated. As we shall see in subsequent chapters, the informal sector plays an important but poorly understood role in Middle Eastern economies.

Third, the use of official exchange rates as the common denominator for international GDP comparisons introduces further distortions. To say that the average annual income in Egypt is US$1,000 evokes the image of an American buying only US$1,000 worth of goods in a year. In fact, however, an Egyptian with the equivalent of this dollar sum, when converted at the official exchange rate, would be able to buy more goods and services than the American because the price of nontradable goods (for example, housing and haircuts) in relation to the price of tradable goods (such as wheat, cars, or textiles) is typically much lower in less developed countries (LDCs) than in developed countries (DCs). Using official exchange rates to compare incomes across countries ignores this difference. Even if Egyptians spent the same percentage of their income on

continues

same time, the average Sudanese lives in poverty as extreme as that in sub-Saharan Africa, and millions of Egyptians, Moroccans, Sudanese, and Yemenis live very close to subsistence.

The diversity of experience with economic growth and structural change is just as wide. At one extreme, MENA contains not only industrialized and developed Israel but also Turkey, formerly the heartland of one of history's greatest empires and a pioneer in industrialization outside of Europe and Japan. Some other important distinctions are found in the rates of growth and structural transformation; the size, efficiency, and diversity of industrial production; the trend in agricultural production; and the composition of international trade.

BOX 2.1. *continued*

nontradable goods as Americans (which is unlikely, given the relative prices), the Egyptians' purchasing power relative to the Americans' would be understated by using official exchange rates to compare them (Kravis, Heston, and Summers 1978). In Figure 2.1, we also depict GDP per capita at purchasing power parity (PPP) prices, and there the disparity between the two measures can be seen. For example, the average Egyptian has the US purchasing power equivalent of $6,140, not $2,662, available to spend. Incomes measured in PPP dollars tend to be more different from straight dollar incomes in poorer countries because their citizens tend to have a larger share of nontraded goods in their consumption baskets.

Fourth, GDP per capita offers no evidence on distribution or happiness. Therefore, one can use increases in GDP as an indicator of increasing social welfare only with great caution. Also, research suggests that increasing GDP (or increasing personal incomes, for that matter) has little impact on how well off people actually *feel* (see, for example, Easterlin 1995; Layard 2005).

Despite these problems and issues, the GDP, employed with caution, offers us the most comprehensive available set of statistics on national income. We take the problems described here as cautionary notes about the concept rather than devastating criticisms, if only because national governments often behave as if increasing (measured) national income is a central policy (and political) goal.

Thus, in assessing the numbers in the following tables and figures, several things should be kept in mind. First, the data are often merely the best guesses of informed observers, and for some of the least developed and poorest countries they are of very poor quality. Second, GDP as a measure of welfare has inherent limitations. Thus, for all countries, data should be taken as indicating orders of magnitude rather than precise "truth." Third, the data are especially noisy in countries where economic growth started from a very low base (Yemen, Oman, Sudan) or where devastating wars led to great destruction and growth collapses.

This chapter describes the evolution of economic growth in the region since the 1960s and explores how it has differed over time and across our three categories of countries. After reviewing the region's performance, we look at its transition from an import substitution model in the 1960s to an export promotion model after the 1990s, describe the contours of this massive policy shift, and evaluate its costs and benefits from an economic and social perspective. We also argue that while the uprisings of 2011 cannot be directly attributed to this shift, its various repercussions laid the basis for the social discontent underlying them.

LONG-TERM GROWTH WITH MODEST RESULTS

Between 1960 and 2010, there was nothing particularly notable about GDP growth in the MENA region as a whole compared to that of other developing regions of the world. The long-term performance of the region has been neither extraordinarily good nor extraordinarily poor—its average long-term rate of GDP growth over the past fifty years stands at 4.9 percent a year, a reasonably solid performance by historical and international standards. The region's long-term average GDP growth over this long period, which is shown in Figure 2.1, is a bit higher than the average for the world's middle-income countries (4.7 percent) and also more than the world's

FIGURE 2.1. Gross Domestic Product per Capita in the MENA Countries, 2010

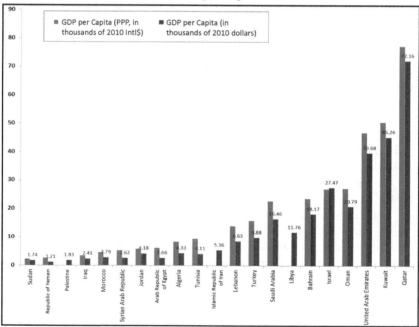

Source: World Bank, World Bank Institute (WBI), and International Monetary Fund (IMF), World Economic Outlook (WEO).

low-income countries' average (3.4 percent). Comparing the MENA region to other regions of the world, we see that it grew at about the same average rate as South Asia (5 percent), at a faster rate than Africa (3.5 percent) or Latin America (3.8 percent), but at a much lower rate than East Asia (7.3 percent).

The average GDP total and per capita real growth rates that are shown in Figure 2.2 are unweighted averages over time and over countries. We use unweighted averages because our goal is to illustrate the performance of an average country of the region, and for each of the three types of countries introduced in Chapter 1, rather than that of the average Middle Eastern individual. If we weighted these figures by the size of each country, the (population weighted) averages would mainly reflect the performance of the larger countries.

It is not surprising that, on average, the MENA region's GDP grew more rapidly than that of other LDCs, given the impact of the oil boom and fast population growth. But averages often hide more than they reveal, and the reality is gloomier when we look at economic performance with greater detail. In particular, there are several reasons why the growth performance of most of the countries of the region was much less positive than implied by a simple average. First, economic growth needs to be compared with population growth in order to evaluate effective economic performance, and population growth has been very rapid in the region.

FIGURE 2.2. Economic Growth in the MENA Region and in Other Regions of the World, 1960–2010

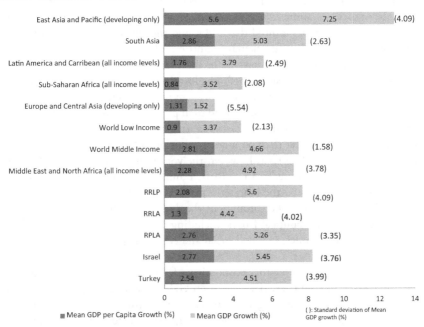

Source: World Bank, WBI data.

Note: Standard deviation of mean GDP growth (%) is in parentheses.

Second, the economic performance differs quite a bit within and among the various types of countries. Third, the variability of growth over time matters, as variability is itself bad for growth and the goal of good economic management is to avoid booms and busts.

Elaborating on the first point, economic performance indeed looks more modest by international standards when it is juxtaposed with the region's high population growth. On a per capita basis, GDP growth was much less impressive. Population growth rates for the region as a whole were on average 2.7 percent a year over the period; thus, one can mechanically compute the average growth rate of GDP per capita for the countries of the region as approximately 2.3 percent over the fifty years. This is quite a poor performance by international standards—below that of the middle-income groups (2.8 percent) and only about half as good as East Asia's stellar performance (5.6 percent). And if we computed GDP growth on a per labor basis, instead of a per capita basis, the region's performance would look even worse, since the labor force grew faster than population until the early 2000s in much of the region. In many countries, and especially when the youth bulge was at its height around 2000, the rate of growth of output was not sufficient to keep up with the growth in the labor force—which was above 3 percent during the 1990s. As a result, average wages in many countries today are at levels not too different from where they were in the 1970s (International Labor Organization 2013b). On the second point, it is striking how extremely variable growth has been over time and across countries. As we discuss in more detail later, there are several causes for this variability, including the relation between economic growth and the price of oil, the costs of socioeconomic adjustments as much of the region moved from state-led to market-led economies around the 1990s, and the devastating effects of various wars on the economies of particular countries. The one period with the lowest economic growth rate was somewhere in the 1980s and 1990s when most of the countries experienced a "lost decade." The lost decade, which was shorter in some cases and longer in others, coincided in most countries with the height of the youth bulge, when the share of labor entrants to total population was at its maximum. In other regions, and particularly in East Asia, this created a demographic dividend: the labor force grew faster than population, thus providing an extra push to GDP per capita. In the Middle East, however, the youth bulge coinciding with rough economic times complicated matters further and led to rising social frustrations. The lost decade depressed the long-term performance of the region in important ways. Moreover, as we argue throughout this book, what happened then on the economic, social, and political fronts, including the rollback of the state and the shift to market economies, initiated social and economic processes that ultimately led to the 2011 uprisings.

In Figure 2.2, we can see that economic performance varied quite a lot among the three types of countries. If we focus on GDP growth, it is apparent that the RRLP group did best, growing at 5.6 percent a year; this is a remarkable average over such a long stretch of time, and the fastest growth rate for any single region besides East Asia. (GDP per capita is low in the RRLP group because the huge influx of foreign workers distorts the "per capita" aspect.) Given the huge contribution of oil wealth to this growth, this performance is not too surprising, but it does stand in sharp contrast with the notion of a "resource curse." More surprisingly, it is the RPLA group that comes in second: its 5.26 percent growth is good performance by global standards, and its per capita performance of only 2.76 percent, while weaker, nevertheless remains around the middle-income average.

The RRLA region, which is rich in both oil and people, comes in a distant third place at 4.4 percent average growth per year (and at only 1.3 percent on a per capita basis). This reinforces the suggestions of Chapter 1 that this group of countries seems to have been hit the hardest by the oil curse. Indeed, the countries exhibiting the lowest performance are those that were once believed to show the greatest promise, as they could combine oil wealth with a large population to develop into industrial giants. Iraq, Iran, and Algeria all had such promise and plans, but they all got mired in internal and external conflicts that ended up undermining their economic potential. Syria has now entered just such a destructive phase.

This brings us to our third point about the variability of growth over time. This variability is partly a result of the dependence of the region on oil revenues—oil prices are determined by international markets and have themselves shown a great deal of variability over time. It is therefore no surprise that the very large variability of growth across periods, especially in the resource-rich countries, is a defining dimension of growth in the region, especially as compared to the rest of the world. We can see this in the coefficients of variation of the growth rate, which are also depicted in Figure 2.2. The standard deviation of growth over the fifty years is about equal in RRLA and RRLP countries, at around 4 percent, and also about equal to East Asia, which, as we have seen, had much larger growth rates. The standard deviation of growth is 3.35 in RPLA countries, which is also larger than the various global averages, with the exception of the East Asia/Pacific region and the region comprising Europe and Central Asia.

One can also see this more directly by looking at the growth rates of our three groups over time in Figure 2.3. Each of these rates varies much more than the rates of the other middle-income countries of the world, and they have a greater tendency to oscillate, more so during some periods (the 1970s and mid-1990s) and less so during others (the 1980s and after 2005). The RRLP countries in particular show an extremely variable growth rate—on a per capita basis, for instance, Saudi Arabia grew at extraordinary rates of around 8 percent a year during the 1970s, shrank to rates of somewhat more than 5 percent a year during the 1980s, and had an essentially flat GDP per capita in the 1990s–2000s.

As noted earlier, these variations over time in economic performance were due in part to oil prices and in part to the effects of the structural adjustment period of the 1980s. The two factors actually interacted in several ways. Oil prices experienced two main periods of boom: one in 1973–1979, and the other more recently, in 1998–2014 (at this writing). In the first two decades after 1960, economic growth and structural change proceeded briskly in the region, initially because statist policies work for a while before running into contradictions, and later because the first oil boom in 1973 allowed states to continue with such policies after they had run their course. The 1980s and parts of the 1990s were marked by the collapse of oil

FIGURE 2.3. Annual GDP Growth Rate for MENA Countries and World Middle-Income Countries, 1960–2010

Source: World Bank, WBI data, and IMF, WEO.

prices, which forced policy adjustments and resulted in lower growth. From the mid-1990s until the uprisings of 2011, growth resumed in most countries, and even when it seemed to start to taper off, it was boosted by a second oil boom in 1998.

Figure 2.4 shows the changes in crude oil prices as well as the changes in regional oil revenues between 1960 and 2010. Oil prices are expressed in constant 2010 dollars, so that they can be compared over time. The two peaks of 1973–1979 and 2007 in regional oil revenues are immediately apparent. The first oil boom had spectacular effects: as oil prices quadrupled between 1972 and 1979, reaching nearly $100 per barrel in 1979, oil revenues in the region jumped from less than $100 billion in 1972 to over $700 billion in 1979—at the time, this represented nearly 50 percent and 90 percent of the GDP of the RRLA and RRLP countries, respectively. The second and more recent boom is equally spectacular, if not more so: it has brought the region over $900 billion in direct oil revenues, which amounted to nearly 40 percent of GDP in both RRLA and RRLP countries in 2010. In between, however, there was a long period when oil prices oscillated between $20 and $40 per barrel and revenues were only around $200 billion a year—less than 20 percent of the region's GDP. These are huge variations with equally huge effects, which will

FIGURE 2.4. Oil Rents for MENA Countries and Crude Oil Prices (in billions of 2010 US dollars), 1960–2010

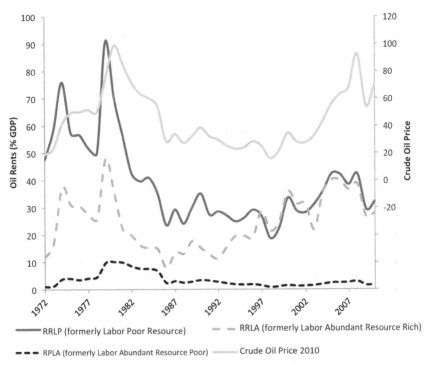

RRLP (formerly Labor Poor Resource)
RRLA (formerly Labor Abundant Resource Rich)
RPLA (formerly Labor Abundant Resource Poor)
Crude Oil Price 2010

Source: World Bank, WBI data, and IMF, WEO.

be discussed throughout the book. Oil production represents an important share of the gross national product (GNP) in both RRLA and RRLP countries. It is interesting to observe that the RRLP countries became more diversified over time, while diversification decreased over time in the RRLA countries.

The oil importers benefited from high oil prices, too, even though they had to pay more when they imported oil. Some countries like Egypt and Tunisia had some oil production, but labor remittances and assistance from oil-rich countries did much to redistribute oil rents across the whole region. Both remittances and aid from oil producers went up and down with oil prices, which explains why the importers' fortunes also followed the same cycle of boom and bust.

Poorer countries, especially those of the Mashrek region (and in particular Lebanon, Jordan, Palestine, and Yemen), benefited from large remittances from their workers who flocked to the oil-producing countries, especially during the 1970s and 1980s (see Table 2.1). The sheer size of the number of migrant workers sets the region apart. For the RPLA countries as a group, workers' remittances have averaged between 10 and 13 percent of GDP since the 1980s, with fluctuations over time loosely connected with the price of oil. Jordan, Lebanon, and Palestine received

TABLE 2.1. External Monetary Flows (as a percentage of GDP) in the MENA Region, 1970s to 2010

Countries		1970s	1980s	1990s	2000s	2010
RRLP countries	**Oil rent**	**62.39%**	**35.26%**	**26.50%**	**35.13%**	**32.30%**
	Net flows of debt	0.00	0.50	3.00	-9.43	5.62
	Total	62.40	35.80	29.50	25.70	37.90
	External debt	20.94	15.21	29.34	32.73	50.09
RRLA countries	**Oil rent**	**27.71**	**14.50**	**27.98**	**34.12**	**28.05**
	Remittances	3.14	7.99	5.54	2.91	2.04
	Grants	2.68	2.88	1.49	3.75	1.63
	Net flows of debt	3.76	3.31	0.66	-0.09	1.12
	Total	37.30	28.70	35.70	40.70	32.80
	External debt	12.72	33.20	80.90	44.90	25.00
RPLA countries	**Oil rent**	**6.76**	**7.00**	**2.65**	**2.84**	**2.59**
	Remittances	8.63	9.96	11.62	13.65	10.22
	Grants	8.12	5.36	4.93	6.83	1.23
	Net flows of debt	7.05	7.19	2.86	2.23	2.17
	Total	30.60	29.50	22.10	25.60	16.20
	External debt	27.40	68.60	78.90	77.90	65.10

Source: World Bank, World Bank Indicators (WBI), and International Monetary Fund (IMF), *World Economic Outlook* (WEO).

between 8 and 13 percent of their GDP from such sources, while Morocco and Egypt received between 5 and 10 percent. Migration to the rich Gulf Cooperation Council (GCC) countries benefited the migrant workers handsomely, but it often deprived the labor-exporting countries of some of their best skills.

Official development assistance (ODA) rose at the same time—especially during the oil booms of the 1970s and 2000s (see Table 2.1)—in part owing to support by GCC countries, with the frontline states of Jordan, Palestine, Egypt (until its peace agreement with Israel in 1982), and Syria being the largest beneficiaries of this aid. Added to this was Western aid, especially from the United States, first to Israel and Egypt, then to Jordan, and more recently to Iraq; the increased involvement of the European Council in the region under the guise of the Southern Mediterranean program; and the involvement of the international financial institutions, with the International Monetary Fund (IMF) most active during economic crises. As a result, most RPLA countries receive generous support to the tune of 5 to 8 percent of GDP. With the notable exceptions of Sudan and Yemen, the poorest members of

BOX 2.2 The Concept of Economic Rent

Economists define rent as the difference between the market price of a good or factor of production and its opportunity cost. Owners of certain assets or providers of certain services enjoy strategic positions in markets that allow them to set prices well above the opportunity cost for what they are providing. When oil prices quadrupled in the 1970s, the new market price reflected neither increases in the cost of production nor new investment. Rather, consumers of petroleum had to accept the new price, and only with the passage of considerable time could they reduce their consumption through improved efficiency in energy use. In the interim, the oil-exporting states of the MENA region reaped enormous rent streams.

A host of ills have been attributed to these rents—which may be referred to as "external"—by analysts of the Middle East. Access to rents has allowed several states to avoid improving the efficiency with which their economies produce anything and has particularly hurt those sectors producing tradable goods. Rents have allowed governments to avoid heavily taxing their own citizenries, thereby breaking that vital, often adversarial link between governments and the people they tax. Out of such links, governmental accountability may flow; in their absence, governments may ignore their citizens.

External rents are not confined to petroleum revenues. Several Middle Eastern nations had continuous access to "strategic rents" throughout the Cold War era. Countries enjoying peculiar geostrategic value in the confrontation between the two superpowers could count on financial flows and aid designed quite openly to buy their allegiance to one side or the other. Israel has been by far the greatest regional beneficiary of strategic rents: by some accounts, US assistance to Israel averaged $14,630 per Israeli over the period 1949 to 2004. Starting from low levels in 1959, assistance climbed to roughly $3 billion per year for the twenty years from 1984 to 2004. By 2004, US aid amounted to some $638 per Israeli. The nearest competitor was Jordan, with $285 in aid per Jordanian. Egypt and the Palestinians lagged far behind in per capita terms, with $30 and $34, respectively. The non-economic rationale behind these transfers is evident.

Not all economic rents are external. The notion of "rent-seeking behavior" refers primarily to the search for strategic privilege in domestic markets. Such privilege is usually bestowed by public authorities through the issuance of import licenses, targeted tariff protection, franchises, and the like. When the privileged are protected from competition in specific markets, revenues and profits are generated without changes in productive efficiency or new investment (beyond the cost of acquiring the privilege). We also refer to this type of rent later in the book as a "regulatory rent"—a type that a state sometimes uses to strengthen its elite coalition when other sources of rents collapse.

the group, the RRLA countries, on the other hand, did not receive large amounts of aid or of remittances—they were too rich to engage massively in labor import, and they were unable or not interested in attracting external support.

THREE PHASES OF DEVELOPMENT

Economic growth in the MENA region was determined in important ways by its development strategy: first, a rising period under import substitution and state activism, which ultimately led to economic contradictions; followed by a period of structural adjustment that saw over a decade of low growth; and finally, a more liberal period focused on export-led growth that saw larger, but still relatively modest, growth rates. These phases were determined, delayed, or exacerbated by the oil cycle, which had important effects on all countries, including importers through remittances and regional aid. Let us now look at each of the three phases in more detail.

The Import-Substitution and State-Led Industrialization Period: The 1960s and 1970s

In the early phase of development post-independence, growth in the MENA region was among the highest in the world. In the 1960s, 1970s, and early 1980s, growth shot up from the relatively low levels experienced during the 1950s as the region benefited from the early phase of the state-led development model (see Chapter 7 for more detail). This period was the height of a movement that had started earlier in the 1950s with the rise of nationalist states and the middle class, investments in human development, and dynamic growth policies fashioned on the Turkish Attaturk model. Economic growth was rapid, at 3 to 4 percent a year on a per capita basis, and reflected high rates of investment and accumulation as well as increased productivity linked to investment in human capital. Oil exporters did particularly well, boosted by the extraordinary rise in oil revenues after 1973. Iran (in the 1960s) and Saudi Arabia (in the 1970s) grew at about 8 percent per capita. But others benefited as well from the regional tide and also grew fast: during the 1970s, Syria was growing at 7 percent a year, Jordan at 12 percent, Tunisia at 5 percent, and Lebanon and Palestine at double-digit rates. For the RPLA countries, per capita incomes tripled from around $500 in the 1960s to about $1,500 in the early 1980s.

The first few decades after independence also witnessed major gains in quality of life indicators. For example, in 1960 the infant mortality rate (IMR) was slightly higher in Arab states (154 deaths per 1,000 births) than in sub-Saharan Africa (151 per 1,000 births). In 2011 the IMR in the Arab world was 30 per 1,000 births while it was 86 per 1,000 births in sub-Saharan Africa. Over a forty-five-year period, the Arab states maintained the highest annualized rate of IMR reduction at 3.6 percent, which was three times faster than Africa (1.2 percent), one-third faster than Asia (2.7 percent), and slightly faster than Latin America (3.4 percent). (We look at progress in health and education in more detail in Chapter 5.) In addition, poverty rates declined significantly in the Middle East more than in other regions of the Global South.

During the 1950s and 1960s, import substitution industrialization (ISI), typically led by a highly interventionist state, was the development strategy of choice in the Arab world, and indeed among most LDCs. Its logic is certainly compelling. ISI is designed to move traditional economies to an industrial footing by engaging in the production of manufactured products for local markets under some trade protection before infant industries have to face the rigors of the international markets once they grow and become more efficient. It was hoped that, through ISI, developing countries could escape the agrarian trap into which they had been thrust by imperialist powers or, more anonymously, by the international division of labor. As industrialization gathered steam and raised domestic incomes, new markets would grow and the infant industries would achieve economies of scale that would make them competitive globally. The process is supposed to be cumulative: the first industries developed will produce backward linkages, stimulating new enterprises in capital goods, basic metals, machine tools, and the like. In Egypt, where this strategy was vigorously pursued during the 1960–1965 period, the hope was that the textile sector, using Egyptian cotton and replacing foreign imports, would give birth to an industry to manufacture spinning and weaving machinery, which itself would utilize steel from the new iron-and-steel complex.

Turkey was the first among Middle Eastern states to pursue an ISI strategy. When Mustafa Kemal Atatürk's republic was founded at the end of World War I amid the debris of the Ottoman Empire, he was determined to transform it into an industrial and "Western" industrialized nation. During the 1930s, the Turkish state began to launch industries in textiles, cement, and basic metals. Next door in Iran, Reza Khan, the founder of the Pahlavi dynasty, was moving in a similar direction. With Algeria's independence in 1962, all major states in the Middle East had won formal sovereignty. With rare exceptions, these states also pursued, to varying degrees and with different ideological underpinnings, ISI strategies. Such a strategy made good sense for the larger economies with important domestic markets that could sustain large industrial units, but ISI made less sense for the small economies. The most determined efforts to follow in Turkey's footsteps were undertaken by Egypt, Iran, Tunisia, Algeria, Syria, Iraq, and Israel. ISI strategies typically rely on publicly owned enterprises, mainly because the initial investments are usually very large and beyond the capacity of local entrepreneurial groups. Public enterprises also confer valuable instruments of social control on regimes that are eager to consolidate power.

In spite of these efforts in the Middle East and elsewhere, ISI experienced widespread setbacks, which stemmed primarily from the degree of protection granted to the infant industries and the proportion of public resources devoted to them at the expense of the agricultural sector. Agricultural sectors were taxed to provide an investable surplus for the new industrial undertakings, while the foreign exchange earned from agricultural exports went to pay for the technologies, capital goods, and raw materials required by the industrial sector. When these income transfers caused slower agricultural growth, the large rural populations could not generate the demand to keep the new industries operating at full capacity. Consequently, idle capacity and production costs rose, but because these industries were protected against cheaper imports by high tariffs and enjoyed monopolies in domestic markets, they had no incentive to keep costs down. In addition, because these industries were generally capital-intensive and did not provide large numbers of jobs, they were unable to meet the challenge of providing jobs for rural workers abandoning a depressed agricultural sector for a livelihood in the cities.

The net result was often high-cost production for the domestic markets (everything from automobiles and refrigerators to fertilizers, sugar, and textiles), in which retail prices needed to be subsidized by the government. Because of their high costs, the new industries could not export their products and earn the foreign exchange needed to pay for imported raw materials and equipment. Thus, the new industries contributed to the growing twin fiscal and balance-payments deficits, which culminated in a series of financial crises that ended the ISI experiments in the 1970s and early 1980s.

The poorer among the Arab countries with large rural populations could have adopted a strategy more focused on the development of their agricultural sector rather than adopt an ISI strategy that taxed the agriculture sector. This opportunity was especially relevant in the 1950s and 1960s, when most of the region's population was still in agriculture, and for countries that had no vast mineral resources and thus little prospect of penetrating foreign markets for manufactured goods (see, for example, Adelman 1984; Mellor 1976). This thinking is still relevant today for the poorer countries of the region with sizable arable land, such as Morocco, Sudan, and Yemen. Moreover, several countries have had, at various points, a strong international comparative advantage in the production of a particular crop, such as cotton in the Nile Valley or wine grapes in Algeria. Improving the productivity of land and/or labor resources could have been a workable way to develop agriculture as a *means* to industrialize. Because of the relatively small size of the local market, the rising agricultural production would have been exported. As the incomes of the farmers rose, the demand for local industrial goods would have increased. Agricultural profits (and exports) would have financed this initial capital deepening, leading to a process of self-sustaining growth (Lewis 1954). However, for better or for worse, reliance on agro-exports was commonly associated in the 1950s with colonialism—cotton cultivation for export to Europe was expanded under colonial rule in Egypt and Sudan, while wine production was introduced and flourished in the settler areas of North Africa. A division of labor between metropole and colony was an integral part of colonial ideology.

The agro-export strategy also faces several real problems. First, commodity prices fluctuate greatly from year to year. Since the point of any agro-export-led growth strategy is to acquire funds for industrialization, such fluctuations can seriously disrupt industrialization efforts. The second problem with this strategy is that it strengthens powerful compradors and oligarchs, who may resent any attempt to impose taxes in order to finance infrastructure for new industries. It is not clear from the historical record of the Middle East whether agro-exporters failed to invest in, eschewed, or generally blocked industrial projects and the rise of infant industries. The Egyptian case is particularly instructive. Wealthy indigenous Egyptian cotton producers often invested in the agricultural sector and provided the bulk of the capital for the initial industrial endeavors of the Bank Misr in the 1920s (Davis 1983; Tignor 1984). But these groups ultimately failed to solve the many pressing domestic political, economic, and social problems facing the country and could not rid the country of the British imperial presence. Their demise as agents of development also spelled the demise of the agro-export-led strategy. A third problem that often arises with agro-exports is the temptation of the government to tax the sector excessively, resulting in declining output. This problem is the reverse of the previous one and arises if the producers are small peasants who are unable to organize collectively to defend their interests. A final problem with this strategy is that it assumes an adequate natural resource base, but in the MENA region the water constraint limits the agricultural production potential of all countries ever more tightly over time. The abuse of natural resources, often induced by misguided policy, is equally rampant. (We look at agriculture in more detail in Chapter 6.)

The period of fast growth in the 1960s could not be sustained. Not all Middle Eastern countries adopted ISI, but for the many that did, the 1970s brought a far-reaching reappraisal of what they had undertaken. As elsewhere in the world (and in particular, Latin America), state-led industrialization strategies that had focused on import substitution faltered after an initial period of fast growth. Shielded from international competition and mired in bureaucratic inefficiencies, labor productivity remained low, and the MENA region did not take advantage of the fast growth in global trade, as East Asia did. For most of the RPLA countries, the moment of truth was the increase in their petroleum import bill after 1973. Many countries of the region attempted to delay adjustment by borrowing, only to face the day of reckoning a few years later. In the 1980s, the debts of the RPLA countries grew immensely as they resorted to international debt in order to delay adjustment. The internationally recognized danger zone for external debt starts at around 50 percent of GDP—at this point, countries become vulnerable to external shocks, sudden stops of capital flows, and financial crises. In both the RPLA and RRLA countries, the average debt-to-GDP ratio stood at over 80 percent in the late 1980s, and in many countries it exceeded 100 percent. In the countries with abundant oil (Algeria, Iran, Saudi Arabia), oil revenues and external borrowings allowed adjustment to be delayed until later in the 1990s. But the mid-1980s collapse of oil prices sounded the death knell of ISI in the region (see Table 2.1).

Adjustment, the Lost Decades, and Export-Led Growth: The 1980s and 1990s

The first countries to start adjustment were Morocco and Tunisia. Jordan followed in the late 1980s, and Egypt and Saudi Arabia began the adjustment process in the 1990s. Public spending was slashed to reestablish macroeconomic balances, and external debts were partially canceled by Western countries and institutions to support adjustment in Morocco, Egypt, and Jordan. As a result, macro-balances were restored over time and economic growth was restarted by the mid-1990s. (Chapter 8 recounts this period of structural adjustment in more detail.)

The transition costs were large, however, and they have marked the political economy of the region ever since, playing an important role in the genesis of the Arab uprisings of 2011. Growth fell deeply in the 1980s and even into the 1990s for some countries. On the whole, the region's "lost decade" was longer than it was in other areas in the world, but there were also significant differences among MENA countries. In the 1980s, GDP per capita growth was -1.0 percent a year in the RPLA countries (Egypt, Jordan, Morocco, Tunisia), -6.0 percent a year for the RRLA countries (Algeria, Iran, Syria, Yemen)—largely on account of the devastation brought by the Iran-Iraq War—and -2.0 percent in the wealthy RRLP countries. Moreover, as we discuss later, countries also slashed public expenditures, thus weakening the welfare state and reducing social mobility.

On the structural side, most of the region started to move in the direction of export-led growth and private initiative. The foreign donor and creditor community pushed for taking this direction, but there was also an independently formulated expectation that the private sector could adjust more rapidly than the public sector to the challenge of reducing costs, improving quality, and seeking out customers abroad for a country's products. This new development model was inspired by the success of South Korea, Taiwan, India, and China, countries that had managed to become the manufacturing hub of the world, earning themselves the epithet of newly industrializing countries (NICs). With world markets as their target, even countries with relatively small domestic markets could achieve economies of scale. (Hong Kong, Singapore, Honduras, and Costa Rica demonstrated the possibilities.) In these countries, local industries were freed from the exigencies of internal demand and allowed to specialize instead in what they did best for sale to the immense global market. Over time, as skills were developed and physical capital was deepened, these countries would move up the quality ladder and improve their position in the international division of labor, shifting from producing simple manufactures to increasingly more sophisticated goods.

To have any chance of success, this strategy requires that factors of production, essentially labor and capital, be moved from inefficient and uncompetitive sectors of production to sectors that would be more efficient and could compete abroad. The Washington Consensus theory was that the reallocation would be best achieved by the market mechanism. As a result, the strategy called for trade to be liberalized, public enterprises to be privatized, the financial sector to be opened up, and national currencies to be sharply devalued to encourage exports.

There were daunting domestic challenges to this strategy. Any "bad habits" that had developed during the ISI phase would need to be dealt with, but possibly at high political cost. Any government contemplating this strategy had to think carefully about the constituencies it would alienate, some of which were part of the state apparatus itself. The owners and managers of import-substituting industries might try to sabotage the new experiment, and they could find tacit allies among the workers who risked being laid off as enterprises streamlined or who faced salary reductions. In addition, urban constituents might see a sharp rise in the cost of living. The negative effects of the new strategy would be felt immediately, whereas the economic payoffs might be years in coming. No politician likes that sort of bargain, and the political difficulties of transitioning from an ISI to an export-driven strategy are compounded when the starting position is one of gross inefficiencies in production, as was the case in the Arab world (as well as in Latin America and Eastern Europe when they started their own reforms). In contrast, ISI had performed better in the East Asian NICs, laying the groundwork for a smoother passage to competitive export.

Despite the risks, some Middle Eastern countries moved in the direction of export promotion and private enterprise. Two of the earliest experiments took place in Morocco and Tunisia, both of which negotiated preferential trade agreements with the European Economic Community (EEC) (the forerunner of the European Union) in the late 1960s. Tunisia was moving away from a period of concerted ISI under state auspices, while Morocco was seeking to diversify its exports beyond its traditional combination of phosphates and citrus. Both hoped to attract light industry from Europe in ready-made apparel, electronics, and consumer-durable assembly. They accelerated these efforts after the mid-1980s, but unfortunately they were hurt by the entry of the previously Communist Eastern European countries into the European market under preferential access agreements in the 1990s, as well as by rising competition from China.

For more than three decades, Turkey has aspired to full membership in what is now the European Union (EU). Since the early 1970s, it has been trying to restructure its economy (after Atatürk's ISI experiment) so as to be able to compete in European markets. The process took on added urgency in the late 1970s as Turkey, without petroleum deposits, absorbed the full impact of rising international prices for fossil fuels at the same time that European labor markets were closing themselves off to migrant Turkish workers. Export-led growth was initiated during a turbulent period marked by political instability, mounting domestic deficits and balance-of-payments crises, and high inflation, ending in a wrenching financial crisis in 2001. The emergence of a centrist Islamist government under the Justice and Development Party (AKP) has produced a long period of macroeconomic stability that has allowed the reforms of the past to be consolidated and has also led to a highly successful export drive for Turkish manufactures that over the past fifteen years has started to transform the country into an industrial giant.

Israel's economy has always been dependent on aid and trade. Like Tunisia and Morocco, and well before them, it negotiated a preferential trade agreement with the EEC, and it had great success in marketing first avocados, citrus, and vegetables in Europe, and later manufactured metal products and high-tech electronics. Equally important is Israel's major role in the international arms trade: the scale and sophistication of its own armaments industry is supported by the development of foreign markets for its weaponry. Despite its relative success in all export sectors, Israel found itself in the early 1980s facing huge domestic deficits, high labor costs that limited the areas in which it could be competitive internationally, the largest per capita external debt in the world, and a domestic inflation rate in 1985 second only to Bolivia's. After 1985, however, Israel simultaneously pursued economic reforms at home and export promotion abroad, with great success. By the early 2000s, it had also established itself as a global hub for high-tech industries.

In the oil-exporting countries, the officially stated goals of an oil-based export strategy tended to be quite similar to those of agro-exporters: to acquire revenue from mineral exports and create an industrial base for sustained development after the natural resource was exhausted. But oil-based growth creates its own types of economic and social challenges, in addition to the political challenges, which we discuss in more detail in Chapter 9. First, export revenues accrue to the state. Second, oil exports lead to a change of relative prices that discourages economic diversification. And third, oil exports depend on oil prices and are therefore highly variable. These three characteristics combine to form a phenomenon known as the "Dutch Disease"—so called because of the experience of the Dutch economy with the large influx of North Sea gas revenues in the 1970s—and thus foster stagnation of the agricultural and manufacturing sectors while government and the building industry boom, at the expense of the manufacturing private sector. In addition, the international movements of oil prices lead to a succession of boom and bust periods.

There is evidence for such effects in the Middle East as elsewhere, most notably in agriculture. But good policy can reverse these nefarious effects. Expenditures can be smoothed by placing revenues in an oil fund, and oil revenues can be used to strengthen the sectors that become weakened. For example, skills and infrastructure can be subsidized to increase the productivity of the tradable sectors. Both the seriousness of the "Dutch Disease" and the "cure" have varied considerably from one country to another. For some oil exporters, such as Algeria, the growth rates of manufacturing and agriculture were greater during the 1973–1983 period than they had been during the previous "cheap oil" decade. Many other countries followed the example of Algeria and subsidized their tradable goods sector. But such subsidies ended up creating problems of their own. The Dutch Disease situation illustrates the argument that state policy both shapes development and responds to its unintended outcomes.

Our typology of resource-rich countries distinguishes between those oil and mineral exporters that have other resources, especially substantial populations (and thus considerable agricultural potential), and those whose economies are entirely dominated by mineral exports. To recall, the first group includes Algeria, Iraq, Iran, and Syria (until recently an average oil producer), as well as Sudan and Yemen, which are newer oil producers; the second set consists essentially of the Gulf states. State-led industrialization may seem like a perfectly reasonable approach for countries with significant nonpetroleum resources, but it is much more difficult to imagine what economic future is in store for the Gulf states after their oil runs out. The absence of arable land, water, and non-oil mineral resources and the presence of a small, poorly educated population suggest that its future without oil may be bleak. Oil exporters in the first group, however, such as Iran, Algeria, and Iraq, should have been able to use their large oil revenues to industrialize. That this simple economic intuition did not turn into reality testifies to the importance of politics in shaping development paths—all three of these countries failed to translate their considerable potential into reality when they were unable to adjust their production structures after state-led growth faltered in the 1980s.

On the other hand, the oil-rich, labor-poor countries (the GCC countries) have had more success, despite what seemed at first like a more difficult situation from a purely economic perspective. Their success arose in part from their ability to ensure high levels of domestic consumption at home through large subsidies, which have brought political benefits in the form of popular support and stability. They have imported labor (their scarcest factor), moved massively into water desalination, and even imported institutions in the form of world-class consultancy firms. Dependent on political stability, this relatively successful strategy was built on four pillars. First, funds were used to expand infrastructure, leading to one of the most massive construction booms in economic history. Despite numerous bottlenecks (which were inevitable given the low level of infrastructure and the size of the projects), roads, schools, hospitals, shopping centers, offices, and other buildings have mushroomed in the GCC countries. Second, monies were invested into wealth funds, a savings account for rainy days. Thus, when GCC countries were hit by the long period of oil slump in the 1980s and 1990s, they had accumulated sufficient financial assets to serve as a shock absorber and a reliable source of income. Third, these countries invested in highly capital- and energy-intensive petrochemical complexes, fertilizer plants, aluminum smelting, and steel production. Instead of creating a future without oil, they opted for increasing the value added in the final output of petroleum- or energy-intensive industries. And finally, they started to diversify away from oil. Today Saudi Arabia is the largest exporter of industrial products in the whole region, and the United Arab Emirates have been able to develop a service sector that is globally competitive.

Recent Growth: 2000 to 2010

Structural adjustment and macro-stability did yield some benefits. Once the macroeconomic situation stabilized by around 2000, the private sector was put in charge of economic growth, and indeed, growth picked up in most of the countries of the region. Between 2000 and 2010, several countries, including Turkey, Egypt, Iran, Jordan, Lebanon, Morocco, Sudan, and Tunisia, grew at more than 3 percent on a per capita basis. Only Israel has grown more slowly, but it had adjusted earlier in the 1980s and therefore saw longer periods of uninterrupted growth, which raised its income levels significantly over time.

Pro-market reforms, which accelerated in the 1990s in most of the region, started to transform the region into private-sector-driven economies. By 2010, the eve of the Arab uprisings, the regional landscape was radically different from that of the 1980s, with the public sector much smaller and the private sector dominant nearly everywhere. But because the new arrangements did not lead to competitive and dynamic markets, growth remained modest. Moreover, the quality of economic growth deteriorated—it was much less inclusive than in the past, the private sector became increasingly informal, monopolies and privileges rather than competitive markets became the rule, there was little trickle-down, and income inequality rose.

The central question of why the Arab region underperformed, given what looked on paper to be impeccable market reforms, has been debated for years. Economists have tended to argue that the market reforms did not go far enough (Noland and Pack 2007; World Bank 2009). A slightly different view is that reforms appear better on paper than they perform in reality: as markets are liberalized, rules that govern the market are applied in a discretionary way that benefits "networks of privilege"—firms with personal and social ties to the political elites (Heydemann 2004). Essentially, the distance between the de jure and the de facto rules has increased. Recently, the World Bank estimated that, based on the experience of countries that, on paper, did as much to reform their economies as the MENA countries, growth in the MENA region should have been one to two percentage points *higher* than its actual growth rate. Policymakers have been preoccupied with understanding the reasons for this shortfall.

The main culprit, then, for the weak performance of Arab economies could very well be the strategy of "economic reforms first, and political reforms later," which led to the rise of networks of privilege (Heydemann 2004) with myopic short-term interests that stifled competition and innovation. Supporting this view has been the evolution of the private sector into a highly dualistic structure, with a few large firms on top and a large informal economy, but very few dynamic firms in the middle. Recent research seems to confirm that the system of political favoritism and the barriers to entry that have emerged in the liberal era have reduced competition and pushed much of private capital to the few large firms that could be trusted by politicians, rather than toward firms that could use capital more efficiently (for a regional discussion, see Malik and Awadallah 2013; on Egypt, see Diwan, Keefer, and Schiffbauer 2014; on Tunisia, see Rijker, Freund, and Nucifora 2013). As we emphasize throughout the book, economic strategies are always shaped by politics. As Karl Polanyi (2001) shows, the construction of markets is not a neutral process but rather entails political struggles and reflects power differentials.

The patterns of growth that emerged after most of the countries in the region undertook structural adjustment programs reflect the low dynamism of their private sectors. For the region as a whole, growth was driven less by the size of total investment—private investment remained modest—than by modest improvements in the efficiency of this investment and by rising labor force participation. As a result, manufacturing remained low, and exports rose only moderately. The following sections go over these aspects of performance in more detail.

From High but Inefficient Investment to More Efficient but Lower Investment

From the 1960s through the 1980s, MENA countries invested as high a proportion of their national output as other LDCs did. Between 1970 and the 1990s, investment rates in the three types of countries were between 25 and 27 percent of GDP—below East Asia's record levels, but higher than in any other developing region (see Figure 2.5). Nearly half of this investment was made by the public sectors

FIGURE 2.5. Public and Private Investment (as a percentage of GDP) in the MENA Countries and in Other Regions of the World, 1971–2010

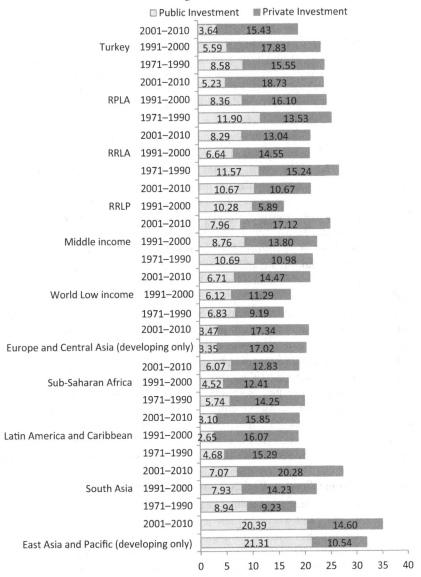

Source: World Bank, WBI data, and IMF, WEO.

of the region. Much of this investment went to public enterprises, and initially they reaped good returns in terms of growth. In some countries, however, returns on these investments were low, especially when combined with import substitution policies. Large and inefficient investments were mainly the problem of oil-rich countries, such as Saudi Arabia in the 1980s, Iran in the 1970s and 1980s, and

Algeria, Syria, and Iraq from the 1960s through the 1980s. In Egypt, too, large investments in heavy industries were not sustainable and did not produce good returns. The Algerian case is a particularly instructive example. For a generation, Algeria relentlessly invested over one-third of its output—one of the highest investment rates in history. By the late 1970s, however, generating an additional dollar of output required twice as much investment as the labor-intensive, rapidly growing South Korean economy required. The opportunity cost of this strategy was twofold: Algeria could have invested scarce national capital in more productive endeavors, and it missed out on the fast export-oriented global economy of the 1980s, which benefited East Asia so handsomely.

In the 1990s, countries with money-losing public enterprises could no longer afford to bail out these enterprises. The rollback of the state hit public investment hardest. By the end of the 1990s, reforms had led to a situation where the return on investment, in terms of growth, was much improved (Noland and Pack 2005). Other factors also improved and contributed to growth, especially higher skill levels. But by then, public investment had collapsed to about 8 percent of GDP in the RPLA countries (see Figure 2.5). Private investment only partly filled the gap—it rose only slightly from its historical levels in RPLA countries, such as reforming Morocco, Tunisia, and Jordan, and in Lebanon after the end of its civil war. However, private investment remained low in Egypt, at between 10 and 15 percent of GDP (though capital flight was high, at 5 to 10 percent of GDP), as well as in RRLA countries, and it even declined in Syria, Yemen, and Algeria. Even though many studies show that in the recent period the efficiency of investment rose, they also recognize that its efficiency was weighted down by rising weaknesses in infrastructure related to reduced spending by governments.

Foreign direct investment (FDI) also remained relatively low. Moreover, both domestic and foreign private investment favored sectors such as mining and real estate rather than labor-intensive sectors. FDI mostly went into the oil sector and nontradables, and technological diversification and technical change remained low. FDI's spillover effects, when they occurred, tended to contribute to the growth of low-efficiency sectors that paid low wages, such as construction, tourism, and trade.

Structural Change: Services Rather Than Manufacturing

Development takes place and incomes rise when labor moves from low- to high-productivity sectors and when productivity increases within sectors. The inability of the economies of the region to achieve a virtuous circle of high-efficiency investment and growth is also reflected in—and indeed, is due to—a stunted pattern of structural change. When agriculture fell but manufacturing did not rise, low-productivity services rose by default. Manufacturing is believed in development circles to be the road to a dynamic economy given its many positive externalities and the possibility of technological upgrading over time. The MENA region invested heavily in the manufacturing sector in the 1970s and 1980s, but much of this investment was washed away when the economy was liberalized in the 1980s and 1990s because the sector could not sustain global competition by more efficient producers. During the oil boom years, growth rates of manufacturing value added

FIGURE 2.6. Manufacturing in the MENA Countries and Other Regions of the World, Value Added (as a percentage of GDP), 1970–2010

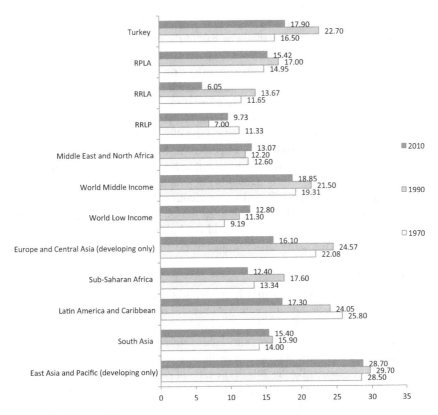

Source: World Bank, WBI data.

(MVA) were respectable but not spectacular; the region boasts no star performers like Korea and Brazil, which grew at double digits (Figure 2.6). Growth rates in Tunisia, Algeria, Egypt, and Saudi Arabia were around 7 percent. The contrast with the years of the oil bust is striking: only in Morocco did the growth of MVA accelerate after 1985, although this growth tapered off in the 2000s. In Algeria and Egypt, MVA as a share of GDP declined. By 2010, MVA in RPLA, RRLA, and RRLP countries averaged 15, 6, and 10 percent of GDP respectively—below the middle-income average of 19 percent of GDP and way below the average of 29 percent of GDP in the East Asian countries.

Manufacturing in MENA is geographically concentrated. Turkey, Egypt, Iran, Israel, and Saudi Arabia account for much of the region's MVA. The pattern of distribution of MVA holds few surprises. Many countries' industries process agricultural outputs or produce textiles. Because of the labor-intensity and relatively well established technology of such industries, most countries concentrate on them initially. The more industrialized countries have gone far beyond this stage, producing significant quantities of machinery, chemicals, and a host of other products. The most industrially diversified countries are Israel and Turkey.

But mostly it is the residual category of "services" that picks up the slack, accounting for one-third to more than one-half of the output in these countries. The share of services has increased by over 50 percent in most countries over the past two decades, with the GCC countries experiencing even higher growth. This has most often happened in the informal sector, which is inhabited by firms that have very low capitalization, sell in easily entered markets, and offer low-paying and insecure jobs. Recent evidence by the World Bank shows that a typical MENA country in 2010 produced one-third of its GDP informally. For example, the share of the informal sector in the economy was 44 percent in Morocco, 33 percent in Egypt, 34 percent in Syria, 30 percent in Tunisia and Lebanon, and 26 percent in Jordan. This share is higher than it is in many other developing countries; in Indonesia and Vietnam, for example, the informal sector accounts for about 21 and 16 percent of the economy, respectively. In the United States, the informal sector accounts for about 9 percent of the economy (World Bank, World Development Indicators 2010). Moreover, informality has continued to expand in the recent past.

Export Performance

Although production is now definitely private-sector driven in all countries, there are important questions about the sustainability of recent growth, which has been mainly fueled by nontradables and oil rather than manufacturing exports and which has made little movement up the quality ladder. Indeed, although exports increased in most countries, performance was generally mixed. Figure 2.7 shows the level and composition of exports. By the 2000s, the ratio of manufacturing exports to GDP averaged 23 percent in the RPLA countries, more than the 10 percent average in the middle-income countries, but much less than the 32 percent average reached by the East Asian exporters. The ratio stood at only 8 percent in the RRLP countries and less than 1 percent in the RRLA countries. The seemingly good average performance of the RPLA countries was due to the big progress made by some countries in the group, and in particular by Morocco and Tunisia, but others, like Egypt, did not manage to raise manufacturing exports. Petroleum exports still dominate the trade (and entire economies) of many countries in the region. The region has three countries that export mainly manufactured goods: Turkey, Israel, and Tunisia, with Morocco and Jordan improving their performance. In the RRLA and RRLP countries, a very small share of exports is constituted of manufacturing goods. Nevertheless, Saudi Arabia's expansion of manufacturing export, while a small share of its overall exports, is remarkable. With over $20 billion in sales of manufacturing goods, it tops all other countries of the region. Rather than diversification away from oil, however, this performance largely reflects the enormous energy subsidies provided by these countries to their industrial sector. Countries such as Egypt, Yemen, and Jordan relied heavily on the export of human labor (international labor migration)

FIGURE 2.7. Export Performance (as a percentage of GDP) in the MENA Countries and Other Regions of the World, 1971–2010

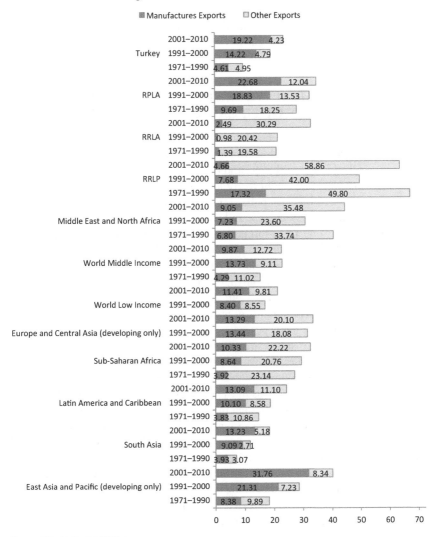

Source: World Bank, WBI data.

for foreign exchange until the Gulf War of 1991, which thoroughly disrupted these flows.

The low dynamism of the private sector could have also been due to other factors—the effects of the "Dutch Disease" may have pushed investment into the nontradable sectors, or perhaps political risk deterred private investment. Moreover, the international economic context created another layer of constraints. Since the 1980s, when the MENA countries began to pursue export-led industrialization, the global economy has become increasingly competitive. It is certainly true that capable states and constructive business-government relations facilitated an economic takeoff in the East Asian countries beginning in the 1960s, but a propitious external environment and available export markets at that time and in the context of the Cold War also ensured that countries such as South Korea and Taiwan had ample outlets for their manufactured exports (Haggard 1990; Stallings 1990).

THE INHERITANCE FROM THE PAST: THE EFFECTS OF FISCAL RETRENCHMENT

The last twenty years have seen a slow transition in the region, not just from state-led to market-driven growth, but also, outside of the RRLP countries, from a very large to a smaller (though still large) and more impoverished state. While the former transformation says much about the process of job creation, the latter has affected the economy differently. Fiscal policy is central for developmental outcomes in several important ways. First, the size and structure of state expenditures have direct and indirect effects on capital formation, infrastructure, skills, and human development, all of which are central to growth. Second, taxation and subsidies affect incentives to invest and to use resources efficiently. Third, developments in the civil service affect the labor market. Fourth, the size and financing of deficits determine macro-stability, as well as the availability of finance for the private sector, both of which are important determinants of growth. Finally, redistribution policies have an important impact on social peace.

A look at the level of state expenditures for the region as a whole and for the three subgroups, from the 1960s to 2010, shows clearly that the rollback of the state began in the 1980s, more than twenty years ago (see Figure 2.8). Government expenditures shot up in the 1970s in the three groups of countries, on the back of rising oil wealth in the region, but fell precipitously in the 1980s before stabilizing in the 1990s at much lower levels. So while state expenditures exceeded those in other global regions during the whole period, unlike all other regions, the MENA region exhibited a downward trend in state expenditures in the past two decades. It is noteworthy that oil-exporting countries started to increase expenditures again during the more recent second oil boom.

Government expenditures decreased dramatically especially in the RPLA countries. On average, state expenditures peaked in the early 1980s at about 50 percent of GDP, but by the early 1990s they were down to about 30 percent of GDP. In these countries, adjustment tended to be slow and gradual because it was supported by the international financial institutions (IFIs) and it only concluded in the late 1990s. This had a dramatic impact on some of the key services offered by the state, and since the 1980s public welfare institutions have declined steadily. This adjustment has affected all segments of the population but has been particularly damaging for the poor, who rely on government services to support their social mobility.

State expenditures exhibit the same pattern of rise and fall for the other two types of countries, the RRLP and the RRLA. In the RRLP group, adjustment

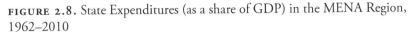

FIGURE 2.8. State Expenditures (as a share of GDP) in the MENA Region, 1962–2010

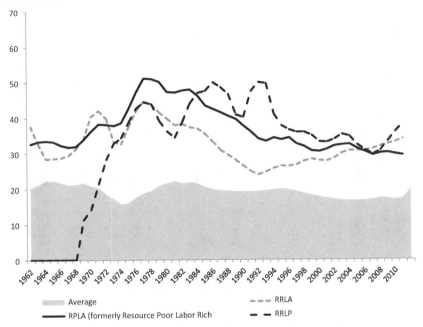

Source: IMF, WEO.

started later, in the mid-1980s, when expenditures stood at over 50 percent of GDP on average. The decline was slower, but expenditures also reached a low of about 30 percent of GDP by the early 2000s. It is noteworthy that the early 2000s also witnessed low oil prices and thus low GDP—so the effect of the low ratio of spending to GDP was compounded by low GDP. In the RRLA countries, the rise of state expenditures came earlier, reflecting the early industrialization push in Iran, Iraq, and Algeria, and the decline started earlier as well, partly because of the effects of a war economy in Iran and Iraq, and partly because these countries received very little international support to smooth their adjustment. In these countries, the expenditure "bulge" was as dramatic as in the RPLA countries, reaching a peak of 45 percent of GDP in the mid-1970s and falling below 25 percent of GDP in the early 1990s. To get a feel for how this enormous fiscal adjustment was achieved, we have constructed Table 2.2, which shows the composition of state expenditures at their peak and at their bottom for each country of the region. For Egypt, the highest level of expenditure was 61.5 percent of GDP in 1982, and its lowest was 25.1 percent of GDP in 1998. The "fiscal bulge"—the difference between peak and bottom expenditure levels—then was enormous at 36 percent of GDP. The rest of the columns show the size of some of the main budget items—public investment, the civil service wage bill, expenditures on health and education, and subsidies—in 1982 and in 1998, that is, at the peak and at the bottom of the bulge. It is thus

TABLE 2.2. MENA Countries' Government Expenditures (as a percentage of GDP) at Their Peak and at Their Bottom, Between 1986 and 2011

Country	Peak Government Expenditures	Peak Date	Bottom Government Expenditures	Bottom Date	Size of "Bulge"	Peak Subsidy	Bottom Subsidy	Peak Public Investments	Bottom Public Investments	Peak Health and Education Spending	Bottom Health and Education Spending	Peak Civil Service Wage Bill	Bottom Civil Service Wage Bill
RRLP	**53.1%**		**30.0%**		**22.5%**	**1.2%**	**1.5%**	**14.8%**	**5.0%**	**9.5%**	**6.5%**	**15.7%**	**9.3%**
Bahrain	53.1	1986	25.1	2000	28.0	na	1.8	na	4.3	7.9	5.4	20.9	13.2
Kuwait	57.2	1986	35.7	2007	21.5	na	4.5	17.6	4.3	11.2	5.6	14.5	8.3
Libya	na	na	26.7	1992	na	na	0.2	na	8.3	na	na	na	12.9
Oman	56.7	1986	30.3	1997	26.4	2.9	0.5	23.7	11.4	8.6	6.6	8.9	8.0
Qatar	51.4	1993	29.4	2003	22.0	0.0	1.9	6.8	7.9	na	na	16.4	7.3
Saudi Arabia	57.6	1987	32.6	1995	25.0	1.8	1.6	16.0	5.0	10.2	8.5	18.0	13.2
United Arab Emirates	27.8	1996	14.7	2006	13.1	0.0	0.0	10.1	6.7	na	na	4.85	2.2
RRLA	**43.3**		**22.2**		**21.1**	**11.4**	**6.1**	**15.6**	**7.7**	**6.5**	**3.8**	**10.7**	**7.5**
Algeria	38.1	1983	25.7	1990	12.4	7.1	5.2	18.9	8.2	na	na	7.8	9.3
Iran	43.6	1980	19.2	1991	24.4	6.9	0.0	10.4	7.5	9.9	5.6	16.2	8.0
Syria	48.2	1980	21.8	1990	26.4	20.2	13.1	17.6	7.4	3.0	2.0	8.1	5.2
RPLA	**53.2**		**27.9**		**25.2**	**9.7**	**1.1**	**14.5**	**6.1**	**6.9**	**5.7**	**12.3**	**9.5**
Egypt	61.5	1982	25.1	1998	36.4	22.7	1.5	20.7	14.1	6.5	5.5	9.7	5.9
Jordan	52.5	1980	29.9	1992	22.6	7.0	2.0	17.7	6.1	5.3	6.2	20.9	12.8
Lebanon	55.7	1994	29.6	2011	26.0	1.6	4.8	9.3	1.7	na	2.7	9.1	8.3
Morocco	51.0	1981	26.2	1996	24.8	5.6	0.6	8.4	3.0	7.8	6.9	12.1	10.4
Tunisia	45.1	1984	28.8	1998	16.2	11.4	0.2	16.5	5.7	7.9	7.1	9.9	10.2
Other	**66.7**		**37.7**		**29.0**	**14.3**	**0.4**	**5.7**	**4.6**	**7.1**	**7.7**	**9.3**	**8.0**
Israel	90.9	1983	41.5	2011	49.4	28.4	0.7	na	na	9.6	11.8	8.1	8.2
Turkey	42.6	1997	33.8	1998	8.7	0.2	0.0	5.7	4.6	4.6	3.7	10.4	7.7

Source: Diwan and Akin (2014).

possible to evaluate how the different sectors bore the brunt of the massive fiscal contraction that took place during structural adjustment.

One of the most deeply affected items was public investment, which collapsed in most countries—from about 14 to 15 percent of GDP in the three types of countries during the 1980s and early 1990s to 6 to 7 percent. The public investment collapse was most marked in Algeria, Syria, Jordan, and Tunisia. This lower investment in infrastructure, schools, and other state assets would have an increasingly negative effect on economic growth, especially in the marginalized regions that were allowed to fall behind—and from where most of the 2011 uprisings started—such as Sidi Bouzid in Tunisia and Daraa and Deir ez-Zor in Syria.

The civil service wage bill was squeezed, too, but less than public investment. Averaging over country types, the reduction in the wage bill was highest in the RRLP countries (from 15.7 to 9.3 percent of GDP), followed by the RRLA countries (from 10.7 to 7.5 percent of GDP), and then by the RPLA group (from 12.3 to 9.5 percent of GDP). The wage bill in the whole region now stands below the developing countries' average (which stands at about 10 percent of GDP). When hiring in the public sector was at least reduced and in most cases frozen, a devastating blow was dealt to the prospects of educated entrants to the job market, the type who had traditionally joined the public sector. In most countries, the overall wage bill fell faster than public-sector employment; as a result, the civil service remains large but is underpaid, a situation that feeds petty corruption.[1]

Government spending on health and education has been the least affected, except in the RRLA countries, where such spending fell precipitously from 6.5 to 3.8 percent of GDP, an extraordinarily low level that mainly reflects low levels of spending in this category in Syria. In the other two regions, it fell from between 7 and 10 percent to about 6 percent of GDP. It is noteworthy that over the same cycle, spending on social services rose in Israel, reaching nearly 12 percent of GDP in 2011. The freeze in budgets going to health and education led to less progress in human development and to the worsening of the quality of services, especially those going to the poor, who could not afford to purchase these services in the burgeoning private sector. A recent United Nations Development Program (UNDP) study confirms this in dramatic ways. The study looks at the evolution of the Human Development Index (HDI), which measured the performance of the health and education systems in all regions between 1990 and 2010 in comparison to the period 1970 to 2010. A slowdown can be observed in all countries of the world, but it is particularly marked in the MENA region. After taking off in the 1970s, the rate of increase in the HDI in the Arab region slowed down markedly (UNDP and ILO 2011). As in other regions, early improvements were easier to achieve, coming from a low base, and increases in the HDI were also boosted by the high expenditures on social sectors in the early period characterized by the rise of the state and the first oil boom. Progress has been more limited in the recent past, partly because incremental advancement is harder, but also in large part because of the fiscal constraints. These themes are explored in greater detail in Chapter 5.

Subsidies on consumer goods were slashed the most during the adjustment episode. In the 1980s, these often took the form of food subsidies and went predominantly to the poor. This line item is measured imprecisely in fiscal accounts, as it is often financed off budget. Nevertheless, our (imprecise) figures in Table 2.2 illustrate the magnitude of the decline in subsidies, especially in the RPLA countries, where they were cut from a height of 9.7 percent of GDP to 1.1 percent of GDP. In the RRLA countries, subsidies started at higher levels and remained high, as this was one of the main ways in which these oil producers transferred some oil income to their citizens (or subjects), a theme we explore in detail in Chapter 9.

With the increase in energy prices in the 2000s, however, and the attempt by many governments to lure the rich and the middle class to continue supporting their weakened hold on power, subsidies on energy and petroleum products rose, further shrinking an already squeezed fiscal space. Energy subsidies grew over time and by 2011 they were much higher in the Middle East than in any other region of the world. In absolute terms, about 50 percent of global energy subsidies are disbursed in the MENA region. In 2010 these subsidies represented about 8.5 percent of regional GDP and 22 percent of total government revenues, which is much larger than in other developing regions (IMF 2013). (Subsidies tend to be negligible in the advanced economies.) Within the region, subsidy levels vary, but twelve of the twenty countries in the region have subsidies above 5 percent of GDP.

About half of all subsidies in the Middle East go to petroleum products, followed by electricity. Government expenditures on these subsidies have gone up in recent years, together with energy prices. This phenomenon is not restricted to oil exporters. For example, in 2011 energy subsidies represented 41 percent of government revenues in Egypt, 24 percent in Yemen, 22 percent in Jordan, and 19 percent in Lebanon, in contrast with "only" 10 percent in Kuwait, 15 percent in the United Arab Emirates, and 18 percent in Saudi Arabia. Among oil producers, Algeria and Iran have particularly large energy subsidies—27 percent and 50 percent of their respective revenues—even *after* the famous Iranian subsidy reforms (Salehi-Isfahani 2013). It is well known that such subsidies are very regressive, as oil products tend to be consumed in much larger quantities by richer people. For example, a study in Egypt shows that 46 percent of the benefits of oil petroleum subsidies accrued to the top quintile in 2008 (Abouleinem, Al-Tathy, and Kheir-el-Din 2009). The sheer size of these subsidies squeezes essential pro-poor expenditures out of the budget. In many countries, they now represent an expense several times higher than total spending on health or education.[2] Once in place, it is almost impossible to reduce or eliminate subsidies because of the threat of political backlash by key constituents.

At the same time, fiscal regimes seem to have become more pro-rich over time. Tax rates have remained relatively low in the countries with large hydrocarbon reserves. In the countries with low per capita natural resources, tax revenues actually fell after structural adjustment, reflecting the lowering of corporate taxes and the rise in untaxed informal markets. Direct taxes now constitute a relatively small share of fiscal receipts. Indirect taxes became a more important component of tax revenue in these countries after the reforms of the 1990s, and they are inherently regressive because they are applied to consumers across the board, regardless of income level (Imam and Jacobs 2007).

The level of spending on security matters is much harder to measure. Typically, military expenditures were also cut, but in many countries spending on security and

police rose as repression increased, in large part to quell the rise in protests and social demands. In several countries, however, the military went off budget to protect
its interests. In Egypt, for example, it is estimated that the military economy ranges
between 10 and 30 percent of GDP, with the army operating its own factories,
housing schemes, and consumer goods distribution (El Badawi and Keefer 2014).

SOCIAL OUTCOMES

The modest improvement in economic growth experienced since the mid-1990s
has not been "jobless," as is often claimed. But most of the jobs created were low-
productivity jobs, mostly in the informal sector, rather than the type of jobs that
could use the skills of the more educated labor force. It is often the unemployment
figures that grab the headlines, but the broader issue in the region is the massive
underemployment of skilled workers. Unemployment has primarily affected the
educated youth who cannot afford lengthy searches for jobs that are in line with
their expectations—this is also the group whose anger seemed most instrumental
in fueling the political unrest. Similarly, much has been made of the youth bulge.
The fear has been that if too many young people are entering the labor market at
times of low growth, many of them will end up unemployed, thus increasing the
risk of social unrest.

The good news is that the region has reached the beginning of the end of the
relentless demographic pressures that prevailed in the past. The bad news is that
the region failed to take advantage of the demographic dividend. Instead, with the
bulge peaking during the "lost decades," what could have been a dividend turned
into a curse, leaving behind a population with low-productivity jobs and a large
stock of unemployed individuals. The more important problem is vast underemployment—that is, productivity has not increased in line with skills owing to a lack
of sufficient complementary capital. We return to these central issues in more detail
in Chapter 4.

In sum, the region has extensive untapped human resources, as reflected in the
underemployment of skilled workers, the high levels of unemployment overall, and
the very low labor force participation rates of women. Although output growth was
relatively higher in the recent two decades compared to the 1980s and 1990s, this
growth has not translated into increases in workers' income. This would suggest
that in recent years poverty stagnated and inequality increased, possibly contributing to the frustrations underpinning the Arab uprisings. We now turn to the
analysis of poverty and inequality to assess whether this was the case.

The Evolution of Poverty

All MENA governments proclaim their desire to reduce poverty and promote equity.
Evaluating their progress in these areas, however, is fraught with both conceptual
and practical problems. Data on poverty and expenditure distribution are scarce and
episodic. We must rely on sample surveys, but these surveys have been conducted
for only a few countries in the region—Algeria, Egypt, Iran, Jordan, Morocco,

TABLE 2.3. World Poverty Rates by Region (percentage living below $2 a day), 1990–2009

	1990–2000	2000–2009
Developing regions	61.0%	46.0%
South Asia	79.0	74.0
Latin America and Caribbean	20.0	12.0
Developing Arab countries[a]	23.0	17.0
Tunisia	8.0	3.9
Morocco	24.0	19.7
Jordan	14.7	13.7
Algeria	22.7	10.5
Yemen	29.0	46.7

Source: Authors' estimates based on Bibi and Nabli (2010) for the Arab region and UNDP/ILO (2013a) for the rest of the world.

Note: The Arab countries included are Djibouti (1996 and 2002), Egypt (1991 and 2009), Jordan (1997 and 2006), Mauritania (1996 and 2000), Morocco (1991 and 2007), Syria (1997 and 2007), Tunisia (1990 and 2000), and Yemen (1998 and 2005).

a. Arab developing countries include Algeria, Egypt, Jordan, and Morocco.

Tunisia, Yemen, and Palestine (Bibi and Nabli 2010). Sudan started collecting data on income and expenditure only in 2009. Moreover, these surveys are not conducted regularly, making assessments of progress (or its absence) over time problematic. The exception is Palestine, which collects yearly data on expenditure and consumption. In addition, the data collected tend to be for expenditures rather than for incomes. Although the former are quite useful for measuring poverty, their exclusion of savings makes them a much less reliable indicator of equity. These surveys are also known to play down inequality as a result of the low response level of the upper end of the income distribution. For these reasons, all statements concerning poverty and distribution in the region should be taken with several truckloads of salt.

Poverty is a relative concept, and the choice of poverty line can have dramatic implications for assessing its severity. Critics point out that the lower poverty line of $1 at purchasing power parity (PPP) fails to meet any reasonable definition of subsistence and is far too low for most countries of the region. The $2 PPP poverty line has more meaning for the region's countries for which data exist. Many analysts suggest, however, that even this benchmark is too narrow a definition of poverty in the MENA region, mainly because many people are very close to the poverty line—with incomes between $2 and $3 a day—and the economic fluctuations that have plagued the region continue to have major effects on poverty (Chaudhry 2005; Iqbal 2006). At $2 a day, about 22 percent of the region's population is under the poverty line—close to the Latin America average until the past decade. (See Table

2.3 for poverty rates for different regions.) These comparisons depend in essential ways on the choice of a poverty line. The poverty rate in the Middle East jumps to 46 percent when the line is pushed up to $3 a day, which is much higher than in Latin America (ESCWA 2013).

In general, poverty in the MENA region is concentrated among the uneducated and socially vulnerable (for example, widows) and in less favored rural areas. In Egypt, for example, even when using the draconian lower poverty line, 34 percent of rural Upper Egyptians are considered to be poor (El Laithy, Lokshin, and Banerji 2003). In Yemen, poverty is related to large family size, illiteracy, and employment in agriculture (Chemingui 2005). The poor have low skill levels and limited access to health services and are excluded from social security coverage. These patterns are roughly similar to those found throughout the Global South. The relatively low levels of *extreme* poverty can be explained by two factors: (1) international migration and remittances and (2) government employment. But while migration expanded greatly from the 1970s to the 1990s, it has since stabilized, if not shrunk, and thus no longer contributes to reducing poverty at the margin. Even if we believe the data that suggest that the region's poverty problems are less severe than elsewhere (and given the data and conceptual issues noted here, we may well *not* believe this), the sustainability of the region's relatively benign performance is still questionable.

There is evidence that poverty increased during the adjustment period of the 1990s. The World Bank estimates that 28 million more people were living on less than $2 PPP per day in 1999 than in 1990 (World Bank 2003). A few comparisons over time are possible for some countries. For Egypt, there is some evidence that poverty fell in the second half of the 1990s, but rose marginally again in the 2000s, and especially after the 2008 global crisis (ESCWA 2013). Reports on Syria indicate that a succession of droughts after 2002 led to a massive rise in poverty in the east of the country and an equally massive migration to the urban centers of Aleppo, Homs, and Damascus—the current centers of the Syrian uprising (IRIN Humanitarian News and Analysis 2012; Mills 2012). For Tunisia, available data suggest that poverty fell over time but became concentrated in marginalized regions. Poverty has likewise declined in Iran, but mobility both out of and into poverty is fairly common in the country (Iqbal 2006; Salehi-Isfahani 2003).

Although extreme poverty has been low in the region and is not as horrifyingly severe as in, say, sub-Saharan Africa, and although some progress has been made, it is reasonable to conclude that progress has recently stalled and that many millions of residents of the region remain below the absolute poverty line with little hope of escape. What is significant is that a sizable portion of the population of many countries has become unable to progress socially in the way previous generations did—through hard work and education—and seem to have been left in a poverty trap by the rollback of state services.

What About Inequality?

Apart from the persistence of poverty, a possible rise in inequality has also been cited as a major factor behind the Arab uprisings.

If the data on poverty are opaque, the data on income distribution (measured by Gini coefficient) are murkier still. As a result, and unlike the case for poverty figures, the evidence to support proposed trends in inequality is scant at best, and some of it is even contradictory. Consumption inequality tends to be low in the region compared to more unequal regions of the world (such as Latin America and Africa) as a result of the "socialism" of the past. There is some notable variation, with inequality highest in Morocco, Jordan, Tunisia, and Yemen (where Gini coefficients are around 40 percent) and lowest in Egypt and Syria (Gini coefficients around 30 percent). However, the hypothesized lower trickle-down of growth, a consequence of the move to a market economy, should result in higher inequality figures. Data for long-term comparisons (covering thirty years) are available only for Egypt, Iran, and Tunisia (Bibi and Nabli 2010; Iqbal 2006). These data suggest that inequality rose everywhere after the reforms of the 1990s, from a low base.

Using survey data, Rana Hendy and Mustapha Nabli (2014) hold that inequality varies between 30 and 45 percent in the Arab region. Their study finds an increase in inequality in Yemen, Syria, and Egypt. Moreover, they show that living standards are the lowest and inequality the highest in the center-west of Tunisia, where the country's revolution was born (in Sidi Bouzid). Yemen, Syria, and Egypt also exhibited a drop in living standards in rural and marginalized parts of these countries. In Syria, poverty is highest in Idlib, Daraa, Hama, and Homs. Mean household expenditure levels were observed to be the lowest in western Yemen (Ta'izz, Ibb, and Abyan). At the same time, Hendy and Nabli's results suggest that protests in countries such as Egypt and Libya, which started in urban areas and in Benghazi, respectively, did not necessarily originate in the poorest or most unequal regions.

These documented trends suggest some rise in income inequality, but the levels of inequality in the region seem low relative to other parts of the world. It may well be that people compare their current situation to their past experience, not to global experiences, and so rising inequality may explain the frustrations underlying the uprisings. But more likely, the figures we have do not reflect realities well. There are several reasons to doubt that the measures we have are adequate: they are based on consumption rather than income; they generally do not include the rich (who rarely fill out consumption surveys); and they do not account for the geographical distribution of income. One distinct possibility is that while inequality between the poor and the middle class has not varied much, the inequality between the middle class and the rich increased substantially after the 1990s (Diwan 2013; Prasad 2013). Indeed, two groups have profited most from the liberal reforms: the top 10 percent of the population who have a household member employed in the formal labor markets, and the top 1 percent who have greatly benefited from their political connections. Thomas Piketty (2014) has shown that these groups control as much as 50 percent of income in the Western countries. In a recent paper on the Arab world, he argues that it is regional inequality that matters and that income inequality in the Middle East region as a whole is by far the highest in the world.

Another recent line of research focuses on a different concept of inequality that is especially relevant for educated youth in the labor market—the inequality of opportunities (Roemer 1998). In a society where individual performance is solely a result of individual efforts, a person's level of education and labor market performance is determined by the supply of education, on the one hand, and the supply of jobs, on the other, and not by the person's own characteristics, such as his or her social class. But access to good-quality education could very well be determined by a person's circumstances, such as social class background and parental education, and thus may reflect a great deal of inequality of opportunity. Similarly, given a certain education level, if a person's circumstances still play a significant role in his or her labor market outcomes, then this could be evidence of imperfectly competitive labor markets in which family connections, social networks, and personal ties make a difference in access to jobs, resulting in inequality of opportunity in the job market.

Recent research has shown that this sort of inequality is extremely high in the MENA region. In particular, recent studies show that building a level playing field in learning requires much more than providing free schools. Ragui Assaad, Djavad Salehi-Isfahani, and Rana Hendy (2013) use survey data from seven MENA countries to understand the relationship between the educational attainment of youth and the circumstances into which they are born—namely, their gender, their parents' education, and the type of community in which they live. They find an alarming degree of inequality of opportunity in educational attainment in most of these countries, but especially in Iraq and Yemen. Salehi-Isfahani, Hassine, and Assaad (2013) estimate the proportion of inequality in test scores that can be explained by variation in family background and community characteristics and find a significant degree of inequality of opportunity for educational achievement in several countries in the region; indeed, in some countries, they find, such inequality has been rising over time. They also find that inequality of opportunity in educational achievement is higher in countries that spend fewer public resources on education and rely more on private tutoring and schools. Family background variables are the most important determinants of this inequality, followed by community characteristics. Their results show that, despite great efforts in past decades to invest in free public education, most MENA countries have less equality of opportunity in educational achievement than European countries, and several have less equality than Latin America and the United States.

Studies focusing on the labor market also show the importance of connections in landing a good job. To illustrate, a typical worker with no experience and twelve to sixteen years of education in Egypt could earn a salary two to three times higher in the formal private sector than in the informal private sector. (The salary in government is somewhere between the two sectors, but the government has stopped hiring.)[3] Where the worker actually lands is determined not by his education but by his connections, known as *wasta* in Arabic.

Ragui Assaad, Caroline Krafft, and Djavad Salehi-Isfahani (2013) studied detailed data on the educational trajectories of individuals in Egypt and Jordan to try to distinguish between the quality of human capital investments and the direct role of family circumstances in labor market outcomes (for example, time to first job, time to first formal job, wages in first job, growth in wages over time, and wages five years after graduation). They find little evidence to support the view that the type of high school, performance in high school, or even type of university (public versus private and other institutions) has an impact on labor market outcomes. Family background explains these outcomes much better than the quality of education received. A recent World Bank study (2013) arrives at similar conclusions: exogenous circumstances play a much more important role than characteristics under an individual's control in determining whether he or she is employed, has a permanent job, or is employed by the formal or public sector. However, this does not mean that public policy is unimportant. Assaad and Mohamed Saleh (2013) examine the effect of an increase in the local supply of schooling on intergenerational mobility in education in Jordan. Their findings show that the local availability of basic public schools does in fact increase intergenerational mobility in education.

From another angle, Assaad, Krafft, Hassine, and Salehi-Isfahani (2012) examine the patterns of inequality of opportunity in health and nutrition outcomes, such as height-for-age and weight-for-height, for children under five in selected Arab countries and Turkey, using Demographic and Health Survey (DHS) data. The results show that different levels and trends are evident across countries in both overall inequality and in the share of inequality of opportunity. Inequality of opportunity is shown to contribute substantially to the inequality of child health outcomes, but its share in total inequality varies significantly, both across and within countries over time.

Given the growing body of evidence for increased inequality of opportunity across the region, rising perceptions of inequality in the region are a plausible and important background factor in the Arab uprisings. In recent World Values Surveys (WVS), more and more people in all Middle Eastern countries where the surveys were carried out expressed support for the statement that "incomes should be made more equal." This shift in public opinion was most dramatic in Morocco, where increased support for income equality (or dissatisfaction with income inequality) jumped from 27 percent in 2001 to 71 percent in 2011; in Egypt, where it rose from 13 percent in 2001 to 69 percent in 2012; and in Algeria, where it increased from 23 percent in 2002 to 44 percent in 2014. The shift in perception was most marked among the middle class, which suggests that it is the increased inequality between the middle class and the rich, as opposed to that between the poor and the middle class, that has been firing up popular frustrations (Diwan 2013).

CONCLUSIONS: PERFORMANCE SINCE THE REVOLUTIONS AND THE ECONOMIC CHALLENGES AHEAD

The uprisings led to a negative economic shock in the "transitioning" countries. Tourism took a hit, capital flight accelerated, exports declined, and investment collapsed in Tunisia, Egypt, and Yemen. As a result, economic growth declined after 2011 and unemployment rose. Initially, governments reacted with expansionary policies to smooth the downturn, but outside the GCC, such policies could not be sustained for long. The expansionary policies carried out were supported mainly by domestic debt levels, as international aid did not rise despite repeated promises. As a result, in Egypt, Jordan, and Tunisia, economic indicators are presently flashing yellow. IMF programs are being developed in these countries, but the "street" may not allow the passage of minimal reform programs that could contain deficits to levels that are financeable (let alone sustainable). By the beginning of 2013, it had become clear that economic recovery could not proceed until political crises were resolved and serious economic reforms initiated. Indeed, a downward spiral may yet ensue if polarized politics exacerbates economic difficulties, in turn leading to more fractious politics.

The main economic challenges will be difficult to resolve in the best of circumstances. The first and most immediate challenge is economic stabilization. How to build a package of measures that reduce expenditures, raise revenues, and command some minimum level of popular support is a tricky endeavor in the best of circumstances, and it will be very challenging in the current hyperpoliticized environment. A more stable political environment, however, also offers the possibility of initiating other important reforms. The second big area of focus should be the modernization of the state and the rehabilitation of public services, especially health, education, and social protection. New governments with broad popular support should be able not only to redirect expenditures toward social services and away from subsidies that benefit the better-off but also to make tax systems more progressive while enlarging the tax base. Improving service delivery and fighting petty corruption will require increased public-sector wages, which will be complicated by the large size of the civil service. The third big ticket item concerns the growth agenda. Priority issues such as improving competition, democratizing credit, and reducing the constraints faced by the informal sector do not have easy solutions.

These are technically, politically, and administratively complicated challenges. In the end, what will make a difference is the process by which solutions adapted to the particular environment of each country are found and implemented. The greatest contribution of the Arab revolutions to these challenges should be in fostering greater popular participation in the policymaking process.

NOTES

1. Although some still claim that public-sector wages are high, these wages tend to be lower than in the formal private sector, especially for skilled workers, but higher than in the informal labor market, especially for more educated workers.

2. For example, spending on energy subsidies exceeds social expenditures by two to three times in Egypt and Tunisia.

3. We made these calculations from wage functions in Egypt (see figure 6 in World Bank 2013, 6).

3

POLITICAL REGIMES IN
THE MIDDLE EAST

We are on treacherous ground but in good company when we try to label the political regimes of the Middle East (see, for example, Binder 1957; Hudson 1977; Henry and Springborg 2010; Lust 2013; Penner Angrist 2013). "Regime" refers not only to a type of government but also to the political elite's guiding ideology, the rules of the game, and the structuring of the polity in a given nation. "Regime change" is no mere changing of the guard or cleaning out of City Hall; it is, rather, profound structural change in all forms of political activity. Regime change may be revolutionary, as in the violent shift from a monarchical to a republican regime in France in 1789 or from Pahlavi dynastic rule to the Islamic republic (some would say "theocracy") in Iran in 1979. Regime change may, however, be relatively peaceful and incremental. Turkey moved between 1946 and 1950 from a single-party, authoritarian regime to a two-party system with openly contested elections. And prior to the uprising in 2011, Egypt had been creeping hesitantly since 1971 from Nasser's single-party, authoritarian socialist regime toward a multiparty system into which private economic interests were increasingly integrated.

There is no dearth of cumbersome labels for Middle Eastern regimes, and both their number and terminological complexity testify to the difficulties that observers encounter in making coherent generalizations about the nature of these regimes. One way to avoid superficial and descriptive labeling is to focus on the dynamics of social and economic change within societies and how these dynamics are reflected in the nature of the regime. This highlights the extent to which regime continuity and change are the products of social and economic developments. For instance, in 1962 there was an abrupt regime change in North Yemen. The quasi-medieval theocracy known as the imamate was overthrown through a military coup d'état and a socialist republic proclaimed. Legally, a profound change had occurred, but Yemeni society had scarcely changed at all. By contrast, one could argue that the downfall of the shah of Iran in 1979 and the proclamation of the Islamic republic came as the result of rapid and profound social change in Iran in the 1960s and

1970s. The large cohorts of literate, urban, and upwardly mobile Iranians spewed forth by the shah's own educational system could no longer be contained within the paternalistic, authoritarian, and repressive regime he had inherited from his father. Although an Islamic republic was surely not the only possible regime alternative to the shah, and the shah's downfall itself was not inevitable, Iranian society was clearly ready for some profound restructuring of the polity.

We therefore focus on both formal and informal dimensions of political regimes. First, we classify the diverse political systems of the Middle East according to formal institutional characteristics—that is, as republics, monarchies, democracies, and so on—and map those onto the main groupings of political economies presented in Chapters 1 and 2. Although the formal rules of allocating power provide only a limited perspective, they affect the distribution of power and resources and, hence, how political actors maneuver and policies are made. As a result, formal institutions at least partially shape economic development strategies and individual efforts to gain access to economic opportunities and to meet social needs. We also delve into the more informal dimensions of political regimes embodied in "political settlements," which arguably have a more important effect than the formal rules on the rule of law, corruption, government effectiveness, and other factors that affect economic and social development.

Next, we provide a brief historical background of the political and social contexts from which new states emerged in the region, focusing on key features of the Ottoman and colonial periods across what is now the contemporary Middle East. We then illustrate the evolution of political regimes across the region in the postcolonial period, organizing these regimes using the three country classifications—resource-poor labor-abundant (RPLA), resource-rich labor-abundant (RRLA), and resource-rich labor-poor (RRLP)—as well as the two Organization for Economic Cooperation and Development (OECD) economies in the region, Turkey and Israel. We look at several key dimensions of governance, such as the rule of law, government effectiveness, and political repression and freedoms, in order to assess patterns across distinct types of political economies and governing institutions. These general configurations and trends in governance among political systems in the region frame subsequent analyses of the establishment and evolution of specific countries in the region. In keeping with the focus on political settlements and their effects on development trajectories, we emphasize the ideological orientations and social coalitions that legitimized and supported rulers across different periods after independence. In subsequent chapters, we focus in more depth on key components of evolving political settlements, including patterns of business-government relations, the role of the military in domestic political economies, and state relations with labor and other social groups.

ECONOMIES, POLITICAL REGIMES, AND GOVERNANCE IN THE MIDDLE EAST

The Middle East is often characterized as a region with a disproportionately large endowment of authoritarian systems (Posusney and Angrist 2004), with twelve

TABLE 3.1. Political Regimes and Resource Endowment Groups in the Middle East

Regime Type

Resource Endowment Group	Authoritarian Republics	Islamic Republics	Monarchies	Transition Countries (post-2011)	Would-Be and Quasi-Democracies
RPLA Countries	Egypt (1952–2011) Tunisia (1956–2011) Yemen Arab Republic (1962–1990) PDR Yemen (1967–1990)		Jordan (1946–2011) Morocco (1956–2011)	Egypt Libya Jordan (2011–present) Morocco (2011–present) Tunisia	Lebanon
RRLA Countries	Algeria Sudan (1969–1989) Syria Yemen (1990–2011)	Iran (1979–present) Sudan (1989–present)	Pahlavi Iran (1921–1979)	Yemen	South Sudan (2011–present)
RRLP Countries	Libya (1969–2011)		Bahrain Kuwait Oman Qatar Saudi Arabia United Arab Emirates		
OECD Members					Israel Turkey

countries classified as "not free" and six deemed only "partly free" according to the 2014 Freedom House evaluations of political systems (Freedom House 2014). At the same time, the region is often associated with economic underperformance vis-à-vis its resource endowments and potential, as reviewed in Chapter 2. Table 3.1 depicts the array of political regimes in the region, including countries categorized by their type at present and as they have evolved since their independence or establishment. In the next section, we provide a brief overview of the political histories of these countries; here we confine ourselves to describing the major patterns that emerge from the table.

As Table 3.1 shows, most authoritarian republics are in the RPLA (resource-poor labor-abundant) and RRLA (resource-rich labor-abundant) categories, with two in the latter group formally classified as Islamic republics. Authoritarian presidents in RRLA countries benefit from higher per capita resource wealth when it comes to maintaining and consolidating their rule because they can redistribute more funds and because they can fund more robust coercive apparatuses. Every Arab country that experienced major uprisings culminating in the overthrow of incumbent rulers, except Libya and South Sudan, were authoritarian republics lacking significant natural resource endowments. Libya, which we discuss in more detail later, is in some ways the exception that proves the rule: increasing repression and inequitable distribution of oil wealth had led to mounting dissatisfaction with the regime of Muammar Gaddafi, but his overthrow and capture in March 2011 probably would not have occurred without the NATO-led bombing campaign against his government. South Sudan, the other country in this category with large resource wealth, is classified as "transitional" because it seceded from Sudan in 2011 to form an independent state.

A second pattern evident in the table is that no resource-rich monarchies fall into the transitional category, and even the inclusion of their oil-poor cousins in this group is debatable. Although most monarchies experienced some unrest and witnessed protests after the Arab uprisings in 2011, thus far no kings, emirs, or sultans have been overthrown. Rulers in all of the Gulf Cooperation Council (GCC) monarchies remain firmly in place, even in Bahrain, where opposition has been strongest.[1] Protests against the Hashemites in Jordan and King Mohammed VI have been far more muted than those against incumbent rulers in the republics, and they have tended to focus on specific policies or politicians; rarely have protesters called for the overthrow of the monarchy.[2]

The virtual absence of mass protests in countries ruled by monarchies in the Arab uprisings might suggest that monarchs are more secure in the face of opposition than presidents of authoritarian republics, and indeed many have remarked on the relative stability of Middle Eastern monarchs (Anderson 1991; Greenblatt 2011; Kirby 2000; Lucas 2004; Ottaway and Muasher 2011). We endorse the claims of Sean Yom and Gregory Gause (2012), who argue that the apparent monarchical exceptionalism has more to do with the structure of patronage and the formation of social coalitions than with innate features of monarchies as regime types. In the next section, our brief discussions of regimes in specific countries illustrate these points in more detail.

This emphasis on structures of patronage and social coalitions points to a third pattern that emerges from Table 3.1, notably the heavy concentration of monarchies in the category of resource-rich countries. Of all monarchies in the region, only Jordan and Morocco do not possess high per capita resource wealth. It is not coincidental that the Gulf monarchies, which all enjoy or have enjoyed high per capita mineral wealth, largely avoided mass protests during the Arab uprisings and that their incumbent rulers have had relatively secure tenures for decades (Heydemann 2002). The only major exception here is Bahrain, where large-scale protests erupted against the ruling family but were suppressed with support from the GCC (see Chapter 11).

Indeed, the alleged "resource curse," which we first discussed in Chapter 1, is one of the most prominent explanations for authoritarianism in the Arab world (see, for example, El Badawi, Makdisi, and Milante 2009; Beblawi and Luciani 1987; Bellin 2004; Chaudhry 1997; Crystal 1995; Ross 2012). The association between oil wealth and enduring authoritarianism, however, does not provide a convincing account of the ascendance of dictatorship in the region. At best, oil has sustained despotism, but it does not explain its initial establishment. Certainly, oil rents enable rulers to co-opt potential opponents and to invest in coercive apparatuses that buttress their arsenals of carrots and sticks to safeguard their rule. But several factors belie the sufficiency of oil wealth as an explanation for Middle Eastern authoritarianism. First, virtually all of the oil-rich countries in the region were authoritarian prior to the discovery and exploitation of oil. Second, MENA countries that lack oil reserves have also enjoyed sustained periods of authoritarian rule, and many continue to do so even after the uprisings. Third, oil wealth is not as robustly associated with authoritarianism in other global regions. Furthermore, the timing of the discovery of oil vis-à-vis state-building efforts (Smith 2007; Vitalis 2006) and the assets of economic elites (Dunning 2006) may mediate the relationship between resource wealth and authoritarian rule. Rather than resource wealth per se, Western support for authoritarian incumbents as well as sustained conflict in the region provide more convincing explanations for the persistence, if not the origins, of authoritarianism in the region as a whole (Bellin 2004).

In addition, a large and growing body of research links governance to development paths and outcomes (see, for example, Acemoglu and Robinson 2012). Governance refers to the combination of political, social, economic, and institutional factors that affect the behavior of organizations and individuals and influence their performance. It relates to macro-level issues such as politics, policymaking, and state-society relations and encompasses multiple dimensions including: (1) administrative procedures such as legislation and regulation; (2) the *rule of law,* or the de facto enforcement of these laws, regulations, and administrative procedures; (3) *voice and participation,* which capture the mechanisms that stakeholders at all levels employ to express their grievances and suggest areas or ways of improvement in economic or political exchanges; (4) *transparency,* or the openness and clarity of the political system; and (5) *accountability,* or the ways in which governments and other actors answer to the public and accept responsibility for their actions (World Bank, WGI). Each of these dimensions of governance has an important bearing on the economic environment in which investors, consumers, citizens, social groups, and other actors interact with each other and carry out economic exchanges. Thus, it is worth investigating the ways in which different countries and country groupings fare on various governance measures as a backdrop to our more detailed discussions of the politics of development across the region.

To facilitate systematic analyses and cross-national comparisons, we use a widely cited set of indicators of governance that taps into related factors such as voice and accountability, political stability, government effectiveness, regulatory quality, the rule of law, and perceptions of corruption (Cingranelli, Richards, and Clay 2014; Kaufmann, Kraay, and Mastruzzi 2010, 4; Transparency International 2013).[3] In Figures 3.1 to 3.10, we depict values for selected indicators both longitudinally for country groupings and cross-sectionally for individual countries within these groupings across time.

Figure 3.1 provides measures of the rule of law over time in the three main country groupings. The stability of legal and regulatory frameworks breeds trust in the political system, encouraging individuals, groups, and firms to invest their scarce resources in local projects and to carry out economic exchanges with each other, thereby contributing to overall growth. As the figure shows, the RRLP countries exhibit the highest scores for the rule of law, followed by RPLA and RRLA countries. Thus, as we have suggested previously, it is misleading to speak of uniform economic patterns across the entire region, even among countries with high natural resource endowments. In the oil-rich countries of the Gulf with small indigenous populations, perceptions of the rule of law are substantially more favorable than in their more populous counterparts. The poorer, populous countries, which lack significant resource wealth, exhibit higher rule-of-law estimates than the equally populous oil-rich countries, but lower estimates than the Gulf monarchies. To contextualize these values, particularly in light of widespread claims that the region suffers from governance deficits, including in the rule of law, we include a measure for all middle-income countries in the world. While the RRLA countries are well below the global average, the other two country groupings are above the benchmark for middle-income countries, calling into question the blanket statement that the Middle East as a whole suffers from an unusual deficit in this realm of governance. This finding is particularly noteworthy for the poorer, high-population countries, given the generally positive correlation between wealth and governance, although it is important to note that governance indicators were declining in the years leading up to the uprisings in these countries.

Figure 3.2 breaks down the rule-of-law estimates by country, using data from 2010, the eve of the Arab uprisings. The figure shows that most countries within each resource grouping conformed to the trends exhibited in the figure; however, each cluster has some notable outliers. For example, among the RPLA countries, Lebanon exhibits particularly low rule-of-law estimates, bringing down the cluster's overall average. Lebanon's low score is undoubtedly a result of the poor *quality* of its democracy, whose power-sharing arrangements and political tensions generate political stalemate. Within the RRLP countries, Libya has markedly lower values for perceived rule of law, which is consistent with general depictions of politics under Gaddafi's rule (Vandewalle 2012) and the fact that Libya straddles the border between the RRLP and RRLA countries based on its per capita value of oil as a percentage of GDP. Within the RRLA group, the rule-of-law values are uniformly low, with all country estimates below zero. In general, the rule of law is higher in the monarchies than in the authoritarian republics. But given the overlap between monarchies and high natural resource endowments, it is not clear that this association results from the effects of the regime type rather than from resources. Furthermore, the two monarchies without oil wealth have markedly lower rule-of-law estimates.

These general patterns hold with respect to measures of state capacity, or the ability of state authorities and institutions to formulate and execute policies and administer state territories effectively. State capacity, which is increasingly invoked as a sine qua non for successful and sustainable economic development, taps into a variety of state activities, such as defending the national territory, making and enforcing rules and regulations, collecting taxes, and managing the economy (Evans 1995; Kohli 2004; Soifer 2008). In Figure 3.3, we depict variation in state capacity

FIGURE 3.1. The Rule of Law by Political Economy Subgroup, 1996–2011

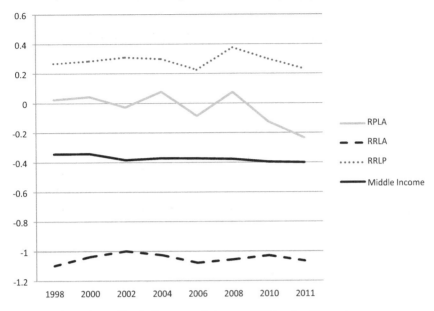

Source: World Bank, Worldwide Governance Indicators (WGI), rule-of-law estimates.

Note: The "rule of law" estimates capture "perceptions of the extent to which agents have confidence in and abide by the rules of society, and in particular the quality of contract enforcement, property rights, the police, and the courts, as well as the likelihood of crime and violence" (Kaufmann, Kraay, and Mastruzzi 2010, 3).

FIGURE 3.2. The Rule of Law by Country, Clustered by Political Economy Subgroup, 2010

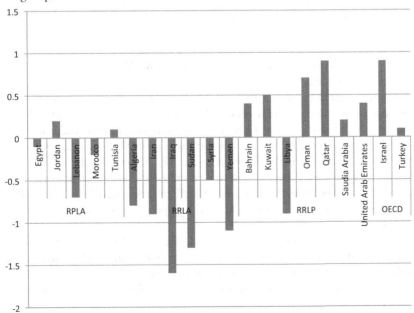

Source: World Bank, WGI, rule-of-law estimates.

FIGURE 3.3. Government Effectiveness by Political Economy Subgroup, 2003–2012

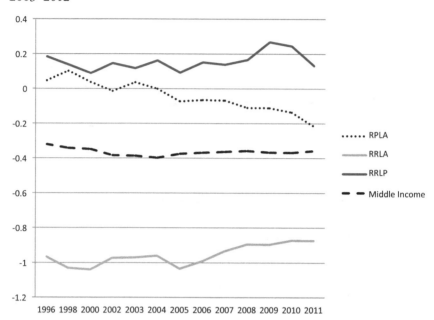

Source: World Bank, WGI, government effectiveness estimates.

Note: Estimates of "government effectiveness" capture "perceptions of the quality of public services, the quality of the civil service and the degree of its independence from political pressures, the quality of policy formulation and implementation, and the credibility of the government's commitment to such policies" (Kaufmann et al. 2010, 3).

across political economy types, as measured by the World Bank's indicator of government effectiveness.

Again, as seen in Figure 3.3, the RRLP countries consistently exhibited the most favorable values across the past decade. The RPLA countries also exhibited comparatively high values, although government effectiveness in these countries began to decline in the mid-2000s. As is true for the rule-of-law estimates, government effectiveness values are markedly lower in the RRLA countries than in the other two country clusters. When compared to middle-income countries, government effectiveness is superior in the RPLA and RRLP countries but inferior in the RRLA countries. Thus, the same patterns hold with respect to state capacity as with the rule-of-law measures.

Similarly, on the country level, the same patterns hold across countries for the two indicators on the eve of the Arab uprisings (see Figure 3.4). In general, the authoritarian republics score worse on government effectiveness, although this tendency is more prevalent among the resource-rich republics. No consistent pattern

FIGURE 3.4. Government Effectiveness by Country, Clustered by Political Economy Subgroup, 2010

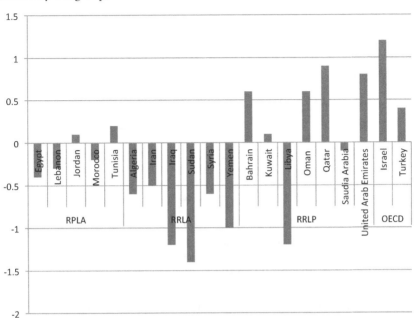

Source: World Bank, WGI, government effectiveness estimates.

can be discerned among the three democracies in the region, Israel, Lebanon, and Turkey, which vary markedly in their levels of government effectiveness. Country size may affect government effectiveness: smaller countries generally have more capable states because smaller national territories are easier to govern and control (Herbst 2000). Yet resource wealth and level of economic development seem to be most consistently associated with the development of more effective governments, a finding consistent with existing research (Beblawi and Luciani 1987; Bellin 2004; Chaudhry 1997; Crystal 1995; Ross 2012).

Much ink has been spilled on corruption and rising cronyism in the Middle Eastern countries (Diwan, Keefer, and Schiffbauer 2013; Henry and Springborg 2010; Heydemann 2004; Hibou 2006; Schlumberger 2008). Scholars have linked the region's economic underperformance to corruption in politics and everyday social transactions and have suggested that privileged access to economic opportunities has disproportionately rewarded regime cronies, who may not run the most efficient firms. What trends and patterns do we see in perceptions of corruption within the region? Figure 3.5 depicts perceived corruption in the three country groupings over the past decade. (Lower scores denote higher perceived corruption.) Again, similar patterns hold: the RRLA countries have the highest reported levels of corruption, while the lowest are found in the RRLP countries. Interestingly,

FIGURE 3.5. Corruption by Political Economy Subgroup, 2003–2012

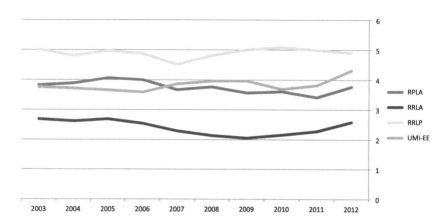

Source: Transparency International, Corruption Perceptions Index (CPI).

Note: In the CPI, "a country or territory's score indicates the perceived level of public sector corruption on a scale of 0–100, where 0 means that a country is perceived as highly corrupt and 100 means it is perceived as very clean." Values are adjusted to a ten-point scale.

perceived corruption declined among the RPLA countries in the first half of the 2000s, but rose slightly in the years leading up to the uprisings in the second half of the decade. Figure 3.5 also suggests that parts of the Middle East are not global outliers with respect to corruption, despite the common refrain that the region is exceedingly corrupt, whether at the level of transactions with petty government officials or with respect to cronyism. Again, although the RPLA and, especially, the RRLA countries have exceeded the average of middle-income countries in perceived corruption in the past decade, the RRLP countries have not fared poorly in broader comparative perspective, exhibiting far lower levels of corruption than the average of all middle-income countries.

On the country level, as shown in Figure 3.6, the most corrupt countries are found in the RRLA grouping, with Iraq scoring the lowest (and therefore being perceived as most corrupt) of all countries in the region. Within the RRLP countries, Libya is again an outlier with particularly high levels of perceived corruption, yet this is not surprising given the country's comparatively low levels of per capita oil endowments. Similarly, Lebanon is perceived as the most corrupt country within the RPLA grouping. With the high correlations between the three dimensions of governance presented thus far—rule of law, government effectiveness, and corruption—these patterns make sense. Nonetheless, their consistency, both over time and at the country level, is striking. Both Figures 3.5 and 3.6 suggest that there is a relationship between political economy type and corruption in light of the relatively similar levels of perceived corruption among countries in the same grouping when compared to those in other groupings.

FIGURE 3.6. Perceived Corruption by Country, Clustered by Political Economy Subgroup, 2010

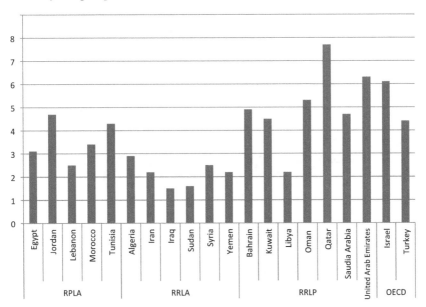

Source: Transparency International, CPI.

Another vital—and immediately tangible—dimension of governance is the degree to which states perpetrate violence and physically repress their populations. Depending on which groups are the targets of state violence, repression is of obvious relevance for development trajectories because it limits the scope for social mobilization and interest group formation. Violence and repression also potentially deter the security of property rights, as investors may live in perpetual fear of governing authorities or, at a minimum, of expropriation and arbitrary enforcement of regulation. Indeed, some analysts link authoritarianism, including physical repression, with poor development outcomes and prospects (Henry and Springborg 2010). Figure 3.7 depicts country scores on the Cingranelli-Richards (CIRI) Physical Integrity Rights Index, which measures physical repression of populations at the country level (see Cingranelli and Richards 1999, 2010). This additive index is constructed from indicators for torture, extrajudicial killing, political imprisonment, and disappearance ranging from zero (no government respect for these four physical integrity rights) to eight (full government respect for these four rights).

The rankings of the country groupings conform to the same patterns as the other governance indicators. The oil-rich, sparsely populated countries had the lowest levels of physical repression (highest scores), while the oil-rich, populous countries employed the highest levels of violence against their people, although 2011 witnessed an increased use of violence against their people in a few RRLP

FIGURE 3.7. Repression by Political Economy Subgroup, 1981–2011

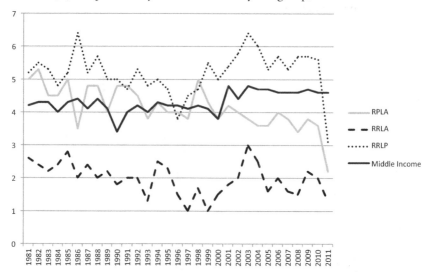

Source: Cingranelli-Richards (CIRI) Physical Integrity Rights Index.

countries in response to the uprisings. If authoritarian rulers deploy a combination of carrots and sticks to buttress their rule, then this patterns seems logical: governments with higher per capita resource wealth at their disposal can afford to invest in more benefits for their populations. But it is noteworthy that, among the high-population countries, those with more per capita resources employed more repression, despite the fact that they had more capacity to co-opt their people through material benefits. This trend may be due to the fact that mineral wealth provides incentives to rulers to gain power and hoard resources, angering deprived populations; thus, more investment in coercion may be required to maintain control. When compared to the average use of repression for middle-income countries, the same general patterns hold, as seen in the measures of the rule of law and government effectiveness. A noteworthy difference, however, is that middle-income countries on average exhibit a lower propensity to repress their people than the resource-poor, labor-abundant countries of the region, a trend that intensified throughout the 2000s.

On the eve of the Arab uprisings, there were relatively consistent patterns with respect to human rights violations across different types of MENA countries. As Figure 3.8 shows, the oil-poor authoritarian republics tended to repress their populations less than their oil-rich cousins, the RRLA countries, but more than the low-population oil-rich countries. Within each political economy grouping, and especially within the RRLA countries, there is some variation. While Iran, Sudan, Syria, and Yemen repressed their populations extensively, Algeria employed less violence against its citizens. The RRLP group also exhibits some cross-national variation, with Libya and Saudi Arabia employing far more repression against their

FIGURE 3.8. Repression by Country, Clustered by Political Economy Subgroup, 2010

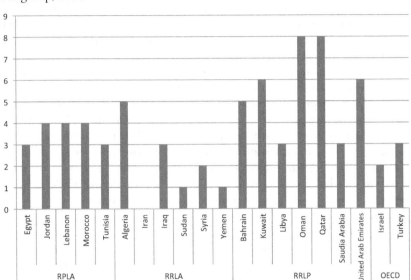

Source: CIRI Physical Integrity Rights Index.

populations than other regimes in this category. As discussed in Chapter 11, the Bahraini government repressed its population extensively after the uprisings erupted in 2011. Interestingly, the quasi-democracies of the region were also quite repressive: Turkey and, especially, Israel violated the rights of their populations at the same level as some authoritarian regimes, or even more severely.

The Middle East stands out in global perspective for its low levels of political freedom, irrespective of political economy type. While repression has either remained constant or increased in most MENA countries since the 1980s, voice and participation have exhibited a downward trend across much of the region, and all subregions fall below the middle-income average on this measure. Figure 3.9 shows the trends in the CIRI Empowerment Rights Index in the three main groupings of regional political economies.[4] Here the relative rankings of political economy types differ somewhat from those seen in all other governance indicators, with the RPLA countries exhibiting higher levels of political freedom than the RRLP countries. As with other dimensions of governance, the RRLA countries permitted the lowest level of political liberties of all three political economy groupings.

The trend toward declining freedom and rights was most marked in the RPLA countries. In fact, the aggregated trend for all RPLA countries masks the sharp declines in this indicator beginning in the mid-2000s for several of these countries, notably Egypt, Jordan, and Tunisia. The upward tick in freedoms in the latter half of the 2000s was largely driven by political developments in Lebanon and Morocco. The RRLA countries also exhibited declining levels of political and civic freedoms, although the trend was less steep than in their more resource-poor RPLA neighbors. The slight upward trend in freedoms in the RRLA countries in the late 2000s was driven by political developments in Sudan. Finally, the RRLP countries, notably the Gulf monarchies and Libya, exhibit consistently low levels of freedoms, albeit not quite to the same degree as the more populous resource-rich countries. It is important to note that this is the only governance indicator in which the values of the RRLP countries are low in comparison with other MENA political economies. This is largely due to the fact that governments in this category have employed patronage rather than repression to control their populations. Furthermore, within this category, however, some countries, such as Bahrain and Kuwait, have generally allowed relatively more freedom of expression than their neighbors in the Gulf, although repression and crackdowns on political and civic liberties rose markedly in Bahrain following the outbreak of the uprisings in 2011. These regional trends contrast to overall tendencies among middle-income countries as a whole, in which freedom and rights generally increased over the past three decades.

Figure 3.10 depicts levels of political freedoms and rights across the countries of the region on the eve of the uprisings. Within each grouping, there is considerable variation with respect to levels of political and civil liberties. Nonetheless, it is noteworthy that the country where the uprisings originated, Tunisia, showed particularly low levels of respect for freedom and rights, the culmination of a steep downward trend that had originated in the 1980s. Egypt and Jordan, too, exhibited relatively minimal levels of empowerment, although the decline in this indicator was far more marked in the former country. Lebanon, which is formally democratic despite serious problems with the quality of its democracy, had the highest levels of respect for voice and participation within the RPLA countries and, indeed, across the region. Among the RRLA countries, Syria and Yemen, where the uprisings have been most intense, displayed the lowest levels of empowerment. The RRLP countries are characterized by the most variation in political and civil freedoms, with Saudi Arabia far and away the most restrictive among this country grouping and across the region.

In sum, an array of governance indicators, including the rule of law, government effectiveness, perceived corruption, repression, and empowerment, point to a consistent pattern: the resource-rich, populous countries exhibit the most inferior outcomes in comparison with the other country groupings in the Middle East. Among the RRLA countries, few if any of them diverge significantly from this pattern within this category. Only Libya, which is formally part of the RRLP group, exhibits comparable values on governance indicators. Conversely, the RRLP countries (with the aforementioned exception of Libya) consistently show relatively high values on all governance indicators except empowerment, although there is more internal variation in this category. This finding contradicts, or at least qualifies, a core tenet of the "resource curse" argument and, more generally, the aggregated depictions of the region as a case of failed development. At a minimum, the alleged "oil curse" does not apply as a blanket rule across the region because it appears to afflict the labor-abundant countries far more than their sparsely populated wealthy counterparts. Thus, it cannot provide a convincing explanation for underdevelopment

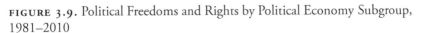

FIGURE 3.9. Political Freedoms and Rights by Political Economy Subgroup, 1981–2010

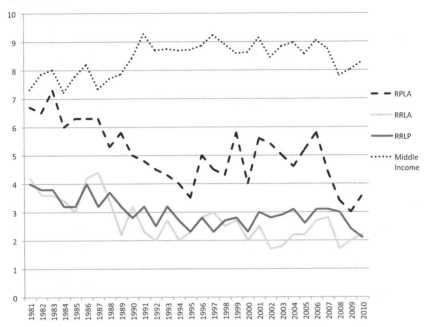

Source: CIRI Empowerment Rights Index.

FIGURE 3.10. Political Freedoms and Rights by Country, Clustered by Political Economy Subgroup, 2010

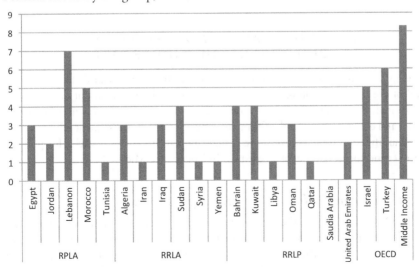

Source: CIRI Empowerment Rights Index.

in the region writ large. Rather, following a variety of institutional approaches to development (Acemoglu and Robinson 2012; Khan 2010; Mahoney 2010), the inferior values of the RRLA countries on diverse dimensions of governance indicate that institutional environments in Algeria, Iran, Iraq, Sudan, Syria, and most recently Yemen are less conducive to longer-term, more stable economic growth and development trajectories than is the case in the RPLA and RRLP countries. Finally, apart from their high levels of repression, the RPLA countries generally fall closer to the middle-income average on most governance indicators than other MENA countries. In the absence of large natural resource endowments, these countries could not sustain the same levels of patronage and had fewer resources to devote to repression than their counterparts in the RRLP and RRLA groupings. As a result, they have permitted greater competition in civic and political life, although this, too, declined in the years leading up to the 2011 uprisings.

A full explanation of these trends is beyond the scope of this analysis, but a few speculative points are in order. Virtually all of the RRLA countries adopted populist policies at independence. Thus, it is worth investigating whether the interaction of oil wealth and populism resulted in worse governance outcomes. Populist commitments facilitated by substantial resource endowments may have eased the pressure on political elites to invest in politically unpopular, long-term development strategies while prolonging their capacity to expand the public-sector labor force and create sinecure posts for key social groups and political allies. As we mentioned earlier, mineral wealth in resource-rich, populous countries may compel rulers to hoard resources and reward more circumscribed social groups or regime allies, which in turn undermines transparency and compels rulers to employ repression against alienated citizens. In short, the apparent association between poor governance and resource abundance in the high-population countries may arise from the incentives available to the rulers of high-population countries in the context of fewer budgetary constraints than some of their neighbors have faced.

THE HISTORICAL FOUNDATIONS OF STATE-BUILDING IN THE MIDDLE EAST

Let us now take a look at the history of state-building in the Middle East. Virtually all of the modern nation-states of the region were either carved out of the former Ottoman Empire or influenced by it in one way or another. The organization of politics and economies under the Ottoman Empire and their subsequent reinforcement or modification under European colonial rule had important legacies for political and economic development in the post-independence Middle East.

Ottoman State-Building and Governing Institutions

The Ottoman Empire, the last great Islamic empire, ruled much of the modern Middle East from the thirteenth through the early twentieth centuries. The empire reached its peak in the midsixteenth century, when it controlled a vast territory from southeastern Europe to the Iranian border through the Levant, parts of the

Arabian Peninsula, and across North Africa to the Moroccan border. Over the course of its existence, the Ottoman Empire developed a sophisticated set of governing institutions to administer its far-flung territories, including a large bureaucracy, a professional army, an elaborate set of legal codes with Sharia—Islamic law based on the Koran—as their key foundation, a large clerical staff to run the courts and educational system, and legal guarantees for other religious communities to worship and control their own communal affairs. In the Ottoman Empire, political authority was highly centralized in some respects, yet very decentralized in other respects.

Several institutions were central to the functioning of the Ottoman Empire and cemented the rule of the sultan.[5] First, during the fourteenth and fifteenth centuries, the Ottomans developed a disciplined corps of professional soldiers, known as the Janissaries. Recruited through the *devshirme,* a system of conscripting and training military slaves, the soldiers were taken as tribute from Christian subjects (especially in the Balkans), converted to Islam, educated in Arabic and Turkish, and trained as soldiers or, on occasion, administrators to run the empire. With the legal status of slaves of the Ottoman sultan, the Janissaries lived in their own barracks and were forbidden to marry or own property. The devshirme not only supplied a stream of military conscripts but also helped to fragment elites, thereby reinforcing the authority of the sultan. By separating traditional landed elites and the devshirme soldiers and administrators, potential challengers to the sultan were divided. This was part of a larger trend toward elite fragmentation, which the Ottoman state helped to foster by "selectively promoting members of each category of elite" (Barkey 1994, 11).

Second, the *timar* system, a land grant system that operated from the fourteenth through the early seventeenth centuries, provided additional methods of obtaining manpower and maintaining social control. In return for service in the military or administration, the sultan made land grants to the *timariot,* or landed elites with timar holdings, who could then derive income or resources from production by peasants. Through this system, the empire maintained some control over local elites, who were permitted to collect a percentage of taxes from their holdings but did not actually own the land. Furthermore, inheritance of the land grants was not automatic, although in practice it was often reassigned to sons contingent on military service. The system also largely ensured that peasants remained tied to a given timar, even though some geographic mobility was possible.

Third, the *millet* system organized subject peoples into religious communities, or millets, with autonomous control over their laws, schools, and general welfare. Community leaders (rabbis, priests, *ulama*) were named by the sultan to mediate between the Ottoman authorities and their communities. By separating communities legally and often geographically and by maintaining control over communal leaders, the system deterred the formation of a united opposition to Ottoman rule by subject peoples. The millet system also had lasting legacies for state and identity formation in modern Middle Eastern states, particularly in countries of the Levant where multiple ethnic and religious communities have long resided and, in some countries, continue to operate under distinct legal codes for some spheres of the law (Karpat 1982).

Differences in patterns of state-building and class formation in Europe and the Ottoman territories highlight the institutional legacies of Ottoman rule for development in the independent states of the Middle East.[6] Europe's structural transformation over a number of centuries from an agrarian to an industrial-urban base has greatly influenced core theories of development but in fact does not provide a model that has been faithfully replicated in developing countries, nor could it be. What, schematically, are the major differences between the Middle Eastern and European experiences of state-building and its effect on society and structural transformation?

The first set of distinctions revolves around the legal institutions of private property so prominent in European history but relatively absent in the Ottoman Empire. As our discussion of the timar system indicates, the Ottoman structure of ownership entailed an absence, in the juridical sense, of private property in land, as well as a state that extracted tribute through appointed intermediaries. The Ottoman state retained the right (but not always the ability) to dispose of landed property as its rulers saw fit, and it would grant temporary rights to appropriate the produce of the land, or usufruct rights. Historians have observed that the state's eminent domain often gave way in practice to what amounted to hereditary access to state-granted land or to the right to collect tribute in the state's name. But as often happened, the arrival on the scene of a powerful sultan would lead to the revocation of those quasi-hereditary privileges. Likewise, local notables could, in the face of a weak or financially constrained sultan, assert "stable" claims to privilege. Between the sultan and his government and the tribute-paying villagers and tribes lay a more or less thick stratum of tax-farmers (*multazims*), tribute gatherers, and rural notables. Some were military figures, such as the Ottoman *sipahis,* charged with raising tribute and troops for the sultan in exchange for timars. Others were tax-farmers pure and simple: the multazims were granted the right to tax a certain population to whatever extent possible in return for turning over to the sultan a predetermined amount.

The Middle East, from the seventeenth century on, was drawn into international trade dominated by the newly industrializing nations of Europe. In addition, Islamic states everywhere (Persia, Moghul India, and Morocco in addition to the Ottoman Empire) dealt with military inferiority vis-à-vis the Europeans. This led to important changes in the relationships of these states to their tribute-paying subjects. The need to raise revenues to pay for an enlarged and modernized military establishment pushed the sultans toward conversion of timar land into hereditary private land, while multazims gained heritable and salable rights to their territories. After a time, local notables began to profit from a lucrative agricultural-export trade with Europe and were allowed to establish commercial estates (*çiftliks*) that were tantamount to privately owned commercial farms.

The question of state revenues is crucial in grasping one of the profound differences between European and Middle Eastern patterns of economic change. The Ottoman system of taxation evolved over time but relied largely on indirect taxation, particularly in the rural sector. During the early expansion of the empire, the Ottomans relied on the timar system, granting the sipahis the right to collect revenues in their domain to support war-making efforts on behalf of the sultan. With the rise of the Janissaries by the fifteenth century, the sipahis morphed into local officials who manned local militias to protect the domains on behalf of the sultan and rarely left to wage war. In the late sixteenth century, the Ottomans adopted the *iltizam* system, which allowed local notables to purchase the right to collect taxes in an agrarian area or in urban industry for a fixed period of time, which gradually expanded to lifetime rights. By the late eighteenth century, however, many regions had established autonomous agricultural policies, and Janissaries and top government officials who owned tax farms effectively operated independently from Istanbul, which reduced the amount of revenues flowing to the center. Many peasant revolts broke out in response to the oppressive policies of local officials, and in many parts of the empire peasants increasingly moved into the cities. Furthermore, the "Capitulation" treaties had lowered taxes for European goods entering the Ottoman Empire, further reducing the Ottoman coffers, while increased customs taxes on imported goods only partially compensated for this loss.[7]

For the most part, then, state revenues in the Middle East were drawn from the agrarian sector in the form of taxes in kind or in cash on land, animals, and huts, despite attempts to reform the system and move toward direct taxation (Issawi 1982, 68–69; Katouzian 1981; Owen 1981, 106). The paradox here is that public authorities did not invest much in improving agricultural conditions so as to maximize production and, derivatively, state revenues. The one partial exception may have been the highly productive irrigated agrarian sector of Egypt, where the state on occasion had to concern itself with flood-control projects and the maintenance of the irrigation infrastructure (Mikhail 2011).

Even had the state fostered rural development more effectively, there is reason to doubt that the kinds of technological breakthroughs in agriculture that occurred in Europe would have been replicated in the Middle East, whose ecology and large nomadic populations would have made any such development difficult. When we consider the vast extent of the Middle East or even its subregions, its rugged terrain characterized by mountain ranges interspersed with large desert expanses, and the prevailing aridity, we can say that it would have been surprising had the Middle East duplicated European agricultural progress. Take Saudi Arabia with its 2.2 million square kilometers, or about four-fifths of the Arabian Peninsula. Although this surface is the equivalent of most of Western Europe, including the Iberian Peninsula and Italy, it is mainly desert. Whereas European governments dealt with compact areas and generally favorable rain and soil conditions, Middle Eastern states faced staggering distances and hostile terrain that defied centralization, the habits of regular administrative practice, and the consistent maintenance of law and order.

The very ecology of the region produced a social phenomenon, the nomads, with no counterpart in Western Europe. The nomads in the Middle East, even into the twentieth century, constituted at least 10 percent of the total population in some areas, particularly in the Arabian Peninsula. They grazed their animals and pitched their tents in the coastal zones, where the few well-watered areas of sedentary agriculture gave way to the desert proper. The nomads' self-image was one of warriors, freemen who had only scorn for peasants enslaved to the land. Like the state, they often preyed on the very populations from which they needed tribute. Not until the twentieth century would the nomads be subdued and the government's control permanently extended over all the territories of sedentary population.

What, then, of the cities and trade as a source of revenue? For millennia, urban centers have been critical features in the political and economic landscape of the Middle East, thriving on the long-distance trade linking Europe to the Far East and, to a lesser extent, Africa. Muslim states were themselves centered in these cities and were able to tax in various ways the commerce passing through them and the crafts and services that were stimulated by overland trade. The cities were the centers as well of Muslim learning and culture. But whereas the state might find in the cities and caravan routes a source of income independent of the fluctuating fortunes of agriculture, its approach to urban business is often depicted as deterring capital accumulation by failing to establish codified rules to govern economic transactions or incentivizing capital holders to funnel their resources into nonproductive investments (Greif 1994; Kuran 2012).

By the eighteenth century, the Ottoman and other sultanic states in the region faced a momentous fiscal crisis resulting from four factors: (1) the diversion of some overland trade to the new sea routes to the Far East; (2) overextension of the administrative capacity of the empire at the expense of settled agriculture; (3) the quest for new revenues in order to undertake military modernization that resulted in the assignation of land and tax-farming rights of a quasi-hereditary nature; and (4) the consolidation of a rural notability engaged in commercial agriculture for export. The privatization of the state's domain that we usually associate with direct colonial rule was well under way before European powers carved up the Middle East.

If we then look at the class "products" of this historical process, we find a relatively undifferentiated peasantry whose surplus was coveted by both the state and the armed nomadic tribes, urban merchants engaged in both overland and internal trade, urban artisans who produced for upper-income urban consumers as well as for peasants and tribesmen, and the legal experts of Islam, the *ulema*. The ulema, along with the soldiers and the bureaucrats of the state, constituted class actors of a sort, but actors who did not necessarily own or directly control property or means of production. Rather, in the name of the state and of Islam, they exercised the authority and, frequently, the naked power to dispose of property and productive means.

The mid- to late nineteenth century was a watershed period in state and class formation in the Middle East. Although processes of monetization, commercialization, and privatization took root prior to that period, they accelerated markedly thereafter as the increasingly industrialized societies of Europe contended for geopolitical and economic advantage in the Middle East. The military threat posed by the European powers, as well as by czarist Russia, had been clear since the seventeenth century, and Ottoman sultans and their governors had begun to transform their military establishments along European lines. Large standing armies, modern industries for manufacturing artillery pieces and firearms, and road and railroad construction to facilitate the movement of troops and goods all required expenditures by the state on an unprecedented scale. The search for revenue led Middle Eastern states into new domestic taxation devices and into external debt to European banks.

By the midnineteenth century, a so-called reform program, the Tanzimat, was under way throughout the Ottoman Empire and was echoed in Qajar Iran and in Morocco (the *nizam aljadid,* or new order). The scope of the reforms was ambitious, affecting most aspects of political, economic, and social life and leading to major reforms of land holdings, the civil, criminal, and commercial legal codes, taxation, welfare regimes, and social structure. The general tendency was to develop the legal infrastructure of private property; the European creditors of the empire argued that stable title to land and wealth would increase productive activity and hence the sultan's tax base. In Egypt, the *khedive,* or Ottoman governor, granted private land titles to anyone who paid five years of agricultural tax in advance. In addition, when the collection of taxes in cash became the norm, cultivators were forced into commercial agriculture in order to acquit their obligations. The process was not at all smooth; the Ottoman *bey* (ruler) of Tunis in 1857 introduced a head tax in cash (the *majba*), which led to a rural revolt in 1864. The tax, which had produced 50 percent of the beylical state's revenues, was rescinded, and Tunis then borrowed its way into an unmanageable external debt (Anderson 1986).

Ultimately, the Tanzimat reforms failed to save the empire for a variety of reasons, including but not limited to a lack of resources to carry out changes on such a vast scale. In addition, the Tanzimat may have been implemented too late to stave off the mounting crisis. Paradoxically, many of the reforms may have furthered the ability of the European colonial powers to undermine the empire. By aligning the Ottoman legal regime with European norms, the reformers facilitated access for European commercial interests to the Ottoman lands and may have enabled them to profit at the expense of the empire. Earlier in the nineteenth century, Muhammad Ali, the Ottoman governor of Egypt and Sudan who became the self-declared khedive of the region he governed, had initiated a similar set of large-scale reforms to build a strong economy, establish a modern bureaucracy staffed by an educated professional class, and construct a powerful military capable of resisting European colonial encroachment. When Muhammad Ali gained control over more and more territory, threatening the very authority of the Ottomans over the empire, Britain and its European allies intervened in 1840 to check his expansion. Although they defeated him militarily, the European powers permitted him to maintain his control in Egypt as a counterbalance to the Ottomans.

A direct consequence of the development efforts of the Middle Eastern state was the promotion, if not the creation, of new propertied interests. The growth of a rural notability through trade and tax-farming was visible everywhere. As land became alienable, it could serve as collateral against loans, bringing more investment into agriculture and, in parts of the Ottoman Empire, efforts to attract foreign capital to export agriculture. Middlemen proliferated and were frequently foreigners or members of religious minorities that were not subject to Islamic strictures on interest—hence the prominence of Greeks, Armenians, Jews, and Coptic Christians. Increasingly, they linked the new squirearchy of commercial agriculture to foreign markets. The squirearchy itself was mainly indigenous, although in Algeria, after the French conquest of 1830, Europeans owned the best lands and dominated the export of wine to France.

In the effort to stabilize rural revenue sources, the state encouraged tribal and nomadic chieftains to settle by granting them titles to what had been quasi-communal lands. State officials, high-ranking military figures, members of the ruling family or dynasty (such as the Qajar aristocracy in Iran or the dynasty of Muhammed 'Ali in Egypt), and even "aristocratic" urban families such as those of the city of Hama in Syria established private titles to what became veritable latifundia. (Iraq, Iran, parts of Syria, and eastern Anatolia were particularly affected.)

Similar processes were at work in the cities. The public bureaucratic function increased in importance, as did the bureaucrats themselves; the military establishment became more elaborate; and a new merchant bourgeoisie, overlapping substantially with the agents of commercial agriculture and just as frequently foreign, took root (see Figure 2.5). These economic and social changes underscore a key analytical point that informs all of our analysis: state authorities can initiate broad-gauged policies that stimulate processes of economic change whose consequences in the creation of new economic actors and class strata are as momentous as they are unanticipated.

European Colonialism

In the late nineteenth and early twentieth centuries, Islamic states collapsed in the face of European imperialism. All of the Middle East except Turkey, Iran, and the Arabian Peninsula fell under European rule. The form and duration of colonial rule varied across the territories of the contemporary Middle East. In some countries, the British, French, and Italians established colonies, which were generally acquired prior to World War I and entailed more unapologetic European control of territory and more unabashed economic exploitation. The Mandates, notably Palestine and Syria, were established after World War I in a different international context with somewhat stricter norms about the nature of European control and a more ostensible obligation to protect the interests of the inhabitants in preparation for independence. Other imperial arrangements were established in the Trucial States of the Persian Gulf, where ruling families signed treaties. The longest duration of colonial rule occurred in Algeria, where the French remained from 1830 to 1962, while Iraq experienced the shortest colonial period (1920–1932). The extent of foreign control also varied across different territories. In the Trucial States such as Kuwait and the United Arab Emirates, Britain controlled foreign policy and port operations (that is, international trade) while local rulers retained significant control over domestic politics. Elsewhere, colonial authority was more extensive. In Morocco, the French controlled domestic affairs by working through indigenous institutions, notably the monarchy. The most far-reaching imposition of European control occurred in Algeria, where the French uprooted and resettled tribes, destroyed domestic religious institutions, confiscated land, settled more than 150,000 Europeans, and formally annexed the entire territory as three separate provinces of France. In line with the social science literature on the long-run effects of colonialism on development, these varied forms of European rule had distinct legacies for state-building and institutional capacity in the different postcolonial countries of the Middle East.

The colonial powers also created new countries out of the former territories of the Ottoman Empire. At the end of World War I, Britain and France signed the secret Sykes-Picot Agreement, which divided up the territories of the Middle East, established modern-day Iraq, Jordan, Lebanon, Syria, Israel, and Palestine, and established their respective political systems. In Iraq and Jordan, the British even chose which kings would rule, although an agreement with the French in 1918 contradicted a prior secret agreement with the Hashemites of western Arabia, who were granted control over Transjordan but were denied control over a large Arab state, as had been previously promised. European imperialism also laid the seeds for the Arab-Israeli conflict by granting support for the establishment of a Jewish state in Palestine while making simultaneous commitments to the Palestinians. European colonialism also increased indebtedness in the region. For example, during the period of British rule in Egypt (1882–1954), colonial policies were aimed at expanding cotton production in the context of a free trade regime, which favored European producers and ensured the British extensive control over the lucrative cotton industry.

The colonial states that were implanted were truly autonomous from the societies they governed. With modern military technology (aircraft, among other things) and administrative practices, they completed the subjugation of territories and peoples that the sultans had begun. Private property, the cash economy, and the tax collector advanced together. The colonial state added two new and vital elements: public education for a limited number of natives and the promotion of a professional civil service. Even though Turkey and Iran escaped direct European control, their leaders attempted—more successfully in Turkey than in Iran—to apply these standards to their own bureaucracies.

The colonial state was in general expected by the metropole to be financially self-sufficient. A modern civil service was necessary to manage roads, railroads, ports, and power, to run the mail and telegraph services, to identify and tax the population, to staff all echelons of local administration, and to assume all the intermediate positions between the colonial authorities and the population for which mastery of both the colonial and the native languages was essential. By the 1930s, a new indigenous protoclass of educated, white-collar, and salaried labor began to assert itself. Its status was dependent not on its ownership of private property—of which it might possess very little—but on its professional attainment. With its bourgeois aspirations and lifestyle, it was the embryo of the "new middle class" in the Middle East (Halpern 1963). Thus, the major achievement of the colonial state in interest formation consisted in consolidating the position of landowners and in midwifing the birth of the new middle class.

Legacies of Ottoman and colonial rule have shaped states, economies, and societies in the newly independent states of the Middle East. First, certain organizational features of the Ottoman Empire persisted in various forms through the colonial era and shaped subsequent political and economic outcomes. In particular, the millet system institutionalized the separate treatment of different cultural and religious groups. In some independent countries, notably Lebanon, these differences have been further institutionalized in the political system through power-sharing arrangements. This reinforcement of ethno-religious diversity may have had delete-rious effects on development. At the national level, identity-based fractionalization has been linked to suboptimal economic outcomes, poor public goods provision, and access to economic opportunities via channels of patronage and clientelism structured along ethnic or religious lines (Alesina, Baqir, and Easterly 1999; Easterly and Levine 1997; Habyarimana et al. 2009). The Lebanese experience certainly confirms this, at least at the national level, although the power-sharing system has arguably enabled the Lebanese political leadership to stave off state breakdown and a full-blown explosion of communal tensions, as have occurred in Iraq and Syria.

Second, the creation of new states out of the former Ottoman territories, espe-cially as a result of the secret Anglo-French arrangements negotiated in the Sykes-Picot Agreement of 1916, created or exacerbated ethno-religious tensions in the region. The perception of some of these states as artificial and illegitimate con-structions created challenges for new rulers in consolidating their control over the national territory. The ensuing difficulties in constructing a shared sense of national political identity may have hindered economic and social advancement, as studies of diversity and development suggest. Furthermore, an enduring source of instabil-ity and conflict was generated when the colonial creation of the new state of Israel resulted in the displacement of the Palestinians.

Third, in some countries, the colonial powers buttressed or even created au-thoritarian ruling regimes and established core state institutions that persisted in the post-independence period and were used to maintain control over populations, such as the military and the bureaucracy. The British or French often struck deals with favored indigenous actors, and usually minorities such as Alawis, who then used their privileged positions to wrest control over the state. In some countries, the European powers even helped to quash emergent democratic initiatives and movements in their current and former colonies (Atallah 2010; Thompson 2013).

Fourth, Ottoman and, more proximately, European colonial rule had deleterious economic effects, which made the task of constructing state and market institutions all the more difficult for postcolonial leaders. The debt spiral and decline of the late Ottoman Empire enabled the European powers to take over its territories, with last-ing implications for economic development in the region. The former lands of the Ottoman Empire entered the post–World War I period in an economically subor-dinate position to the colonial authorities, and that paved the way for the European colonial rulers to take control over their finances and gain leverage over indigenous economies for the profit of the home country. Britain and France used their colonies as export markets for cheap European manufactured goods, damaging local econo-mies, and extracted raw materials such as cotton and wheat from imperial holdings to their profit. The economies of the newly independent Middle Eastern countries were initially integrated into global markets as exporters of primary products, raw materials, and agricultural goods; thus exposed to world market volatility, they had to build their own manufacturing capabilities from a limited base. Industrialization was all the more difficult because these newly created states lacked the requisite institutional capacity to guide a long-term development strategy (Chaudhry 1993).

Atatürk's Turkey

The 600-year-old Ottoman Empire and the Islamic caliphate ended in 1923, when the Treaty of Lausanne established formal international recognition of the new Republic of Turkey. Under the leadership of Mustafa Kemal Atatürk, an officer in the former Ottoman Army and the father of modern Turkey, the newly established republic served as a model for many countries adopting similar forms of government at independence. Nationalism, etatism, republicanism, revolutionism, populism, and secularism were the watchwords of the Turkish experiment. Atatürk and his lieutenants sought a society in which all class conflict and parochial loyalties would be subordinated to citizens' functional or occupational roles. The political guarantor of the nation's integration was to be a single party, to mobilize the citizenry rather than to compete for power against other parties, which were only sporadically tolerated. The Republican People's Party, while the creation of the regime, became an important organization in its own right.

The Turkish experiment put the state center stage. This was to be an activist, interventionist state rather than a set of agencies and bureaucracies over which political factions fought for control. Together with the military, the Turkish state rose above society and sought to reshape it in the image that Atatürk and his lieutenants thought desirable (see Trimberger 1978). This understanding of the proper role of the state and of the uses of public power spread throughout the Middle East in the post–World War II era and was at the heart of the socialist republican experiments.

Many other Middle Easterners, while seeing much to admire in republican Turkey, were disturbed by Atatürk's vehement secularism. Tunisia's Habib Bourguiba, among the Arabs, came closest to emulating Atatürk's ideas and practices, but few other Arab leaders dared try to separate national from religious identity or "church" from state. The strengthening of Islamic challenges to many Middle Eastern states stemmed in part from the conviction that these states failed in their mission and lacked a compelling ideological project.

POLITICAL REGIMES IN THE POST-INDEPENDENCE MIDDLE EAST

We now turn to a more in-depth discussion of political regimes as they emerged and evolved in the post-independence period, organized by the major groupings of political economies that we use throughout the book—RPLA, RRLA, and RRLP. For each grouping, we use examples from specific countries to describe the formal structure of power institutionalized in the various branches of government, political parties, and interest groups and how they have evolved over time, particularly after structural economic reforms were adopted beginning in the late 1970s and 1980s.

To understand the actual nature of political settlements in the MENA countries, it is equally, if not more, important to address the more informal aspects of state-society relations, in particular the legitimizing principles employed by rulers and the codified and uncodified social contracts forged between the state, societal elites, and the broader population as well as their position in the international political order. Across distinct regime types in the region, rulers' embrace of varied modes of legitimation and the distinct international alliances they forged shaped the types of development approaches and policies they adopted in the early years after independence and to some degree constrained subsequent reforms through path-dependent processes.

The RPLA Countries

All RPLA regimes initially pursued a modernization agenda, but the rhetoric about the means to achieve this goal varied. In general, the presidents of authoritarian republics legitimized their rule with promises of redistribution, social mobility, and a radical reworking of the social order that had prevailed in the colonial-era systems. In some countries, and especially authoritarian republics such as Egypt, rulers officially adopted quasi-socialist policies and employed such language to justify their policies. Others were more amenable to liberal economics, notably the authoritarian monarchs of Jordan and Morocco, who tended to reject the quasi-socialist ideology of their republican counterparts and left more space, at least in theory, for the private sector. In all cases, these ideological principles were more rhetorical than real, as all regimes viewed their supremacy, and thus the suppression of liberties, as an essential tool for mobilizing the masses for their overriding social project. In all MENA countries, government spending was high and the state took a prominent role in the economy, irrespective of regime type and formal ideological commitments. As we discuss in subsequent chapters, government investment in basic infrastructure and services brought about marked improvement in social development in both the republics and the monarchies in the initial decades after independence. By the 1980s, however, the sense of purpose that these ideologies engendered had diminished as it became clear that state-led modernization had failed.

In the late 1970s and 1980s, virtually all RPLA countries experienced fiscal crises that compelled them to undertake structural economic reforms with support from international financial institutions. As we show in Chapter 5, investment in human capital and social services was cut substantially in the 1980s and 1990s. With shrinking government budgets and the increasing privatization of state-owned assets, the social foundations of the state narrowed and underlying political settlements changed. Public-sector employment and benefits could no longer fuel upward mobility, while newly introduced markets were often not truly competitive, enabling a relatively small segment of the private sector with close ties to ruling elites to benefit disproportionately. With more and more segments of the population effectively sidelined in the new, post-adjustment political settlements, many governments increased repression while Islamist movements gained popularity, particularly among the marginalized middle classes.

The RPLA Authoritarian and Transitional Republics

Of all the regime types that have characterized the Middle East since World War II, the republic was the most prevalent and, until recently, demonstrated considerable longevity (see Table 3.1). Egypt and Tunisia, as well as their more oil-rich counter-parts Algeria, Iraq, Syria, and Yemen,[8] all replicated to varying degrees the Turkish republican model, particularly in terms of economic growth strategies, patterns of state intervention in the economy, and the adoption of redistributive rhetoric.

The authoritarian republics, in both RPLA and RRLA countries, shared certain institutional and sociopolitical commonalities. First, all were characterized by single-party dominance and generally had less tolerance for organized societal interests. Second, they adopted more explicitly secular rhetoric and policies, although some presidents invoked religion and established ties to religious authorities and groups when it suited their purposes. This tendency toward secularism, however, left the leaders of authoritarian republics more vulnerable to attacks from opposition Islamist movements, which at times questioned the religious credentials of incumbent rulers in order to discredit them among pious populations. Finally, as noted previously, the republican leaders tended to adopt more populist rhetoric and redistributive policies, but when the state began to decline in the late 1970s and 1980s, they were forced to cut back the programs and policies that had promoted social development.

Unlike the RRLA and RRLP regimes, however, rulers in RPLA countries were compelled to tolerate greater competition in society because they lacked sufficient rents to repress or buy the loyalty of all. If they were unable to deliver economic improvements, they were equally unable to maintain power by sheer repression, exposing their essential fragility, which was most evident by 2011. Rulers in RPLA countries adopted more selective strategies aimed at buying the allegiance of the middle class and repressing the poor while using first the suppression of leftist opponents and later political Islam as a dividing tool to scare away potential supporters of these opposition movements.

The experience of Egypt illustrates the kind of political settlements that were established, with slight variations, across the oil-poor republics in the first decades after independence and that then unraveled in the wake of structural adjustment from the 1980s onward. In July 1952, the Free Officers, a group of Egyptian military officers, seized power and ended the monarchical rule of the descendants of the old Ottoman governor in Egypt, Muhammed 'Ali (1804–1841). All existing political parties were abolished in 1953, and the Muslim Brotherhood (*al-Ikhwan al-Muslimun*) was abolished in 1954 after one of its members attempted to assassinate Colonel Gamal Abdel Nasser, a member of the Free Officers who took the helm of the state in 1956 and ruled until his death in 1970. Having swept the political arena clean, the new regime sought to build its own monopoly political organization from the top down through the construction of a single dominant party.

In 1956, after the acquisition of extensive economic assets from the British and the French, a socialist ideology gradually took shape. After the abrupt nationalizations of 1961, the regime committed itself to socialism and used the monopoly party, then called the Arab Socialist Union (ASU), to organize the citizenry along functional lines, including the peasants, workers, intellectuals and professionals, national capitalists, and troops. As in Atatürk's Turkey, the rhetorical emphasis was on unity, cohesion, devotion to the national cause as defined by the state, and the peaceful resolution of class differences by the redistribution of national wealth through state policies. At the same time, land reforms as well as serious investment in human capital afforded significant social mobility among poorer rural and urban segments of the population, partly at the expense of former economic elites.

When Nasser died in 1970, his vice president, Anwar Sadat, took over as president of the Egyptian Republic. Under Sadat, Egypt experienced a significant reorientation of politics and the economy. In the economic realm, Sadat deemphasized socialism and introduced limited economic liberalization (*infitah*), creating a new class of import-export traders and generally providing greater scope for the development of a local, protected private sector. These changes did not represent major structural reforms, however, as the state was still the preponderant actor in the economy and welfare programs remained intact. Politically, Sadat permitted more room for civil society than Nasser had done, allowing some independent political parties to operate. As part of a larger strategy to crush the leftist opposition while permitting religious groups greater scope, the Sadat regime tolerated (but did not legally recognize) the Muslim Brotherhood. As a result of these shifts, Islamist influence grew in society and particularly in professional associations. Ironically, Sadat was assassinated by a member of an Islamist organization, the Islamic Jihad, in 1981. Hosni Mubarak, his vice president, took power in his stead. These shifts in the underlying political settlement during Sadat's rule reflected both the failure of Arab nationalism as a guiding principle and the move toward a new arrangement in which capitalist elites occupied a more central role. Despite these important changes in state-society relations, the regime did not open up the political system as a form of compensation for the resultant stagnation of social mobility facing the emergent middle classes.

The Mubarak regime generally distrusted human rights and women's groups while his security forces decisively crushed militant Islamist groups. At the same time, mounting economic difficulties in the 1990s compelled him to allow greater scope for development and charity organizations to provide welfare, including Islamist charitable networks. In 1991 the Egyptian government adopted stabilization and structural adjustment programs with support from the IMF and the World Bank. Economic reforms accelerated markedly in the 2000s. In 2004, under the administration of Prime Minister Ahmed Nazif, the Egyptian government adopted new, deeper reforms to cut government spending and speed up privatization. These reforms fueled economic growth, but this trend was largely due to increased gas exports, earnings from transit fees through the Suez Canal, and sales of state-owned enterprises rather than to the establishment of a competitive industrial sector or rising exports. Throughout the 2000s, corruption, cronyism, and government repression increased while poverty rates stopped declining despite rising macroeconomic growth. By the turn of the twenty-first century, the underlying political settlement in Egypt had shifted markedly. An increasingly narrow elite with close ties to Mubarak benefited disproportionately from the so-called market-oriented reforms, while the traditional middle-class base of public-sector employees, professionals, and formal-sector workers received a smaller and smaller portion of the economic pie. With the defection of the middle classes from the state's social support base, Egypt became ripe for revolution (Diwan 2013).

Since Mubarak was ousted in February 2011 in the wake of massive popular demonstrations, Egypt has undergone a roller-coaster ride of political changes. As of this writing, however, strong elements of continuity with the Mubarak era have reemerged and are becoming increasingly entrenched. The roots of the radical shifts in post-Mubarak Egyptian politics can be traced to intense power struggles among the army, Islamists, and the liberal opposition, with shifting alliances and maneuvers along the way. Throughout the transitional period, the army retained its pivotal role within the political system, albeit often behind the scenes. Indeed, the army's decision not to side with Mubarak in the face of mass protests paved the way for the downfall of the dictator.

In March 2011, Egyptians approved a package of constitutional reforms aimed at paving the way for new elections, which were held in several rounds in December 2011 and January 2012. In the run-up to the elections, opposition groups of all ideological stripes struggled over the electoral rules with the Supreme Council of the Armed Forces (SCAF), which was serving as the interim ruling body. Islamists dominated the first post-Mubarak elections held in several rounds from November 2011 to January 2012, permitting the Muslim Brotherhood and the Salafist Al-Nour Party to dominate the legislature. The Muslim Brotherhood's control continued with Mohammed Morsi's narrow victory in the two rounds of presidential elections in May and June 2012. However, in the face of mounting popular dissatisfaction with the rule of the Muslim Brotherhood, the military, led by General Abdel Fattah Al-Sisi, removed Morsi. The military government led by Al-Sisi has since become increasingly intolerant of opposition, compelling even some supporters of Morsi's ouster to regret their decision to ally with the army against the Brotherhood. A court banned the Muslim Brotherhood from carrying out any activity in Egypt, ordered the confiscation of its assets, and officially designated the group a "terrorist organization." New laws have been introduced restricting protests, and the government has increasingly cracked down on human rights activists, some of whom were among the most prominent leaders of the Tahrir Square demonstrations that led to Mubarak's ouster. The new military government quickly drafted a new constitution, which was overwhelmingly approved in a national referendum in January 2014. In May 2014, Al-Sisi handily won presidential elections.

A brief overview of the founding and evolution of the core political settlement in Tunisia, the birthplace of the Arab uprisings, reveals similarities to Egypt's situation. At the same time, important differences in the social coalitions of the Egyptian and Tunisian regimes, among other domestic and external factors, help explain the distinct political trajectories of the two countries since their authoritarian rulers were overthrown in 2011. The origins of the post-independence regime in Tunisia were far different from those of Nasserist Egypt. Habib Bourguiba, a young lawyer from Monastir in Tunisia, founded a mass-based party, the Neo-Destour (New Constitution) Party. The party came to mobilize organized labor, white-collar professionals, the intelligentsia, provincial merchants, and commercial farmers into a powerful coalition. The Neo-Destour helped win independence from the French in 1956, and Bourguiba served as president for thirty-one years until he was deposed in the fall of 1987.

Like Atatürk's vision for Turkey, Bourguiba's vision for Tunisia was republican (he ended the old quasi-monarchical institution of the bey), secular, populist, and—even more so than Atatürk's—imbued with a kind of French rationalist version of the state. Socialism was only briefly part of Bourguiba's plan, though redistributive policies were certainly included. Bourguibism was resolutely nonmilitarist on the grounds that Tunisia could never be a credible military power and that the building of a large military establishment would only consume scarce investment and even thrust Tunisia into the cycles of military intervention in politics that had plagued the rest of the Middle East. This is a key difference with Egypt, where the military was always a central actor, if not the dominant actor, in the domestic political economy and social foundation of the regime.

Twenty years after independence, most observers saw Tunisia as one of the best-organized and most legitimate polities in the Arab world (Hudson 1977, 378). But in 1975 the National Assembly proclaimed Bourguiba president for life, an action that foreshadowed a breakdown in the rationality of the regime—the reinforcement of the cult of the indispensable leader, a violation of the ideal of meritocracy and political accountability. In 1987, Bourguiba, in his eighties and senile, was ushered into retirement by General Zine El Abidine Ben Ali, the man he had appointed minister of defense.

President Ben Ali changed little in the Bourguibist system except to rename the party the Democratic Constitutional Rally (RCD by its French acronym). The new order was no less corporatist, and only slightly more liberal, than the old order. And given the man at its head, the new regime was far more wedded to the military and security than Bourguiba's had ever been. Under Ben Ali, the state became increasingly repressive, brooking virtually no independent sources of social organization. In the 1990s, the Islamist Al-Nahda Party was a key target of state repression—its leaders and supporters were killed, imprisoned, or exiled.

As in Egypt, the core political settlement shifted substantially when the state adopted and deepened market-oriented reforms. During Ben Ali's rule, the social base of the state increasingly narrowed as a small group of elites with close ties to the families of the President and his wife benefited disproportionately from the spoils of privatization and new economic opportunities. This marked a sharp contrast to the Bourguiba era, when political leaders and their associates largely refrained from monopolizing the economic pie and corruption was relatively low by comparison. As in Egypt, the narrowing of the underlying political settlement was not accompanied by an opening up of the political sphere. Instead, the regime increasingly relied on repression as a tool for social control.

Rewriting the basic political institutions of the state is a critical juncture in the history of any polity. The overthrow of authoritarian rulers and the initiation of a democratic transition incite a scramble over who gets a seat (and the size of that seat) at the table where the new rules of the game will be written. In comparative perspective, that process has gone far more smoothly in Tunisia than in Egypt. In part, this is due to the fact that the military is less influential in Tunisian politics, and so competing liberal and Islamist factions have been able to broker a kind of power-sharing deal directly with each other. As of this writing, an array of political groups and actors have set aside their ideological differences to renegotiate the political transition, while Egypt has experienced a return to de facto military rule and growing repression under Al-Sisi.

Soon after the departure of Ben Ali from Tunisia in January 2011, the transitional government, headed by Béji Caid Essebsi, appointed a political reform commission to draw up electoral rules for the elections to the Constituent Assembly, with initial membership gradually expanded to include a wide array of representatives of political and civil society groups. Elections for the Constituent Assembly were held on October 23, 2011, when the Islamist Ennahda secured a resounding victory (41.5 percent of the votes cast), with 51 percent of eligible voters casting ballots. The party won 89 of 217 seats in the Assembly, which translated into a slightly higher proportion than its percentage of votes received given the nature of electoral rules (see Table 12.1). Three parties, including the secular Congress for the Republic (CPR) and Ettakatol, formed a coalition with the Ennahda Party.

During the course of Ennahda's time in power, tensions ratcheted up to great heights between Islamist and liberal forces, leading to increasing instability, violence, and a seemingly intractable political deadlock (see Chapter 12). The deteriorating security situation, the reduced credibility of the government, and the overthrow of the ruling Islamists in Egypt created an opening for the opposition National Salvation Front coalition to demand that Ennahda step down in favor of a nonpartisan government of technocrats (Wilson Center 2014). Following mass demonstrations, a rapprochement was brokered between Rashid al-Ghannushi, the head of Ennahda, and Essebsi, who spearheaded an opposition coalition, with the two sides agreeing to a road map for power transfer in October 2013 and settling on a compromise caretaker prime minister by late December (Gall 2014).

The agreement restarted the Tunisian political process, and the parliament finally adopted a new constitution in January 2014, with the support of 200 out of 216 votes. Nevertheless, the caretaker government continued to face extremist violence and popular unrest in the country's south ahead of parliamentary and presidential elections held in fall 2014, even as the economic situation has continued to deteriorate. The resolution of the political gridlock helped to secure significant loans in the interim—a second $500 million tranche of the IMF loan (Saleh 2014) and $500 million in loan guarantees from the United States (Project on Middle East Democracy 2014)—and economic growth was expected to pick up again in 2014 and 2015 as a result of the calmer political environment (Reuters 2013).

In Egypt, Islamists also dominated the first elections held after the uprisings, although their margin of victory was even higher than in Tunisia and they made no pretense of governing in coalition with non-Islamist parties. During its time in power, the Muslim Brotherhood was the dominant partner in the alliance with the Salafi Al-Nour Party and increasingly alienated both its onetime Islamist ally and liberal opponents (see Chapter 12). Once in office, the Muslim Brotherhood proved incapable of enacting reforms and bringing about tangible improvements in the lives of ordinary Egyptians.

On the political front, the Morsi government's critics accused it of excluding its opponents from decision-making processes and attempting to push through its own agenda with little attempt to gain broader consensus over sensitive points, while the Morsi administration accused the state bureaucracy, the judiciary, and opposition parties of obstructionism. The standoff reached a fever pitch in November 2012, when President Morsi issued a constitutional decree preventing the Egyptian judiciary from dissolving the Shura Council or the Constituent Assembly. (The Constitutional Court had previously dissolved the People's Assembly on technical grounds.) Some argue that this event constituted the real turning point by making the return of the army almost inevitable (Roberts 2013). Despite protests, the Islamist-dominated Constituent Assembly approved a draft constitution in December, which boosted the role of Islam and restricted freedom of speech and assembly in the polity. The document was quickly approved by referendum, despite vocal objections from liberal groups. An opposition coalition, the National Salvation Front—which included former head of the International Atomic Energy Agency (IAEA) Mohamed ElBaradei, Nasserist presidential candidate Hamdeen Sabahi, and former Arab League secretary General Amr Moussa—increasingly mobilized against the government. Meanwhile, though the Salafi Al-Nour Party had supported Mohammed Morsi in the runoff round of the presidential elections, the passage of the constitution marked a growing rift between the Salafis and the Brotherhood, with the Al-Nour Party wary of the Brotherhood's growing power (al-Anani 2013).

In March 2013, a court ruling halted Morsi's plans to hold parliamentary elections to replace the dissolved People's Assembly, a plan that the emerging opposition front opposed. After months of rising tensions and deteriorating conditions, the Tamarod (rebellion) campaign arose in Egypt, calling for the departure of President Morsi, and it soon received backing from a number of opposition groups. In the face of mass demonstrations calling for his ouster, the military deposed Morsi in July 2013. The circumstances surrounding his ouster remain contested, with even some of his critics terming his ouster a military coup. Morsi's ouster incited mass protests by his supporters, who called for his reinstatement. A government crackdown on pro-Morsi demonstrators resulted in clashes that left more than 2,200 people dead.

As the military government led by Al-Sisi has become increasingly intolerant of opposition, some proponents of Morsi's ouster have come to regret their decision to ally with the army against the Brotherhood. A court banned the Muslim Brotherhood from carrying out any activity in Egypt, ordered the confiscation of its assets, and officially designated the group a "terrorist organization." By July 2014, over 16,000 Brotherhood members had been jailed, while over 700 supporters and members of the Brotherhood had been charged with the crime of inciting riots in the city of Minya and sentenced to death, though many of the sentences were later commuted (Loveluck 2014).

The RPLA Monarchies

Monarchs, like republican presidents, have espoused the cause of economic development, marshaling state resources and large technocracies to pursue them. All have paid lip service to an even distribution of national wealth. What, if anything, makes the monarchs different? In our view, there are two main factors. First, all monarchs claim some degree of divine right to rule—they do not rest their legitimacy on the expression of popular will or sovereignty—and use this to justify hereditary rule. Although it is debatable whether this confers legitimacy, it certainly eases the succession problem that nonhereditary rulers face, although in practice republican presidents have effectively treated their offices in a similar manner (Brownlee 2007).

The second factor has to do with how monarchs handle diversity and pluralism, especially in the RPLA monarchies where rulers lack the resources to buy social peace across the board. Monarchs might decry the fractious elements in society that impede national unity, but they do not deny these elements legitimacy so long as they behave according to the rules of the game as defined by the monarchy. What the monarchs in resource-constrained countries want is a plethora of interests—tribal, ethnic, professional, class-based, and partisan—whose competition for public patronage they can arbitrate. None of these elements can be allowed to become too powerful or wealthy, and the monarch will police and repress or entice and divide factions that become too entrenched. But monarchs must have both the factions and the squabbles, as it is their role of arbiter and supervisor of the distribution of patronage and state resources that makes them relevant to the political game.[9] By positioning themselves above the contending forces in the political arena, monarchs have found it less risky than the leaders of the socialist republics to allow contested elections and some modicum of democratic practice. That said, their populations have not always believed in their indispensability, and monarchs have been overthrown in the region, including King Farouk of Egypt in 1952, King Faisal of Iraq in 1958, the Imam of Yemen in 1962, King Idris of Libya in 1969, and the Shah of Iran in 1979. Yet, since the Iranian revolution, monarchies have been relatively resilient.

The two RPLA monarchies, Morocco and Jordan, exhibit some similarities that partly help to explain their apparent durability in the face of the regional wave of uprisings since 2011. The monarchy of independent Morocco emerged out of the French protectorate (1912–1956). The nationalist Independence Party had used King Mohammed V as the symbol of the nationalist struggle, but with independence the king took his distance from the party, abetted its scission, and encouraged the formation of rival parties. Mohammed V died in 1961 and was succeeded by his son, Hassan II, who assiduously followed the divide-and-rule tactics of his father and presented himself as the final protector of all interests. This "balancing role" continues to be the official pose of his son and successor, Mohammed VI, who took over after his father's death in 1999.

In Jordan, King Hussein (1952–1999) straddled the cleavage between a majoritarian, highly educated Palestinian population and a largely Bedouin minority that dominated the Jordanian armed forces and key government positions. The Bedouin looked to King Hussein to protect their privileged position and to "contain" the Palestinian intelligentsia and entrepreneurial bourgeoisie. King Hussein took the risk of holding parliamentary elections in 1989 and 1993, the latter following the Declaration of Principles (DOP) establishing peace between the Palestinians and Israelis. Both elections were free, although the electoral system used in 1993 favored individual candidates at the expense of parties, especially the Muslim

Brotherhood. The Islamic vote was strong but not dominant in both elections, and many Palestinian voters abstained. King Hussein's son, Abdullah II, acceded to the throne upon his father's death in 1999. The new king has followed his father in making skillful use of the social cleavage between the Palestinian majority and East Bankers of Bedouin origin. During King Abdullah's reign, parliamentary elections were held in 2003, 2007, and 2013. In the 2003 and 2007 elections, the Islamic Action Front (IAF) and the Jordanian Muslim Brothers contested the elections, but the vast majority of seats went to tribal candidates and others closely linked by patronage with the Hashemites, a result facilitated by the structure of the electoral rules. The IAF boycotted the 2013 elections, claiming that the system continued to favor tribal candidates.

As in the RPLA republics, the social foundations of the Moroccan and Jordanian states have increasingly narrowed since the 1980s in the context of economic crises. In Morocco, where the "500 first families" have historically dominated the economy, the ownership of major economic assets has become even more concentrated in the past two decades, with the monarchy dominating the major holdings in the country. Well-connected elites have also benefited under economic liberalization in Jordan, where some business elites assert that the royal family is claiming a larger share of the spoils than under King Hussein. Furthermore, the decline of the public sector has had a larger toll on the Transjordanian population, which has disproportionately occupied positions in the military and civil service.

The relative pluralism in the Moroccan and Jordanian political systems, albeit constrained, partly explains the limited spread of the Arab uprisings in these countries (see Chapter 11). In February 2011, protests erupted in the major cities of Morocco but fizzled after the king disseminated a new constitution that acceded to key demands of the protesters and ostensibly set the country on a path toward a true constitutional monarchy. In addition, in November 2011, the king permitted the head of a major Moroccan Islamist party, the Justice and Development Party (PJD), to assume the premiership of the government after his party won the plurality in national elections (see Chapter 12). However, the jury is still out on the true degree of change in the political system—a close reading of the document shows that in reality it makes few real concessions (Benchemsi 2012). In Jordan, protests in the wake of the Arab uprisings have also been relatively limited and have tended not to call for the dismantling of the monarchy. Unlike Morocco, however, Jordan has seen popular demonstrations continuing unabated. Importantly, the monarchy's core social base of East Bankers is increasingly disgruntled as economic conditions have declined and perceptions of cronyism have mounted.

Despite important differences across the RPLA republics and monarchies in the nature of political contestation and the role of the executive in the political system, these countries share some important commonalities. All RPLA countries began by undertaking significant redistribution for at least formal-sector workers, particularly in the military and civil service, which fueled tangible gains in social mobility. Beginning in the 1980s, however, fiscal crises compelled them to cut government spending, limiting the prospects for advancement of key constituents while well-connected elites enjoyed a greater and greater share of the economic spoils.

The RPLA Democracy: Lebanon

Lebanon exhibits economic characteristics similar to those of the other RPLA countries, notably its relatively low levels of oil endowments and high population size vis-à-vis its territorial footprint. However, two factors differentiate Lebanon from the other RPLA countries, and indeed from many other MENA countries. First, by design, the economic elites who founded Lebanon ensured that state intervention in the economy, and thus efforts to promote state-led development, would remain minimal. Second, with its history of formal democratic rule, Lebanon does not fit neatly into either of the categories—RPLA authoritarian republic or RPLA monarchy—discussed earlier.

Lebanon's consociational democracy emerged from the French protectorate when the authorities organized and consolidated politics and society along sectarian and confessional lines. Seats in parliament were initially distributed in a ratio of six-to-five between Christians and Muslims; that ratio was later adjusted to an even split, and then subdivided among the several sects in both religious communities. The 1943 National Pact, elaborated by the principal leaders of the Maronite and Sunni sects, consecrated the French arrangement. Henceforth, presidents of the republic would always be a Maronite Christian, prime ministers would always be a Sunni, and presidents of the Chamber of Deputies would always be a Shi'a. Positions in the civil service and the armed forces are similarly distributed along confessional lines, while electoral districts allocate seats according to sectarian quotas. Lebanon quite literally enshrines religion in politics. People run for office or vote, win jobs or lose them, and occasionally come to blows as members of specific sects. Yet the press is free, debate is open and vigorous, and elections are held on a regular basis (although not without tampering and delays).

The fragility of the confessional balance soon became apparent (see especially Hudson 1968) and ultimately contributed to the outbreak of civil war, first in 1958 and later from 1975 to 1990. The influx of mostly Muslim Palestinian refugees after they were expelled from Jordan in 1970 touched off fears of a further demographic imbalance, particularly among Christians, despite the fact that the refugees could neither vote nor seek formal employment in occupations. As offices and spoils were distributed strictly along confessional lines, these lines became even more rigid. Except at the elite level, there were few crosscutting alliances, although candidates did have to seek votes outside their own confessional constituencies. The rigidity of the sectarian quotas in the political system became a constant source of friction. For example, although population growth and migration gradually transformed them into a minority, Christians continued to control the presidency and a larger number of deputies than its shrinking demographic weight might warrant.

Also contributing to confessional friction was the fact that the fruits of Lebanon's booming merchant economy were not equally shared. The oligarchs of the economy came from all sects but were dominated by the Maronite banking elite. Yet the sharing of economic interests among the very wealthy cut across confessional lines, and the oligarchs saw it as to their advantage to promote confessional conflict so that class-based politics might be avoided.

The civil war, which ended after the Ta'if Accord was signed in 1989, brought a halt to Lebanon's democratic processes and further weakened the state. After the war, the Syrian military presence in Lebanon was essentially given an open-ended lease. When Lebanon held its first postwar parliamentary elections in 1992, many Maronite Christians boycotted them in protest of Syria's continued presence. But candidates loyal to Hezbollah, the dominant Shi'a militia in the south, participated in these elections and did well. Although all militias were to be disarmed, Hezbollah, enjoying Iranian and Syrian backing, has remained fully armed to this day, even after the Israeli withdrawal from southern Lebanon in 2000.[10]

Lebanon's brand of sectarian democracy not only is a periodic source of instability, with its built-in tensions over confessional quotas and susceptibility to foreign meddling, but also contributes to ineffective governance. Critics of power-sharing arrangements contend that this form of political system is conducive to securing ceasefires but poses serious obstacles to governance; the mundane business of policymaking, they argue, is often stymied (Roeder and Rothchild 2005). Lebanon's chronic political stalemate supports this critique (Cammett 2014; Zahar 2005). Lebanon has managed to weather, with some difficulty, the dramatically heightened regional tensions of the past decade, but the future remains uncertain—particularly after the spread of tensions from the ongoing Syrian crisis into Lebanon and the rise of the Sunni-Shi'a divide, which has mobilized Sunni extremists in the country.

The RRLA Countries

Among the RRLA countries, post-independence economic and political trends have been less coherent than among the more resource-poor RPLA group. Notwithstanding important differences in the underlying political settlements of these countries, which we discuss later, a common theme has emerged since the 1980s: virtually all of the RRLA regimes have been unable to bring tangible and sustainable gains to their population and have failed to introduce a new ideological "project" to mobilize citizens, despite their resource wealth. As in the RPLA countries, the recent histories of the RRLA countries reveal track records of failed industrialization, bankrupt ideological programs, growing indifference of state elites to society, and decreased political voice. In most cases, the RRLA countries have employed their relative resource wealth to invest in their coercive apparatuses and have exhibited declining state capacity, contributing to poor economic and social performance despite greater availability of resources than in the poorer labor-abundant countries.

For over three decades, the RRLA countries have all been republics, although two are formally "Islamic" republics in which religious authorities are central actors in the political system. Only in Iran has there been regime change, with the 1979 revolution that overthrew the Pahlavi monarchy and replaced it with a republic dominated by clerics.

Algeria

Brief analyses of the post-independence evolution of the RRLA countries show the diversity in their underlying political settlements. In Algeria, the National

Liberation Front (FLN) led the nationalist struggle against the French colonial occupiers, culminating in independence in 1962. The FLN was a heterodox coalition of all the major participants in the war for liberation. In the early years of independence, the socialist wing of the organization was able to promote worker self-management on agricultural land taken over from departing Europeans and in abandoned or nationalized factories. But alongside the articulate and cosmopolitan radical intelligentsia were other major forces far less committed to the radical transformation of Algerian society. This faction's principal spokesman was Houari Boumediene, who seized power from Ahmed Ben Bella, Algeria's first president, in June 1965. Boumediene ushered in an era that was in many ways Nasserist, launching Algeria onto the path of state-led heavy industrialization. Although the FLN was increasingly marginalized while the army and bureaucracy became the real seats of power, Boumediene's statist, technocratic socialism and his efforts to remake the Algerian economy ultimately enjoyed considerable legitimacy (Leca 1975; Roberts 1984).

After Boumediene died in 1978, Chadli Bendjedid took over as president and led a profound political and economic transformation of his country until 1992, when he was deposed. Economic crisis in the mid-1980s necessitated a thorough overhaul of state expenditures and macroeconomic policy, which in turn opened the way to political transformation. Algeria was hard hit by declining international prices of oil and gas and squeezed by the closing-off of European labor markets, where many Algerian migrants had found work. Algeria had no choice but to undertake stringent austerity measures, and these were the proximate cause of violent cost-of-living riots in October 1988, which signaled the delegitimization of the regime and of the FLN. At the same time, Bendjedid introduced limited political liberalization and, after a referendum, introduced a new constitution that allowed for greater civic and political liberties but omitted any mention of socialism and any reference to the state as guarantor of the citizens' well-being (Quandt 1998).

Bendjedid also moved Algeria rapidly toward its first democratic elections. In 1992, with an impending victory for the newly legalized Islamic Salvation Front (FIS by its French acronym), the senior military deposed Bendjedid and dissolved the FIS. After Bendjedid's replacement, Mohamed Boudiaf, was assassinated, Algeria sank into civil war, which ended in 2002 thanks to brute force and the passage of an amnesty law.[11] In 1999, after a series of leaders drawn from the military, Abdelaziz Bouteflika was elected president, a post he has maintained through three subsequent elections, the most recent in April 2014. In February 2011, the government lifted the state of emergency that had been in place since 1992. However, the government remains unresponsive to popular demands. Algeria has witnessed ongoing demonstrations calling for regime change and improved economic conditions as part of the Arab uprisings, but protests are localized and sporadic, in part because the political system is already relatively open and Algerians have little faith in formal organizations (Parks 2013). The diverse factions of the military-business complex that dominates and monopolizes the political arena largely neglect popular demands while preserving their own interests and their control over the governing apparatus.

Iraq and Syria

Iraq and Syria, though also RRLA countries, have institutional arrangements and underlying political settlements that are quite distinct from Algeria's. Beginning in 1963, both Iraq and Syria were ruled by national branches of the same Arab nationalist party, the Ba'ath or Arab Renaissance Party. (In Syria, the Ba'ath is still in power, while the US invasion of Iraq in 2003 ousted Saddam Hussein and led to the dismantling of the Ba'ath Party in Iraq.) After 1968, an intense rivalry developed between Ba'athist Syria and Iraq that was related to geopolitical rivalries more than to doctrinal differences. However, the structures of the two Ba'athist regimes were similar. In both countries, popular support for the party was narrow and military officers largely controlled it (Helms 1984, 87; Hinnebusch 1979, 21).

Both Iraqi and Syrian politico-military elites tended to be drawn from regional and sectarian minorities, a practice that colonial powers also employed in the Middle East, Africa, and South Asia as a governance strategy. In Syria, first Hafez al-Assad and now his son, Bashar al-Assad, who took over after his father's death in 1999, have favored members of the Alawite sect, an offshoot of Shi'ism, particularly from the poor hinterland of the Latakia region. Although Alawis occupied most positions in the state and party, the ruling family reached out to Sunnis, especially in the urban business class, and built a broad coalition of public and private, civilian and military, and Sunni and Alawite economic interests. In addition to the harsh repression of opponents, the construction of this cross-sectarian elite coalition helps to explain the apparent resilience of the regime in the face of mass protests and an armed insurgency. Over time, however, the underlying political settlement forged by the ruling Assad family increasingly narrowed. The move to an ostensibly market-based economy and the abandonment of rural development in favor of the urban sector and an export economy promoted under Bashar al-Assad marked a major shift in the political economy of Syrian authoritarianism and led to the economic and social marginalization of large segments of the population (Haddad 2012).

Saddam Hussein officially became president of Iraq in 1982 but had been the de facto power broker in the country since 1968, when the Ba'ath returned to power through a military coup. Saddam and other stalwarts of the regime were from central Iraq, specifically the provincial town of Tikrit, and were bound by shared blood, their home region, and the fact that they were Arab Sunni Muslims. The Tikriti clan in Iraq became the functional equivalent of the Alawite clan in Syria. Saddam's state, like Assad's, rested on the pillars of the armed forces, the police, the bureaucracy, the party, and his clan. Like the regime in Syria, the Iraqi regime redistributed income, promoted growth, spread literacy, and for a time improved the economic lot of its citizens, while transforming Iraq into a police state. The eight years of war with Iran (1980–1988) deepened the culture of repression and fear and subordinated all economic activity to the war effort.

The end of the Cold War and Russia's dwindling support for its Ba'athi clients in Syria and Iraq produced different responses from the two regimes. Assad exploited

Syria's crucial role in the Arab-Israeli peace process and in the anti-Saddam coalition during the First Gulf War to attract international financial support. Consequently, Assad could proceed with cautious economic liberalization (Heydemann 1992) while blocking any meaningful political liberalization. By contrast, Iraq alienated itself from the West. By the end of the Iran-Iraq War, Iraq had amassed a large foreign debt, most of it owed to Kuwait and Saudi Arabia. In the summer of 1990, after it was clear that the Gulf states would not forgive Iraq's debt and would not invest heavily in Iraq, Saddam seized Kuwait in order to control his neighbor's large oil reserves and infrastructure and to obtain greater access to the Persian Gulf and infrastructure.

Operation Desert Storm, the military operation by the US-led coalition in response to Iraq's invasion of Kuwait, shattered Iraq's infrastructure and reduced its military capabilities. The Kurds were placed under a kind of UN trusteeship, and the southern part of the country was beaten into submission by Saddam's Republican Guard after an aborted Shi'ite insurrection. As a result of more than a decade of war, there was no longer a unified national economy, nor was there an administration present and functioning in all parts of the country. Because of international sanctions imposed as a result of its occupation of Kuwait, Iraq could not market its oil. While the regime and its allies lived off contraband and billions of dollars stashed away before the invasion in foreign bank accounts, the population suffered tremendously. Saddam's regime hunkered down in the central part of the country and played on Sunni Arab fears of Kurdish or Shi'ite domination should Saddam be overthrown.

In 2003 the United States again invaded Iraq, ostensibly to rid the country of chemical weapons and promote the establishment of a new democracy regime. Even with far less international support than in the First Gulf War, the United States toppled the Ba'athist regime and helped to establish new political institutions, which ironically have been dominated by Shi'ite political parties close to Iran. After more than a decade, Iraq has still not established stable political institutions, corruption is rampant, political factions are engaged in intense struggles within and across sectarian communities, and political violence remains a daily fact of life for many Iraqis. Although a series of elections have been held, the case of post-Saddam Iraq underscores that elections do not solve all problems and may even exacerbate them. The inability of political factions within the three main ethnic groups, the Sunnis, Shi'ites, and Kurds, to agree on a new political settlement that entails a formula for sharing political power and resource wealth has helped to fuel the recent descent into civil war in the country.

In March 2011, the Arab uprisings spread to Syria in the form of peaceful protests calling for regime change and greater economic opportunities. When the regime responded with a brutal crackdown, elements of the opposition gradually took up arms, and later militant groups, some of which were linked to al-Qaeda and extremist Islamist organizations, entered the fray, even as much of the indigenous, localized opposition maintained its peaceful tactics. Despite more than three years of anti-regime mobilization and intense fighting in key parts of the country, the regime has thus far remained intact. Meanwhile, deep differences within the international community on the appropriate strategy vis-à-vis the Syrian crisis have prevented the mobilization of a foreign invasion to promote regime change, as occurred in Libya (discussed later in the chapter).

Yemen and Sudan

In Yemen and Sudan, post-independence rulers initially pursued policies that were to some extent Nasserist in their structures and programs, but the societies onto which these regimes were imposed were (and remain) different from the other RRLA republics. In both countries, much of the population was rural and tribes were important forms of social organization. The former North Yemen was largely a tribal society, with basic agriculture and very little industry, and it was divided between the mainly Shi'ite tribesmen and the urban Sunni Muslims. In the former South Yemen, an avowedly Marxist regime came to power in 1968 but proved unable to impose its ideology on its tribal base, and the dominant Marxist elite was itself divided along tribal lines. When the Soviet Union collapsed and abandoned its international commitments, South Yemen was obliged to integrate with North Yemen. Unity was proclaimed in May 1990, and despite tensions and all-out war in 1994, a unified Yemen was restored, with Ali Abdullah Saleh as its head, buttressed by military force.

Sudan, like Yemen, is still overwhelmingly rural and agricultural; its approximately 41 million inhabitants (in 2010) are scattered over the largest country in Africa in terms of surface area. In the southern region, one-third of the population consists of tribes who, for the most part, are neither Muslim nor Arabic-speaking, while the rest are of mixed Arab and black African stock and Sunni Muslims, many of whom speak Arabic.[12] For more than a decade after Sudan gained independence in 1956, various civilian and military leaders held power, but ultimately all of them failed, largely because of ongoing fighting in the south. In May 1969, Colonel Jaafar al-Nimeiri seized power and established an explicitly Nasserist regime with central planning and heavy investment in state-owned enterprises. Nimeiri also negotiated an end to the fighting in the south and granted local autonomy to the three southern provinces. As in Yemen, tribal and regional loyalties to brotherhoods and religious leaders were very much alive, and Nimeiri eventually became absorbed in elaborate games of patronage, payoffs, and the balancing of rivals that sapped the regime of much of its socialist energy. His one achievement, ending the civil war in the south, was undone by his penchant for the strategy of divide-and-rule, which eventually alienated his own supporters among the southern populations.

Beginning in the early 1980s, Sudan increasingly incorporated religion into the political system. Nimeiri became a kind of "born-again" Muslim, threatening to apply Sharia throughout the country, including the non-Muslim south, sparking further revolts and eventually his overthrow in 1985. The civil war raged on under his successors, who were reluctant to rescind the promulgation of Sharia. In 1989, Lieutenant General Omar al-Bashir succeeded Nimeiri after yet another military coup, and Sudan was officially proclaimed an Islamic republic, a regime type we discuss in more detail in the next section.

The RRLA Islamic Republics

There are two Islamic republics in the Middle East: Iran and Sudan, both of which enjoy large oil reserves. Sudan's leader, Bashir, relied on Hassan al-Turabi, the founder of Sudan's Muslim Brotherhood, for spiritual and political guidance. Turabi cast himself as the dominant voice of political Islam in the Muslim world after the death of Ayatollah Ruhollah Khomeini in Iran. The Islamic regime prosecuted the war in the south with ferocity, and again more recently in Darfur in the west of the country. In 1999 a "soft coup" reshuffled personnel and led to the ouster of Turabi by Bashir and his allies.

Under Bashir, the economy became marginally less state-dominated than under Nimeiri, but this was an inevitable result of the enfeeblement of the state by two decades of economic crisis and the military campaign in the south. Moreover, after the time of Nimeiri, Sudan lost access to IMF and World Bank funds, and rapprochement with the West remained problematic in the post-9/11 era. However, the reshuffling of the government, the signing of the Comprehensive Peace Agreement in 2005 with the Sudan People's Liberation Army (SPLA) from the south, and the discovery and export of oil marginally improved the situation outside of Darfur and other conflict zones. In 2011, South Sudan officially declared independence after a referendum in which almost 99 percent voted for secession (Dagne 2011, 1). Within the newly established country, however, the political situation deteriorated as bloody clashes broke out among political factions in December 2013, leading to thousands of deaths.

The other Islamic republic in the region, Iran, was established in the 1979 revolution under the guidance of the Ayatollah Khomeini, sending tremors throughout the region. The 1979 revolution caused the complete dismantling of the shah's political regime, the remaking of Iran's foreign policy and alignments, and a cultural transformation. However, it did not bring about a full social or economic revolution. Years of war had fattened a class of profiteers and speculators, a phenomenon common to nearly all war situations, while the regime allowed many of its own to live off sinecures in the public sector and the state-owned foundations. In some Iranian cities in the mid-1990s, when the regime tried to bulldoze shantytowns, the reaction was the same as it had been under the shah—riots and violent confrontation. In addition, the public-enterprise sector, with its center of gravity in petroleum extraction, refining, and petrochemicals, remained large. There has been little talk of privatization. Much of the property and assets taken over from the Pahlavi family and those accused of collaboration with the old regime remain grouped in state-owned foundations that spin off handsome revenues for the cronies of the new power elite.

Although pluralism is officially condemned, the new regime does share one characteristic with the monarchies of the region—denying the principle of popular sovereignty. Sovereignty is God's alone, and although the people elect their representatives, those who rule are ultimately responsible to God rather than to the people. Unlike the monarchies, however, the regime does not allow rulership to be inherited; rather, it is the duty of the council of the foremost clerics to judge and select the best-qualified leaders. The Constitutional Council reviews all parliamentary legislation to ensure that it conforms to Sharia and to the Iranian constitution. The overarching principle is the "trusteeship of the jurisprudents" (*vilayet al-faqih*): the elite of the clergy who, on the strength of their learning, ensure that the people, in practicing Islamic democracy, do not stray from "the straight path."

The regime has been plagued with equity issues made all the more acute by eight years of war with Iraq. It has not rolled back the shah's land reform measures, and it has invested significantly in rural infrastructure and power generation. But the majority of Iranians are urban wage earners, and the inflation generated by the war lowered their standards of living dramatically. Unemployment among educated male youths is high, and a significant portion of the workforce survives in the informal sector.

When the Ayatollah Khomeini died in June 1989, the heroic, romantic phase of the Iranian revolution came to an end, and the mundane task of postwar reconstruction and economic reform began. The new and uncharismatic president, Akbar Hashemi Rafsanjani, took up this task. In 1997, Rafsanjani was succeeded by the liberal cleric Mohammad Khatami, who sought, vainly, to liberalize the system; he was succeeded by the hard-line populist Mahmoud Ahmadinejad in 2005. The 2009 elections, in which Ahmadinejad was reelected, were widely viewed as rigged, sparking mass uprisings in Tehran known as the Green Revolution, which spurred a brutal crackdown by the state. When Ahmadinejad's term expired, the 2013 elections ushered in an apparent turn to "moderation" under the newly elected President Hassan Rouhani, who reinitiated talks with the West over Iran's nuclear capabilities.

Iranian presidents, however, do not wield the powers of American ones. The man who took on the role of the revolution's spiritual guide after the death of Khomeini, 'Ali Khamenei, is the real head of state. The mullahs control the major institutions of the state, the parliament, the Foundation for the Disinherited, and the Revolutionary Guard. Although there is some evidence that younger Iranians have begun to lose faith and interest in the Islamic regime, it is doubtful that we shall soon see a retreat of the clergy from politics.

For someone who was male, Muslim, and loyal to the notion of an Islamic polity and who revered the memory of Ayatollah Khomeini, Iran was a vibrant and relatively contentious place, at least until the controversial 2009 elections. Iranian political cleavages array around foreign policy issues, notably the country's relationship with the West, as well as economic and social issues. On the one hand, the so-called radicals, both clerical and lay, want to confront the West, especially the United States, and spread the revolution. This faction is linked to many of the military and paramilitary groups that have flourished after the Islamic Revolution. These actors only partially overlap with social and economic radicals who want to tax the rich, punish the speculators, and redistribute wealth to the poor and who opposed the economic reforms unsuccessfully advocated by Rafsanjani. President Ahmadinejad, whose support base lay with more marginal groups in poorer regions, was representative of this tendency. On the other hand, aligned against them are so-called pragmatists, some of whom seek a more conciliatory policy toward the West in order to attract investment and promote trade and incorporate more liberal interests in the economy. Pragmatists may or may not condone the support extended to allies in Lebanon, Sudan, and Palestine, but they are apt to respect private property, to want to encourage the private sector to invest, and to be prepared to work with Western creditors, including the World Bank, to control government expenditures, reduce inflation, and deregulate the economy. Finally, there are voices, even among the clergy, who suggest that the mullahs have had their day in power, made a hash of it, and should if possible gracefully retreat to their *madrasas,* where they enjoy some comparative advantage.

As of 2014, none of these tensions within the political establishment have been resolved, but the issues are being debated in a remarkably open way. Iran has not fallen under the total control of a religious police state, and it is not ruled by the military. There are possibilities for a peaceful transition to a postmullacracy, though these tendencies are unlikely to be fostered should there be a military confrontation with the West, since in Iran, as elsewhere, the "nationalist card" may easily trump all others. Competition with the Saudis for regional influence also shapes Iranian foreign policy and further embitters relations with the United States and other Western powers, which have close alliances with many of Iran's regional rivals.

The RRLP Countries

Recent history has seen more continuity among the last grouping of political economies in the Middle East, the oil-rich, low-population countries. Relatively high per capita resource wealth enables these governments to cushion the effects of economic shocks on their citizen populations. Their relative capacity to spread the wealth—at least among citizens—has enabled rulers in RRLP countries to ensure that their populations do not feel marginalized in the face of a narrowed elite. The RRLP countries also differ from their poorer RRLA cousins in that they have managed to avoid or minimize the negative economic consequences of the "resource curse." Some Gulf countries have promoted globally competitive firms and fostered islands of efficiency in their economies. They may also have learned from the first oil shock of the 1980s and are now saving more and spending less. Some countries—notably Saudi Arabia, which has a higher population than the other RRLP countries—have even implemented austerity programs. Thanks to relatively high per capita resource wealth, these regimes can place tight restrictions on political voice and generally do not resort to high levels of repression, while avoiding the scale of corruption and state institutional weakness found in regimes in RRLA and RPLA countries.

As one of the world's largest oil producers, Saudi Arabia dominates oil production within the region. As in the other RRLP monarchies, natural resource wealth plays a vital role in the country's political economy, in part by enabling the royal family to maintain power directly, through co-optation and repression, and also by ensuring that the West maintains an interest in the regime's stability. Since the 1920s, the Kingdom of Saudi Arabia has been run by and largely for the sprawling Al-Saud family, which now numbers in the thousands. Commoners are incorporated into the political establishment through co-optation, often on the basis of technical merit and competence but not as the result of electoral victories. Despite Saudi Arabia's crucial geopolitical significance and place in US strategic thinking, the monarchy has periodically come under some pressure to put on a more liberal face. It has generally responded by creating various consultative councils, which are charged with advising the sovereign but not legislating. At the same time, the monarchy has resorted to conservative Islamic clergy to fend off a growing political Islamic challenge from within.

Other RRLP monarchies have more open political systems, most notably Kuwait. Kuwait first introduced a parliament, in which the country's wealthy merchants were represented, in the 1930s (see Crystal 1990). Once the Kuwaiti state and the Sabah family had control of the country's increasing petroleum rents after World War II, the need for merchant support dwindled. The rescue of Kuwait after the First Gulf War came at a price: both domestic constituents and external backers pressured the Sabahs to take steps to reestablish democracy. In October 1992, elections for the National Assembly were held in which only about 70,000 male Kuwaitis of proven Kuwaiti ancestry, out of some 625,000 native Kuwaitis, were allowed to vote (Gause 1994, 188–189). Multiple parliamentary elections have been held since then, most recently in 2013, and women gained the right to vote in 2005. With the significant exception of the disenfranchisement of long-term resident alien workers, Kuwait has a reasonable claim to be called a liberal monarchy.

Since 2011, Saudi Arabia has played an influential counterrevolutionary role in the region by actively blocking the overthrow of its allies (i.e., Bahrain) and even helping to restore military rule in Egypt at the expense of the Muslim Brotherhood while bankrolling some opposition groups fighting against the Assad regime in Syria. At home, fearing a regional diffusion of protests, the royal family extended financial incentives to its citizens and suppressed domestic protests, which were geographically limited or played out in online forums. Other RRLP countries, such as the United Arab Emirates (UAE), Qatar, and Kuwait, also deployed their vast resources to increase subsidies and extend other benefits to citizens in a preemptive effort to block dissent.

Many of the RRLP monarchies straddle social and regional cleavages within their domestic territories. In Saudi Arabia, these include the Shi'a minority in the east of the country, the Hijaz, which contains the holy cities of Mecca and Medina and is the home of Saudi Arabia's traditional trading and merchant families, and, more important, the Najd, from which the royal family comes. The Sabah ruling family of Kuwait, too, finds itself astride major cleavages, including a Shi'a minority that is sometimes seen as a fifth column for Iraqi or Iranian interests. Sunni-Shi'a tensions have been most politicized in Bahrain, where the Sunni al-Khalifa family rules over a population that is over 70 percent Shi'a. In February 2011, the predominantly Shi'a opposition initiated massive protests against the monarchy, prompting a brutal crackdown from the monarchy, with Saudi support. On the surface, tensions in Bahrain look sectarian in nature—an interpretation promoted by the regime, which often accuses Iran of whipping up anti-Sunni sentiment in its borders. In reality, the conflict is largely political and centers on the distribution of resources and opposition to political repression. Beyond sectarian cleavages, the distinction between citizens and "guest workers" constitutes another important social division across the Gulf. For decades, the RRLP countries have used their oil wealth to import a large pool of migrant laborers, both skilled and unskilled, who do not enjoy the same rights as citizens. Unskilled workers in particular often face harsh working conditions and restrictions on their freedoms.

Within the RRLP countries, Libya has been unique in its formal and informal rules of the political game. In 1969 then-Captain Muammar Gaddafi overthrew the Libyan monarchy and proclaimed an Arab republic modeled on that of Nasserist Egypt. In 1977 he introduced what he called the Jamahiria, or "mass state," the intent of which was to abolish all intermediaries between the people, or masses, and their leaders. There were to be no political parties or mass organizations, and all agencies, enterprises, and places of work were to be run by the employees themselves, through revolutionary people's councils. The blueprint was breathtaking, but its implementation was not visible. Key bureaucracies built around the oil and banking sectors seemed little affected by massism, and the armed forces were hardly controlled by the revolutionary councils. The idea of the mass state seemed hollow when, much like Saudi Arabia and Kuwait, 40 percent of Libya's workforce was foreign, as was 50 percent of its managerial and professional personnel. Foreigners could not be members of revolutionary councils, and it was inconceivable that they would not be paid wages. In the end, Libya was simply another rentier state with an idiosyncratic and autocratic leader. After 2003, when Gaddafi agreed to decommission Libya's chemical and nuclear weapons programs, relations with the West improved. After the United States removed Libya from the list of state sponsors of terrorism in 2006, the Libyan economy began to open up, with increasing privatization of state-owned industries. However, parallel political reforms were not adopted, and given that Libya straddles the border between the RRLP and RRLA countries, it is perhaps not surprising that governance patterns resemble those in the more populous resource-rich countries.

In February 2011, protests erupted in the eastern city of Benghazi and soon spread to other cities, eliciting a harsh crackdown from the government. In the following month, the UN Security Council authorized a NATO-led no-fly zone over Libya and air strikes to protect civilians. For months, various militias battled progovernment forces, but after Gaddafi was captured and killed in October 2011, it was the Libyan National Transitional Council (NTC) that declared that Libya was officially "liberated." In the following July, elections were held for the 300-member General National Council (GNC), which replaced the NTC and was tasked with forming a constituent assembly to write a permanent Libyan constitution to be approved by referendum.

Since the overthrow of Gaddafi, Libya has been labeled a "transitional" state, and it is questionable whether or not democratic institutions are taking root. Elections for national councils and the constituent assembly tasked with writing the new constitution have been held. But thus far the new government has faced growing lawlessness and has failed to gain control over the national territory and to build effective state institutions. Militias operate with impunity in much of the country, movements for autonomy have pressed their claims on the state, and extremist groups, some with linkages to al-Qaeda, have emerged. In addition to mounting insecurity, Libya is suffering increasing economic problems owing to the disruption of oil exports and the control of pipelines by militias demanding concessions from the central government. As a result, even the capital city in this oil-rich country has been experiencing power cuts.

The OECD Economies of the Middle East: Turkey and Israel

On both economic and political grounds, the last two countries covered in this book, Turkey and Israel, do not fit into our main categorizations of MENA political economies. Their membership in the OECD, a club of wealthy countries committed to market-based economies and democratic rule, signals their differences from the other MENA countries. First, the two countries have more developed economies than most MENA countries, with greater economic diversification and higher social development indicators, and therefore they face distinct opportunities and constraints in their domestic economic environments and global economic engagements. Second, Turkey and Israel have comparatively long histories of democratic rule, albeit with important caveats. Turkey oscillated between freewheeling electoral politics in the 1950s and 1970s and military rule in the 1960s and early 1980s. In 1983 another attempt was made to revive civilian electoral politics, and so far it has been successful, despite mounting political tensions in the past few years. Beyond domestic factors, Turkish aspirations to someday join the European Union have provided another external pressure to democratize. Since its creation in 1948, Israel has maintained a continuously democratic regime, but that distinction must be qualified by its strict policing of the Arab populations it inherited in 1948 and its continued occupation of the Palestinian Territories.

In recent decades, both countries have undergone significant economic transformations that have made them far more competitive in the global economy than other countries in the region. As discussed earlier, Turkey was a pioneer in the region in adopting statist developmental policies. During the 1970s, however, instability and a series of fractured governing coalitions hindered Turkey's ability to pursue a coherent economic policy. In 1980 the military staged a coup, in part to put a stop to perceived economic mismanagement under the rule of the Justice Party and the Republican People's Party, which had become more overtly socialist than at any time under Atatürk. After the banning of most parties functioning before the 1980 coup, new elections were held in 1983, and Turgut Özal's Motherland Party won a narrow majority. Under Özal, whose party remained in power until November 1991, Turkey embarked on a liberalization of its economy.

In the 1990s, important shifts in domestic politics and the structure of the private sector became increasingly apparent. In 1994 the Welfare Party, a thinly disguised Islamic party (the constitution prohibits the formation of openly religious or ethnic parties), swept municipal elections in several cities, including Istanbul and Ankara. Although the military forced the party from power and the Turkish Constitutional Court banned it and a successor party several years later, its supporters regrouped to form the Justice and Development Party (AKP), which swept the Turkish national elections in November 3, 2002. This moderate Islamist party, committed to joining the EU, was the first single party to be able to form a government in fifteen years. Since 2002, the AKP has won three successive rounds of national elections and increased its share of representation each time while increasing its control over society, prompting its critics to proclaim that Turkey is becoming authoritarian via democratic channels.

Under AKP rule, the state carried out far-reaching economic reforms, which were designed under the preceding government but never implemented. An economic crisis in 2001 and increased political unity after the Islamist party gained majority power facilitated the enactment of these politically risky reforms. In addition, the interests of a key social base of the AKP compelled the party to push for economic opening and privatization with renewed vigor. The "Anatolian Tigers," a new breed of export-oriented entrepreneurs based in provincial cities who emerged in the 1980s, were closely associated with the rise of the AKP.

For a time, the AKP was widely acclaimed for promoting civil and political liberties, reining in the military, and generally bringing Turkey closer to fulfilling the conditions required for EU accession. In recent years, however, the party and its head, Prime Minister Recep Tayyip Erdogan, have exhibited increasingly authoritarian tendencies with restrictions on the media, a zealous crackdown on its secular opponents in the army in what has come to be known as the Ergenekon scandal, and most recently efforts to quash its former allies, the Islamist Gulen Movement. The outbreak of the Gezi Park protests, initially sparked by opposition to the government's plans to build a shopping mall and mosque on a park in central Istanbul, also called into question the AKP's democratic credentials.

Israel's democracy is vigorous and even older than the Turkish democratic system, but it has exhibited important changes over time. As in Turkey, old political coalitions such as the center-left Israel Labor Party (MAPAI), which dominated Israeli politics in the first two decades and favored redistributive policies, have broken down and reassembled. Now the major cleavage in Israeli Jewish society is between secularists with some commitment to socialism and a strong welfare state and a growing conservative coalition increasingly characterized by an aggressive religious nationalism. The Likud alliance, which dominated Israeli politics from the mid-1970s to the mid-1980s, has been home for Israelis favorable to private-sector growth, religious claims to the occupied territories, and repressive policies toward Israel's Arab minority. The bulk of Likud's following has come from Oriental and Sephardic Jews, who tend to be somewhat less educated and lower-income than the dominant Ashkenazi elites. After some ups and downs during the 1990s and 2000s, since 2009 the Likud, under the leadership of Benjamin Netanyahu, has once again dominated Israeli politics.

Two main issues have preoccupied the Israeli political scene. A major question dominating Israeli politics for many years has been whether the system can absorb a large, possibly majority-non-Jewish population and still preserve the logic of one citizen, one vote. There are today about 1.7 million Arab citizens of Israel, dating from 1948; 2.7 million Palestinians in the West Bank and East Jerusalem; and over

1.6 million Palestinians in Gaza. How to address the Israeli-Palestinian conflict has been a major topic of debate within Israeli society.

Increasingly, economic issues have dominated the Israeli domestic sociopolitical scene. The economy initially followed a state-led development model, which was gradually dismantled. As in many neighboring Arab countries, the resultant cuts in public spending on social programs and growing inequality have fueled rising tensions (Rivlin 2010). Thus, as the Arab uprisings spread across the region and the Occupy movement spread across the globe, Israeli witnessed its own mass protests. Since 2011, the Israeli "social justice protests" have compelled hundreds of thousands of protesters to oppose the rise in housing costs and the decline of public health and education services.

A brief discussion of the Palestinian Territories finds its logical place here because Israel exerts extensive direct and indirect control over Palestinian politics and economic conditions. After the June War of 1967, Israel occupied Gaza, the West Bank, the Golan Heights, and East Jerusalem. In 1989, Yasser Arafat and the Palestine Liberation Organization (PLO) accepted the existence of Israel and declared their readiness to live in peace with Israel on the basis of UN Resolution 242, calling for Israeli withdrawal from the occupied territories. After secret talks in Oslo, Norway, Israelis and Palestinians ironed out the details of what became the Declaration of Principles, and the historic handshake of Prime Minister Yitzhak Rabin and Chairman Arafat happened at the White House in September 1993. The DOP called for a transition period and direct negotiations toward a final settlement. As a result, Israel withdrew from parts of the West Bank but maintained control over certain areas deemed priority security zones, and in 2005 Israel disengaged from Gaza. Since then, the peace process has deteriorated, and in 2000 a second Palestinian *intifada,* or uprising, against Israeli occupation broke out. In reality, Israel still maintains extensive control over both the West Bank and Gaza by controlling their borders, maintaining checkpoints that restrict movement within the West Bank, and limiting the movement of people and goods outside of the Palestinian Territories. As a result of the Israeli occupation, the Palestinian Territories have experienced a trend toward "de-development," or a "process which undermines or weakens the ability of an economy to grow and expand by preventing it from accessing and utilizing critical inputs needed to promote internal growth beyond a specific structural level" (Roy 1987, 56; see also Roy 2001).

Internal Palestinian politics have also deteriorated. Formally, the Palestinian Territories are governed by a democratic system: elections have been conducted regularly, voter turnout has been high, and international observers agree that the elections have been free and fair. In some ways, this is unsurprising. The long years of the first (unarmed) intifada prior to 1991 and its reinforcing of Palestinian civil society, the distance of its leaders-in-exile, and the high levels of literacy and political awareness among its population have enabled the Palestinians to move beyond the paternalistic authoritarianism of other Arab regimes—a paternalism shared by Yasser Arafat, the long-exiled PLO leader who won the presidency handily after the first elections were held in the Palestinian Territories in 1993. Despite Arafat's popularity, Hamas, the Palestinian branch of the Muslim Brotherhood, gained increasing appeal. In the second Palestinian legislative elections held in January 2006, Hamas won 56 percent of the total seats. (Owing to the electoral structure, Hamas's share of the legislative seats was greater than its share of the popular vote, which was 44 percent.) Hamas's victory owed as much, if not more, to the failure of the peace process to yield tangible results and rising corruption in the Fatah-controlled Palestinian Authority (PA) as it did to a positive expression of support for the Islamist party. The PA seemed to have succumbed to the classic dilemma facing the RPLA regimes, notably the tension between the inability to repress or buy off populations and the resulting need to institute economic reforms in order to deliver material improvements. Israeli and American officials' refusal to deal with the Hamas-led government contributed to the breakdown of the democratic system. Armed clashes between Fatah and Hamas led to a split, with the former controlling the West Bank and the latter controlling Gaza. Tensions ratcheted up further between the two sides during the Israeli siege of Gaza in 2009, when Hamas officials accused the Fatah-led government in Ramallah of doing little to alleviate the situation. The fragmentation of power in the Palestinian political system as well as the enduring Israeli occupation in part explain the limited scope of protests during the Arab uprisings.

In April 2014, Fatah and Hamas leadership formally announced efforts to reach a rapprochement. The Israeli blockade as well as reduced regional aid had greatly reduced Hamas's access to resources, compelling the Palestinian Islamist group to offer major concessions to its rival as part of the deal. In response to the agreement, Israel announced its withdrawal from the peace talks on the grounds that it would not negotiate with Hamas, which it regards as a terrorist organization. Indeed, the Israeli attacks on Gaza in July 2014, known as Operation Protective Edge, were widely regarded as an attempt to undermine the power-sharing agreement between the two Palestinian factions. The ensuing war between Israel and Hamas resulted in more than 2,000 Palestinian deaths, overwhelmingly of civilians, and the deaths of 66 Israeli soldiers, 5 Israeli civilians, and one Thai guest worker.

CONCLUSIONS

In this chapter, we integrated political regime type into our typology of political economies in the region. The RPLA group of countries includes the most diverse array of political regimes. Until the uprisings, Egypt, Tunisia, and the two Yemens (before the unified Yemen began to exploit oil in the 1990s) were RPLA authoritarian republics; today Egypt is drifting back into this status several years after its dictator was overthrown. Jordan and Morocco are RPLA monarchies, while Lebanon has a long history of democratic rule, however imperfect. Despite the diversity of regime types and informal political settlements underlying their political formal institutions, the countries in the RPLA group share some important commonalties that partly explain why many of these countries have witnessed the most extensive and persistent levels of social mobilization in the region since the Arab uprisings broke out. First, all implemented statist economic policies in the first decades after independence but were forced to cut back public investment sharply in the 1980s, leading to rising poverty as well as declining prospects for social mobility for their key constituents in the middle class, especially those in public-sector positions. Second, in all RPLA countries, structural adjustment narrowed social coalitions and cronyism expanded as a small group of elites profited the most from lucrative economic opportunities. Finally, their low oil endowments gave them fewer resources to invest in co-optation and repression than their neighbors had. It is perhaps no accident that protests have been less pervasive in the monarchies, where hereditary succession and greater pluralism have muted calls for total regime change. Lebanon has witnessed the lowest levels of social mobilization, in part because the power structure is highly fragmented in its consociational system, inhibiting opponents of the system from focusing their protests on a single political office or leader.

The RRLA countries are all authoritarian republics, with Algeria, Syria, and Yemen as its secular variants, and Iran (post-1979), and Sudan (post-1989) classified as Islamic republics. Despite substantial diversity in their political institutions and underlying political settlements, some common patterns have emerged among these countries. In the post-independence period, most RRLA countries embarked on a statist development project, leading to the expansion of public employment and heavy investment in public enterprises. Given their high populations, their substantial resource endowments did not cushion them from the economic crises beginning in the 1980s. In response to the failure of their development strategies, none of the RRLA countries has been able to launch a new ideological project that could mobilize the masses, and as in their oil-poor republican cousins, economic liberalization has been characterized by cronyism and the exclusion of the poor and middle classes from the social contract. Since the 1980s, rulers in some of these countries, such as Syrian and Iran, have increased repression, while in others, notably Algeria, popular protests have increased while state elites remain indifferent to societal demands. Yet the RRLA countries have thus far remained relatively stable—only in Iran has there been regime change.

Finally, the RRLP countries, which include the Gulf monarchies and Libya, have exhibited the most continuity since their establishment or independence from colonial rule. In part, their relative stability arises from their high per capita resource wealth, which enables rulers to maintain a modicum of support among their citizen populations. With its revolution in 2011, Libya is an exception, but Gaddafi's neglect of key groups and growing repression as well as the NATO bombing campaign had already set this country apart from the Gulf monarchies. Despite their oil wealth, which has cushioned them from making major changes in their founding political settlements, in recent decades the small oil-rich Gulf countries have exhibited some gradual transformations. In particular, in some countries, such as the United Arab Emirates, islands of quality in their public- and private-sector institutions have emerged, and other countries, notably Saudi Arabia, with its relatively high population, have even been forced to undertake austerity programs.

In the remainder of the book, we explore the economic and political developments presented briefly in Chapters 2 and 3 in more detail to show how shifting economic circumstances and political developments contributed to the wave of changes across the region in recent years.

NOTES

1. Of course, external intervention from Saudi Arabia as well as tacit US support were key factors reinforcing the rule of the al-Khalifa family in Bahrain.

2. In 2011–2012, the GCC countries considered the possibility of inviting Jordan and Morocco to join their club. For the time being, this initiative seems to have fizzled.

3. But see Thomas (2010), who casts doubt on the construct validity of the governance measures used in the World Bank's World Governance Indicators data set, which is based on the measures developed by Kaufmann, Kraay, and Mastruzzi (2010).

4. Cingranelli and Richards (2010, 418) define this measure as an "additive index constructed from the Freedom of Movement, Freedom of Speech, Workers' Rights, Political Participation, and Freedom of Religion indicators." This index ranges from zero (no government respect for these five rights) to ten (full government respect for these five rights).

5. This section draws on Barkey (1994), Itzkowitz (1972), and Kafadar (1995).

6. On Ottoman state-building and its differences from the European experience, see Barkey (1994).

7. Betty Anderson, Department of History, Boston University, personal communication, September 28, 2014.

8. Until 1990, Yemen was divided into two countries, the People's Democratic Republic of Yemen in the South and the Yemen Arab Republic in the North. After the fall of the Soviet Union, the two countries reunified.

9. Increasingly, Middle Eastern monarchs, like the presidents of Arab socialist republics, pose as the sole bulwark against Islamist parties. The claim of divine right to rule is a decidedly two-edged sword.

10. Hezbollah claimed that the ongoing dispute with Israel over the Shebaa Farms area, a small village located at the intersection of the (disputed) Lebanese, Syrian, and Israeli border, made it necessary to retain its militia. Occupied by Israel after 1967, the area is claimed by both Syria and Lebanon.

11. The FIS was blamed for Boudiaf's death, but many Algerians remain convinced that the military eliminated him because of his efforts to crack down on corruption in the government and military.

12. Many Muslim Sudanese in Darfur, for example, are not native speakers of Arabic.

4

THE IMPACT OF
DEMOGRAPHIC CHANGE

The so-called youth bulge has been cited as an underlying cause of the Arab uprisings (Amin et al. 2012; LaGraffe 2012; Mirkin 2013; see also Dhillon and Yousef 2009). Middle Eastern populations are young, and even a quick glance around the major metropolises of the region reveals the high number of unemployed or underemployed young people, many of them sitting around in cafés. In Algeria, they are known as *hétistes,* a combination of the Arabic word for "wall" (*heta*) and the French suffix-*iste* to refer to one who leans against a wall. A closer inspection of demographic trends, however, calls for a more nuanced interpretation of the role of youth in the uprisings. Indeed, the region's youth bulge peaked in the late 1970s in North Africa and in the early 1990s in the Middle East. If the youth bulge explains the propensity to revolt, then why did the Tunisian revolution erupt in 2011 rather than in 1979? Demographic trends must be contextualized within larger socioeconomic settings if they are to be related to major political events or movements. In the Middle East, the mismatch between the kinds of jobs generated by labor markets and the aspirations of relatively educated youth, rather than demography per se, help to explain grievances among populations (ILO 2012; Al-Nashif and Tzannatos 2013; see also Bricker and Foley 2013).

The majority of modern demographers agree that population growth is at least partially the result of social conditions and economic incentives (that is, that crude Malthusian "population determinism," which holds that rapid population growth dooms development, is silly, but is not *solely* determined by economic conditions (and therefore family planning programs have an independent impact on fertility). Understanding the determinants of fertility and population growth and the impact of policies is thus a first goal of this chapter. To reduce fertility, policymakers can respond directly by promoting family planning programs and indirectly by altering the incentives for couples to have children. Both sorts of instruments can be politically controversial. Contrary to prevailing stereotypes, however, governments in Muslim-majority countries—even Islamist rulers—do not always adopt pro-natalist policies, and some have even launched successful family planning initiatives.

While we are doubtful that the youth bulge directly "explains" the uprisings, we also believe that fast population growth exacerbates development problems, particularly the ability to provide adequate education and employment for the young. In line with these views, we think that rapid population growth may have retarded the development process in some countries, a theme we develop in the second section of this chapter.

We also believe that rather than the youth bulge itself, it was the inability to take advantage of the rise in the labor force, which peaked during the "lost decade" in most Arab countries, that explains many of the grievances that fueled the uprisings, a theme we explore in the last part of the chapter. Deceleration of population growth presents both opportunities (for example, a decline in the dependency ratio, leading to the so-called demographic dividend, discussed in more detail later in the chapter) and challenges (such as the increasing burden of caring for an aging population). Policymakers must confront such difficulties.

COMPARATIVE DEMOGRAPHIC PATTERNS

Several demographic developments in the Middle East stand out (see Table 4.1). In the second half of the twentieth century, population growth accelerated for nearly forty years. The population growth rate rose to 2.8 percent and then to 3.6 percent for the 1980s. In the late 1980s, however, population growth reached a peak and then began decelerating, falling to 2.6 percent during the 1990s, rising to almost 3 percent in the 2000s, and then dropping again to about 2.4 percent in 2011. In all of those periods, the MENA region had the highest population growth rate in the world until 2011, when sub-Saharan Africa surpassed it. In the simplest terms, population growth accelerated because the birthrate declined more slowly than the death rate. Since no one advocates population control by raising the death rate, population policy analysis focuses on the birthrate.

The Determinants of Fertility

The most revealing statistic for tracking population growth is the total fertility rate (TFR), which tells us roughly how many children the "average woman" will have during her lifetime.[1] By this measure, Middle Eastern women were the most fecund in the world in the early 1950s and were second only to sub-Saharan African women by the early 1980s, when Middle Eastern women were still bearing an average of six children each (National Research Council 1986). In the early 1990s, the Arab region's women were still giving birth to, on average, just under five children each. These figures have gone down rapidly over time, but fertility is still high in the MENA region in general at 2.8 children per woman, and the Arab countries of the region have an especially high fertility rate at 3.2, the second-highest rate after sub-Saharan Africa. Fertility has been decreasing since the 1980s: in the Arab world, it fell from 5.79 to 3.16 (a 44 percent decline), and in the MENA region as a whole it fell from 4.16 in the 1990s to 2.8 in 2011 (a 33 percent decrease). In fact, in some countries in the region (such as Iran and Lebanon), fertility among educated women has fallen to, or below, replacement levels.[2] Since the early 2000s, the rate of decline in fertility in the MENA region has been the fastest in the world (UNICEF 2005). As Table 4.1 shows, the Arab world has experienced the highest decline in fertility rates, followed by East Asia.

In 1950–1955, the regional crude birthrate (CBR, defined as the quotient of the number of births and the total population) was the highest in the world at 50.5 per 1,000. The CBR fell continuously over time, from 45 in 1970 to 25.4 in 2011. The decline in the birthrate is a worldwide phenomenon: the CBR for the total world population fell from 33 in 1970 to 19.3 in 2011, and for less developed countries (LDCs) it fell from 39 to 24 over the same period. Even the CBR of sub-Saharan Africa declined—from 48 in 1970 to 37.2 in 2011. Although the decline in fertility in the MENA region has been large, the region's CBR remains the world's third highest, above the LDC average, which was 19.3 in 2012 (World Bank, World Development Indicators [WDI]).

There has also been a striking change in the relationship between fertility and income during the recent past. Formerly, fertility rates in the region were high in relation to incomes. The relationship between fertility and income for several MENA countries in the early 2000s is illustrated in Figure 4.1 and shows fertility falling with increases in per capita income. The relationship is not a simple one and reflects complex behavioral adjustments. Indeed, if everything else remains the same, higher incomes may lead to more children, since poor health due to low income levels may limit a woman's ability to bear children. The inverse relationship can be thought of as the outcome of a highly complex social process in which new attitudes, new preferences, and new habits are generated. One theory of economic demography holds, in effect, that parents start to substitute "child quality" for "child quantity" as they become richer (see, for example, Schultz 1981). Increased incomes *alone* are unlikely to reduce fertility; additional socioeconomic change is required.

Up to the 1990s, MENA fertility rates exceeded what would have been expected, given per capita incomes in the countries of the region, with the exceptions of Egypt, Tunisia, and Turkey. The disparity was most notable for major oil-exporting countries but was not limited to them. However, the relation between income and fertility has changed profoundly in some countries over the past decade: today fertility rates in roughly half of the MENA countries are now *below* what we would expect on the basis of income alone, while rates in some relatively wealthy countries remain stubbornly high (see Figure 4.1).

How can these differential fertility changes be explained? Demographers do not agree on the precise determinants of fertility. All concur that economic conditions play some role and that the social position of women is highly significant. In addition, all concede that high infant mortality is correlated with high fertility rates. But different analysts accord varying weights to these and to other factors. The decision to have a child is so complex and the available data are so open to various interpretations that dogmatic positions are out of place.[3] We survey some of the plausible explanations for varying fertility rates in the Middle East without offering a firm conclusion. Nonetheless, we maintain that both the social position of women and

TABLE 4.1. Demographic Indicators in the Middle East and in Other Regions of the World, 1980–2011

Country/ Region	Population Growth Rate				Crude Birth Rate (per 1,000 population)				Crude Death Rate (per 1,000 population)				Fertility (children per woman)			
	1980s	1990s	2000s	2011	1980s	1990s	2000s	2011	1980s	1990s	2000s	2011	1980s	1990s	2000s	2011
Algeria	3.04	1.98	1.49	1.43	38.60	25.83	20.60	19.81	8.89	5.76	4.95	4.85	5.99	3.63	2.44	2.22
Arab world	2.96	2.40	2.22	2.06	39.03	31.56	27.09	25.39	10.31	7.38	6.03	5.59	5.79	4.46	3.48	3.16
Bahrain	3.37	2.71	6.36	4.77	32.08	25.19	20.85	18.94	3.87	3.23	2.89	2.73	4.45	3.18	2.62	2.50
Egypt	2.37	1.77	1.81	1.73	36.70	28.33	24.47	22.83	10.56	7.28	5.39	5.11	5.03	3.78	3.01	2.69
Iran	3.43	1.73	1.27	1.10	41.59	25.73	17.83	16.78	13.73	6.06	5.35	5.40	6.09	3.45	1.87	1.64
Iraq	2.83	2.93	2.82	2.86	39.06	38.10	36.92	34.92	10.31	5.56	5.86	5.51	6.28	5.64	4.98	4.64
Israel	1.76	3.04	1.99	1.85	23.38	21.48	21.34	21.40	6.75	6.38	5.55	5.30	3.07	2.87	2.93	3.00
Jordan	3.75	4.26	2.32	2.19	38.73	33.19	27.32	24.51	6.17	4.75	4.13	4.02	6.78	4.85	3.74	3.70
Kuwait	4.65	1.77	3.52	2.93	32.18	20.90	19.04	17.91	3.17	2.82	3.09	3.05	4.31	2.54	2.34	2.28
Lebanon	0.39	2.39	1.23	0.75	28.25	23.83	17.05	15.16	7.43	7.09	6.92	6.94	3.65	2.86	2.01	1.78
Libya	3.73	1.89	1.93	1.05	38.67	23.99	23.96	22.57	8.45	4.17	3.99	4.04	6.49	3.79	2.84	2.50
Morocco	2.43	1.57	1.05	1.01	34.87	25.73	20.55	19.21	9.90	6.90	5.90	5.81	4.98	3.38	2.45	2.42
Oman	4.76	2.29	1.89	2.26	46.55	30.79	20.36	17.51	7.32	3.78	3.43	3.87	8.11	5.55	2.79	2.24
Palestine		4.05	2.65	2.99		43.52	37.04	32.79		5.58	3.98	3.52		6.19	4.86	4.38
Qatar	8.16	2.14	10.24	6.13	29.90	21.25	16.29	12.19	2.83	2.16	1.75	1.51	5.06	3.71	2.70	2.23
Saudi Arabia	5.26	2.27	3.07	2.28	40.72	31.98	23.64	21.50	6.82	4.74	3.98	3.71	6.68	5.05	3.30	2.74

Region															
Sudan	2.87	2.54	2.36	2.10	42.82	39.53	35.15	32.38	15.12	12.72	9.87	8.81	6.24	5.69	4.87	4.32
Syria	3.35	2.67	2.51	1.81	40.97	31.91	25.08	22.40	6.17	4.15	3.56	3.55	6.39	4.47	3.25	2.87
Tunisia	2.47	1.72	0.99	1.17	32.50	21.59	17.29	18.60	7.58	5.62	5.74	5.70	4.61	2.81	2.05	2.13
Turkey	2.09	1.64	1.35	1.21	31.19	23.97	19.23	17.50	10.03	7.17	5.58	5.47	3.79	2.76	2.20	2.06
United Arab Emirates	6.11	5.28	8.66	4.93	29.35	21.15	15.02	12.75	3.45	2.35	1.56	1.36	5.06	3.53	2.13	1.72
Yemen	4.02	4.09	3.04	3.06	56.08	46.48	39.27	37.77	14.56	10.87	7.69	6.26	9.08	7.71	5.79	5.09
MENA Average	3.62	2.61	2.98	2.36			23.73	21.88						4.16	3.10	2.82
East Asia and Pacific		1.22	0.76	0.65	22.65	18.73	14.30	13.46	7.16	6.77	6.79	7.11	2.83	2.17	1.84	1.74
European Union	0.29	0.23	0.36	0.23	13.01	11.18	10.55	10.41	10.43	10.30	9.79	9.59	1.75	1.51	1.52	1.57
High income	0.72	0.71	0.71	0.65	14.55	13.08	11.81	11.31	8.81	8.69	8.39	8.35	1.85	1.74	1.70	1.69
Latin America and Caribbean	2.07	1.68	1.26	1.11	29.56	24.50	20.34	18.17	7.52	6.37	5.96	5.92	3.73	2.92	2.41	2.18
North America	0.95	1.21	0.95	0.75	15.66	15.06	13.75	12.53	8.53	8.53	8.19	7.98	1.84	1.97	1.99	1.86
South Asia	2.40	2.04	1.58	1.44	35.38	30.30	24.85	22.63	11.69	9.91	8.37	7.83	4.67	3.82	2.99	2.69
Sub-Saharan Africa	2.85	2.67	2.51	2.53	45.35	42.48	39.24	37.16	16.94	16.14	14.08	12.32	6.52	5.95	5.28	4.88
World	1.76	1.49	1.21	1.15	27.22	23.63	20.32	19.32	9.76	9.04	8.42	8.12	3.52	2.94	2.55	2.42

Source: United Nations (UN) Population Division (2013), World Population Prospects.

FIGURE 4.1. Per Capita Gross National Income and Fertility Rates in MENA Countries in the Early 2000s

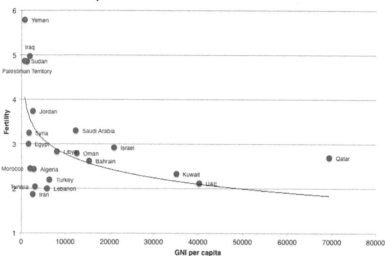

Source: World Bank, World Development Indicators (WDI).

national policymaking are central to any satisfactory explanation for the varying levels of MENA fertility rates.

One hypothesis is that poor health conditions raise fertility rates. Much evidence suggests that high infant mortality stimulates fertility. The logic is clear: for both economic and emotional reasons, parents are interested in *surviving* children. If many infants die, people will, on average, tend to have more children to compensate. One study found that more than one-third of the decline in fertility was "explained" (in the statistical sense) by health improvements (Dyer and Yousef 2003). Several changes lead to faster decline in fertility rates: delayed marriages, wider acceptance of and access to family planning services, and female education. Strong cultural values attached to the family and traditional marriage and childbearing practices delayed the transition to lower fertility in the MENA region (Roudi-Fahimi and Kent 2007). Although infant mortality rates in the region are high relative to those of advanced industrial countries, they have come down very sharply in the past several decades—from 128 per 1,000 births in 1970 to 92 in 1980, 59 in 1990, 45 in 2003, and about 21 in 2012. MENA infant mortality is below the average for sub-Saharan Africa (63.8), South Asia (46.6), and LDCs in general (57). Studies of Iran stress the role of improved health in that country's dramatic fertility decline (Abbasi-Shavazi 2001; Roudi-Fahimi 2002; see also Box 4.1). Conundrums appear among countries in the region. For example, in 2011 Turkey and Syria had nearly the same infant mortality rate (see Table 5.2), yet fertility in Syria (2.9) was above that of its northern neighbor (2.1) (World Bank, WDI, 2011).

Economic analysis provides a useful perspective on fertility. Although any couple's decision to have a child is a complex product of social norms and personal psychology, some insights can be gained if one views the decision as similar to any other economic decision—as a balancing of "cost" and "benefit," neither of which are exclusively monetary. This view suggests that since most people like children, they will tend to have *more* of them as they become richer, just as they buy more clothes, meat, radios, and entertainment. How, then, are we to explain the observed correlation between higher incomes and lower fertility? Economic analysts of demography argue that the key is the rising *opportunity cost of having children* as family incomes rise. This rising cost has two major components: the increased amount of money that parents wish to spend on each child, and the higher opportunity cost of parents' time. If rising incomes do not generate enough to meet these costs, increased wealth may do little to reduce fertility.

An important component of the opportunity cost of having children is their economic activity: the earlier children can perform productive labor, the sooner their net contributions to the family budget will be positive. In most peasant societies, including those of the Middle East, children can and do perform numerous tasks, ranging from caring for younger children to harvesting cotton. In general, the more child labor is performed in agriculture, the lower the opportunity cost of having many children and therefore the higher the fertility rate. This aspect of the argument that low levels of development engender high fertility is certainly reasonable and is confirmed by evidence from the region. This relationship is much less evident in urban areas. Consequently, rapidly increasing urbanization may facilitate fertility declines.

Similarly, children perform an important function as "pension funds"—as the providers of income and care in old age. If, as in the MENA countries, such a burden falls on the sons, and if child mortality is high, an average peasant or urban poor family will rationally want to have seven births to ensure that two sons survive to provide for them in old age. Here, too, the MENA countries resemble most developing countries, and therefore the "insurance" motive for having children cannot explain the relatively high fertility levels in half of the MENA countries—especially those with higher per capita incomes.

A critical component of the economic analysis of fertility is the opportunity cost of *women's* time, since women have primary responsibility for child care everywhere in the world. If women are illiterate, and if they are more or less systematically excluded from alternative employment, the opportunity cost of their time will be low. When such considerations are combined with and reinforced by social pressures on women to have many children, the result is likely to be a high fertility rate.

The socioeconomic status of women is therefore crucial to fertility. Despite important improvements, the adult literacy figures for women in the Middle East remain low in international comparative perspective (see Table 4.2). There is much evidence that higher education is correlated with lower fertility. Educated women both want to have fewer children and are more likely to use birth control to achieve their desired family size. However, anomalies remain: within all countries, more educated women have fewer children than their less educated counterparts, but the variation across countries is large; for example, illiterate Moroccans have fewer children, on average, than university-educated Palestinians (Ouadah-Bedidi, Vallin, and Bouchoucha 2012).

Women's employment also lowers fertility, provided that it is outside of the home. Although many Middle Eastern rural women do participate extensively in crop and

TABLE 4.2. Youth and Adult Literacy Rates in the MENA Countries and in Selected Global Regions, circa 2013

Country	Youth Literacy		Adult Literacy (total)	Adult Literacy Rate (females as % of males)
	Male	*Female*		
Algeria	94%	89%	92%	73%
Bahrain	100	100	100	91
Egypt	88	82	85	66
Iran	99	99	99	85
Iraq	85	80	83	78
Israel			95	96
Jordan	99	99	99	92
Kuwait	99	99	99	94
Lebanon	98	99	99	90
Libya	100	100	100	89
Morocco	87	72	79	56
Oman	98	98	98	87
Palestine	99	99	99	95
Qatar	98	98	98	95
Saudi Arabia	99	97	98	86
Sudan	89	83	86	70
Syria	96	93	94	84
Tunisia	98	96	97	78
Turkey	99	97	98	91
United Arab Emirates	94	97	95	90
Yemen	96	72	84	62
MENA	93	87	90	75
World	92	87	89	84
Industrialized countries	100	100	100	99
Sub-Saharan Africa	77	67	72	62
South Asia	85	72	79	61
LDCs	75	66	70	58

Source: World Bank, WDI.

livestock production, such work is typically integrated with child care and thus creates little pressure to reduce fertility. Egyptian surveys showed that women who worked for cash outside of the home had an average of 3.2 births, compared with 4.9 for women who did not (USAID 1992). Women's participation in work that is more directly competitive with child-rearing is, with a few exceptions, relatively low in the region (see Chapter 5). In the Arab countries, the female labor force participation rate increased modestly from roughly 21 percent in the 1990s to about 22.9 percent in 2011 (World Bank 2012). However, as Chapter 5 shows in more detail, different Arab countries had different trends. For example, the female labor force participation rate increased in countries such as Bahrain, Jordan, Kuwait, Oman, Qatar, the United Arab Emirates, and Yemen. In others, such as Syria and Turkey, women's participation in the labor force declined. Despite the general trend toward improvement, on average, women's participation in the labor force in the MENA region, and especially in many Arab countries, remains the lowest in the world.

These considerations pose the question of how "culture" affects fertility and, in particular, what role Islam plays in promoting population growth. It should be obvious that the answer to the broadly stated question "Does culture affect fertility?" must be "Of course!" The social norms regulating the sexual division of labor and, indeed, all aspects of relations between the sexes powerfully shape individual actions. Specifying the precise ways in which culture influences reproductive behavior is extremely difficult, but we can offer a few general points. It is important to remember that, until the 1970s and early 1980s, most MENA countries were largely peasant or herder societies. There are *no* peasant societies in which women are treated equally with men; in all such societies the norm has been women's "social marginalization and economic centrality" (Meillassoux 1981). In most peasant societies, whether Muslim or non-Muslim, family life is important, there is social and economic pressure to bear sons, and women's sexuality is strictly controlled. Therefore, at least part of the subordination of women (and consequent high fertility rates) may be due to their peasant status as much as their Muslim faith.

But this can hardly be the whole story. After all, China remains overwhelmingly a peasant society, yet its fertility rate has plummeted over the past several decades. Furthermore, to an outsider, Muslim societies seem especially socially restrictive for women (Fish 2002; Donno and Russett 2004; Norris and Inglehart 2002). There are stringent practices of female seclusion and segregation of the sexes, and Islamic law defines women as juridical minors. Men can easily divorce women, whereas the reverse is not true; the father, not the mother, typically gets custody of the children. Some Muslim women may try to have large families as a kind of "insurance policy" against divorce: a man might be more reluctant to divorce the mother of six than the mother of an only daughter.

International evidence suggests a positive correlation between Islam and fertility: Albania (a majority-Muslim country) has the highest fertility rate in Europe, and Muslims in Malaysia have higher fertility than other religious groups in Malaysia. In Israel, Muslim women's TFR in 2000 was 4.5, whereas the rate for Christians was 2.35 and that for Jews was 2.53 (Courbage 1999). In India, Sri Lanka, and elsewhere, adherence to Islam has been shown to have an independent and positive impact on fertility (Mishra 2004). Not all studies find such a correlation, however;

in parts of sub-Saharan Africa, notably Cameroon and the Central African Republic, Muslim fertility was not higher than adherents of other religions, while the fertility rate among Muslims is slowing down in Southeast Asia. On average, the fertility rate of Muslim-majority countries has dropped over time, as in all regions of the world (Pew Research 2011).

One must avoid essentialism here. Islam is a living religion, and there is much debate in the Muslim world over personal status questions or those related to familial relations, such as marriage, divorce, child custody, and inheritance. Many Muslim scholars believe that many of the practices that Westerners label "Islamic" are in fact corruptions of Islam, derived from other sources such as '*urf*, or customary law. They are horrified by practices such as female genital cutting (also widely practiced in non-Muslim Africa and more rarely in West Asia) and regularly denounce them. This debate is critical: only internal change that is consistent with people's beliefs has any chance of affecting such deeply personal issues as the regulation of family life. When we say that "Islam" promotes the subordinate status of women and thus high fertility, we mean "Islam as currently practiced by (many) Muslims." Inconveniently for essentialists, the most rapid fall in fertility in world history occurred in the Islamic Republic of Iran (see Box 4.1). Furthermore, while the personal status codes of Middle Eastern countries vary widely, those in Morocco (since 2005), Tunisia, and Turkey provide relatively strong protections for women's rights in family law.

More generally, all cultures are flexible; they can accommodate wide-ranging changes in economic, political, and social life. For example, one might summarize this discussion by saying that Islam places great stress on family life and considers women's primary place to be in the home. But then, of how many cultures could one say otherwise? Few would try to argue that family life is marginal in Chinese culture, yet fertility rates in China declined precipitously in the past several decades. Before the 1950s, the status of women in Chinese society was lower than in the poorest Muslim society: a married Chinese woman could own no property distinct from her husband's, divorce was even easier for men than in Muslim societies, and women were essentially the property of their husbands. Yet governments as diverse as that of the People's Republic of China, Taiwan, and Singapore have all succeeded in educating women, raising their legal status, and dramatically lowering fertility rates. "Culture" is not immutable.

The question is not whether "culture" or "belief systems" affect behavior, but whether they would continue to produce high fertility *even after* substantial changes elsewhere in social and economic life. For example, it is clear that early marriage contributes to higher fertility. Few children are born outside of marriage in the Middle East; if couples are formed early in life, fertility will be higher. Demographic historians have shown that postponing the age of marriage was the principal mechanism for limiting fertility in preindustrial Europe and Japan (Mosk 1983; Wrigley and Schofield 1981; World Bank 1984). Early marriage is common in some Islamic countries and receives social sanction and reinforcement. In the early 1980s, about one young woman out of three was married before her nineteenth birthday (Lapham 1983). However, the median age at first marriage has risen in every Arab country since then. One study found that changes in nuptiality (marital status) were the key

BOX 4.1. The Fertility Revolution in Iran

Iranian family planning has undergone two sharp reversals. In 1965 the shah instituted a family planning policy that, like most such programs at the time, stressed the "supply side": the availability of contraception. The program collapsed after the Islamic Revolution, since the new regime associated it with both the shah and the West, which had helped to finance it. Notwithstanding the fact that the Ayatollah Khomeini issued a *fatwa* permitting contraception and family planning, social traditionalism and the war with Iraq combined to produce a pronatalist policy. The minimum age for marriage was reduced, the High Council for Coordination of Family Planning was disbanded, contraceptives became harder to get, and the government provided large families with special housing and food subsidies. These policies contributed to the reversal of fertility decline. The TFR rose from 6.5 in 1976 to 7.0 in 1986 (Omran and Roudi 1993). The rate of natural increase rose from 2.9% between 1966–1967 and 1976–1977 to 3.9% between 1976–1977 and 1986–1987; the total fertility rate in 1994 was 6.2 (Bulatao and Richardson 1994).

The census of 1986 served as a "wake-up call" for planners, and the end of the war with Iraq in 1988 provided them with their opportunity. Fertility had already begun to fall, but only slightly, and it remained unacceptably high. The government completely reversed course, establishing a Population Committee in the Ministry of Health and Medical Education. The committee set a goal of reducing the TFR to 4.0. Contraceptives were reintroduced into the primary health care system, which covered Iran's vast rural areas as well as the cities, a crucial factor according to most analyses (Abbasi-Shavazi 2001; Roudi-Fahimi 2002). In 1990 the government legalized female sterilization, and both male and female sterilization were offered without charge (for any man or woman with three or more children). Seminars and the media have been, and are, extensively used to promote family planning. In May 1993 the *majlis* (Iranian parliament) passed a law requiring the withdrawal of some subsidies from families that had a fourth or higher-order child after May 1994.

The results of these policies, combined with increasing female literacy and (probably) economic hardship, have been dramatic. The country's total fertility rate fell to 2.8 by 1996, and today it is between 2.0 and 2.1—below replacement level! Rural fertility fell exceptionally swiftly: from 8.1 in 1976 to 2.4 in 2000 (Roudi-Fahimi 2002). Whereas some 37% of married couples practiced contraception in 1976, 74% did so by 2000. Fertility fell in every province and among all ethnicities. Iran's fertility decline has been one of the fastest in history. Policy matters—greatly.

force lowering fertility in Tunisia, Morocco, and Algeria (Rashad and Khadr 2002). Significant changes in this area also occurred in Jordan and Syria. Contraceptive prevalence has also risen in all countries reporting data (except Iraq). At least one-half of married women in Algeria, Egypt, Iran, Jordan, Lebanon, Morocco, Tunisia, Turkey, and the United Arab Emirates use contraception (UNICEF 2013).

Family Planning Policies

State policy can have a dramatic impact on fertility rates. A wide range of policies exist in the region, both those that affect desired family size (sometimes called "indirect" policies), such as health and education programs, and those that affect the number of children a couple actually has (birth control). Policies in the MENA countries have eschewed coercion and have only lightly relied on disincentives (for example, higher taxes for larger families). The main family planning policy approach (when there has been one at all) has been to subsidize birth control technology and disseminate information through government health networks and the media.

Turkey and Tunisia have followed a consistent policy of promoting family planning since 1965. The Tunisian government has pushed for universal female schooling, raised the legal marriage age, made divorce more difficult, and ensured that birth control technology is widely available. The percentage of teenage women who were married fell from 42 percent in 1956 to only 6 percent in 1975 and to 3 percent in 1994. In the late 1990s, the average age at marriage for women was about twenty-nine years. Fertility rates fell from over 7 at independence to 3.8 in 1992 to 2.0 in 2003, but rose slightly to 2.13 in 2011 (see Table 4.1); until recently, fertility rates were below replacement level. In Turkey, reforms of family law were part of Atatürk's broader developmental vision for the country. After 1965, the Turkish government promoted family planning with subsidies and propaganda without significant interruption, although recent statements by Erdogan are calling into question the AKP governments commitment to this policy.

Other countries have displayed on-again, off-again family planning policies. Both Egypt and Iran fall into this category. Egypt launched a family planning program in 1965 that focused on the supply of birth control technology. The program languished, however, under Sadat. The slogan of the time was "development is the best contraceptive," and the focus—in theory but not in practice—was on, among other things, better health and increased female school enrollment. Gad Gilbar (1992) argues that this shift was political—that Sadat tried to use the Muslim Brotherhood and other Islamists against the pro-Soviet left (see Chapter 12) and accordingly yielded to the pronatalist views of the Islamist group. Mubarak's government reversed this position, however, and with considerable donor assistance, launched a sustained program of family planning that began to show results in the early 1990s. Iranian policy reversals have been still more dramatic (see Box 4.1).

Most countries in the region now have some kind of family planning program (see Table 4.3). Algeria, Yemen, Iraq, Jordan, Lebanon, Morocco, Turkey, Tunisia, and Sudan have all adopted official government policies to promote decreased fertility. At present, only Israel and Iran have explicit initiatives to promote fertility, although the latter country had previously implemented a highly successful program to reduce

TABLE 4.3. Types of Family Planning Programs in the MENA Region

	Raise Fertility	Maintain Fertility	Lower Fertility
Direct Support	Iran	Bahrain, Qatar	Egypt, Algeria, Yemen, Iraq, Jordan, Lebanon, Morocco, Turkey, Tunisia, Sudan
Indirect Support	Israel	Saudi Arabia	
No Support			Oman

Sources: UNFPA (2012b); UNICEF and UNFPA (2008); Roudi (2012); UN Women Watch (2006); Ouadah-Bedidi and Vallin (2013).

fertility. In general, only countries whose leaders feel beleaguered—by war (Iran in the 1980s and again very recently; Iraq under Saddam Hussein) or by the weight of numbers of unfriendly neighbors (Israel)—have explicitly pronatalist policies.

Apart from politically motivated pronatalism, there are several reasons why governments neglect family planning policy. First and probably most important, the benefits of reduced population growth accrue in the future, and here, as elsewhere, myopia characterizes most government policy. Second, some governments believe that rapid population growth is not a problem; these pronatalist countries want more people. To evaluate this position, one must consider the economic consequences of population growth and the politics of ethnic differences in population growth (discussed later). Third, many believe that changing economic conditions will reduce population growth and so the problem will take care of itself. This argument, however, ignores the considerable evidence that the availability of family planning exerts an independent negative pressure on fertility rates.

Perhaps the critical point here is to ask, not whether governments can affect fertility (they can), but rather, how hard they have to try—what it costs them politically. We should also ask what role religion plays in these costs. The legal age of marriage is still only fifteen in Jordan, Kuwait, and Palestine, and as of this writing, Yemen has no legal minimum age for marriage, although this may change soon. Raising the legal age of marriage prompts opposition from Islamic revivalists, as in the mass demonstrations against King Mohammed VI's plan to increase the legal age of marriage for girls in Morocco to eighteen. It is probably not accidental that Moroccan television did not begin showing family planning information until 1982, when economic crisis left little choice. But the politics here are complex. In Morocco, the king prevailed, and the legal age of marriage changed from fifteen to eighteen in January 2004. Meanwhile, the first change in the Turkish Family Code since 1926, raising the legal age of marriage and increasing women's rights in marriage and divorce, occurred under the moderate Islamist government of Recep Tayyip Erdogan. Each government, and each political party, maps its own strategy.

Such stories strongly suggest that high fertility levels are the result of political, not cultural, problems in the Middle East.

THE ECONOMIC CONSEQUENCES
OF DEMOGRAPHIC CHANGE

How does demographic change affect economic development? In the 1950s and 1960s, the United States and other developed nations urged the LDCs to adopt national programs of family planning and population control. Many in the developing world saw these urgings as racist in nature—as white fear of the rising tide of blacks, browns, and yellows. Moreover, it was an era of grandiose development plans and optimism in the Third World. High rates of economic growth suggested that ever-larger numbers of people would be provided for and employed. It was assumed that larger cohorts of the young could be educated and trained so that they could contribute to the growth effort rather than be a drain upon it. A striking example of this outlook is provided by President Houari Boumediene, who delivered a speech on June 19, 1969, that squelched a campaign for family planning that had been quietly building in Algeria. Inaugurating a huge steelworks at Annaba, he said (as quoted in Waterbury 1973, 18):

> Our goal . . . over the next twenty years is to assure that our people, who will number 25 million souls, will have a standard of living which will be among the highest of the modern peoples of the world of tomorrow. I take this opportunity to say—concerning what is called "galloping demography"—that we are not partisans of false solutions such as the limitation of births.

Few leaders in the Middle East today would be prepared to make such a statement. Indeed, most leaders have come to see the need to lower birthrates.

Pressure on Development Efforts

Population growth is neither an exogenous force nor the sole cause of development problems. It is merely one (albeit important) variable in the ensemble of relationships in the political economy. But the rapid growth of population has slowed economic development in the region, and it has also created particular political problems.

A critical feature of the demography of Middle Eastern countries is the large proportion of the total population that is young. A comparison of age pyramids for Algeria, Egypt, and the United States is instructive (see Figure 4.2)—a much larger share of the population is young in Egypt compared to Algeria, and a much larger share of the population is young in Algeria compared to the United States.

About 65 percent of the population in the Middle East is younger than twenty. There is near-consensus among demographers that rapid population growth leads to a reduction in the amount of money spent per pupil (see the discussion in National Research Council 1986). This usually takes the form of reduced teacher salaries and higher pupil-teacher ratios. As we shall see in the next chapter, most countries try very hard to fund education adequately. A country committed to educating its

FIGURE 4.2. Distribution of Population by Age and Sex in Algeria, the United States, and Egypt, 2012

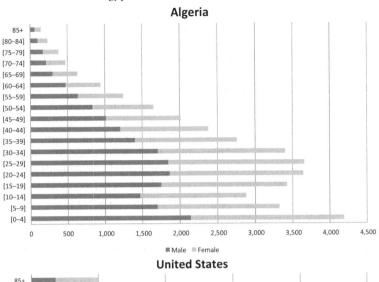

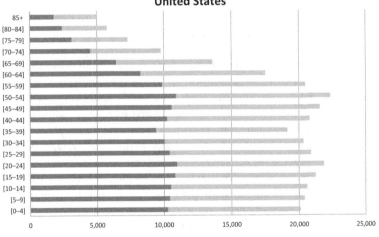

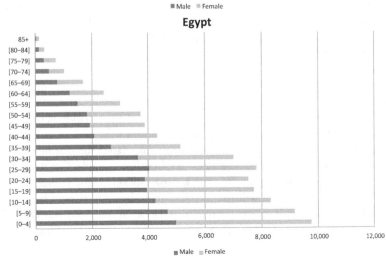

Source: US Census Bureau, international database.

children will find it more difficult to offer primary education to all if their numbers are growing rapidly, as well as when the share of the youth is large relative to the share of the working population. For example, although the total number of Algerian children enrolled in primary school nearly quadrupled from 1962 to 1978, there were still more than 1 million school-age children not in school in 1978 (Bennoune 1988). Today almost all Algerian children enroll in primary education, but fewer than half of them continue into secondary education. Similarly, although education absorbs about 16 percent of the Yemeni government budget, nearly half of the country's girls are still not in school and two out of three girls are illiterate (UNICEF Yemen 2014). In 1999 one study projected that the number of young Palestinians requiring education would rise by about 50 percent, and by about 45 percent in Yemen by 2020 (Courbage 1999). Rapid population growth swamps even the most determined attempts to diffuse education.

Rapid population growth exacerbates other development problems as well. Investable funds are diverted not merely from "capital deepening" but from any form of job creation to social-overhead investment (for example, housing and water and sewage systems). Some investment may be necessary simply to repair the damage caused by population growth, such as the rehabilitation of ecologically degraded areas. Rapid population increase contributes to the very rapid growth of cities, which are expanding at roughly twice the rate of the overall population in the region. Such rapid urban population growth strains the administrative capacities of governments and generates political problems. Rapid population growth contributes to a soaring demand for food in the region and increases pressure on already scarce water supplies (see Chapter 6). Finally, by increasing the supply of labor relative to capital and by raising the ratio of unskilled to skilled labor, rapid population growth probably worsens the distribution of income.

A rapidly expanding labor force compels the diversion of investment to providing jobs with a given amount of capital per worker. Since increasing the amount of capital per worker is typically necessary to raise worker productivity and therefore incomes, rapid population increase slows the growth of per capita incomes, if all other factors remain unchanged. Rapid population growth means that money must be spent just to create jobs, rather than to improve those that already exist or to create more productive ones. It is particularly difficult to create the entry-level jobs that the young labor force requires, especially when skilled older workers are so scarce. The problem is particularly acute in states without oil resources: where funds for investment remain scarce, rapid population growth slows the pace of growth and development.[4]

Although population growth is falling, every year the population of the Middle East and North Africa continues to grow. Populations will continue to expand as long as fertility remains above replacement levels. Population forecasting is fraught with difficulties, but even optimistic demographers (for example, Courbage 1999) have projected the regional population to be 562 million by 2025. Others project that the region's population will rise to 692 million by 2050 (Roudi-Fahimi and Kent 2007). By comparison, the regional population in the 1950s was about 100 million and numbered approximately 430 million in 2007 (Roudi-Fahimi and Kent 2007) (see Figure 4.3).

FIGURE 4.3. Years to Double MENA Populations at 2000–2010 Average Growth Rates

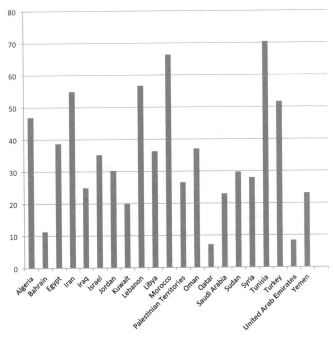

Source: United Nations Population Fund (UNFPA) (2012a).

Population growth remains very high in the richest Arab countries of the GCC and in the poorest (Sudan and Yemen). In the richest countries, fast population growth makes the current development model based on patronage unsustainable (see Chapter 9). In the poor countries, fast population growth creates a poverty trap and makes it very hard to attract the kind of investment needed to raise the productive capacities of the whole population.

HOW LABOR MARKETS ADJUSTED IN THE FACE OF LARGE POPULATION GROWTH

Much has been made of the "youth bulge." The fear has been that if there are too many youth entering the labor market at times of low growth, many of them will end up unemployed, increasing the risk of social unrest. But on the positive side, the economy can also benefit when population growth starts falling. Just as accelerating population growth poses serious development problems, the recent deceleration in population growth may offer an important economic opportunity. The decline in fertility automatically leads over time to a decrease in the "dependency ratio": the number of people (under fifteen and over sixty-five) who must be supported by the working-age population. In effect, the labor force rises faster than the population during the demographic transition, until the population growth rate stabilizes. This has two positive effects: the income per capita is boosted, since workers have to support smaller families; and the national saving rate rises, since people save during their working lives, whereas children and the retired do not (or they save at a much lower rate). The demographic dividend accounts for well over one-third of economic growth in East Asia.

The demographic dividend occurs as long as the labor force grows faster than the the population, a phenomenon that started to take place in the region in the mid-1990s and will continue until the 2020s. So the good news is that the region has reached the beginning of the end of the relentless demographic pressures that prevailed in the past. Indeed, the improvements we see in labor outcomes in the 2000s are largely due to a combination of declining labor force growth and rising GDP growth. But ultimately, whether this demographic pattern actually yields a positive dividend depends on the larger socioeconomic context within which it occurs. The bad news is that the region has failed to take advantage of the demographic dividend. Instead, as Figure 4.4 indicates, because the bulge peaked during the "lost decade," the potential dividend turned into a curse: the decade left behind a population with low-productivity jobs and a large stock of unemployed individuals.

Rapid Increase in the Number of Job-Seekers

The problems that a burgeoning number of young people create for society are not limited to educational difficulties. The impact on the job market is equally profound. Indeed, the rapid increase in the number of job-seekers may be *the* key challenge facing the region's political economy. Everywhere in the region, the labor force is growing much more quickly than the demand for labor. Despite the recent deceleration (which tracks the deceleration in population growth, with a lag), the rate of growth of the labor force will remain the highest in the world through at least 2020. The total number of new job-seekers has risen steadily: 47 million for the four decades from 1950 to 1990; about 18 million during the decade of the 1990s; and over 33 million from 2000 to 2010.

Two forces drive labor force growth: (declining) population growth rates and (rising) female labor force participation rates. Since past population growth rates have changed differentially, the future rates of growth of the labor force vary considerably across countries. In some cases (for example, Yemen and Palestine), growth is accelerating; in others (Tunisia), it is decelerating; in still others (Morocco), it has stayed roughly the same. Iran now faces a surge in labor supply. Oil-producing countries are experiencing surges in labor force size largely because of the influx of migrant workers into the Gulf. The labor forces of the Gulf countries have been growing at a very high pace, especially in Saudi Arabia and the United Arab Emirates. Some analysts (Courbage 1999; Fargues 1997) use the deceleration in past fertility rates to predict the year when additions to the labor force will be just matched by those reaching retirement age (defined as sixty to sixty-five). The predicted year is 2015 in Tunisia, 2020 in Morocco and Algeria, 2025 in Egypt, and even further in the future in Syria. These analysts note that the number of new job-seekers entering the labor market every year will range from an increase of 40 percent of the 1990

FIGURE 4.4. Demographic and Labor Force Participation Trends in the MENA Region, the 1990s Through the 2010s

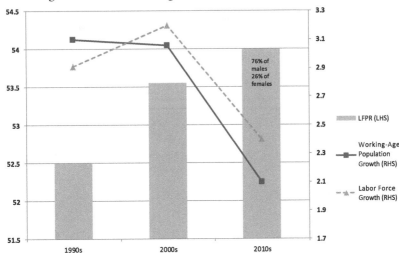

Source: International Labor Organization (ILO) (2012).

Note: LFPR = Labor Force Participation Rate; LHS = Left-Hand Side; RHS = Right-Hand Side. LFPR corresponds to country average.

level in Tunisia to an increase of 125 percent in Syria. The general conclusion that the Maghreb is in considerably better shape than the countries farther east seems valid, but even the best performer, Tunisia, faces a demographically driven tidal wave of young job-seekers for at least the near future.

Unemployment and Labor Force Participation

From the late 1990s until 2011, unemployment rates had actually slightly declined in the region, although they remained among the highest in the world, averaging in 2010 around 8 percent for males and 18 percent for females across the region (see Table 4.4). Today the employment problem may be the most politically volatile economic issue facing the region. With the increase in the labor force over the past decade, the absolute number of unemployed in the MENA countries has grown and now exceeds 13 million people (Al-Nashif and Tzannatos 2013). Unemployment mainly affects young, semi-educated people, who are prime participants in political unrest. In some countries, unemployed youth provided fertile ground for the revolutionary fervor that led to the Arab uprisings (al-Momani 2011).

Some estimates of national unemployment rates are shown in Table 4.4. Unemployment was highest in recent years in Tunisia, Iraq, Yemen, Jordan, and Algeria; in these countries, over one-third of the youth and nearly one-half of the women were unemployed. The outlines of the situation are clear. First, unemployment is often greater in cities than in the countryside because poorer rural populations simply

TABLE 4.4. Female and Male Unemployment Rates in the MENA Countries, 2010

Country	Female				Male			
	Total	Primary	Secondary	Tertiary	Total	Primary	Secondary	Tertiary
MENA	17.6%				7.8%			
Algeria	17.4	25.3%	27.5%	46.5%	10.0	68%	18.9%	10.5%
Bahrain	20.0	20.6	44.0	29.5	5.6	45.0	38.1	9.8
Egypt	22.6				4.9			
Iran	16.8	14.2	32.5	52.3	9.1	50.7	30.4	14.9
Iraq	22.5				16.2			
Israel	6.5	13.6	53.9	30.5	5.7	30.3	42.2	25.8
Jordan	21.7				10.4			
Kuwait	1.8	7.4	47.2	19.4	2.0	29.7	33.6	6.6
Lebanon	10.1	32.2	18.6	45.7	8.6	50.7	19.9	23.6
Morocco	11.5	36.6	23.9	33.5	10.8	57.7	21.7	16.2
Palestine	23.8	9.7	5.7	82.4	26.5	36.5	16.0	12.9
Qatar	2.6	13.6	53.8	31.6	0.2	28.4	50.7	10.8
Saudi Arabia	13.0	2.3	22.3	75.4	3.5	25.6	52.0	11.3
Syria	24.2	35.6	45.1	8.1	8.3	52.0	18.5	3.1
Tunisia	17.1	36.8	34.4	14.2	13.2	44.8	37.1	6.0
Turkey	11.6	34.5	34.9	24.9	10.7	59.6	22.5	9.5
United Arab Emirates	12.0	8.8	46.7	43.0	2.0	36.5	36.4	17.9
Yemen	40.9				11.5			

cannot afford to be unemployed and because female labor force participation is higher in agricultural communities. For example, in Turkey women's participation in the workforce is higher in rural areas (33 percent) than in the country as a whole (26 percent) (IFAD 2011). Rural-to-urban migration also plays a role in the increasing pressure on urban labor markets in many countries. Rural populations are growing much less rapidly than urban populations, despite the (generally) higher fertility rates in the countryside. Everywhere in the world, increasingly educated young people seek to leave rural areas. In a sense, unemployment is "exported to the cities," where it has significantly different political consequences from what would be expected if it were found mainly in rural areas. Many sociological studies have found that the people most likely to become members of Islamist groups are recent immigrants from the countryside who have some education (see, for example, Ayubi 1991, 158–177; Ibrahim 1994; Kepel 2002, 66–69; Mandaville 2007, 96–101; Roy 1994).

Second, unemployment is mainly an affliction of the youth who spend a long period searching for adequate jobs. Although this is a universal phenomenon, it is particularly salient in the MENA region, which has the highest rate of youth unemployment (25 percent) in the world (IMF 2012). More than half of the region's unemployed are younger than twenty-five years old. The percentage of youth contributing to the total unemployed is highest in Syria, where it approaches 48 percent (IFAD 2012). In Morocco, where urban unemployment is about 20 percent, youth unemployment stands at 30 percent (World Bank 2013). Egyptian unemployment rates for young men (ages fifteen to twenty-four) are some *seven times* higher than for men over thirty (El-Kogali 2002). In Iran, youth unemployment rates exceed rates for those over thirty by a factor of four (about 20 percent compared with less than 5 percent) (United Nations 2003). Unemployment is particularly severe for youth with intermediate levels of education. Among university graduates, rates of unemployment vary considerably among countries. In Egypt, the rate of unemployment among university graduates is approximately half that of those with only a secondary education (see Table 4.4), but this is not the case in Algeria, Morocco, and Jordan (Bourdarbat 2005; Nabli and Keller 2002; World Bank 2004). The World Bank (2004, 90) goes so far as to say that "unemployment [in the region] is essentially a labor market insertion problem for youth."

Third, educated workers are more likely to be unemployed than uneducated ones because their aspirations for a good job are higher and they typically spend more time searching—in some countries, the average search time for a first job extends for over five years, especially in countries where "insiders" in labor markets are more protected. High rates of unemployment among the youth translate into high rates of unemployment for the labor force, given the demographic weight of this group within the working-age population.

Fourth, unemployment rates for women exceed those for men by several magnitudes. This is especially the case in the countries that have stopped hiring in the public sector and where light manufacturing industries have not been developed, as both are sectors usually dominated by women. And finally, because unemployment rates peaked in the 1990s, job creation has had to contend with a large stock of unemployed workers for a fairly lengthy period (Al-Nashif and Tzannatos 2013).

The root causes for the politically volatile unemployment problem in the MENA region vary. In the RPLA countries, there has been much debate on the cause of the high unemployment rates, especially among educated youth. One line of thought holds that much of the problem is due to the unemployed themselves, notably their high reservation wages and their willingness to wait until public-sector jobs open up (see Assaad 2013). There is certainly some truth to this in the richer GCC countries, but the evidence for such phenomena in the poorer countries is scant. The more convincing argument in the RPLA countries is that the lack of good jobs is due to the excess demand for jobs, which is connected to the low dynamism of the private sector (Tzannatos 2014).

Data on unemployment come from surveys, and although countries try to conform to international definitions, the frequency and coverage of surveys are far from uniform. "Unemployed" means "without a job and looking for work" and is measured by the percentage of the labor force that is unemployed. Because high unemployment discourages workers from looking for jobs, measured unemployment can be a serious understatement of the problem. A better measure of how much people work is given by the labor force participation rate, which measures the share of those in the working-age population who work or are unemployed and looking for a job.

Labor Force Participation

Labor force participation has remained low in the region compared to other regions of the world, but it has expanded a bit in the past decade (Table 4.5). Men participate as much as elsewhere in the world, except in the GCC countries, where their participation is extremely low. Women in all MENA countries participate in the labor markets much less than women in the rest of the world—only one in four Arab women are in the labor force, compared to a global average of 51 percent. As a result, the region has not been able to take advantage of the potential "women's gift," or the "increased potential savings resulting from increased female labour force participation, which leads to growing per capita income and potential savings, even where population growth rates are not slowing down and labour productivity remains constant" (Moghadam and Karshenas 2006, 14).

The low participation rate of women in the labor force is due to several factors, some of which are cultural or related to the large size of families. Others are more structural: two traditional employers of women, the state and light manufacturing, have been subject in recent years to rollbacks and lack of development, respectively (Moghadam 2000; Ross 2012). The underlying trends, however, are positive, and the expansion in total participation is largely due to the fact that *educated* women have increased their participation, and indeed, the proportion of women who have become educated has risen.

Better-educated women tend to want fewer children *and* a job outside the home. Increasingly, growth in the labor force will be driven by this social (rather than purely demographic) force. Philippe Fargues (1997, 169) suggests that a critical determinant of women's labor force participation in the region is the *gap* between a husband's and a wife's education: "It is the husband, and not the children, who keeps the woman out of the labor market." When measured by enrollment ratios, men's education in the region is about a generation ahead of women's. Given the rapid increase in female enrollment ratios during the past three decades, the current younger generation has a smaller gap than older-age cohorts. For example, the gap between male and female enrollment was about 10 percent by 1999 compared to a gap of 15 percent in 1990 (World Bank 1999). Accordingly, Fargues argues, younger men today will be less likely to try to keep their wives out of the labor market. Rising female labor force participation will increasingly displace demography as the engine of labor force growth in the Middle East. The combination of rising unemployment among urban males, especially men who are not only young and relatively well educated but also unmarried, and rising female labor force participation creates intense psychological pressure.

TABLE 4.5. Female and Male Labor Force Participation Rates in the MENA Countries, 1990 and 2010

Country	Total		Female		Male	
	1990	2010	1990	2010	1990	2010
Algeria	41.9%	43.3%	9.9%	14.7%	74.2%	71.7%
Bahrain	64.4	70.5	27.9	39.2	87.9	87.2
Egypt	50.2	48.8	26.5	23.5	74.2	74.2
Iran	44.7	44.3	9.7	16.1	80.1	71.8
Iraq	39.8	41.4	10.9	14.3	71.0	69.3
Israel	51.8	57.3	41.3	52.5	62.6	62.4
Jordan	38.9	41.1	8.9	15.3	65.3	65.4
Kuwait	58.5	67.7	34.7	43.3	78.3	82.2
Lebanon	41.7	45.7	16.7	22.5	69.5	70.8
Libya	47.6	53.8	18.2	30.4	73.1	76.9
Morocco	52.7	49.5	26.2	25.9	80.0	74.7
Oman	54.9	60.0	17.4	28.0	80.6	79.9
Palestine	39.3	40.8	9.9	14.7	68.4	66.3
Qatar	80.6	86.4	43.4	52.1	94.2	95.2
Saudi Arabia	54.1	50.0	14.5	17.4	80.4	74.2
Sudan	52.9	53.6	27.4	30.8	78.7	76.5
Syria	49.0	42.3	17.9	12.9	80.4	71.6
Tunisia	48.1	47.4	20.8	25.3	75.5	69.7
Turkey	57.9	49.5	34.5	28.1	81.6	71.4
United Arab Emirates	72.6	79.1	25.0	43.7	91.2	92.0
Yemen	44.5	48.2	16.3	24.8	74.4	71.7

Source: World Bank, WDI.

The Evolution of Employment and the Rise of Informality

Across the MENA region, the gap between labor force growth and job creation—especially the creation of good jobs—is one of the central issues facing policymakers. This is certainly true of most RPLA countries, including Algeria, Iraq, Iran, and Yemen. On the other hand, most of the GCC countries seem to have taken off recently with increased diversification.

Economic growth affects the labor market through the impact of structural transformation. A successful structural transformation entails a shift of workers from low- to high-productivity jobs. In addition, sector productivity rises as a result of investment and technological change. Together, these two sources of productivity improvement lead to higher productivity and growth. Unfortunately, developments in the MENA region have not conformed to this pattern. As elsewhere, the share of the labor force working in agriculture has declined considerably in all countries over time. The share has fallen by nearly twenty percentage points in the last twenty years, with large declines in all regions, and more so in the GCC countries and the Mashriq than in North Africa. Whereas in 1950 between one-half and two-thirds of the workforce was in agriculture, by the early 2000s only Morocco, Sudan, Turkey, and Yemen had more than one-third of their labor force in agriculture. Although part of the labor force previously employed in agriculture redeployed to industry, much more of the labor force moved to the service sector. Industry now often employs between one-fifth and one-third of the labor force in many MENA countries. However, employment in manufacturing has increased more than the expansion of manufacturing's share of GDP in the industrial sector, resulting in lower productivity over time. In general, well over half of the workers in the region's industrial sector are employed in small establishments with fewer than twenty people. Much of the expansion has been in the informal sectors, such as construction, and in sectors with low value added, such as labor-intensive manufacturing.

Growth-enhancing structural transformation is about valuable jobs being created to replace less productive jobs being destroyed. But the structural adjustment of the 1980s destroyed what were considered "good" jobs in the public sector and in import-substituting manufacturing because these sectors were unsustainable and needed to be shrunk in order to restore macroeconomic balances. However, no serious engine for growth has replaced them. What grew instead were jobs in low-skill manufacturing and services, mainly in the informal sector. With the exception of the GCC countries, the formal private sector has remained small throughout the region, and the expanding informal sector has absorbed most of the labor force moving away from agriculture. As of 2010, the informal sector had come to dominate the region, with nearly 70 percent of the labor force employed in this sector in a typical MENA country (World Bank 2013).

Urban labor markets can be divided into three major sectors: public, private formal, and private informal. The public sector is composed of bureaucracies and state-owned enterprises. Public employment is very secure—it is almost impossible in many cases to lose one's job. Until recently, the public sector provided the first jobs for the growing masses of educated and semi-educated young men. Only in the Gulf countries does this remain true for nationals.

The role of the public sector in these transformations has been significant. Until the 1980s, the public sector was a large creator of good formal jobs that absorbed most of the educated entrants to the labor market, and thus it was a major factor in fostering social progress. In the past two decades, however, the public sector shrank, and all the new jobs began to come from the private sector—and more specifically, from the informal private sector. As new hiring in the public sector was reduced and in most cases frozen, educated entrants to the job market who would have joined the public sector in the past suffered a hard blow. The legacies of historical hiring trends have kept public-sector employment high in the region, but as can be seen

TABLE 4.6. The Share of Public-Sector Employment in Selected MENA Economies in the 1990s vs. the Latest Available Year

Country/Economy	2005–2010	1990s
Algeria	30%	58%
Egypt	27	32
Iran	16	
Iraq	54	
Jordan	34	49
Morocco	11	26
Palestine	21	20
Syria	21	29
Tunisia	22	32

Source: For the 1990s, World Bank (1995). For 2005–2010, Egypt's Labor Force Survey (LFS), 2010; Iraq's Household Socio-Economic Survey (HSES), 2006; Jordan's Labor Market Panel Survey (LMPS), 2010; Morocco's LFS, 2009; Tunisia's LFS, 2010; the United Arab Emirates' LFS, 2009; Palestine's LFS, 2008; and Laborsta (2012).

in Table 4.6, the share of the labor force working for the state has declined in many countries.

The civil-sector wage bill was squeezed, too, but typically much less than public investment. As shown in Table 4.7, the reduction in the wage bill was highest in the RRLP countries (from 15.7 to 9.3 percent of GDP), followed by the RRLA countries (from 10.7 to 7.5 percent of GDP), and then by the RPLA group (12.3 to 9.5 percent of GDP). Compared to the average developing country, where the wage bill stands at about 10 percent of GDP, the wage bill in RRLA and RPLA countries still stood below these global averages in 2010. In these countries, the overall wage bill fell faster than public-sector employment, resulting in an underpaid (though still large) civil service, which in turn fed petty corruption. The large and underpaid state sectors pose enormous challenges in these countries, including the negative effects on the state's ability to deliver basic services to the population. Budgetary pressures are largely to blame, but among public-sector workers the situation also encourages absenteeism, the delivery of poor-quality care, and moonlighting in the private sector. (For more on labor markets in the labor-poor and labor-abundant oil economies, see Chapter 9.)

The private formal sector can vary greatly in size among the MENA countries, but it is often the smallest of the three sectors. Typically, a minimum of ten to fifty workers is required to classify an enterprise as belonging to this sector. Additionally, workers in the private formal sector are assumed to have some job security, although less than in the public sector. Employers in the private formal sector are responsible for paying their workers' payroll and social protection taxes. The formal private sector constitutes only about 10 to 15 percent of the labor force in

TABLE 4.7. Peak, Low, and Recent Peak Wage Bills (as a percentage of GDP) Among the MENA Countries, 1990–2010

	Peak Wage Bill	Lowest Wage Bill	Recent Peak Wage Bill	Bulge (peak to lowest)	Average Wage Bill: 1990s	Average Wage Bill: 2000s	Average Wage Bill: 2010s	Public Employment: 2005–2010 (% of Labor Force)
RRLP	15.7%	9.3%	13.4%	4.9%	12.5%	8.3%	9.7%	62.3%
Bahrain	20.9	13.2	14.6	7.7	15.7	12.2	10.5	33.9
Kuwait	14.5	8.3	8.1	6.3	16.3	11.1	10.1	80.1
Libya		12.9	34.8		14.1	9	23.4	65.0
Oman	8.9	8.0	7.8	0.9	8.6	7.6	6.8	47.1
Qatar	16.4	7.3	6.1		15.5	6.6	4.7	86.7
Saudi Arabia	18.0	13.2	19.0	4.8				49.9
United Arab Emirates	4.9	2.2	3.5		5.0	3.0	2.8	73.3
RRLA	10.7	7.5	7.3	3.2	7.6	6.7	11.0	22.3
Algeria	7.8	9.3	8.8	-1.5	8.9	7.2	11.0	30.0
Iran	16.2	8.0	7.7	8.1	9.4	7.8		16.0
Syria	8.1	5.2	5.5	2.9	4.6	5.0		21.0
RPLA	12.3	9.5	10.3	3.3	9.9	9.6	9.9	22.3
Egypt	9.7	5.9	6.8	3.8	6.1	6.7	6.4	27.0
Jordan	20.9	12.8	15.3	8.1	14.5	13.8	13.7	34.0
Lebanon	9.1	8.3	6.9		8.1	5.8	8.1	17.6
Morocco	12.1	10.4	11.7	1.7	10.6	11.4	11.3	11.0
Tunisia	9.9	10.2	10.6	-0.3	10.0	10.1	10.1	22.0

Source: IMF, World Financial Statistics.

Egypt, Yemen, Morocco, and Tunisia, and a slightly larger share at 22 percent in Jordan, where the formal labor market is less regulated. Despite its relatively small size, this sector of the labor market has disproportionate access to credit, starving the informal sector.

In much of the region, particularly outside of labor markets for GCC nationals, the informal sector is the biggest component of the labor market. The definitions of this sector vary considerably in the literature. Sometimes the term is used as a euphemism for slum dwellers or the poor. Most commonly, the sector is defined as including all self-employed persons plus those employed in firms with fewer than ten workers. Sometimes the unskilled, casual laborers employed by larger firms are included. Virtually by definition, the informal sector offers the most insecure employment conditions.

This taxonomy of the distinct segments of labor markets is useful for evaluating the oft-repeated claim that the region's economic growth has been "jobless." In fact, the improved economic growth since the mid-1990s has generated a healthy employment response, so that even though the region's labor force grew at the most rapid rate in the world, the region's employment "elasticity" was still among the highest in the world (see IMF 2013). As a result, growth has not been jobless, as it is often claimed; instead, job creation occurred more in some sectors of the labor market than in others. The jobs created were low-productivity jobs, biased toward the informal sector, and thus were also unprotected and vulnerable. Moreover, labor markets have exhibited a rising level of inequality of opportunities (see Chapter 2).

The informal sector includes small-scale manufacturing, handicraft workers, itinerant and jobbing artisans like carpenters and masons, providers of personal services like servants, porters, and watchmen, car washers, street vendors, and garbage collectors (Abdel-Fadil 1983). Many of these jobs, although not all, are found in the services sector, which in part explains the relatively high share of service-sector employment across all three country groupings in the MENA region (Table 4.8). While services account for the largest share of value added and employment in virtually all Middle Eastern countries, service-sector employment in the informal sector is especially high in the RPLA countries.

A defining feature everywhere of this informal sector is that "firms" are unregistered and untaxed. Typically, there are few or no barriers to entry in the informal sector. Capital per worker is very low, and incomes fluctuate considerably, both seasonally and annually. The sector usually employs a higher proportion of women, children, and young adults than other sectors. Few aspire to employment in the informal sector, which has less job security, fewer benefits, and fewer legal protections and tends to discriminate against women in earnings (Wahba 2009).

How large is the informal sector? Because its activities are unregistered, much uncertainty surrounds the answer to this question. Most estimates hold that the sector accounts for anywhere from one-fifth to one-third of national output across the region, and for a low of about two-fifths of non-agricultural employment (Syria) to highs of about 51.0 percent (Egypt) and 58.5 percent (Palestine) (ILO 2011). Notably, in many other Third World countries, the sector's share in non-agricultural employment is even higher (for example, 75.1 percent in Bolivia, 83.5 percent in India, and 81.8 percent in Mali). The share of this sector in employment has grown under the impact of economic reform in Algeria, Egypt, and Morocco. The change in Egypt has been especially striking: there the informal sector created only about one in five jobs for new workers in 1970, but by 1998 it was creating six in ten new jobs (Wahba 2009; World Bank 2004). The informal sector is also the main entry point for employment in Syria—it currently employs 48 percent of the poor labor force in rural parts of the country, 80 percent of whom have a low level of education. Although the share of informal-sector employment declines with age, the share for older women is still around 57 percent (IFAD 2011; ILO 2014). According to one report, the self-employed constitute 31.7 percent of workers in Algeria, 42.5 percent

TABLE 4.8. Value Added and Labor Force in Various Sectors of the MENA Countries, 1970, 1990, and the 2000s

	Share of Sector in Total Value Added								Share of Sector in Total Labor Force					
	Agriculture		Industry Without Manufacturing		Manufacturing		Services		Agriculture		Industry		Services	
	1970	2000s	1970	2000s	1970	2000s	1970	2000s	1990	2000s	1990	2000s	1990	2000s
RRLP	**3.2%**	**1.8%**	**8.7%**	**9.5%**	**11.3%**	**18.0%**	**76.8%**	**70.7%**	**11.8%**	**9.1%**	**28.3%**	**35.8%**	**59.8%**	**54.4%**
Bahrain	1.0	1.0	7.0	6.0	13.0	19.0	79.0	74.0	2.0		29.8		68.2	
Kuwait	2.0	2.0	5.0	5.0	5.0	6.0	88.0	87.0	1.3		24.7		74.0	
Libya	na	na	na	na	na	na	na	na	18.9	17.0	33.7	23.0	47.4	59.0
Oman	5.0	3.0	4.0	11.0	6.0	25.0	85.0	61.0	44.5		23.8		31.6	
Qatar	1.0	0.0	7.0	9.0	18.0	23.0	74.0	68.0	2.7	0.2	32.0	80.1	65.4	19.7
Saudi Arabia	8.0	4.0	10.0	9.0	13.0	22.0	69.0	65.0	5.7	12.0	27.4	25.0	66.9	61.0
United Arab Emirates	2.0	1.0	19.0	17.0	13.0	13.0	66.0	69.0	7.8	7.0	26.8	15.0	65.4	78.0
RRLA	**22.3**	**17.6**	**28.6**	**33.5**	**11.7**	**11.0**	**41.5**	**41.1**	**17.9**	**35.4**	**28.2**	**21.8**	**57.8**	**43.5**
Algeria	11.0	10.0	28.3	33.0	15.0	10.0	31.0	47.0	17.3	14.0	36.7		46.0	62.6
Iran	24.0	17.0	28.2	33.0	12.0	13.5	48.0	48.0		23.0		34.0		43.0
Iraq	7.4	5.4	56.7	67.7	5.9	0.9	27.5	12.0	13.6	17.0	19.1	1.8	67.3	63.0
Sudan	43.6	39.0	7.0	9.0	8.0	9.0	42.0	46.5		80.0		7.0		13.0
Syria	24.0	26.5	24.5	26.0	20.0	25.0	51.5	48.0	22.9	30.0	28.8	27.0	48.3	43.0
Yemen	24.0	7.7	27.0	32.0	9.0	7.5	49.0	45.0		48.5		15.1		36.4
RPLA	**19.0**	**11.0**	**21.3**	**16.5**	**15.0**	**15.3**	**55.6**	**61.4**	**28.9**	**21.3**	**24.8**	**20.4**	**46.3**	**58.3**
Egypt	29.4	17.0	28.5	32.0	18.0	15.8	47.0	51.0	39.9	32.0	21.4	17.0	38.7	51.0
Jordan	8.0	4.5	13.0	10.0	11.3	16.0	64.0	68.5	6.2	5.0	17.9	12.5	75.9	82.5
Lebanon		5.6		14.8		8.4		71.2						
Morocco	19.0	16.0	29.5	13.0	17.0	18.0	55.0	55.5	43.4	40.0	25.7	15.0	30.9	45.0
Palestine										11.8		24.6		63.6
Tunisia	19.7	12.0	14.1	12.7	13.5	18.4	56.5	61.0	26.2	17.7	34.1	33.0	39.7	49.3
Israel									6.3	2.6	30.8	31.7	62.1	65.7
Turkey	40.2	9.7	10.0	9.0	16.5	18.5	43.0	63.4		35.9		22.8		41.2
MENA	**15.8**	**10.1**	**18.8**	**19.4**	**12.6**	**14.9**	**57.4**	**57.8**	**17.2**	**23.2**	**27.5**	**25.3**	**55.8**	**51.6**

in Egypt, 37.9 percent in Iran, 35.3 percent in Lebanon, and 31.3 percent in Syria (OECD 2009). However, the formal private sector remains small everywhere.

THE POLITICS OF YOUNG POPULATIONS

Generational Tensions

In countries with moderate or low population growth rates, political leadership is generally drawn from an age pool that contains a significant proportion, if not the majority, of the population. In North America, Western and Eastern Europe, the former Soviet Union, and Japan, not only are most citizens legal adults (about 73 percent of the US population is twenty years old or older; US Census Bureau 2012), but the populations as a whole are aging. There is in these countries a much more profound sharing of experience between leaders and their major constituencies than is to be found in societies experiencing rapid population growth. Political generations are often depicted as having been shaped by national crises. For example, Churchill, Roosevelt, Truman, Stalin, and de Gaulle all spoke for a generation that shared the trauma of the worldwide Depression and World War II. In 1980 there were 57 million Americans, or 26 percent of the population of the United States, who were born before 1925, grew up during the Depression, and were at least teenagers during World War II. That experience provided them and their elected leaders with a common language and a set of symbols that were drawn from their own lives.

The situation in the Middle East, as in many developing areas, is radically different. In 2000, two-thirds of the Algerian population was under thirty years old. Although the Algerian population is aging—in 2003, only 55 percent of the population was under thirty—young people still make up over half of the population. These demographic trends have political implications. First, only about 56 percent of the population are adults in the legal sense, that is, entitled to vote and to stand for election. Also, more than 88 percent of all living Algerians were born after independence in 1962. They had no direct experience of the French colonial presence or of the seven years of war and devastation that preceded independence. By contrast, *all* of Algeria's presidents since 1962—Ahmed Ben Bella (1962–1965), Houari Boumediene (1965–1978), Chadli Bendjedid (1979–1991), Mohamed Boudiaf (January–June 1992), Ali Kafi (1992–1994), Liamine Zéroual (1994–1999), and Abdelaziz Bouteflika (1999–)—have been of the generation shaped by the revolutionary war. Their legitimacy, such as it is, stems directly from their role in the struggle against France, but for most Algerians that struggle is history, not a living memory or a shared experience.

One could go on with examples of the enormous disparities in age and experience of leaders and followers in the Middle East. There is evidence that Islamic movements across the region have been successful in mobilizing young people hitherto kept on the fringes of political systems that claim to represent them. Since at least the early 2000s, however, youth movements have been on the rise, even if their centrality in the 2011 uprisings is contested, and youth factions have even split from or openly disagreed with the leadership of the Egyptian Muslim Brotherhood.

Some analysts contend that populations with a greater proportion of youth are more prone to violence (Kaplan 1994; Marcus 1998; Urdal 2004). Various causal mechanisms have been proposed to explain this apparent empirical association, such as the lower opportunity cost for violence among youth, who tend to have lower-wage jobs than their elders, to be rebellious in general, and to defy the efforts of older cohorts to control them, among other characteristics. More recent work, however, suggests that the correlation between youth bulges and violence holds only under certain socioeconomic conditions. For example, Bilal Barakat and Henrik Urdal (2009) argue that youth's access to education reduces the likelihood of conflict. By contrast, Noah Bricker and Mark Foley (2013) find that as the ratio of youth (defined as ages seventeen to twenty-six) to the total labor force increases, the propensity for violence rises. This suggests that labor market conditions mediate the relationship between youth and conflict.

The Politics of Differential Fertility

In defining the rights and obligations of citizens, the constitutions of most Middle Eastern states are blind to their ethnic or religious origins. But in policy terms, the ideal of the homogeneous nation-state in which every citizen is equal to every other is something of a myth. In a de facto sense, the relative weights of religious and ethnic communities are important in the political calculus of each state's leadership. There is an unstated expectation that the flows of public patronage will reflect communal weights. If the pattern of income distribution, particularly the locus of poverty, corresponds closely to ethnic or religious boundaries, then a potentially explosive situation may develop.

The only way to know the population of various ethnic communities is through the national census. Censuses are carried out under the control of the national authority and can be manipulated to reflect its interests. In Turkey, where there have been repeated assertions of Kurdish separatism in eastern Anatolia since the 1920s, the national census provides no head count of the ethnic Kurds. In Iraq, where ethnicity (Kurd/Arab) cuts across religious sect (Sunni/Shi'a Muslim), regimes before 2003 were dominated by Sunni Arabs. Periodically there was talk of autonomy for regions in which Kurds predominate, but to delimit these regions required a census. While negotiating over conducting a census, the regime of Saddam Hussein resettled Arabs in Kurdish areas and Kurds, who are Sunni Muslims, in Shi'ite areas in order to achieve a desired census outcome. (Under the American occupation, these trends were reversing, often violently.) In Egypt the problem is one of adjusting census results. The Coptic Christian minority there has always protested that it has been undercounted by some 50 percent in Egypt's national census.

The problem of ethnic and sectarian head counting is acute in Lebanon. The system of political representation in Lebanon, cobbled together by the French after World War I, was founded on sectarian communities. Representatives in parliament competed for seats that were allocated in proportion to the numerical strength of each religious group in the population. The basic ratio consisted of six Christian seats in parliament for every five Muslim seats. After 1989, when fourteen years of civil war finally came to an end, the ratio was adjusted to five-to-five.

The Shi'ites were historically the poorest of all the religious sects, but beginning in the 1960s, a new set of communal leaders, notably the Imam Musa al-Sadr and later other groups, mobilized the community, bringing about important socioeconomic gains for the Lebanese Shi'ites. Today Sunnis, particularly in the north, constitute the poorest group in the country. Precise estimates of the sectarian breakdown of the population remain elusive, but by some estimates Christians are only about 35 percent of the population now. Regional conflicts have also altered the composition of the resident population. Lebanon now hosts about 500,000 Palestinians, more than 1 million Syrian refugees, and about 200,000 foreigners from other Arab countries, Africa, and Asia.

Kuwait, the United Arab Emirates, Qatar, and Saudi Arabia face politically perilous demographic situations as well. They are home to large numbers of residents without citizenship. For the most part, these are migrant workers and professionals from the oil-poor countries of the region and from India, Pakistan, and points farther east. Kuwait also had a substantial community of Palestinian refugees before 1991. In these countries, not only is most of the workforce foreign, but nearly half the resident population may also be foreign (see Chapter 13). Moreover, because they are worker-migrants, they are adults and preponderantly male. Although the economic life of these countries is dependent upon these workers, they have been excluded from political life. To date they have not exploited their strategic economic position to express political demands, but the possibility that they might do so is sufficiently alarming that all of the host states are actively pursuing policies to diminish their numbers.

It is perhaps in Israel that questions of ethnic and religious numbers are most sensitive, as communal boundaries correspond to highly differentiated socioeconomic and political status. The question is not as simple as how many Jews and non-Jews live in Israel. The Jews themselves are divided between the Ashkenazim, of East European origin, and the Sephardim (or more accurately the Oriental Jews) of Middle Eastern and Spanish origin. Israel's political establishment has been dominated since independence by the Ashkenazim. As a group, they are highly educated and relatively wealthy, and they tend to have small families. The Oriental Jews, by contrast, occupy lower socioeconomic positions in Israeli society and are seen as more traditional. Birthrates among the Oriental Jews are higher than among the Ashkenazim, but even though the Oriental Jews and their Israeli-born offspring have become a majority of the Jewish population, they have yet to inherit the political kingdom.

Far more crucial is the question of Israeli Arab birthrates. Over the period 1950–2000, the Israeli Arab community grew at the extraordinary rate of more than 4 percent per annum, or from 160,000 to 1,892,000 in 2010, out of a total population of 7.6 million in 2010. Non-Jews thus represent about one-quarter of the total population. Even with significant in-migration from abroad, the Israeli Jewish population over the same period grew by only 2.6 percent per annum during the second half of the twentieth century. Jewish rates of natural increase and of immigration declined over time, although the influx of Soviet Jews after 1989 marginally reversed that trend.

Since the June War of 1967, Israel has occupied the West Bank, formerly under Jordanian control, and Gaza, formerly under Egyptian control, and it has annexed East Jerusalem and the Golan Heights. In 2010 there were some 4.1 million Palestinians in the West Bank and Gaza. Israel's dilemma is twofold. First, if present trends continue, Israeli citizens of Arab origin will come to constitute nearly 25 percent of the population. A minority of that size, if not fully reconciled to the Israeli state, could severely test its democratic system. Second, if Israel decides, for security or religious reasons, to annex the West Bank and Gaza, that would raise the proportion of non-Jews in Israel to more than half (see Figure 4.5).

On political grounds alone, few Jewish Israelis were historically prepared to accept that. In a more profound sense, it would constitute the abandonment of the Zionist quest for a Jewish state. There are three alternatives: (1) expel the Palestinian populations from the West Bank; (2) concede sovereignty over the West Bank and Gaza to some sort of Palestinian entity through negotiations; or (3) unilaterally withdraw from selected areas. In 1993, after years of *intifada,* Israel and the Palestine Liberation Organization (PLO) signed the Declaration of Principles that seemed to cast the die in favor of the second alternative. In 2005 the Israelis unilaterally withdrew from Gaza, which was never considered a core territory for most Israelis, even for ardent Zionists. Nevertheless, since the second intifada broke out in 2000, the Israeli-Palestinian peace process has become increasingly elusive, at best.

CONCLUSIONS

Our analysis yields two major conclusions. First, high population growth has often overwhelmed the capacities of economies and administrations to provide good health, education, and infrastructure in much of the region. In the next chapter, we examine the record of the Middle East on these fronts in more detail.

Second, while better health and education can make people more productive, such enhancements can materialize only if labor markets can match these healthier, better-trained individuals with jobs that utilize their skills. If no jobs or the wrong kinds of jobs are created, some combination of unemployment and low real wages will follow. The region has now extensive untapped human resources, reflected in the underemployment of skills, high levels of unemployment, and women's very low labor force participation rates. This conclusion explains why in the recent past poverty stagnated and inequality increased while at the same time aspirations were rising, contributing to the social frustrations that fueled the 2011 Arab uprisings (see Chapter 2).

More than fifty years ago, Manfred Halpern (1963, 62–66) wrote of the new middle class and the would-be middle class in the Middle East and North Africa. He had in mind those educated Middle Easterners who had moved into the white-collar ranks of the civil service and the professions as well as the educated Middle Easterners who aspired to those ranks but could find no room in them. Part of the

FIGURE 4.5. Share of Israeli Jews and Palestinian Arabs in Israel and in the West Bank and Gaza, 2005 and 2010

2005

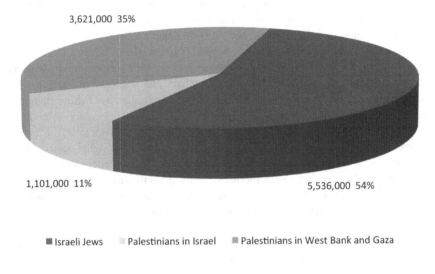

3,621,000 35%

1,101,000 11%

5,536,000 54%

■ Israeli Jews   Palestinians in Israel   ■ Palestinians in West Bank and Gaza

2010

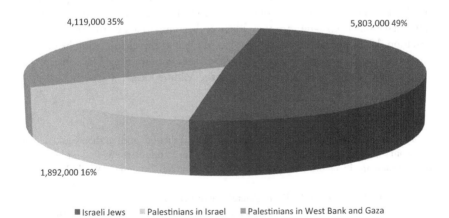

4,119,000 35%

5,803,000 49%

1,892,000 16%

■ Israeli Jews   Palestinians in Israel   ■ Palestinians in West Bank and Gaza

Source: Courbage (1999) for 2005 data; US Census Bureau for 2010 data.

danger that Halpern foresaw was the formation of a kind of intellectual proletariat made up of upwardly mobile but frustrated young men and women.

Over the past three decades, the structural problem that Halpern sketched has become far more acute. Today there are roughly 143 million Middle Easterners between the ages of fifteen and thirty out of a total population of over 506 million. Most of them have some education. Until the 1950s, a high school diploma would have qualified the recipient for a comfortable if unglamorous white-collar job, a decent standard of living, and a modicum of prestige. That is no longer the case. The young Middle Easterners recruited into the civil service and professions during the 1960s are only now retiring. They have enjoyed rapid promotion, and some have risen to the top of their administrative hierarchies. Yet behind them are new, even larger cohorts of men and women with equal aspirations and sometimes better professional credentials. They are being offered make-work jobs (if they are offered a job at all), salaries that lag behind inflation, and low social status. Their numbers are growing and will continue to grow for at least a generation. It is hard to see how and where they can be productively absorbed into the workforce. Because they are literate and politically aware, denying them material security is risky. In fact, this very class may have constituted the backbone of the uprisings in Egypt and elsewhere (Campante and Chor 2012; Diwan 2012).

It is reasonably clear that this age group contributes significantly to various kinds of radical movements, from the street fighters of Baghdad to the Islamic militants of Cairo, Gaza, and Tunis. One would be wrong, however, to attribute common political attitudes to an entire age cohort. Its members are just as likely to be worker-migrants to the Gulf states or to be following conventional career paths in the bureaucracy or service sector as they are to be political activists. Yet the opportunities for them to achieve their aspirations have narrowed as their numbers have increased. They have not been—nor are they likely to become—passive in the face of this situation. Until the rate at which jobs can be created comes into equilibrium with the rate at which this generation is growing, these young people will constitute an important source of political instability in the Middle East.

NOTES

1. That is, "the total fertility rate represents the number of children that would be born per woman, assuming that she lives to the end of her childbearing years and bears children at each age in accord with prevailing age-specific fertility rates" (World Bank 1984, 282).

2. The replacement level TFR is generally assumed to be 2.1.

3. A sophisticated statistical analysis found that 38 percent of the variance in regional TFRs was "unexplained" (Dyer and Yousef 2003, cited in World Bank 2004, 51).

4. This conclusion would be invalidated only if more rapid population growth either increased the domestic savings rate or stimulated additional capital inflows from abroad. Little evidence supports either conjecture.

5

HUMAN CAPITAL: HEALTH AND EDUCATION

In the first two decades after independence, governments across most MENA countries made human development a policy priority. The statist development models adopted throughout the region involved major government investment in social sectors and public infrastructure. Populations across the MENA region enjoyed significant advances in social development and tangible social mobility, thanks in no small part to the establishment of basic public welfare programs and the expansion of government employment. The fact that the marginal costs of improving social indicators are relatively low in the initial stage of investing in human development also facilitated these early gains.

In the 1980s and 1990s, with the rollback of the state and the gradual decline of public welfare infrastructure, human development slowed and, in some areas, even stalled or declined. The increased marginal costs of achieving additional gains in later stages of social development exacerbated these trends. After the "lost decade" of the 1980s, all but the well-to-do lived increasingly tenuous and precarious lives. For the middle classes, who had been the prime beneficiaries of expansive government employment programs, aspirations of social mobility were increasingly out of reach. For the poor, cuts in subsidies as well as the deterioration of public services limited their prospects for rising out of poverty. Middle Eastern societies were increasingly characterized by sharp inequalities of opportunity. Against the backdrop of major advances in human development in earlier decades and the rise of an ostentatious and well-connected super-elite with economic liberalization, these trends in social outcomes were particularly egregious.

In this chapter, we review the major developments in health and education. In so doing, we present some key building blocks in our argument about the role of real and perceived inequalities in fueling the uprisings. This overview of social sectors also contributes to a better understanding of the distinct context within which the various subregions of the Middle East have pursued economic and social development.

SOCIAL SECTORS AND SOCIAL SERVICES

The necessity of ameliorating health conditions and educating people as widely as possible—of investing in human capital—is a rare point of consensus in social science. First, all agree that good health and universal literacy are ends in themselves. A society that fails to educate its children and to eradicate preventable disease may be justifiably accused of neglecting the general welfare. Second, analysts believe that healthier and better-educated people are more productive. There are important "virtuous circles" among education, health, fertility decline, and labor productivity. Neoclassical economists point to high rates of return on investments in human capital, while Marxists stress the need for socialist regimes to liberate the productive potential of the masses. It is rare in the field of development studies to find such substantively similar conclusions emanating from such radically different perspectives. Human capital issues are particularly important for the MENA countries because, with the obvious exception of oil, the region is relatively poor in natural resources. Therefore, many argue that development of human resources should lie at the center of national development plans.

Although performance varies widely by country, in general, the region made dramatic progress during the past two generations. Life expectancy in the region has improved markedly: a child born today in the Arab countries is expected to live seventy-one years on average, eighteen years longer than a child born in the 1970s (see Table 5.2). Massive improvements in education have taken place, with youth illiteracy nearly eradicated and the male-female education gap closing. In some countries in the region, female school enrollment exceeds that of males. The importance of women's education is not restricted to empowerment and gender equality; research has shown that female education has positive consequences for children's health and the overall well-being of the household because family income increases when women are able to work outside the house, and home production also increases when women are educated (Semba et al. 2008; UNESCO 2011). Such positive changes provide a welcome contrast to the sea of other, more somber news about the region's political economy.

Today most countries in the region continue to make some progress; however, there are still significant national, regional, gender, and social class gaps in access to the basic human rights of health and education. Despite real gains, the "ultimate resource" of human beings continues to be wasted far more than the region can afford. In addition, labor markets function inadequately and are generally unable to absorb educated Middle Easterners, while unemployment plagues individuals, families, and entire nations. Whatever skills they acquire often go unused, and as a result, they move into the informal sector (see Chapter 4). The expansion of education, coupled with rapid population growth, has created a potent political force: secondary- and university-level students who often cannot find jobs consistent with their aspirations.

The last two decades have seen a slow transition in the MENA region, not just from state-led to market-driven growth, but also from a very large to a smaller (but still large) and much impoverished state (with the exception of the RRLP countries).

While the first transformation has directly affected the process of job creation, the second has affected the economy and human capital formation through the fiscal channel. With the shrinking of the fiscal gains of the 1970s oil boom era, government spending on health and education has been less affected than other sectors,[1] except in the RRLA countries, where it fell precipitously from 6.5 percent of GDP in the early 1980s to 3.8 percent in the early 1990s, an extraordinarily low level that mainly reflects low levels of spending in this category in Syria. In the other two regions, it fell from 7–9 percent of GDP to about 6 percent, but more recently it rose again in the Gulf Cooperation Council (GCC) countries, reaching high levels of 12 percent of GDP in Saudi Arabia, for example (see Table 5.1).

The freeze in budgets going to health and education led to less progress in human development and to the worsening of the quality of services, especially those

TABLE 5.1. Expenditures on Health and Education (as a percentage of GDP) in the MENA Countries, 1990s to 2010s

	Peak Health and Education Spending	Lowest Health and Education Spending	Recent Peak Health and Education Spending	Bulge in Health and Education Spending (peak to lowest)	Average Health and Education Spending: 1990s	Average Health and Education Spending: 2000s	Average Health and Education Spending: 2010s	Human Development Index Rank Average (1990s, 2000s, 2010s)
RRLP	9.5%	6.5%	7.8%	3.0%	7.5%	6.1%	6.1%	
Bahrain	7.9	5.4	6.3	2.5	6.1	6.0	6.2	38 (40, 38, 48)
Kuwait	11.2	5.6	6.9	5.6	9.7	7.3	7.3	31 (41, 39, 51)
Libya								
Oman	8.6	6.6	6.9	2.0	6.8	6.4	6.0	145 (158, 169, 84)
Qatar			5.9			4.7	4.9	21 (32, 32, 37)
Saudi Arabia	10.2	8.5	12.7	1.7				
RRLA	6.5	3.8	5.6	2.7	6.4	5.4		
Algeria			8.3		10.4	6.8		70 (81, 84, 93)
Iran	9.9	5.6	2.9	4.3	6.1	3.9		75 (86, 75, 75)
Syria	3.0	2.0		1.0	2.8			64 (83, 90, 115)
RPLA	6.9	5.7	6.5	1.2	6.1	6.4	6.0	
Egypt	6.5	5.5	5.7	1.0	5.4	6.0	5.1	81 (92, 91, 111)
Jordan	5.3	6.2	7.8	-0.9	7.5	8.1	6.9	59 (72, 77, 99)
Lebanon		2.7	3.6		3.5	3.4	2.8	137 (151, 163, 74)
Morocco	7.8	6.9	8.3	0.9	6.7	7.2	8.0	85 (99, 107, 130)
Tunisia	7.9	7.1	7.3	0.8	7.7	7.3	7.2	72 (85, 80, 92)

Source: International Monetary Fund (IMF), World Financial Statistics.

FIGURE 5.1. Average Rate of HDI Gains of the MENA Countries, 1970–2010 and 1990–2010

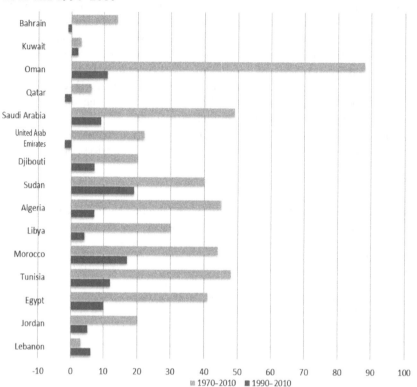

Source: United Nations Development Program (UNDP) (2011).

going to the poor, who could not afford to purchase these services in the burgeoning private sector. A recent United Nations Development Program (UNDP) study confirms this in dramatic ways. Analyzing the evolution of the Human Development Index (HDI), the study measured the performance of the health and education systems in all regions during 1990–2010 and compared it to the performance of the health and education systems during 1970–2010. As can be seen in Figure 5.1, HDI gains have slowed significantly since the 1990s in countries across the MENA region.

After taking off in the 1970s, the rate of increase in the HDI in the Arab region slowed down markedly. As happens elsewhere, early improvements were easier to achieve, coming from a low base, and with the rise of the state and the first oil boom in the early period, they were also boosted by the high expenditures on social sectors. Progress has become more constrained in the recent past, partly because incremental advancement is harder, but also in large part because of the fiscal constraints.

In the next two sections, we review trends in health conditions and educational performance. As the literature on the social determinants of health tells us (see, for example, Marmot and Wilkinson 2005), health care and health spending are only one small set of factors that affect the health outcomes of individuals; their social status and social conditions are often far more consequential. To some degree, similar points can be made for education: parental social status has an important impact on both educational achievement and future employment prospects. Thus, spending on social sectors is only one part of the equation shaping health and educational outcomes, and of course, how the money is spent matters greatly.

That said, the fiscal context is consequential for public welfare, particularly for the poor. Access to public health and education is the main avenue that allows the poor to escape from their poverty trap over generations. There is evidence that poverty reduction, which was robust during the oil boom period of the 1970s and 1980s, has essentially stagnated since the early 1990s. Many millions of residents of the region have become unable to progress socially in the way previous generations did—through hard work and education—and the rollback of state services seems to have trapped them in poverty (see Chapter 2).

HEALTH CONDITIONS

Although most countries have significantly improved their citizens' health, it still falls short of ideal. "Good health" is a multidimensional phenomenon, and therefore measuring it is difficult. Two assessments are widely used as indicators of health conditions: life expectancy at birth (LEB) and the infant mortality rate (IMR). LEB may be the single most robust indicator of national health conditions. Based on age-specific mortality rates, it tells us how long, on average, a newly born child can expect to live. It summarizes health, nutritional, and other welfare factors in a single, easily understood number. LEB figures for the region are shown in Table 5.2. IMR is a second key indicator of a country's overall state of health (see Table 5.2).

Avoidable infant deaths are not only especially poignant but also symptomatic of wider health problems such as malnutrition, polluted water, poor infant feeding practices, and, more generally, an underdeveloped public health system. As we discussed in Chapter 4, high infant mortality fosters high fertility and rapid population growth. From a demographic perspective as well as from a simple humanitarian one, understanding the causes of and remedies for high infant mortality is critical.

Health Levels and Rates of Change

Our evaluation of Middle Eastern health performance varies depending on whether we compare it with conditions in other less developed countries (LDCs) or with conditions in more developed countries. Furthermore, a focus on health *levels* yields different conclusions than an analysis of *rates of change* in those levels. With regard to the first perspective, infant mortality rates in the region as a whole (19 infant deaths per 1,000 live births) and in the Arab countries (34 per 1,000) are below both world (37 per 1,000) and LDC (64 per 1,000) averages. Within LDCs, the

164

TABLE 5.2. Basic Health Indicators: Life Expectancy at Birth and Infant Mortality, 1970–2011

Country	Life Expectancy: 1970s	Life Expectancy: 1980s	Life Expectancy: 1990s	Life Expectancy: 2000s	Life Expectancy: 2011	Infant Mortality: 1970s	Infant Mortality: 1980s	Infant Mortality: 1990s	Infant Mortality: 2000s	Infant Mortality: 2011
Arab world	53	60	65	70	71	108	72	52	40	34
Algeria	56	63	68	72	73	114	69	47	32	26
Bahrain	67	71	73	74	75	43	21	14	9	9
Egypt	53	59	65	71	73	141	87	50	27	18
Iran	54	53	67	71	73	106	60	41	28	21
Iraq	60	60	70	69	69	68	43	36	33	31
Israel	72	75	78	81	82	20	13	8	5	4
Jordan	64	69	71	73	73	61	39	28	21	18
Kuwait	69	72	73	74	75	38	21	12	10	9
Lebanon	66	67	70	72	73	40	32	22	12	8
Libya	55	64	70	74	75	68	41	27	17	13
Morocco	54	61	66	70	72	107	78	55	37	28
Oman	55	65	73	74	73	98	52	27	12	7
Palestine			70	72	73	86	49	30	23	20
Qatar	69	73	75	78	79	33	21	14	8	6
Saudi Arabia	57	66	70	73	74	93	50	26	13	8
Sudan	47	51	54	59	61	89	83	72	62	57
Syria	63	69	73	75	76	65	39	24	16	13
Tunisia	57	65	71	74	75	96	54	33	19	14
Turkey	53	60	66	72	74	128	80	45	20	12
United Arab Emirates	66	70	73	76	77	51	26	15	8	6
Yemen	43	53	57	66	65	167	108	81	65	57
MENA average						81.52	50.76	33.67	22.71	18.33
World	60	64	66	67	70	86	68	57	44	37
OECD	70	74	76	78	80	35	22	14	8	6

Source: World Bank, WDI.

FIGURE 5.2. Infant Mortality Rates in Various World Regions, 2011

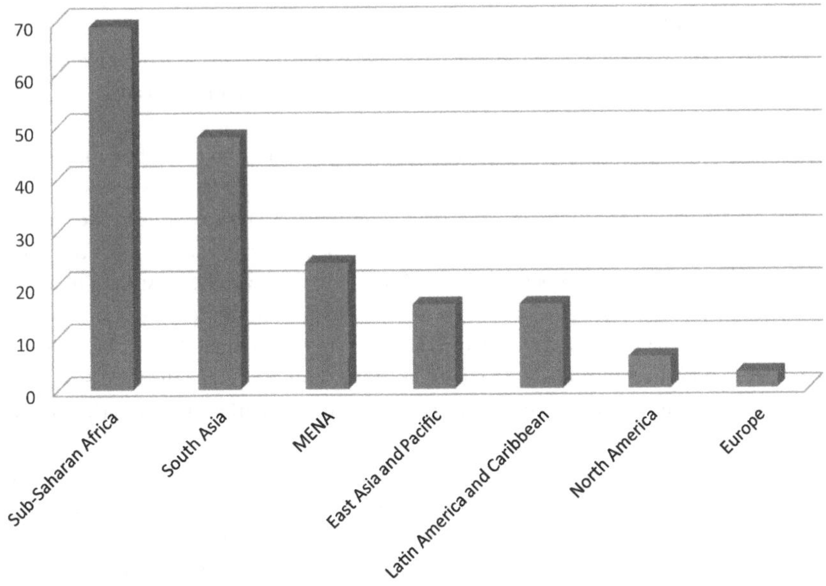

Source: World Bank, WDI.

infant mortality rate of the MENA region is lower than the rates of sub-Saharan Africa and South Asia, but higher than those prevailing in East Asia and Latin America (see Figure 5.2).

As with all LDCs, health conditions in the MENA countries are far worse than conditions in industrialized countries; for example, nearly six times as many infants die in the MENA region as in more developed countries. And within the region, there is much heterogeneity: rates in Lebanon, Israel, and the GCC countries are at the same level as the industrialized countries, whereas Sudan and Yemen have very high infant mortality rates. And heterogeneity is not restricted to the national level: the national numbers shown in Table 5.2 conceal considerable regional and social class variation. For instance, rural infant and child (under five years old) mortality rates routinely exceed those of urban areas throughout the region. In Egypt, children born in an urban setting are 25 percent less likely to die as compared to their rural counterparts (Lara and Pullum 2005). Class position has an even greater impact than urban or rural residence: babies born to poor Egyptian parents are nearly three and a half times as likely to die before their first birthday as the children of rich Egyptians (El-Saharty et al. 2005).[2] There is evidence that the gap between the rich and the poor widened in Egypt from the late 1980s to the late 1990s (Minujin and Delamonica 2003). Nearly one-third of children in Khartoum squatter settlements die before their fifth birthday, a child mortality rate more than three times the Sudanese average (Eltayib 2003). In the Middle East, as elsewhere, the poor watch more of their children die than do the rich.[3]

BOX 5.1 Iraqi Child Mortality, 1991 to the Present Day

Before Saddam Hussein's invasion of Kuwait in 1990, and even during his brutal war with Iran, Iraqi progress on health indicators was, on average, better than elsewhere in the MENA region. The infant mortality rate fell from 117 deaths per 1,000 births in 1960 to 90 in 1970, 63 in 1980, and 40 in 1990. In 1992 the IMR for the region was 58. But the First Gulf War in 1991, the sanctions regime of 1990–2003, and the Anglo-American invasion and occupation from 2003 on dramatically transformed the health situation of the country.

The six weeks of coalition air attacks in 1991 destroyed more Iraqi economic infrastructure than did the entire eight years of war with Iran (Tripp 2000). In particular, power facilities and water-pumping stations were devastated. In the spring of 1991, the UN Security Council continued the sanctions regime created in the run-up to the Gulf War in order to force Saddam Hussein to dismantle his nuclear, biological, and chemical weapons programs. By most accounts, this was the most thorough sanctions program in history. Food and medicines were theoretically exempt from the embargo. However, constant conflict between the Iraqi government and the UN Security Council, led by the United States, created shortages of both. Additionally, prohibitions on the imports of so-called dual-use items (for example, many chemicals and spare parts for power, water, and sanitation systems) crippled attempts to repair infrastructure.

Although sanctions may well have achieved their political goal—the denial of weapons of mass destruction to Saddam's regime (Lopez and Cortright 2004)—the cost in human lives was appallingly high. During the 1990s, a highly charged political debate over sanctions emerged. In hindsight, the outlines of the situation have become clear: beginning in mid-1991, hundreds of thousands of Iraqi children died who would not otherwise have perished. A number of different studies (not all of which agreed with each other) showed that child mortality in Iraq during the 1990s was very much higher than what one would have anticipated without the sanctions regime (see, for example, Garfield 1999; UNICEF 1999; for a review of UN studies, see Rowat 2000).

After a UN Food and Agriculture Organization (FAO) mission to Iraq in 1995, two team members published a letter in the British medical journal *The Lancet,* asserting that "excess deaths" of children in Iraq from 1990 to 1995 were about 567,000 (Zaidi and Smith-Fawzi 1995).[1] This number—usually rounded off to 500,000—was widely disseminated by critics of the sanctions regime, not least by the Iraqi government. A 1999 study by Richard Garfield of Columbia University Medical School surveyed different data and estimated excess deaths at roughly half that figure, or approximately 227,000. UNICEF then conducted a child and maternal mortality survey in 1999 and estimated excess deaths for the years 1991–1998 at about 500,000 (UNICEF 1999). Then, in 2002, Garfield revised his estimate of excess deaths, based on all of the research conducted up to that time. He calculated that between 343,900 and 529,000 excess deaths of children under age five occurred from August 1991 to June 2002 (Global Policy Forum 2002). Garfield (1999, 45) described the unusual nature of this health crisis in his 1999 study: "Sustained increases in young child mortality are extremely rare in this century. Such a large increase as that found here (227,000) is almost unknown in the public health literature. . . . Living conditions in Iraq . . . represent a loss of several decades of progress in reducing mortality."

The proximate causes of child death were diarrhea and respiratory illness. Contaminated water, inadequate breast-feeding, and the absence of supplies in the curative medical system killed many. The isolation and austerity of the 1990s had a strong impact on the educational system. Elsewhere in the MENA region, the younger the age group the higher the literacy rate. But this is not the case in Iraq: the 71 percent literacy rate for fifteen- to twenty-four-year-olds who grew up in the 1990s is *lower* than the 75 percent literacy rate for twenty-five- to thirty-four-year-olds (UNDP and Iraq Ministry

continues

BOX 5.1. *continued*

of Planning and Development Cooperation 2005, 32). Mortality was highest in the southern, largely Shi'ite-inhabited provinces (the poorest and least-educated region), in rural areas, and among the poor and uneducated (Garfield 1999). A vicious cycle of ignorance, child death, and high fertility—with more child deaths—was instigated under the sanctions regime. Whereas multiple, mutually reinforcing forces drove down child mortality elsewhere in the region, in Iraq these same forces were essentially reversed.

The Anglo-American invasion and occupation of Iraq ended the sanctions regime. After March 2003, the debate shifted to total excess deaths (that is, including adults). A study published in *The Lancet* using cluster sample survey methodology estimated the most probable number of excess deaths since the invasion to be 98,000, most of which were due to violence (Roberts et al. 2004). In the spring and summer of 2004, the Norwegian Statistical Agency and the Iraqi government carried out a sample survey by which they estimated the total number of violent deaths at 18,000 to 29,000 (UNDP 2005).[2] Between May and July 2006, researchers from Johns Hopkins University and their Iraqi colleagues again deployed the standard epidemiological methodology of a cluster sample survey to estimate excess deaths since the invasion in April 2003 (Burnam et al. 2006). They estimated that, "as of July 2006, there have been 654,965 (392,979–942,636) excess Iraqi deaths as a consequence of the war," the vast majority of which (over 600,000) were violent deaths, most commonly due to gunfire (Crawford 2013).[3] Child malnutrition, which had fallen to 4 percent in 2002 (UNICEF 2005), climbed to 7.7 percent. That is, roughly 400,000 Iraqi children suffered from chronic diarrhea and dangerous protein deficiencies. The country's water and sewage systems remained in disarray; the Norwegian survey observed standing sewage in the streets in front of 39 percent of houses (Garfield 2005; Vick 2004). Meanwhile, after the invasion, 34,000 doctors fled and hundreds have been killed. As a result, only 16,000 doctors remain, leaving only 5 doctors for every 10,000 Iraqis (Dewachi 2013).

Women and children are the most vulnerable under the current conditions in Iraq. Many pregnant women are unable to reach hospitals for delivery, immunizations are severely reduced, the delivery of medical supplies is disrupted, and electricity is cut at the hospitals. There has been a serious increase in the maternal mortality rate since 2003, rising from 47 to 84 per 100,000 live births, and a 150 percent increase in infant mortality rates between 1990 and 2005—the world's worst retrogression in infant mortality (Dewachi 2013).

The invasion of Iraq also created a massive refugee crisis, which has abated somewhat in recent years. The total number of Iraqi refugees is estimated to be higher than 3.2 million, of whom 1.5 million are internally displaced persons (IDPs), 1 million are in Syria, and 500,000 are in Jordan. The war has also severely damaged the Iraqi health care system. As a result, Iraqis who can afford to do so travel abroad to receive proper health care. Many arrive at late stages of their sickness, in part because they have been misdiagnosed in Iraq and also because in Iraq they are required to pay their health care costs out of pocket. Recently, the Iraqi government has contracted with hospitals in neighboring countries to treat Iraqis with government financial support, opening up additional opportunities for corruption and discretionary access to care (Dewachi 2013).

1. The term "excess deaths" is defined as the difference between observed mortality and the prewar, pre-sanctions level of mortality, or what is presumed to have been the pre-1990 trend. Since child mortality fell dramatically in the region during the 1990s, the second assumption seems the more reasonable standard of comparison.

2. Their number excluded deaths from "criminal murder." In the absence of political authority whose legitimacy is widely recognized, it is not at all clear what this phrase might mean.

3. The figures in parentheses denote, respectively, the lower and upper bounds of the 95 percent confidence interval.

There are several grim exceptions to the general trend toward improvement shown in MENA human development indicators over the past several decades— the children in Iraq, the victims of famine in Sudan, and, most recently, the victims of the crisis in Syria. Iraq presents what had previously been a historically unprecedented case: fifteen years of war and economic sanctions dramatically reversed earlier progress (see Box 5.1). The Syrian conflict has generated another major humanitarian crisis in the region. The United Nations estimates that the number of official Syrian refugees exceeds 3 million, as of September 2014. Syrian refugees are spread out across the region and are mainly in Lebanon (1.2 million), Jordan (620,000), Turkey (850,000), Iraq (215,000), and Egypt (140,000) (UNHCR 2014). In Jordan and Turkey most refugees live in camps, whereas in Lebanon, Iraq, and Egypt they live with local host families or in public spaces such as schools and parks. The vast majority of refugees, having arrived with little more than the clothes on their back, are dependent on aid and are not entitled to obtain legal work permits. In addition to financial hardship, refugees are at greater risk for exploitation, underage marriage, and human trafficking and are often the victims of discrimination.

Gender differentials in life expectancy are less striking in the region than in other LDCs (particularly in South Asia). LEB for women exceeds that for men by 3.6 years. The highest gender differential is in Iraq, where women live on average 6.3 years longer than men, perhaps the result of protracted war and conflict, whereas in Qatar male life expectancy surpasses that of women by 0.5 years. In countries of high human development, however, women live as much as seven years longer than men (UNDP and AFESD 2002). Maternal mortality remains tragically high in the MENA region, where it is now almost on par with Latin America but five times higher than in the high-income countries in North America and Europe (see Figure 5.3). Nevertheless, infant mortality today is much lower—and therefore LEB is much higher—than it was even twenty years ago. Of course, LEB also varies widely by country. Israel and Qatar have the highest life expectancies—eighty-two and seventy-nine, respectively—and they are at the same levels as the OECD countries. The life expectancy of a Sudanese child, however, is the lowest in the region at sixty-one years, well below the world average (see Table 5.2).

Since the fall in IMR and the associated increase in LEB has been a worldwide phenomenon, we need a comparative perspective. We know that medical advances potentially affect all nations; for any given income level, IMR falls and LEB rises over time. However, the MENA region has done relatively well in improving health as measured by IMR and LEB in comparison with other regions of the world. Most notably, *the decline in its infant mortality rates from 1980 to 2000 was the fastest of any region in the world* (Cornia and Menchini 2001). During the 2000s, IMR dropped by almost one-third, compared to a 20 percent drop for the world average. In 2012 the Middle East ranked third in the rate of reduction of infant mortality (3.3 percent annual drop), after Latin America (4.8 percent) and East Asia (4.7 percent) (UNICEF 2012). Unlike the situation a decade ago, Middle Eastern health conditions are no longer much worse than would be predicted on the basis of incomes. Nonetheless, although LEB is somewhat better than would be predicted

FIGURE 5.3. Lifetime Risk of Maternal Death Around the World, 2010

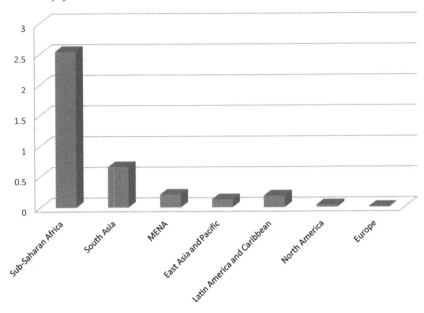

Source: World Bank, WDI.

on the basis of income, IMR remains, in several countries, worse than would be expected (see Figure 5.4).

We know that economic growth improves health. Carcinogenic industry notwithstanding, there is a clear positive correlation between LEB and per capita income; for a set of over one hundred countries, 45 percent of the variance in LEB (the dependent variable) can be attributed to variation in per capita income (Cornia and Menchini 2001). For example, the GCC countries spend billions on health care and advanced medical technology, which are heavily financed by governments. At the same time, obesity has reached near-epidemic proportions in the GCC, increasing the prevalence of chronic diseases and hence driving up health care costs (Ng et al. 2011).

Although no single variable other than income plays so important a role in explanations of cross-country differences in LEB, over half of the variance remains to be explained. The recent experience of countries such as China and Sri Lanka shows that increased income is not a necessary condition for improving health—both countries' LEB is comparable to the LEBs found in advanced industrial countries, even though the World Bank considers them LDCs. Conversely, a highly inegalitarian pattern of economic growth may reduce infant mortality only very slowly.

Explanations for Health Performance

Total spending on health provides only a very partial explanation for health improvements. For example, on average, the countries of the MENA region devoted a

FIGURE 5.4. Infant Mortality in the MENA Region as a Function of Gross National Income per Capita, 2011

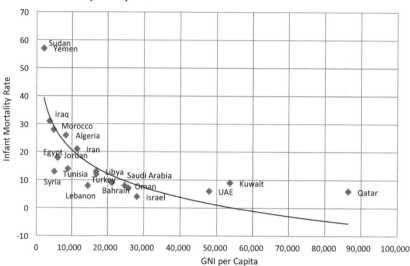

Source: World Bank, WDI.

higher percentage of GDP to health during the 1990s than East Asia did, yet they had significantly poorer health conditions (World Bank 2002). More recently, in 2012, average health care expenditure in the Middle East (4.6 percent) was lower relative to other regions: it was substantially lower than in East Asia (7.1 percent), Latin America (7.7 percent), and sub-Saharan Africa (6.5 percent), though it still exceeded expenditures in South Asia (4 percent). Average life expectancy in the Middle East could be higher, particularly in light of the region's substantial wealth, but it is by no means the lowest among all developing regions. In 2012 average life expectancy was about seventy-two in the Middle East, which was lower than East Asia and Latin America (both seventy-five) but higher than South Asia (sixty-seven) and Africa (fifty-six), both areas hit hard by HIV/AIDS.

Money alone does not solve public health problems. The key issue is how the money is spent. One approach to this problem is to ask what diseases kill young children (the "proximate" causes of death) and why they contract these diseases or are not swiftly cured (the "underlying" causes). A great deal is known about both of these. The tragedy of high infant mortality rates is that most children in the Third World die from diseases that can be prevented, often at very low cost. With the partial exception of malaria, common diseases that kill children, such as diarrhea, diphtheria, measles, tuberculosis, and whooping cough, can be prevented with proven methods at relatively low cost.

Middle Eastern countries have had a mixed experience with practices such as growth monitoring, breast-feeding, and immunization, which reduce infant mortality. The problem is that their adoption often requires that mothers visit clinics. There are typically too few of these in most countries of the region, and the staff is too poorly paid, leading to significant delays, long waiting times, and under-the-table payments, even where citizens have the legal right to free health care. Many countries in the region, even outside the oil-rich Gulf countries, provide free health care to those in need. Some, such as Egypt and Syria, provide constitutional guarantees to health care. In practice, however, public health facilities are often underutilized because of staff absenteeism, the unavailability of basic supplies and infrastructure, and widespread perceptions of poor quality of care.[4] Consequently, many (especially poorer) residents use them only as a last resort, when a child is already sick and perhaps beyond simple treatment (US Institute of Medicine 1979). In addition, in many countries such clinics are more abundant in urban areas than in rural areas. Regional variation is wide: even today, in many countries, rural outpatient clinics remain scarce. In Yemen, for example, less than one-fourth of the rural population has access to a clinic (USAID 2003) and six women die every day from pregnancy-related complications (World Bank 2014).

There has been a regional revolution in child immunization during the past quarter-century. In 1980 most children in most countries failed to complete the three shots of the DPT (diphtheria, pertussis, tetanus) series. During the 1980s the percentage immunized rose dramatically in all countries; the change in Yemen (from 1 percent to 84 percent) may have been the most striking, but others performed impressively as well. Progress continued, albeit at a somewhat slower pace, for the next fifteen years. Only Algeria, Iraq, Turkey, and Yemen faltered during the 1990s (UNICEF 2006). Significantly, immunization among the poor improved dramatically in some regions; for example, in the six years from 1992 to 1998, the percentage of immunized children in rural Upper Egypt, the poorest region of the country, rose from just over 50 percent to 90 percent (UNDP 2002, 109). Improving immunization rates remains a major objective for some MENA countries. Sudan and Yemen, which are on the UNICEF priority list in part owing to their comparatively high rates of deaths from measles, implemented programs for supplementary immunization in 2006. By the mid-2000s, measles immunization had risen to 89 percent across the MENA region as a whole (UNICEF 2007).

Three other measures are essential for reducing infant mortality, the so-called three Fs: family spacing, food supplements, and female education. There is a strong correlation between infant health and the length of time between births. Too little time between births weakens the mother, thereby threatening her own health and that of her children. The MENA region has the highest prevalence of short birth intervals in the world (Aoyama 2001, 42), and at least in Egypt, birth intervals are shorter among younger women and those living in rural areas (El-Zanaty and Way 2006). The consequences are grim: in both Egypt and Yemen, the IMR for births occurring less than twenty-four months after the birth of a sibling is more than twice as high as the IMR for births occurring two to three years after the birth of a sibling (Aoyama 2001). A minimum spacing of two years is recommended to reduce the risk of adverse maternal, perinatal, and infant outcomes (WHO 2006). Short interbirth intervals are clearly the result of the failure to practice contraception, since, in contrast to practices in many sub-Saharan African societies, prolonged sexual abstinence after the birth of a child is not common in the region.

Food supplements are designed to break the synergies between malnutrition and disease. Not only does malnutrition reduce resistance, but disease can also engender malnutrition by impeding the body's ability to absorb or properly utilize ingested nutrients. Compared with other Third World regions, Middle Eastern countries have done well here. UNICEF estimates that only 8.3 percent of the people of the region receive "insufficient calories for an active working life," that is, less than 90 percent of the caloric intake recommended by the Food and Agriculture Organization (FAO) and World Health Organization (WHO), as compared with 12.2 percent in East Asia and the Pacific, 21.1 percent in sub-Saharan Africa, and 33.1 percent in South Asia. Latin America performs better here—only about 3.3 percent of the population in this region meets this definition of malnourishment (see Figure 5.5).

Nonetheless, child malnutrition ("stunting") afflicts 20.2 percent of the region's children.[5] Three MENA countries suffer from critical malnutrition problems: Iraq, Sudan, and Yemen. The latter two rank especially high on the list of stunting and malnutrition for children in the world. In Yemen, 58 percent of children suffer from stunting and 43 percent are underweight; in Sudan, 40 percent are stunted and 27 percent are underweight (World Bank 2013). Children in these countries also tend to have lower birth weights. Egypt and Iraq share this problem but, like other countries in the region, suffer simultaneously from obesity problems. Throughout the region, rural areas with scarce arable land appear to be worse off than urban areas, where extensive food subsidy systems prevail.

Significant class biases also exist. Typically, it is a lack of purchasing power rather than a failure of national (much less global) food supplies that causes hunger everywhere (Sen 1981; World Bank 1986). Malnutrition is a problem for all Egyptian children regardless of social and economic background; however, children from poorer families (and with less educated mothers) tend to have lower micronutrient intakes (Aran and Ersado 2013). As elsewhere, within disadvantaged groups the members suffering most severely from malnutrition are children and pregnant and lactating women. This is where food supplements could have a dramatic impact in reducing infant mortality rates. Few Middle Eastern governments have supplementary feeding programs, although most have sharply reduced malnutrition through extensive, untargeted, and costly consumer food subsidy systems. However, blanket subsidy programs are suboptimal because they often fail to help the poor while causing large budget deficits (IMF 2012). Targeted subsidies or cash transfers to the poor are increasingly popular policy recommendations to address these problems, yet corruption may divert their benefits away from the neediest.

Female education may be *the* key to health conditions in the region. John Caldwell (1986) surveyed ninety-nine countries and found that the best predictor of both infant mortality rate and life expectancy at birth was the 1960 female primary school enrollment rate. He argues that nations with "exceptionally good" performances (China, Sri Lanka, the Indian state of Kerala, Costa Rica) had relatively

FIGURE 5.5. Malnutrition in the Major World Regions, 2011

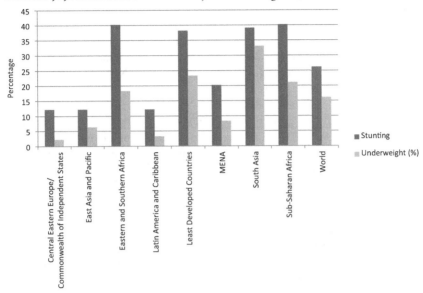

Source: WHO and UNICEF Joint Global Nutrition Database (2011).

high degrees of "female autonomy" and that nine of the eleven worst performers were Middle Eastern Muslim countries. Since in all Third World countries women have primary responsibility for child care, it is essential that they be sufficiently well educated and accustomed to taking the initiative on their children's behalf. They must recognize early warning signs (such as a child's failure to grow properly), understand disease origins and prevention, and be ready and able to act immediately to seek remedies. All such behavior, of course, presupposes female literacy. Caldwell argues that this kind of basic education is only a necessary, not a sufficient, condition for such autonomy. If a woman is educated but is not in the habit of venturing out of her home unaccompanied, child health will still suffer.

Much evidence supports this reasoning. A 10 percent increase in girls' primary school enrollment has been shown to decrease infant mortality by 4.1 deaths per 1,000 live births, while a 10 percent rise in secondary school enrollment decreases infant mortality by another 5.6 deaths per 1,000 live births (Aoyama 2001). In Egypt in 2000, the child mortality rate for women with no education was 89, while the rate for mothers who had completed primary education was 55 and the rate for those with at least a secondary education was 38 (Roudi-Fahimi and Moghadam 2003).

For assessing current health, the key statistic is literacy among women ages fifteen to twenty-four ("youth literacy"). Since today's Middle Eastern mother is typically young, such a number is a proxy for basic health knowledge. Over 84 percent of Arab women in this age group are literate, while nearly all (98 percent) young female Turks and Iranians can read and write. This is a profound, albeit quiet, so-cial revolution; as recently as twenty-five years ago, when Alan Richards and John Waterbury first began thinking about writing this book, for example, fewer than two out of five young Iranian women were literate. Even the poorest countries have made important, rapid progress: only 35 percent of young Yemeni women were lit-erate twenty years ago, compared with 74 percent today (UNESCO 2005). Millions of children's lives have been saved as a result.

In recent years, some prominent scholars—for example, Bernard Lewis (2002)—attempting to explain the political strife in the region, have asked, "What went wrong?" in the Middle East. With respect to the education of young women and its positive impact on health conditions, the answer evidently is, "Less than you think!" Neither culture (still less religion) nor type of political system seems to be a critical factor in explaining improving health conditions. The recent increase in female enrollment in primary school and the decline in infant mortality have been rapid under both regimes espousing a socialist ideology (the People's Democratic Republic of Yemen [PDRY], Iraq, Libya, Syria) and more conservative governments (Tunisia, Turkey, Pahlavi Iran). With the exception of the former PDRY, none of these regimes has ever been officially non-Muslim, while the Islamic Republic of Iran now has enrolled all girls in primary school. Indeed, the performance of that Islamist-governed country in both education and health is one of the best in the region. There is little doubt that most regimes dominated by male Muslims (which is to say, all regimes in the MENA region except Israel and, to some extent, Leba-non) have rapidly expanded the enrollment of girls in school and the education of young women. This progress has had critical, positive impacts on both health and fertility (see Chapter 4).

EDUCATIONAL SYSTEMS

As with health conditions, how we assess Middle Eastern progress in education depends very much on whether we look at the current situation or at the speed of change. On the one hand, present levels of literacy in the Middle East are not as high as would be expected, given income levels; on the other hand, most nations have expanded educational opportunities rapidly in the past few decades.[6] Edu-cational levels vary considerably by country, region, gender, and social class. The education of women has also advanced markedly in recent years—from a very low starting point. Finally, the rapid *quantitative* expansion of school systems, partic-ularly when combined with fiscal austerity, has generated serious *qualitative* defi-ciencies in education.

Literacy Rates

In international comparative perspective, MENA rates of adult literacy have im-proved in the past decades but remain unjustifiably low in some countries (see Table 5.3). Bahrain, Israel, Jordan, Kuwait, Palestine, Qatar, Turkey, and the United

TABLE 5.3. Adult Illiteracy in the MENA Region, 1980–2010

Country	1980	1985	1990	1995	2000	2005	2010
Algeria	63.4%	55.1%	47.1%	39.7%	33.3%	27.4%	
Bahrain	28.8	23.3	17.9	14.8	12.5		8.1%
Egypt	60.7	56.8	52.9	48.9	44.7	28.6	27.9
Iran	50.3	44.1	36.8	30.0	24.0	17.6	14.9
Iraq	68.4	66.3	64.3	62.5	60.7		21.8
Israel	13.9	11.2	8.6	6.7	5.2		
Jordan	30.8	24.4	18.5	13.5	10.2	8.9	7.5
Kuwait	32.2	27.9	23.3	21.0	18.1	6.7	6.1
Lebanon	27.6	23.7	19.7	16.7	14.0	10.4	
Libya	47.3	39.2	31.9	25.5	20.1	13.9	10.8
Morocco	71.4	66.5	61.3	56.1	51.2	47.7	43.9
Oman	63.8	54.5	45.3	36.3	28.3	18.6	13.4
Palestine						7.7	5.1
Qatar	30.2	25.6	23.0	20.8	18.8	11.0	3.7
Saudi Arabia	49.1	40.8	33.8	28.8	23.8	17.1	13.4
Sudan	65.8	60.3	54.2	48.5	42.3		28.9
Syria	46.7	40.6	35.2	30.1	25.6	19.2	16.6
Tunisia	55.1	47.4	40.9	35.3	29.0	25.7	22.4
Turkey	31.6	26.1	22.1	18.2	15.0	11.8	9.2
United Arab Emirates	34.6	31.2	29.0	26.6	23.8	9.9	
Yemen	80.0	74.1	67.3	59.9	53.6	45.3	36.1

Source: World Bank, WDI.

Arab Emirates have literacy rates above 90 percent, and several other countries are approaching this rate. Only Morocco, Yemen, and Egypt have serious literacy problems: a little bit less than half the population is illiterate in the first two, and one-third of Egyptians are illiterate. In these countries and others in the region, female illiteracy remains a problem, especially where religion and conservative social norms persist. Female literacy in Morocco and Yemen is around 45 percent, almost on par with much poorer countries like Nepal and Pakistan. Sudan and Egypt also have high rates of illiteracy (higher than 30 percent) among their female populations. Surprisingly, in Tunisia, which is reputed in the region to be progressive when it comes to women's rights, a considerable portion of women, almost 30 percent, are illiterate. These unsatisfactory statistics should not mask the positive trends in female literacy in the region. Youth female literacy rates are much higher. On average, female literacy for young Arab women is around 80 percent, and Syria

FIGURE 5.6. Adult Illiteracy in the MENA Region as a Function of Gross
National Income per Capita, 2010

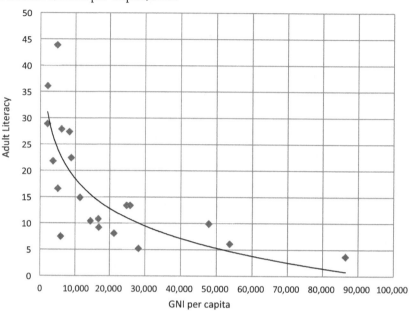

Source: World Bank, WDI.

and Tunisia have risen above 90 percent. Even in Morocco and Yemen, almost 75 percent of young women are literate. Thus, low overall female literacy rates reflect the low levels among women born prior to the 1980s, when schooling for girls was still not widely acceptable among conservative populations.

As elsewhere in the LDCs, both male and female illiteracy in the Middle East is concentrated in rural areas and among the poor. In Yemen, only 17 percent of the urban population is illiterate compared to 44 percent of their rural compatriots and about 62 percent of rural women. There are various historical and sociological reasons for these disparities. In Yemen, where tribal and religious values still predominate, social norms deter female education in some areas, while in Aden, the capital of the former socialist republic of South Yemen, literacy rates are the highest in the country. Egypt suffers from similar disparities, with about twice as many illiterates living in rural versus urban areas.

These statistics are sobering, and a global comparative perspective affords only partial comfort. As before, three types of comparison seem appropriate: with other regions, with respect to per capita incomes, and with the recent past. If adult literacy is our standard, the Middle East has room for improvement. Regional adult literacy, now at 79.2 percent, exceeds that of sub-Saharan Africa (59.8 percent) and South Asia (61.6 percent), but more than nine of ten adults in Latin America and East Asia are literate. Adult literacy rates in the MENA region are also below what we would predict on the basis of per capita incomes alone (see Figure 5.6). These human capital deficiencies place the region at a disadvantage in competing in international markets with countries from Eastern Europe, the former Soviet Union, Southeast Asia, and Latin America.

A historical perspective partially mitigates this pessimistic picture. One must remember that Middle Eastern countries launched their educational efforts from an extremely low base. The anciens régimes of the region did essentially nothing to educate most of their people. In some cases, education for the rural poor was actively discouraged, as on the estates of wealthy Egyptians under the Farouk monarchy (Adams 1986; Nyrop 1983). Arab and Berber children in North Africa were either entirely excluded from education or channeled into segregated schools under French colonial rule.[7] These countries faced severe difficulties in expanding their educational facilities after independence. Algerian teachers, nearly all of whom were Europeans, departed in a mass exodus in 1962—27,000 of 30,000 teachers left—and only one-fifth of the 20,000 new Algerian teachers were qualified (Bennoune 1988, 220). Many countries have come a long way since colonial days, when two-thirds to three-quarters of the people of the region were illiterate. By way of comparison, when South Korea shifted its development strategy to export-led growth in the early 1960s, over 70 percent of the population could already read and write. However, historical legacies alone do not explain persistently high adult illiteracy. With the exception of Iraq, Algeria, and the former PDRY, Middle Eastern countries have largely ignored the problem of illiterate adults, choosing instead to concentrate resources on educating children. Here the record is considerably more encouraging, although some countries of the region still have much unfinished business (see Table 5.4).

As with health conditions, change over time is better than static levels of achievement in global comparative perspective. Consider primary school enrollments. One of the UNDP's Millennium Development Goals for 2015 is to "achieve universal primary education." One benchmark for achieving this goal is a net enrollment ratio (NER) of 95 percent or better.[8] Most Middle Eastern countries have worked to improve school enrollments, and many have already reached the 95 percent target level, although Sudan and, to a lesser degree, Yemen are notable exceptions. In Oman, where education was restricted to a limited elite (about 3 percent of the population) until the 1970s and enrollment is now nearly universal, schooling made a miraculous improvement (Halliday 1974).[9]

The most dramatic change in primary enrollments occurred from 1970 to 1990. By 1990, the NER for Arab boys was 82 percent and 67 percent for girls. By 2003, 85 percent of boys and 78 percent of girls went to school in Arab countries (UNESCO 2013). Interestingly, for both Iran and Turkey, data from UNESCO suggest lower NERs in 2003 than in 1991. (It is worth noting that the United States had the same experience: the US NER fell from 97 percent to 92 percent during the same time period.) For the Middle East as a whole, the news is good: NER rates are improving and the gender gap in enrollment is closing, with the exceptions of Iraq,

TABLE 5.4. Gross Primary School Enrollment in the MENA Countries, 1971–2010

Country	1971		1990		2000		2010	
	Female	Total	Female	Total	Female	Total	Female	Total
Algeria	67.4%	76.1%	86.0%	94.6%	97.2%	107.8%	104.5%	110.2%
Bahrain		107.7	100.7	111.4	107.1	106.8		
Egypt		63.9		87.3	88.1	97.8	102.3	106.1
Iran	63.2	71.6	104.3	108.2	93.3	100.5	106.7	107.7
Iraq	47.2	69.9	94.5	108.3	98.7	95.36		
Israel		103.2		95.4	102.6	106.0	108.6	104.3
Jordan	115.0	102.7	94.6	101.5	105.8	97.9	96.1	91.9
Kuwait	48.9	88.1		91.2	105.4	103.3		105.6
Lebanon		127.6		95.9	94.8		105.8	104.6
Libya	108.0	109.4				119.9		
Morocco	34.9	51.5	55.9	68.2	109.7	92.4	108.9	111.4
Oman		2.8	71.8	78.9	90.7	90.74	103.2	105.2
Palestine						98.4	91.2	90.8
Qatar	87.1	109.8	63.4	99.7	109.2	100.8	106.9	102.9
Saudi Arabia							106.3	106.0
Sudan	34.9	35.9		47.9	41.7	47.8	75.4	72.6
Syria		81.8	101.3	107.4	112.2	109.2	116.9	117.8
Tunisia	69.7	100.4	96.3	112.0	102.4	115.0	107.3	110.0
Turkey		100.8	89.7	102.0		101.0	106.4	104.0
United Arab Emirates		80.9	107.4	107.8	96.1	89.6		
Yemen					63.2	78.3	96.2	87.3

Source: World Bank, WDI.

Note: Gross enrollment is defined as total enrollment in primary education, regardless of age, expressed as a percentage of the population of official primary education age.

Sudan and Yemen (see Figure 5.7). However, the extremely difficult task of reaching children in remote areas is still proving problematic. In providing universal primary education, the last few miles of the long race are not easy.

In contrast to the total number of illiterate persons, the total number of children not in school has declined in most countries since 1960. Illiteracy is increasingly a phenomenon of older people (see Table 4.2). More than 90 percent of fifteen- to twenty-four-year-olds can read in every country reporting data except Egypt (87.5

FIGURE 5.7. The Gender Gap in Primary School Enrollment in the MENA Countries, 2007

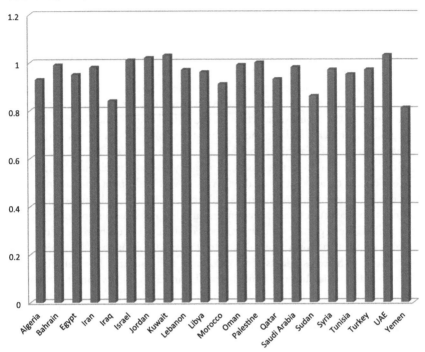

Source: World Bank, WDI.

percent), Iraq (82.6 percent), Morocco (79.5 percent), Sudan (86.6 percent), and Yemen (85.2 percent). (World Bank, World Development Indicators [WDI]).[10]

Educational Quality

To judge the quality of educational systems in the Middle East, we must look beyond literacy to the academic performance of students in the region as well as other features of the educational system more generally. Middle Eastern students tend to score lower than their peers in other regions on international standardized tests such as the Trends in International Mathematics and Science Study (TIMSS), which measures fourth- and eighth-grade outcomes and is administered every four years internationally to a large sample of countries, and the Program for International Student Assessment (PISA) of the OECD (World Bank 2013). In the 2007 TIMSS, students in the Middle East fared poorly in comparison with their counterparts in countries with similar per capita income levels. The wealthy Gulf countries scored particularly low in light of their high per capita income, but the poorer countries of the region also underperformed. While eighth-grade-level students in Malaysia received average scores of 474 in math and 471 in science and Bulgarian students scored 464 in math and 470 in science, their peers in Egypt obtained average scores of 391 in math and 408 in science. Even in Tunisia, where the public educational system was historically much stronger, students scored only 420 and 445 in these subjects, respectively. Jordan is a partial exception: there, students scored 482 in science on average (TIMSS 2007). Social inequalities also affect educational achievement in the region. One study found that in some MENA countries, notably Egypt, Iran, Jordan, Turkey, and the United Arab Emirates, inequality of opportunity (conceptualized as circumstances beyond individual control, such as gender, family background, ethnicity, and community membership) negatively affects achievement in math and science (Salehi-Esfahani, Belhaj, and Assaad 2014).

Beyond evidence from test scores, commonly voiced complaints about Middle Eastern education are that its quality is very low, that dropout rates are high, and that too few students master technical subjects, especially math and science. Class size does not seem to be cause for concern and has not been a significant problem in Middle Eastern primary education. Indeed, there is at best mixed evidence that learning or future performance is linked to class size (Colclough 1982), which varies from twelve to fifteen students per classroom in rich countries like Bahrain, Israel, Qatar, Saudi Arabia, and the United Arab Emirates to twenty-nine to thirty students in the poorest countries (Sudan and Yemen) (UNESCO 2013). Clearly, something other than class size affects educational achievement, as average class sizes in China and the Republic of Korea, whose students regularly shine in international comparative testing, are rather large. More important than class size are pedagogical methods, teacher quality, and morale. Far too often, education in the MENA region mimics traditional *madrasas* (Islamic schools where boys memorize parts of the Qur'an), with their emphasis on rote learning rather than problem-solving, writing skills, and creativity (Alayan, Rohde, and Dhouib 2012; World Bank 2008, 42, 89, 182). Few teachers, especially in poorer areas, have access to any materials besides simple textbooks and paper, and even these may be in short supply. Teachers in the Middle East do not enjoy markedly high social status, and rural posts are too often assigned to those with the worst academic performance. Teachers receive low pay, as do all civil servants, and lack proper training. The upper end of the Egyptian teachers' salary scale exceeds the national poverty line by only 10 percent (UNDP/INP 2005). One study estimates that 60 percent of parents hire private tutors, further sharpening the inequalities between Egyptians (Chatham House 2012).

Much of the money spent on education goes to teachers' and administrators' salaries; very little is left over to spend on books, equipment, or other educational materials. Between constricting budgets and exploding enrollments, educational quality has been crushed. In Egypt, for example, salaries consumed 64 percent of primary and secondary spending in 1982–1983 and 71 percent in 1998–1999 (UNDP/INP 2005). A recent report on Yemen also notes that teachers' salaries consume the bulk of the public education budget (Brookings 2013). These fiscal realities play a large role in the rote memorization approach to learning from kindergarten to university throughout the region.

The costly regionwide effort to expand secondary and university education (discussed later) has to some extent backfired because it has proved impossible to maintain exacting standards of instruction at the same time. In poorer countries like Morocco, schools, whether urban or rural, are primitive—drafty and cold in the winter, ovenlike in the spring. They are run-down because of inadequate budgets for maintenance—besides having either no or very little artificial lighting, there may be broken windows, missing blackboards, primitive and insalubrious plumbing, and classrooms crowded with benches and desks that look like relics from a war zone.[11] The students who suffer through this are often ill clothed and ill fed and must return to homes where there is no place to study and perhaps little understanding among the older generation of what modern education is all about.

Under such circumstances, morale is very low among both the students and the teachers. For the latter, pay is low, student-teacher ratios are high, and support equipment is nonexistent. That teachers resort to rote learning punctuated by long periods of chanting and calisthenics in what passes for the schoolyard is hardly surprising. Nor is their absenteeism. Young male teachers, thrust as bachelors into village schools, face long periods of sexual and social frustration. The teaching profession, like the diplomas it produces, has lost much of its prestige. Normal schools attract the least capable university students. It is a miracle that the system functions at all.

Given the working conditions in the poorer countries, it is hardly surprising that many teachers sought employment in the oil states during the 1980s. At present, unofficial estimates indicate that Egyptian schoolteachers can make twice their domestic salaries in Saudi Arabia, although the salaries they make there are below average for Saudi Arabian teachers; small wonder that tens of thousands of teachers work abroad, while many thousands more seek to leave. Indeed, one of the difficulties with maintaining, much less advancing, the educational systems of countries such as Sudan and Yemen has been the departure of the small number of trained teachers to the Gulf states. Yemeni and Sudanese teachers in the Gulf suffered the same fate, however, as their fellow nationals during the First Gulf War of 1990 and 1991—expulsion.

Migration had several important effects on the educational systems of both sending and receiving countries. Given the extremely low levels of adult literacy in most of the major oil-exporting countries at the onset of the oil boom, rapid expansion of their primary enrollments required large-scale importation of teachers. Such teachers had to be fluent in Arabic, and therefore Egyptians, Jordanians, and Palestinians were prominently represented. These migrant teachers usually dramatically improved their private welfare. There is little evidence that such emigration outflows exceeded the recruitment and training of new teachers; as noted earlier, pupil-teacher ratios continued to fall during the 1970s in Egypt, Jordan, and other countries that were major suppliers of teachers. Although this implies that the export of teachers had few negative consequences in countries with high enrollment ratios, the same argument is much weaker in Egypt and Sudan. After all, the favorable pupil-teacher ratios were achieved in part by slow growth of the numerator— that is, by sluggish improvement in the (low) percentage of Egyptian and Sudanese children in school. The Gulf crisis opened up new opportunities for Egyptian and Syrian teachers, thanks to the expulsion of Palestinians, Jordanians, and Yemenis.

Educational Allocation Decisions and Their Effects

The MENA countries have made strenuous efforts to improve education. Most governments allocate a relatively high percentage of expenditure to education: shares range from a low of 7.1 percent in Lebanon and Qatar to a high of 25.7 percent in Morocco. During the austerity of the 1980s, however, real spending slowed and in some cases declined. In Egypt, for example, educational spending had only just regained 1980 levels by 1990, and although educational spending's share of the government budget rose from 10.2 percent in 1991 to about 17 percent in 1999, real government educational spending actually fell in the first half of the decade (UNDP/INP 2003). This was a regional pattern: per capita educational expenditures in Arab countries fell during the second half of the 1980s. Arab countries continue to spend more per pupil than other LDCs, but this advantage has been narrowing since 1985. Meanwhile, the (large) gap between Arab countries and the industrialized ones doubled from 1985 to 1995 (UNDP and AFESD 2002).

This picture grows grimmer when we consider how the money is spent. Gender, class, and rural/urban biases (the last, however, to a decreasing extent in some countries) remain factors in many countries' educational allocation decisions. As is true everywhere in the world, there are class biases in educational expenditures and enrollment profiles in the Middle East. In Morocco, children from upper-income families are twice as likely to be enrolled as children from low-income families. Rural enrollment rates are still lower than urban rates in the large, relatively poor countries of Egypt, Morocco, and Yemen. The gap has narrowed but not yet disappeared. For example, in the late 1970s, while over 90 percent of urban Egyptian children were in school, only 70 percent of rural delta children and 60 percent of rural Upper Egyptian children were enrolled (Nyrop 1983). By 2000, the gap for boys[12] had all but vanished (88 percent of rural boys enrolled versus 89 percent of urban boys), but the rural/urban gap remained high for girls, with 92 percent of urban girls enrolled in school but only 75 percent of rural girls enrolled (El-Zanaty and Way 2001). Similar gaps in the rural/urban rates of school enrollment for girls were found in Yemen (Watkins 2000). To counteract the role of conservative social norms and practices in depriving girls from access to education, the Yemeni government implemented a policy of training female teachers and providing financial incentives to families to allow their daughters to attend school in rural areas. In response, female enrollment in rural Yemen has improved (World Bank 2013).

Promoting rural education is challenging. The children of widely dispersed rural families often live far from any school. Countries that insist on separate schools for girls and boys multiply the costs of schooling, and it is especially difficult to attract women teachers to rural areas. At the same time, many rural families see no point in educating all of their children. It is quite common in the MENA region for rural families to make sacrifices to educate at least one son. One study of Turkey found that the highest rates of return to investment in education were obtained by the sons of farmers attending primary school (Özgediz 1980), while observers of rural Egypt often note that peasant families try to educate at least one son through high school in the hope that he will obtain a secure government job. Educating all their children, and especially all their daughters, is expensive and therefore a lower priority. Children in rural areas can, and do, contribute to their family income at young ages by tending animals, helping with processing, harvesting cotton, weaving rugs, and so forth. And peasant attitudes toward women's status die hard: Upper Egyptian peasants asserted to one researcher in the 1980s that sending girls to school was "shameful" (Adams 1986, 142). Such attitudes are slowly changing, however, as the steady increase in school enrollments and the steady decline in youth illiteracy attest.

Secondary education consumes a larger portion of public education budgets than primary education in most MENA countries, a phenomenon observed in most countries where data are available. While many more students are enrolled in primary schools, the cost per student is greater in secondary education.[13] Spending on tertiary education varies widely from country to country. University education, which is far more expensive to fund than other levels of education, gobbles up anywhere from 15 percent of educational budgets in Morocco to 31 percent in Lebanon (UNESCO 2013). Such allocations are extremely difficult to justify economically; much evidence suggests that if educational spending is (properly) treated as an investment, the social rate of return is highest for investment in the lower grades.[14] However, private returns increase with investment in higher education. And so politics, not economics, dictates the bias in favor of secondary and, especially, higher education.

The politics of this all-too-common distortion in the allocation of human capital spending is not hard to understand. First, there is some complementarity between diffusing primary education and widening more advanced educational opportunities. Someone has to teach the children, and a growing, industrializing economy needs more advanced skills as well as basic literacy and numeracy. This need is especially acute in countries that inherited little skilled labor from colonial regimes and are eager to defend their independence. Given the "national project" of Arab Socialist, Atatürkist, and other early developmentalist regimes in the region, it is hardly surprising that they have vigorously promoted the development of university training.

Second, the urban middle classes have had a disproportionate influence on policy. Planners themselves typically come from such backgrounds, and regimes have sought to open up more room at the top—through greater access to higher education—as a mechanism of income redistribution. And since the private rate of return due to investment in higher education remains very high, middle-class families press for space in the universities. Regimes wishing to mollify this social group have responded by rapidly expanding secondary and higher education. Vested interests, created by past state policies (by history), may be the main obstacle to more socially rational and equitable allocations of educational resources (see Box 5.2).

BOX 5.2 The Misallocation of Educational Resources in Egypt.

Egypt provides perhaps the most striking case of class bias in education. Fifty years after Nasser's revolution, 44% of adult Egyptians could not read and write, while the country boasted 21 public and 12 private universities. Nearly one-third (31.5% in 1999) of educational spending is allocated to universities, which enroll perhaps 6% of students at all levels. (In East Asia, universities receive about 15% of total educational spending.) The current proportion, although high, is lower than the 37% of educational funding universities received at the beginning of the 1990s (UNDP/INP 2000).

How did this happen? Between 1952/1953 and 1976/1977 the number of secondary school students in Egypt rose from 181,789 to 796,411, or at a rate of 14% per annum. Primary school enrollments rose at exactly half that rate, and university enrollments rose at an extraordinary 32% per annum. Higher education enrollments doubled in only four years (1971–1976) and then increased another 50% by 1984 (to over 600,000). In fiscal 1984/1985 higher education consumed nearly 38% of all spending on education. Meanwhile, nearly one-quarter of girls were not enrolled in primary school. The proportion of science students declined from 55% in 1971 to 25% in the mid-1980s, and at all levels the quality of education was dominated by rote memorization.

These trends were unintended consequences of the worthy goal of democratizing education, a process that had started even before the military seized power in 1952. The main nationalist party, the Wafd, controlled the government and parliament in 1950 and, in what Kerr termed "a demagogic bid" (1965, 176), not only opened the secondary schools to anyone who completed primary school but also made instruction tuition-free. After the abolition of the monarchy and the establishment of the Egyptian republic, the Free Officers continued these policies. In 1957 an unusually tame Egyptian parliament rose up against an attempt to restrict admission of secondary school graduates to the university and imposed a policy of tuition-free admission to universities for any Egyptian in possession of a secondary school diploma. The fatal sequence was thus established: all primary school graduates could go to secondary school, all secondary school graduates could go to university, and all university graduates were entitled to a government job.

Much of the demand for secondary and higher education was a demand for the credential necessary for a government job. Over half of university graduates and more than half of secondary school graduates sought jobs in the public sector (Fergany 1991). From 1976 to 1986, 90% of new jobs for Egyptians came either from the government or from emigration abroad (Handoussa 1989).

continues

BOX 5.2. *continued*

The government made university education especially attractive by heavily subsidizing students and by guaranteeing government jobs to all graduates, thereby greatly increasing the private returns to university education. It is privately rational for a family to sacrifice to get a member through the university; the graduate can then join the job queue for government employment (effectively lifetime), which can easily be combined with a second job and provides a kind of "income insurance." The educational system thus interacts with labor-market policies to misdirect social spending and to generate unemployment (since graduates tend to wait for government jobs). Even ignoring the fact that many of these graduates acquired only marginally useful skills, the country's development would have been better served by shifting resources away from more advanced education toward primary schooling.

During the past fifteen years there have been some important policy shifts. These have mainly involved large increases in total educational spending (up 90% in real terms during the 1990s) and a shift of investment spending away from higher education toward secondary and primary. Primary enrollment is nearly universal now (see text), and in the late 1980s, university enrollments actually declined by about 100,000. Enrollment growth resumed in the early 1990s, with enrollments in 1995 approaching those in 1985 (roughly 850,000) (World Bank 2000). By the end of the decade, enrollments totaled some 1.2 million (Said 2001). This expansion occurred even though the government's job guarantee was in practice being ignored. Basically, the jobs of those already employed in the government have been preserved by a tacit suspension of the job guarantee to the young (World Bank 2004c). Vested interests and political calculations have kept the law on the books, however. A study found that the private rate of return on education for males was 8.3% for primary education (contrast this with 39% in Asia), 31.7% for secondary education, and a whopping 62% for higher education (UNDP/INP 2000, 80). Misguided educational policies can have profound, long-lasting effects.

Secondary Education and Colonial and Postcolonial Politics

Prior to direct European control and the consolidation of large bureaucratic state systems, literacy in the Middle East was a skill limited to a relative few and, among Muslims, one valued for providing access to the sacred text of the Qur'an more than for its contribution to everyday life. As the range of government activities grew, so did the need for literate, white-collar staff—clerks, accountants, and managers (although not many). After World War I, nationalist movements throughout the Middle East put mass education at the top of their list of demands. Their concerns were twofold. First, nationalist leaders believed that Europe's strength in large measure stemmed from its educational systems and educated citizenries. As long as Middle Eastern societies were deprived of such systems and citizens, they would remain backward and subjugated. Second, these same leaders decried the elitism inherent in the new school systems promoted by colonial powers in the Middle East. Secondary education was limited to a narrow stratum of the population, often the offspring of the indigenous well-to-do, whom the colonial authorities wished to keep on their side. The object of the systems was to produce the clerks necessary to staff the colonial administration itself and the banks and businesses that sustained the economic links between the colony and the metropole. The nationalist leaders who criticized the elitism and manipulativeness of these policies knew of what they spoke. Overwhelmingly, they were among the elite and cogs in the colonial administrations' wheels. Only a handful of Middle Easterners ever received a university education. With the exception of Cairo University, universities in Istanbul and Ankara set up by the independent Turkish republic, and the American University of Beirut, there were no universities in the region. The very fortunate could go to the United Kingdom, France, Germany, or even the United States for advanced studies. In Algeria on the eve of the revolutionary war in 1954, out of a native population of 10 million, only 7,000 were in secondary school and only 600 had gone on to university-level studies. Although the elitism of the Algerian situation was more pronounced than elsewhere, it was a difference in degree, not in kind.

In the interwar years a number of ideas became rooted in the popular mind, among them the belief that education and literacy were rights of all citizens rather than privileges. Once independence was achieved, nationalist leaders were held to this notion. In addition, the link between secondary education and stable, respectable white-collar employment was firmly established. From peasants and tradespeople to craftspeople and manual laborers, all saw their children's education as the key to moving upward in society and also as a hedge against the day when they would be too old or infirm to work.

The new states of the Middle East kept their promises in various ways. There was the temptation to yield to popular (middle-class) pressure and open wide the gates of secondary and university education. In most cases the financial costs of such a policy appeared prohibitive. Typically, per student outlays in secondary school are two to three times higher than in primary school, and university outlays may be ten times higher. The demands for and costs of teacher training for secondary education are also commensurately higher. Alongside these concerns was the realization that the economy needed skilled craftspeople, technicians, and low-level supervisory personnel as much as or more than it needed civil servants. As a result, secondary education has become much more widespread in the past thirty years (see Table 5.5), and the increasing flood of secondary school students into the labor market has become a critical challenge facing economic policymakers and political strategists.

In general, countries with the lowest secondary enrollment ratios are also the poorest, like Sudan and Yemen. The richest economies tend to have higher enrollment ratios, but Jordan and, especially, Egypt appear to be exceptional performers in comparison with their per capita incomes. Despite this apparently excellent performance, only Iraq before the Anglo-American invasion and Israel have had net secondary enrollment ratios that compared with those in advanced industrial countries, at 91 and 89 percent, respectively.[15] However, Palestine, Qatar, and Jordan are not too far behind. Egypt's ominous scenario, as described in Box 5.2, is similar to the situation in a number of other states, especially those that followed programs of state-centered socialism (Syria, Iraq, Tunisia, and Algeria in particular).

The Economic and Political Roles of the Universities

Prior to the twentieth century, the Middle East had no modern public universities. There were a few higher institutes of Islamic studies, such as the Qarawiyyin in Fez, Morocco, and Egypt's prestigious Al-Azhar. The first university on the Western model in the region was the American University of Beirut, which was private and established as part of the Protestant Mission in Lebanon. By 1925 Cairo University had been chartered as a fully public institution, and national universities were started in Turkey and Iran. The Hebrew University was founded in Jerusalem, in Mandate Palestine, in 1925. These aside, there were no universities in the region until the 1950s and 1960s.

With full independence throughout the region, there was an explosion in the establishment of universities and in the number of students attending them. Algeria, which had no universities in 1962, now has 130 universities and colleges. In 1994 there were only two universities in Yemen, in Aden and Sana'a. Today, however, there are nine public universities and around fifteen private institutions. Tehran University was founded in Iran in 1934, and by the mid-1970s another eight universities had been established, with total enrollments of around 60,000. Ten years later, enrollments had more than doubled (to over 145,000). Today there are more than 1.5 million Iranian students attending more than fifty public universities and more than two hundred private institutions. By the end of the 1980s, Turkey had an equivalent number enrolled in universities. In the region as a whole, the proportion of eighteen- to twenty-three-year-olds attending institutes of higher learning grew from 4 percent in 1960 to 10 percent in 1980, 15 percent in 1993, 20 percent in 2006, and 31.4 percent in 2011. In addition, tens of thousands of Middle Easterners pursued university educations abroad (see Table 5.5).

The institutional expansion within the region necessarily sacrificed educational standards. For many years the growing economies and governments of the Middle East could absorb all the graduates produced by the universities almost regardless of the quality of their preparation. By the late 1970s, however, administrations were clogged with fairly young civil servants, the expansion of public-sector enterprises had slowed, and, except in the Gulf, the construction booms of the 1960s and 1970s were over. The formation of a "dangerous" class of the educated unemployed had begun.

Universities and institutes of higher learning exhibit a greater degree of class bias than secondary schools. They have undoubtedly witnessed a certain measure of democratization, as we saw with respect to the University of Damascus, with members of the lower-middle class in particular bettering their position through access to a more open educational system. Still, findings from a survey of university

TABLE 5.5. Male and Female Enrollment, Secondary and Tertiary Education, in the MENA Countries, 1971–2010

Country	Secondary Education					Tertiary Education				
	1971	1980	1990	2000	2010	1971	1980	1990	2000	2010
Algeria	0.41	0.63	0.77		1.01					1.45
Bahrain	0.72	0.84	1.00	1.08		1.44	1.01	1.38	1.77	
Egypt	0.48	0.58	0.76	0.92	0.96	0.37	0.44	0.53		0.91
Iran	0.53		0.71	0.94	0.95	0.36	0.49		0.86	1.01
Iraq	0.42	0.46	0.63	0.62		0.30	0.46	0.59	0.54	
Israel		1.10	1.10	1.00	1.02	0.84	0.94	0.98	1.44	1.29
Jordan	0.58	0.91	1.00	1.04	1.05	0.49	0.87	1.28	1.15	1.16
Kuwait	0.81	0.90	0.90	1.03		1.14	1.73	1.33	1.90	
Lebanon	0.67		1.10	1.09	1.12	0.32	0.56	0.92	1.05	1.19
Libya	0.23	0.73		1.06		0.13	0.36	0.85	0.97	
Morocco	0.42	0.59	0.71	0.79	0.86	0.18	0.34	0.60	0.73	0.87
Oman		0.30	0.72	0.99	0.98		0.08	0.94	0.94	1.39
Palestine				1.04	1.11				0.89	1.33
Qatar	0.67	1.20	1.30	1.20	1.09		3.41	3.62	3.04	5.38
Saudi Arabia		0.58			0.89	0.09	0.39	1.00	1.26	1.12
Sudan	0.40	0.54	0.79	0.96	0.88	0.15	0.36	0.69	0.92	
Syria	0.34	0.57	0.72	0.92	0.99	0.26	0.40	0.64		
Tunisia	0.38	0.61	0.76	1.03	1.05	0.25	0.44	0.63	0.96	1.48
Turkey	0.42	0.48	0.59	0.73	0.91	0.25	0.32	0.51	0.67	0.82
United Arab Emirates		0.95	1.23	1.10			2.02	4.08		
Yemen				0.36	0.62				0.21	0.27

Source: World Bank, WDI.

applicants carried out in Turkey in the mid-1970s may be applicable throughout the region (Özgediz 1980, 507). Only 30 percent of all applicants were from rural areas, while 47 percent were from the three major cities, Istanbul, Ankara, and Izmir. The success rate in passing entrance exams was three times higher for applicants from upper-income strata than for those from lower-income groups.

The first universities were all located in major cities. Cairo alone has three major public universities and well over 200,000 students. No regime likes to see that kind of concentration of potentially volatile, young, educated people in one place.

Since the 1960s and 1970s, Algeria, Egypt, Iraq, and Syria, all of which had post-independence regimes that espoused populist rhetoric, built campuses all across their national territories. In recent years, there has been a general move throughout the Middle East to establish provincial campuses, although in rural provinces the quality of education may be lower, in part owing to the difficulties of obtaining qualified personnel in outlying areas. In the last three decades, there has also been a surge of private universities across the region. In Iran during the 1980s, the private Azad Islamic University opened branches all over the country and now has four hundred institutions, some of which are located outside of Iran in Lebanon, Armenia, and the United Arab Emirates. Many of its campuses are in remote areas. In the past decade, the Gulf countries have also experienced a surge in private universities, such as the American University of Dubai (AUD) and American University of Sharjah (AUS) and various campuses opened by American universities (Cornell, Northwestern, and Texas A&M, among others).

This policy serves several purposes. It demonstrates to more remote regions the government's interest in making higher education directly available to the population. It helps satisfy the relentless demand from all sectors of the population for university education. And it eases the concentration of students in economic and political capitals, where their agitation is highly visible and disruptive. The strategy does not always work. For over twenty-five years the University of Assiut in Upper Egypt has been a hotbed of clashes among Islamic student groups, other students, university authorities, and the local police. Many of the provincial universities dispense a thoroughly mediocre education. Even more than the older universities, provincial universities are understaffed, underfinanced, underequipped, and overpopulated. Most of them are monuments to political expediency.

Middle Eastern universities are preeminently and self-consciously political. Various elements within them claim to speak for the nation's intelligentsia as well as for the generation that will furnish the nation's leaders. By its very organization the university, in its research and instruction, touches upon all the issues that are of great moment to the nation as a whole. All the political currents of the nation are manifested within the university. There is a constant battle within its walls for control over the institution, and particularly in the authoritarian systems that typify the region, the conduct of that battle is seen as a bellwether for the entire polity.

Student elections of one kind or another may be more hotly contested and less easily controlled than other elections in a given society. In the absence of other indicators of shifts in public opinion or in the relative weights of political forces, such elections are closely scrutinized. Every regime has its own tame student association or union enter the fray. In single-party regimes, such as those of the Ba'ath in Syria, the RCD in Tunisia, or the FLN in Algeria, the student union has often been directly affiliated with the party, as are associations of professors and administrators. In this way the university is supposed to remain a place of learning, subordinate to the regime, but it seldom works out that way in practice. Although student and faculty activists may be a minority of the university population, they are ubiquitous, visible, and highly motivated. For this reason, rulers and their security apparatuses tend to keep a close watch on campus politics.

In the more repressive countries in the region, the freedom of teaching and research is highly circumscribed. There may be subjects that cannot be researched and questions that cannot be asked. Classes typically have their share of police informers. Some regimes have resorted to strong-arm tactics, with party-affiliated toughs enforcing the proper line, breaking up unauthorized meetings, and intimidating student leaders. Since 1967, Israeli authorities have engaged in a running battle with Palestinian students and faculty at Birzeit University and An-Najah University on the West Bank. Still, the spirit of the university as an institution with a peculiar responsibility for the fate of the nation is kept alive, and university students are often prepared to take great risks to make their views known. The best among them will in all likelihood be the nation's future leaders. In fact, student militancy has often been the stepping-stone to high official position, as incumbent leaders identify their challengers and set about co-opting them. It is for all these reasons that in national power struggles contenders may see capturing the university to be as strategically important as capturing the armed forces.

Vocational Training

In recent years in many parts of the Middle East, there have been reassessments of mass educational policies and sometimes timid, camouflaged attempts to slow the rate of increase in secondary school enrollments and to restrict admission to universities. Such attempts are usually accompanied by efforts to orient primary school students and those who fail general secondary school exams toward vocational training institutes. Such institutes have been regarded as dead ends, and students and parents alike have gone to great lengths to avoid them.

All governments of the region have for years stressed the need for vocational and technical training for their youth. Egypt's goal in 1985 was to provide primary and preparatory education to all children and then orient 60 percent of secondary students toward vocational and technical training. The remaining 40 percent would follow the traditional secondary school curriculum, with admission to university as the final target. Egypt is a long way from achieving this distribution, as are all other states in the area. Again, if we take Egypt as representative, we find that most of the vocational students are being trained in commerce, probably simple accountancy, and relatively few in industry and skilled trades. As in many developing countries, there is still a marked preference for white-collar, desk-bound employment. Even when herded into vocational education, Middle Eastern students opt for potentially white-collar skills in accountancy rather than certifying themselves as electricians, mechanics, or plumbers. Governments in the region are trying to promote vocational and technical education but without much success. Egypt has the highest enrollments, with 31 percent, followed by Jordan (19 percent) and Lebanon (14 percent). Tunisia initiated a plan in 1995 to improve vocational training and to promote it among students by showcasing promising career trajectories in the private sector with a degree from a vocational institute (World Bank).

These attitudes, however, may be changing. The great construction boom of the 1970s in the Gulf states created a heavy demand for masons, carpenters, electricians, and the like. Wages for these trades rose rapidly, not only in the oil-rich countries importing labor but in the sending countries as well. Within a few years, plumbers and mechanics in Egypt could earn far more than a university-educated civil servant. Moreover, in addition to the oil boom, a technological transformation of the region was taking place. In the cities, elevators in high-rise buildings needed maintenance, as did air conditioning systems in workplaces and private homes, and so did tractors and diesel pumps in the countryside. In short, a booming market for skilled repair persons emerged in the 1970s, and their relative wages seem to have been unaffected by the oil bust.

It is not at all clear that a bigger public effort to promote vocational training would remove these bottlenecks. The quality of vocational education in Egypt seems to be poor on average, and graduates often must be retrained by their employers. In fact, it may make more sense for public authorities to help employers design their own on-the-job training. For many trades this takes place anyway through the traditional system of master and apprentice. In any auto mechanic's workshop or alongside any plumber on a job, the person carrying the tool bag is likely to be a boy learning the trade. Whether he also goes to school is irrelevant. He may be paid little more than subsistence, but working side by side with the master, he becomes familiar with a range of real-life situations—such as dismantling five different kinds of automobile engines—that the vocational trainee will not face. Given the structure of labor markets in the region (see Chapter 4), it is unsurprising that publicly funded vocational training has largely failed.

Privatization and Class Bias in Education

Given the perceived deterioration of education quality and the historic premium placed on education as the means for social mobility, the privileged classes have reproduced themselves in part through their ability to put their children through an educational process that gives them career advantages and excludes most of their compatriots of a similar age. Thus, despite the professed ideal of the region's governments that an educational system must be developed and maintained that is free and open to all, a number of practices have developed that have maintained its class bias.

One avenue is offered through private schools, which have expanded rapidly over the past decade. Private education varies from one country to another in the region (see Figure 5.8). In Lebanon, private schools outnumber public schools, whereas Algerian law bans private schooling. In some countries, such as Lebanon, not-for-profit providers enable students from beyond the elite to enroll in private schools. Although many private schools in the region are run by for-profit institutions, charitable and religious groups also play a key role in education in some MENA countries. On average, however, enrollment in private education in the region is lower than in the other middle-income countries (World Bank, WDI).

A second prop for the protection of privilege comes through the acquisition of foreign languages, especially English. Whether one is headed toward a career in industry, foreign trade, or banking and finance, mastering English, German, or

FIGURE 5.8. Private-Sector Share of Total Enrollments in Selected MENA Countries, Early 1990s

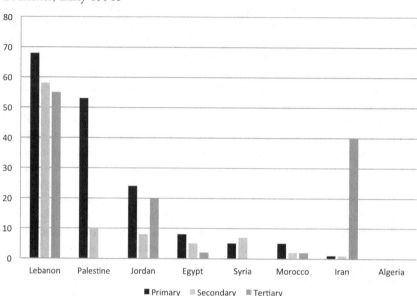

Source: World Bank (1999), 16.

French may be requisite to rising to the top. This brings us to the consequences—perhaps unintended, perhaps not—of Arabization, or Persianization, or Turkishization. Having all one's young citizens learn the national language is a logical and laudable policy, a strong foundation for democratization and cultural revitalization. But those who learn only Arabic, Turkish, or Persian will be able to rise only so far in the civil service, in professions such as medicine and engineering, and in modern industry and finance. Some critics have seen in the efforts to Arabize curricula and texts a plot on the part of the privileged to keep control of the commanding heights, for they can afford to send their children to secondary schools with quality instruction in foreign languages and their children are likely to do their university studies abroad or in disciplines that require foreign-language competency.

This question is most relevant for the Maghreb, formerly French North Africa, where indigenous civil service and professional elites were educated almost exclusively in French. Even after independence, French continued to be the official language of the government and the military. Such a situation was seen as absurd, as the local populations were very largely Arabic-speaking and thus unable to share the discourse of those who governed them. The governments of Tunisia, Algeria, and Morocco began to Arabize primary and secondary school curricula and then university curricula while slowly promoting Arabic as the main language of government. In theory, a North African today, monolingual in Arabic, has an equal chance with one who knows more than one language to achieve any position in society. In practice, it is probably still the case that entry into the technocratic and intellectual elites requires a mastery of French or English. The offspring of incumbent elites are the most likely to have that competency.

In many Middle Eastern societies the public school system may be the only one available to the well-off. Facilities and teaching quality are supposed to be uniform throughout the system. Everywhere it is the central government that finances school budgets, so the local tax base is not relevant to school quality. Still, schools in urban areas are better equipped and better staffed than schools in rural areas, and schools in wealthier districts tend to have lower student-teacher ratios and an atmosphere more conducive to learning. These kinds of variations in what are supposed to be systems of uniform quality are common throughout the world. One may add to them the fact that although the public system is free to all eligible children, the well-off can afford books, pens and pencils, decent clothing, and decent food and housing for their offspring, giving them a range of material advantages over the poor.

Going well beyond these types of class bias is the phenomenon of tutorials. Most of our evidence is drawn from Egypt, but the logic of the phenomenon is so compelling that we believe it is likely to be found elsewhere as well. In Egypt, students sit for a general exam at the end of the secondary cycle. The scores obtained on the exam determine the university faculties to which they will gain admission. Engineering and medicine require the highest scores and are, indeed, the most sought-after faculties. In short, high scores on the secondary school exam determine access to the faculties that will produce the next generation of elites.

Enter the underpaid teacher and the anxious middle-class parent. The teacher wants to supplement his or her meager income, and the parent wants to give his or her child a leg up. The result is fee-based private tutorials to prepare for the exams. Depending on the subject matter and the number of students in the tutorial, the fees can be very high, sometimes more than a low-income Egyptian earns in a year. An Egyptian teacher can earn ten times as much from tutoring as from his or her government salary; anxious Egyptian families spend about 7 billion Egyptian pounds (LE) on these services (UNDP/INP 2005, 84). Thus, an informal parallel educational system, based on fees, has arisen—a system that favors the rich and penalizes the poor. The parallel system helps ensure that the children of the well-to-do accede in disproportionate numbers to those professional disciplines that will be most highly rewarded in terms of income and prestige.

Education and Social Mobility

Having stressed educational strategies that reflect class bias, we must even more strongly emphasize that the mass educational systems set up in most Middle Eastern countries have been catalysts for real social mobility. The evidence for this assertion is fragmentary; systematic studies of the socioeconomic background of secondary- and university-level students have not been carried out. We do not know how profound the democratization process has been in higher education. All indications, however, point in the same direction, to wit, that the children of the lower-middle-income strata—the petty bourgeoisie of craftsmen and service providers, the clerks, the teachers, and the agrarian smallholders—seized the educational opportunities offered to them and moved well beyond their parents in status and wealth at least until recently.

The phenomenon was first observed in the 1930s, when in various countries admission to institutes of higher education and, most important, to officers' candidate schools was determined by competitive examination. Hardworking, ambitious, intelligent offspring of the lower-middle class outperformed all others and entered educational and professional domains that had been reserved to the upper classes. Gamal Abdel Nasser, the son of a rural functionary, and a number of others who overthrew the Egyptian monarchy in 1952 entered the military academy between 1936 and 1938 and attained the rank of colonel in the postwar years. A similar process got under way in Syria a few years later and yielded Hafez al-Assad and other officers of rural, lower-middle-class background.

This democratization process in education only accelerated post-independence. One of the most striking examples is that of Damascus University, where in 1968 half the student body was of rural origin and only 65 percent of the students had fathers with a university education (Hinnebusch 1979, 28–29). Rapidly expanding public bureaucracies, educational systems, state enterprises, and military establishments provided a growing job market for these young people. They also became functionaries in some of the more coherently organized political parties, such as the Republican People's Party in Turkey, the Ba'ath Party of Syria and Iraq, and the Neo-Destour (New Constitution) Party of Tunisia—now known as the Democratic Constitutional Rally (RCD). However, it would appear that the offspring of peasants, salaried workers, and common laborers—that is, the majority of the low-income strata—have not gained access to secondary and university education in numbers that come near to being proportional to their weight in society.

Schools also play an important socialization role and may constitute a breeding ground for political activism, as alluded to earlier with regard to secondary and tertiary education. Some of the region's better-known political leaders came out of the teaching corps or received their political baptism as secondary school students. Probably the single most important Muslim political leader of the first half of the twentieth century was the Egyptian Hassan al-Banna, monolingual in Arabic and a primary school teacher, who founded the Muslim Brotherhood in 1929. Of a very different political persuasion were Michel Aflaq and Salah al-Din al-Bitar, the Syrian secondary school teachers who founded the Ba'ath Party that continues to rule in Syria. Several of the nationalist movements in the Middle East, such as the RCD Party of Tunisia, the Istiqlal Party of Morocco, the National Liberation Front (FLN) of Algeria, the Wafd Party of Egypt, and the Ba'ath Party, relied to some extent on schoolteachers and students to develop the local infrastructure of their organizations. Whether we consider the adolescent Gamal Abdel Nasser experimenting with the Young Egypt Party (Misr El-Fatah) in the 1930s or the lycée student Hocine Aït Ahmed, who was a militant in the Algerian People's Party (PPA) and later one of the six historic chiefs of the Algerian revolution, we see a pattern of the political awakening and active political involvement of secondary school students from the 1930s on.

Leaders of the newly independent countries of the region were acutely aware of the strategic importance of both students and teachers. Habib Bourguiba of Tunisia was able to harness them to his Neo-Destour Party but lost some of them to his more militant rival in that party, Salah Ben Youssef. After 1963, the shah of Iran tried to mobilize students and teachers in literacy campaigns in the countryside, while Houari Boumediene, president of socialist Algeria, put them to work in 1972 on a survey of landholdings prior to an agrarian reform (Leca 1975). Kemal Atatürk and his successor, Ismet İnönü, saw secondary school teachers as the vehicles for promoting the secular values of the Turkish republic. Village institutes were created to train rural youth to be teachers and to carry the message of republicanism, secularism, and statism to the traditional rural populations. People's houses, functioning as local cultural centers, were set up to propagate the new credo to people outside the school system. In Egypt, during its most pronounced socialist phase in the mid-1960s, the single party, the Arab Socialist Union, relied on local schoolteachers, veterinarians, co-op officials, and other white-collar functionaries to break the influence of local landowning groups (Harik 1974, 81–100). However, these efforts at co-optation often rang hollow among the targeted groups, partly because of the yawning gap in age between the political elites relative to the students they were trying to control. The co-opters lacked credibility. In addition, as we argue throughout this book, the period of austerity from the mid-1980s to roughly 2000 made access to jobs something of a lottery in which the majority of students drew a losing ticket.

Islamic movements have exploited this situation to their advantage. They have always viewed the educational system as a crucial battleground, control of which might yield influence over the hearts and minds of students. In some ways political Islamic groups seek political power, not for its own sake, but rather because it would provide them with control—so they believe—over the cultural and educational institutions and the mass media. To the young, these groups offer leadership that has generally been closer to them in age and spirit than the aging leadership of the status quo, as well as values that stress probity, the separation of the sexes, and religious faith. Islamist political groups move along three tracks: (1) assaults, direct or indirect, on the bastions of political power; (2) infiltration of the public education system; and (3) the establishment of private schools under their direct control. During Algeria's civil war, the struggle was violent and waged extralegally by the Islamic Salvation Front (FIS). In Turkey, the Welfare Party waged its struggle at the ballot box, a struggle continued with great success by the Justice and Development Party. The Muslim Brotherhood has used the same strategy in Egypt. In Palestine, the Islamic Resistance Movement (Hamas) does both.

CONCLUSIONS

Nearly all post-independence Middle Eastern governments promised their citizens health, education, and jobs. Progress in health and education was rapid and real, and starting from such low bases, these improvements in basic living conditions were transformative for earlier generations of Middle Easterners. That said, the progress was not commensurate, by international standards, with the average levels of income and per capita GDP of these countries. Moreover, the rapid increase in population in the region made the effort to catch up extremely costly. In countries without sizable oil resources, fiscal crises and economic adjustment beginning in the 1980s led to major cuts in public-sector employment, which was the main ticket to social mobility for the new, post-independence middle class. At the same time, public investment in the social sectors stalled or froze, which was especially damaging to the poor.

The region has witnessed major gains in human development: nearly all children are in school in most countries; literacy rates have increased rapidly, even among women; and infant mortality, while still high in some places, has plummeted. Paradoxically, the initial gains and especially the emergence of a middle class composed of civil servants and professionals may have sowed the seeds of discontent in a later period, when aspirations for social mobility would be increasingly thwarted.

NOTES

1. For a comparison of shifting public expenditures across multiple sectors, see Table 2.2.

2. Rich and poor are defined, respectively, as the bottom quintile and the top quintile of the income distribution.

3. For a sobering analysis of this phenomenon worldwide, see Farmer (2003).

4. Reports published by the WHO Eastern Mediterranean Regional Office document these trends.

5. Stunting is defined as "the proportion of under-fives falling below minus 2 and minus 3 standard deviations from the median height-for-age of the reference population" (UNICEF 2001).

6. Unless otherwise stated, in this chapter "literacy" means adult literacy.

7. Segregation in Algerian schools formally ended in 1948, but the system remained strongly biased in favor of *colon* children until independence.

8. NER is defined as the number of children of a certain age group in school divided by the total number in that age group. The other commonly used measure, gross enrollment ratio, divides the total number of children in school (whatever their age) by the total number of children in the age group. The latter number, typically higher, would include in the numerator, for example, thirteen-year-olds still in the sixth grade, whereas the net enrollment ratio would not.

9. There was some dispute about Saudi enrollment figures. A UN report (United Nations 2002, 15) asserts, "Primary school enrolment ratio registered 96.1% in year 2000, resulting from a male enrolment of 97.3% and 94.8% rate for females." It appears that this figure refers to the gross enrollment rate. However, the World Bank gives a less sanguine picture. Using the same indicator, the World Bank reports that in 2002 the overall gross primary enrollment rate was 67 percent: 69 percent for boys and 67 percent for girls.

10. Sudan does not report such data, and indeed, it is unclear what such data would mean, given the violent conditions plaguing large regions of the country outside of the Nile Valley.

11. In Yemen, as recently as a decade ago, nearly half of primary schools had neither electricity nor water, and over 40 percent had no toilets (Al-Amri et al. 2003).

12. Defined as ten to fourteen years of age.

13. In part, this difference may be due to the higher marginal costs of teaching secondary school students.

14. The social rate of return on an investment is the internal rate of return, calculated using international prices (as opposed to distorted domestic prices) and taking into account externalities. A crucial—and dubious—assumption of these studies is that wages accurately reflect productivity.

15. For example, in 2002–2003 the ratio in the United States was 88 percent, in Japan 100 percent, in Germany 88 percent, and in South Korea 87 percent.

6

WATER AND FOOD SECURITY

The Middle East has been squeezed by a combination of rising global food prices and increasingly difficult environmental conditions that constrain agricultural production. Some analysts point to rising food prices, increasing food insecurity, and protracted drought conditions in some countries, such as Syria, as grievances underlying the Arab uprisings (Breisinger, Ecker, and Al-Riffai 2011; Femia and Werrell 2013, 27; Harrigan et al. 2012; Johnstone and Mazo 2011; Nasser, Mehchy, and Ismail 2013, 20). To compound these challenges, escalating demand and limited supply response have made it the least food-self-sufficient region in the world. But both public and private responses to the food deficit have failed to restore food self-sufficiency. Despite its political appeal, food self-sufficiency is actually physically impossible and economically undesirable in much of the region.

The water constraint exposes populations to increased risks, raises the probability of domestic and international conflict, and dooms dreams of self-sufficiency in the region, with the situation growing more serious by the day. Annual renewable water resources have fallen from 4,150 cubic meters per capita for the entire region in 1960 to only 1,280 cubic meters today. Population growth ensures that these numbers will fall further in coming decades; the World Bank projects that annual supplies will drop 50 percent by the year 2050 (World Bank 2007b). Water use already exceeds 100 percent of renewable water supplies in seven countries and threatens to do so in several more, while other countries are plagued by water quality problems. Fifty-six million people in the region lack access to safe drinking water, and 72 million people lack access to proper sanitation (UNICEF and WHO 2011).[1]

The rising demand for water is due to population growth, rapid urbanization, and expanding irrigation. Water used by households and industry has a much higher economic value than water used in agriculture—overwhelmingly the largest water user in the region (see Figure 6.1 and Table 6.1). As water's scarcity increases, agriculture will have to get by with less. For example, Israel and Jordan have little choice but to save water by cutting back on irrigated agriculture, increasingly using recycled wastewater for farming and investing in expensive technologies such as desalination. Although there is scope for greater efficiency in irrigation, there is

FIGURE 6.1. MENA Water Use by Sector, 2013

Source: World Bank, World Development Indicators (WDI).

simply not enough water in the region to permit anything remotely approaching food self-sufficiency.

Food self-sufficiency, however, is a very different concept from food security. Ensuring food security means guaranteeing that consumers are reasonably certain of being able to eat properly. Nevertheless, for decades policymakers have all too often conflated food security with food self-sufficiency. The resulting policies have transformed agricultural production and the relationships between both rural and urban citizens and their states throughout the region. By now the necessity to import "virtual water"—the water contained in food—is quietly recognized by many policymakers,[2] and the inevitability of reliance on food imports is much more widely recognized today than it was decades ago. Still, local policymakers more commonly view water as a social good that is vital to the livelihood of a large proportion of the population than as an economic good. Further, current water users—particularly well-to-do farmers—often constitute a politically potent lobby (Olmsted 2003; Richards 2002).

At the end of the day, any nation can obtain its food in only three (not mutually exclusive) ways: by producing it (national production), by buying it (imports), or by being given it (food aid). The first two are overwhelmingly the most important ways for all but the very poorest (usually disaster- or conflict-wracked) countries. Any country is likely to use both domestic production and imports to meet its food security goals. Each of the MENA countries faces significant constraints, and each faces political, economic, and social challenges to meeting food security goals.

In this chapter, we focus on the evolution of agricultural strategies in the MENA region and then explore the impact of increased water scarcity on its future.

THE FOOD GAP

Any description of the facts of food security at the national level must distinguish between two different periods: the oil boom of the 1970s, when the "food gap"

TABLE 6.1. Renewable Water Resources in the MENA Countries, 2013

Country	Withdrawals m3/person/year[a]	Usage Agriculture	Domestic	Industry
Algeria	182.0	64%	23%	14%
Bahrain	386.0	45	50	6
Egypt	973.3	86	8	6
Iran	1,306.0	92	7	1
Iraq	2,616.0	79	7	15
Israel	282.4	58	36	6
Jordan	166.0	65	31	4
Kuwait	441.2	54	44	2
Lebanon	316.8	60	29	11
Libya	796.1	83	14	3
Morocco	428.1	87	10	3
Oman	515.8	88	10	1
Palestinian Territories	112.1	45	48	7
Qatar	376.9	59	39	2
Saudi Arabia	928.1	88	9	3
Sudan and South Sudan	683.4	97	2	1
Syria	867.4	88	9	4
Tunisia	295.8	76	13	4
Turkey	572.9	74	15	11
United Arab Emirates	739.5	83	15	2
Yemen	162.4	91	7	2

Source: Food and Agriculture Organization (FAO) AQUASTAT (2013); World Bank, WDI.

a. Cubic meters per person per year.

exploded, and the decades that followed, when policymakers implemented a variety of strategies to narrow this gap. Particularly in the past decade, the region's countries have struggled in their efforts to expand domestic food production at a rate that outpaces population growth.

The Exploding Food Gap of the 1970s

During the 1970s, rapidly increasing populations and oil rents fueled per capita income growth, sharply raising the demand for food. The impact of income growth on food demand depended on the specific foodstuff. Demand for cereals for direct food consumption (as opposed to use as livestock feed) grew at approximately 3.7 percent per year from 1966 to 1980; although this growth was mainly due to burgeoning population, increasing incomes accounted for roughly 25 percent of it. Demand for cereals for livestock feed grew more rapidly still (4.8 percent per year); about one-fourth of all cereals consumed in the region were eaten by animals (Paulino 1986, 26). Income growth particularly stimulated the growth of consumption of meat, dairy, fruits, and vegetables, as happens elsewhere when people get richer.

The domestic supply response was sluggish in the 1970s in part because of the "Dutch Disease"—when foreign exchange and imports become cheaper—and in part in response to policies that excessively taxed investment in the agricultural sector (see Chapter 2). Cereal production was especially weak, caught between rising labor costs, marginal rainfall, and government-imposed price disincentives. By contrast, the production of higher-value crops such as fruits, vegetables, and livestock did much better. Almost everywhere, the food gap could be plugged with imports; abundant foreign exchange and improving terms of trade permitted a dramatic increase in food (and especially cereal) imports.[3]

The levels of dependency on food imports in the 1970s alarmed policymakers, many of whom became obsessed with the risk of a politically motivated food embargo. Heavy reliance on food imports, particularly for basic foodstuffs like wheat, entails political risks, and threats of embargoes raised the perceived political risk of relying on imports for food security. Egyptian policymakers were acutely aware of this risk: by the mid-1980s, Egypt was purchasing nearly 50 percent of its wheat and wheat flour—*the* staple food in the country—from the United States.[4] Such dependence, even on friendly countries, makes policymakers nervous. Indeed, no country in the world—least of all the United States or the European Union—relies exclusively on comparative advantage and market forces in its food system. To reduce risks, states focused on diversifying their exports (thereby increasing the stability of their foreign exchange earnings) and at the same time launched programs to increase the proportion of domestic supplies to total consumption. Increasingly, the water constraint has forced most countries of the region to increase their reliance on the former approach. In the 1970s, however, few were prepared to undertake the kind of economic policy reforms that an import-oriented food security strategy would have required.

Partially Redressing the Balance: 1980–2012

During the 1980s and 1990s, regional economic growth collapsed and turned negative in many countries. But as population growth also slowed down, the implied deceleration in the demand for food provided a respite for harried agricultural planners, who succeeded in formulating and implementing significant policy shifts. In the early 1980s, subsidies of inputs were retained and in some countries even increased (although this had begun to change by the end of the decade), while taxation of output through price policies typically eased. Governments often began to allocate a larger share of investment to agriculture, and many urban entrepreneurs entered the production of horticultural crops, poultry, and livestock. Today these

FIGURE **6.2.** Per Capita Agricultural Growth in the MENA Countries, 1980–2010

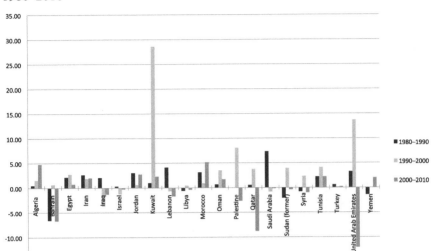

Source: FAOSTAT (2013).

entrepreneurs constitute a significant "farm lobby" in most countries, a fact of considerable relevance for water policy, as we discuss later in the chapter.

In part because of these policy shifts, most countries' agricultural sectors managed at least to keep up with population growth during the 1980s. During the 1990s, growth remained strong, with ten countries experiencing accelerating growth in per capita food production; only four fell back from previous levels. Data from the Food and Agriculture Organization of the United Nations (FAO) on the growth of per capita food production over time are shown in Figure 6.2.[5] During the 1980s, fifteen countries' output kept up with population growth (sometimes just barely), while in five others' output lagged behind. In the 1990s, per capita growth decelerated in four countries and even turned negative in four, but it accelerated in thirteen others, including the largest Arab country, Egypt. For the region as a whole, the trend in per capita food production was (just barely) positive for each decade: the population-weighted average grew at an annual rate of 0.5 to 0.7 percent (Lofgren and Richards 2003). Perhaps the safest conclusion to draw from these disparate studies is that food self-sufficiency at least did not deteriorate during the 1980s and 1990s.

Output gains required using additional inputs. While growth in total cultivated area has slowed, a higher percentage of land than ever before is under irrigation (some 28.7 percent across the region); most countries that saw strong agricultural growth over the past decade also greatly expanded their land under irrigation, particularly Jordan and Yemen (see Figure 6.3). Fertilizer use generally increased during the 1980s, slowed during the 1990s, then held steady or declined for most

FIGURE 6.3. Cultivated Land Under Irrigation in the MENA Countries, 1980–2011

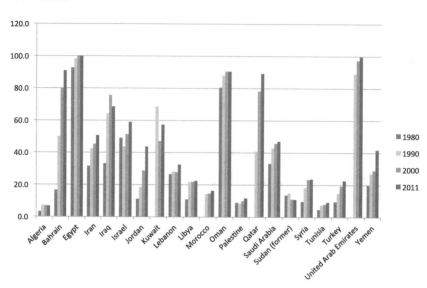

Source: AQUASTAT (2013) and FAOSTAT (2013).

countries over the past decade, with the exception of a few major producers such as Egypt (FAOSTAT); World Bank, World Development Indicators [WDI]). The mechanization of farms, as seen in the expanded use of diesel-powered tractors, continued throughout the region during the 1980s and 1990s, though growth began to slow in the early 2000s. In Egypt, for example, the number of tractors in use rose by 58 percent between 1980 and 1990 and then by 51 percent between 1990 and 2000, though it had only risen a further 19 percent by 2008 (FAOSTAT). The farm labor force either continued to grow or resumed growing after an oil boom–induced decline in most countries. The oil boom of the 1970s had drawn labor out of agriculture; in Algeria, Iraq, Jordan, Libya, Syria, and Tunisia, the adult male farm labor force actually declined during the 1970s. However, the 1980s largely reversed this Dutch Disease phenomenon in all but Iraq, Jordan, and Libya. In short, agriculture in the MENA region used more land, more water, more fertilizer, more machines, and more labor—all just to keep up with population growth.

Droughts, the 2008 Global Food Crisis, and the Fading Mirage of Food Self-Sufficiency

The welcome resumption of modest income growth in the 2000s intensified the challenge of the growing demand for food, which combined with rising global food prices to increase pressure on Middle Eastern consumers. In this context, and given the increasing scarcity of water, more and more policymakers now recognize that food security must take precedence over food self-sufficiency.

There is some evidence of deceleration in both output growth and input usage during the past decade. Again, country experience is highly varied. From 2000 to 2010, only a few countries (Algeria, Jordan, Morocco, Yemen) achieved significantly higher rates of growth, with production declining outright in most of the GCC countries while stalling in major producers such as Egypt (see Figure 6.2). Input use seems more ambiguous: in the Near East, for example, the major producers Egypt, Sudan, and Turkey continued to expand fertilizer usage over the past decade, though the trend was far from universal. In the Maghreb, however, fertilizer use declined in the largest agricultural economy, Morocco, though it expanded in Tunisia and Algeria (World Bank, WDI 2013). Growth in tractor usage slowed or turned negative for several countries.

The common conflation of food security with self-sufficiency assumes that domestic production is a less risky mode of satisfying domestic demand than dependence on international trade. To be sure, international trade poses risks, both economic (price fluctuations) and political (US-led embargoes and sanctions). Yet relying on national production is also risky. In much of the Middle East, agriculture is inescapably a gamble on the rains. About 75 percent of the arable land in the region is classified as "semi-arid," which means that it receives on average only 200 to 400 millimeters of rain each year (Hazell 2007). Cereal production remains highly variable in the region, as weather shocks disrupt staple food production. Only Egypt, with its entirely irrigated agriculture, is relatively safe from the effects of repeated weather shocks. Elsewhere in the region the situation is far worse. In Syria, for example, food production has fallen by 5 percent or more roughly every third year over the past three decades (FAOSTAT 2013). As a result of these shortfalls, planners in the Maghreb must find supplementary foreign exchange to buy "unusual" amounts of food four years out of ten.

The devastating droughts in the Maghreb and in Sudan underscore the climatic threat. In Morocco, production of wheat fell by nearly 40 percent from 1976 to 1977, while in Sudan millet and sorghum output fell by 38 percent and 58 percent, respectively, in 1982 and 1983 and continued to fall the following year (FAOSTAT). The social, economic, and political impacts were severe: some 4 to 5 million northern Sudanese were forced from their homes, moving either into the Nile Valley or farther south to less severely affected areas. The wrenching population movements, combined with various power struggles among ethnic factions in the region, led to the politically driven mass killings of today's Darfur (see Box 6.1).

Serious drought returned to the Maghreb in the 1990s and has remained a pressing concern ever since. In the 1995 drought, Moroccan cereal production fell to 1.8 million metric tons, down from 9.6 million the previous year (Hazell, Oram, and Chaherli 2003). The drought of 2005 was the worst in six decades. In 2012 yet another drought caused grain production to plummet some 40 percent from the previous year's harvest, prompting the government to offer emergency subsidies and price supports to hard-hit farmers (USDA/FAS 2013a, 2013b). Meanwhile, in Sudan, the drought that affected much of East Africa in 2011–2012 cut cereal production by an estimated 50 percent, prompting food security concerns for some 4.2 million people (FEWS NET 2012).

Nor has the Mashreq been spared. The drought in 1999–2000 reduced Syrian sheep flocks (a crucial source of livelihood for the poor) by up to 80 percent (IFAD 2001). Subsequently, drought conditions in the country reached peak intensity in the 2007–2009 growing seasons. By then, some 75 percent of farming households experienced nearly total crop failure, with thousands of families forced to move to

---

BOX 6.1. Food Insecurity and Ethnic Cleansing: Darfur, Sudan

The ultimate in food insecurity is what is variously called a "food emergency," a "humanitarian emergency," or simply a "famine" (see Devereux 1993; de Waal 1989; Prunier 2005; and the seminal work of Sen 1981). There is now a consensus that such human disasters are fundamentally caused by politics rather than by agricultural practices or climatological events. This has certainly been the case in the MENA region. Extreme food insecurity (as in Iraq, Sudan, or Yemen) typically reflects political instability and conflict, which, as we argue throughout this book, are linked to failed processes of economic development. Explaining famines also requires that we identify the critical social actors. In keeping with the argument of Chapter 1, the relationship is reciprocal: politics helps to cause famines, and famines, in turn, foster political destabilization. In the worst-case scenario, such a spiral can lead to genocidal massacres.

The current horrors of Darfur provide such a scenario. This vast (150,000 square miles), remote (Darfur's capital, El Fasher, is a dusty road trip of more than 600 miles from Khartoum) northwestern province of Sudan was neglected by the British administration (starting in 1916) and by successive independent Sudanese governments in Khartoum. The experience of Darfur supports the perspective that extreme food emergencies are fundamentally political.

Most analyses of the current crisis begin with the severe drought and famine of 1984. Tellingly, this was called *maja'a al-gutala,* "famine that kills," as opposed to the quotidian dearth of food that normally plagues this extremely poor region. Many authorities assert that more people died of disease than outright starvation (Devereux 1993), although, given the interactions of nutrition and disease resistance, it is likely that food deprivation contributed to the estimated 95,000 deaths (out of a population of approximately 3.1 million) (Prunier 2005).

For any attempt to explain today's violence, perhaps the most important aspect of the events of 1984 was the further destabilization of the symbiotic, partly conflictual, yet also partly cooperative relationship between the social groups that relied mainly on livestock herding and those that relied mostly on farming. Older mechanisms of conflict resolution came under great stress owing to drought, population growth, and the bankruptcy and incompetence

continues

cities in search of work. During this time period, Syria's livestock herds dropped by 24–33 percent, according to various estimates, while wheat and barley yields dropped by 47 and 67 percent, respectively (Erian, Katlan, and Babah 2010).

Still more ominously, there is increasing disquiet that global warming may be exacerbating and intensifying droughts, particularly in the region (Hazell, Oram, and Chaherli 2003). One study suggests an increased frequency in short-term droughts (four to six months) by the end of the twenty-first century, with long-term droughts (greater than six months) becoming nearly three times as common (Sheffield and

---

BOX 6.1. *continued*

of local government, which was nominally beholden to national authorities in Khartoum (de Waal 2004).

Transnational forces likewise stirred the pot. An ongoing civil war in neighboring Chad spilled over into Darfur, flooding the area not only with Kalashnikov rifles and other modern weapons but also, perhaps even more lethally, with an imported racist ideology of "Arab" supremacy (de Waal 2004; ICG 2004; Prunier 2005). (The definition of the concept "Arab," particularly in Sudan, has a long and highly complex history; for an extended discussion, see Prunier 2005.) Further, the Islamist regime in Khartoum, which came to power in 1989, as well as the Libyan government, armed many Darfuri "Arabs" and used them as *murahiliin,* or irregular forces, to fight the Sudan People's Liberation Army (SPLA) in southern Sudan and to terrorize southern civilians. An interplay of war between the SPLA and the Khartoum government, infighting among various Islamist politicians, and escalating violence among increasingly polarized, heavily armed Darfuri ethnic groups continued through the 1990s.

Ironically, it was the approach of peace between the SPLA and the Khartoum government, combined with a revolt in Darfur, that launched the current round of horrors. Threatened by rebellion from Muslim Darfuris, and particularly suspecting their ties with out-of-power Islamist politician and former president Hassan al-Turabi, the Khartoum government armed and abetted the *janjaweed* ("evil horsemen"), militias based in the nomadic "Arab" population. These militias then embarked on a horrifying campaign of ethnic cleansing against "Africans," mainly agricultural speakers of Fur, Tunjur, and Masalit, as well as Zaghawa-speaking pastoralists. This campaign, labeled "counter-insurgency on the cheap" (de Waal 2004), has killed hundreds of thousands of Sudanese civilians. At least 400,000 people have died and over 2.5 million people have been displaced (see, for example, United Nations Human Rights Council 2014). In addition to outright murder and rape, janjaweed depredations made foraging for "famine foods," or edible wild plants—which saved many lives in the 1984 famine—much too dangerous. Violent political insecurity thus produced food insecurity (de Waal 2004).

Wood 2008). Rising temperatures undermine agricultural production by reducing levels of soil moisture as precipitation becomes increasingly concentrated into short, intense bursts of rain. In addition, the majority of global climate change models predict a reduction in rainfall for the MENA region this century (Christensen et al. 2007).

Fundamentally, arid zones like the Middle East cannot escape geography: water is scarce in the region and will become scarcer. Thanks to the water requirements for photosynthesis, there are serious constraints on domestic food and agricultural production anywhere outside of Turkey or (potentially) Sudan. We have seen that agriculture uses over 85 percent of the region's water. Water problems are especially acute in the Mashreq and the Arabian Peninsula, where unsustainable rates of usage are common. Increasing pollution of water is also a growing problem. The region now uses 56 percent of its renewable water supplies annually, compared with 9 percent globally (FAO AQUASTAT 2013). By 2050, per capita water availability for all purposes could be as low as 550 cubic meters per year (World Bank 2007b).

The recent spikes in global food prices, most notably in late 2007 and early 2008, have hurt consumers, especially among the poor, but they also strengthened incentives for local production. The 2007–2008 crisis saw global food prices increase some 83 percent over 2005 levels, owing to a variety of factors, including rising food demand among developing nations, shortfalls in key grain harvests, the diversion of crops to the production of biofuels in developed nations, and an increase in fuel prices (Bush 2010; Harrigan et al. 2012). Given the region's heavy dependence on cereal imports and the fact that many of the MENA region's poorer populations spend as much as 40 percent of their annual income on securing food, the non-oil-producing countries of the RPLA group and the poorer, more populous labor exporters experienced the highest levels of food insecurity. In Yemen, the percentage of the population reporting inadequate food supplies increased from 24 percent to 59 percent between 2006 and 2008 (World Bank 2009b). This spike in vulnerability helped to spur demonstrations and riots against high food prices and low wages across the Middle East. In response, governments employed short-term "firefighting" measures, such as increasing food and fuel subsidies, raising public-sector wages, and reducing import tariffs—many of the same tactics they would later employ during the Arab uprisings and their aftermath.

In recent years, Middle Eastern rulers have placed less emphasis on food self-sufficiency, though there are exceptions. For example, Syria pursued self-sufficiency in wheat extensively prior to the onset of civil war in 2011, at great cost to its water supplies (Haddad 2011). And in 2013, ousted President Mohammed Morsi in Egypt declared his intention to promote self-sufficiency in wheat production and to cut imports (McFarlane 2013). The government of President Abdel Fattah Al-Sisi has expressed similar goals (Reuters 2013). If the high level of international food prices persists, such policies will become more popular again. This is especially the case for the poorer countries of the region that have little potential outside of agriculture and, in the middle-income countries, for the rural regions that were left behind by the reforms of the 1980s, such as Sidi Bouzid, the birthplace of the Arab uprisings.

POLICY CONSTRAINTS ON OUTPUT GROWTH

We can (loosely) divide the policy constraints on food production into two parts: (1) skewed access to land and other "property rights" problems, and (2) limited incentives for farmers. Farm output growth is also constrained by investment problems, which we discuss in the context of the key physical constraint, limited water supplies.

Land Tenure

Although there is significant diversity across MENA countries, we propose five generalizations concerning land tenure and property rights in the region: (1) pre-reform land tenure more nearly resembled the bimodal pattern of Latin America than the small peasant systems of East Asia; (2) the state has been exceptionally active in shaping patterns of land tenure; (3) land reforms implemented roughly between 1953 and 1975 reduced but did not eliminate the inequalities inherited from the past; (4) the state has had mixed success in substituting itself for the expropriated landlords as marketing agent, crop selector, and so forth; and (5) since the 1980s, states have retreated from land reforms and especially from public-sector agriculture, a retreat that is part of a wider trend toward increased reliance on the private sector. States have created social actors through land reforms and other policies with regard to property; the actors so created now often constitute an important force-shaping policy—a farm lobby.

During the nineteenth and early twentieth centuries, large landholdings emerged in many MENA countries. Relations between the state and local social groups and expanding markets for crops provided opportunities for private aggrandizement. States typically resisted this process; rulers tried to remove intermediaries between themselves and the tax-paying peasantry. The success or failure of such policies depended on local, regional, and international political forces.

The intrusion of European colonialism always fostered bimodalism, a land-tenure system that combines a small number of owners holding very large estates with a large number of owners holding very small farms. The pattern was most striking in the Maghreb, where agrarian changes resembled those of Latin America: foreign conquerors seized the best agricultural land for themselves, relegating the indigenous inhabitants to marginal areas for subsistence farming, to wage labor on the European modern farms, or, commonly, to both (see Box 6.2). "Indirect" colonial rule generated a similar result in Iraq and Egypt. Charles Issawi (1982, 138) has aptly summarized the pre-reform land-tenure systems: "Large estates, accounting for a quarter to four-fifths of privately owned land and in the main tilled by sharecroppers; a huge number of very small peasant proprietors, often with highly fragmented holdings; short and precarious leases; high rents . . . large debts, rising land values; and a growing landless proletariat earning very low wages."

Land reform swept through the region in the quarter-century after World War II. Echoing David Ricardo, critics charged that wealthy landlords were economic drones who failed to invest their profits and rents domestically. Although historians

---

BOX 6.2. Colonialism and Land Tenure

Colonialism helped to concentrate landownership in the hands of a few across the region. In Algeria between 1830 and 1880, *colons* and the French state seized nearly 900,000 hectares of land; by 1962, 30 percent of the cultivated area was owned by colons, of which some 80 percent was held in large farms consisting of more than 100 hectares (Smith 1975). By 1914, nearly 20 percent of the arable land in Tunisia was in European hands, and over half of it belonged to only sixteen extremely wealthy absentee owners. By 1953, Europeans held nearly 1 million hectares in Morocco, concentrated in the fertile, well-watered plains of the west and north. The Italian Fascists seized some 500,000 hectares of land in Cyrenaica in Libya. The dispossessed indigenous population was forced onto more marginal lands, while the European farms enjoyed privileged access to government loans and other favors (Abun-Nasr 1971; Nouschi 1970). Population growth shortened fallows, extended cultivation into ever more marginal land, and reduced the amount of land available to each peasant family even as large estates continued to expand (van der Kloet 1975).

The British in Iraq shored up the *sheikhs* and *aghas* as counterweights to (nationalist) urban groups and to the king (Batatu 1978, 78–100; Dann 1969, 4). By confirming the registration of formerly tribal land in the names of sheikhs, the British, and later the independent Iraqi government, placed vast amounts of cultivated land in a few hands. By 1953, 1.7 percent of landowners held 63 percent of the land, while nearly two-thirds of the population held less than 5 percent. Over three-fourths of the rural population was landless (al-Khafaji 1983, ch. 7).

In Egypt, Muhammad Ali had attempted in the early nineteenth century to eliminate all intermediaries between the state and the peasants. When internal economic difficulties and British pressure forced him to decentralize, he granted land to court favorites, military officers, and the like. These actions created a class of large, typically absentee landlords known as *pashas*. By 1900, large farms—over 50 feddan (1 feddan = 0.42 hectares = 1.03 acres)—covered 40 percent of the cultivated area of the country (Baer 1962; Owen 1986; Richards 1982).

---

have rejected this portrait (Davis 1983; Tignor 1984), there is little doubt that the land-tenure systems fostered huge social inequities and impeded human capital formation. The real impetus behind land reform was political. Reformers expropriated their enemies: Nasserists dispossessed the family and friends of King Farouk; Syrian Ba'athists (often Alawi or Druze) took away the lands of urban (typically Sunni) merchant absentee landlords; the Algerian National Liberation Front (FLN) seized the farms of fleeing *pied noir* colonists; and Iraqi nationalists and Communists dispossessed the sheikhs, who had often supported the deposed Hashemite monarchy. Even the shah of Iran, shortly after he was reinstalled by the United States in 1953, agreed to launch land reform, mainly because he believed that this would weaken his opponents, such as the friends of Prime Minister Mohammad Mosaddegh (himself a landowner) or the Shi'i *ulema* (Hooglund 1982; Katouzian 1981). Large landlords have ceased to exist as a political force in any MENA country that had a significant agrarian reform.[6]

The contributions of land reform to equity and economic growth were mixed. The Egyptian agrarian reform, which became the model for other Arab regimes, affected only 12 percent of the land area. Landless workers were excluded, since only tenants were believed to have the necessary agricultural experience. This pattern was repeated in Algeria, where the permanent workers seized the estates of the departed *colons*. When the land seizures were institutionalized under *autogestion* (self-management), temporary and seasonal laborers received nothing (Zghal 1977). Subsequent reforms of the 1970s affected some 30 percent of the rural population (Tuma 1978).

The administration of land reforms often created serious production problems. Governments sometimes removed large landowners—who often had supplied credit and seed to tenants—without replacing them with anyone else. This was a function of continual political upheaval, as in both Iraq and Syria during the 1960s, and of the lack of sufficient cadres, a problem that was more serious in Iraq than in Syria and that had become less acute by the late 1970s (Springborg 1981). Most land reform beneficiaries were obliged to join government-sponsored service cooperatives. Peasants farmed their own lands as private property, but input supply, marketing, and often crop choices were regulated by the cooperatives. The cooperative system, pioneered in Egypt, also appeared in Tunisia, Algeria, Syria, Iraq, and the former People's Democratic Republic of Yemen (PDRY). Such cooperatives became the principal instrument for channeling resources out of agriculture toward industrial projects. Land reform was the handmaiden of state-led industrialization strategies. Some scholars have argued that the disappearance of the large owners in Egypt removed a powerful lobby on behalf of all farmers, leaving the farm sector exposed to the significant taxation increases that such growth strategies entailed (Hansen 1991). However, few countries succeeded in mobilizing the agricultural surplus for industrial investment through land reforms and cooperatives.

Land reforms throughout the region greatly reduced the gross inequities in land tenure that had been inherited from the pre–World War II era. But the limited scope of land reform, the use of state-supported cooperatives to distribute and subsidize inputs, and the lingering legacy of the colonial era often combined to generate a "new class" of rural rich, the more prosperous sections of the peasantry. Large landlords had been eliminated, while official cadres relied on the wealthy peasants for information and for social activities. Such farmers dominated their areas and ensured that government policies and cooperatives favored or at least did not threaten their own interests (Adams 1986).[7]

At the same time, the extensive experience with large-scale state farms has been disappointing throughout the region. Whether in Tunisia in the 1960s, in Iraq and Syria in the 1970s, or in newly reclaimed lands in Egypt, wholly public-sector farms have been abandoned. In Algeria, 2,000 "self-managed" farms were subdivided into 6,000 smaller and more specialized units, while "other land is being leased to state farm workers or coop members who want to farm privately" (USDA 1987, 23). One of the last holdouts for collective, public-sector farming, Syria, dissolved its remaining public-sector farms along the Euphrates Basin (about 70,000 hectares), distributing the land among 5,000 individuals (Ababsa 2010). Privately owned large farms have fared little better: in Pahlavi Iran, for example, the large "farm corporations" set up by the shah not only disrupted rural society but also failed to outproduce medium-sized peasant holdings by any of several measures (Moghadem 1982).

More recently, however, large corporations based in and financed by the wealthy countries of the GCC, such as Saudi Arabia's Tabuk Agricultural Development Company, encouraged by high global food prices, have made substantial agribusiness investments in countries such as Sudan and Ethiopia (see Box 6.3). This is part of the "land grab," a global trend that is seeing millions of hectares fall under the control of large global corporations. The risks are enormous, from displaced populations to environmental damage. But the opportunities for enhancing rural productivity and raising millions of farmers above poverty levels also exist, especially when mechanisms are used that rely on small farmers for production and on MNCs for the provision of inputs and marketing services, as in contract farming and other out-grower schemes (Diwan and Osire 2013).

Over the past two decades, the trend has been toward much greater reliance on private farming and on market incentives in agriculture. The turn toward the private sector and a greater role for market forces has sometimes stimulated rural social conflict. In a pattern that any student of rural politics in Latin America or India will recognize, landowners have used police and private security guards to drive unwanted tenants off the land, often with considerable brutality, while human rights activists have protested, petitioned, and sued in court. In Egypt, for example, Law 96, passed in 1992, loosened Nasser-era restrictions on farm size and tenancy contracts. In particular, the law made it easier to raise rents and to dismiss tenants. Under the old laws, the landowners retained de jure ownership, but because tenants could not be removed, they held a de facto property right to the land. Law 96 abolished that de facto right. As usually happens when property rights are redistributed, violence surged. An Egyptian non-governmental organization (NGO), the Land Center for Human Rights (LCHR), reported "at least 107 deaths and 565 injuries" in conflicts over Law 96 in 1998–1999 alone (LCHR 1999; see also Bush 2002). Over ten years later, another Egyptian NGO, Sons of the Soil, reported 270 deaths due to land-related violence in a single year (Viney 2012). In Yemen, where rising land and irrigation prices have helped consolidate landholdings in the hands of the few, the government acknowledged in 2010 that land and water disputes resulted in some 4,000 deaths each year. This is probably more than the total annual number of deaths from southern secessionist violence, northern armed rebellions, and al-Qaeda-linked terrorism combined (Small Arms Survey 2010).

Despite such upticks in rural social conflict, as the food security problem loomed ever larger, governments from Algeria to Iraq turned to the private sector to solve their domestic agricultural supply problems. For example, Morocco passed twin agricultural laws in 1995 to aid the government in collectivizing and privatizing millions of hectares of what was previously collective grazing territory (Davis 2006). Since 2000, the Moroccan government has leased out over 100,000 hectares to private investors, hoping to help satisfy internal food demand as well as boost agricultural exports (Pfeiffer 2012). For these strategies to succeed, however, incentives must be provided. The results here have been mixed.

Price Signals

Heavy taxation slowed agricultural growth in the MENA region. The mechanisms chosen to transfer resources out of the farming sector distorted farmers' incentives and misallocated scarce resources. Two types of price policies were particularly problematic: (1) direct or sectoral taxation, in which government marketing agencies enjoying monopsony power offered farmers prices well below those prevailing on world markets; and (2) the indirect or macroeconomic taxation implicit in an overvalued real foreign exchange rate. Both types of taxation originated in import-substituting industrialization (ISI) programs; the choice of such a development strategy thus implied bias against agriculture (Johnston and Kilby 1975; Little, Scitovsky, and Scott 1970; Timmer, Falcon, and Pearson 1983). Both of these forms of taxation were used extensively, and both had the predictable effect of slowing production growth. Consequently, as food security fears increased, such taxation mechanisms were gradually reformed in some countries.

The first mode of taxation typically relied heavily on government marketing monopolies. These were extensively used by governments in Algeria, Egypt, Morocco, Sudan, and Tunisia throughout the heyday of ISI economic development strategies and were closely linked to the land reform/cooperative systems described earlier. Indeed, such "cooperatives" are best understood as taxation devices rather than as cooperatives in the American or European sense.

Sectoral price policies engendered inefficiencies and may have retarded output growth. Farmers are highly responsive to price signals *among* crops. Because some crops are more heavily taxed than others, farmers reallocate land, labor, and purchased inputs toward less taxed, more profitable crops. The resulting distortions can be extensive. For example, Egyptian farmers fled from cotton and rice into horticultural crops, and from wheat into clover, whereas Sudanese farmers in the Gezira switched their land and labor away from heavily taxed cotton toward sorghum, peanuts, and wheat. In Algeria, value added in (taxed) cereals stagnated between 1974 and 1986; during this same period, value added in vegetables grew at 7.4 percent per year and that of fresh fruit at 4.3 percent (World Bank 1987; FAOSTAT).

Such static resource misallocations mattered. In Egypt, the value of the allocative distortions amounted to some 7 percent of total GDP and fully 30 percent of agricultural GDP (Dethier 1989; Hansen 1991). In Sudan, the incentive bias against cotton reduced the average yield of that crop by roughly 50 percent between 1974 and 1980–1981 (World Bank 1985). Since cotton is that country's largest export, farmers' responses to such policies exacerbated the country's severe balance-of-payments problem. In the early 1980s, some 15 percent of the value of Moroccan agricultural GDP was transferred out of the sector (Tuluy and Salinger 1991). Even as Tunisia liberalized its trade regime in the mid-2000s, tariffs and centrally set profit margins promoted growth in uncompetitive sectors such as beef, milk, and potatoes at the expense of citrus fruits and olive oil, which might have been sold to newly opened EU markets. The resulting distortions imposed a 4 percent cost-of-living increase on Tunisian consumers (World Bank 2006).

Overvalued exchange rates also blunted farmers' incentives. Such overvaluation creates excess demand for foreign exchange, which is then usually rationed by (often complex) government regulations. These policies lower the value of exports and raise the value of imports, while also increasing the prices of nontraded domestic goods relative to products that are traded internationally. The first effect hurts producers of export crops (such as cotton, rice, and vegetables) as well as producers of the major import-competing crop—cereals. Furthermore, government rationing of scarce foreign exchange usually favors industrial and military users; farmers are often last in line, where they find that they must pay higher prices for inputs or consumer goods—if, indeed, they can get them at all. The increase in the relative price of nontradables to tradables also hurts farmers because a large portion of the sector's costs is in nontradable inputs such as land and labor, while its outputs are, of course, tradables. All of these effects reduce farmers' incomes.

In Egypt, for example, exchange rate overvaluation increased the taxation of agriculture by 50 to 200 percent, depending on the year, between 1970 and 1985 (Dethier 1991). The overvalued Turkish lira more than compensated for the sectoral subsidies that politically active Turkish farmers were able to obtain during those fifteen years.[8] A similar phenomenon occurred in the Islamic Republic of Iran, which also combined sectoral subsidies (input credits, price supports) with a seriously overvalued real exchange rate.

As usual, the variation in countries' experiences with both direct and indirect agricultural taxation was wide. Although foreign exchange largesse was supposed to be detrimental to agriculture in models of the Dutch Disease, countries with surplus capital often found ways to offset such problems. Their hefty oil rents eliminated the need to transfer resources from agriculture to other sectors, their demand for food was growing the most rapidly of all the countries in the region, and their food security fears were acute. In response, major oil-exporting governments lavishly subsidized their farmers. The most extreme case of this was the experience of Saudi Arabia (see Box 6.3).

As food security fears mounted, more and more countries began to reform their price policies. Already in the 1970s, four countries (Jordan, Morocco, Libya, and Saudi Arabia) subsidized their wheat producers even when taking exchange rate overvaluation into account. In the 1980s, Moroccan cereal farmers came to enjoy increasing protection (in the form of subsidies) (Tyner 1993), while the Syrian government paid farmers producing wheat, maize, and other crops prices that were about 30 percent more than the international price (World Bank 1986). Syrian wheat farmers continue to receive prices above international levels (World Bank 2001). Some countries' farmers may enjoy "natural protection" due to transportation barriers; for example, farmers in the Yemen Arab Republic (YAR) in 1982

BOX 6.3. Sowing Oil Rents in Saudi Arabia

Saudi Arabia paid farmers from five to six times the international price of wheat during the early 1980s while simultaneously subsidizing inputs; the effective rate of protection (the combined impact of protected output prices and subsidized inputs) may have reached 1,500 percent in the late 1980s (Wilson and Graham 1994). Saudi government loans to farmers rose from under US$5 million in 1971 to over US$1 billion in 1983; from 1980 to 1985, the Saudi government spent some US$20 billion on agriculture, mostly in the form of subsidies (*The Economist*, April 6, 1985). The results were spectacular for the key food security crop: wheat output rose from less than 3,300 tons in 1978 to over 3.9 million tons in 1992. The kingdom became the world's sixth-largest wheat exporter, though not without cost: the Saudi government spent at least $85 billion from 1984 to 2000 purchasing domestic wheat that would have cost it only $20.4 billion on the open market.

Kuwait, Qatar, and the United Arab Emirates also offer generous farm incentives. These policies have been, to put it mildly, dubious both economically and ecologically, but food security concerns and the vested interests of subsidy recipients (often well-placed ruling family members) have swept these concerns aside.

Reality sank in during the early 1990s, however, with the economic burdens of higher government spending and falling oil prices in the wake of the First Gulf War. In 1993 the government cut the wheat area eligible for price supports to 25 percent of previous levels. Thanks to this change in policy, the amount of water pumped from nonrenewable aquifers fell by nearly half (46 percent) (Abderrahman 2001). The area planted in wheat continued to fall in the 1990s, but some 624,000 hectares were still planted in wheat in 2002 (World Bank 2003). It took until 2008 before the Saudi Arabian government decided to abandon the program altogether, reducing production by about 12.5 percent each year until 2016, when wheat production will cease entirely (Elhadj 2008; McFerron 2013).

---

received cereal prices that were, on average, 360 percent above those prevailing on international markets (World Bank 1986).

By the late 1990s, many countries had moved toward greater reliance on market forces. In Egypt, Morocco, and Tunisia, governments reduced levels of protection, permitted private traders greater leeway, and reduced input subsidies. Even Syria began gradually freeing up prices in the early 1990s, with farmers bound to state-determined prices when selling to state agencies but permitted to export crops abroad at market prices (Ababsa 2010). Shifts in macroeconomic management were also implemented in order to reduce the real exchange rate overvaluation. Adherence to World Trade Organization (WTO) agreements and bilateral agreements with the EU reduced rates of protection in agriculture as well. Although these results may have improved efficiency, some initial studies suggest that the efficiency gains were small relative to the redistribution effects (Chemingui and Thaber 2001).

The impact of these price distortions on aggregate farm output (and on sectoral growth) is less clear than their impact on the cropping pattern. As Hans Binswanger (1989) has pointed out, the basic argument for inelasticity of aggregate farm output was made over forty years ago (by Johnson 1950): aggregate sectoral output can increase only if more resources (land, labor, and capital) are utilized or if there is technological change. Binswanger reviews a series of econometric studies of aggregate supply response from around the world; although he finds the usual methodological debates and conundrums, his conclusion is clear: aggregate supply elasticities are very low in the short run, usually below 0.2 and often below 0.1. Several studies of Egyptian agriculture indicate that the responsiveness of the entire sector to shifts in its terms of trade is rather low (see, for example, Alderman and von Braun 1984). As usual, however, the longer the time period the greater the response: price distortions may inhibit technological change and/or bias its direction in socially undesirable ways (Valdes 1989). Even if *elasticities* are low, a large *output response* can occur; for example, if prices rise 100 percent, then output could rise by 10 to 20 percent—a result that regional policymakers would certainly welcome (Braverman 1989).

Price reform is probably a necessary but not sufficient condition for agricultural growth. In some cases, complementary price policy shifts and technological innovations have led to dramatic output gains, as the Egyptian example shows (see Box 6.4). The available evidence strongly suggests, however, that technological and physical constraints are likely to be at least as important as price policies over the medium and long run. The deceleration of output growth in the 1990s, the decade when the price reforms typically became effective, is consistent with this view. However, a case may be made that the price policy changes were necessary to prevent further deceleration, as the natural resource constraints, above all of water, began to bind ever more tightly. The changes in price policies implemented in the past three decades were probably necessary, but not sufficient, to promote food security at the national level.

WATER AND THE IMPERATIVE OF A NEW FOOD SECURITY STRATEGY

Five key water problems face most nations of the region in the coming decades.

1. Water is increasingly scarce, whether measured by some simple indicator such as supplies per capita or by more sophisticated projections of water demand.
2. Water quantity problems are exacerbated by water quality problems, which become increasingly serious as nations seek to solve water quantity problems through reuse of water. Technologies exist to do this safely, but they require considerable funds and careful management, and neither is abundant in the region.
3. From an economic perspective, the burden of adjustment to increasingly scarce water must fall on the agricultural sector because the economic value of water is much lower in farming than for domestic or industrial use. Politically,

BOX 6.4. Egyptian Price Policies

The Egyptian government has used its monopolies over domestic marketing (implemented through the cooperative system) and over international trade to pay farmers prices below international levels. In the 1970s, regulations and controls affected cotton, wheat, rice, sugarcane, beans, and winter onions. All of these crops were taxed. Livestock products, in contrast, were protected because of consumers' preferences by explicit tariffs and the complex bureaucratic hurdles placed before importers until 1987. Horticultural crops (fruits and vegetables) were entirely unregulated.

As a result of these policies, and despite area controls, cotton yields stagnated, and the area planted in wheat declined in favor of *birsim,* or Egyptian clover. Farmers had ample incentives to divert variable inputs (labor, fertilizer) away from (heavily taxed) crops like cotton and wheat. Finally, foreign exchange scarcity in the mid-1980s led to the restriction of nonwheat agricultural imports, which increased the degree of protection of crops that competed with cotton (Dethier 1991). Egyptian price policies not only robbed the country of the foreign exchange that it could have obtained through exporting cotton (in which the country has a strong comparative advantage) but also exacerbated the food gap by retarding wheat production.

Egypt began dismantling these policies in the late 1980s and accelerated the process after the First Gulf War. By 1995, only cotton and sugarcane retained controls. Particularly dramatic was the case of wheat. The combination of the release of a new variety along with decontrol of the wheat market was highly effective: wheat production tripled from 1980 to 2010, while the farmland used for planting wheat increased by 126 percent (USDA/FAS). A 50 percent increase in wheat yields per acre planted was partly due to new high-yielding varieties; their adoption had been retarded by the earlier policies, which had made wheat straw nearly as profitable as wheat grain (Kherallah et al. 2003). Since high-yielding varieties produce less straw, the shift in the relative price of straw and grain in favor of the latter was not independent of price policies. Although there is a debate about the accuracy of national wheat data, it seems very likely that wheat production responded well to price policy shifts.[1] However, the production of Egyptian wheat, a strategic crop, has increasingly benefited from government procurement prices above the market rate—some 33 percent higher than world prices in 2013 (Abaza 2013).

Total food production nearly quadrupled between 1980 and 2012, but with population growth and changing consumption patterns, over 40 percent of Egyptian cereal consumption is still imported (FAO/GIEWS 2014). Cotton followed the opposite path: since price supports were removed in 1997, production of cotton has fallen by over 70 percent, while the area of land devoted to cotton production has fallen by nearly two-thirds (USDA/FAS; World Bank 2007a).

1. Timothy Mitchell (2002) has argued that much of the increase in wheat production may be a statistical artifact. He asserts that many *fellahin* (peasants) simply concealed their wheat production from the authorities under the compulsory quota system; when this system was abolished, they were more forthcoming about their production. Since measured wheat production tripled, such a practice can explain the entire increase in measured wheat production only if one assumes that fellahin were hiding two bushels for every one they admitted to producing.

however, such a shift is very difficult; past government programs to reclaim or redistribute land and increase domestic agricultural production have created powerful interest groups that will oppose reallocation of scarce supplies away from their farms.

4. Government water management systems suffer from lack of funds and are geared to a situation of relatively abundant water.

5. Most water resources in the region are rivers and aquifers that cross international frontiers. There is a sharp clash between, on the one hand, economic and engineering logic, which would favor managing a river basin as a unit, and on the other, political considerations, which are often marked by fear and distrust of neighbors.

Water Quantity

Since water supplies throughout the region are essentially fixed (with a few exceptions), the total amount of water per capita declines as population grows. But such information is not sufficient to answer the question of whether there will be enough water, since much depends on *how* the water is used. Of the various empirical measures of water scarcity, one of the most popular is that developed by Malin Falkenmark (1989), who has estimated that a country is "water-scarce" if it has less than 1,000 cubic meters per person per year of available water supplies. The calculation includes an allocation for agriculture as well as estimates for domestic and industrial use.

However, the "Falkenmark indicator" has been criticized for ignoring regional variations in water usage and the differences between various water shortages. Alternative measures have been proposed. One example is the "criticality ratio," which compares each country's water demand to its available resources. Per this ratio, water-scarce countries withdraw 20 to 40 percent of their annual supplies for human use and anything beyond that is considered severe water scarcity. Another example is the comprehensive but complex and time-consuming metric developed by the International Water Management Institute (IWMI), which takes into account a wide variety of factors to try to predict a country's potential to meet future water demand. A similar "water poverty index," developed by the Global Water Forum, aims to take into account access to water, quality of resources, and environmental factors, but it may be more suited to local than national studies (White 2012). A comparison of these rough indicators with the estimates of the water resources that will be available in 2025 illustrates the dimensions of the emerging challenge.

Discussions of water quantities often refer to "water needs." Since water is necessary for life, there is some amount of water that is a basic need or a human right, but that amount is very small in relation to most uses of water. In the United States, for example, water for drinking and cooking accounts for only 1.6 percent of residential use (AWWA Research Foundation 1999). And as Figure 6.1 and Table 6.1 show, most of the water in the region, as in most countries, is used not by households directly but by farmers.

In consequence, water economists typically split the demand for water into two parts: a small amount treated as a "merit good," a basic need to which everyone is entitled, and the rest of water use, better viewed not as a "need" but as a "demand." Water for large domestic use (such as watering lawns) or for industry and agriculture is to be treated as a commodity like any other: as a good the demand for which depends on its price, people's incomes, and the prices of substitutes and complements. Considering water *demands* instead of water *needs* complicates the simple picture of population growth pressing against fixed supplies. First the bad news: water is like food—people demand more of it as their incomes rise. From this perspective, the water situation is, if anything, even more serious than the food situation.

The key concept to understand here is the *economic value* of water. Like any commodity, water must be scarce to have an economic value. If water is scarce, the "shadow price" of water is the amount by which one additional unit of water (say, one cubic meter) will increase our use of it. Put differently, we should be willing to pay a price for water that is just equal to its contribution to our goals. Willingness to pay for water on the part of industrial and agricultural users is determined by the marginal value product of water. Water is an input into industrial and agricultural production processes. Farmers are willing to pay a price for water that is just equal to the marginal physical product of water (for example, the amount of additional cotton made possible by one more cubic meter of water) multiplied by the price of that output. Industrial values are lower than what domestic users are willing to pay, but higher than what farmers are willing to pay. Consequently, agriculture is the "residual user" of water, and within agriculture the residual users are those producing crops with low marginal value products. (A cubic meter of water used for Egyptian sugarcane production produces only about 0.1 Egyptian pounds.) In addition, price policy reforms that raise crop prices also necessarily raise the demand for water. Thus, farm price liberalization without reform of the water system exacerbates water shortages.

Fortunately, the demand approach also offers good news: the demand for water, although price-inelastic, is by no means completely unresponsive to price. A recent study estimated that the price elasticity of domestic water demand was around -0.45 (Hung and Chie 2013); a study of Tunisian irrigation water estimated price elasticity of demand for irrigation water at -0.44 (Belloumi and Matoussi 2007). Everywhere in the region, water use is heavily subsidized. In many countries, not even the costs of operations and maintenance of water systems are recovered, though irrigation charges now cover these costs in Tunisia, and partially in Morocco (World Bank 2007b). Only in Syria are farmers charged any portion of the capital cost of providing water supply (Salman and Mualla 2008). The marginal cost of water for most surface irrigation users in the region is effectively zero, since water use charges are typically a fixed charge that varies only by the area planted, not by the amount of water used.[9] Mechanisms to raise the private cost of water to users may well be critical to the management of increasing scarcity. But creating such mechanisms, particularly equitable mechanisms, faces formidable institutional, managerial, technological, and political challenges.

A particularly acute problem in the region (as in the world) is overpumping of groundwater. Groundwater provides vital irrigation to farmers because the reliability of private pumps greatly exceeds the reliability of surface-flow systems, particularly for farmers at the tail end of canal networks. Being able to water crops at critical moments in their growing season has a dramatic impact on crop yields (Shah et al. 2000). But everywhere in the world, overcoming groundwater overuse is a serious problem, and MENA countries are no exception. In Syria, for example, under the stimulus of food self-sufficiency goals, the area irrigated with groundwater more

---

BOX 6.5. The Political Economy of Groundwater Overuse in Yemen

Yemen may offer the most serious case of groundwater overuse in the world. The total area of irrigated land rose from 37,000 hectares in 1970 to 407,000 in 2004, with some 40 percent of irrigation water supplied by deep groundwater aquifers (Lichtenhaler 2010). Government policy strongly encouraged this development. Until 1995, diesel fuel, which is used to power the irrigation pumps, was priced at around US$0.02 per liter, while international prices ranged from $0.15 to $0.20 per liter. Agricultural borrowers also enjoyed generous interest subsidies, paying 9–11 percent compared to market rates of 50–60 percent. Consequently, water was priced at $0.04 per cubic meter, although the marginal costs of extraction were three to five times higher. The government also protected the domestic fruit and vegetable market and did nothing to restrict the boom in *qat,* a mild narcotic, whose cultivation consumes as much as 37 percent of all agricultural water in the country (Lichtenhaler 2010). Unsurprisingly, experts describe the groundwater situation in the country as a "basket case." Water tables have fallen dramatically as wells have been deepened two to four times in the Sa'adah Basin (Lichtenthaler and Turton 1999). Extraction now exceeds the recharge rate by 33 percent for all water resources, and by as much as 70 percent for groundwater resources (Ward 2007).

The high growth rate of Yemeni agriculture during the past decade (over 5 percent total annual growth from 2000 to 2010) is probably unsustainable (FAOSTAT). This has serious negative implications for Yemen's welfare, since roughly 71 percent of the labor force works in agriculture. During the past two decades, the Yemeni government, faced with a large balance-of-payments crisis in the wake of the expulsion of Yemenis from the Gulf during and after the First Gulf War, has embarked on a process of economic reform, including reforms that aim to enhance water conservation. The path, however, has been rocky.

In the Sa'adah Basin of North Yemen, communal systems of land use prevailed until the mid-1970s. Escalating conflict between herders and farmers over the use of runoff water was adjudicated by religious scholars; a decision in 1976 (unanimously accepted by all tribes) induced many tribes to privatize their land. Subsequently, merchants and other tribesmen of comparative wealth were able to capture most of the groundwater by investing in pumps (Lichtenthaler and Turton 1999).

When hundreds of thousands of Yemeni workers were expelled from Saudi Arabia and other Gulf states in 1990–1991, the resulting precipitous fall in

continues

than doubled from 1988 to 1998. By 2000, 60 percent of irrigated farmland used groundwater, all of which was privately developed. However, nearly 50 percent of the wells were illegal, leading to the inevitable result of severe overpumping and pollution problems (World Bank 2001). The problems in Yemen are still more serious; indeed, by some accounts, the problem there is the worst in the world (see Box 6.5).

BOX 6.5. *continued*

remittances exposed deep structural weaknesses in the Yemeni economy. To cope with the post–Gulf War economic crisis, Yemen slowly raised the price of diesel fuel, which is used in pickup trucks as well as in water pumps. Then, after the civil war that ultimately reunited the country, the government embarked in 1995 on a stabilization and structural adjustment policy. In addition to the increases in diesel fuel prices, the end of credit subsidies and the lifting of import bans on fruits and vegetables were intended to provide significant incentives for greater water conservation and more efficient agricultural use of water (Ward 2000). The Yemeni government managed to raise the initial price of diesel fuel by 75 percent in the wake of the civil war, and then by a further 100 percent in 1995–1996 (IMF 2013). The Yemeni government further reduced subsidies in 2011–2012, doubling the price of diesel fuel, presenting this as necessary to ensure adequate supplies amid shortages brought on by political unrest.

Such changes are likely, however, to exact a political price. In 1993, the public rejected the government's first proposal to raise diesel fuel prices. By 1995, the government's cumulative price increases had tripled the cost of diesel fuel, sparking riots in which twenty people were killed (Ward 2000). Similar government actions triggered further riots in 1996 and 1998; after the 1998 disturbances, Islamic activists emerged as the opposition leaders to the government and denunciations of "foreign interference" in the economy became more widespread. The protests were not specifically focused on water issues. Rather, protesters were galvanized by the related increases in fuel and food prices as well as by the issues of governmental corruption and lack of transparency in the entire process (*Yemen Observer,* January 10, 1999). The turmoil continued in the 2000s. When the cabinet removed diesel fuel subsidies in 2005 and prices rose from 17 to 45 rials per liter, riots broke out all over the country and at least twenty-five people were killed (*Al Jazeera,* July 21, 2005). A 2010 initiative to reduce fuel subsidies also triggered deadly riots.

While the initial demands raised in the 2011 Yemeni uprisings did not directly stem from concerns over water and food security, the political instability that followed prompted a major food and fuel crisis. From January to July 2011, fuel shortages caused by ruptured pipelines helped drive up the black market price of fuel by 567 percent and food commodities by 43 percent (IRIN 2012). Though mass infusions of foreign aid and a GCC-backed political transition plan ultimately helped ameliorate the crisis, fuel shortages have provoked mass demonstrations as recently as June 2014, while political unrest and terrorist attacks have pushed water issues far down the government's list of priorities.

Unsustainable groundwater use plagues the entire region and poses an increasingly serious challenge to policymakers.

One approach to dwindling per capita water supplies is to recycle water. But to safely increase the reuse of water requires not only treatment technologies but also institutions and management systems that work. The recycling of water and greater water use efficiency can certainly reduce pressure on supplies, but doing so will require significant changes in behavior and incentives at all levels of the water system. In turn, this will require effective public regulatory capacity, which is underdeveloped in many MENA countries (see Figure 3.4).

Agriculture as the Residual User

Increasing water scarcity is forcing farmers to make do with less and less water for irrigation. This is becoming increasingly apparent in very water-scarce countries such as Israel, Jordan, and the West Bank and Gaza. In Jordan, the main water authority has been promoting greater water efficiency by steadily decreasing the amount of water allocated to agriculture since 1999, following a two-year drought. In Palestine, without the financial resources to promote more efficient practices, and with most available water supplies governed by restrictive agreements with Israel, the share of agriculture in the Palestinian economy has dropped from 13 percent in 1994 to just 4.6 percent today (Hatuqa 2012). Forecasts in Israel, meanwhile, suggest that agriculture will have to obtain over 50 percent of the water it needs from recycled wastewater by 2020. Economic logic strongly suggests that agriculture, as the marginal user, will bear the brunt of increasingly limited water supplies. The implications for food security strategies are obvious: food security cannot be achieved through domestic production alone, and thus food imports are becoming more important.

As is so often the case, however, the political calculus yields a very different answer. The region's states have sponsored irrigation expansion for decades, in some cases (Egypt) for over 150 years. The interests that have been created, including national bureaucracies and prosperous farmers, are formidable indeed. Farmers can invoke nationalism as a defense for subsidized water. In Israel, irrigated farming is closely connected to the Zionist dream of "making the desert bloom"; meanwhile, the Jordan Valley Authority aims to strengthen Jordanian farmers along the border with the West Bank. In Egypt, various ambitious irrigation plans, such as in Toshka in upper Egypt, seem motivated by political desires to support rich investors as much as a need to create new jobs for graduates—indeed, not many have turned out to be interested in becoming farmers.

States have invested in irrigation in the hopes of reducing national food dependency, but irrigation has also provided the state with an opportunity to extend its authority in the countryside and pursue its "vision" of development. The Egyptian government has pursued land reclamation and concomitant irrigation expansion to the fringes of the Nile Valley. However, most studies show that the returns to water in such uses are very low. The Moroccan government has used irrigation development partly as a kind of substitute for land reform and partly as a mechanism for bestowing benefits on the rural notables who constitute such an important source of political support (Leveau 1985; Swearingen 1987). Morocco continues to be firmly committed to irrigation expansion (see Box 6.6). Dam construction has continued throughout the region, with annual dam construction from 2000 to 2007 on par with the number of dams commissioned during the 1990s (FAO/AQUASTAT 2013).

However, state interests in agriculture and irrigation have been tempered in recent years by the realities of water scarcity and political instability. The Jordan Valley Authority, for example, has been increasingly willing to privilege urban consumers of water over agricultural users when faced with drought-induced shortages, while Israeli farmers have been partially placated by new water supplies in the form of reclaimed wastewater and drainage water.

The consequence of past irrigation expansion is that powerful vested interests block adoption of better management strategies for coping with scarcity. Farmers oppose the imposition of operations and maintenance charges, often claiming (with some justice) that the quality of service is so poor that they should not have to pay for it. But changes in water policy are possible, as the Israeli case demonstrates. The drought of 1986 forced the Israeli water commissioner to cut water to farmers, but the lobby's strength overturned this decision. After the country suffered three additional and consecutive drought years, the cuts were reimposed in 1991 and the agricultural sector's water allocation was slashed a whopping 65 percent. Although much of the water was restored after the drought ended, the sector nevertheless wound up with 25 percent less water than it had in 1986. Part of the explanation was the shift in economic (and political) clout in Israel as the country underwent a rapid transformation into an industrial and skill-intensive services economy.[10] Yet farmers did not lose all of their subsidies: in return for acceding to the policy establishing agriculture as the "residual user" of water in the event of a drought, farmers were granted a price of US$0.20–$0.25 per cubic meter for irrigation water, far lower than the real cost of delivery, which was $0.65 (Allan and Karshenas 1996).

Although water use in Israeli agriculture rose again during the 1990s, freshwater use in farming dropped dramatically during the subsequent decade—from around 950 million cubic meters annually in 1998 to around 500 in 2010—owing to the substitution of wastewater and reused drainage water (Ben-Gal 2010). As a result, the Israeli government was able to reduce allocations of freshwater to the agricultural sector during drought conditions in 2000–2009 with little backlash from farmers. Water conservation in Israel was thus a product of political negotiations, technological development, and pressures brought on by drought.

Farmers strongly oppose water charges. This is understandable. Water once had a zero price, but as it has become scarcer its value has been capitalized into the value of land. Farmers reasonably view the imposition of water fees as an expropriation; they feel that they have already paid for the water. The pricing of water also raises religious (and therefore political) objections in Muslim countries. For these reasons, some analysts recommend granting farmers tradable water rights. Such a system would give the rents of water to farmers rather than to the government and simultaneously create incentives for water conservation (Rosegrant and Binswanger 1994). The concept is intriguing, but so far attempts at following this approach have

BOX 6.6. Irrigation in Morocco

The commitment of the Moroccan government to irrigation has deep roots. A drought that began in 1935 and lasted for more than two years in southern Morocco deprived several hundred thousand Moroccans of food, and half a million people became entirely dependent on government food distribution. The experience led to the creation of the first major irrigation perimeter in which land was allocated to Moroccans rather than to French *colons*. There was worse to come: in 1945 Morocco was hit by the most severe drought of the twentieth century. For eight months there was no rain whatsoever. Half of Morocco's livestock perished, and a massive relief operation was undertaken to distribute grain brought in from the United States, Canada, and Argentina. Because of weaknesses in the distribution system, relief stations could distribute only six to nine kilograms per person per month; since an average person needed about fifteen kilograms per month, widespread starvation ensued.

With this historical background, it is hardly surprising that the government of Morocco is so committed to the development and extension of irrigated agriculture. Irrigation development has another attractive feature: it allows the government to reward its friends and to strengthen its support among leaders in rural communities. Ever since 1961, its rural development programs have sought, successfully for the most part, to strengthen rural elites, who have long been among the key supporters of the monarchy (Leveau 1985). In the mid-1980s 9,000 to 9,500 large landowners owned some 2.2 million hectares, or nearly 30 percent of the country's farmland (Swearingen 1987, 187). They continue to constitute a critical constituency for the palace, as do the much larger number of smaller farmers who know perfectly well that their relative wealth is in large measure the result of public investment.

Public investment in large dams and infrastructure has been the key. According to Will Swearingen (1987), from 1912 to 1956 (the French Protectorate period), fourteen dams were constructed. In the first ten years of independence (1957–1967), three dams were built. In 1968 the government proclaimed a *politique des barrages*, designed with the assistance of the World Bank, and by 1991 fourteen more dams had been completed. The goal, originally proclaimed by the French Protectorate, was to bring the total area under irrigation to one million hectares. Although this goal has been achieved, current plans call for continued dam construction. The Al Wahda Dam on the Ouergha River in the Sebou Basin, completed in 1996, is the second-largest dam in Africa, smaller only than the Aswan High Dam in Egypt. A further fifteen dams have come into operation since.

More recently, projects such as the National Irrigation Water Saving Program, launched in 2009 with financing by the African Development Bank, have sought to expand and revitalize Moroccan irrigation networks, providing more efficient drip agriculture technology to thousands of farmers.

been limited to a few, localized efforts, such as informal markets for water in Bitit, Morocco, and Ta'izz, Yemen.

Another proposal, noted by the Arab Forum for Economic Development, would be to expand support to local water users' associations, or organizations of local water users tied to a shared resource (such as a branch canal or irrigation system) to which public water agencies would delegate some level of control over water distribution (Abdel-Dayem et al. 2012). In theory, these associations could reduce state costs and responsibilities for administering water and irrigation systems, while promoting more efficient use of available resources within local areas. However, they often lack the authority and financial backing to make and enforce local water rules.

Financial and Managerial Constraints

The financial challenge of providing water is daunting. A report from Global Water Intelligence predicted that the entire MENA region would invest some $120 billion in various water projects during the ten years ending in 2015. In the GCC countries, Israel, and North Africa, considerable sums are being invested in desalination plants. Even though political instability has delayed projects in Egypt and Libya, the GCC countries alone have planned $100 billion worth of desalination projects for the next five years. Enthusiasm for dam construction remains high, with FAOSTAT figures on dam construction showing around thirty-three new dams commissioned annually during the early 2000s. Yet even as new dams require substantial new funds, many smaller dams in the region are increasingly threatened by siltation of reservoirs, while canal maintenance often lags behind need (FAO 2003).

Financing will mostly come from either international donors or national governments. The strain that this places on national budgets is not helped by the fact that all countries heavily subsidize water use, particularly water for agriculture. Water charges rarely cover operations and maintenance costs, much less the opportunity cost of water in alternative uses. Only in prewar Syria did water charges even begin to capture some of the investment costs needed to provide additional water, with farmers paying additional service charges for building and maintaining irrigation networks (Salman and Mualla 2008).[11] Still, it is unclear whether merely reducing such subsidies would automatically spur greater water use efficiency. Given that investments in more efficient irrigation practices are out of the financial reach of the region's poorer farmers, any increase in water pricing without significant investments in rural infrastructure could further contribute to rural poverty, already a concern in countries such as Egypt and Morocco (Sowers, Vengosh, and Weinthal 2011).

The managerial constraints are no less severe than the financial constraints. The current system of centralized public-sector management of water systems predominant across the region breaks the link between suppliers' incentives and users' needs. Under some conditions, the privatization of municipal water systems could greatly improve not only access to capital but also managerial efficiency and responsiveness to users' needs. Yet privatizing water supply systems has often led to significantly increased costs for drinking water, thereby jeopardizing attempts to meet the basic needs of the poor. Furthermore, the politics of water privatization can be fraught, undermining its effectiveness.[12] Water bureaucracies in the region suffer from the many ills of public-sector management (see Chapter 7). Poor pay and performance and haphazard ministerial coordination (in most countries, a number of ministries have responsibility for different aspects of water systems) are among the most serious. The past decade has seen some efforts to address this problem through the formation of high-level coordination bodies, such as the Water and Wastewater Holding Company established in Egypt in 2004, or the regrouping of Lebanon's twenty-two separate water authorities under four regional entities. Still, even a study that cited these examples as "best practices" of bureaucratic reform in the region noted that these agencies generally lacked the "institutional capacity" to deliver on promised efficiency gains (Khashman 2011).

International Hydropolitics

However serious the domestic political impediments to the management of scarcity, they pale beside the international political complications. Many countries in the Middle East depend for much of their water supply on sources that are either outside of their boundaries (rivers) or shared with other countries (aquifers). The major international rivers in the region are the Nile, the Jordan, and the Tigris-Euphrates. Internationally shared aquifers include the Eastern Erg (Algeria and Tunisia), the Nubian Sandstone Aquifer System (NSAS) (Egypt, Sudan, and Libya), the Saq-Disi formation aquifer (Jordan and Saudi Arabia), the Ras al-'Ain aquifer (Turkey and Syria), and the Yarkon-Taninim and coastal aquifers (Israel and Palestine).

Sharing water resources with one's neighbors can lead to severe problems in water quality and quantity. We have seen how water is used and reused. Water can be diverted or polluted by upstream states, leaving downstreamers with either less water or poorer-quality water or both. International law is generally unhelpful, and in any case, only two of the rivers are governed by even limited agreements (the Nile Agreement of 1959, signed by Egypt and Sudan, and the Israeli-Jordanian Peace Agreement of 1994, which contains a water protocol). Beyond accords to share flow data, there are no agreements governing the other international water resources.

Needless to say, in the volatile political environment of the MENA region, the sharing of water resources holds the potential for international conflict. From an engineering and economic perspective, water basins and aquifers are best managed as units. However, political leaders are very reluctant to entrust their water supplies to other nations. It does not help that upstream and downstream states often have serious political differences over other issues (for example, Turkey, Syria, and Iraq; Israel and Jordan; Israel and Syria; Jordan and Syria).

Shared water resources have emerged as a key point of contention in the Israeli-Palestinian conflict. During the official, direct occupation of Palestine (1967–1993), the Israeli occupation administration developed shared aquifers to primarily benefit Jewish Israelis and particularly Israeli settlers, at the expense of Palestinian users. The signing of the Oslo Accords raised hopes of more equitable water distribution, particularly when promises of additional water rights for Palestinians were made in the 1995 Oslo II agreement and the creation of a cooperative Israeli-Palestinian Joint Water Committee (JWC) to manage resources. However, the existing water supply network's bias toward Israeli users, the financial burden on Palestinian authorities to carry out further developments, and prohibitions in the Accords against infringing on water supplies to Israeli settlements have perpetuated the preexisting inequities in water distribution through to the present day (Jayousi 2010; Selby 2003). In the years following the Oslo Accords, Israel has annually drawn on more than 80 percent of the available water resources it shares with the West Bank. A 2009 World Bank report argued that Israel's authority within the JWC to reject or delay approval of Palestinian water projects and the deteriorating security and economic situation in Palestine have combined to keep water withdrawals per capita in the West Bank to some 25 percent of the levels in Israel, while only 5–10 percent of water in the Gaza aquifer is currently fit for human consumption (World Bank 2009a). In response, Israeli authorities have claimed that the JWC already provides the West Bank with the amount stipulated by the Oslo II agreement, while charging Palestinians with violating water agreements through the illegal drilling of wells and failure to appropriately manage wastewater.

Even Egypt and Sudan, which have normally enjoyed reasonably cordial relations, have confronted the specter of conflict over water: as accusations and counter-accusations flew between Cairo and Khartoum in the wake of the assassination attempt on President Hosni Mubarak in 1995, Sudan threatened to "cut off Egypt's water." The fact that the Sudanese lack the engineering capacity to do such a thing did little to dampen hysteria in the Cairo press.

More serious tensions have recently broken out between Egypt and another country of the Nile Basin, Ethiopia. Along with other upstream countries, Ethiopia has long contested the 1959 Nile Agreement, which reserved all water usage rights for the downstream countries of Egypt and Sudan. Though these countries have proposed various alternative frameworks for dividing the Nile's waters, their efforts have been consistently rejected by Egypt, which has claimed veto power over any upstream developments on the river (Yohannes and Yohannes 2013, 198). Beginning in 2011, the Ethiopian government directly challenged this claim by laying the first stone of the $4.8 billion Grand Ethiopian Renaissance Dam, aiming to boost economic development through hydroelectric power and earn foreign currency through exporting electricity to neighboring countries. Egypt, which views its stake in the Nile's waters as a vital issue of national security, has issued increasingly stern warnings to Ethiopia over the construction of the dam. Egyptian officials mentioned the potential use of force against the project in the summer of 2013, and tensions remain high despite subsequent diplomatic engagement between the countries' foreign and water ministers (Aman 2013).

Two additional important points need to be emphasized. First, the increasing pressure on surface water and aquifers among the sovereign nations of the region has introduced into foreign policies and interstate bargaining a range of issues that have traditionally been seen as domestic and none of the business of one's neighbors. For example, the on-field efficiency of water use in a given agricultural sector may be scrutinized by neighbors who contest the status quo or the "real" needs for water of a state with which they share a river or aquifer. Even the selection of crops with different crop-water needs may appear on the international bargaining agenda.

Second, the reluctance of sovereign states to put their claims to water at risk by integrating storage and delivery infrastructure across international boundaries may stymie any future attempts to create regional water markets. The only way in which quantities of water could be transferred among riparians in an international basin is through dams, reservoirs, pumping stations, irrigation grids, and pipelines running across boundaries. Narrow concerns for national and food security may prevent such integration even at the cost of suboptimal solutions such as overexploitation of limited national water resources or investment in costly desalination technologies (see Box 6.7).

BOX 6.7. Was the Aswan High Dam Worth It?

Egypt's agriculture had been dependent on the Nile flood for millennia, but the country's irrigation system underwent a fundamental transformation in the nineteenth century with the transition to year-round irrigation, a transformation that concluded in the 1960s with the completion of the Aswan High Dam.

There are certain inescapable facts about Egyptian irrigation development.

1. Summer irrigation made possible the production of cotton on a substantial scale and was thus an important part of Egypt's integration into the international economy during the nineteenth century.
2. Year-round, dependable irrigation makes it possible for Egyptian yields to be among the highest in the world; for example, the Aswan High Dam allowed maize (until very recently the main rural foodstuff) yields to increase by over 70 percent.
3. The expansion of irrigation not only redistributed land, especially in the nineteenth century, but also increased the role of the state in the countryside.
4. Political forces have determined the pattern and timing of irrigation investment, with the result that the technological externalities that often accompany irrigation development were ignored and neglected (Waterbury 1979; Richards 1982).

The debate on the merits of the high dam at Aswan has raged for at least thirty years. Although its problems were and are serious, the achievements of the dam are too often overlooked. First, there is no doubt that some form of "over-year storage" for Nile water was absolutely necessary to provide increased irrigation water to keep up with the country's expanding demand for food. Egypt's food security problem would have been much worse much earlier without the dam. When the annual Nile flood was unusually low in 1972, the

continues

CONCLUSIONS

For a few MENA countries, agricultural development may be a compelling approach to economic growth (see, for example, Adelman 1984; Mellor 1976). This strategy is most appropriate for poor countries and poor regions that have most of their population still in agriculture, that have no vast mineral resources, and that have little prospect of penetrating foreign markets for manufactured goods. This is especially the case for poorer countries like Sudan and South Sudan (which remain water-rich), rural Morocco, and Yemen (which, however, is starting to experience acute water scarcity). Agriculture is the most labor-intensive of any industry; increasing output per unit of land also raises the demand for agricultural laborers,

---

BOX 6.7. *continued*

country's agriculture suffered relatively little—thanks to the dam. The devastating droughts that ravaged Ethiopia and Sudan in the early 1980s would have severely affected Egypt as well had it not been for the dam. Even with the dam, disaster has been narrowly averted; the level of Lake Nasser was only 147 meters in August 1988 (at 145 meters, the turbines of the dam would have had to be shut down). Second, there was really no alternative to the dam; all other technically feasible approaches faced insuperable political obstacles. It is hardly surprising, given the need and given the alternatives, that the Aswan High Dam was constructed.

The technological externalities, however, were severe. Some of these were unique to the dam: problems of shoreline erosion (because all silt was trapped behind the dam), decline in fish catches in lakes and in the Mediterranean, scouring of the Nile banks, and high evaporation losses of the water stored in Lake Nasser. The most serious problems, however, were really not qualitatively different from problems that had repeatedly plagued the extension of year-round (i.e., summer) irrigation in Egypt for more than half a century: inadequate drainage and disease. The incidence of schistosomiasis and ancylostomiasis in Egypt is very ancient but was certainly exacerbated by earlier (khedivial and British) irrigation works just as it was by the Aswan High Dam.

From the point of view of agricultural production, however, the main problem with irrigation expansion has always been the neglect of drainage. The ecological consequences of such neglect are straightforward: all water contains soluble salts and minerals, and even if farmers use water with maximum efficiency, inadequate drainage permits these salts to accumulate, dramatically lowering soil fertility. By the late 1970s, this problem afflicted some two-thirds of Egypt's cropland. While massive investments into improved drainage systems funded by the World Bank have since largely alleviated the problem, this remains an ongoing concern.

usually the poorest people in any country. Furthermore, farmers spend a high proportion of their increased incomes on labor-intensive domestic manufactured goods such as housing, furniture, and bicycles. In turn, agricultural productivity growth, which augments farmers' incomes, raises the demand for industrial labor. Increases in agricultural output can be obtained at a relatively low cost. Finally, activities that improve agricultural infrastructure (roads, irrigation and drainage systems) are also typically very labor-intensive. This strategy takes advantage of the agricultural production function and farmers' tastes to create "virtuous circles" of increased food production, improved health, steadily growing labor absorption, and relatively equitably rising incomes.

But the future of the MENA region lies largely in non-agricultural development. There is simply not enough water available for countries to become self-sufficient in food, even if they are willing to bear the (considerable) costs of such an economically inefficient strategy. They will increasingly have to export in order to eat, to reform and revamp their water allocation mechanisms, and to find new, often unpalatable ways of cooperating with their neighbors. Nonetheless, some of their exports may well be high-value agricultural products for niche markets. Policies in support of such value-added exports have led Egypt to become the fourth-largest exporter of strawberries in the world. Such shifts, in turn, will require a rather dramatic change in the role of the state in the economy.

Policymakers now generally acknowledge that achieving food security by combining export promotion with food imports is the most viable strategy for most MENA countries. Export-oriented production is necessary to buy the food in order to save the water, as well as to provide the jobs needed for the rapidly growing labor force (see Chapter 4). Middle Eastern political economies will have to emulate other economically successful but agriculturally resource-poor nations to achieve food security in the years ahead. Unfortunately, the spectacle of harsh US-led sanctions against Iraq, as well as US trade sanctions against Iran and Libya until 2005, raised the perceived risk of the trade option for food security.[13] Furthermore, the implementation of credible economic reforms faces formidable political obstacles (see Chapter 8). Nevertheless, because of policy and, still more, physical constraints on increased food production, the countries of the region will increasingly have to export in order to eat.

At the same time, as water becomes increasingly scarce, all governments will have little choice but to devise mechanisms for choosing which consumers do *not* get all the water they want. Whether this is done by administrative edict, by differential taxing of land planted in water-using crops, by volumetric pricing of water, or by tradable water rights, *some* mechanism for rationing scarce water resources will have to be found. The course of these changes will be central to the region's political economy in the decades ahead.

NOTES

1. It is important to note that the UNICEF/WHO Joint Monitoring Program statistics for "improved water sources" do not fully capture all aspects of water quality, as

argued in Shaheed et al. (2014). A World Bank (2007b) study, for example, points to the high rates of illness and death from diarrhea as evidence of extremely poor water quality across the Arab world, save Libya and the countries of the Gulf Cooperation Council (GCC).

2. Food imports are, among other things, imports of water (see, for example, Allan 2001).

3. In 1970 a barrel of oil would buy roughly one bushel of wheat; by 1980 the same barrel would purchase six bushels, and even in May 1986 a barrel of oil priced at US$14 would buy over three bushels. At the post-1973 nadir of oil prices in December 1998, a barrel would still buy 2.7 bushels. By early 2006, a barrel would buy *over thirteen bushels* of wheat.

4. Such concerns finally led the government to raise wheat prices to farmers, with dramatic results (see Box 6.4).

5. As usual, there are questions about the accuracy of the data. Different sources often conflict; for example, FAO and World Bank data often differ from data from the Arab Organization for Agricultural Development (AOAD). Studies in Egypt have shown significant differences between data from national sources and data extrapolated from sample interviews with farmers (Kherallah, Minot, and Gruhn 2003).

6. The shah's land reform provoked Ruhollah Khomeini to attack the policies so vociferously that he was forced into exile in Iraq, thus beginning the long saga that culminated in the revolution of 1978–1979.

7. For a portrait of rural social life in Egypt in the 1970s, see Yusuf al-Qa'id's *War in the Land of Egypt*, which was first published in Arabic in 1978.

8. Sectoral policies (such as price supports) transferred *into* agriculture a nominal sum equal to 1.3 percent of GDP, but when the impact of exchange rate overvaluation is included, 3.8 percent of GDP was transferred *out of* agriculture between 1961 and 1985 (Hansen 1991).

9. However, this is not true for all users. Urbanites who buy drinking water from water vendors typically pay the full cost of water provision, while farmers who pump groundwater pay both the capital and the operation and maintenance costs of such services—unless fuel is subsidized. The current situation, in which some users pay the full costs while others pay nearly nothing, is both inefficient and inequitable.

10. By 1997, agriculture accounted for only 2 percent of Israel's GDP, compared with 17 percent for industry and 81 percent for services (CIA 2000).

11. That is, only Syria charges farmers part of the long-run marginal cost of water—the cost of supplying an additional unit of water (in this case, the cost of extending irrigation networks), which water economists regard as the efficient price. In Syria, the World Bank estimates, perhaps 40 percent of the capital costs are covered by charges to farmers.

12. On the conditions under which the privatization of water can be effective, see Post (2014).

13. As argued by a Muslim Brotherhood delegate in Jordan's parliament in February 1994.

7

THE RISE AND FALL OF
STATE-LED DEVELOPMENT

Our concern in this chapter is to document the prodigious growth in the economic functions of the Middle Eastern state up to the 1980s, look into the economic contradictions that emerged and weakened state-led development, and analyze the political forces that created resistance to reforms up until the late 1980s, when they became inevitable in most of the region.

Middle Eastern states were big until the structural adjustment policies of the 1980s and 1990s started chipping away at the dominance of the public sector. They employed large numbers of people as civil servants, laborers, and managers. These states monopolized resources; they controlled large investment budgets, strategic parts of the banking system, virtually all subsoil minerals, and basic infrastructure like roads, railroads, power, and ports. Whether size and resources translated into strength is a question to be examined on a case-by-case basis. Certainly the potential for strong states was there, especially when resources were coupled with control by the military. There is, unsurprisingly, abundant contrary evidence that size spawned red tape and administrative paralysis, that resources were diverted into corruption and patronage, and that authoritarian leaders could not easily discipline administrative agencies in order to improve their performance.

Though attenuated after years of economic stagnation and reforms, the legitimacy of an interventionist state has long been widely accepted in the Middle East. Not that most Middle Easterners accept the legitimacy of the particular state under which they live—they frequently do not. Rather, it has been conceded in the abstract that the state and its leaders have a right and an obligation to set a course for society and to use public resources to pursue that course. Therefore, to some extent, there has been an acceptance of a high concentration of power—economic, administrative, and military. It can be argued that in Muslim society political authority is legitimate only insofar as it promotes the interests of the community of believers, the *Umma*. This yields an organic image of society, a living community whose "health" the state must maintain.

Religious and cultural antecedents notwithstanding, it is our conviction that it is more the politics of decolonization and development than cultural norms that accounts for the interventionist, organic state in the Middle East. The caretaker states of the colonial era, concerned with law, order, and taxation, logically evoked the opposite—states that impinge upon all aspects of their citizens' lives. Moreover, the postcolonial state has seen as its duty the reparation of all the economic damage resulting from colonial policies. It has had to mobilize human and material resources on an unprecedented scale. The goal has been to overcome "backwardness" and build a prosperous, educated citizenry, a diversified economy, and national power. These tasks and goals are culture-blind. Hence, we find basic similarities in the goal orientation and interventionism of states in societies as widely varied in cultural origins as Indonesia, India, Brazil, and Ghana.

THE STATE AS ARCHITECT OF STRUCTURAL TRANSFORMATION

In the postcolonial era, the leaders of Middle Eastern states saw themselves as engineers and architects, in charge of designing new societies. Ideologies varied, but not the perceived need for state intervention.[1] The point of departure for the state was backwardness—a condition imposed on the region by imperial powers, it was alleged, and characterized by three major components: (1) an economy mired in the production of cheap agricultural commodities requiring an unskilled workforce; (2) the perpetuation of this system of production by denying education and the acquisition of modern skills to all but a privileged few; and (3) the forcible integration of this backward agrarian economy into an international division of labor. To remedy backwardness required a supreme effort, a kind of military campaign on three fronts. Only the state could coordinate the campaign and mobilize the inherently scarce resources needed to carry it out.

The area had an inadequately educated, poor population and an agricultural system characterized by small pockets of high productivity in a landscape of low yields and by the inefficient use of scarce capital. However ironic it may seem in retrospect, the leaders of the state saw the need for intervention in order to avoid wasting scarce resources. The comprehensive and rational planning effort anticipated required an inventory of available resources, a strategy for their development and utilization over time, and, in light of the profound structural changes that would take place in the economy and society as the plan unfolded, the construction of the economic levers needed to implement the plan.

Throughout the region it was assumed that the private sector could not be relied upon to undertake this kind of resource mobilization and planning. The least critical saw the private sector as too weak financially, too close to a commercial and trading past rather than an industrial one, and too concerned with short-term profit to be the agent of structural transformation. More severe critics emphasized the greed and exploitativeness of the private sector, its links to interests in the metropole, and its tendency to export capital rather than reinvest profit. Private sectors might be tolerated, but nowhere, save in Lebanon, did they enjoy legitimacy. Reliance on private entrepreneurs and on the law of supply and demand to allocate scarce resources would be wasteful, it was believed, and would not extricate the economy from its trap.

As important as efficiency for the state leaders was equity. Gross inequalities in the distribution of assets in Middle Eastern societies, not to mention absolute poverty for large segments of the population, were associated with the colonial system of exploitation. A more equitable distribution of assets within society became a universal goal throughout the area—again, regardless of ideology. Some states pursued redistribution with greater conviction than others, but all espoused it as an ideal.

Powerful interventionist states with large public sectors and the groups that dominate them grew out of the need to promote the structural transformation of their "backward" economies and a kind of class vacuum in which a temporarily dominant class emerged on the strength of its education and competency rather than its property. The process of state intervention has contributed directly to the demise of some classes (large landowners, traditional trading bourgeoisies, craftspeople) and promoted others (capitalist farmers, bureaucratic middle classes, a small-scale manufacturing bourgeoisie).

State interventionism in the Middle East was driven by two different motivators and strategies, both aiming at structural transformation of the economy. The two processes of accumulation are not mutually exclusive and may, in fact, fluctuate over time. With the first, the state nurtures and strengthens the private sector, in several ways. The state provides roads, railroads, ports, and electrical power to stimulate economic activity in general. It provides raw materials (coal, oil) and semimanufactured goods (iron, aluminum, chemicals, synthetic fibers) through its basic industries and mines, which feed directly into private production. It provides cheap credit and protective legislation. The state may also take over failing private enterprises. In this process of accumulation, the state transfers surpluses on its own operations, profits if any, and external rents to the private sector and tries to absorb all major risks for that sector.

This has been the predominant process of accumulation in the Middle East, although it is important to remember that it is frequently interrupted and that within the state sector itself there are always powerful lobbies that decry the handmaiden role. It is also worth noting that the state, when it gains access to an increased volume of external rents, has used those rents to expand its own activities with little regard to the private sector, as Iran and Morocco did after 1973–1974 and as Tunisia did after its oil revenues shot up in 1977. Structural crises may also provoke episodes in which the state sector mobilizes resources by and for itself, as did Egypt and Syria in the 1960s. By and large, however, we see the handmaiden process at work in Turkey since 1950, in Egypt since 1974, in Tunisia since 1969, in Morocco since 1956, in Iran since 1963, and in Sudan since 1972. Israel also fits somewhat awkwardly into this schema. Leftist critics of the Ba'athi experiments in Syria and Iraq are wont to attribute the same role to state intervention in their economies (see, for example, al-Khafaji 1983; Longuenesse 1979), but our view is that in both countries there were dominant coalitions committed to state power and, to some extent, to a socialist vision of society such that the private sector was encouraged only insofar as it remained subordinate to the state, the party, and the plan.

The second process of accumulation is one in which the state undertakes all the resource mobilization and infrastructure development functions already mentioned, but captures the surplus of its own activities, a substantial portion of private-sector profits, and external rents in order to finance its own expansion. Its goal is to dominate all aspects of resource allocation and to seize, once and for all, the commanding heights of the economy. The term "socialist transformation" has generally been used to describe this process. Turkey flirted with this strategy in the 1930s. Egypt explicitly adopted it with the Socialist Decrees of 1961 and then gradually dropped it after 1974. Algeria has described itself in those terms since 1962, although after Boumediene's death in 1978 the regime became more attentive to private-sector interests. Between 1964 and 1969, Tunisia adopted and then abandoned the strategy. Syria has adhered to it since 1963, as did Iraq until 2003. Finally, it may be that Libya, since 1975, has gone further than any country in the region, outside the Marxist regime in the former People's Democratic Republic of Yemen (PDRY), in strangling the private sector.

Initial calls for reform in such systems are concerned with making the public sector more efficient, reducing the deficits of specific enterprises, increasing monetary incentives for workers, allowing price increases, linking budgetary support and banking credit to performance, and perhaps even reducing the personnel list. The shift here is toward state capitalism. That shift began in Egypt in 1965, when Nasser first denounced the inefficient performance of the public sector; it began in Algeria sometime between 1967 and 1969. Discipline, productivity, and profitability become the watchwords of the new era, but frequently they remain slogans more than effective guides to improved performance.

Whether driven by socialism or the handmaiden motive, the Middle Eastern state took upon itself the challenge of moving the economy onto an industrial footing, shifting population to the urban areas, educating and training its youth wherever they lived, raising agricultural productivity to feed the non-agricultural population, redistributing wealth, building a credible military force, and doing battle with the international trade and financial regimes that held it in thrall. These were goals widely held if poorly understood by the citizens at large. There were no impediments, then, to the expansion and affirmation of the interventionist state.

ATATÜRK AND THE TURKISH PARADIGM

The Republic of Turkey has been an example, if not a model, for many of the other states in the Middle East. Because it achieved real independence in 1923 after successful military action against European forces (Italian, French, and Greek) that were bent on dismembering all that remained of the Ottoman Empire, Turkey showed what could be done to thwart imperialism. It possessed an inspiring leader, Mustafa Kemal Atatürk, "Father of the Turks," who built a secular, republican, nationalist system in Anatolia. His sweeping reforms, from the abolition of the caliphate to the introduction of the Latin alphabet, have been too well studied to require treatment here (see, inter alia, Lewis 1961). For our purposes, it is important that by the late 1930s Turkey was endowed with a credible military structure, the beginnings of a diversified industrial sector, and a rapidly expanding educational system.

Atatürk's contemporaries, including Reza Khan of Iran, who was to found the Pahlavi dynasty, looked on with varying degrees of admiration.[2] So, too, did the Arab nationalist politicians, such as Habib Bourguiba of Tunisia, who would lead their countries to independence. There were also students and young army officers in the turbulent 1930s who learned from the Turkish experience lessons that they would come to apply in the 1940s, 1950s, and 1960s.

In April 1931, Atatürk issued a manifesto that contained the principles of etatism (a term taken from the French that means "statism" and that retains a strong Bonapartist flavor), populism, and revolution, which would be later embodied in the 1937 Constitution of the Republic. Etatism provided legitimation for a strongly interventionist state. Populism meant that the masses were the object of political and economic policy and that distributive issues were at the top of the policy agenda. The revolution lay in Turkey's rejection of empire along with the sultanate and caliphate, its militant republicanism, and its confrontation with the imperial powers of Europe. Within a few years of the enunciation of these principles, Turkey, led by the Republican People's Party (RPP), embarked on an economic experiment that was to be emulated in several countries following World War II.

Turkey's trajectory toward this experiment was erratic, and there is no question that the world depression in the 1930s forced it to revise profoundly the strategy that had prevailed in the 1920s. It is important to review these antecedents. First, Turkey was in a shambles after World War I. The empire itself had been destroyed, and the Arab portions had fallen under French or British control. The basically agricultural economy had been badly damaged, especially in the fighting against the Italians, French, and Greeks. Then, after the signing of the Treaty of Lausanne in 1923 between Turkey and the major war victors, an enormous exchange of population took place. By 1926, perhaps 1.3 million Greeks had left Anatolia, taking with them vital skills in commerce and trades. In their place came 400,000 Turks, mainly peasants from Thrace, whom the rural areas could absorb only with difficulty.

Atatürk was determined from the outset to promote Turkey's industrialization and to liberate its economy from dependence on the West. In contrast to what was to transpire after 1931, the republic's early strategy was to rely on private-sector initiative and to avoid taxing the peasantry in order to finance industrial growth. With the founding of the İç (Business) Bank in 1924 to finance private enterprise, the state showed its willingness to foster the growth of an indigenous capitalist class (Ahmad 1981; Boratav 1981).

In 1934 Turkey embarked on its First Five-Year Plan, which was a blueprint for import substitution industrialization (ISI), emphasizing local industry. A major part of the program lay in developing the textile industry, utilizing Turkish cotton, and selling to a large domestic market. This kind of thrust is often associated with the so-called easy phase of ISI. Other industries of a similar nature are food processing, sugar refining, and simple assembly. But Turkey went further, launching projects in basic chemicals, cement, iron, and paper. Atatürk headed a coalition of interests and ideological perspectives within his government and party. Left-of-center figures who had been behind the scenes during the 1920s were now given much more prominence. There was much more talk of the "Kemalist Revolution," and the private-sector strategy of the earlier years was abandoned. Rather than the state acting as handmaiden of a growing private sector, the state would now seize the "commanding heights" of the economy and bend the private sector to its will.

Even prior to the First Five-Year Plan, the Turkish state owned several enterprises; the plan added some twenty new enterprises to the public patrimony. The State Office for Industry was set up to enforce price and wage controls. In 1933 the Sümer Bank was created to supervise state-owned enterprises, plan new projects, and invest in other projects coming under the plan. By 1939 Sümer Bank's holdings accounted for 100 percent of production in artificial silk, paper, cardboard, iron, and superphosphates, 90 percent of shoes, 80 percent of steel and lubricants, 70 percent of coke, 62 percent of leather, 60 percent of wool, and 55 percent of cement (Hershlag 1968, 92). The İç Bank went well beyond private-sector financing to invest in a number of joint ventures. The Eti Bank was set up in 1935 to finance mineral exploration, extraction, and marketing. In this way the state in the 1930s had the financial leverage to orient all economic actors in accordance with plan priorities.

The Second Five-Year Plan was adopted in 1938, just before Atatürk's death. Over one hundred new enterprises were planned, and the first efforts at "industrial deepening" were formulated. The Zonguldak-Karabük region was slated to become a pole of heavy industrial growth, built around coal, steel, and cement and serviced by its own Black Sea port. A major effort was to be made in power generation, basic chemicals, engineering, and marine transport. Part of the plan was to disperse industry in order to benefit backward areas, especially eastern Anatolia.

Some of the seemingly inevitable side effects of this sort of big-push strategy began to make themselves felt during the 1930s. The government ran a growing deficit that was due in large part to an outsized bureaucracy—the civil service reached 184,000 in 1945 (Karpat 1959, 129). About 35 percent of the budget went into their salaries. But the level of investment was modest by postwar standards; the government was investing annually about 5 percent of national income, with another 5 percent coming from the private sector.

World War II interrupted the Second Five-Year Plan, and a period of severe privation ensued. Import substitution continued out of necessity, as Mediterranean shipping was disrupted during the hostilities. A major shift in the political domain occurred after the war, leading to a two-party system and the victory of the Democrat Party. Led by Adnan Menderes and Celâl Bayar, the Democrat Party rejected etatism in favor of a liberal economic policy to benefit commercial farmers and the industrial bourgeoisie. Nonetheless, during the 1950s eleven new state-owned enterprises were started, the initial objective of selling off some public enterprises was abandoned, and the share of public in total investment rose from 38 percent in 1952 to 62 percent in 1959 (Roos and Roos 1971, 43).

The brief military takeover in 1960 ushered in another period of national planning and state-led ISI. This thrust was modified in the 1968–1972 Five-Year Plan to put a greater burden of investment on private industry. Subsequently, the Republican People's Party, under Bülent Ecevit, resurrected the statist strategy and stressed intermediate and capital goods industries with the 1973–1977 Five-Year Plan (Walstedt 1980, 85–87; Hale 1981, 198–200). By the end of the 1970s, the state sector remained the economy's center of gravity. Public investment in the manufacturing sector had risen from 34 percent in 1965 to 65 percent in 1980, and employment in state-owned enterprises had grown from 362,000 in 1970 to 646,000 in 1980, or the equivalent of 16 percent of the non-agricultural workforce. Overall government spending had risen from about 18 percent of GDP in the 1960s to 35 percent of GDP in the early 1980s.

REPLICATING THE PARADIGM

It would be an exaggeration to say that other states in the Middle East slavishly imitated the Turkish experience. In fact, state-led ISI spread throughout the developing world in the years after 1945 and, as a strategy, had a logic independent of any single country's efforts. We shall see that among Middle Eastern states, the tremendous growth in publicly owned assets and the development strategies associated with them had varying sources of inspiration, some external and some internal.

We are distinguishing here between public-sector enterprise and other governmental agencies that employ the bulk of the civil servants. Generally, public-sector enterprises have their own statutes, personnel policies, and salary and wage scales. They are companies in the legal sense that they make and sell products or deliver services for a fee. They enter the national marketplace directly and usually with great impact.

If we look at the developing world as a whole around 1980, we find impressive statistics on the weight of public sectors in their economies. On average, the output of public-sector enterprise, exclusive of financial institutions, accounted for 8.6 percent of GDP; these enterprises, on average, employed 47 percent of the manufacturing workforce in the organized sector, utilized 27 percent of all manufacturing investment, and ran deficits equivalent to 5.5 percent of GDP (World Bank 1995). State-owned manufacturing enterprises frequently accounted for 25 to 50 percent of value added in manufacturing. Some Middle Eastern states, especially Egypt, Algeria, and Syria, were well above these averages: Egyptian state-owned enterprises accounted for around 60 percent of value added in manufacturing and Syrian ones for 55 percent. The output of Algeria's and Egypt's state-owned enterprises reached 13 percent of GDP, while Syria's was close to 11 percent. In 1980 Turkey's state-owned enterprises were producing about 8 percent of GDP and accounted for 25 percent of value added in manufacturing.[3]

Parallel to the rise in their productive capacity, states also undertook the financing of health, education, and other social programs. A look at the level of state expenditure for the region as a whole and for the three subgroups (RRLP, RRLA, RPLA) shows the rise of state expenditures from 1960s to the mid-1980s (see Figure

2.8). Government expenditure shot up in the 1970s in all three groups of countries, on the back of rising oil wealth in the region, reaching 53 percent of GDP in the RRLP and RPLA countries and 43 percent of GDP in the RRLA countries.

Arab Socialism

One set of Arab states adopted the Turkish paradigm and went well beyond it. These states' strategies were explicitly socialist and populist, hostile to the indigenous private sector and to foreign capital, and aimed at far-reaching redistribution of wealth within their societies. The strategy has not always been sustained and on occasion has been officially abandoned (for example, Egypt after 1974, Tunisia after 1969, and Sudan after 1972). The principal experiments with the Turkish paradigm were Egypt from 1957 to 1974, Algeria from 1962 to 1989, Syria from 1963 to the present, Iraq from 1963 to 2003, Tunisia from 1962 to 1969, Sudan from 1969 to 1972, and Libya from 1969 to the present. What all these had in common was a blueprint for the radical transformation of their societies and economies. In these states, the campaign for growth, equity, and national economic sovereignty was no mere metaphor. Indeed, Habib Bourguiba of Tunisia likened his country's quest for development to a *jihad* and said that Tunisians should be dispensed of the obligation to fast during the month of Ramadan just as if they were warriors.

A number of basic assumptions underlay these experiments. The first was that profit and loss should not be the primary criterion for assessing public-sector performance. Rather, the creation of jobs, the provision of cheap goods of first necessity, the introduction of new economic activity to remote or poor regions, and the achievement of self-sufficiency in goods of a strategic or military nature were more appropriate tests of success. Second, it was assumed that the operation of supply and demand was inferior to planning and the application of administered prices. Third, the large-scale private sector was seen as untrustworthy. Most of the regimes nationalized the private sector or sharply curtailed its activities. Entire "strategic" sectors, such as basic metals, chemicals, and minerals, became reserved exclusively for public-sector enterprise. Finally, foreign investment was viewed with suspicion. The favored form of collaboration with foreign capital was through turnkey projects and management contracts in which foreign investors acquired no equity in the host country. Socialist Algeria, in the 1970s, was able to do billions of dollars' worth of business with the United States, France, Japan, and other countries through such formulas.

The setting up of closed sectors for public-sector enterprise underscores another assumption: that there is nothing inherently inefficient about monopolies. State-owned enterprises often enjoyed monopolies in entire lines of production or were the sole purchasers (monopsonists) of certain inputs (raw cotton or sugar beets). Egypt, after 1961, took matters further, putting the entire banking, insurance, and foreign-trade sectors under public ownership. For all this to succeed in promoting overall growth, industrialization, and a more equal distribution of income, the planners needed to anticipate accurately the complex interaction of all the economic variables, the managers needed to pursue efficiency even while protected by tariffs and monopoly status, and the civil servants needed to put in an honest day's work. By and large none of those requirements were met.

Egypt

Egypt was the first Middle Eastern country in the postwar era to adopt a strategy of radical transformation. In many ways it was far more integrated into the world economy than Turkey since Muhammad Ali's big push in the 1860s, financed by an expansion in cotton production when international cotton boomed as a result of the US Civil War. It had been one of the leading exporters of raw cotton for nearly a century. The British occupation after 1881, the economic dependency on Britain that ensued, and the role of the Suez Canal in world trade made Egypt's a classic colonial economy. As in Turkey, the world depression and World War II set Egypt on the path toward ISI. It was the Egyptian private sector, partly indigenous and partly foreign, that led this effort.

In 1952 the Egyptian monarchy was overthrown by a military coup led by Colonel Gamal Abdel Nasser and a group of his colleagues known as the Free Officers. From 1952 to 1956, Egypt promoted public-sector growth but did so, as Turkey had done in the 1920s, either to help the private sector or to undertake projects that the private sector could not finance or manage. The old Aswan Dam was electrified to augment Egypt's power supply, and it was decided to promote a new giant dam at Aswan to increase hydropower generation several-fold and to ensure a predictable supply of irrigation water to the agricultural sector. Work was begun on an iron-and-steel complex at Helwan and on a large fertilizer plant at Aswan. That year also saw the initiation of land reform to redistribute large estates to small farmers.

It was not until the Suez War of November 1956 that the public sector grew at the expense of the private. Because of the participation of Britain and France, along with Israel, in a direct attack on Egypt, all assets owned by the former two in Egypt were taken over by the Egyptian government. The attack itself had been provoked by Egypt's nationalization in July 1956 of the Suez Canal Company. With the war-time sequestrations of banks, trading companies, insurance companies, utilities, and some manufacturing enterprises, the Egyptian state found itself in possession of a very substantial patrimony. It was only then that the term "socialism" was intimated and that left-of-center voices in Nasser's coalition gained greater prominence. In 1957 Egypt contracted its first loan for economic assistance from the Soviet Union, followed in 1958 by a Soviet loan to help build the Aswan Dam. In 1957 Egypt began its first five-year industrial plan, with strong emphasis on state enterprise. By 1960 it considered itself ready for a five-year plan for the entire economy.

After 1956, there was some evidence of private-sector disinvestment and profit-taking and of growing suspicion between the private sector and the regime. The privately held Misr Group and Bank Misr had been essentially taken over by the state by 1960. The new Ministry of Industry was empowered to license and regulate all private industrial activity. The elaboration of the First Five-Year Plan was carried out without consulting the private sector, although the latter was called on to mobilize about 55 percent of all investment over the five-year period.

The failure of the private sector to do so allegedly provoked a wave of nationalizations through the Socialist Decrees of 1961. In one fell swoop, the Egyptian state took over most large-scale industry, all banking, insurance, and foreign trade, all utilities, marine transport, and airlines, and many hotels and department stores. The bulk of agricultural property remained in private hands, but new desert reclamation projects were owned by the state.

The First Five-Year Plan embodied a straightforward ISI strategy, combining aspects of the easy (textiles, sugar, automobile assembly, pharmaceuticals) and hard (heavy engineering, steel, chemicals, fertilizers). It generated 1 million new jobs and growth rates of 6 percent per annum. Yet in 1965 it ended in crisis. The Achilles' heel of ISI, whether under public or private auspices, is the economy's ability to earn foreign exchange. For the major oil exporters that at one time or another pursued an ISI strategy (Iran, Algeria, Iraq), this was not a major problem, but for Turkey, Egypt, and Syria it certainly was. Egypt's new industries were designed to market their products in Egypt. They did not have the economies of scale and basic operating efficiency required to export to other markets. Thus, although they needed to import capital goods and raw materials to function, they could not generate the foreign exchange to pay for them.

To finance its Second Five-Year Plan, Egypt had little choice but to try to borrow more heavily abroad. Egypt was not very successful in this endeavor, and even the Soviet Union was reluctant to extend new lines of credit. The Second Five-Year Plan, which, like Turkey's, would have led to industrial "deepening," had to be abandoned for want of adequate financing. Then came Egypt's disastrous defeat in the June War of 1967 and Israel's occupation of the Sinai Peninsula. Egypt lost its oil fields there, the Suez Canal was closed to traffic, and tourism was badly disrupted. Egypt went into severe recession. Its strategy for radical structural transformation through public-sector enterprise had to be revised.

President Nasser died in 1970, and his successor, Anwar Sadat, cautiously pursued a policy of economic liberalization aimed at reforming and streamlining the public sector, stimulating the private sector, attracting foreign investment, and promoting exports. Public-sector enterprise was subjected to sharp criticism for its chronic inefficiency and huge operating deficits. Although Egypt continued to produce five-year plans, they had clearly lost their mystique, and the notion of socialist transformation was downplayed.

Even though heavily criticized, Egypt's public sector continued to grow throughout the 1970s. Entering the 1980s, it included 391 companies, employed about 1.2 million workers with a wage bill of over 20 percent of GDP, and accounted for 22 percent of total value added in the economy. The return on its total investment was only 1.5 percent per annum. Counting the public authorities that ran everything from the Suez Canal to the Aswan High Dam, along with the civil service, the public and governmental sector in the early 1980s, before the structural adjustment effort began, had 3.2 million employees—more than 40 percent of the total workforce. Total public expenditures in 1980 represented 61 percent of GDP, total government revenues were 40 percent of GDP, and the public deficit was 20 percent of GDP—an extraordinarily large imbalance by international standards.

Algeria

Algeria is one of the few less developed countries (LDCs) to rival Egypt in terms of the weight and extent of its public sector. Independent Algeria emerged in 1962 out of seven years of revolutionary warfare against the French. Many of the leaders of the National Liberation Front (FLN) were committed socialists. The nature and intensity of their struggle made it inevitable that Algeria would confront France and the imperialist world in general. International business interests and the Algerian private sector itself were seen as likely enemies of Algeria's revolution (Leca 1975, 124). At no time did the state see its role as helpmate to the private sector as did Turkey during the 1920s or Egypt up to 1957.

From 1966 to 1989, the commanding heights of the economy were reserved to the state. Collaboration with foreign firms was extensive, but it was carried out on a contract basis involving turnkey projects, technical assistance, and purchase of technology. Direct investment was carefully avoided. Like all states in the region, Algeria was the exclusive owner of all subsoil minerals. French companies that had developed the country's petroleum and natural gas deposits were nationalized between 1969 and 1971, giving the state exclusive control over their production, refining, and marketing. The hydrocarbon sector, after the surge in world petroleum prices in 1973, came to represent over 30 percent of GDP.

In many ways Algeria could not have avoided heavy state intervention even if its official ideology had not been socialist. On the eve of independence, nearly all of the French settler community in the country, nearly 1 million strong, packed up and left. This was an exodus even more devastating than that of the Greeks from Turkey in 1922–1923. The French settlers had dominated modern farming, the skilled trades, the small industrial sector, and government services. Inheriting agricultural, industrial, and residential property, the state gave over the first two to "worker self-management" units. In the agricultural sector, over 2 million hectares were cultivated by about 130,000 permanent workers on 2,000 farms. The state owned the farms, but in theory the workers had full control over their operations. The same formula was applied to industrial units, which consisted of about 400 enterprises, with a workforce of 15,000.

In the early years, when Ahmed Ben Bella was president, the experiment in self-management was seen as putting power in the hands of the working people and constituting a barrier to the emergence of a dominating and domineering bureaucracy and technocracy. The period 1962–1965 was one of near-romantic populism and socialism, but already one could see government agencies arrogating basic decision-making power in all spheres of production. The FLN, which had seen many of its militants absorbed into the civil service, could do little to defend the populist experiment, and the workers themselves soon reverted to apathetic clock-punching.

The romantic period came to an end in June 1965 when the minister of defense, Houari Boumediene, overthrew Ben Bella and ushered in an era of "rational" top-down planned development that implicitly saw the masses as a source more of disruption than of revolutionary support. Worker self-management was paid lip service but deprived of any effective autonomy. With its First Four-Year Plan, 1969–1973, Algeria launched a program built on heavy industry. Oil and natural gas were to serve two ends: first, they would be the feedstock for a modern petrochemical sector producing fertilizers and plastics; second, the earnings from their export would pay for the import of plant and capital goods for steel manufacture and vehicle assembly. It was expected that the agricultural sector would be an expanding market for the new products (fertilizers, irrigation pipes, tractors). The local private sector was regarded as irrelevant to the effort, and foreign firms were seen mainly as providers of technology. The slogan was "Sow oil to reap industry."[4]

By the time Algeria initiated its Second Four-Year Plan, world petroleum prices had quadrupled. In contrast to Egypt, Algeria faced no financing problems in the mid-1970s, and the Algerian state was able to invest the equivalent of 25–30 percent of GDP annually. In that sense, its experience emphasizes some of the inherent weaknesses of state-led ISI, for by the late 1970s important elements of the strategy had been called into question. Rather than the agricultural sector's generating demand for new industrial products, there was a general decline in agricultural production, especially in the self-managed sector. Algeria became a major importer of food. Insufficient domestic demand meant that public-sector industries operated below capacity and at high cost. They had little hope of exporting except to some of their East European creditors. Finally, some of the imported technologies, for example, in natural gas liquefaction, were so sophisticated that costly units were frequently shut down for technical reasons.

Boumediene died in 1978. His successor, Chadli Bendjedid, a former liberation army commander, was elected president in 1979. During his tenure, which ended in 1991, Algeria's public sector was extensively overhauled. However, it still dominates the Algerian economy. In the late 1980s, there were some fifty public-sector companies and twenty authorities employing 80 percent of the industrial workforce and accounting for 77 percent of industrial production. Add to this 260,000 civil servants and 140,000 teachers and other employees of the educational system and one has 45 percent of the non-agricultural workforce on the public payroll. The collapse of international petroleum prices in 1984–1985 forced Algeria to question the very premises of the strategies it had followed since the mid-1960s.

Syria and Iraq

Beginning in 1953, Syria and Iraq fell under the domination of the same pan-Arab party, the Ba'ath, or Arab Renaissance Party. Since its founding in Syria after World War II, this party has called for Arab unity and socialism and has tried to propagate its message throughout the Arab world. The major obstacle to its spread was perceived by its leaders to be Nasser's Egypt, especially when that country entered its socialist phase after 1961. Many of the policies of state intervention implemented by the Ba'ath in Syria and Iraq sprang in part from its socialist ideology, but just as important were the fears of Ba'athi leaders that Egypt's socialist transformation would dazzle the radical youth of the Arab countries.

Both Syria and Iraq, in contrast to Algeria, had substantial indigenous trading and landowning bourgeoisies and no foreign settler communities (see, inter alia, Batatu 1978 and Khoury 1983). Prior to the Ba'aths coming to power, both countries pursued policies whereby the state helped the private sector through the development of infrastructure and banking credit. Neither country had made significant advances in industrial production, although Iraq enjoyed the revenues from a sizable oil sector.

In the 1950s, under the Iraqi monarchy, oil revenues gave the state tremendous leverage in the economy. Most of these revenues were invested in infrastructure to boost agriculture. It was this policy that required deferred consumption and contributed to a situation in which elements of the Iraqi armed forces overthrew the monarchy in July 1958. Almost immediately the new regime, led by Abd al-Karim Qasim, operated a major shift in investment toward industry. The newly created Ministry of Industry was empowered to promote public-sector projects and to supervise and license private-sector activities (Penrose and Penrose 1978, 253).

The new regime, however, was not Ba'athist. Qasim was merely a nationalist army officer with leftist leanings. He tried, unsuccessfully, to balance Nasserist, Communist, and Ba'athist forces within his coalition, contend with Kurdish dissidence, and implement far-reaching agrarian reform. All the contenders battled for the hearts and minds of the officers' corps, and in February 1963 a group of Ba'athi officers overthrew and killed Qasim and set up a government presided over by Colonel Abdul Salam Arif. This new regime moved in early 1964 to nationalize all banks, along with thirty-two large industrial and commercial firms. With these moves, the state's share in large manufacturing concerns rose to 62 percent of gross output and 46 percent of employment. Once more the state had captured the commanding heights (Batatu 1978, 1031; al-Khafaji 1983). It was not, however, until 1972–1975 that full nationalization of the petroleum sector took place, under the leadership of the Ba'ath Party, which took over through a military coup in 1968.

The nationalization coincided with the first big increase in world petroleum prices. With the oil sector under state ownership, the state's share in GDP rose to 75 percent in 1978, although if the petroleum sector is excluded, the state's share was a more modest 23 percent. By 1977, there were some 400 public-sector enterprises, employing 80,000 workers. They absorbed over 60 percent of all industrial and commercial investment (Stork 1982, 36; al-Khafaji 1983, 36). Total government employment in 1977 reached 410,000, or nearly half of Iraq's organized workforce. Adding to this 250,000 members of the armed forces (a figure that rose to over 1 million in the 1980s), 175,000 in the Ba'ath militias, 260,000 in the police, 120,000 pensioners, and thousands of schoolteachers, we find that by 1980 one in four Iraqis was on the state payroll (Batatu 1978, 123). Saddam Hussein, who took over in 1982, organized the public sector in a far more sinister aspect. Not only was it heavy with police and intelligence personnel, but it is estimated that it came to employ about one-quarter of the workforce as part-time paid informants (al-Khalil 1989, 38).

Iraq faced continuous disaster in the following decades owing to several major conflicts—the Iran-Iraq War, the Kuwait invasion, and then the First Gulf War. The Iran-Iraq War between 1980 and 1988 deeply affected the Iraqi economy as up to 21 percent of the labor force was drafted into the army and military expenditures came to consume as much as 60 percent of GDP in 1986. Oil production was deeply reduced as a result of the destruction of oil-exporting facilities in the south of the country. Abbas Alnasrawi (1986) has estimated that the loss of production and oil revenue, plus the costs of reconstructing lost infrastructure, amounted to more than $400 billion, which represents more than 100 percent of GDP for every year of the war. Iraq emerged from the war in 1988 with a GDP per capita lower than in 1975 and with external debts of $86 billion—when it started the war, it had reserves of about $50 billion.

With no prospects for recovery, Saddam decided to invade Kuwait with the hope of expanding oil production and becoming more influential in dictating high oil prices. The cost of the Kuwait adventure turned out to be equally disastrous. The loss of production during the long embargo imposed following UN Security Council Resolution 661 in 1990 led to incalculable human suffering and death, refugees, and a sharp deterioration in health conditions that increased death rates among infants and children. After 1991, when GDP per capita stood at $546—comparable to levels it had reached in the 1960s (Alnasrawi 1992)—Iraq had to institute food rationing until 2000. Then the Anglo-American invasion of Iraq in 2003 destroyed $20 billion in assets, by some estimates. When all losses related to the three wars are added, the total reaches nearly $1 trillion—thirty times Iraq's GDP in 2001 (Rivlin 2009).

Between 1958 and 1961, Syria had been a member, along with Egypt and North Yemen, of the United Arab Republic (UAR). In those three years, under Egyptian pressure, land reform measures were undertaken as well as some steps toward expanding public-sector enterprise. Egypt's Socialist Decrees of 1961 alarmed the Syrian private sector, which feared that the decrees would be applied in Syria. In league with sympathetic army officers, these elements brought off a coup d'état that took Syria out of the UAR and installed a somewhat conservative, pro-private-sector military regime in Damascus.

In March 1963, a month after the Ba'ath had come to power in Iraq, yet another military coup brought the Ba'ath to power in Syria. A year later, in May 1964, the regime took over the country's banks, and in the wake of private-sector protests in Hama, seven enterprises of "reactionary capitalists" were nationalized. Then, in January 1965, the regime undertook far-reaching nationalizations, and the public-sector share in industrial production rose from 25 percent to 75 percent. Part of the motive was to demonstrate to organized labor that Syria's socialist experiment was as radical and devoted to workers' welfare as Egypt's (see Chatelus 1982; Hannoyer and Seurat 1979; Longuenesse 1985). In fact, Syria structured its public sector exactly on the Egyptian model, using general organizations to supervise production in specific sectors such as textiles, chemicals, and metals.

A more radical wing of the Ba'ath seized power in 1966, but its militancy was manifested mainly in confronting Israel and sponsoring Palestinian guerrilla attacks. This faction's image was battered in the June War of 1967, and in 1970, after an internal trial of strength, Hafez al-Assad, the minister of defense and commander of the air force, took power. The shift to some extent resembled that from

Ben Bella to Boumediene. Hafez al-Assad was an organization man, mistrustful of the masses and of revolutionary adventures. He relied on the large power structures of the country—the armed forces, the bureaucracy, the Ba'ath Party, and the public sector, perhaps in that order—to control, preempt, and police rather than mobilize.

Between 1970 and 1982, the largely politicized public sector rose in importance. Employment in public-sector enterprises rose from 57,000 to 119,000, or half the industrial workforce. In just two years the public-sector wage bill doubled, from 3.5 percent to 6 percent of GDP. In 1979 Syria's total workforce was about 2.1 million, of which about one-third were engaged in agriculture. Combined public-sector and civil-service employment probably totaled 350,000. There may have been 230,000 Syrians in uniform and perhaps 200,000 members of the Ba'ath Party, although these two categories may have overlapped to some extent (Drysdale 1982, 5–7). Some 220,000 workers, in both the public and private sectors, were unionized and under Ba'athi supervision. Again, as we have found in all the preceding experiments, the state not only owned the major means of production but controlled through the payroll, the party, and the armed forces the most strategically situated elements of the workforce.

This dominance in Syria and elsewhere was achieved at the expense of economic efficiency. The strategic sectors became used to their privileges and to low levels of performance. In 1985 the state was responsible for over 60 percent of total investment, mainly through money-losing public enterprises that received subsidies from the state budget, even as they benefited from monopoly power. The manufacturing sector remained one of the smallest in the Arab world, producing about 6 percent of GDP in the late 1980s. The Syrian economy operated until the late 1990s in large part as an autarchic economy, isolated from the rest of the world.

In the mid-1980s, the volume of remittances and Arab aid fell dramatically, bad harvests had a severe impact on the economy, and growth rates fell sharply. The state had to adjust to its new budget constraint, but little was changed on the structural side, since it hesitated to alienate its main constituencies by asking more of them or paying them less. This held true especially for the military: in the late 1980s, Syrian defense outlays were cut but remained above 10 percent of GNP (down from over 30 percent in the late 1970s), placing it among ten nations worldwide to spend more than 10 percent of GNP on defense. After 1976, army and intelligence institutions, which were grossly underpaid, were allowed to benefit from Syria's occupation of Lebanon in the form of various types of "protection" rents, legal and illegal trade between Lebanon and Syria, and involvement with the drug trade in the Beqaa Valley.

Syria's occupation of Lebanon benefited the economy in other ways as well. Up to 1 million Syrian workers sent home an estimated $1 billion in remittances per year. In many ways the Lebanon occupation also provided some breathing space that allowed Syria to avoid reforms—much as Hong Kong provides breathing space for China. Lebanese banks were used while the Syrian banking system remained sclerotic, and contraband flowing through Lebanon allowed the trade system to remain officially closed, to the benefit of rent-seekers mainly associated with the security forces. Moreover, oil production, which took off late relative to other countries in the region—Syrian oil production rose from US$330 million in 1986 to US$2.5 billion in 1995—provided the state with some room to maneuver. Syria adjusted to its budget constraints by tightening autocratic rule and expanding its foreign adventure in Lebanon, managing to avoid pressures to reform its economy. The Syrian economy remained in a low-growth trap even as Bashar Al-Assad, succeeding his father in 2001, undertook a short-lived series of modernization measures. The cost of this immobilism has been Syria's low GDP per capita (US$2,623 in 2010), less than one-third of Lebanon's (US$8,628 in 2010), in spite of the fact that Lebanon went through a wrenching civil war and Syria benefits from self-sufficiency in agriculture and some oil reserves.

Tunisia

After its independence in 1956 and up to 1987, when General Zine El Abidine Ben Ali deposed Habib Bourguiba on the grounds that he was medically unfit to govern, Tunisia maintained uninterrupted civilian rule. Bourguiba had founded the Neo-Destour (New Constitution) Party in the 1930s; rallied the small-scale trading and commercial groups, the professionals and intelligentsia, and the trade unions; and led the coalition to power (Moore 1965). Nonetheless, during the years of civilian rule Tunisia had also built an interventionist state system that resembled those of Egypt, Turkey, and Algeria. From the outset, much as in Turkey in the 1920s, Bourguiba built a powerful state apparatus, to some extent gutting the Neo-Destour of its best cadres, subordinating the trade unions, and using the state to mobilize capital and raw materials to stimulate private activity. The state's role in resource mobilization was, until the 1970s, overwhelming.

Although the French settler community in Tunisia was smaller than that of Algeria, it nonetheless dominated the modern private sector. At independence there was no such mass exodus of settlers as had occurred in Algeria, but the fact remained that there was no indigenous industrial bourgeoisie upon which the new state could rely to promote the country's structural transformation.

Tunisia in the 1960s was quite literally boxed in between the Arab world's two most ostentatious socialist experiments—Algeria's to the west and Egypt's to the east. In 1962 Tunisia launched its First Three-Year Plan, followed by a series of four-year plans. By 1964, Bourguiba had decided that it was necessary to give a more radical cast to the Tunisian strategy. In October 1964, the Neo-Destour Party became the Socialist Destour Party and called for the "coexistence" of the public, private, and cooperative sectors. The First Four-Year Plan, 1965–1968, was to embody a socialist transformation of the economy: cultivators were to be grouped into agricultural cooperatives, and state enterprise would spearhead the industrialization drive. A young intellectual, Ahmed Ben Salah, active in the Neo-Destour and the unions prior to independence, was made secretary of state for planning and national economy and was the driving force behind the experiment.

This strategy, however, alienated much of the regime's petty capitalist and small landowning constituency. In 1969, in a dramatic shift, the statist experiment was overhauled, and Tunisia adopted a strategy of stimulating its private sector and promoting exports to the European Economic Community (EEC). Still, the Tunisian state remained, until the late 1980s, a dominant force in the economy and, through its modest oil exports, had substantial revenues at its disposal. Those rents explain the rising share of the state in gross fixed capital formation after a decline in the early 1970s. In 1981 state-owned enterprises accounted for about 60 percent of the value of manufacturing output and employed 180,000 persons, or over 11 percent of the workforce. The budgetary burden of state-owned enterprises increased to 4 percent from 1978 to 1981. Private investment was largely limited to consumer goods production and tourism. Even for consumer goods, the government continued to manage large firms, often trying to attract joint-venture partners.

As elsewhere, the approach before 1986 was mainly one of streamlining the existing economic strategy of state-led growth, in which the government dominated the commanding heights of the economy, supplying the intermediate goods that private industry needed. The complex of controls over prices, investments, trade, credit, and foreign exchange remained in place—as did its corollary, misallocation of resources.

Events in the 1980s made this policy unsustainable. The government tried to "grow through" external shocks such as the international recession of the early 1980s, drought, rising European protectionism, and falling oil prices. Tunisia's debt continued to mount, however, rising from 38 percent of GDP in 1980 to 63 percent in 1986. Because of strong internal demand, an overvalued currency, and deteriorating terms of trade, the current account deficit widened from 5 percent of GDP in 1980 to 11 percent in 1985–1986. The government's budgetary deficit reached 5.2 percent of GDP in the five years before 1986, while the resource gap averaged 9 percent from 1981 to 1985. The Mohammed Mzali government instituted some halfhearted reforms, including the changes in consumer subsidy programs that provoked the riots of January 1984. The government then retreated, but the problems became even more severe: by the summer of 1986, the country had only a few days of import cover left.

Libya

The Jamahiria ("mass state") of Libya represented the unacknowledged combination of romantic revolutionary and Islamic programs with a kind of cynical authoritarianism. As in all the major oil-exporting nations, the state dominated the economy by the simple fact of owning the petroleum and controlling the proceeds of its sale. That was the case under the Idrissid monarchy, and it remained the case after 1969, when the monarchy was overthrown by then-Lieutenant Muammar Gaddafi. He eventually elaborated a new theory of the Jamahiria in which all productive units and all workplaces were to be directly governed by popular congresses. Bureaucratic hierarchies, top-heavy party structures, and elaborate command channels were all depicted as antithetical to true popular democratic control. Libya's experiment, on paper, was one of worker self-management with a vengeance (see Fathaly and Palmer 1980).

Beginning in 1979, Gaddafi led an assault on private-sector interests unrivaled anywhere in the Middle East. He expropriated all private industry. In 1981 all bank deposits were seized without warning, and a program to abolish retail trade by replacing it with state-owned supermarkets was begun. By this time, three-quarters of the workforce was on the public payroll (Anderson 1986). The Libyan state and regime never really relinquished effective control of production and administration to popular committees. The oil and banking sectors were kept under tight state control, as were the 60,000–70,000 men and women in the armed forces. Like other countries we have considered, Libya had multiyear development plans, and the leadership did not allow the "people" to question—much less change—any of the plans' major parameters.

The "Liberal" Monarchies

It may be that socialism entails a significant public sector, but the converse is not true. The monarchies of pre-1979 Iran, Jordan, and Morocco all professed liberal economic credos in which the private sector was to be the leading force. The role of the state was, once again, that of handmaiden to the private sector. Yet if we look at statistical indicators of state activity, we see that these three countries possessed public sectors of a size and weight equal to those of the socialist countries. The experience of these monarchies highlights the general point that we should not confuse state ownership with socialism. Some "radical" regimes have waved the flag of public ownership to demonstrate their socialist bona fides, while "liberal" regimes have passed over in silence the substantial assets they control through state ownership.[5]

Iran

Next door to Turkey, a would-be Atatürk appeared on the scene following World War I. Colonel Reza Khan of the Persian Cossacks had de facto taken over the Iranian state by 1924. After having himself crowned Reza Shah Pahlavi, he set about building a nation in the ethnically and geographically fragmented society he inherited from the Qajars. The state apparatus and the armed forces grew side by side, and as in Turkey, the depression pushed the Iranian state into ISI. The private sector benefited from credit provided through the state industrial bank as well as from high tariff walls against imports. But the state did not wait to see how the private sector would respond to these incentives: by 1941, there were public enterprises in textiles, sugar, cement, and iron and steel. Through consumption taxes and trade monopolies, the Iranian state, over the period 1926–1940, was able to invest some US$400 million in industry and infrastructure, a very substantial sum for that era. Another US$120 million was invested by the private sector. All this was done with very little foreign borrowing. The modest revenues from the sale of oil in those years were turned over to the military (Issawi 1978). Iran was neither populist nor revolutionary, but it was just as etatist as Turkey.

Reza Shah was sent into exile in 1941 by the Allies, who feared his collaboration with the Axis. His young son, Mohammad Reza Pahlavi, became the new shah. He did not consolidate his grip on power until his showdown in 1953 with the prime minister, Mohammad Mosaddegh, a nationalist leader who brought under state ownership the British-controlled Anglo-Iranian Oil Company. After that, Iran's economic strategy marched on three legs: petroleum exports, continued ISI, and a division of labor between the public and private sectors. State enterprise undertook the deepening process in iron and steel, copper, machine tools, aluminum, and petrochemicals, while a dynamic private sector, sometimes in joint ventures with foreign capital, moved into finished metals and special steels, synthetic fibers, paper, automobile assembly, and sugar. Iran in 1944 established a Plan and Budget Organization and launched its first national plan. In this respect, it was well ahead of all countries in the region except Turkey.

This kind of division of labor was what one would have expected—it reconciled the regime's professed economic liberalism with a strong state presence in the economy. But in the 1970s a very significant shift in the division of labor occurred, one that contains lessons about the logic of public enterprise in the Middle East. With the first great surge in petroleum prices in 1973, the shah's state had at its disposal a tremendous volume of rents. Neither the shah nor his advisers nor the state technocracy proposed investing these rents in private-sector growth. Rather, the new funds allowed the state to expand and consolidate in an atmosphere in which public authorities either disregarded or were actively hostile to the private sector (Razavi and Vakil 1984, 66; see also Katouzian 1981, 237).

By the end of the 1970s, government investment and consumption represented 43 percent of GNP and military expenditures had risen to 10 percent of GNP. One-quarter of the non-agricultural workforce—1.5 million people—were on the public payroll.

Regardless of the ideology of the regime, one of the major incentives to expand the state's economic role is the *control* it offers the nation's leaders over resources and people. State ownership also denies resources and people to other contenders for power. In this sense it is doubtful that the shah ever wanted a powerful and autonomous private sector to develop in Iran. A prosperous, subordinate, parasitic private sector, yes; a true national bourgeoisie, no. When given monopoly over Iran's external rents in the 1970s, the shah showed the real content of his liberalism (Esfanani and Gurlakar 2014).

Has the Islamic Republic of Iran reversed this pattern since 1979? The constitution of the Islamic republic is explicit on the role of the public sector, which is to include "all major industries, foreign trade, major mines, banking, insurance, power, dams, major irrigation systems, air, sea, land and rail road transport." Shortly after Khomeini's return to Iran, a wave of nationalizations took place in June and July 1979 involving twenty-seven banks, insurance companies, and heavy industries. By the end of 1982, the National Industrial Organization controlled about 600 enterprises, with 150,000 employees. In addition, the Foundation of the Disinherited (Bonyad e-Mostazafan) was created to take over the assets of the Pahlavi family, the Pahlavi Foundation, and the expropriated property of the shah's entourage (Bakhash 1984, 178–184). In the next decade, the *Bonyads* (foundations) would become the most influential agents in the Iranian economy, and under President Mahmoud Ahmedinejad, they would come to be the main beneficiary of government privatizations (Harris 2013).

There was, then, no rollback of the state under the Islamic republic, yet it is clear that the new regime was deeply divided on the issue of state ownership and intervention in the economy. The Guardianship Council, whose duty it is to monitor the constitutionality of legislation, in 1982 declared unconstitutional land reform measures passed by the parliament, but a law was passed giving the state a monopoly in key industries and in foreign trade. At the same time, an important faction of radicals in the parliament sought to use the state to engineer a far-reaching redistribution of wealth in Iranian society. In early 1988, when Iran emerged from the Iran-Iraq War with staggering losses and a weakened economy, Khomeini's pronouncements showed that he was leaning in the direction of the more radical, statist elements. His death left the tension unresolved, and his successors were left to deal with an economy in shambles and a heightened level of expectations throughout society for better living conditions.

The Kingdom of Jordan

The Jordanian economy is small and, since the Israeli occupation of the West Bank in 1967, severely truncated. It is dynamic and growing but highly dependent on external assistance. In 1976–1977, for example, when GNP stood at US$1.7 billion, external assistance exclusive of military aid stood at US$500 million.

The Jordanian state has controlled the economy in three ways. First, as the direct recipient of external assistance, it has been able to channel investment in the ways it sees fit. This channeling has taken the form of large-scale joint ventures with state, foreign, and local private capital in fertilizers, cement, petroleum refining, and so forth. State pension and social security funds, as well as the Housing Bank and the Industrial Development Bank, have been the conduits for substantial public finance. In 1980 the state had a significant equity stake in private firms in mining (42 percent), manufacturing (23 percent), tourism (27 percent), and transportation (20 percent). The state also owned 90 percent of the shares of the Jordan Phosphate Mines Company, 100 percent of the Jordan Automatic Banking Company, and 99 percent of the Agricultural Products Manufacturing Company (Rivier 1980, 111, 206). The second lever in the hands of the state has been the phosphate sector, the country's single largest export and foreign exchange earner. The third lever has been the defense budget, which stood at US$763 million in 1988, or 15 percent of GNP; the army is a major employer for the East Bankers, who constituted the traditional base of support of the regime. By the mid-1970s, about one-half of Jordan's labor force worked for the government in a civilian or military capacity (Rivlin 2009).

The Jordanian economy grew rapidly and in double digits during the first oil boom, from the mid-1970s to the mid-1980s, fueled by generous support from the Gulf states and by labor remittances. By 1986, about 10 percent of the labor force, or about 300,000 Jordanians, worked abroad, and phosphate revenues boomed with rising commodity prices.

The Jordanian private sector, a large proportion of which is of Palestinian origin, has been given the lead in promoting exports of fruits, vegetables, and manufactured goods to Arab and regional markets. Given its small population and narrow resource base, it would have been impossible for Jordan to pursue an ISI strategy. If it were not so internally divided between Palestinians and non-Palestinians, Jordan would have been a good candidate for an export-led growth pattern à la Hong Kong or Singapore. Its relatively well-educated and hardworking population and its no-nonsense political leadership might have been sufficient to attract foreign investment and technology.

However, the rentier state model collapsed when the oil boom ebbed in the mid-1980s. Support from the Gulf, workers' remittances, and phosphate exports shrank. Budget and balance-of-payments deficits increased, and Jordan had to start borrowing abroad to avoid deep reforms. Growth turned negative during 1985–1989, while at the same time Jordan's foreign debt quadrupled. When, in 1989, debt could not be serviced anymore, Jordan had to turn to the International Monetary Fund (IMF) for support. The removal of subsidies on basic commodities and a 50 percent devaluation led to food riots. The crisis led to further decline in economic growth and a rise in poverty. King Hussein sided with Saddam Hussein when he invaded Kuwait, and thousands of Jordanian and Palestinian workers were thrown out of the country during the ensuing First Gulf War. It was only after the 1994 peace treaty with Israel that Jordan managed to improve its relations with the United States and develop a more reformist program, which received generous support from the IMF and other Western donors.

The Kingdom of Morocco

Morocco and Iran up to 1979 followed similar development strategies. Morocco, like Iran, had a substantial trading bourgeoisie that was never totally eclipsed by French economic interests during the protectorate, 1912–1956. The country's economic ideology has always been liberal and pro-private sector. Yet, like the shah, King Hassan II may have been reluctant to see a national bourgeoisie with its own resource base gain an undisputed foothold in the economy. Finally, although Morocco is not an oil exporter, it has been the world's leading exporter of phosphates, and through the giant public holding company the Cherifian Phosphates Office (OCP), it controls the most important sector of the economy.

The state's control of the economy has taken the form of direct ownership of assets (mines, railroads, dams, sugar refineries) and equity positions through public holding companies. The OCP and the Cherifian Foreign Trade Office (OCE) own assets themselves and have a controlling interest in a host of affiliated enterprises. The OCE, for example, between 1965 and 1975 helped launch twenty-five branch operations involved in citrus exports and wound up controlling about US$5 billion in assets. In addition, the state controls a number of special investment agencies such as the Caisse de Dépôt et de Gestion, which handles social security and pension funds, and the National Bank for Economic Development, which has been a favored channel for World Bank credits.

The post-1973 surge in world petroleum prices was followed closely by a large jump in world phosphate prices. The Moroccan state found itself in control of windfall rents and used them, just as Iran did, not to invest directly in the private sector but to expand the public sector. The 1973–1977 plan was revised midcourse, with public investment targets rising from 11 billion to 29 billion dirhams (about US$6 billion), destined mainly for the steel, sugar, cement, and chemical sectors. The number of public-sector firms increased from 137 in 1970 to 238 in 1976, and state equity in them from 700 million to 2.2 billion dirhams (el-Midaoui 1981, 234–238; el-Malki 1982, 175). The share of the government and the public sector in total gross fixed capital formation reached 19 percent in 1977. The Moroccan state employed well over 400,000 persons in the civil service and public sector. There were at least another 150,000 in the armed forces and police. At least one-quarter of the non-agricultural workforce was on the public payroll.

Even at the height of the boom, state expansion was partly financed by foreign borrowing. Expansion continued into 1976 even as phosphate prices collapsed (falling by 47 percent), swelling the budget deficit to 20 percent of GDP (Morrison 1991). Expenditures rose with the beginning of the Saharan War (Morocco's military involvement in this war would cost the country on average US$300 million per year for a decade), the increased cost of consumer subsidies (rising from 1 percent of GDP in 1973 to 6.9 percent in 1974) (Horton 1990), the unwillingness to cancel investment projects, and the political fear of canceling public-sector salary increases. Although some initial steps toward stabilization were taken in 1977, the Moroccan government, along with many others, hoped that the adverse price shock was temporary and tried to "grow through" the recession. Accordingly, its foreign debt rose from 20 percent of GDP in 1975 to nearly 60 percent (at US$10 billion) in 1980, when service payments consumed 32.7 percent of exports.

As the burden of debt became increasingly unmanageable, the Moroccan government was forced to undertake stabilization measures. It was obliged to restrict its current expenditures and investment and to revert to its pre-1974 policy of stimulating the private sector and luring in foreign investment. Although the number of enterprises in which it had a majority stake increased, the share of the state in the total equity of these companies declined. By 1983, however, foreign creditors refused to continue to finance budgetary deficits, forcing the country to turn to the IMF for assistance. As usual, the initial impetus for stabilization came from outside: in Morocco, as in other countries of the region, the first key agent of change was external.

Because of the high political costs of austerity, most countries of the region have found adjustment policies difficult to sustain. On initial examination, Morocco's situation seems similar. Beginning in 1978, it reduced public spending on investment, increased taxes, restricted civil servants' salary increases, and slowed the growth of credit to private companies. It retreated in 1979, however, granting a 10 percent rise in civil servants' salaries and a 30–40 percent increase in the minimum wage. It also expanded food subsidies even as the prices of imported farm products rose. A second attempt at implementing a stabilization program was aborted when an extremely sharp rise in consumer prices (50 percent) and the government's decision to reduce subsidies on food products led to major rioting in Casablanca in the spring of 1981.

In the two years following the Casablanca "bread riots," Morocco pursued an expansionist policy by borrowing more and more from abroad. Foreign public debt continued to rise, reaching US$11.8 billion (84 percent of GDP) in 1983. Drought added to the difficult situation, accelerating rural-to-urban migration and increasing the need for food imports. The number of state-owned enterprises rose to 700 in 1984. By 1981–1982, the current account deficit had risen to 12.6 percent of GDP (from 8 percent in 1980). By the middle of 1983, currency reserves were almost exhausted, forcing the government to institute emergency measures to restrict imports.

The Princes and Kings of Oil

The most conservative regimes in the Middle East, the princedoms of the Gulf and the Kingdom of Saudi Arabia, are also those with the largest state sectors. They are conservative in the sense that they share nonrepublican forms of government, a concern for the protection of Islamic values, a fierce anticommunism throughout the Cold War era, and dominant classes with roots in older maritime and trans-desert trading communities.

These regimes combine small populations (Saudi Arabia is by far the biggest, with about 21 million inhabitants of local origin), little or no agriculture (with the exception of Saudi Arabia; see Chapter 6), no tradition of manufacturing, and a common resource, oil, that has generated tremendous rents. The share of the oil sector in the GNPs of these countries reached the following levels in 1980: Saudi Arabia, 66 percent; Kuwait, 51 percent; the United Arab Emirates, 65 percent; and Oman, 69 percent (World Bank 1995). Kuwait's lower figure merely signals that its rents had diversified and that the country had begun to draw significant revenues from its foreign investments.

With this kind of financial clout at the disposal of the state, it was inevitable that all new investment programs would fall within the state sphere.

The civil administration grew prodigiously in all these countries. Kuwait's expanded from 22,000 in 1963 to 146,000—of whom 90,000 were foreigners—in 1980. Saudi Arabia's grew from 37,000 in 1962 to 232,000 in 1981, to which we should add another 81,000 part-time or nonclassified employees (Ayubi 1985; see also Chatelus 1982, 23; Islami and Kavoussi 1984). The entire native Saudi workforce in 1980 totaled 1.5 million, and there were 800,000 foreign workers in the country.[6] Nazih Ayubi (1985) saw this expansion as a function of increased educational output unaccompanied by significant industrialization. Public employment serves the purpose of political control of the educated. It also serves as window dressing: "a respectable and modern looking tool for distributing part of the oil revenues and for 'disbursing' largesse camouflaged in the language of 'meritocracy and national objectives.'"

Saudi Arabia has gone further and established a giant public-enterprise sector, with more than forty corporations in housing, storage, agriculture, and basic industries. In the plan period 1976–1980 alone, Saudi Arabia disbursed US$290 billion, which went into infrastructure, port development, and new industrial cities at Jubail and Yanbu. The 1980–1985 development plan, although less spectacularly funded, was designed to put Saudi Arabia on an industrial footing. The oil minister at the time, Ahmed Zaki Yamani, prophesied that Saudi Arabia would soon rank alongside Argentina, Brazil, and South Korea as a semi-industrialized country (*Middle East Journal,* March 1984, 25–27). Whereas the goal was to shift some of the burden of industrialization onto the private sector, the industrialization that did take place mainly involved public-sector joint ventures with foreign capital.

When oil revenues collapsed in the 1980s, Saudi Arabia reduced its expenditures by about half the reduction in revenues, and it financed the deficit through mostly internal borrowing. Over time the public investment program was sharply curtailed, but hiring in the public sector and the provision of public services actually rose. It was only in the late 1990s, after running eighteen years of deficit in a row and sustaining negative economic growth for much of this period, that the government decided to start implementing serious structural reforms to put the economy on a more solid footing.

Israel

Israel, for obvious political, social, and religious reasons, is a case apart, but in the structure of its economy, the weight of the state, and some of its ideological predispositions, it has shared many features with the socialist states of the Arab world and with Turkey. These similarities are all the more striking in that before there was any Israeli state at all, the Zionist community in Palestine had well-organized party and union structures and cohesive farmer-soldier communities in the *kibbutzim.* That a powerful and somewhat autonomous state grew out of such a highly structured civil society says much about the logic and attractiveness of the interventionist state.

It was David Ben-Gurion, the first Israeli prime minister, who developed the doctrine of etatism (in Hebrew, *mamlachtiut*) and subordinated to the state his own socialist Labor Party, the MAPAI, and its powerful trade union affiliate, the Histadrut. The Histadrut included in its membership about 70 percent of Jewish wage earners in Palestine. In addition, the new Israeli state asserted its control over the Zionist defense force, the Haganah, which had fought successfully to achieve and then defend Israeli independence.

What Ben-Gurion did in absorbing the labor movement into the state sector, robbing the kibbutzim of their most dynamic leaders, and putting the MAPAI and the Israeli Defense Forces (IDF) under state control, was not unlike the process undertaken by another charismatic civilian—Habib Bourguiba in Tunisia after 1956. As Gabriel Ben-Dor (1983, 109) pointed out, "There was an overwhelming paradox in a man trying to use his party as a base of power from which to destroy the party-state linkage."

However, a number of factors made Israel's experiment in state building unique. First, there was the "acquisition" by the state of all the property previously owned by Arab Palestinians who had left their homes during the hostilities of 1948 (similar to what happened in Turkey in 1923 and in Algeria in 1962). Second, the Jewish immigrant population of Israel doubled between 1948 and 1952, most of the newcomers were "Oriental," and the state had to undertake their economic, cultural, and social integration into what had been a predominantly Ashkenazi society. Third, Israel, like Jordan, has been dependent on external assistance and financial flows, and it is the state that controls their disbursement. Between 1950 and 1974, for example, such assistance totaled US$19.5 billion. Finally, the state runs Israel's military-industrial complex. Defense outlays were about 17 percent of GNP in 1972 and 30 percent in 1979, probably the highest proportion in the world at that time (Arian 1985; Kimmerling 1983; Rosenfeld and Carmi 1976).

What had emerged in Israel by the late 1960s was a large, paternalistic welfare state with vaguely socialistic objectives and extensive public ownership. In this system, "the citizen would be perceived as an object available for the activities of the state and its bureaucracy, this latter serving as [a] paternalistic body deciding what was good for the citizens and for the collectivity as a whole. By definition, the reasoning of the authorities was better than and took precedence over the individuals and groups" (Kimmerling 1983, 99).

The Israeli variant of statism was given practical effect by state-owned or state-controlled enterprise. The Histadrut in the 1970s had 1.5 million members, or 80 percent of the employed workforce. It in turn had controlling interests in several corporations: Solel Boneh in construction; the Koor holding company, with 250 industrial, financial, and commercial firms under its control (Koor was one of the Fortune 500); Bank Hapoalim; and others. There were 200 corporations in Israel in which the government had at least 50 percent equity. In addition, there were some 450,000 persons on the public payroll, including the professional military, teachers, and municipal employees. Asher Arian (1985, 36) estimated that in the late 1970s about 52 percent of the Israeli workforce was employed by the state and the Histadrut, with the remaining 48 percent in the private sector. By 1983, government expenditures were improbably high at 91 percent of GDP.

The Israeli economy paid a heavy and familiar price for mamlachtiut. After the Labor Alliance lost power to the Likud in 1976, the government made important modifications to the Ben-Gurion formula and tried to contain government expenditures and promote exports through devaluation. However, in the years after the 1973 Yom Kippur War, growth slowed down considerably, resulting in Israel's own "lost decade," and further weakened state finances. The government increasingly had to resort to printing money to finance its budget deficits.

Huge government deficits resulting from indexing wages to the cost of living, heavy defense expenditures, and various forms of subsidies led to a rise in inflation. By 1984, inflation was reaching an annual rate close to 450 percent and was projected to reach over 1,000 percent by 1985. Despite flows of concessional aid and grants, Israel's external debt had risen to US$12.5 billion in 1980, or 62 percent of

GNP, one of the highest ratios in the Middle East. In response, a major economic stabilization plan was devised in 1985 under the leadership of Professor Michael Bruno. Starting in 1986, Israel implemented a determined inflation reduction program, cutting government expenditures, temporarily freezing prices and wages, and increasing tax receipts. Structural adjustment came later in an attempt to get the economy going again, and over time the reforms led to a major reorientation of both the economy and politics, with a much larger role for the private sector.

CONTRADICTIONS OF STATE-LED GROWTH

In many respects, state-led growth achieved a great deal. Both absolute and per capita national output grew at respectable rates in most countries of the region even before the massive infusion of oil rents during the 1970s and early 1980s (see Table 7.1). Structural transformation, whether measured by the share of industry in output or by employment, also proceeded at rates that were not unfavorable in international comparative perspective (see Chapter 2). This performance was no mean achievement considering the rapidity of population growth, the heavy burden of defense expenditures, the limited natural resource base apart from oil, the initially low levels of literacy, and the perennial political instability of the region.

However, industry was seldom internationally competitive, and many "infant" industries never grew up. The stress on heavy industry and import substitution failed to create sufficient jobs for the rapidly expanding workforce, and the relative neglect of agriculture until the late 1970s contributed to the widening food gap. Finally, many countries continued to rely on external sources of investment capital and to accumulate large external debts. The goals of both social justice and national economic independence proved elusive.

It is now widely acknowledged that state intervention in the economy and the public-enterprise sectors have, by and large, malfunctioned financially and economically. Other than in oil, public enterprises have failed to generate profits, and they constitute a net drain on state resources; to remain afloat they have required subsidized credit and inputs, foreign exchange at preferential rates, and constant flows of working capital and new investment. At the same time, public enterprises have not solved many of the social and economic problems they were designed to address.

Too often, the wrong price signals led state managers and private economic actors to produce the wrong things with the wrong combination of inputs. Heavy industry grew rapidly, while agriculture and light industry were relatively neglected. International comparative advantage was often ignored. For example, two of the leading industrial nations, Egypt and Algeria, heavily invested in industries in which profitability was actually negative if international prices were used for the calculation. Furthermore, the multiple goals of state-owned enterprises (such as supplying cheap inputs to other industries and providing jobs for the rapidly expanding labor force) often gave the managers of these industries little incentive to minimize costs, even with a given technology. Capacity utilization was often poor, leading to

TABLE 7.1. Growth in GDP per Capita in the MENA Countries, per Decade and Across Political Economy Subgroups, 1961–2010

	1961–1970	1971–1980	1981–1990	1991–2000	2001–2010	Standard Deviation, 1960–2010	Average, 1960–2010
RRLP countries	8.22%	2.56%	-1.67%	0.96%	0.33%	3.75%	2.08%
Bahrain	4.20	4.70	-1.49	2.92	-0.94	2.90	1.88
Kuwait	2.50	-3.10	-3.12	-1.58	1.92	2.72	-0.68
Libya			0.20	1.78	2.32	1.10	1.43
Oman	18.62	1.10	4.28	2.64	2.65	7.22	5.86
Qatar					0.84		0.84
Saudi Arabia	4.77	7.86	-5.23	0.55	0.13	4.98	1.62
United Arab Emirates	11.00	2.26	-4.66	-0.56	-4.63	6.47	0.68
RRLA countries	3.02	3.88	-6.47	3.98	2.06	4.41	1.30
Algeria	2.08	3.07	-0.21	-0.18	2.22	1.50	1.40
Iran, Islamic Republic of	8.31	0.86	-1.15	1.99	3.79	3.59	2.76
Iraq	3.20	8.00	-30.00	14.92	-1.53	17.27	-1.08
Sudan	-0.77	0.70	-0.11	3.13	4.39	2.20	1.47
Syria	2.29	6.76	-0.87	2.46	2.37	2.72	2.60
Yemen				1.59	1.14	0.32	1.36
RPLA countries	3.03	6.16	0.00	2.44	2.38	2.21	2.80
Egypt	2.82	4.32	3.04	2.50	2.97	0.70	3.13
Jordan		11.74	-1.58	0.99	3.89	5.77	3.76
Lebanon	4.00	7.00	-9.10	4.61	3.93	6.38	2.09
Morocco	2.09	2.65	1.52	1.00	3.80	1.08	2.21
Palestine		6.10	5.00	2.47	-3.74	4.40	2.46
Tunisia	3.21	5.14	1.11	3.10	3.46	1.43	3.20
Israel	5.26	2.99	1.76	2.67	1.17	1.57	2.77
Turkey	3.01	1.89	3.14	2.07	2.62	0.56	2.54
Overall MENA	4.79	4.11	-1.97	2.45	1.56	2.66	2.19

Source: World Bank Indicators

higher unit costs. For example, the Algerian steel plant at El Hadjar operated at only 40 percent of capacity in the early 1980s (Nelson 1985, 208).

Many countries of the region tried to invest more resources than were saved domestically. The resource gap—gross domestic investment (GDI) minus gross domestic savings (GDS)—was large for some countries and during particular periods, but more generally, there has long been great variability in this indicator across countries and over time (see Table 7.2). Unsurprisingly, during the oil boom the oil-exporting countries typically saved more than they invested. Indeed, this phenomenon led to the creation by the World Bank of a new category of developing country, "capital-surplus oil exporters," composed, prior to the collapse of oil prices in the mid-1980s, of Saudi Arabia, Libya, Kuwait, and the United Arab Emirates. Other oil exporters, principally Iran, Iraq, and Algeria, had adequate national savings to meet investment.[8] Another group of countries—Sudan, Morocco, Tunisia, Egypt, Syria, Turkey, and Israel—had resource gaps in 1985 ranging from 2 to 11 percent of GDP. Two other countries, the former Yemen Arab Republic and Jordan, had massive gaps, 36 and 34 percent of GDP, respectively.

Mainly because of heavy debt repayments, domestic savings exceeded domestic investment in all middle-income countries from 1980 to 1985.[9] There were several reasons for this resource gap, but the inefficiencies of the state-owned enterprises certainly contributed to it. For example, the "budgetary burden," or net deficit, created by these enterprises was 4 percent of GDP in 1978–1981 in Tunisia and 3.5 percent in 1978–1980 in Turkey (Floyd 1984). The failure to develop internationally competitive industrial (and agricultural) exports, combined with rapidly expanding domestic incomes and demand, exacerbated the deficit of the balance of trade. The public sector, originally created in part to generate foreign exchange, too often simply absorbed it.

Finally, just as the goals of efficiency, growth, and national independence were only partially achieved, the ideal of increasing equity also proved elusive. While millions of good jobs were created, and the provision of social services fostered some social mobility and helped create a new middle class, these equity gains had a high efficiency cost, as in expensive consumer subsidy programs or the swelling ranks of redundant public-sector employees. Over time, in order to protect the privileges of what would become an elite labor, the interests of new entrants to the labor markets would have to be sacrificed, creating a fault line between insiders and outsiders. At the same time, as the budget constraint became more binding, the education and health systems deteriorated and became unable to continue promoting the equalization of human capital and the expansion of social mobility.

THE RESISTANCE TO REFORMS

By the 1980s, the process of state-led intervention has resulted in deep-seated crisis in the state sector itself and in the economy in general, calling into question the feasibility of continued domination of the economy by the state. In time, this crisis led to the retreat of the state and a gradual weakening of the state bourgeoisie. In

TABLE 7.2. MENA Resource Gaps, 1975, 1985, 1995, 2003

	Gross Fixed Capital Formation (% of GDP)				Gross Domestic Savings (% of GDP)				Resource Gap (% of GDP)			
	1975	1985	1995	2003	1975	1985	1995	2003	1975	1985	1995	2003
Algeria	39	32	29	24	36	31	28	45	-3	-1	-1	21
Bahrain	-	34	17	20	-	48	26	39	-	14	9	19
Egypt	25	25	16	16	12	15	12	14	-12	-11	-4	-2
Iran	28	17	21	29	34	21	21	43	6	3	0	15
Israel	29	19	25	18	-3	6	12	11	-33	-13	-13	-6
Jordan	-	19	30	21	-	-15	8	-2	-	-34	-21	-22
Kuwait	12	20	14	9	67	30	25	25	55	10	12	16
Lebanon	-	-	36	20	-	-	-18	0	-	-	-54	-20
Libya	28	-	12	-	41	-	19	-	13	-	7	-
Morocco	25	23	21	24	15	16	14	20	-10	-7	-7	-4
Oman	36	-	15	16	52	40	23	35	17	-	8	18
Saudi Arabia	17	22	19	18	69	15	29	42	51	-7	10	23
Sudan	-	11	-	18	10	3	-	14	-	-7	-	-4
Syria	27	26	27	23	14	13	20	26	-13	-13	-7	3
Tunisia	26	28	24	23	26	24	21	21	0	-4	-4	-2
Turkey	15	15	24	15	11	13	21	19	-4	-2	-3	4
UAE	31	25	28	22	76	53	36	37	45	28	7	15
WBG	-	-	35	3	-	-	-8	-37	-	-	-43	-39
Yemen	-	-	21	16	-	-	15	12	-	-	-6	-4
LDC average												
Low & middle income	24	22	24	23	23	25	25	26	-1	3	1	3
Middle income	25	22	24	23	25	26	26	27	0	4	2	4
Upper middle income	24	20	20	18	24	25	23	23	0	5	3	5

Resource Gap equals gross domestic savings minus gross fixed capital formulation.

Source: World Development Indicators, Online.

some countries, such as Algeria, this retreat was driven by an effort to rationalize state intervention and make it more efficient. In other countries, such as Turkey, an assertive private entrepreneurial sector was ready to take over from the state the role of leading the development process. Falling in between were countries like Egypt and Tunisia, where economic liberalization measures were introduced in the absence of strong, self-assured private sectors. By 2010, on the eve of the Arab uprisings, most countries of the region had resolutely moved to a system in which most of production took place in the private sector.

The states in the Middle East did not confine themselves only to regulating market economies. They also put themselves in a position to provide privileges to preferred entrepreneurs and exclude those they did not favor from operating with the same conditions. Thus, when the confidence that leaders and the led once placed in the efficacy of state intervention changed—and changed dramatically (in fact, that confidence was largely gone by the late 1980s)—reforms were not initiated even when the inefficiency of the system became apparent. It was not always possible to discern which groups, organizations, or class interests carried the most weight in promoting or defending the state's role in the economy. But after thirty or more years of strong state intervention in the economy, there were a multitude of powerful bureaucratic, managerial, and political interests that stood in the way of any diminution of state economic activities.

Organized labor was generally a staunch opponent of reform because of relatively high wage levels and benefit packages and, above all, because of job stability and relatively light workloads. In many ways, unions in the public sector constituted a labor aristocracy (the unemployed in many Middle Eastern countries outnumbered those in the public-sector labor force two-to-one by the end of the 1980s) and defended their privileges in the name of socialism and the toiling masses. When regimes began to promote state capitalism, the unions found themselves in a difficult position. They sensed that the public sector was under fire and sought to defend it against its critics. Yet they did not want to pay the price of greater efficiency, which would entail higher productivity: more output per hour of work for the same pay. The unions also resisted the introduction of incentive systems that would reward individual or group performance and insisted that pay and promotion be based on seniority systems, thus sapping the very logic of the state-capitalist thrust. Union leaders generally knew that this was a dangerous game: if public-sector performance did not improve, its critics would inevitably call for privatization, an even worse outcome for the unions than state capitalism.

The managers of public assets also resisted efforts at reform. Frequently they had formed alliances of convenience with labor that led to low productivity and high enterprise deficits. Managers preferred periodic bailouts from the state to the harder option of exacting higher levels of performance from the workers and from themselves. They were generally drawn to the public sector by its salaries and "perks," which were better than those found in the civil service and even in parts of the private sector. Although these salary advantages eroded in the 1980s, when inflation rates were high throughout the area, public-sector work remained less demanding and jobs and promotions more secure than in the private sector. Individual managers may have had good prospects for shifting into the private sector, but most public-sector managers preferred their quasi-sinecures. Moreover, the opportunities for side payments and moonlighting compensated for deteriorating salary levels.

For some twenty years up to the early 1980s, the external donor community showed some predilection for public enterprise and direct state intervention in the economy. The attractiveness of public-sector enterprise to donors lay in the possibility of bypassing cumbersome entrenched bureaucratic agencies in order to promote specific projects (such as fertilizer industries) or programs (for example, the diffusion of new varieties of wheat). For bilateral donors there was also the attraction that large public-sector enterprises could become important purchasers of equipment and technology from the donor's home economy. Although bilateral donors would become the major proponents of public-sector reform and privatization, particularly after the advent of Margaret Thatcher in the United Kingdom and Ronald Reagan in the United States, it is important to note that they supported public-sector expansion not so long ago.

Parts of the private sector frequently found it in their interest to have a large public sector alongside them. Large public enterprises in basic metals, plastics and petrochemicals, and other semi-manufactures such as cotton yarn could support private-sector manufacturers with a regular and cheap supply of inputs—Turkey, Algeria, and Iraq were all notable in this respect. Likewise, the public sector was a reliable and not very cost-conscious purchaser of private-sector goods, from automobile components to army uniforms. Several observers have concluded that the stirrings and growth of the private sector in several Middle Eastern countries, notably Turkey and Egypt, were an assertion of class interests and that a strengthening private sector was the principal force behind the gradual abandonment of state regulation of the economy. Private interests, sustained over decades by state contracts and protection, allegedly were sufficiently powerful to force the state into retreat, or at least to put the state more directly at the service of the private sector. Doubtless, some private interests would benefit from the process of liberalization. We do not believe, however, that private class interests caused such policies. Indeed, the private sector remained weak politically as a class, all the way until the 2011 uprisings (Hertog, Luciani, and Valeri 2013).

Did the system produce a state bourgeoisie that also resisted reforms? There is a compelling logic to the *assumption* of a dominant state class given the size and strategic importance of the assets owned by the state. The state does constitute the major means of production, except in the agrarian sector, where it nonetheless has the means to orient production. It stands to reason that the professional managers of public assets could develop the attributes of a class, standing as they do in a similar position in relation to the means of production and sharing a common set of interests and goals, that is, class consciousness. The existence of such a class is all the more plausible in that conventional class actors are weak or in decline. The old landowning classes have long since been destroyed by land reform, while an industrial bourgeoisie has yet to emerge.

However, the paradox in the identity of the state bourgeoisie is that it cannot really ensure its reproduction as a state class. Members of the state bourgeoisie have no legal title to their offices—they cannot transfer them, and the higher they are in the state hierarchy the less likely it is that they will hold their own positions for very long. The survival of the members of this class is dependent on three factors: (1) their ability to move from position to position within the state hierarchy; (2) their technical competency, which makes them marketable in *any* milieu; and (3) their ability to build nest eggs (farms, businesses, investments, foreign bank accounts) outside the state sector. Seen in this light, the state bourgeoisie is a strange class indeed. Bertil Walstedt (1980, 187) saw that in Turkey "a self-perpetuating power group was born, linking bureaucrats, labor unions, and local politicians, that was far more powerful than any private capitalist power blocks operating in Turkey." John Waterbury (1983, 260) saw 200,000 to 300,000 members of the state bourgeoisie in Egypt. Over time this class and its offspring became one of the backbones of the private sector, often in coalition with old money, as well as with security interests and foreign investors, often from the Arab Gulf.

DELAYING REFORMS AND THE POLITICAL ECONOMY OF STRUCTURAL ADJUSTMENT

The failures arising from mismanaged ISI and public enterprise experienced across all the countries in the region were no doubt exacerbated in those countries with no or very limited oil reserves by the increase in world oil prices in the 1970s. The increase in world oil prices also led to lower levels of official assistance (especially in Egypt and Jordan) and later, reductions in workers' remittances. Growing import bills coupled with stagnant exports led to burgeoning trade deficits that had to be financed by foreign borrowing, both commercial and multilateral.

MENA countries filled their very large resource gaps for the most part with continued foreign borrowing and with aid from the United States, the EEC (the precursor of the European Union), and the capital-surplus oil exporters of the Gulf. The net amount of borrowings rose in the RPLA countries from close to zero in the 1960s to around 7 percent of GDP during the 1970s and 1980s. The failure of state-led growth to close the twin gaps between domestic savings and investment and between exports and imports contributed in time to the accumulation of very large foreign debts. In most cases, there was a marked increase in external indebtedness and a rise in the debt-service ratio (debt repayment as a percentage of export revenue). Although these debts were not nearly so large in absolute terms as those of Latin American debtors like Brazil (US$125 billion) or Mexico (US$100 billion), they were large enough to narrow the options for policymakers and to increase the influence of international lending agencies in the policy process. In the RPLA countries, the debt-to-GDP ratio nearly doubled, from an average of 45 percent in 1980—an already large ratio by international standards—to 92.5 percent in 1990. The financial situation in Egypt, Jordan, Morocco, and Tunisia in particular became unsustainable, forcing structural adjustment as the only alternative to default.

TABLE 7.3. External Debt over GDP in the MENA Countries, 1970–2010

	1970	1980	1990	2000	2010
Low income	0.0%	28.7%	63.1%	67.1%	29.6%
Middle income	0.4	21.7	39.0	39.6	22.8
RRLA	0.0	24.4	64.9	58.4	25.0
Algeria	0.0	45.9	45.5	46.4	4.5
Iran, Islamic Republic of		5.0	7.8	7.9	
Iraq	na	na	na	na	57.5
Sudan	0.0	68.0	119.4	130.9	34.3
Syrian Arab Republic	0.0	27.6	139.0	115.0	8.9
Yemen, Republic of	na	na	77.7	49.9	19.8
RPLA	1.1	45.6	92.5	78.8	65.1
Egypt, Arab Republic of	0.0	83.4	76.6	29.3	16.6
Jordan	0.0	47.2	207.2	131.2	63.3
Lebanon	5.4	5.3	19.2	124.1	167.2
Morocco	0.0	51.7	96.9	56.2	29.0
Tunisia	0.0	40.4	62.5	53.0	49.5
Turkey	0.0	27.8	32.7	43.8	41.0

Source: International Monetary Fund (IMF), World Economic Outlook (WEO).

The timing, pace, and content of structural reform efforts in the MENA region have varied widely across countries, but in all cases, reforms were resisted and delayed as long as possible. The common elements of the reform efforts that have had major political consequences include restraining public expenditures, holding in check if not reducing the size of the public-enterprise sector, stimulating private enterprise and investment, and removing subsidies on consumer goods, agricultural and industrial inputs, and credit. In addition, there have been efforts to liberalize foreign trade, to reduce the tariff protection of domestic producers, and to stimulate the export sectors of the economy. Each of these moves produces winners and losers. Combining them all at once in reform efforts would have been likely to send shock waves through well-established coalitions of economic interests and beneficiaries of the status quo.

The major risk, at least as it is perceived by political leadership, is that austerity will provoke violence, especially among urban populations. As it is, cost-of-living rioting in Middle Eastern cities has severely tested the regimes of Morocco in 1965, 1982, and 1984, Tunisia in 1978 and 1984, Egypt in 1977, Algeria in 1988, Jordan in 1989, Yemen in 2005, and Sudan, where it may have been the catalyst for the overthrow of Jaafar al-Nimeiri in March 1985.

There are basically two kinds of response to economic pressures that national leaders can adopt. The first is rejection of structural reform; leaders who choose this response generally cite the deleterious consequences for equity and the likelihood of economic stagnation. A common variation is to adopt a posture of rejection of some or all of the recommended reforms but quietly to pursue "just enough reforms" to keep the system afloat. In Egypt from 1976 on, both Anwar Sadat and Hosni Mubarak followed this tactic to some extent, as we discuss further later. The second option is to accept the reforms and take the lead in devising reformist programs purely out of domestic concerns and because they make sense.

The first strategy is illustrated by the way Turkey managed one of its gravest economic crises, in the late 1970s. It was governed at the time by fragile and chang-ing political coalitions, dominated by the Republican People's Party (led by Bülent Ecevit) and the Justice Party (led by Süleyman Demirel). Neither of these protago-nists could afford to promote economic austerity for fear of alienating a significant part of the electorate. The result, according to Merih Celasun (1983, 11), was that despite the oil crisis and related external shocks, Turkey attempted to preserve its growth momentum under its Third Five-Year Plan (1973–1977) through rapid re-serve decumulation and massive external borrowing.

Most other countries of the region initially replicated this scenario, at least as long as they could borrow their way to delay reforms, although Turkey was unique in the nature of its party-competitive political system. In the end, foreign resources were more often used to pay for current consumption rather than to increase pro-duction. Eventually, as foreign debt snowballed, new borrowing was used to some extent to cover payments on past debt, leading to a mounting debt trap. But debt financing was not sustainable in the absence of deeper structural reforms. In the early and mid-1980s, Turkey, Egypt, Sudan, Tunisia, and Morocco were all wres-tling with structural adjustment programs.

The strategy was typically taken up as long as countries could avoid adjustment, because they could count on oil revenues, such as Iran and Algeria, or strategic rents, such as Egypt. In Iran, the oil boom of the 1970s allowed the shah to finance large capital-intensive projects in the public sector, to continue to neglect agricul-ture, and to generate high rates of inflation in an overheated economy. His failure to use Iran's petroleum rents for structural adjustment set the economic stage for his own downfall. As Henry Bienen and Mark Gersovitz (1985) argued, stabiliza-tion and structural adjustment programs may be at least as likely to contribute to political stability as to undermine it. Indeed, other oil-producing countries that had experienced no severe balance-of-payments problems, such as Algeria and Iraq, had nonetheless spontaneously moved in the direction of mild reforms because of problems of food security, unemployment, and poorly integrated domestic markets.

In Egypt, the challenge of structural adjustment was first posed unequivocally in 1976. The country had fallen in arrears on payments on its commercial debt; in addition, the government deficit and domestic inflation were growing in lockstep, the public sector was riddled with idle capacity and large aggregate losses, and price disincentives were preventing agriculture from taking up the slack. Egypt entered into a standby agreement with the IMF in the spring of 1976. Part of the reform package was to reduce the level of subsidies of several consumer goods in order to lower the deficit. When the price increases were announced, three days of severe rioting ensued in Alexandria, Cairo, and several other Egyptian cities. Sadat immediately revoked the price increases, and the stabilization program was shelved. That Egypt's economy did not then founder was the result of great luck and some skillful political maneuvering. In the fall of 1977, Sadat made his historic trip to Jerusalem in search of a peace that might, among other things, enhance Egypt's image as a home for foreign investment and lighten the burden of military expenditures on the economy. In fact, the Camp David Accords of March 1979, which established formal peace between Egypt and Israel, led to Egypt's ostracism from the Arab world and a drying up of Arab aid and private investment in the Egyptian economy.

In the late 1970s, however, other processes, unplanned and unanticipated, were in train and brought Egypt large amounts of unexpected foreign exchange. The booming oil economies of the region needed manpower at all skill levels to implement their gargantuan development plans. By 1980, hundreds of thousands of Egyptian migrant workers were remitting to the home economy upwards of US$3 billion per year. Moreover, the recovery of oil fields in the Sinai Peninsula after years of Israeli occupation had coincided with a second surge in international oil prices, and Egyptian oil exports were earning the country US$4.5 billion per annum. The surge in oil prices also was reflected in increased transit fees in the Suez Canal. Finally, the peace between Israel and Egypt did stimulate tourism, which in 1980 generated US$700 million in revenues.

These external resources could have been used to cushion the impact of the measures needed to reform Egypt's economy. But when President Hosni Mubarak came into power in 1981 after the assassination of President Sadat by Muslim extremists, he was only too aware of the depth of alienation of large segments of Egypt's youth, who faced a soaring cost of living and a shrinking domestic job market. To take on structural adjustment reforms at the very moment when external markets for Egyptian labor were beginning to contract must have seemed as politically suicidal as it was economically inevitable. He searched, successfully from a political perspective, for a way to do just enough to keep the economy afloat without destabilizing the system, and he avoided deep reforms as long as he could.

Rather than use the rise in external resources to make structural adjustment less painful, Mubarak decided to use these resources to pay for increased consumption, mainly in the form of imports and increased consumer subsidies, thus avoiding structural adjustment. By the mid-1980s, however, a global oil glut was manifest, and the bottom dropped out of international oil prices. Egypt's oil earnings plummeted, the demand for Egyptian labor in Arab oil-exporting economies slackened and the flow of remittances began to diminish, tanker traffic through the Suez Canal tapered off, and numerous terrorist incidents in 1985 and 1986 scared away tourists. Ten years after first nibbling at the bullet, Egypt was once again faced with bankruptcy.

Several other Middle Eastern states have, to varying degrees, shared in Egypt's distress. For example, in 1985 *The Economist* surveyed Israel and noted the following symptoms: an inflation rate of 180–200 percent per annum, the highest per capita foreign debt in the world (US$6,200 per person), unemployment running at 10 percent of the workforce, an absolute decline in the standard of living, and an annual growth rate of GNP of about 1 percent (*The Economist,* July 20, 1985). The causes of the disease were seen as lying in a defense establishment that annually absorbed 20 percent of GNP, a massive welfare state, subsidies of basic consumer goods, the indexing of wage increases to the cost of living, a "huge socialist bureaucracy—encompassing not only trade unions but also banking, transport, farming, insurance, [and] education," the dampening of private initiative through public quasi-monopolies, and "irresponsibly disbursed American aid." The public-sector deficit in 1984 was at about 16 percent of GNP. The trade deficit had reached US$2.5 billion.

The second strategy, "taking the bull by the horn," is best illustrated by the reform programs implemented by Turkey in 1980 and, to a lesser extent, by Tunisia and Morocco in the mid-1980s and Jordan in the late 1980s. In Turkey, even before the military seized power in 1981 in the midst of escalating civil violence, the civilian government had introduced sweeping policy changes in January 1980. These policy changes included sharp increases in the prices of public-sector goods, elimination of a wide range of price controls, major currency devaluation, export incentives, favorable legislation for foreign investors, and curbs on government spending. It is moot whether this program could have been implemented with the same force had the military not intervened to put an end to civil violence as well as to open democratic life. The trade unions and universities were muzzled, and the return to civilian government in November 1983 was under the strictures imposed by Turkey's senior officers. In Morocco, too, the reforms were pushed by an autocratic government, but a political opening was created in the late 1990s by the government of longtime opponent Abderrahmane Youssoufi. In contrast, reform in Jordan was preceded by a political opening that brought the Muslim Brotherhood into government in an attempt to create "moderation through participation" (Schwedler 2013).

The new Turkish government announced a sweeping stabilization and structural adjustment policy with devaluation of the currency, fiscal austerity moves, and trade and parastatal reform. A crawling peg was adopted for the currency, tariffs were cut, and many quantitative export restrictions were lifted. Parastatal institutions were reformed; management obtained the authority to set prices and was required to phase out subsidies. From 1981 to 1985, exporters received tax rebates and subsidized credit while non-exporting firms faced sharper increases in the real cost of borrowing. Average tariff rates fell precipitously (Öniş and Webb 1994). Turkish manufactured exports responded very strongly to this new policy environment. Manufactures jumped from one-third to three-quarters of exports between 1980 and 1985, with continued strong performance thereafter. There was considerable diversification of manufacturing, both by sector and geographically (Anatolian towns did particularly well), and the sector's efficiency rose. Turkish consumer durables became competitive in the discriminating markets of the European Union and the Gulf. During the 1990s, exports continued to be upgraded and to pull economic growth, with automobiles and non-electrical machinery leading the way (ERF and IM 2005).

Turkey in the 1980s and 1990s was for the most part governed by a center-right coalition in which business interests that were economically strong but electorally weak (because they were few in number) sought allies among losers from structural adjustment (Waterbury 1992). The parties spent large sums of public money not only to foster exports but also to compensate losers. In such a fragmented democratic polity, it proved very difficult to implement the classic structural adjustment package. Turgut Özal, the prime minister from 1983 to 1989, forged a center-right coalition to support the initial push for market reforms, incorporating key business leaders and also, as junior partners, various Islamist political elements. He institutionalized this coalition in his Motherland Party. However, this grouping soon splintered. It is true that the institutional structure of Turkish politics supported Özal's key role; the state bureaucracy had long been far more powerful than any set of interest groups, which tended to take direction from the state rather than vigorously press their own demands. Thus, the reform effort benefited from determined, skillful leadership operating within institutions that magnified its power.

Tunisia adopted a variation of the second strategy, which consisted of not delaying reform but instead implementing it over time and in small doses. Tunisia offers a striking exception to the generally weak economic reform performance of Arab socialist republics. Although it had difficulty privatizing—for the same reasons similar regimes experienced this difficulty—its history of pragmatism in development since 1969 paid off. Tunisian reform had four advantages. First, the government not only started its reform effort early but very carefully lived up to all of its commitments. Second, it worked very closely with the IMF and the World Bank in constructing and implementing reform programs. Third, President Ben-Ali, after 1987, visibly backed the decisions of the Western-trained and -oriented technocrats whom he placed in charge of economic policymaking. The generally high level of competence of the Tunisian civil service helped to ensure adequate implementation of reform measures. Fourth, the country's strong performance in human capital formation made it relatively more plausible to embrace a strategy of opening up to foreign competition, while redeploying capital and labor to areas of comparative advantage.

CONCLUSIONS

By the early 1990s, Middle Eastern societies and LDCs as a whole had come to the end of a major historic developmental phase. State-led growth had brought about a certain amount of structural transformation, but rapid population growth and the collapse of oil prices overwhelmed the income-raising effects that such transformation was presumed to yield. The state overextended its capacity to manage and guide increasingly diversified economies. It was able to give a big push to industrialization but was unable to deal with the complexities of industrial "deepening" (the efficient use of labor and capital) or the need to export in highly competitive world markets. Adding to the complexity and diversity brought about by state intervention was the creation of new social actors and interests that benefited from state policies (land reform beneficiaries, for instance, or the recipients of subsidized credit) or from state business (the whole range of subcontracting). Over time these groups became entrenched in their economic niches, absorbing resources and saving and investing in such a manner that they developed some economic autonomy and the means to lobby effectively vis-à-vis the state.

Although multiple forces were blocking reforms, in the end public sectors and big government seemed to have mostly preserved their dominance in Middle Eastern economies, seemingly regardless of the ideologies of individual regimes. What Middle Eastern states have in common that helps explain this perpetual dominance are an unwillingness to open up politically and the extraordinary power the public sector offers their political leadership to preempt resources from actors outside the state system and to control strategic sectors of the workforce. It does not surprise us to see leaders of self-proclaimed socialist regimes defending their public sectors, but at first blush it seems odd to see large public sectors in nominally liberal or liberalizing economic systems such as those of Egypt, Jordan, or Tunisia. To the leaders of these countries, however, the economic risks of inefficient public enterprise may not outweigh the political risks of giving up the leverage over resources and people that public enterprise provides.

It is the political calculus of these two kinds of costs that determines how political elites respond to the poor performance and fiscal burdens of public enterprise. To some extent, equity (in the form of redundant labor, relatively high remuneration, and low productivity) and inefficiency have been combined and paid for through deficit financing and borrowing abroad. But when foreign creditors refuse to advance new lines of credit until the fiscal mess is cleared up, the painful day of reckoning can no longer be postponed.

NOTES

1. In this regard, the goal of the US Coalition Provisional Authority, which governed Iraq for two years, was no different: use state power to reshape society and its institutions.

2. It is important to remember that for many Muslims, Atatürk is probably the most despised leader of the twentieth century precisely because he abolished the caliphate and tried to subjugate the Islamic establishment in Turkey.

3. A number of advanced industrial nations, especially Austria, Italy, France, and the United Kingdom, revealed similar proportions in the 1980s.

4. The strategy owed a great deal to the French economist G. Destanne de Bernis (1971).

5. Recall again that we are using "liberal" in an exclusively economic context in this chapter. While far from the worst offenders, no monarchy in the region could be described as "liberal" in the conventional political sense of being concerned with human rights and the role of civil society.

6. As noted earlier, the fear that time was running out impelled Bourguiba to delegate broad powers to Ahmed Ben Salah in Tunisia's version of the big push.

7. By 2006, foreign workers numbered approximately 5.5 million (CIA, *World Fact-book,* 2006).

8. Iran and Iraq joined their poorer brethren in facing a resource gap once they embarked on their mutual slaughter, but there were no international data on this issue for these two countries during and immediately after their war (1980–1988). Unofficial estimates placed Iraq's debt at as much as US$90 billion, while Iran had entirely depleted its accumulated reserves at the end of the war (*Middle East,* July 1988).

9. In that year, the difference between domestic savings and domestic investment was 4 percent for all middle-income countries, 21 percent for lower-middle-income countries, and 5 percent for upper-middle-income countries.

8

STRUCTURAL ADJUSTMENT
AND THE RISE OF
CRONY CAPITALISM

The economic imbalances caused by years of the unsuccessful state-led strategy of import substitution industrialization (ISI) made the status quo no longer viable unless countries could borrow indefinitely from abroad the resources that they could not generate at home. Without some sort of "biting the bullet," some form of fundamental restructuring of the basic parameters of the economy, the vicious circle described in Chapter 7 would lead to debt default and economic collapse. At the very least, those governments whose countries' oil rents were limited or nonexistent, being unable to continue to borrow internationally to finance the twin deficits of the government budget and the external current account, would have to live within their means. By itself, however, stabilization is not a strategy for growth, let alone for regime preservation. In this chapter, we look at the systems that emerged from the restructurings undertaken in the RPLA and the RRLA countries in the 1990s. Chapter 9 focuses on the richer RRLP countries of the Gulf Cooperation Council (GCC).

So, if state-led growth did not work as a development model, what would? In the early 1990s, most economists agreed on what needed to be done to revive growth in the countries of the Global South: let the invisible hand of the market allocate factors of production to their best use. The collapse of the Soviet Union in the 1990s further discredited centrally planned economies—and supporters of the status quo in the Middle East. At the same time, globalization had become a formidable force (Henry and Springborg 2010). The challenge for the mostly autocratic governments of the Middle East was thus twofold: getting growth going, and maintaining control over society.

A common economic policy prescription to address the accumulation of macroeconomic imbalances and other contradictions associated with state-led growth was formulated by the international financial institutions (IFIs) in the 1990s. This was known as the "Washington Consensus," and its recommendations centered on three pillars: (1) macroeconomic stability (especially price stability and real exchange rate devaluation); (2) relying on the market mechanism to allocate finance, labor, and inputs and relying on the private sector to drive growth; and (3) a greater openness to international trade and export-led growth. By "getting the prices right" and "getting the state out of the way," it was hoped that (private) capital would flow into productive investment, thereby producing exports and creating jobs while also stimulating efficiency, thus enhancing international competitiveness. This would foster a virtuous circle of inflows of foreign (and domestic) direct investment, bolstering financial soundness and, in turn, creating more investment, more exports, more jobs, and more wealth.

The logic of this prescription for economic reform seemed unassailable—it was backed by intellectual developments as well as political change in the West. Thus, it was only a question of time before MENA countries would bow to internal and external pressures and embrace a new model of political economy. Between the mid-1980s and the 1990s, with the support of the World Bank and the International Monetary Fund (IMF), most of the countries of the region had adopted many of the Washington Consensus policies. By the end of the 1990s, the region's macroeconomic imbalances were reduced and its economies were much more private sector–driven compared to the past—or so it seemed. As we shall see in the rest of the chapter, what came into being was quite different from the neoliberal model imagined by the architects of the Washington Consensus, as happened repeatedly elsewhere in the world, and in particular during the economic opening of the FSU and Eastern Europe.

The economic path of the RPLA and RRLA countries diverged further after the 1980s. In the RPLA countries—Tunisia, Morocco, Egypt, and Jordan—exhausted political regimes needed to find a way to consolidate their rule and at the same time get the economic growth process restarted. From their perspective, structural adjustment programs (SAPs)—the loan programs and economic policies developed by the World Bank and IMF—offered the means to switch from the old social contracts with bureaucrats, farmers, and workers and toward a new alliance with business elites. Ultimately, however, SAPs did not deliver sufficient growth. Undoubtedly, part of the explanation for the low growth performance of the MENA countries was related to the more competitive nature of export markets after the 1980s, when Asian exporters had established an unassailable lead and competition from the newly liberalized economies of Eastern Europe was rising. But in addition, the politically connected firms that replaced public enterprises as the drivers of growth performed poorly and reduced the beneficial aspects of competition, and this form of capitalism would be rejected by the popular movements of 2011.

In the RRLA countries, on the other hand, very little structural adjustment was undertaken, as regimes simply would not tolerate the emergence of economic actors outside their direct control. Indeed, they did not need to do so as much anyway, given that their rule relied more on oil-financed repression than on the promise of economic prosperity. From Iraq to Algeria and Syria, these regimes became increasingly more repressive and relied on a narrowing alliance with security forces and cronies, which led to even lower economic growth amid rising political instability, although there is notable heterogeneity within the RRLA group on this score. The level of repression fell in Algeria as the use of patronage increased there with the advent of the second oil boom, but repression rose in Sudan, Yemen, and Syria—they became the most repressive regimes of the whole region (see Figure 3.8).

THE WASHINGTON CONSENSUS

The World Bank, in cooperation with the IMF and other multilateral lenders, developed the economic strategies and multiyear loan programs known as structural adjustment programs to address the issues of restructuring the economy. These programs were not designed to deal with a particular balance-of-payments crisis or short-term disturbance in economic performance; instead, they were focused on the basic assumptions of development strategy. And whether they were SAPs leveraged by the World Bank and other donors or other structural adjustment plans that evolved spontaneously out of domestic considerations (India has been notable in this latter respect), these strategies struck at the very heart of structural transformation. International capital markets also exerted pressure for change, advocating the downsizing of the public sector of the economy, expanding foreign trade, and increasing integration into the global economy.

Successful adjustment was thought to have several essential components: reduced government spending; a shift of investment resources from the public sector to the private sector; a move away from a planned economy to one in which the market would play a major role in allocating resources; and a move to an economy in which equity concerns might be "temporarily" sacrificed to prioritize efficiency, at least in the first version of the Washington Consensus. Based on these requirements, ten key elements of the Washington Consensus were initially identified (see Box 8.1).

Typically, countries took the first steps toward austerity and restructuring in the wake of balance-of-payments crises. A country would turn to the IMF in order to borrow in excess of its quota. The IMF would then disburse these funds in "slices" (tranches) as the country took a sequence of steps to prevent a recurrence of the balance-of-payments shortfall. Between 1984 and 1995, Algeria, Egypt, Israel, Jordan, Morocco, Tunisia, and Turkey entered into such agreements.

A major element of these structural adjustment loans (SALs) was a focus on balancing the books in order to reduce macroeconomic imbalances, inflation, and the accumulation of foreign debts. There are several steps in this process. First, government deficits need to be reduced to some target level—say, 4 percent of GDP. To do this, governments might implement salary and hiring freezes and slash investment budgets and subsidies, as discussed in Chapter 2. Such measures may undermine the state's role as employer of last resort, deny public-sector enterprise the flows of investment to which it has become accustomed, and reduce the quality of public services—imposing hardship on the poor and reducing the employability of the educated middle class.

The second step is to streamline the public sector and stimulate the private sector. This may require measures to reduce administrative interference in pricing mechanisms and allow supply and demand to determine price levels. Public-sector enterprises, which must start competing with the private sector, will need to increase productivity, reduce costs, let go of redundant labor, and stop relying on government financing of their deficits. At the same time, new sources of commercial credit may be opened to the private sector, and it could be the private rather than the public sector that is tasked with leading an export drive to reduce the country's balance-of-payments problems. Over time, public-sector enterprises will be privatized. Structural adjustment programs generally also seek to stimulate national savings by raising interest rates and liberalizing the financial markets to ensure that capital flows to where it is needed most. The end of cheap or subsidized credit in the long run encourages more careful project selection and a more efficient utilization of capital, but the short-term effect may be to put many firms out of business and many people out of work. In addition, state banks will need to be privatized.

BOX 8.1. The "Washington Consensus"

The basic concept of the "Washington Consensus," a term coined by John Williamson (1990) of the Peterson Institute for International Economics in Washington, DC, was that markets promote growth better than states. For countries enmeshed in the fiscal imbalances generated by ISI policies and the various international shocks of the 1970s (oil price increases, a rise in international interest rates, recession in the OECD countries), the view was that "stabilization" (of the macro economy) had to precede and then be followed by "structural adjustment," or more microeconomic change, such as price liberalization and privatization. Williamson (1990) summarized the perspective as consisting of the following ten points:

1. Fiscal discipline
2. Reorientation of public expenditures
3. Tax reform
4. Interest rate liberalization
5. Unified and competitive exchange rates
6. Trade liberalization
7. Opening for direct foreign investment
8. Privatization
9. Deregulation
10. Securing property rights

As experience around the world with the adoption of such policies wore on during the 1980s and 1990s, many were disappointed in the results. One response was so common that it became known as the "Post-Washington Consensus." This view continued to advocate the original ten policy changes, but added ten more (Rodrik 2004):

continues

Third is the encouragement of engagement in international trade and finance, which usually involves a devaluation of the national currency as well as trade reforms. Before the long-term benefits of devaluation and tariff reductions are felt, however, the short-term effects can be devastating. The objective of devaluations is to promote exports, but all imports will also become more expensive, hurting the industries that rely on imported raw materials and capital equipment as well as urban consumers who are used to cheap food imports. Devaluations also make servicing the international debt more onerous in terms of local currency. With lower tariffs, local industries will feel the impact of foreign competition and lose their local market share unless they can become more competitive. The government will also lose access to easily collected custom revenues and be forced to institute new taxes to replace them.

BOX 8.1. *continued*

11. Corporate governance
12. Anticorruption efforts
13. Flexible labor markets
14. Adherence to WTO disciplines
15. Adherence to international financial codes and standards
16. "Prudent" capital-account opening
17. Non-intermediate exchange rate regimes
18. Independent central bank/inflation targeting
19. Social safety nets
20. Targeted poverty reduction

Implementing all twenty components simultaneously would, of course, be essentially suicidal: any government asked to do so would offend all entrenched interests at once. Accordingly, much ink was spilled concerning the timing and sequencing of such a daunting list, but as Dani Rodrik puts it, in practice the approach is "do whatever you can, as much as you can, as quickly as you can" (Rodrik 2004, 12).

Rodrik persuasively (to us) advocates a more nuanced and a more historically and politically grounded approach. He argues that "there are some general, first-order principles of economic policy that all successful countries have more or less adhered to": (1) achieving macroeconomic stability; (2) integrating into the world economy; (3) providing investors with effective protection for property rights and contract enforcement; and (4) maintaining social cohesion, solidarity, and political stability (Rodrik 2004). He points out that such principles have been met through a wide range of institutions, governance structures, and political systems. It is this perspective that seems to us most useful for understanding the recent past in the Middle East and for thinking about the future.

This process is inevitably painful. The goal of structural change is to free up capital and labor resources from inefficient activities, especially in government and in protected sectors, and to direct these newly freed resources toward the more efficient private sector. While the loss of jobs in the uncompetitive sectors is immediate, the gains in new jobs are contingent upon a "supply response," which theoretically comes over time. The supply response itself is subject to the credibility of government policy, which militates for rapid reforms. But it also depends on social and political stability, which militates for gradualism and the creation of safety nets and retraining programs in order to move factors of production to areas where they can be more useful while minimizing social pains.

In an ideal world, structural adjustment would take place without sacrificing growth, but the reality is that this process requires austerity and adjustment costs for important segments of the population. Even so, two kinds of policy design pitfalls must be avoided. The structural adjustment "medicine" must not be so powerful as to lock the economy into a downward spiral of contraction, business liquidation, unemployment, and slack demand, as is happening in the European countries gripped by "austerity" since the euro crisis of 2011. Judicious government pump-priming and foreign borrowing to keep the economy expanding will certainly be needed, something that is lost on the budgetary hawks in the United States and Europe today. The second pitfall is related directly to seeking that delicate balance between austerity and growth. The application of stabilization and structural adjustment programs cannot be so diluted that they achieve the worst of both worlds—a deterioration in standards of living for important segments of the population without the structural reforms that would set the stage for further growth.

Such redistributive policies may lead to a decline in standards of living for people on fixed incomes and/or low- and middle-income urbanites and the erosion of wages and benefits for previously privileged labor unions. In addition, educated and skilled youth may face an economy that generates very little skilled employment. Short-term economic contraction, proponents of these policies argue, is the price that must be paid to ensure future sustained growth. However, getting from the short term to the long term has often proved politically perilous, if not fatal, unless careful social engineering to compensate the losers, such as developing a targeted safety net, is put in place at the outset of the reforms. Such efforts were not considered to be pressing, however, until the Consensus evolved in the 1990s (see later discussion).

These measures, then, led to mighty changes in the social and economic environments of the MENA countries, unleashing all kinds of political forces to defend established interests or take advantage of perceived new opportunities. In other circumstances, such as in Latin America, Africa, and Eastern Europe, these profound changes were accompanied by an opening of the political space and the introduction of competitive politics. By 2010 in the Middle East, however, the political economy systems remained recognizably the same as they had been prior to the introduction of the Washington Consensus principles. Elegant theories of social engineering rarely survive protracted contact with human reality, as famously noted by Karl Polanyi (2001) as early as 1944.[1] Just as the orthodoxy of an earlier generation, ISI, failed to deliver on all of its promises, the career of the Washington Consensus in the MENA region has been a decidedly checkered one.

CRITICS OF THE WASHINGTON CONSENSUS
AND ALTERNATIVES AROUND THE WORLD

As the policies advocated by the Washington Consensus took root and became more established in various developing countries around the globe, dissenting views and heterodox practices began to emerge. Some economic historians noted that the Washington Consensus policies were very different from those adopted by the now-advanced industrial countries (see, for example, Chang 2002). In fact, these countries had relied extensively on protectionism and state controls earlier in their histories. This critique, however, could be dismissed by arguing that although ISI might indeed have been a phase of development, its historical moment had now passed. But still, the countries that grew the fastest in the 1970s and 1980s did not by any means fully adopt policy prescriptions like those laid out in the Washington Consensus.

Political scientists have noted, since at least the defining work of Polanyi (2001), that although there are some policy principles that favor economic growth, these can be stated only in a very general way. How these general goals are achieved in practice will be locally, institutionally, politically, and historically specific (see, for example, Chaudhry 1993). In this vein, Dani Rodrik (2004) offers a useful perspective, particularly for understanding the complex and uncertain economic *and* political challenges in the MENA countries. States need to become more accountable, market mechanisms need to function more effectively, and greater involvement in the global economy is essential, but the institutional specifics of *how* these general goals can be achieved are wide indeed (see Box 8.1). Other prominent economists, such as Joseph Stiglitz (2003, 2004) and William Easterly (2011), have made the same point: without local adjustments, the Washington Consensus does not seem to lead to the kind of growth its advocates confidently predict, nor has it been either necessary or sufficient for growth accelerations. This failure has been particularly marked in two aspects: a governance failure to develop the checks and balances needed to make markets work, and economic market failures particularly associated with the growth-reducing effects of private monopolies and the destabilizing effects of capital mobility.

The star performers since the 1970s, the countries of East Asia—the "Asian Tigers"—clearly took a different path from the kinds of policies advocated by the Washington Consensus during particular parts of their development trajectory. Taiwan and Korea, two of the larger "Tigers," relied extensively on state intervention throughout the postwar era (Amsden 1992, 2001; Fishlow et al. 1994; Wade 1990). The secret of their success seems to lie in their export orientation and the disciplined management of state favors to firms that could respond with high levels of economic performance. Only after economic growth had raised income levels to the level of upper-middle-income countries did they start to liberalize their polity. The country whose record of sustained economic growth and poverty reduction is unmatched anywhere in the historical record, the People's Republic of China, obviously did not embrace a number of the allegedly critical criteria of good policy according to the Washington Consensus. In its first phase of reform, China liberalized its economy only at the village level, but this created sufficient economic momentum, while preserving social and political stability, to lead in time to the growth of the manufacturing coastal regions that would become the export powerhouse of the country. As of 2014, Chinese banks remained publicly owned, the financial system was heavily repressed, and state-owned enterprises still produced nearly half of China's GDP. And China remained a staunchly autocratic state dominated by its Communist Party.

But autocratic state-led reforms are not a sure recipe for success. The example of Russian privatization has been less than encouraging to many observers. Although Russia's privatization process has its defenders, most observers agree that its privatization in the absence of a functioning judiciary has simply transferred vast wealth from the state to a small cadre of insiders—a classic case of crony capitalism. The huge upsurge in poverty in Russia has also been disquieting. As Stiglitz (2003, 133) notes, "The middle class has been devastated, [and] a system of crony and mafia capitalism has been created." Although many of the Washington Consensus reforms were supposed to decrease rent-seeking and other forms of corruption, there is considerable skepticism about how much improvement has actually been made (Öniç and Senses 2003). This uncompetitive form of privatization in which public assets and wealth are transferred only to a small group of insiders is known as *nomenklatura* privatization, and it has been a marker of the MENA experience as well.

Although ultimately Latin American countries that embraced a more liberal and outwardly oriented political system experienced increased growth, countries as diverse as Mexico, Brazil, and Argentina also suffered a long "lost decade" before growth picked up. Problems surfaced related to the functioning of markets. The private sector often did not respond dynamically to the reforms, and private investment did not always rise—or it did not rise sufficiently to take the place of the public sector as an engine of growth. State monopolies were often replaced by private monopolies, which, unlike their predecessors, did not care about social welfare and took full advantage of their market dominance to reap monopoly profits. Large firms circumvented labor laws by hiring temporary workers to reduce their costs, thus further weakening the role of unions in negotiating outcomes more favorable to labor.

It is widely agreed that the way in which capital markets were liberalized played a significant part in the Asian financial crisis of 1996, the Turkish financial crisis of 2000, and the global financial crisis of 2008. These financial crises contributed to regime change in Indonesia and Turkey and more recently in European countries. In all these cases, private and poorly regulated banks took large risks with depositors' funds and concentrated their loans in the real estate sector and the large corporate sector, depriving small and medium-size firms and farmers of access to credit. Malaysia, on the other hand, used capital controls extensively and weathered the storm with the lowest social cost. Many economists, including staunch supporters of free trade, now argue that capital market liberalization should come only at the very end of the reform process.

Another assumption of SAPs is that countries will build up their export sectors, especially in manufacturing but also in services. But the success of this strategy is contingent at least in part on the availability of rising global markets. Global conditions were far more propitious in the 1970s, when East Asia paved its way to development via exports, than in the 1990s, as there was much less global competition in the earlier period. By the 1990s, it was already much harder for MENA firms to tap into world markets the way East Asia had done a decade or two earlier. At the same time, the hope that the delocalization of industry in Europe would benefit the Mediterranean periphery faded away once the Eastern European countries started to join the European Union in the 1990s.

In response to these and related difficulties, a revised consensus, often dubbed the "Post–Washington Consensus," emerged after the 2008 financial crisis. In the new consensus, all of the original elements remained, but new reforms were added (see Box 8.1). The early Washington Consensus saw the state as the problem, because it creates rent-seeking opportunities. So the policy recommendation was to liberalize as much as possible to move economic activity away from the state and toward an idealized market. But over time, as deficiencies of governance (a technocratic word for "politics") became the focus of attention, the Post–Washington Consensus began to advocate changes that were more political in nature. The development community turned its attention to the central role of institutions in development. Various pathologies, from replacing a public monopoly with a private oligopoly to banking crises, were now explained by "deficiencies in the rule of law" and similar governance issues, which is really just another way of restating the essential necessity of market regulation. It became increasingly apparent that for the state to withdraw from the economy, a *stronger* state, not a weaker one, is needed in order to regulate markets and provide the public goods that allow them to function. As Rodrick (2012, 10) summarizes the relationship between the state and markets:

> Markets depend on non-market institutions. That is because they are not self-creating, self-regulating, self-stabilizing, or self-legitimizing. Anything that goes beyond simple exchange among neighbors requires: investments in transport, communications, and logistics; enforcement of contracts, provision of information, and prevention of cheating; a stable and reliable medium of exchange; arrangements to bring distributional outcomes into conformity with social norms; and so on. Well-functioning, sustainable markets are backed up by a wide range of institutions that provide the critical functions of regulation, redistribution, monetary and fiscal stability, and conflict management.

This second-generation policy advice, driven by the disappointing results of the first wave of reforms, focused on governance and the establishment of institutions to regulate the market and build state capacity to do so. Policy advisers had realized that markets influence power relations, and thus reforms could not be conceptualized separately from the evolution of politics (Chaudhry 1993). Most of the MENA states were in crisis in the mid-1980s, with leaders facing rising opposition and losing the levers of ideology, state spending, and state-owned enterprises that had allowed them to rule uncontested for decades. These leaders would need to boost their legitimacy in order to survive, but structural adjustment was unable to do that for them. In some countries in Latin America, Africa, and Eastern Europe, the wholesale economic change went hand in hand with a new political openness and democratization. But rulers in the MENA region were unwilling to open up their political systems. And while foreign donors and governments became more involved in advocating internal political changes, such as accountable, democratic governance and the rule of law, Western powers were too happy to see their autocratic allies battling the forces of political Islam to want to push them to change in any serious manner. Also, Western interests in oil and the geostrategic importance of the region were additional factors deterring the Western powers and IFIs from pushing MENA states to open up so rapidly as to threaten regime stability. Out of this mix of contradictory signals emerged a Middle Eastern form of state-led capitalism that allowed aging autocrats to survive for another two decades—until the uprisings of 2011.

THE DEVELOPMENT OF CRONY
CAPITALISM IN THE MENA REGION

By 2011, it was clear that the economic reforms had failed to transform the region. A principal weakness of the new economic regime that emerged was the low demand for skilled workers. Governments stopped hiring, but these jobs were not replaced by a strong private-sector demand. Looking at the structure of employment in the region from 2005 to 2010 (Figure 8.1), one sees that while the public sector had declined since the 1970s, the size of the formal private sector in the region remained marginal—a mere 10–15 percent of the labor force in Morocco, Tunisia, and Egypt, and much lower in Iraq and Yemen. The region's star performer turned out to be Jordan, which benefited most from Western largesse owing to its geostrategic value and where nearly 20 percent of the labor force held formal private-sector jobs.

The private sector's lack of dynamism is also seen in its low rates of investment. The idea of state retrenchment was to make resources available for the private sector to invest, according to price signals. But as public-sector investment collapsed, private investment did not rise sufficiently to pick up the slack (see Table 8.1). In the RPLA countries, public investment plummeted to 5.2 percent of GDP in the 2000s, from nearly 12 percent of GDP in the 1970s. At a mere 18.7 percent, however, private investment in 2010 was only about 5 percent higher than in the 1970s; this level of growth was neither high enough to compensate for the rollback of the state nor sufficient to create the type and numbers of jobs needed in the region. Except in Lebanon, coming out of its long civil war, total investment actually decreased everywhere. Private-sector performance in Egypt, where private investment remained around 10 percent of GDP in the 2000s, and in Jordan and Morocco, where it was slightly higher but flat at close to its historical levels, was particularly disappointing.

Can the Arab region's economic underperformance be attributed to the type of state-business relations that have developed since the "liberal" reforms that began in the 1980s? Some economists have rightly argued that the reforms have not gone far enough (for example, Noland and Pack 2007), and political scientists have pinpointed the rise of "networks of privilege" and "crony capitalists" with

FIGURE 8.1. Employment Composition by Sector in Selected Economies in the MENA Region, 2005–2010

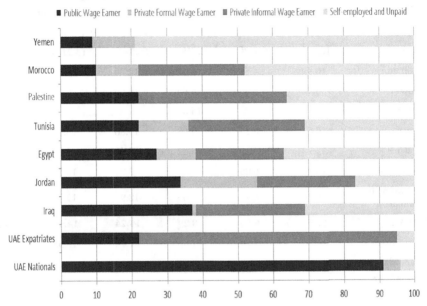

Source: Based on Egypt's Labor Force Survey (LFS), 2010; Iraq's Household Socio-Economic Survey (HSES), 2006; Jordan's Labor Market Panel Survey (LMPS), 2010; Morocco's LFS, 2010; Tunisia's LFS, 2010; the United Arab Emirates' LFS, 2009; Palestine's LFS, 2008; and the Republic of Yemen's Household Budget Survey (HBS), 2005.

Note: Formal employment, defined as employment affiliated with social security, is not available among private-sector firms in Palestine or for migrant workers in the United Arab Emirates.

myopic short-term interests as the central reason for low economic growth (Henry and Springborg 2010; Heydemann 2004; Owen 2004; Sadowski 1991). A study of corporate performance in the Middle East (World Bank 2009) shows that while economic reforms in the Middle East look impeccable on paper, a differentiated application of policy has led to a rising difference between de jure and de facto rules. Building on recent studies of Egypt and Tunisia (Diwan, Keefer, and Schiffbauer 2014; Rijkers, Freund, and Nucifora 2013), a 2014 World Bank report documents the mechanisms used to dispense privileges and ascribes the weak supply response from the private sector to the fact that MENA states grant privileges only to a select few, thus reducing the competiveness and dynamism of the economy. In Egypt, the trend accelerated in the last decade with the "businessmen" cabinet headed by Prime Minister Ahmed Nazif from 2004 to 2011. In Tunisia, the Ben Ali and Trabelsi families monopolized business opportunities and even expropriated the real estate and business holdings of wealthy elites (Kaboub 2014). Similar stories about favoritism and insiders abound in Syria, Yemen, and Algeria, where political

TABLE 8.1. Public and Private Investment (as a percentage of GDP) in the MENA Region, 1971–2010

Country	Public Investment			Private Investment		
	1971–1990	*1991–2000*	*2001–2010*	*1971–1990*	*1991–2000*	*2001–2010*
RRLP	**11.18%**	**6.92%**	**7.75%**	**10.98%**	**13.21%**	**14.13%**
Bahrain	10.99	4.59	6.47	12.74	8.17	16.50
Kuwait	6.96	6.59	5.94	10.50	9.96	9.94
Libya			14.89			3.18
Oman	10.51	8.24	9.08	15.86	13.07	15.45
Qatar	13.78	9.19	8.82	5.68	15.55	23.84
Saudi Arabia	18.09	6.06	5.42	2.09	13.28	12.82
United Arab Emirates	6.75	6.85	3.65	18.99	19.22	17.17
RRLA	**11.57**	**6.64**	**8.29**	**15.24**	**14.55**	**13.04**
Algeria	11.86	7.24	11.86	22.74	18.38	12.22
Iran, Islamic Republic of	13.08	10.28	9.60	15.14	16.43	17.94
Sudan	4.96	0.93	4.79	8.07	10.51	16.85
Syrian Arab Republic	15.01	10.75	10.36	10.27	12.01	10.05
Yemen, Republic of	7.18	3.99	6.78	3.32	15.44	10.40
RPLA	**11.90**	**8.36**	**5.23**	**13.53**	**16.10**	**18.73**
Egypt, Arab Republic of	18.46	13.98	8.25	9.62	5.58	10.30
Jordan	13.49	9.27	7.29	15.93	17.61	17.04
Lebanon	1.70	5.50	2.68	16.10	22.82	22.32
Morocco	6.87	4.18	14.36	15.43	18.23	13.92
Tunisia	14.04	8.85	3.42	12.32	16.26	19.89
Turkey	8.58	5.59	3.64	15.55	17.83	15.43
Overall MENA	**10.81**	**6.88**	**6.23**	**13.82**	**15.42**	**15.33**

Source: World Bank Indicators.

cronies seem to control large chunks of the private sector (Haddad 2012; Alley 2010; Tlemcani 1999).

Economic reforms posed existential challenges to the ruling elites. A main concern for all the autocratic rulers in the region, given that there was little in the way of parallel political reforms, was continuing to exercise power as they gave away important tools—ownership of state-owned enterprises, large investment budgets, large civil services, large military and security spending—that had allowed them to maintain effective control over beneficiaries and potential sources of opposition. Sfakianakis (2004) argues that privatization in Egypt was politically managed by the government "to allocate patronage to a narrow circle of supporters that it trusted." In this respect, the lack of transparency in the privatization process was an inherent part of a political process to reach the government's goals (Kienle 2002).

Analysts of the MENA region have come to conceptualize markets as political spaces, with reforms seen as processes of reregulation (Heydemann 2004). Political logic infuses markets no less than other domains, not only in terms of concerns about redistribution but also in terms of reorganizing rent-seeking in ways that preserve power and maintain political stability (Chaudhry 1993). So while in the early 1990s analysts of reforms in the Middle East had focused on the tension between winners and losers, they increasingly shifted their focus to the formation of new coalitions between rulers and parts of the business community—a marriage of old money, the state bourgeoisie, and elements of the security establishment. They began to see the underpinning of the politics of structural adjustment as a process of forming new networks of privilege driven by the logic of power preservation. Rent-seeking was back in a big way.

Recent social science literature about the region makes cronyism the central mechanism that resolved the contradictions created by the gradual liberalization of the economy in countries where political power remained highly autocratic. These analyses highlight the "imperfections" in the economic liberalization programs: "deals rather than rules," they argue, allowed weakening regimes to redefine the rules of the game by building alliances with the business elite in order to dominate the business sector and use it as a new source of patronage. Middle Eastern states needed to come up with new rents once oil-related revenues stopped flowing, and in the RPLA countries they had no choice but to turn to regulation rents, which are created by erecting barriers to entry that exclude opponents and provide privileges to a small coterie of allies (Malik and Awadallah 2013). Roger Owen (2004, 243) describes the economic regimes that emerged after economies were liberalized:

> Instead of encouraging more plural political systems, the Arab regimes . . . [produced] an Egyptian, or Tunisian, or Jordanian version of "crony capitalism" in which competition was stifled and entrepreneurs with close connections with the regime were able to obtain most of the major contracts, as well as to bend or break planning laws and other legal constraints when it suited them.

The private sector had diverse interests, but business elites adapted once it became clear that things had to change. The new arrangements tended to balance the gains and losses of the elites. For example, in Jordan and Morocco, when import tariffs went down, corporate and income taxation was also reduced to offset the increased cost advantage of international competitors. In some countries, like Tunisia, tax exemption was given to sectors that would lose the most from trade liberalization. In several countries, firms were allowed to avoid taxation if they contributed directly to funding projects and supporting constituencies important to the ruling interests (Cammett 2007). In Tunisia, high-level bureaucrats and members of the Ben Ali clan bought many of the firms that were privatized. Some firms from the old elite in the trade or import substitution sector moved into new sectors with high potential, but they were given special access to privileges that would allow them to make the adjustment more easily, such as subsidies, nontariff barriers, or loose application of the regulations. Sometimes they made deals with new entrants to slow down the reform so as to create win-win opportunities (as in the Moroccan garment and textile sector; see Cammett 2007). Jordanian and Egyptian elites often went into banking, another means by which to keep competitors at bay.

This new system rested on the distribution of privileges to those who could be trusted not to trespass beyond political red lines. Clement Henry and Robert Springborg (2010, 205), writing on Egypt, put the "political management of capital by all means, including using intimidation and managed predation," at the center of the "active efforts by political elites to strongly discourage potential manifestations of political behavior by business elites." In this context, "support for the opposition was a red line punishable by closure and expropriation." The rising bourgeoisie was not allowed to develop a sense of class interest—its members typically dealt bilaterally with the state to ensure their privileges. Moreover, in most countries, businesses with privileged access to resources and other advantages perceived the continuation of autocracy as being in their interest (Hertog 2013). When business interests became too autonomous, politically driven readjustment took place, such as anticorruption campaigns in Morocco and Algeria, the closing down of Islamist financial institutions in Egypt, and the tax inspections to drive out successful businessmen with a rising interest in politics in Tunisia.

Other constituencies also mattered for political stability. Consumers and workers were typically losers in the short term, and the fear of street action, as in the 1980s, pushed governments to resort to selective co-optation mechanisms to keep some core constituencies in the autocratic alliance and increase repression measures for all the other groups outside it. The fight against political Islam was used as a divide-and-rule tactic to scare elements of the middle class away from supporting the opposition. A large literature has developed to explore how regimes managed to survive by using these sticks and carrots (see, for example, Henry and Springborg 2006; King 2009; Lust 2005; Posusney and Angrist 2005; Schlumberger 2007).

Western governments continued to support autocrats, often by providing aid, especially when these autocrats were implementing policies that, however unpopular at home (such as fighting Islamists, being friendly to Israel or unfriendly to Iran), were valuable to the West. For example, reform conditions became less strict in Egypt after it participated in the First Gulf War in the 1990s and in Jordan after it signed a peace deal with Israel in 1992, thus introducing new or enhanced sources of rent into the region. Such "strategic rents," which are most available in some of the RPLA countries (Egypt and Jordan more than Morocco or Tunisia), alleviated the need for reforms by allowing these countries to attract donors' funds and profit from their geostrategic importance (rather than resource endowments).

Cronyism entailed practices such as granting monopoly rights to close associates of the rulers, selling public firms and land at reduced prices, and manipulating the financial markets for the benefit of a few insiders. Large swaths of the population increasingly came to see cronyism and corruption, both petty and grand, as the hallmark of economic liberalism and the source of many ills, including the job deficit, the rise in inequality, and the perpetuation of authoritarian rule. Indeed, the perceived "corruption" of the political and business elites was a driving force of popular discontent. Many indicators point to the rising concerns with corruption. A Pew survey reveals that in 2010 corruption was the top concern of Egyptians, with 46 percent listing it as their main concern even ahead of lack of democracy and poor economic conditions (Pew 2011). Also, changes in the corruption ratings of Arab countries in Transparency International's Corruption Perceptions Index (CPI) confirm this popular perception. In 2005, Egypt ranked 70th, Tunisia ranked 43rd, Libya ranked 117th, and Yemen ranked 103rd out of 158 rankings on the index. Perceived corruption increased markedly in the following three years. In 2008, Egypt dropped to 115th, Tunisia to 62nd, Libya to 126th, and Yemen to 141st out of 180 rankings on the CPI. A recent study of Gallup data during 2009–2012 in eighteen Arab countries reveals that the perception about state corruption was highly correlated to perceptions about business corruption (Diwan and Nabli 2013; see Figure 8.2). We now know that this was not just about perceptions. In both Tunisia and Egypt, the ongoing trials of leading businessmen are starting to shed light on the ways in which influence was wielded for private gain.

A SURVEY OF COUNTRY EXPERIENCES

In our overview of the structural adjustment experiences of different countries, it is useful to start with Turkey, a country that has managed to find a path of economic growth that supported the democratization of its political system over the past decade and a half. Turkey's story serves both to contrast the experience of the Middle Eastern countries and to highlight the limitations of the Turkish model, which became the main reference for aspiring democracies in the region after the Arab uprisings of 2011.

Turkey: The Benefits and Challenges of a "Messy" Democracy

Just as Turkey pioneered the adoption of ISI, so, too, did the country lead in embracing the policy shifts of the Washington Consensus. It was the first country in the region to embrace reforms in the early 1980s, transforming its development strategy from import-substituting industrialization to export-led growth. This strategy had its ups and downs, at times causing tremendous pain, but over time it was enormously successful. Exports exploded from $3 billion in 1980 to $13 billion

FIGURE 8.2. Perceptions of Corruption in the Public and Private Sectors in Selected MENA Countries

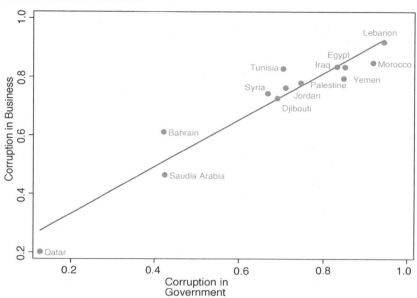

Source: From Gallup data cited in Diwan and Nabli (2013).

in 1990, $30 billion in 2003, and $163 billion by 2014. The country continued its long-term policy of increasingly tight integration with Europe by joining the European Customs Union in 1996 and becoming a candidate for accession to the European Union (EU) in 1999; talks on Turkey's accession began in October 2005. Wide-ranging liberalization touched most sectors of the Turkish economy, and powerful entrepreneurial energies were unleashed throughout the society (Keyder 2004). Since the early 1980s, Turkish per capita income has increased by an average of 2 to 3 percent a year, resulting in growth by a factor of nearly three by 2014.

But at least until 2002, growth was highly uneven and erratic; growth rates were negative in the crisis years of 1994 (-6 percent), 1999 (-6 percent), and 2000 (-9.4 percent). During the 2001 crisis, more than 1 million Turkish workers lost their jobs (ERF and IM 2005). The "stop-and-go" pattern of growth both created and was created by unstable governments. Throughout the 1980s and 1990s, successive coalition governments often found it impossible to maintain budgetary discipline. The Turkish experience highlights the difficulties of consolidating economic reform in a politically fragmented parliamentary democracy.[2] Persistent budgetary deficits were fueled by parastatal borrowing and by public spending that greatly increased just before elections. Eliminating subsidies proved very difficult—until after 2001. Kurdish policy cost Turkey some US$500 million per year in the 1990s. The budgetary drain—not to mention the human and political cost—was heavy.[3]

Budgetary deficits were not the sole cause of the ensuing financial crises of 1994, 1999, and 2001; the way they were financed also played a crucial role. Critically, in 1989, the Turkish government liberalized the capital account. Public banks continued to suffer so-called duty losses, as they were used by the state as an instrument of subsidization (for example, to extend often nonperforming agricultural loans). With capital convertibility, real interest rates soared, averaging 20 percent during the decade (Keyder 2004). Banks shifted their portfolios, taking on ever larger amounts of government debt by buying government bonds, which they financed by entering the global capital market. Banks were thus exposed to the risks of both interest rate and exchange rate changes, which were greatly magnified by government regulatory failures. In response to the first financial crash of 1994, the government guaranteed 100 percent of deposits, thereby creating a severe moral hazard problem for banks. (If banks gambled on interest and exchange rate differentials and lost, they were protected, since the government would bail them out.) Bank concentration, corruption, and lack of transparent bank oversight completed the witches' brew, which erupted in the financial crashes of 2000 and 2001. The entire process led to short-term, unsustainable, and highly uneven growth, as populist political patronage was financed by the government borrowing from banks that borrowed from international capital markets, a process caustically known in Turkey at the time as the "chain of happiness" (ERF and IM 2005). The state debt reached 150 percent of GDP by the end of the decade, while external debt was some 75 percent of GDP. Interest payments consumed half the government budget. The real exchange rate appreciated, the current account deficit widened, and interest rates soared. In 1999 Turkey fell victim to the aftershocks that radiated out from the Russian financial crisis and deeply felt the impact of the Marmara earthquake on output and confidence that same year. Worried international lenders called in their short-term Turkish loans, leaving Turkish borrowers in an untenable position. The resulting crash slashed output and employment and greatly magnified already considerable public discontent with the ruling parties.

These crises led to some important economic turning points. An emergency IMF loan of some $16 billion was issued in 2000, and an austerity program was instituted. The program was implemented by a coalition government led by the Democratic Left Party of Bülent Ecevit, whose economics minister, Kemal Derviş, was a former vice president of the World Bank. While recessions typically strengthen popular opposition to belt-tightening, the sheer depth of the financial crisis, the worst in postwar Turkish history, gave the state a unique window of opportunity to implement far-reaching reforms as it became clear that the previous policies had led to a state of near-bankruptcy of the Turkish economy, thus dramatically weakening popular resistance to Washington Consensus policies as well as to "Euroskepticism" in Turkey (Öniç 2004). The crash and ensuing reforms paved the way to a significant restructuring of the Turkish political economy.

A small clique of hugely rich financiers was widely perceived by the Turkish public as the beneficiaries of the 1990s "debt boom" years. Displays of conspicuous consumption by such interests did little to enhance their public reputation. Politicians were seen as being intimately involved with this clique and "in league with bank owners, plundering the state treasury" (Keyder 2004). As the decade continued, accelerating inflation, continued heavy rural-to-urban migration, public bickering within the political elite, and the weakness of social services opened a wedge for the

Islamic Welfare Party to win mayoralties in Istanbul, Ankara, and elsewhere. The party gained support among the export-oriented Anatolian manufacturers, who had long felt excluded by the statist, ISI-focused big businessmen of Istanbul and the Aegean coast. Through a coalition government, Necmettin Erbakan, head of the Welfare Party, became prime minister in 1996. In the following year, the Turkish military, alarmed by the government's embrace of Islamic reforms, forced Erbakan to step down through what some have called a "postmodern coup" (Boratav et al. 2000). The Welfare Party and its successor, the Virtue Party, were subsequently banned (see Chapters 10 and 12 for more details).

After the dramatic austerity measures from 1999 to 2001, a watershed election was held in November 2002. Benefiting from public disgust with corruption, mismanagement, and economic crisis, as well as the long-standing popular resentment of the Turkish elite and the "deep state,"[4] the moderate Islamist Justice and Development Party (AKP) won a sweeping victory. Led by the successful mayor of Istanbul, Recep Tayyip Erdogan, the AKP won 34 percent of the popular vote and 367 out of 550 parliamentary seats—a definitive majority.[5] The party had managed to forge a coalition of globalization's winners (Anatolian export capitalists) and losers (farmers, many workers) that led to a long period of growth with electoral successes and political stability unseen in Turkish history (Öniş 2004). The new Anatolian "tigers," whose emergence owed much to Prime Minister Turgut Özal's programs of support for exporting small and medium enterprises (SMEs), promoted a new model of pious and politically active entrepreneurs. As a result, the Anatolian SMEs came to play a much larger role in the economy and polity over time (Atiyas et al., forthcoming). Importantly, they increasingly became more efficient and started to compete with the large conglomerates that had monopolized state favors in the past, accounting for a sizable part of the rise in new exports (Atiyas 2014), as illustrated in Figure 8.3.

The AKP maintained fiscal discipline: deficits, not counting interest payments, were slashed to the point that the government ran a surplus from 2002 to 2004 amounting to approximately 6.5 percent of GDP (BSB 2005; ERF and IM 2005). Inflation fell to 7.7 percent in 2005, the lowest inflation rate for a generation. The 2000 financial crisis was so profound that the electorate came to support financial discipline in its aftermath. As a result, the AKP rigorously followed the austerity program that the previous government had developed with the IMF and vigorously pursued further integration with the European Union. In stark contrast to the past, maintaining macroeconomic stability became a priority for the AKP, one valued by its new constituency. When Turkey was hit hard by the global financial crisis in 2008 (GDP fell by 7.9 percent), the government adopted a conservative rather than expansionary posture, and the economy rebounded in 2009 owing to the government's enhanced credibility (Ersel 2013).

There was more good news. Growth resumed, privatization picked up, and the extensive institutional and policy changes needed for a bid for EU membership accelerated. Agricultural subsidies fell from $6 billion in 2002 to $1.5 billion in 2005. From 2001 to 2004, exports doubled, as did imports. By this point, tariffs had essentially become a non-issue in the Turkish economy, since nearly all manufactured goods from the EU entered without duties. Nontariff barriers remained,

FIGURE 8.3. Regional Distribution of Exports in Turkey, 2002–2012

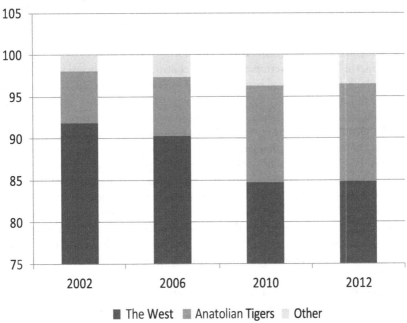

Source: Atiyas (2014).

but the Erdogan government successfully dismantled a series of these in such sectors as telecommunications, banking, and electricity. By 2005, Turkey had adopted most of the EU regulations covering these sectors, and there is evidence that at least some independent regulators have managed to instill effective competition in key sectors of the economy (Atiyas 2012). Foreign direct investment (FDI) soared. These changes produced a new sense of hopefulness in Turkey, which was further bolstered by the large reductions in both poverty and inequality during this period (Keyder 2004). Between 2003 and 2006, poverty declined rapidly, especially in urban areas, falling from 22.3 to 9.4 percent of the population. At the same time, urban inequality also fell, with the Gini coefficient falling from 33.4 to 28.4 (Aran et al. 2010).

Daunting challenges remain, however. First, the growth in the 1990s and 2000s can be characterized as "jobless growth." During the two decades, employment rose by less than non-agricultural output (ERF and IM 2005), and unemployment continued to hover around 10 percent, with higher rates among the youth. The unemployment rate would have been still higher if "discouraged workers" had been included. The stagnant job market led to a dramatic fall in the labor force participation rate, from 57 percent during the early 1990s to 48.2 percent in 2012.

Second, the Turkish economy has continued to suffer from inflation, and the budgetary deficit was purchased at the expense of increasing appreciation of the real exchange rate. Such appreciation is widely viewed as unsustainable (ERF and

IM 2005). Although exports have boomed, the current account deficit has widened, reaching close to 10 percent of GDP during 2011–2014. Turkish debt remains high, at about 40 percent of GDP. Although the government has maintained fiscal discipline, households have reduced their savings, and it is to finance private investment and household borrowings that banks now borrow externally.

Third, the Turkish government does not control all of the critical variables. Turkey has long followed the reform strategy of "Ulysses and the Sirens," that is, "tie yourself to the mast" (Elster 1979). For Turkey, the mast is closer integration with the EU and the global economy. By entering into treaty commitments with the EU and the World Trade Organization (WTO), Turkish policymakers are "tying themselves to the mast," thus enhancing the credibility of policy change. Unfortunately, however, the mast itself may wobble—or even snap. Not only is Europe in crisis, but it is also showing distinct signs of "enlargement fatigue," and Muslim–non-Muslim relations in the EU have worsened. For several decades, there has been a consensus in Turkey that the country should join the EU. In recent years, however, this consensus has weakened and there has been a revival of a new Ottoman policy of turning toward the East, but that, too, is not seen as viable given Turkey's fiasco on the Syrian and Iraqi fronts and the weakening of Islamic parties in the region after 2013.

Although the AKP government's initial record was very promising, and although it managed to considerably weaken the position of the army (see Chapter 10), negative signs of its long tenure in power started to show. Increasingly, state contracts went mainly to the politically connected firms, the massive construction boom turned out to rest on shaky financial foundations, and there was rising opposition to overbuilding. After the Gezi Park protests, Erdogan was perceived as increasingly autocratic as he attempted to muzzle the media, intimidate business groups he considered disloyal (using tax audits and penalties), and push for constitutional changes that could prolong his tenure. The growing divisions in the ruling party with the Gulenist movement have exposed further the rising cronyism of recent years and seem to be jeopardizing the very institutional foundations that supported high growth in the 2000s.

While the dominance of the AKP does not seem to be at risk in the coming years, and indeed the AKP was just reelected despite the media coverage of corruption scandals, it will be presiding over a society becoming increasingly polarized. It is worth remembering that modern Turkish history is strewn with the debris of good starts gone bad. If modern Turkish history is any guide, the future is likely to hold wrenching surprises as well as increasingly sophisticated responses to these surprises.

The Experiences of the RPLA Countries

In all the RPLA countries, autocrats needed to boost economic growth in order to have a chance at survival. To do so, it was crucial for them to support private-sector development in ways that would deliver growth without empowering potential opponents. As Henry and Springborg (2006) note, "These regimes favored trusted individual capitalists, rather than the capitalist class as a whole." In other words, these autocrats felt that they needed to embrace some private firms, while excluding others. This tension applied equally in all RPLA countries, but as we discuss in this section, the experiences of Egypt, Tunisia, and Morocco illustrate vividly how this dilemma played out in different contexts.

Egypt

On the eve of the First Gulf War, the Egyptian economy was in shambles. Growth had turned negative in the late 1980s. Real wages of unskilled workers had plummeted by 40 percent in four years, while civil servants were earning only about half of their 1973 salaries (Richards 1991). The level of open unemployment had roughly doubled during the decade. The quality of government health, transportation, and educational services had declined precipitously from already dismal levels. By 1990, the country's debt-GNP ratio of roughly 150 percent was arguably the highest in the world, and debt service payments consumed over 25 percent of exports. The situation in the early 1990s could fairly be characterized as one of crisis, in which foreign exchange for wheat imports was hard to locate and only last-minute help from the Gulf states narrowly averted an American aid freeze for failure to service military debt.

At the core of Egypt's macroeconomic crisis were three macro-imbalances: gaps between domestic savings and investment, between imports and exports, and between government revenues and spending. In the mid-1980s, total public expenditures were 60 percent of GDP, total revenues were 40 percent of GDP, and the public-sector deficit was 20 percent of GDP. There were very few, if any, developing countries in the world with such high proportions. By 1991, expenditures had begun to be cut back, but revenues also fell with the collapse of oil receipts. Spending was downwardly inelastic for the usual political reasons: blockage by vested interest groups that feared losing their cushy jobs and economic rents, and dread of popular wrath over subsidy cuts. As new foreign lending dried up in the latter half of the 1980s, the deficit was increasingly financed by the local banking system, crowding out investment and fueling inflation. Moreover, investment was inefficient and capital-intensive, creating few formal-sector jobs, and the mounting losses of public-sector companies undermined public savings. The rise of inflation led to the usual results: further distortion of price signals, sharply negative real interest rates that further exacerbated the savings-investment gap, and, thanks to fixed nominal rates, a steadily increasing overvaluation of the exchange rate. Such underpricing of increasingly scarce foreign exchange discouraged the production of traded goods and favored imports over exports, worsening the trade gap. Negative interest rates fueled capital flight, which hovered around 5 percent of GDP, increasing the gap further (see Figure 8.4).

The First Gulf War created an entirely new situation. The government struck a bargain: in exchange for massive debt relief, the government would adopt a reasonably conventional stabilization and structural adjustment package, endorsed by the IMF. The government embraced reform by leveraging strategic rent. Such a bargain was attractive both economically and politically. Economically, the reduction of up to US$20 billion of debt cut yearly interest payments by US$2 billion for the next

FIGURE 8.4. Public and Private Investment in Egypt, 1985–2011

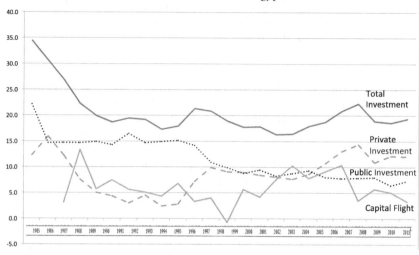

Source: WBI

ten years. Politically, the deal was an easy sell at home since Egypt's strong bargaining position with the financial institutions enabled it to choose the speed and manner in which it would implement the various parts of the package.

The reforms envisioned by the World Bank and IMF were meant to shrink the twin deficits and start moving Egypt's economy from central planning toward more reliance on market-based mechanisms. At the heart of the stabilization package was a large adjustment that would bring the fiscal deficit down through a substantial reduction of public investments. Additional reforms involved the following:

1. The reduction of consumer subsidies, which were running at about 7 percent of GDP, and of energy subsidies. Petroleum products in Egypt were priced at about 16 percent of the world prices, costing the Egyptian economy US$2.5 billion per annum.
2. The elimination of the multiple exchange rate system, exchange rate devaluation, and export promotion.
3. The implementation of tax reform to increase revenues.
4. The liberalization of interest rates and the removal of limits on lending to the private and public sectors.
5. The application of agricultural production policies to improve the terms of trade between the agricultural and non-agricultural sectors and to promote agricultural production.
6. The deployment of public-sector reforms that would give state-owned enterprises greater autonomy and require them to sell their products and/or services at their real market value and pay market wages to attract skilled labor, but also while shedding redundant unskilled labor. At this stage, the World

Bank did not recommend privatization or divestiture, though a later phase of reforms witnessed the privatization of some public enterprises but not the financial sector, which could have contributed to a more efficient mobilization of savings (Al-Mashat and Grigorian 1998; Posusney 1997).

The contrast between the situation in the late 1980s and the adjustment period in the late 1990s before the Second Gulf War was striking. Macroeconomic stabilization had done quite well. Fiscal restraint and debt relief were the keys here. Thanks to the banking reform package, Egyptians turned dollar holdings into Egyptian pounds, generating current account surpluses. International reserves soared, rising close to US$20 billion by the mid-1990s. With the help of reduced interest payments, the government deficit was slashed to 2 percent of GDP in 1993, and it remained at that level until the late 1990s. Inflation came down. As a result, GDP grew at an average rate of almost 5 percent between 1994 and 2000, with a peak of 6.1 percent in 2000 (from 2.8 percent in 1991–1993).

At first glance, Egypt looked like the poster child for the Washington Consensus. The reality, however, was more complex. First, consider the sources of growth. Although the Washington Consensus projected that macro-stability and deregulation would stimulate export-led growth, Egyptian growth was in fact largely driven by public investment in huge infrastructural projects, such as the New Valley, or Toshka, irrigation projects. Second, the growth of exports—particularly job-creating manufactured exports—was unimpressive, partly because of sluggish reform efforts. Private investment remained around 10 percent of GDP (Figure 8.4), and exports stayed flat at about 21 percent of GDP. Job creation continued to lag behind additions to the labor force, while employment became increasingly "informalized." Third, the balance of payments remained dependent on the old reliables like Suez Canal revenues and workers' remittances. By the early 2000s, balance-of-payments difficulties had arisen again, owing to a series of external shocks—the East Asian crisis, falling tourism revenues due to insecurity exacerbated by the attacks of September 11, 2001, and the slowdown of world trade in 2001. Shortages of foreign currency resulted in a cumulative devaluation of more than 30 percent by 2003. As a result of the rising imbalances, economic growth fell to around 2.4 percent in 2003.

Following the Second Gulf War, an aging Mubarak, who had overseen a reduction in state expenditures from its height of 60 percent of GDP down to 30 percent of GDP, empowered his son Gamal to lead a new drive to get economic growth going by opening up the economy further. Working closely with a group of young economic experts and ambitious businessmen, Gamal Mubarak started to redefine the political program of the aging ruling party. After the socialism of Nasser (1958–1968), the first opening of the economy by Sadat in the 1980s, and a long transition with stabilization efforts and timid liberal reforms from Hosni Mubarak's first term up to the early 2000s, a new and vigorous effort was under way to modernize Egypt's private sector—or so the official narrative went. This effort was managed by the "businessmen" cabinet headed by Ahmed Nazif (2004–2011), and it included a push to create an internationally competitive corporate sector in the midst of a renewed effort at privatization that included the banking sector, trade reforms, drastic cuts in income tax rates and a streamlining of tax administration, and a costly financial-sector recapitalization and liberalization in 2005 (World Bank 2007). These macroeconomic policies, coupled with an improved external environment, have contributed to higher growth (6–7 percent between fiscal year 2005 and fiscal year 2008, up from an average of 3 percent between fiscal year 2001 and fiscal year 2003). Large FDI inflows—8.1 percent of GDP in fiscal year 2008—which went principally to the energy, real estate, and tourism sectors, were accompanied by a rapid credit expansion, leading to an investment boom. The privatization program gained momentum and was extended to the banking sector. In an overall favorable external context, reserves were at over US$36 billion in 2011, on the eve of the Arab uprisings.

By 2010, however, it was clear that the big push was not delivering the expected results. Growth was not trickling down. Poverty—defined as income of less than $2 a day (in purchasing power parity, PPP)—was still very high at about 40 percent of the population. Unemployment rates were not coming down, in spite of sharp reductions in real wages following the 2008 global crisis, which had led to a further devaluation of the Egyptian pound. Employment in the formal private sector barely grew—in 2010, 25 percent of the labor force worked for government as compared to 35 percent a decade earlier, while only 12 percent worked in the formal private sector, barely more than the proportion a decade earlier. Moreover, real wages in the late 2000s were at the same level as in the late 1980s (Beinin and Vairel 2011). With the strike of industrial workers in Mahalla in April 2006, labor unrest started to rise sharply (Beinin and Vairel 2011) (see Chapter 12 for more detail).

This lackluster economic performance has been attributed to the crony nature of private-sector development in Egypt constraining the growth of the private sector. The 1990s had seen the emergence of a new class of capitalists connected to the state. After the mid-2000s, a few well-established insider firms were joined by new enterprises more closely connected with Gamal Mubarak. These connected firms took on the modernization of the economy. As they spearheaded the development of new sectors and the modernization and expansion of old ones, they were backed by state favors and international and Arab finance and were prime beneficiaries of an invigorated privatization drive. Not only were the rising businessmen well connected, but they also occupied important posts in government, the ruling party, parliament, and various boards and committees (see Osman 2010) that allowed them to influence economic policy directly.

Two iconic cases illustrate the nature of these privileges. The first is that of Ezz Steel. Ahmed Ezz, a very successful businessman who dominated the steel industry after 2000, is currently accused of having lobbied on behalf of his firm on issues related to raising external tariffs, increasing protection in the steel sector, and relaxing antimonopoly constraints. A prominent member of the National Democratic Party (NDP), the dominant party in the Egyptian political system, Ezz was extremely well connected. Ezz held influential positions such as chair, as a member of parliament, of that body's Budget Committee, which oversees the work of the Competition Commission and trade policy, among other things. He was also a member of the NDP's influential Policy Committee (chaired by Gamal Mubarak) and NDP secretary for organizational affairs. A second example is that of Palm Hill Corporation, the second-largest real estate developer in Egypt. The main owner of Palm Hill, Ahmed El Maghrabi, was minister of housing in the Nazif cabinet; he has been accused of exploiting his ministerial position to sell the company large tracts of land in various parts of the country at exceptionally cheap prices, giving his firm a big advantage over competitors.

Critics increasingly came to realize that reforms were not proceeding as expected. Although the liberalization of banking and of interest rates did lead to an increase in household savings, to 18 percent of GDP (a reasonable figure by international standards), the banks' lending patterns became extremely concentrated, as they were more interested in lending to the government and to large firms than to SMEs. The twin deficits rose again under the weight of rising energy subsidies (which mainly benefited well-to-do households and connected businesses), rising fuel and food prices, and anemic exports. Although tariff rates were reduced, nontariff barriers rose to replace them, especially in the industries dominated by connected businesses (Diwan et al. 2014). In many ways, the regime of crony capitalism was not delivering.

Recent studies have started to examine in detail the magnitude, performance, and impact of cronyism in Egypt (see, for example, Chekir and Diwan 2013; Diwan, and Schiffbauer Keefer et al. 2014). These studies were made possible by the revelations following the Arab uprisings in 2011 and the court cases brought against the "cronies." Ishac Diwan, Philip Keefer, and Mark Schiffbauer (2014) identify around five hundred firms controlled by thirty-two businessmen closely connected to Gamal Mubarak, most of whom also occupied political posts in the mid-2000s, like Ezz and El Maghrabi. Between 2000 and 2010, these firms came to dominate the Egyptian corporate landscape and monopolized most profitable new economic opportunities among themselves, including massive housing projects and construction, tourism at coastal areas, the oil and gas sectors, the banking sector, and telephony, as well as local distribution of international consumer brands. By 2010, these firms received close to 90 percent of the credit going to the private sector, and they earned 60 percent of the overall corporate profit in that sector, even though they employed only 11 percent of the labor force in the formal private sector.

Government decisions were instrumental in all of these areas: tourist resorts were built on formerly government-owned land; investments in oil and gas required government approval; and new banks or factories in specific manufacturing sectors such as cement required government licenses. In exploring the mechanisms of privilege, Diwan and his colleagues (2014) show how connected firms benefited from protection from foreign competition through the growth of nontariff barriers in the sectors where they were active, preferential access to energy subsidies and to land, and preferential regulatory treatment.

There is significant evidence that cronyism led to stagnant economic growth and poor job creation through both direct and indirect channels. While their advantages allowed connected firms to increase their profits, they were also run less efficiently than their competitors, partly because they were more capital-intensive and partly because they were shielded from competition. This contributed to the misallocation of scarce national savings (bank loans and state subsidies), which starved the rest of the corporate sector, including SMEs, of much-needed capital. Equally important, Diwan, Keefer, and Schiffbauer (2014) find that sectors that were dominated by a few crony firms were less dynamic—they were less competitive, saw lower firm entry, had a larger "missing middle" of medium-size enterprises, and overall did not create many jobs compared to more competitive sectors. These effects add up to a sizable aggregate impact of cronyism on growth. The social effects were also problematic: cronyism led to the emergence of a very rich "1 percent," and the slow growth of the formal private sector exacerbated labor market dualism, increasing the inequality of opportunities faced by young graduates (World Bank 2013).

Such crony capitalism was clearly not a part of the Washington Consensus plan, but in Egypt, as elsewhere, it seems to have been the outcome of the policy changes of the 1990s. The Mubarak regime successfully utilized strategic rents to jump-start an economic reform process, which then proceeded at the government's own pace. The market mechanism was more widely utilized and there was improved economic growth to show for it, but it was not inclusive. At the same time, exports responded sluggishly as globally uncompetitive crony capitalism became entrenched. While the reforms provided neither needed jobs to the rapidly rising number of young job-seekers nor the foreign exchange needed to sustain macro-balances, it did satisfy foreign patrons and donors, who supported the government's hold on power until the social explosion of 2011.

Between the uprisings in Egypt in 2011 and 2014, the political scene became particularly volatile, with six parliamentary, constitutional, and presidential elections marked by economic populism and a lack of serious reforms. Political instability and deadlock blocked the adoption of serious efforts to chart a way out of the mounting economic and social problems, generating further political instability that put Egypt at risk of becoming locked into what could be termed a transition trap. The state of the economy in 2014 strangely resembled that of the early 1990s. The government deficit was approaching 15 percent of GDP, and reserves had reached a record low of US$13 billion, reflecting sustained efforts to defend the national currency, which was allowed to depreciate by only 20 percent despite the significant drop in foreign exchange earnings. Foreign currency deposits made by neighboring Gulf countries, estimated at around US$15 billion since May 2012, had helped the Central Bank of Egypt stabilize the situation. The government deficit had ballooned owing to increased public-sector hiring and a rising energy subsidy bill (again largely benefiting the well-to-do). As a result, public debt had risen to 70 percent of GDP. This debt was primarily financed by domestic banks, thus constraining the banks' capacity to lend to the private sector. Owing to the size of the debt and rising sovereign spreads, public debt service consumed a good one-third of government expenditures. Public investment was dismally low and private investment anemic. The crony capitalists were heavily indebted to the banking sector, but most of them lived abroad, awaiting better times to come back. Meanwhile, Egyptians continued to flock to the informal sector to scrape out a living. President Abdel Fattah Al-Sisi, elected in May 2014, started his term with Egypt facing enormous economic and social challenges. How he chooses to tackle them will mark not just his legacy but also the development path of the country and the welfare of millions of its citizens.

Tunisia

Like other countries hit by crisis, Tunisia had tried to borrow its way through various external shocks, including the international recession of the early 1980s, drought, rising European protectionism, and falling oil prices. A rising twin deficit led to a piling up of debt, which reached 63 percent of GDP in 1986. The Mzali government instituted some halfhearted reforms, including changes in consumer subsidy programs that provoked the riots of January 1984. The government then retreated, but the problems became even more severe; by the summer of 1986, the country had only a few days of import cover left. At that point, the government had little choice but to turn to the IMF and accept the standby agreement that it had proudly avoided for so long.

In August 1986, Tunisia embarked on an IMF-funded program. As in other countries, devaluation of the currency, export promotion, reduction in import protection, liberalization of banking and prices, budgetary austerity, and privatization were the key elements of Tunisia's structural adjustment program. Because the macroeconomic imbalances were not as large as in other countries of the region, most of the reforms were structural in nature. Most targets were met, and the economy's performance improved significantly. Economic growth for 1987 to 1992 was 4.3 percent, compared with 2.8 percent for the previous five years. Exports of manufactures grew at 15 percent per year, and workers' remittances rose until the First Gulf War. Private savings rose, as did FDI, which increased from US$75 million in 1989–1990 to US$215 million in 1992 and US$316 million in 1993. Inflation fell to 8 percent, and the balance of payments improved despite the adverse shock of the Gulf War. Debt accumulation decelerated markedly in the second half of the decade. In 1991–1992, Tunisia achieved a positive food trade balance for the first time in twenty years. In addition, the efficiency of investment improved: the incremental capital-to-output ratio (ICOR) fell from 7.7 in 1980–1984 to 3.8 in 1988–1991. During 1993–1994, the government made the dinar convertible, adopted a unified investment code, and took some limited steps to institute a stock market.

Financial liberalization was less ambitious. The Central Bank is often accused of excessive regulatory intervention, and as a result, a truly modern, competitive banking sector has yet to emerge. There are persistent reports of collusive behavior among bankers, especially through the Association Professionnelle des Banques (Henry 1996). Two of the largest four banks are owned by the state, and public banks hold over half of the nonperforming loans in the country. Although there have been some regulatory changes (for example, increased discretion in lending decisions by bank management), as well as some privatization (such as the 2003 privatization of the Union Internationale des Banques), the state has retained a dominant role. Indeed, after three years of stimulus following the Jasmine Revolution of 2011, one of the main threats to the Tunisian economy is once again the very high number of nonperforming loans carried by the state banks (IMF 2012).

Privatization has also moved slowly. Although the government announced goals to privatize all holdings (except for "strategic industries"), privatization has largely been limited to profitable ventures, including textile companies, hotels, and small banking subsidiaries. The General Confederation of Tunisian Workers (UGTT) successfully lobbied the government to move slowly on privatization and trade liberalization, thereby protecting jobs. Other state-owned enterprises in mining, construction, and transport were given performance contracts. The government divested parts of its ownership of the large state companies by selling shares on the stock market. In 2004 the government sold 35 percent of Tunisie Telecom, the most profitable state-owned enterprise, for a record price. However, as the regime continued to lose legitimacy and to rely increasingly on sheer repression to survive, it hesitated to open the door for full economic and political competition. Over time the privatization and government subcontracting deals became monopolized by Ben Ali's inner circle, ushering in a period of large-scale corruption (Kaboub 2014). By 2009, when a third telecom network was put out for competitive bids, the two finalists were both sons-in-law of Ben Ali.[6]

There were hopes that the reform process would be revived with the signing of an association agreement with the EU in 1996. This agreement tied Tunisia to the "mast" of a free-trade agreement with the world's largest economy. By 2002, 40 percent of imports from the European Union entered Tunisia without tariffs, and the average tariff rate fell steadily, but it remained high, reaching 23.2 percent by 2002 (Bechri and Naccache 2003). Several other features of the agreement also promoted the reform agenda, but their halfhearted implementation reduced their effectiveness. First, the agreement's provisions were phased in gradually: free trade would not occur for twelve years. Second, both the World Bank and the European Union provided considerable funds to support the project. But the EU-financed technological upgrading program (Programme de Mise à Niveau) was not terribly attractive to manufacturers and did not manage to upgrade their export capabilities, in large part because supporting services remained plagued with inefficiencies. The food processing industry was the main beneficiary of the Mise à Niveau programs, though construction, textiles, and electrical parts also received subsidized loans and technical assistance to upgrade their technology.

In 2005 the cumulative FDI in Tunisia was at US$14.3 billion, most of which was concentrated in export-oriented manufacturing; some 235,000 jobs had reportedly been created through this foreign investment (USDS 2005). Tunisia would be heralded by the World Bank and the World Economic Forum as the Arab model to emulate, but despite what appeared to be a solid success (before the 2011 Arab uprisings), the employment situation in Tunisia became problematic. More than 90 percent of Tunisian exports remained labor-intensive manufactures, largely textiles, automotive parts, electrical machinery components, and niche processed agricultural goods (such as olive oil), even though the labor force was becoming more skilled. The lack of demand for skilled workers led to rising levels of skilled unemployment and, as elsewhere in the Middle East, rising levels of frustration among educated youth. Moreover, the creation of offshore export-oriented zones allowed domestic import-substituting manufacturers to remain inefficient. In addition, because all inputs had to be imported, domestic manufacturers became increasingly unable to compete against cheap Chinese and Eastern European products and the linkages in the Tunisian economy were diminished, stunting job creation.

The Tunisian economy remained a case of "state-led growth." The government continued to direct the economy, but it did so using indirect rules of regulation as opposed to the direct involvement of the ISI era. Regulation is prone to rent-seeking risks, however, and it is rarely applied in a politically neutral way in countries that lack democratic checks and balances. Ever since independence, Tunisian governmental elites have sought to emulate the rich countries of Western Europe, and so they naturally have moved toward a regulated economy, along the French top-down model. They have also perceived the way forward as one of gradual integration with the global economy, and particularly with the EU. Unfortunately, these ambitions were being pursued through the ruthless suppression of human rights. Economic liberalization did not foster "democracy," and this had negative implications for the type of capitalism that developed over time. Indeed, while the state gradually gave up its direct control of productive assets, it increased its control over the economy through state regulation (Bellin 2002). All large government contracts had to be approved directly by the president's office (Kaboub 2014), and declining tariffs were replaced by rising nontariff barriers of all sorts. The government did create a "one-stop shop" for foreign investors, the Investment Promotion Agency, and a 1994 investment code permitted foreigners to own 100 percent of new capital investments, though they needed to have special permits from the cabinet. As a result, private investment remained sluggish, rarely exceeding 15 percent of GDP (Rivlin 2009).

Following Ben Ali's ouster, the new government faced the challenge of finding the estimated $17 billion appropriated by Ben Ali, his family, and his closest cronies. In addition, the new government expropriated the assets of the Ben Ali family in Tunisia, valued at an estimated $13 billion, or about one-quarter of Tunisia's 2011 GDP. The confiscation affected 117 individuals—including Ben Ali himself and his relatives and in-laws—and 400 enterprises. These firms, which were accused of illegally profiting from political connections, were predominantly in the real estate, industrial, telecom, air transport, and banking sectors, and all were in the onshore market.

Bob Rijkers, Caroline Freund, and Antonio Nucifora (2013) examine the benefits of political connections for firms by looking at the financial success of the expropriated firms that had been owned by Ben Ali and his family. These firms accounted for a whopping 21 percent of all net private-sector profits in 2010, although they produced only about 3 percent of private-sector output and employed 1 percent of the labor force. The number of sectors requiring licenses expanded under the Ben Ali administration, and the connected firms were primarily found in sectors with investment restrictions—those that required licenses to operate or were closed to FDI—since it was in these sectors that firms were most likely to benefit from government connections. The study finds evidence that the Ben Ali clan had a hand in manipulating investment laws to increase exclusionary regulations in sectors where they planned to invest.

Hamouda Chekir and Claude Menard (2012) focus their more ethnographic study on the unconnected firms. They conducted interviews at about thirty firms in all sectors to try to understand how political connections affected their behavior. They find that while the offshore sector was preserved from predation and open to international competition, the onshore sector was constantly confronted with expropriation pressures by the Ben Ali clan and their cronies. This predation evolved over time. Under Bourguiba, it was limited to putting pressure on businesses to remain uninvolved in politics, a practice that also characterized the first half of Ben Ali's rule. The Ben Ali clan's predatory behavior became more pervasive in the early 2000s, when the regime became more repressive in the face of rising opposition. They pressured the business community to co-invest with the clan, controlled all the businesses that required authorizations from the state, and held a quasi-monopoly on the acquisition of profitable state assets. Their predatory practices sometimes took an extreme turn to include harassment and threats. They even expropriated occasionally private businesses and property.

All these distortions had considerable impacts on the firms' behavior. Firms adopted an attitude of hiding below the radar, overfocusing on highly sophisticated businesses generally shunned by the clan, and working exclusively with foreign partners. Compared to their peers in other countries, this defensive position kept Tunisian corporations small and family-led. The predatory behavior of the Ben Ali clan created severe barriers to entry and, above all, to the development of Tunisian firms, keeping them below their production potential. The challenge for future governments will be to find ways to reverse the trend and help usher in a dynamic private sector that can create the type of skilled jobs to which young and increasingly educated Tunisians aspire.

Morocco

Morocco provides a striking case of a country that seemingly systematically implemented a wide array of Washington Consensus policies and seemingly overcame political obstacles to reform in the 1980s and 1990s—but that like Egypt, which eschewed rapid reforms, and Tunisia, which implemented halfhearted reforms, had very little in the way of growth or employment creation to show for it.

By mid-1983, Morocco's currency reserves were almost exhausted, forcing the government to institute emergency measures to restrict imports. In 1984 Morocco was one of the first countries in the region to turn to the IMF. The ingredients of the new policy package were familiar—nominal exchange rate devaluation, budgetary discipline, tariff reduction, real interest rate increases, and privatization. By 1992, Morocco was being held up as a textbook case of successful economic reform. On the macroeconomic side, the government achieved stability through orthodox means: contractionary fiscal and monetary policy and floating the dirham in 1985. Budgetary deficits, which had exceeded 15 percent of GDP in the late 1970s, steadily fell to around 2 percent. Inflation had declined to about 3 percent by the late 1990s. Such achievements, however, masked some important issues. First, improved budgetary balance on the expenditure side was largely achieved by cutting government investment; personnel costs rose as a percentage of GDP, reaching nearly 12 percent of GDP by the late 1990s (Denoeux 2001).[7] On the revenue side, tax collection was hampered by evasion (which historically was very common), sluggish growth, and reductions in customs revenues. The budget was largely balanced through the proceeds of privatization, and so over time the deficit rose again. Real exchange rate management was likewise mixed.

Many analysts also gave Morocco high marks for structural reforms. Prices were liberalized—all goods except flour, sugar, and tobacco were at market prices (World Bank 2006a). Trade reforms reduced tariffs as Morocco joined the WTO in 1995 and entered into free-trade agreements with the EU in 1996. The banking sector was liberalized, prudential regulation was strengthened, and positive (although low) real interest rates were maintained. The government announced its intent to privatize a wide range of companies. As with macro-management, however, a closer look at structural change reveals a spottier picture. The effective rate of protection remained high,[8] and so did nontariff barriers.[9] The course of privatization has likewise been far from smooth. First, actual privatizations have fallen well short of the bold pronouncements of the early 1990s. The usual suspects are involved: union resistance, government wariness, and investor reluctance (Denoeux 2001). Second, as elsewhere, many observers allege that sales were often made to the politically well-connected, who enhanced their market share and weakened domestic competition (Bergh 2005; Hibou 2004). More generally, big financial groups maintained control and blocked new entrants, including in new financial markets (Henry 2003).

Initially, the results of these policy shifts were encouraging. GDP expanded at an average annual rate of 4 percent during the 1980s, with manufacturing growing slightly faster (4.1 percent). The export response was also initially strong, with exports rising from 18 percent of GDP in 1965 to 26 percent in the 1990s. The composition of exports also shifted markedly away from a sole reliance on phosphates, with large increases in farm and factory goods. In particular, garment exports to Europe boomed. But the results since the late 1990s have been disappointing in relation to the effort. GDP growth has been slow, roughly 1 percent per year on a per capita basis from 1995 to 2000, and nearly 4 percent on per capita terms in the 2000s, below the estimated 6 percent growth rate needed to create adequate jobs for the growing labor force and to reduce unemployment and poverty. Importantly, growth has remained low in comparison to one of the highest investment rates in the region, now in the neighborhood of 35 percent of GDP (much of it, directly or indirectly, state-led in mega-projects such as the Tanger Med industrial corridor, investments to boost capacity in phosphates, and large infrastructure projects).

A key failure since the late 1990s has been the sluggish growth of exports. Export-to-GDP continued to rise, reaching 32 percent in the mid-2000s, but much of this is explained by the rising price of phosphates, which constitute about one-third of total exports. The problems may be divided by product type—roughly, "old" manufactured exports (textiles and leather) and the development of "new" exports (ready-made clothing). Basically, the growth of the former has stagnated, after an initial boom in the 1990s, owing to inherited inefficiencies, increasingly severe competition from Asian countries and Eastern Europe, exchange rate over-valuation, high unit labor costs, and the end of the multi-fiber agreement in 2005, which ended any Moroccan textile trade advantages in the EU. Meanwhile, a com-bination of market and government failures has inhibited the development of newer exports. Problems include monopoly power (particularly of those closely connected to the *makhzen*[10]), credit access difficulties for smaller enterprises, and poor labor productivity and skills (and weak government support of industrial restructuring and training) (Cammett 2007; Denoeux 2001; Hibou 2004; World Bank 2006b). Labor-intensive exports have so far failed to provide the "engine of growth" of out-put and jobs that Washington Consensus advocates had anticipated. Instead, much of the labor released from agriculture has moved into low-productivity sectors such as trade and construction. Morocco remains ill equipped to compete globally, much less to even keep up with foreign competition in its home market.

As a result, the balance of trade has continued to be under pressure—its deficit rose from -6.0 percent of GDP in 1996 to -13 percent in 2004, and to the alarming level of -23 percent in 2013 as investment and imports continued to rise much faster than exports. Until now, this has not caused serious balance-of-payments problems, thanks to tourism, workers' remittances, a rising level of external debt, and some FDI, but the situation is not sustainable. In the past two years, the popular leader of the moderate Islamist Justice and Development Party (PJD), Prime Minister Abdelilah Benkirane, has had to implement an austerity program, with the help of a $6.2 billion precautionary line of credit from the IMF, to protect Morocco from further external shocks—namely, an economically depressed Europe, high oil and food prices, and low export growth.

Morocco enjoyed a number of political advantages that helped it carry out its reforms. Both Hassan II and his successor, Mohammed VI, provided crucial leader-ship and visibly supported the key technocrats, who, moreover, enjoyed considerable longevity in their posts. Broad segments of the business and agrarian elite supported the kings' programs. Many policy changes (including strategic delays) were de-signed to provide the elite with benefits and thus ensure their support. Finally, as elsewhere, the Moroccan government "tied itself to the mast," at first through the IMF, and then with its association agreement with the European Union. Although the ropes in such programs tend to be rather loose—countries consistently find ways to evade implementation of reforms or find workarounds—such a constellation of interests and state structures helps to explain the rapid macroeconomic stabilization program (for all its faults) and the relatively gradual implementation of structural changes (Mansouri et al. 2004).

Morocco has one of the highest rates of inequality in the region, with Gini co-efficients of about 40.0. Nevertheless, the kingdom benefits from a good measure of political stability, owing in no small measure to the sustained gains in poverty reduction achieved in the recent past. Between 1990 and 2008, the share of the population living on less than $2 a day (in PPP) shrank from 30.4 to 8.1 percent; at the end of the period, the poor represented 14.2 percent of the rural population and only 3.4 percent of the urban population. This remarkable achievement has been connected to several factors: a sharp drop in fertility rates from 5.5 to 2.3 children per adult woman, which relieved pressures on budgets; infrastructure investments in isolated rural areas in water, energy, and roads; the expansion of micro-credit; and the dynamism of the nongovernmental organizations (NGOs) active in rural development (Achy 2010). Although Morocco still faces the challenges of high illiteracy, inequality, and volatile economic growth, the progress on poverty reduction has allowed the kingdom to enjoy a relative measure of social peace (see Chapter 2 on social outcomes). This is undoubtedly part of the reason why the February 20 Movement fizzled in Morocco in 2011. In comparison, there was less progress in reducing rural poverty in the marginalized areas of Tunisia, such as Sidi Bouzid, where the Tunisian uprising started.

Organized labor, unemployed youth, and Islamist reformers are important interest groups active in Morocco. The balance of political forces also helps to explain the difficulties. First, organized labor has long been a force in Morocco. Although, as elsewhere, labor unions do not (and cannot) represent the vast number of workers employed in the informal sector, they are strong in larger enterprises and in the public sector. Keeping the social peace requires at least their acquiescence. This helps explain budgetary difficulties (such as high and rising public-sector wage bills), slow privatization (which the unions have often opposed), and rigid labor market structures (which have slowed the development of export industries). As elsewhere, the "labor aristocracy" of organized and public-sector workers has benefited, while those forced into the informal sector, unemployment, or emigration have fared less well. But few governments, faced as Morocco has been since the mid-1990s by strikes, street protests, massive rural-to-urban migration, and rising opposition forces (mainly Islamist), would risk alienating such a key urban constituency as organized labor. Occasional protests by educated unemployed youth culminated in large-scale demonstrations during the 2011 uprisings and have kept the pressure on, resulting in a new constitution meant to placate the protesters. However, although the new constitution grants more powers to the prime minister and parliament, the king retains veto power over most government decisions (see Chapter 3).

But these are hardly the only interest groups active in Morocco. Employers and industrialists play a still more important role. The more established, highly interconnected oligopolistic interests associated with the older, import-substituting industries, such as textiles, constitute a powerful political force. Some observers attribute the slow change of trade regime in Morocco to their influence. In a manner reminiscent of the Turkish experience, these entrenched interests met important opposition from the newer money investing in export industries such as ready-made clothing (Cammett 2004). The powerful interests in the core of the state (*makhzen*) were able to make good use of this division—as well as more traditional tools of patronage and "planned corruption" (Waterbury 1973) to maintain firm control over the entire process of economic policy change (Hibou 2004).

As in Tunisia, the Moroccan state has had an active industrial policy, but efforts have been fragmented, and some observers suggest that much of the state support to industry is dissipated in rent-seeking by influential economic agents. Between 2000 and 2007, there was a donor-driven patchwork of some thirty different support services intended to support SMEs, including the EU-funded Programme de

Mise à Niveau. All of these programs had diverse eligibility criteria determined by the specific objectives and areas of intervention of each donor, resulting in an overall effort that was dispersed, overlapping, and unfocused. At the same time, the Hassan II Fund and its follow-up funds focused on large firms and used privatization proceeds for funding; this was a powerful tool for the distribution of favors, and had low oversight. In recent years, support for enterprises has evolved in the form of the "Emergence" program. Eight sectors have been selected as drivers of growth: French- and Spanish-language offshoring, the agro-food industry, the seafood industry, textiles, and the automotive, aeronautics, and electronics industries. These sectors are supported through the establishment of free zones. In spite of these efforts, structural change has been slow.

Morocco remains at an early stage of development—the share of labor in agriculture still accounts for nearly half of GDP. An important strategy for growth, then, is to ensure that labor moves from agriculture to sectors with higher productivity. However, as we noted earlier, labor movement from low-productivity sectors to manufacturing has been slow compared to lower-productivity sectors such as petty trade or construction. It is important to understand why this would be. Recent studies suggest that a key weakness of the growth process is the low dynamism of the private sector, which is itself connected to the concentration of market power. That is, the sectors dominated by large firms tend to be less dynamic, and they also experience lower gains in productivity (Sekkat and Achy 2007). This suggests that one result of market concentration by a few large firms is that small firms tend to stay small (and the favored large firms stay large), creating a "missing middle," the component of the private sector in other countries that tends to exhibit a greater degree of innovation. The question, then, is why does size provide an unfair competitive advantage?

The advantages of being large may reflect various market imperfections, especially in the capital market, where the need for collateral creates barriers to entry. Large firms may also have an unfair advantage, simply because of their size, in lobbying for better treatment by the state and regulators. That these types of privileges for large firms are prominent can be seen in the public perception of corruption. The recent Gallup polls cited earlier in the chapter (see Figure 8.1) show that the perception of corruption in business and government in Morocco is among the highest in the region. Another way in which size might lead to an advantage is the unpredictability in the implementation of government regulation—a hypothesis supported by the results of a recent World Bank Enterprise Survey (WBES). Figure 8.5, based on the WBES, shows that 60 percent of firms in Morocco state that rules are not applied consistently; such unpredictability generates uncertainty for firms that do not have sufficient influence. This is one of the worst scores in the region.

The continuity of governance structures in Morocco is striking. When the World Bank pressed for tax reform in the mid-1990s, the makhzen obliged, but governance hardly became more transparent as a result. In fact, "at the heart of [the makhzen's] method of exercising power was the preservation of confusion" (Hibou 2004, 205). Discretion has been maintained in many other ways; for example, the funds from

FIGURE 8.5. Percentage of Firms in Selected MENA Countries and Cities That Agree That Government Officials' Interpretations of the Laws and Regulations Are Not Applied Consistently

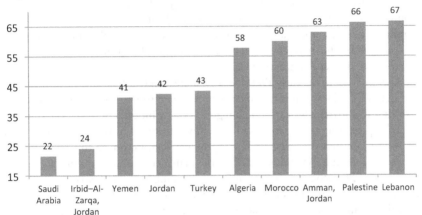

Source: World Bank Enterprise Surveys (WBES).

some of the largest privatizations have gone into the coffers of the Hassan II Fund, which is entirely unaccountable to the legislature or any other public body.

Many observers lament the failure of economic changes to produce any significant governance change (see, for example, Denoeux 2001; Hibou 2004; Layachi 1999). Morocco is far from alone in this response to economic changes. One can certainly argue that "social dialogue" is more advanced in Morocco than in Tunisia or Algeria (Denoeux 2001). The young king, Mohammed VI, is certainly popular (Hegasy 2007), and he has managed to build a popular image of himself as "the king of the poor," compared to his more severe father. He is forward-looking, and his technocrats are undoubtedly able. But the history of the Moroccan state, its governance structures and style, its ambivalent relationship with Europe, and the inheritance of some of the region's worst human capital indicators continue to matter. During the past two decades, unemployment, emigration, and poverty have all increased. It is small wonder that the Moroccan state continues to preserve its discretionary powers, since it will very likely need them in the years ahead.

The Experiences of the RRLA Countries

We review here the cases of Algeria and Iran, two of the larger RRLA economies of the region. After the industrial push failed in the 1980s, both countries' leaders have preferred to depend on a narrow circle of cronies as a strategy for regime preservation and to rely more on patronage based on oil revenues when possible, and on sheer repression when necessary, than on growth and job creation. As a result, economic growth has tended to be lower and private-sector activity more severely repressed than in the RPLA countries (with some variation).

Algeria

Despite oil rents and rapid growth, Algeria could not escape the contradictions of its statist, inward-oriented development strategy. The key failings of the Houari Boumediene era were excess capacity, overcentralization, unemployment, massive rural-to-urban migration, and a seriously neglected agricultural sector. These problems elicited halfhearted reform measures that helped delegitimize the government, but failed to deliver a restructured economy.

The situation in the early 1980s became increasingly difficult. Two-thirds of Algerian basic food was imported, and unemployment rose to 16 percent in the cities. Housing was extremely scarce. The regime slowly, inexorably sowed the dragon's teeth by providing young men with incentives to move to the cities, where they found no jobs and no housing. These problems can be traced to the strategy of concentration on heavy industry and to the management problems of state-owned enterprises. The economic argument for developing heavy industry was based on linkage effects: these industries were to provide the basic materials for other industries that would supply the population with its needs. It is true that basic metals and energy industries have high forward linkages, but they are also very capital-intensive and create relatively few jobs. Worse, in Algeria they were run as monopolies, which gave enterprise managers little reason to be efficient. Furthermore, the location of these industries in and around the major cities of Algiers, Constantine, and Oran further stimulated rural-to-urban migration, which was already massive because of rapid population growth and the neglect of agriculture. This exacerbated the severe problems of the cities.

Reform in Algeria in the 1980s was fundamentally an attempt by Boumediene's successor, Chadli Bendjedid, and his reform-minded technocrats to overcome the Boumediene legacy while maintaining state control of the economy. It was a classic case of reform as survival strategy. Much of the impetus for Algerian reform was the mounting pressure of servicing the country's international debt. Bendjedid's team argued that reform was necessary to avoid rescheduling the debt, but in marked contrast to its Maghreb neighbors, Algeria deliberately avoided entering into an agreement with the IMF. Beginning in 1982, Bendjedid's regime embarked on a "structural adjustment with a nationalist face" reform program, designed in part to avoid the perceived humiliation of "losing sovereignty" to the IMF.

By 1985, some 66 huge state-owned enterprises had been broken up into 474 smaller companies. Successive decrees were issued that were intended to decentralize decision-making in state enterprises. Other changes included the reallocation of public investment away from heavy industry, incentives to attract foreign investors, and measures to revive the agricultural sector. Management's autonomy was strengthened, and capacity utilization rose from an average of 30–40 percent in the late 1970s to 75 percent in 1984. Industrial workers received bonuses linked to productivity.

Bendjedid's regime tried to encourage both domestic and foreign private investment. The private sector, whose activities continued to be concentrated in light-industrial products, accounted for about one-fourth of manufacturing output in 1985. As elsewhere in the region, private entrepreneurs had a symbiotic relationship with the public sector, obtaining inputs from the public sector and/or selling their output to the giant monopolies. The 1982 investment code reduced the tax rate on profits and expanded credit for industries that were likely to generate foreign exchange (for example, tourism). The amount of foreign currency that such firms could legally import was doubled, and the establishment of some 660 new private firms was approved. Private FDI rose from virtually zero to US$280 million in 1984. Whereas previously nearly all contracts with foreign companies had been turnkey arrangements, for the first time foreign firms were allowed to operate facilities (in joint ventures) in the country. The two most visible were in telecommunications (Sweden's Ericsson Company) and automobiles (Italy's Fiat Corporation).

However, the restructuring of the economy under Bendjedid failed to alleviate debt or reduce unemployment. Although labor force growth accelerated, output growth declined to 3 percent during the 1980s. Urbanization accelerated; the urban population growth rate rose from 4.1 percent in the 1970s to 4.8 percent in the 1980s (Bennoune 1988). International debt continued to mount, reaching US$26.5 billion in 1991, by which time a vicious civil war was well under way. Algerian perestroika had failed.

Bendjedid's attempt at reform was fundamentally flawed. Poor conceptualization was accompanied by poor implementation. Large sections of the ruling National Liberation Front (FLN) never accepted the need for reform, and middle- and lower-level functionaries impeded the shift to the market at every opportunity. Suspicion of market activities remained high in these quarters, and even as legal changes dictated from the top removed obstacles to private-sector activity, bureaucratic resistance blocked their realization.

After the riots of 1988, reform intensified, an agreement was made with the IMF in 1989, and there were continued changes until 1993. However, economic reformers increasingly had to vie with hard-liners, who were arguing that the reforms were responsible for the rise of the Islamic Salvation Front (FIS) and the Islamist insurgency. After the assassination of Mohamed Boudiaf in June 1992, the government of Belaid Abdessalam abandoned reform and reverted to a more traditional, FLN-style policy of favoring state enterprises. The government persisted in this approach until the spring of 1993, when the Bank of Algeria could no longer service the country's international debt; at that point, the government was forced to begin serious negotiations with the IMF. By then, internal violence had increased considerably.

Le pouvoir (the ruling elite of army generals and crony capitalist allies) managed to retain power and weather the storm of civil war, enriching itself, while failing to address the deep contradictions of the inherited state-centric development model. In 1994 the state played the "strategic rent" card to strike an agreement on debt rescheduling with the international community, which was led by the IMF.[11] At the same time, the state acceded to the usual array of Washington Consensus policy changes.

As in Egypt, the macroeconomic performance was respectable. Inflation dropped from 39 percent in 1994 to less than 5 percent by the early 2000s. The fiscal deficit, at nearly 9 percent of GDP in 1993, was first cut in half and then fell to 2.5 percent by 1997 (Chemingui and Ayadi 2003). Foreign exchange reserves had been restored to more than $16 billion by 2001, and the debt service ratio fell from 86 percent in 1988 to 49 percent in 1994 to 21 percent in 2000. GDP growth recovered, reaching 3.4 percent in 1995–2000. High oil prices after 2000 allowed the twin deficit to remain under control and brought down inflation and foreign debt. External reserves, which stood at nearly $200 billion by 2014, allowed the state to defuse social tensions after the February 2011 street demonstrations by extending patronage. Public spending rose by 20 percent, including increased food and energy subsidies, which now approach 20 percent of GDP (Khan and Mezran 2014). Rising oil prices allowed Algeria to delay political and economic reforms while retaining control, a key difference with the RPLA countries that did not have such a choice available to them when the productivity of their economic system declined.

Because of such differences in Algeria, the microeconomic and, especially, institutional changes were far more hesitant than they were even in Egypt. The difficulties were classic ones. The process of privatization was opaque, with regime insiders benefiting greatly from the privatization of some banks, import-export companies, and construction firms. Privatization in Algeria was nomenklatura privatization—even more so than in Egypt or Morocco. At the same time, the rents engendered by the wedge between international and domestic prices had already led to the development of a "parallel economy" composed of shady traders, marginalized youth, and corrupt public officials. A number of observers (for example, ICG 2001; Lowi 2005; Martinez 1998) have documented how such networks fueled the violence on both sides of the civil war as economic conflict between competing mafias merged with—and, in some accounts, increasingly replaced—ideological struggle. Although the worst violence ended in 1999 (after some 150,000 Algerians had perished) with the amnesty offered by President Abdelaziz Bouteflika, popular distrust, even hatred, of *le pouvoir* has remained intense. The common cry is against *hogra,* the contempt that the elite have long shown for ordinary Algerians. Although the Algerian regime has regained macroeconomic balance and is now considerably aided by increased oil prices, the system remains very far from that envisaged by the Washington Consensus.

Unemployment remains acute, housing shortages are severe, and popular alienation from the state is intense. Economic growth since 2000 has fluctuated between 3 and 4 percent—not enough to reduce the unemployment rate, which is officially at about 10 percent, with youth unemployment fluctuating around 20 percent for males and 30 percent for females, despite ambitious public spending. The economy remains dominated by oil revenues, which constitutes 34 percent of GDP, 65 percent of government revenues, and 98 percent of exports. Non-oil industries have continued to shrink, reaching 4.3 percent of GDP in 2013, down from 9 percent in 1998. Algeria's economy also remains dominated by the state, and successive Bouteflika governments have shown little interest in seeing an independent private sector develop. On the other hand, the informal economy has boomed and employs nearly 50 percent of the labor force (IMF 2013). The banking system remains dominated by six state-controlled banks that control 90 percent of the market (African

Economic Outlook 2014). Algeria ranks 153rd out of 189 countries in the World Bank's ease of doing business ranking.

On the positive side, the private sector has grown and now represents 52 percent of total non-oil value added (African Economic Outlook 2014). But, as in Egypt, the Algerian private sector is made up of small, mostly informal SMEs and larger, politically connected firms. Crony capitalism and corruption remain firmly entrenched even as the networks of privilege have evolved over time. While army-connected interests—and later FIS-connected businessmen—monopolized economic opportunities between 1984 and the late 1990s, President Bouteflika has built his own support network over time, relying on the entrepreneurs who rose in the bazaar economy of the 1990s (Boubekeur 2013). This has resulted in a broadening of the business elite. But in the absence of a credible political project, uncertainty over future control of rents remains high and patronage is still a risky bet. So while President Bouteflika's reelection campaigns of 2004, 2009, and 2013 were heavily supported by various business leaders and interests, private investment has remained timid. It remains to be seen whether, over time, the rising economic actors will become more active in supporting policy reform and political change. So far, *le pouvoir* appears to have weathered the storm of the 1990s, containing popular dissatisfaction through patronage, divide-and-rule tactics, and violence. However, ordinary Algerians have gained little.

Iran

The Iranian economy declined precipitously after the 1979 revolution. At the end of the Iran-Iraq War in 1988, per capita GDP was one-half of its 1977 level. Per capita incomes did not regain their pre-revolution peak until 2004. A combination of revolution, war, and collapsing oil prices ensured that the 1980s would see sharp declines in output and the 1990s would see only modest economic growth.

These failures need to be weighed against the dramatic improvements in a variety of human development indicators. Private consumption fell less than half as rapidly as per capita output (23 percent versus 50 percent) during the period 1977–1988 and grew more rapidly during 1997–2004 (4.6 percent per year) than during the boom years of 1960–1977 (Salehi-Isfahani 2009). The poverty rate fell from 47 percent in 1978 to 15.5 percent in 2001, by which time half of the poor were covered by various government social safety net provisions (World Bank 2001). As documented in Chapter 5, there was a boom in school enrollments of girls, including rural girls, infant and child mortality rates plummeted, and gaps between rural and urban human capital indicators narrowed. Iran also witnessed the largest rate of reduction in fertility rate in the world (see Chapter 5). These improvements were driven by public investments in drinking water, schools, rural (and urban) health clinics, and public food subsidies (Salehi-Isfahani 2009).

The poor economic performance of the 1980s and early 1990s had three sources: the revolution itself, low oil prices, and the usual problems of statist, inward-oriented policies. The revolution and ensuing war can be blamed for political interference in management, labor strikes, the exodus of managerial skills, and electrical power shortages. Since more than 80 percent of all Iranian exports are oil products, world oil markets delivered heavy blows to the economy when oil prices collapsed in the mid-1980s. Inward-oriented policies such as tariffs and a grossly overvalued exchange rate insulated firms from competition, permitting inefficiency to flourish and creating a vested interest in the continuation of these policies. The Iran-Iraq War greatly stimulated the centralization of economic decision-making as the basic statist economic structures, already well advanced under the shah, were markedly enhanced during the 1980s. The government implemented price controls, rationing of consumer goods, strict quantitative regulation of imports, and tight controls over banking. The revolution greatly increased direct state management of Iranian industry. In its wake, most medium-size and large-scale enterprises were nationalized, and most are still run by public or quasi-public institutions. By 1991, public enterprises accounted for 73 percent of industrial value added, 72 percent of employment, and 65 percent of investment (Amuzegar 1983).

At the time of the revolution, the opposition to the shah seems to have been as widespread as Polish opposition to Communist rule. Like Solidarity (the Polish antibureaucratic social movement), the initial coalition led by Khomeini was very broad indeed. Over time it has narrowed, but the regime still rests on an uneasy alliance of two very different sets of interests: populist lower and lower-middle classes and prosperous clergy and business associates. The first group, the "populists," includes economically dependent mullahs of mainly poor, provincial origin; left-wing elements who had infiltrated the high ranks of the bureaucracy; and the many radical groups ushered in by the revolution, such as the foundations, or *Bonyads,* that took over the assets of the Pahlavi family and groups associated with the Revolutionary Guards Corps (IRGC). The second group, the "reformers," includes a collation of landlords and the urban bourgeoisie who tend to support economic reforms, as they would benefit from more space being afforded for private-sector growth (Amuzegar 1983, 32). Wealthy *bazaaris,* who enjoy monopoly power as holders of quotas and licenses, also often support this group.

Such a configuration of interests, particularly in a context of oil price instability, strongly suggests that economic policy will oscillate. When oil prices fall, pressures for market-oriented change become acute. Although such pressures are partly accommodated, there is also resistance to them. Political resistance limits the extent of the reforms, problems reemerge, and the cycle continues. Iran certainly has followed this pattern. At the beginning, the populists seemed to have had the upper hand, and a number of their views were incorporated into the constitution, which severely restricts the private sector's fields of activity. The reformers first took charge in the early 1990s during President Akbar Hashemi Rafsanjani's tenure (1989–1996), but they had to retreat in the face of strong opposition. The reformers regained their ground during the government of Mohammad Khatami (1997–2005), but then rising oil prices allowed for a reversal of reforms under President Mahmoud Ahmadinejad, who swung the balance again toward the economic interests of the radical populists.

The government of Rafsanjani, who sought to encourage private-sector growth, announced various reform plans, such as unification of the exchange rate, privatization, and some dismantling of price controls. As is common in the aftermath of wars, state investment for reconstruction increased; the investment rate rose from 25 percent of GDP in 1986 to 35 percent in 1991, and imports exploded. The classic twin gaps—between imports and exports, and between saving and investment—emerged with a vengeance in the first half of the 1990s. The government first plugged these gaps in the classic manner—with monetary expansion and external borrowing. Inflation rose, although the presence of numerous price controls insulated consumers to some degree. The government also increased external borrowing, and external debt rose from $4 billion in 1990 to $22 billion in 1994 and continued to rise, leading to a mini–debt crisis in the mid-1990s (World Bank 2001). Since then, the exchange regime has been tightly controlled and very complex, with several different exchange rates. In 1993 the free-market price of foreign exchange was *twenty times higher* than the official rate. Macroeconomic instability combined with interest group pressures, especially those grouped around the Bonyads,[12] to oppose any turn toward economic liberalism. During Rafsanjani's eight years at the helm, the economy grew by only 10 percent per capita over the whole period (and 25 percent overall). Manufacturing output stagnated during the 1980s. Some industries fared far worse than this: automobile production in 1996 was a fraction of its pre-1979 level.

The upward surge of oil prices since 1999, together with these gradualist reforms, led to significant improvements in the economy. During President Khatami's eight-year term (1997–2005), GDP per capita rose by 25 percent over the period (World Bank 2006b). But the growth surge was almost entirely due to the increase in oil prices, and productivity showed no increase (Mojaverhosseini 2003). Thanks to the huge surge of entrants into the job market, job creation, even during booms, has not made a significant dent in unemployment (although it has prevented it from getting worse), which stabilized at around 10 percent. More than two-thirds of new jobs created during the 1980s and early 1990s were in the public sector. The US embargo has impeded investment in the petroleum sector; Iran has managed to attract only some $10 billion of investment in this sector, far below what is needed to maintain existing capacity.[13]

The governments of Rafsanjani and Khatami made important changes, but without altering the basic configurations of power within the polity. They stabilized the economy, liberalized trade somewhat, and introduced a more transparent management of the exchange rate, but they were unable to push the privatization agenda. Instead, they followed a strategy of allowing a new private sector to develop alongside the large public and quasi-public large enterprises (Harris 2013). The reforms were both accelerated and implemented to the benefit of the radicals rather than the private sector during President Ahmadinejad's term from 2005 to 2013.

Ahmadinejad presided over a period of record oil revenues, until the US sanctions were tightened in 2012. A populist, he was intent on reversing the economic liberalization of his predecessors in ways that would benefit the poorer segments of the population and strengthen the radical groups. Initially, he sharply cut public investment and redirected foreign exchange toward consumer imports "to bring oil to the people's dinner table"—his main presidential campaign promise. Over his presidency, he also pushed subsidized loans to support SMEs. His major achievements were in areas that he attacked as a candidate: the removal of the energy subsidy and the initiation of a major privatization program. In both instances, Ahmadinejad displayed a large degree of pragmatism and opportunism that disarmed his opposition and allowed him to strengthen his hold on power. Indeed, in both cases, the structure of the reforms ensured that their main beneficiaries were his supporters.

Subsidies had been large in Iran since the 1979 revolution (Salehi-Isfahani 2013). Subsidies on food, medicines, and other items have typically oscillated around 4 percent of GDP. Far worse is the huge implicit subsidy for energy consumption, estimated at over 15 percent of GDP in 2010. The price of gasoline in Iran in 2005 was $0.09 per liter ($0.34 per gallon), stimulating inefficiently high use of energy, horrendous air pollution in Tehran, and rampant smuggling to Pakistan, where the price was nine times higher (IMF 2006). The reform bill, approved by parliament in 2010, called for sales prices to be within 90 percent of the international oil price. In parallel, a system of refunding 50 percent of the fiscal gains to *all* Iranians was put in place. Since the oil subsidies benefited mainly the rich, the flat distribution was very progressive (Salehi-Isfahani 2013).[14] For the poor, the cash transfer represented about 40 percent of their income. The rest was used to support industry and agriculture, which were also beneficiaries of these subsidies. The implementation of the reform led to a bubble of inflation, which was countered with increased price controls, but there were no riots, and unlike outcomes elsewhere in the region, the reform initially stuck. It is not clear, however, that these gains will be sustainable politically. When industry suffered from the combination of higher energy costs and controlled output prices, the result was layoffs and a rise in unemployment, which required the reinstatement of some subsidies to industry. Over time, energy prices to consumers were not adjusted sufficiently to keep up with inflation, but the cash payments remained, leading to renewed fiscal pressures.

Privatization was the second area of reform on Ahmadinejad's agenda. Under his predecessors, there had been only modest privatization—assets amounting to some 0.5 percent of GDP were sold on the Tehran Stock Exchange in 2000–2001, and other shares were distributed to workers. By contrast, between 2006 and 2010, the government divested some $80 billion of state-owned assets in 370 state-owned enterprises. But only 13 percent of the shares ended up with the private sector; the rest went to parastatals, including military firms, state-connected investment and holding companies, and the recipients of what came to be called "justice shares" (Harris 2013). The bottom two deciles of the population were offered justice shares to buy at half their face value, while the third to sixth deciles could buy them at face value, but payable over ten years. The program was then expanded to various groups close to the regime, including low-income villagers and nomads, public-sector retirees, beneficiaries of the Imam Khomeini Relief Committee, and families with martyr status. The Iranian Parliament Research Center has estimated that, overall, 68 percent of the share of privatized firms went to the justice shares. Critics contend that privatization served as a way to reward the supporters of the regime, such as the Basij militia, for their loyalty and support (Habibi 2013). The rest of the shares, which were intended for the private sector, ended up being mainly bought by semi-state agencies and the Bonyads, partly because of the private sector's lack of interest in coming in as minority shareholders.

Army-connected economic interests, which were created during Rafsanjani's era, blossomed under Ahmadinejad, benefiting interests connected with the Islamic Revolutionary Guards Corps and the Basij. Government contracts were preferentially allocated to such firms, especially after the US embargo prevented foreign firms from operating in Iran. Over time, the IRGC became active in mega-construction projects, housing development, and the oil and gas sector. Kevan Harris (2013) documents how the Telecommunication Company of Iran was sold to a conglomerate linked to the IRGC Cooperative Foundation, a large service company and service contractor. The auction was limited to two bidders, the second linked to the Basij investment cooperative. The IRGC commander became oil minister in 2011, at which point twelve out of twenty-one ministers had ties to the IRGC (Habibi 2013). State banks were also forced to provide large amounts of credit to such parastatals, including financing their expansion in the area of foreign trade (Habibi 2013).

Despite record oil revenues, economic growth was low during 2005–2012, at about 10 percent per capita for the seven years taken together. The policy of cheap foreign exchange, and later expensive energy, severely reduced the competitiveness of Iranian production, and unemployment rose considerably, from 15 percent in 2005 to 20 percent in 2011 for males, and from 22 to 28 percent for females. Young workers were hit the hardest, with youth unemployment at about 35 percent in 2012 (Salehi-Isfahani 2013). By some estimates, the Iranian economy did not create any new jobs on a net basis between 2006 and 2011 (Salehi-Isfahani 2013).

The tightening of the US sanctions sharply reduced the state's foreign exchange earnings, and the government had to cut its budget by 20 percent between 2011 and 2013. The Iranian riyal collapsed by about 50 percent, leading to a burst of inflation. It is quite likely that the dire economic situation contributed to the Iranian regime's motivation to participate in nuclear talks with the United States. But paradoxically, the devaluation, which made imports more expensive and thus reduced imports and consumption (imports were cut from $80 billion to $50 billion during 2012), also made Iranian products more competitive, leading to a rise in production and non-oil exports.

On the whole, while the conservatives were strengthened during Ahmadinejad's presidency, the fundamental features of the political economy created by the Islamic revolution have remained intact, but the society has become more polarized. Unemployment has risen, and with it youth discontent. The contested 2009 elections showed that the Iranian electorate was deeply unhappy with the management of the economy, not to mention the lack of liberties. But at the same time, the vast network of patronage represented by the Bonyads, the IGRC, and other security-connected parastatals has flourished—and with it a dense web of patron-client relations extending into towns and rural areas. Clouding the horizon are the conflict between Iran and the West over Iran's nuclear capability and the Syrian and Lebanese situations. The election of President Hassan Rouhani in 2013 holds the promise of a period of reforms that will focus on the removal of sanctions and the reintegration of the Iranian economy into the global economy. Such plans are unlikely to be in the interest of the radical group, however, and it is not clear at the time of writing whether Rouhani will be able to win over the opposition from within.

CONCLUSIONS

Although the problems and contradictions of state-led growth are real enough, there is no simple, much less universal, set of institutional changes that can overcome them. The problems of economic growth and structural change are intractable, complex, murky, and deeply, inescapably political. Sweeping "reform packages" are always suspect, if for no other reason than that it is political folly for autocratic governments, especially after they have lost their legitimacy, to open up their economy to forces that they cannot control and that could someday support the opposition. It is also dangerous to offend everyone at once—which is what the economic logic of the Washington Consensus has often implied. As it has turned out, the benefits of the partial reforms that were implemented in the end tended to be mixed and unequally distributed, but still, as evidenced by the 2011 uprisings, profoundly destabilizing.

As we discussed in Chapter 7, much of the impetus for change came from the accumulation of debt and fiscal imbalances. Although these problems arguably had been building for some time, they became acute when oil prices collapsed in the mid-1980s. The decline of rents was widely noted at the time, and many analysts (including the authors of this book) thought that such a development provided an opportunity for real institutional change. As a simple generalization, one can say that many MENA governments have markedly improved their macroeconomic management but have postponed or simply balked at more complex reforms, such as privatization, regulatory reform, and development of the rule of law. On the structural side, certain changes certainly took place: many economies are now more open to trade, and the private sector in the region is more active than before.

It is hardly surprising that regimes implemented economic policy changes gradually and selectively. Most countries have reacted to the reduced external rents by working hard to generate new forms of domestic rents, especially by creating privileges for friendly private actors and by developing regulatory and other mechanisms to exclude actors perceived to be threatening to their interests. The result has been a very mixed picture in which regimes have embraced some economic reforms; on the whole, however, the private sector that emerged remained either too close (the "cronies") or too far (the large informal sector) from government. The results of economic reform were thus disappointing. Although in some countries economic performance in the mid to late 1990s was considerably better than in the previous ten years, in no country has growth been strong enough to lower unemployment or significantly raise real wages and living standards in ways that could satisfy the rising tide of educated youth cohort joining the labor market.

In the end, only Turkey has made sweeping institutional changes. Other regimes have been able to manage the appearance of reforms but made little real change, and even in Turkey daunting challenges remain. The MENA economies survived the lean years of the 1990s,[15] regimes did enough to stay afloat, and repression did the rest, especially in the RRLA countries, where the second oil shock reignited old traditions of patronage politics. No regimes fell until 2011, but during the Arab uprisings the street massively rejected the system of privileges that had emerged over the past twenty years. In the future, the challenge of creating a form of capitalism that is workable enough and dynamic enough to create the good jobs required by the more educated population, as well as respectful enough of the elementary forms of social justice to which they aspire, remains as daunting as ever.

NOTES

1. See, for example, the discussions of this viewpoint in Scott (1998) and Gray (1998).

2. And in this sense, Turkey provides a useful lesson for the transitioning Arab countries, where political polarization and unrest have hindered the adoption of clear social and economic policies to address the very problems that at least partially spurred the uprisings in the first place.

3. At least 1,500 villages were destroyed and some 30,000 people lost their lives amid widespread human rights abuses by both the Kurdish rebels and the Turkish government (Keyder 2004).

4. A Turkish phrase (*derin devlet*) covering the key players in the military, security services, courts, and other Atatürkist public institutions.

5. The discrepancy is partly explained by the Turkish rule that a party must garner at least 10 percent of the popular vote to receive any representation in parliament.

6. The bid was won by a company held by Marwan Mabrouk and his wife, Cyrine Ben Ali, a daughter of the deposed president. After gaining the telephone network, Mabrouk was named president of the board of Orange Tunisia and obtained an interest-free loan from institutions linked to the state. The company was under investigation in 2013 (Beauge, 2011).

7. Some of the increase, however, went to improving teachers' salaries, which can be viewed as a form of investment in human capital.

8. The effective rate of protection includes the impact of tariffs on inputs, and hence costs, to domestic producers.

9. The Overall Trade Restrictiveness Index (OTRI) measures "the uniform tariff that, if imposed at the border, would have the same effect on aggregate imports as the current structure of trade measures." Morocco's OTRI is 0.51, Tunisia's 0.37, China's 0.20, and Turkey's 0.12 (World Bank 2006b, 43).

10. The traditional term for the Moroccan royal state apparatus.

11. When defending their abrogation of the 1991–1992 elections and asking for financial and other assistance, Algerian authorities asked members of the French government, "Would you accept that oil rent fell into the hands of the Islamists?" (Lowi 2005, 15).

12. The largest foundation, Bonyad e-Mostazafan (the Foundation of the Deprived), officially controls some $3.5 billion in assets (other sources cite much higher figures) and manages more than 400 companies in sectors ranging from food processing to metals to construction materials, financial institutions, and five-star hotels. Such companies employ over 400,000 people (World Bank 2001; Devaux 2003).

13. A US law passed in 1996 provides for US sanctions against any company investing more than $20 million in Iran.

14. For example, Djavad Salehi-Isfahani (2013) calculates the following ratios of expenditures of people in the top to the bottom deciles: gasoline, fourteen-to-one; heating, six-to-one; and electricity, five-to-one.

15. Of course, the fall of the Ba'athist regime in Iraq had essentially nothing to do with the issues discussed in this chapter.

9

THE EFFECTS OF OIL ON DEVELOPMENT AND THE RISE OF THE GULF COOPERATION COUNCIL

As we have noted throughout this book, the presence of large oil revenues has profoundly affected development paths in the region. In this chapter, we explore some of the effects of oil on development in greater depth, and we examine the extent and nature of recent developments in the Gulf states. The long period of decline in oil prices during the 1980s and 1990s was all about adjusting budgets downward. However, the second oil boom, beginning around 2000, has reopened the question of how oil revenues affect development prospects when such revenues are plentiful. As can be seen in Figure 9.1, oil revenues not only boomed but flowed at unprecedented levels into the coffers of the Gulf Cooperation Council (GCC) countries as well as those of Iran, Iraq, and Algeria, between 2004 and 2014 when the second boom seemingly ended.

As historian Roger Owen (2008) reminds us, the story about the place of oil in the region can be told in many different ways, depending on one's point of view. The triumphalist story of oil irrigating development, for example, focuses on the metropolises emerging in the deserts of the Emirates. There is also the story of oil interests exploiting local populations and disrupting their traditional way of life. The nationalist story of OPEC leaders, including Mosaddegh, Gaddafi, and Saddam, is one of confronting major oil companies, telling them to pay more for oil, and ultimately nationalizing said companies. A popular story is the narrative of Western powers supporting the Arab autocrats in order to defend the West's oil interests in the region. All these stories have some elements of truth, and the contradictions they contain reveal the complexity of the oil phenomenon in the region.

There have also been abundant academic writings, mostly Western, on oil as a "resource curse" that distorts countries' development paths by unbalancing economies, strengthening the rule of autocrats, and generally stunting social development

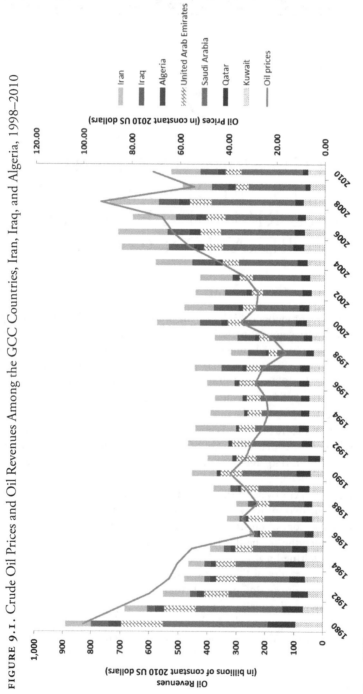

FIGURE 9.1. Crude Oil Prices and Oil Revenues Among the GCC Countries, Iran, Iraq, and Algeria, 1998–2010

Source: WBI

and favoring distributional over productive societies. These concepts have often been developed by Middle East area specialists who have subsequently exported them to other regions, and so reviewing these "models" in light of the economic takeoff in the GCC countries and the economic stagnation in the RRLA countries is likely to yield interesting insights both about the region and about these theories.

This chapter focuses on the phenomenal rise of the GCC economies, which now produce nearly two-thirds of the Arab region's GDP. We compare the GCC's development performance to that of the RRLA countries in order to explore the reasons for the differences. Given the predominance of the political impact of oil, we begin by looking at the development implications of the variations in the political mechanisms for power preservation between the two groups: the ways in which the wealthy "rentier" states of the GCC have secured themselves and consolidated power by extending ownership and rentier status to their citizens, in contrast to the strategy used in the RRLA countries, which has been more focused on developing large state policing and security apparatuses and repressing the opposition, while doling out patronage to a more select and narrow group of allies. We argue that these two governance configurations have affected state autonomy, state capacity, and social development differently, leading to different development outcomes.

Next, we look at how oil revenues complicate economic management and possibly depress economic growth. The three main challenges that can depress economic growth are the economic diversification challenge, the economic volatility challenge, and the challenge of promoting private-sector growth. We also review a unique feature of the GCC economy: its massive import of labor from the global market—more than one-third of the GCC population is made up of expatriate workers. This unique phenomenon has massive political and economic implications. Finally, we examine the sustainability of the GCC developmental model and discuss how it may evolve over time.

THE DIVERSE EFFECTS OF OIL ON GOVERNANCE

Prior to 2011, the Middle East was often thought of as the most oil-rich and least democratic region of the world. A confluence of factors has encouraged the consolidation of authoritarian forms of governance in many Middle East countries: rentier wealth from oil, patrimonial forms of state governance, and the benefits of Western state strategic alliances (as guided by antiterrorism interests) (Bellin 2004). As discussed in Chapter 3, some political scientists have argued that oil wealth fosters autocratic rule, while others maintain that oil wealth tends to entrench the status quo.

The broader question that interests us here, beyond the association between oil and democratic rule, is determining the conditions under which large oil revenues in the Middle East have been associated with governance outcomes that are either favorable or not favorable to development. A few developing countries, such as Botswana, Chile, Mexico, and Brazil, have managed to develop fast, initially under autocratic rule, and then by transitioning to democracy after incomes reached a relatively high level (see, for example, Rosser 2006). In the MENA region, we have seen that, in general, while all oil-producing countries have remained staunchly autocratic, the RRLP countries have done better than the RRLA countries, not just in terms of economic growth but also in measures of state capacity, rule of law, and (lack of) repression. Thus, we want to look here at the economic, political, and social factors that enabled some of the resource-rich countries of the region to utilize their resources to promote development, while others were not able to do so.

Rentier state theory supposes that the accrual of state revenue from foreign sources effects a particular configuration of the state vis-à-vis society. The theory began as an attempt to explain how rapid GDP growth following the initial oil booms of the 1970s and 1980s did not seem to prompt the transformation and modernization of society in the oil economies. Over time, this sprawling literature has pinpointed three important channels through which oil can affect development outcomes: (1) oil can foster the rise of autonomous states that are little influenced by their society; (2) oil can undermine the development of state capacity; and (3) oil can foster social fragmentation and prevent social development. These three effects are at play in the MENA region in varying degrees, depending on the type of governance arrangement that has taken shape in each country over time.

One of the main difference in governance arrangements between RRLP and RRLA countries, which we have described in Chapter 3, is the different mix of repression and co-optation used by their leaders to stay in power (see, for example, Bellin 2004; Posusney and Angrist 2005). As we have seen, while the two strategies have typically been used in parallel, the relative dependence of regime survival on co-optation versus repression has depended partly on factor endowment and partly on pre-oil history. Theoretically, when oil production per capita is very high, as in RRLP countries, regimes will tend to prefer survival strategies that depend more on rentierism than on sheer repression, whereas if oil per capita is modest, as in the RRLA countries, a strategy of repression is theoretically preferable (Ali and Elbadawi 2012; Malik and Auty 2013). The intuition for this assertion can be related to what Douglass North, John Joseph Wallis, and Barry Weingast (2009) call "limited order arrangements": when resources are plentiful, ruling coalitions can afford to be broader, and broader coalitions produce more stable and less violent orders. On the other hand, when resources are more constrained, ruling coalitions tend to be narrower, and they will accept the trade-off of higher payoffs for some amount of insecurity, even if this reduces the size of the economic pie. This conforms to the picture we painted in Chapter 3, where we found that repression is much higher in the RRLA countries and lower in the RRLP countries, as compared to regional averages.

But we also recognized that beyond the rather sordid cost-benefit calculus, which provides only a first-cut account, albeit a compelling one, regime types are also determined by history and geography—or more specifically, by the nature of the political settlements that have been shaped by these factors. There are indeed salient historical differences between RRLA and RRLP countries. The emergence of the modern Gulf states—generally around the same time as the twilight of colonial empires worldwide—coincides with the discovery of oil reserves in the Gulf.[1] The initial development of an oil production industry at this nascent stage of statehood allowed old structures of (patrimonial and monarchical) governance in the Gulf not only to endure but to prosper—a relationship that has continued into the present. The necessary development of a centralized extraction infrastructure fits neatly into the type of clan-based, consolidated patrimonial rule that had developed since the eighteenth century in Arabia (Luciani et al. 2012). Oil, in other words, consolidated a system of interlocking interests, privileges, and monopolies already in place prior to its discovery (Owen 2008; Vitalis 2007). On the other hand, the republican RRLP countries were born out of more violent political processes that put at the helm groups that espoused radical departures from the past—as embodied, for example, in Ba'ath ideology in Iraq and Syria, Islamism in Iran and Sudan after the 1980s, socialism in Algeria, and Gaddafi's particular ideology, which combined elements of Arab and pan-African nationalisms with a peculiar form of "populism." In these countries, oil supported a more benign form of autocratic rule in the beginning, within a modernist nationalistic phase of fast development and industrialization. The second, more violent and repressive phase emerged later, after the failed industrialization drives of the 1960s and 1970s, coupled with the humiliating defeat in the 1967 Arab-Israeli War, which put the core legitimacy of the frontline states into question. Oil allowed these states to finance large armies and security forces and also to remain somewhat independent of foreign patrons (Posusney and Angrist 2005).[2]

History also points to a more geographically based explanation of the differences between the two groups. In addition to benefiting from relatively small labor populations, the GCC states were notably only lightly incorporated into both the Ottoman Empire and the European empires, compared to many other states in the MENA region. Several analyses correlate the legacy of colonial-era extraction economies with the weakness of post-independence state institutions, the prime examples being Iraq and Algeria (Acemoglu, Johnson, and Robinson 2000). This colonial legacy and Ottoman history in Iraq through the early twentieth century may partly account for how relatively slowly state institutions became stable in these countries, as compared to the largely uncolonized Gulf region.[3]

In examining oil's impact on the development process over time through its influence on state autonomy, state capacity, and social development, it is helpful, following Steffen Hertog (2010a), to go beyond an analysis that simply focuses on state and society and to focus instead on institutions and social forces at the macro-, meso-, and micro-levels. Here "macro" refers to the level at which rulers operate, where decisions move in a top-down fashion through formal and informal institutions. "Micro" is the social level, where operators such as brokers and the private sector operate. The "meso" level is that of intermediate institutions, such as business associations and labor unions, where society can aggregate preferences and voice its concerns in ways that can be effective; this level of institution is sorely missing in many of the oil producers. Rentierism centralizes power at the macro-level and tends to fragment society at the meso-level, but it typically cannot extend its control to the micro-level. Thus, regimes that practice rentierism generally remain constrained—outside periods of fast rise in the oil rent—in terms of margin of maneuver. As a result, the efficiency of public administration and the general economy are constrained because the absence of meso-level political and institutional forces exposes the private sector to predation and leaves public policy open to the risk of incoherence and inefficiencies.

State Autonomy: Distributive and Repressive States

Large oil revenues confer to the state a certain autonomy from society in both RRLP monarchies and RRLA republics. State autonomy can be good or bad for development. On the positive side, relative autonomy could theoretically, allow the state to adjust more rapidly to external shocks, which could be good for development given how costly reform avoidance could be. On the negative side, autonomous states, whether distributive or oppressive, are not compelled by their society to develop administrative capacity and more generally to respond to social demands and change, which are mechanisms that allow more complex societies to evolve. This idea that despotism leads to underdevelopment is old—it dates to Karl August Wittfogel's *Oriental Despotism* (1957) and Marx's theory of the "Asiatic Mode of Production" (Marx 1932/2012). This idea was developed to account for the failures of development in eighteenth-century Egypt and in the Ottoman Empire.[4]

The classic case linking oil, state autonomy, and underdevelopment has been made in terms of taxation (Beblawi 1987; Gray 2011). Because rents have allowed governments to avoid taxing their own citizenries, the vital, often adversarial link between governments and the people they tax has been broken. Such links encourage governmental accountability, but in their absence governments may ignore their citizens. It is true that the distributive oil countries tend to have low taxation—taxes in the GCC states are minimal. But as with every theory, critical voices have expressed doubts as to the applicability of the tax argument to the region. For one, other countries in the MENA region did tax their citizens but did not become democratic (Waterbury 1997). More to the point, what is at the heart of GCC governance systems is patronage, a system of *negative taxation* in which the oil rent is extended to the population. The way in which patronage has been exercised has shaped in many ways state autonomy and capacity.

Throughout the last seventy years of Gulf state development, the imbricated relationship between oil production and monarchical rule has endured, and as such we need to understand the hierarchical, or vertical, structuring of the state and its mirroring in society. The concept used in the literature to explicate the mutually beneficial yet unequal relationship between state and society is *neo-patrimonialism,* or *clientelism.* Although neo-patrimonialism has been applied broadly to explain the political-economic developments across the Arab world (Schlumberger 2008), Saudi Arabia's development is a particularly good example of it. The population has benefited from patronage through the provision of social services, subsidized energy, water, and housing, and state employment. The private sector, which initially consisted of trading families associated with the rulers, benefited from some exclusivity and protection, state contracts, massive energy subsidies, and, importantly, a free flow of foreign labor.

Like Iraq and Jordan, Saudi Arabia emerged from Britain's influence in the early twentieth century as a monarchy. Unlike other modern Arab states, however, Arabia did not draw on a shared ethnic identity or populist nationalistic rhetoric to consolidate the state. The leader known as Ibn Saud instead invoked his own patrimonial inheritance: a claim to rule extending from an earlier (though much smaller) Saudi state founded in the eighteenth century, and in particular a brief phase of expansion through a Saudi-Wahhab pact that ultimately united much of the peninsula. Ibn Saud established the Kingdom of Saudi Arabia in 1932 (styling himself as King Abdulaziz) and thus oversaw the discovery of oil in 1938. The paternalist "spirit" of the nation's founding in 1932 evolved into a broad system of patronage that has been the hallmark of the Saudi state's structural development through the present.

Prior to the discovery of oil, Abdulaziz's "clientelist" strategies were only partially successful. On the one hand, incorporating functionaries into the government through personal hierarchical structures allowed Abdulaziz to utilize existing power structures, like co-opting vanquished tribal leaders into regional-level government posts. However, the state faced significant financial constraints in its first years, and the Al-Saud family was forced to recruit financial patronage from elite merchants, thus subjecting themselves to their influence and forcing their incorporation into the state system as partners (rather than clients). The influx of oil rents by the 1940s largely curtailed the need for such internal strategic financial alliances. The deal Abdulaziz struck with the elite families involved protecting their interests by restricting property and business rights to nationals. He also co-opted the *ulema* into the state bureaucracy, making religious leadership partners with the state throughout the subsequent decades.[5]

During the oil boom, when patronage was expanded significantly, some of the benefits flowing to the population were programmatic, but most circulated down through networks of patron-client relations operated by the various princes as they took it on themselves to expand their networks of influence. They developed sprawling administrations, such as the National Guards and the Ministry of Defense, which function as a mini-state, providing all kinds of advantages and privileges to their members. Over time, this system of expanded but fragmented government has both constrained the Saudi state's effectiveness and underlain its successes.

Like Saudi Arabia, the smaller emirates—seven of which combined to form the United Arab Emirates (UAE) in 1971—developed social contracts that include direct patronage to the population as well as significant control over the private sector. The difference is one of degree—being much richer on a per capita basis, the Emirates provide more largesse than Saudi Arabia to their small populations. Here, too, to reward clients, the state offers direct income, land, and other privileges. In parallel, a system of social privileges has allowed elite merchant families to secure close relationships with the ruling class that endure in today's business environment in the UAE. To safeguard local interests, the UAE also instituted restrictive property and business ownership laws. By becoming clients, however, property and business owners had to give up the influence they enjoyed in pre-oil times, when they were partners in governance. Similar *wasta* systems have developed in Qatar and Kuwait (see Crystal 1990).

Thus, it does seem that oil had conferred a certain level of autonomy to the monarchies initially. Over time, the system that evolved in the GCC was built on a generous extension of rentier status to both the business elite and the population as a whole. But as patron-client relations developed, this autonomy must have become increasingly constrained by the expectations of the beneficiaries of state largesse. In the RRLA countries, however, the failure of the republics to deliver on their modernization utopia in the 1970s and 1980s pushed them to develop survival strategies built on repression, since they could not afford generous forms of patronage; as a result, the base of these regimes became narrower over time, at the same time making them more fragile, but also increasing their margin of maneuver.

State Capacity

State capacity is central for development, whether state-led or market-led. Although capacity may be boosted in the initial phases of development by a dynamic leader, later growth requires a demand for capacity expressed as political pressure, either as a demand from society and the middle class for better government services or as a demand from the business class for more enforcement of the rule of law (Levy and Fukuyama 2010). We have seen that "capacity" and "rule of law" were at relatively good levels in the RRLP countries relative to their income, but were abysmally low in the RRLA countries (see Figures 3.1 and 3.2). This section investigates the reasons for these differences.

The classic argument, which was alluded to earlier, relates to the organization of tax collection, which in the history of state development has led to the creation of bureaucracies that become the instrument of productive states. Alternatively, the exploitation of oil in conjunction with the construction of state institutions may obviate the need to establish efficient tax bureaucracies because rulers have substantial income at their disposal (Smith 2007). But the oil-rich countries generally constructed political institutions in conjunction with their exploitation of oil resources, often with substantial foreign influence (Chaudhry 1997; Vitalis 2006). Indeed, many of the Emirates, for example, have imported new institutions wholesale in the form of foreign consulting companies. Moreover, while it may be true that it was not taxation that prompted oil states to develop their administrations, other motives seem to have led to the same result. In particular, it was the development of a welfare state in Saudi Arabia that led to the development of a large bureaucracy (Hertog 2010a).

However, in Saudi Arabia and the rest of the GCC, paternalistic management created problems for the state's development over time. Abdulaziz's commitment to personalized patron-client relations led to a great segmentation and fragmentation of the government. Competing branches would sometimes arrive at contradictory policies (Hertog 2010a). Bureaucratic overreach led to sprawling services that could not be controlled through systems of vertical accountability. Yet horizontal forces were unable to develop at the meso-level to push for better performance, or even to lobby for the delivery of top-down decisions in an integrated way. There were also too many veto players in the system, especially when policies cut across many "fiefdoms" and ministries.

Various forms of adjustment took place over time to deal with these institutional weaknesses, some initiated at the macro-level and some developed organically in society at the micro-level. At the macro-level, the state discovered that it could go around inefficient state institutions by creating new institutions that served the role of protected "islands of bureaucratic efficiency" (Hertog 2010a). These institutions represented an exception to the narrative of bureaucratic bloat under rentierism, and they evolved a critical independence from the bureaucratic clientelistic network; structured as such, they thrived. An influx of returning young Saudis with Western degrees, as well as highly paid foreign advisers, changed the character of many institutions; these new managers strategized to insulate and isolate certain sectors of the government from clientelism and its nefarious effect on institutional performance. Such institutions included the central bank SAMA, the oil company Saudi Aramco, the industrial manufacturer SABIC, and the Saudi Ports Authority. The first two set the standard. SAMA was created in the 1950s by an American adviser to the state and was run by American and Lebanese technocrats and accountants. Since the private sector was weak in the 1950s, SAMA received its entire capital from the government and generated revenue by charging the government fees. Similarly, Saudi Aramco inherited and maintained the management structure first developed by its American partners (Hertog 2010a). The Gulf states have also become exemplars for the development of state-controlled, private-public development investments. Saudi Arabia's Basic Industries Corporation, Industries Qatar, and the UAE logistics provider DP World and telecom provider Etisalat are all successful state-owned enterprises that provide basic state services and garner smaller but more reliable profits than those from oil rents (Hertog 2010b).

At the micro-level, the inefficiencies of the bureaucracy became a new source of rent for well-connected individuals. Brokers emerged who could use their connections to resolve problems such as getting labor permits for foreign workers or licenses to operate for foreign corporations. Thus, citizens who remained outside government employment could plug into various patronage networks of localized sponsorship—of guest labor in particular—and clientelist relations could be extended throughout the micro-level of society. The *kafala* visa sponsorship system (common to varying degrees across the Gulf states) allowed natives to leverage their citizenship to authorize foreign workers and entrepreneurs to reside and work in their country. In this way, the native population conformed to a broad "rentier class," while foreign labor was imported to meet production demands (Davidson 2012).

In the RRLA countries, state capacity has mainly developed around repressive security apparatuses. Repressive states like Algeria, Iraq, and Syria inherited large bureaucracies from their socialist pasts, an inheritance itself related to their oil endowment. These states worked at developing an "efficient" repressive apparatus—Saddam's spies, Syria's *mukhabarat,* and Iran's Revolutionary Guard—to become the pillars of autocratic durability. In these countries, security interests and the mandate of regime survival at all costs have dominated the "civilian" institutions (Henry and Springborg 2008) (see Chapter 10 for a more detailed discussion).

These two types of regimes are also characterized by very different capacities for sustaining shocks. In the distributive GCC states, gradual reforms that preserve political stability can be financially viable given these countries' deep pockets. The oil boom in the 1970s generated a period when rulers had a great deal of autonomy and agency in the choices they made, but these choices imposed on these rulers political obligations that they could not easily escape. As the revenues were spent, new domestic actors emerged (contractors, agents, recipients of subsidies, government bureaucrats) who, in turn, began to limit the state's freedom of maneuver (Chaudhry 1997). Even at the hardest times during the period of low oil prices in the mid-1980s, the RRLP states refused to consider reducing their rate of hiring in the public sector or cutting the welfare state, which, indeed, kept expanding even as resources had to be borrowed. In many ways, the legitimacy of rulers had come to be based on a functional system of patronage to all nationals, and any attempt at curtailing what was now perceived as entitlements would be strongly resisted. In the end, fluctuating petroleum prices were absorbed largely by adjusting public investment. The economic system was not affected until the late 1990s, when Saudi Arabia's ruler decided, after running deficits for eighteen years in a row, and with the rise of Dubai as proof of the potential of a private-sector approach, that fundamental economic reforms were needed to create the jobs that the public sector could not deliver alone. Thus, while state autonomy is constrained by political considerations, the state retains an ability to strategize for the long term, and it can afford the slow and gradual reforms that transform society over time. This ability to both strategize for the long term and find some space alongside patronage-focused institutions to act on those strategies is the essential characteristic of the RRLP countries. For these states, the real question is whether more productive models can be found over time that do not undermine their autocratic rule. With the onset of the Arab Uprisings of 2011, reforms took a back seat. The Gulf states reacted to the Arab uprisings by massively increasing their patronage, reducing their savings, shifting expenditures toward recurrent support (wages and subsidies), and thus abandoning reforms.

The RRLA countries did not have pockets as deep as Saudi Arabia's, and thus they could not smooth shocks over long durations. Moreover, unlike Saudi Arabia and other GCC countries, RRLA countries never saw the development of the private sector as an attractive alternative to state-led development, as it would threaten regime durability at its core, given the smaller size of the spoils that could tie the private sector to the regime. Moreover, these regimes' history of radicalism, including the nationalization of much of the private sector, made it harder for them to find workable arrangements for private-sector growth. As a result, while these countries were more flexible in imposing top-down changes, their alternatives were severely curtailed. In many of these countries, levels of repression rose as the state retreated and was replaced by a very narrow form of cronyism closely associated with the regime. In some cases, as notoriously illustrated by Iraq's invasion of Kuwait, foreign adventurism was an attempt to replenish "strategic rents." In addition, myopic interests connected with the fragility of their autocratic rule explains why these states tended to be the hawks in the Organization of the Oil-Exporting Countries (OPEC), pushing for increased international oil prices even at the risk of falling global demand.

In Algeria, the attempt at reform after the first oil shock led to the events and calamities that still mark the sociopolitical scene today. Under the guise of increased repression and the fight against Islamists, army interests came to dominate a stagnating private sector. In Syria, low oil prices (together with falling reserves) led to a rapid economic adjustment that reduced dramatically state involvement in the peripheral regions from which the 2011 uprisings emerged. The country's intervention in Lebanon in 1976 was largely predicated on extracting rents. The economic reforms led to the increased concentration of economic powers among the elite, from cousins of the president to the sons of generals (see Chapter 12). Foreign policy, too, was dominated by the search for increased strategic rents—from the Gulf, Iran, or Russia—and Syria carefully avoided becoming accountable to a single foreign patron. Iraq, coming out of the war with Iran with a huge foreign debt and destroyed infrastructure, sought to invade Kuwait as a way to shore up its economy, with dramatic consequences for the Iraqi people. Iraq lost most of its oil revenues during its war with Iran when its export facilities at Shatt-el-Arab were bombed, and again when it was under sanctions; in both cases, the country went through wrenching and socially calamitous adjustment periods.[6] In Sudan, the fight over dwindling resources led to the disaster of Darfur, and the state's pursuit of oil revenues culminated in a deal with the Sudan People's Liberation Army (SPLA) that led to the division of the country. In Yemen, the fight over newly discovered oil led to a civil war and the forced unification of the country.

Social Fragmentation

As discussed earlier, social development plays an important role in supporting economic development through two important channels: as incomes rise, the interest of the private sector as a group increasingly leans toward the development of a predictable system of rule of law; and civil society becomes more and more inclined to hold the civil service and government accountable for their performance in delivering public services. As we saw in Chapter 3, however, society's "voice" has been equally low in both RRLP and RRLA countries—indeed, the suppression of this "voice" is the main instrument of regime survival and the main goal of the autocratic instruments of co-optation and repression.

In the distributive GCC states, the government's successful "clientization" of society fragmented the native population into a series of vertical networks, all reliant on a combination of subsidies and government employment. This fragmentation has severely restricted the development of a class-based social structure and, more broadly, of any special associations at the meso-level that could push for accountability at the macro-level. That the development of oil production forestalled the development of typical class structures and related patterns of popular dissent and calls for representation is due in part to the efficiency of oil extraction and in part to policies of massively importing labor from abroad. Compared to other forms of energy resource extraction, such as coal, oil production requires far less labor. Whereas, historically, labor movements drove the push toward "mass democracy" in industrial countries such as the United States, such labor organizations were less viable in the oil-rich Gulf (Mitchell 2011).

The only form of social organization that has started to emerge in the GCC, besides the controlled religious groups, is the business association. Business associations have been encouraged to form in order to support rulers' decisions to engage in economic reforms. Consultations on visions and plans for the future and on particular reforms (for example, WTO accession, financial market reforms, or the "nationalization of labor") have increasingly involved such groups, which seem to have become at least a veto player, though they refrain from activism. Their power is likely to continue to rise, however, at least as long as their collective interests and the interests of the rulers converge.

One of the main weaknesses of the private sector that prevents it from playing a more activist political role is its restricted relation with the native middle class. The private sector itself is dualistic, divided between a capital-intensive element that responds to generous energy subsidies and a labor-intensive element that takes advantage of cheap foreign labor and invests in low-productivity activities, and not in growth opportunities based on knowledge acquisition and innovation. Neither element creates the type of jobs that natives need, and they tend to operate as enclaves with few connections to local societies. Kuwait, which has a parliament, has tended to be much less oriented toward the private sector than the United Arab Emirates, where natives have much less voice (Herb 1999). This disconnect with society reduces the legitimacy of the private sector and thus its potential to play an active national role (Hertog 2010a).

Dissent is rare in the absence of meso-level organizations, but the risk of major popular conflagrations remains. Rulers tend to be wary of public opinion, as reflected in their efforts to suppress dissent expressed on social media, for example, or in the exaggerated response of Gulf leaders to the Arab uprisings. As citizens become more educated, they tend to hold higher expectations of the performance of their leaders, and issues such as corruption are now more often publicly debated. One defining issue that hurt the legitimacy of Gulf rulers was their inability to face Iraq's aggression without the support of the US Army. In Saudi Arabia, military spending has typically eaten up a large part of state budgets—around 30 percent of government spending.[7] The First Gulf War made it all too clear that the mighty army built with hundreds of billions of dollars was more a tool of patronage than of national defense, something that average Saudis found humiliating.

The massive influxes of foreign workers of all types have had social and political consequences as well. Labor immigration, more than the capital-intensity of oil extraction, has completely severed the expected link between economic growth and structural change and severely stunted class formation (Hanieh 2012). With much of local labor working for the government, the importation of foreign labor allows for the development of a private sector, without the risk of labor movements demanding more of a voice in decision-making. Native Saudi Arabians usually avoid manual labor and work instead as merchants, soldiers, and bureaucrats. Some fear the long-run impact of the identification of hard work with foreigners. To be sure, immigrants from poorer countries do the hard, dirty, and dangerous work in all rich countries, but only in the Gulf states do the foreign menials outnumber the indigenous leisured.

There have been a host of other social costs to the open immigration policies. For instance, immigration posed a serious political challenge to the Saudi and Kuwaiti regimes during the First Gulf War. Much of the animus against the Gulf states that was so visible in popular demonstrations from Morocco to Pakistan during the fall of 1990 derived from these states' denial of citizenship rights and benefits to fellow Arabs.[8] Large-scale influxes of foreigners have made national security agencies nervous, especially after the Grand Mosque incident of 1980.[9] As a result, several GCC countries have beefed up enforcement by importing foreign police experts, soldiers, and policemen, such as the Pakistani police and military personnel in Oman and Saudi Arabia.[10] The Gulf states have also tightened labor importing rules, for instance, by denying family reunification. *Hajj* (pilgrimage) rules have also become more stringent in Saudi Arabia. Finally, the Gulf states have resorted extensively to devices for controlling imported labor such as the use of turnkey construction contracts, in which the general contractor supplies the workers and guarantees their subsequent departure.

As illustrated by the controversy over Qatar's treatment of the workers building the facilities for the 2022 World Cup, observers around the world now see the ways in which the Gulf states handle foreign workers as infringing on their human rights; as a result, they are losing international legitimacy at a time when they are trying to open up to the world (Gardner 2010). The absolute exclusion of such foreigners and their descendants from citizenship status and the system of sponsorship in which workers are regularly denied the freedom to seek alternative employment within the country or advancement within their organization have both ensured that meso-level institutions of representation, such as voluntary associations, do not arise. Even in Kuwait, which is an exception in the Gulf in terms of civil liberties (which include elected representation in government and substantial rights for women by Western standards), the regulation of trade and labor unions by the state and their financial dependence on the state weaken the organization of political activity (Tétreault 1993).

Gender equality is another salient aspect of social development in oil-producing countries, where female labor force participation is especially low. In the Middle East, female labor force participation is around 30 percent in non-oil-producing countries such as Morocco, Lebanon, and Syria; lower, at around 20 percent, in the RRLA countries like Iran, Iraq, Egypt, and Jordan; and as low as 10 percent or less in Algeria, Saudi Arabia, and the rest of the GCC (see Chapter 4). On the one hand, the underdevelopment of the manufacturing sector, which tends to be a top hirer for women globally, reduces the opportunities for female employment. But on the other hand, the rise of female education has improved the hiring of women in the public sector in countries where the civil service is still growing (as in the GCC). Nevertheless, patriarchal values still prevail in these societies (Moghadam 1999; Ross 2012).

In RRLA countries, the fragility of power precludes the normal development of social organizations—both civil society groups and independent private-sector operators are severely repressed. But they exist, often underground, to a significantly greater degree than in the Gulf, and some even manage to be active. Repression fosters the emergence of a violent opposition, often in the form of political Islam, as the only form of organization that is viable in such conditions (outside of Iran and Sudan). Ironically, despotic regimes have developed a relation of complementarity with such movements, as was apparent during Algeria's dark years: the presence of such an opposition has helped regimes pursue a divide-and-rule strategy that draws the domestic middle class and Western powers to their side. The entrenchment of the elite helps to explain why the "bunker states" reacted to the Arab uprisings with such violence, which led to civil wars of varying magnitudes in Syria and Libya and, to some extent, in Sudan and Yemen. Algeria's exhaustion is probably the reason why it did not partake in this wave of contestation.

An analytical frame that is useful for understanding the stark policy difference between the RPLA countries and the RRLA countries is the idea of "violence traps," recently developed by North and his colleagues (2013) to explain the persistence of violent regimes in developing countries. They posit that the political-economy "equilibrium" can include violence when authoritarian elites, though mindful that better outcomes can be achieved by cooperation with the opposition, also know that they would lose out if concessions were made because they cannot trust that deals entered with the opposition would be respected in the future. For the GCC states, such system-improving deals are possible with their private sectors, and these are politically safe from the point of view of the governing elite as long as the rest of society remains fragmented into controllable clientelistic networks. The RRLA countries, however, cannot trust the business community to grow more powerful, because it does not share the economic rents. As a result, implementing pro-growth reforms is seen as a form of political suicide by ruling elites.

THE ECONOMICS OF OIL

A sudden influx of foreign currency can lead to a phenomenon known as the "Dutch Disease," so called because of the experience of the Dutch economy with the large influx of North Sea gas revenues in the 1970s. The term was coined by *The Economist* in 1977 to describe the effects of natural gas export on the Dutch manufacturing sector. As we discussed earlier in Chapter 2, the "Dutch Disease" posits that a large influx of oil disturbs the process of development in important ways and can make an oil-producing country worse off than it was without the oil. The arguments for this are both economic and political: oil-producing countries are less diversified, and they also tend to be autocratic, both of which characteristics can lead to less growth.

While it is hard to believe that Saudi or UAE citizens would be richer in the absence of oil, it is more plausible to think that Iraq (or Nigeria) could have been better off without it. There was a widespread belief in the 1980s and early 2000s that oil, in most circumstances, is bad for economic growth. Today one would be more circumspect. Looking back at the studies done in the 1980s and 1990s, most of which followed and deepened the evidence presented in the classic Sachs and Warner piece (1995), one would conclude that their results on the economic performance of oil producers was very much biased by the long oil price slump of the 1980s and 1990s. During this period, the collapse of oil prices following the first oil boom had deeply depressed many developing countries' economies, as these countries had found it costly (and difficult) to adjust to much lower revenues after they had greatly expanded state expenditures.

More recent studies using data over the longer period 1960–2010, however, have produced more balanced results (Ross 2012). In fact, over longer periods of boom and bust—for example during the period 1960–2010—average economic growth in an average oil economy has been historically slightly higher than average growth in an average non-oil economy. However, when we focus on particular historical windows, it is possible to claim, based on historical evidence, that the oil countries have grown either faster than the non-oil economies (for example, if one considered the period 1972–1982) or slower (if one considered the period 1982–2000) (Ross 2012).

So while the evidence shows that the "average" oil-producing country has not been made worse off by the presence of oil, the question remains as to why the RRLP countries have not grown significantly faster than non-oil countries, and why the RRLA countries have grown much more slowly than the RRLP countries. Even as oil supports growth, does it also generate other effects that hurt growth, so that, on net, the advantage of oil producers over non-oil producers is not that great? If so, what are the sources of economic weakness, or the special challenges, that oil brings?

There is now a wealth of work that documents how natural resources affect the structure of economies and thus determine their overall performance (Auty 2001; Corden and Neary 1982; Gelb 1988; Sachs and Warner 1995). Oil revenue is different from other sources of income in three main ways, each of which exerts a negative influence on the process of economic development. First, the expansion of the oil sector reduces the price of foreign currencies, thus hurting the productive sectors exposed to foreign competition. Second, the accrual to the state of large oil revenues can hinder the development of an efficient private sector. And third, the boom-and-bust cycles created by oil revenues, which tend to be highly variable over time, hurt the growth process.

Through the effects of these three channels, countries that rely on natural resources can suffer from various ills: they risk performing poorly on agriculture and manufacturing; they have high levels of macroeconomic instability and inflation; they have oversized states and private sectors that lack dynamism; and they have low levels of job creation and high levels of unemployment. In the following section, we examine the impact of these three channels and the effects they have had in the MENA region.

Let us stress at the outset that particular economic policies can mitigate the negative economic effects of each of these ills. So while the economic management of large oil revenues is challenging in many respects, economic policies are technically available to ensure that oil becomes a blessing rather than a curse. Such policies include sensible macroeconomic policies of stabilization to smooth the cycle, policies to avoid excessive external debts, policies that slow down spending to control inflation, policies that support the growth of the private sector, and policies of investment in sectors that can diversify the economy and push it toward dynamic growth. More extreme proposals include the privatization of oil and the distribution of oil revenues directly to the population, which the state can then tax according to its revenue needs (Sala-i-Martin and Subramanian 2003; Weinthal and Luong 2006). All of these recommended policies tend to include restraints on public-sector spending; thus, the main problem with them is their political feasibility or desirability.

The Effects of Relative Price Change and Labor Migration

The presence of large oil revenues affects, sometimes in major ways, one key price in the economy—the exchange rate. This seems intuitive enough: because oil is sold abroad, the government gains access to large amounts of foreign exchange, thus raising the supply of foreign exchange in the local market and strengthening the relative price of the local currency. The appreciation of the exchange rate makes the economy less competitive internationally, and as a result the economy's level of diversification is reduced.

While one can think of the exchange rate as the price of local to international currency, as is done in the macroeconomic tradition, a more precise characterization from the microeconomic tradition is the price of traded to nontraded goods. Consider, for simplicity, that the world consists of two types of goods—those that are traded internationally and those that are not traded internationally. Prices for goods traded internationally are determined by the international market, and prices for goods that are not traded internationally are determined by local demand. A country whose income is boosted by oil revenues will spend more on nontraded goods, whose prices will thus rise, and it will therefore have a higher real exchange rate. Such a country will become less competitive internationally at producing traded goods—unless it manages to lift its efficiency in line with costs.

Let us trace more precisely the impact of oil revenue on the real exchange rate. Initially, it is government spending of oil revenues that rises, with the government buying more tradables (such as wheat) and nontradables (for instance, hiring more civil servants). For most small countries, the supply of tradable goods is perfectly elastic and the supply of nontradable goods is not. Therefore, increased spending bids up the price of nontradable goods relative to tradable goods (in the above example, local wages relative to wheat). This effect is compounded when government spending is concentrated in nontradables, such as services and construction (as in the oil-exporting countries during the 1970s and 1980s).

This real exchange rate appreciation deeply affects economic incentives. It leads capital and labor to shift from the production of tradable goods to nontradable goods production, where returns are now higher. This shift fosters stagnation of agriculture and manufacturing (tradable goods), while the sectors that benefit from larger government revenues—typically the main nontradables are civil service employment and the building industry—are booming. International competition holds down the prices of, say, food and manufactures, while wages and costs in domestic agriculture and industry rise, catching local producers in a profit squeeze. It becomes cheaper to import agricultural and manufacturing goods than to produce them at home. The Dutch Disease contributes to the rural exodus, as farm workers abandon the countryside in search of construction and other service jobs in the cities. Manufacturing also becomes less competitive and shrinks.

There are several well-documented examples of this aspect of the "oil curse" both inside and outside the MENA region. After the first oil boom, the Dutch Disease hurt the agriculture and manufacturing sectors in Algeria, Colombia, Ecuador, Nigeria, Trinidad, and Venezuela (Gelb 1988). In the region, there is evidence of a loss of economic diversity, most notably in agriculture. For example, Tunisian agriculture grew at a 4.1 percent average annual rate from 1970 to 1981, but at only 1.6 percent from 1973 to 1983, when oil production was at its highest. More generally, the Middle East has become the least food-self-sufficient area in the world (see Chapter 6). Demand for food rose by 4–5 percent per year during the 1970s, driven by rapidly rising per capita incomes and by population growth rates that were surprisingly high given national incomes. Supply was constrained: scarce water resources, urban bias, and the Dutch Disease all contributed to the relatively sluggish supply response. In the 1980s and 1990s, growth in food demand slowed as incomes fell, but supply increased modestly as the Dutch disease weakened and improved policies were put in place. Food and agriculture imports accounted for nearly one-third of all imports in Algeria from 1993 to 1999 (Lofgren and Richards 2003).

Evidence of the Dutch Disease can also be seen in the low levels at which manufacturing expanded in the region. As discussed in Chapter 2 manufacturing value added in the RPLA countries has not grown over time, and the manufacturing value added in RRLA countries has actually shrunk relative to GDP (after a short period of increase in the 1980s). By 2010, subregional averages were at 15.42 percent of GDP among the RPLA countries and at only 6 percent of GDP among the RRLA countries, below the average of 19 percent of GDP for middle-income countries (Figure 2.6). The effect of the real exchange rate appreciation on industrial growth is neatly illustrated in Iran when it was subjected to an oil embargo. In the past decade, and especially after the second oil boom, the manufacturing sector was flooded by cheap imports.[11] When foreign exchange became scarcer, the Iranian riyal depreciated deeply. The result was to strengthen the national industrial sector, which regained competitiveness, and despite the embargo, Iran's manufacturing exports actually rose. In effect, the embargo, while costly to Iran, compelled Iranians to consume fewer imports, but also provided incentives for firms to produce more and thus create new jobs (Salehi-Isfahani 2013).

What is wrong with an economy dominated by services rather than agriculture or manufacturing? After all, as these societies become richer, it is only natural that these structural changes will occur. However, there are two types of problems that might be generated by this type of transformation. First, if the oil boom is temporary, resources will be exhausted, and when the economy is forced to move back to producing tradable goods in the future, structural change will be hard to reverse. For example, people do not easily go back into agriculture, and it is hard to move back into industry, a sector where productivity improves with learning by doing. Several countries in the region have faced this type of problem. Tunisia exhausted its oil in the 1980s but has managed to diversify into industry. Bahrain, Oman, and Syria are on their way to losing their oil revenues in the next decade, and so the industrialization challenge is now acute. Yemen and Sudan have small reserves and cannot count on oil as a source of long-term growth. Second, the manufacturing sectors tend to be more dynamic than the services sectors, and so losing manufacturing can make overall growth less dynamic. Manufacturing's dynamism comes from several factors: it has more linkages with the rest of the economy; it employs a large number of skilled workers; and it presents more potential to adopt more efficient technologies and move up the production frontier. (Much of growth operates this way—as an attempt to catch up to countries that use more productive technologies.) Some countries, in particular Algeria and Saudi Arabia, do not want to lose industry and see it as part of their diversification strategy to retain and develop industrial sectors. Third, for a variety of reasons, some countries may want to protect their agriculture: they may consider food security a strategic issue; perhaps they fear the social costs imposed by a rapid urban migration; or they may want to build a comparative advantage in this sector. Iraq was such a case in the 1950s; more recently, Libya and Saudi Arabia have extended huge support to their agriculture sectors, in very costly ways (see Chapter 6).

For some oil exporters, especially Iran and Algeria (and to some extent Egypt, which produced more oil in the past), the growth rates of manufacturing and agriculture were in fact greater during the 1973–1983 period than they had been during the previous "cheap oil" decade. The reason for the discrepancy between this evidence and theoretical predictions was that Middle Eastern and other oil-exporting governments intervened directly to counteract these relative price shifts in various ways. Both the seriousness of the disease and the cure have varied considerably from one country to another, illustrating the argument that state policy both shapes development and responds to its unintended outcomes. Whether they were running out of oil or did not want to lose their agriculture or industry sector, governments have looked for ways to offset the push away from tradable goods. One important strategy has been investment of large shares of oil revenues in ways that can boost national productivity to offset the relative price change, typically through a combination of increased public-sector investment and support for the private sector. We review this strategy further in the next section.

Here we focus on a unique strategy employed by the GCC countries more than any other region of the world: the massive importation of foreign labor, which has become the signature policy of this region. The goal of this strategy is to remove the key bottleneck that constrains growth, that of labor and skills—factors of production that are in short supply domestically—to prevent wages from rising when the economy grows. Besides unskilled labor, international construction firms, international financial and insurance services, foreign teachers, and so forth, have been imported massively. Demography and sociopolitical factors have constrained

TABLE 9.1. The Labor Force in the Gulf States, 2010

	Population		Labor		*Natives Working in Public Service*	*Natives Working as Civil Servants*	*Expatriates in the Private Sector*
	Total	*Expatriates*	*Total*	*Expatriates*			
Bahrain	727,000	40.7%	599,016	77%	34%	79%	83%
Kuwait	2,867,000	65.1	2,058,852	84	80	69	96
Oman	2,567,000	24.4	1,095,528	75	47	85	84
Qatar	813,000	78.3	1,260,239	94	87	41	99
Saudi Arabia	24,573,000	25.9	8,793,812	62	75	97	87
United Arab Emirates	4,496,000	71.4	3,000,000	91	73	49	97
All GCC countries	35,862,000	35.7	16,807,447	78	66	70	91

Sources: Hodson (2013); for Saudi Arabia, Hertog (2012).

domestic labor supply. The Gulf states and Libya have long had small and young populations: generally, at least 40 percent of the indigenous populations of these countries is younger than fifteen, and more than half are under twenty. Consequently, the economically active population and the domestic labor supply were and remain limited. Limited female participation in the labor force has further exacerbated the shortage of domestic workers. Many males of working age are illiterate and unskilled, and the few who are skilled are attracted to public-sector employment, especially in the armed forces. Foreigners are needed, and they have come in unprecedented numbers. The situation has not changed much in the nearly fifty years since the first oil boom.

The Gulf region is unique in the world for the immense scope of its imported labor. Migrants as a percentage of the workforce in GCC countries range from 62 percent in Saudi Arabia to over 90 percent in the United Arab Emirates and Qatar (see Table 9.1).[12] During the second oil boom, nationalist rhetoric notwithstanding, this dependence has only grown, even though the source of the demand is now much more often the private sectors than the governments. The reliance of the Gulf states on foreigners for labor has no parallel in modern economic history. The private sectors have also boomed, but a GCC private sector is mainly a sector for expatriates. Around 2010, it has been estimated, there were more than 12 million migrant workers in the GCC countries, constituting nearly 80 percent of the overall labor force, 91 percent of the labor force in the private sector, and about 36 percent of the population (see Table 9.1).

The GCC ranked third (after the United States and the European Union) as an immigration region in 2010, and the influx of cheap labor continues to underwrite infrastructural development in the Gulf countries. Moreover, Gulf-based businesses are clamoring for cheap labor, often claiming that the availability of cheap foreign labor is key to their success (Shah 2008) and their ability to be competitive globally. In effect, the GCC is the only region of the world where wages are truly set by a global labor market, ensuring that it gets the cheapest wage-to-skill ratio in the world. Perhaps in no other region would domestic labor accept such "unfair" competition by foreign labor. Normally, domestic workers might feel entitled—and rightly so—to benefit from oil booms. They accept the policy of free labor movement, which benefits mainly rich private entrepreneurs, only because (and as long as) they get their share of the oil pie in the form of state patronage, free social services, cheap energy and water, subsidized housing, and, importantly, employment by the government at much higher wages than those that prevail in the labor market. This quid pro quo—open labor imports to satisfy the private sector against generous patronage to satisfy local labor—is at the heart of the social contract in the Gulf between the rulers, the private sector, and the middle class.

Besides an open labor market that dampens wages, the GCC countries have also developed a strategy that dampens domestic demand, which is yet another way to neutralize the Dutch Disease: they do not allow foreign labor to take up long-term residence, which encourages a free flow of remittances. As a result, a large share of the labor earnings go abroad and do not augment the domestic demand for nontradable goods—the outflow of labor remittances from GCC countries stood at 6–10 percent of GDP in 2010. A (negative) example of how restrictions on foreigners dampen prices for nontradables is the housing sector in Dubai, the only such sector in the GCC that was opened to foreign investment: prices zoomed up initially, in the mid-2000s (only to crash during the global financial crisis of 2008).

As a result of these policies, the Dutch Disease's effects have been, at most, quite muted in the GCC countries. Raphael Espinoza, Ghada Fayad, and Ananthakrishnan Prasad (2013) estimate that there has been no exchange rate overvaluation at all in the GCC countries. The same cannot be said of the RRLA countries, such as Iran, Algeria, and Iraq, which do not have important labor inflows and cannot afford a strategy of isolating their national labor from the effect of the labor market. Libya is an intermediate case, with large informal labor flows from sub-Saharan Africa and neighboring North African states. Unemployment rates are high in these countries, and many of the youth entering the labor markets have to join the ranks of the low-productivity informal service sector. Algeria and Iran especially are cases in point: unemployment rates among Algerian and Iranian youth are over 25 percent. As discussed later, however, even though the GCC countries do not suffer from the Dutch Disease, and even though they have had more success in developing private sectors and diversifying their economies, their unemployment rates are also rising (albeit at lower levels), if for entirely different reasons.

The model of imported labor was not so much designed as it grew out of need and circumstances (see Box 9.1). Bringing in foreign workers for the early infrastructure programs of the 1970s made sense. Soon local trading families who had become contractors were lobbying for more visas to attract workers who would help them deliver on their state contracts. As these contractors evolved into commercial and industrial businesses, they continued to hire pliant foreign labor. The boom encouraged governments to hire all employable natives in government. The Kuwait parliament, under pressure from the street, voted to deny foreign workers the right to citizenship and restricted business dealings to natives. Thus was the GCC model born, and it has since flourished. The question is, how long can this system remain workable and sustainable?

The civil administration in the GCC countries has grown prodigiously. Kuwait's expanded from 22,000 in 1963 to 146,000 in 1980 and to 392,000 in 2009. Saudi Arabia's grew from 37,000 in 1962 to 312,000 in 1981; today an estimated 2 million Saudis are employed in the civil service and in security-related institutions (Hertog 2013a). Altogether, of the 4.2 million Gulf native workers in the labor force, most work in the public sector; the average share of the native workforce employed in the public sector is 66 percent for the GCC as a whole, ranging from 34 percent in Bahrain to 75 percent in Saudi Arabia and 87 percent in Qatar (Table 9.1). The main reason nationals work predominantly in the public sector is that the wages they earn there tend to be many times greater than what is offered in the unregulated private-sector labor market—two to four times as much in Saudi Arabia (four times as much for the lowest skills) and about two times as much in Bahrain (Espinoza, Fayad, and Prasad 2013).[13] Indeed, current rates of national employment in the private sector in the various GCC countries range from 1 to 4 percent (in Qatar, Kuwait, and the United Arab Emirates) to 10 to 15 percent (in Saudi Arabia, Bahrain, and Oman) (see Table 10.3). Unless the gap between private and public compensation narrows dramatically, natives are simply not employable in the private sector. In addition, other conditions will also have to improve: Gulf workers will have to acquire the type of skills demanded by the market and adapt their work attitudes and expectations to the realities of the market.

Whenever the Gulf states have tried to reduce hiring in the public sector—as happened in the late 1990s at the low point of oil prices—this effort has been met by a rise in youth unemployment. Whenever unemployment coincides with large-scale immigration, political criticism of immigration rises. Replacing foreigners with unemployed locals, however, is no easy matter. Because of the wage differentials and the lack of job security and prestige, locals do not want to take the kinds of jobs that many foreigners accept. Every country in the Gulf has embarked on a "nationalization" campaign aimed at reducing the employment of immigrants and reducing national unemployment. Such campaigns have been most successful in the public sector, which has become much more "nationalized." Countries have also tried to impose restrictions on private-sector hiring, as when Saudi Arabia attempted to restrict the jewelry retail trade (formerly dominated by Yemenis) to Saudis. There have been limited successes here. The private sector does not like these policies, and it can resist them by slowing down implementation. Many locals prefer to remain unemployed, hoping for a public-sector job down the line (Yousef 2005). Despite all these efforts, only in Saudi Arabia, which recently implemented a quota system, has the foreign percentage of the labor force declined somewhat—and even there, foreigners still fill more than half of all jobs.

As education levels rise, the pressure on the state to employ natives only intensifies. A good share of the oil revenues has been spent on education in the GCC countries, with the goal of making national labor more efficient. In recent years, a larger share of budgets has gone into social services as public investment has fallen. Human development indicators, while still below what would be suggested by these countries' high incomes, have improved considerably since the 1980s, and in 2010 Qatar, Bahrain, Saudi Arabia, and the United Arab Emirates ranked among the top thirty globally on the Human Development Index (see Chapter 5). The question remains, however, as to how this increase in skill levels will benefit the national economies as long as national labor remains shut off from the private sector.

A related, and grave, political challenge is the rise of educated unemployment. Depending on the source one consults, unemployment in the Gulf states varies between 5 and 12 percent, with higher figures reported for educated youth. It may well be that youth unemployment in the RRLP countries is as bad as it is in the RRLA countries. Although the underlying problems are very different—there are no jobs in the RRLA countries, while there are plenty of jobs in the RRLP countries, but they are all for foreigners—the effect is the same. As long as there are no

---

BOX 9.1. On Labor Migration

The modern history of migration in the Gulf region can be divided into four phases. During the first phase, the period prior to 1974, more than 80 percent of immigrating workers were Arabs, mainly Egyptians, Syrians, Yemenis, and Palestinians. The major characteristics of the Gulf labor market at this time were the relatively narrow wage differentials between sending and receiving countries and the high skill level of many migrant workers, who were mainly teachers, accountants, and engineers.

The second phase began with the oil price increase of 1974. The number of expatriates working in the Gulf states rose dramatically, from 1.1 million in 1975 to 2.8 million in 1980 (Girgis 2002), to 4.1 million in 1985. At the same time, the number of migrant workers in Iraq, locked in the long war with Iran, had increased more than ten times, to about 750,000, and the number of expatriate workers in Libya had risen from just under 50,000 in 1973 to more than 400,000 (Sherbiny 1984). Two other trends stand out during this period. First, the share of Arab migrant workers in the total expatriate workforce started to decline as Indians, Pakistanis, Sri Lankans, and other Asian workers flocked to the region. Not only was the wage gap even greater for these countries than for some of the poorer Arab countries, but the Gulf states increasingly preferred these workers. As non-Arabs, they were believed to be less likely to stay in the Gulf and were perceived as politically safer than potentially recalcitrant Egyptians, Yemenis, Lebanese, and Palestinians. Second, the growth of demand for unskilled labor slowed as major infrastructural projects were completed, while that for skilled workers to operate the completed projects accelerated. When the fall in oil revenues by the 1980s curtailed demand, the growth of immigration

continues

mechanisms to motivate natives to work in the private sector, the pressure to hire them in the private sector will remain, and the pressure on the budget will increase, since oil revenues cannot possibly increase as fast as the labor force in the long run (now growing at about 4 percent a year). Because more and more new entrants to the labor market are educated, they also hold higher expectations. For example, three-fourths of current students in Saudi Arabia are in university. The limits of the patronage-driven model is most keenly felt by young Saudis, whose "waithood" period keeps getting longer as they are forced to queue for public-sector jobs, housing, or loans in support of SME development (Hertog 2013a).

By comparison, diversification and employment challenges are even more acute in the RRLA countries. The RRLP countries' problem is essentially a political one: the jobs exist, but the challenge is convincing the local private sector and labor to work together. In the RRLA countries, however, the jobs do not exist, and the private sector is extremely weak and dominated by a narrow range of cronies and a few dysfunctional public enterprises. As a result, not only is unemployment high, but as

---

BOX 9.1. *continued*

slowed down—by the end of the 1980s, there were about 5.2 million foreign workers in the Gulf (some two-thirds of the labor force).

The third phase began with the Iraqi invasion of Kuwait in August 1990. Operation Desert Storm tore asunder the web of intraregional labor flows—some 2 million workers were directly affected by the crisis. An estimated 1 million Yemenis, 200,000 Jordanians, and 150,000 Palestinians were expelled from Saudi Arabia and the Gulf, and nearly all of the Sudanese in Saudi Arabia were expelled. In addition, some 700,000 Egyptians fled Iraq, Kuwait, and Jordan. Jordan, Sudan, and Yemen, as well as the Palestine Liberation Organization (PLO), which backed Iraq, paid dearly for opposing the Saudis and the Americans.

The fourth phase encapsulates the past ten years, when migration flows to the Gulf have matured and the two trends that began with the expulsions of 1990—the Asianization and nationalization of the labor force—have continued. The inflows of foreign workers decelerated and the composition of immigrants continued to shift. Of the estimated 8–12 million migrants in the GCC countries, more than 7 million are Asians, mainly from India (3.2 million), Pakistan (1.7 million), Bangladesh (820,000), the Philippines (730,000), and Sri Lanka (705,000). Even with the influx of Asians, large numbers of nonnational Arabs are employed in the Gulf. Nearly 1.5 million Egyptians, 250,000 Sudanese, 480,000 Jordanians, 265,000 Syrians, and perhaps 1 million Yemenis work there today (Kapiszewski 2004). Unskilled work and domestic service in the Gulf are largely performed by Asians, while Arabs tend to be found in the semiskilled and skilled tasks. For example, roughly 40 percent of Egyptians employed in Saudi Arabia today are scientific and technical workers (Baldwin-Edwards 2005).

we have seen earlier in the chapter, the economies have become *less* diversified over time. Despite their large endowment of oil and labor, the economies of the RRLA countries are becoming dominated by three things: oil, some public employment for the lucky ones, especially in the security forces, and a huge unproductive informal sector for all the rest. If the RRLP countries do not manage to find a more productive development model before their population sizes start catching up with their oil revenues, the RRLA experience shows the risks ahead.

The Private Sector's Development Challenge
When Revenues Accrue to the State

Oil revenues accrue to the state. If the state is myopic, or if the population is impatient, oil rents can end up largely consumed rather than invested. This situation is sustainable as long as oil rents can grow at least as fast as the population. For most of the countries of the region, however, this condition does not hold true. The problem is not related to the level of reserves per se: these are extremely large and can sustain higher oil production for the foreseeable future. In Kuwait, the United Arab Emirates, and Iraq, proved reserves stand at over one hundred years, while the reserves of Iran, Qatar, and Saudi Arabia stand at between fifty and eighty-three years (see Figure 9.2).[14] These countries know that they need to diversify their economies over time because oil will dry up in the long run. In addition, oil prices may plunge for good if other technologies are invented or a tax on carbon emissions is created. But the main risk for the GCC countries is in the nearer future, and it concerns having insufficient income to sustain their costly systems of patronage, since if all countries pump out more oil, global prices will fall, and thus more production does not necessarily result in higher income (see Chapter 13 on cartel dynamics). Indeed, an oil glut developed in late 2014 due to global conditions of low demand and lush supply, and prices plunged from over $100 per barrel to $60 to $70.

Oil revenue continues to dominate budgets, exports, and GDPs in the region. In 2010 the share of the oil sector in their GNPs reached 47 percent in Saudi Arabia and 48 percent in Kuwait, 18 percent in the United Arab Emirates, 36 percent in Oman, and 16 percent in Qatar. In 1980 these percentages had been, respectively, 66, 51, 65, 69, and 60 percent. These figures show that some countries have had some success at diversification, against all predictions, especially Saudi Arabia and Oman. Oil receipts, however, remain the lifeline for these countries, as oil exports constitute between 42 percent (for the United Arab Emirates[15]) and 93.5 percent of exports (88.2 percent for Saudi Arabia), and oil revenues constitute between 60 percent (for Qatar) and 88 percent (for Saudi Arabia) of government revenues. The relatively low figures in the United Arab Emirates and Qatar are due to the fact that these countries have begun to draw significant revenues from their foreign investments (see Figure 9.3).

Thus, to increase the chances of maintaining future incomes, the oil-producing countries must transform oil capital, at least in part, into other forms of productive capital, such as physical or human capital, which can supplement oil revenues and generate further income streams down the road. Both monarchies and republics have devoted great efforts to developing long-term plans, such as the GCC major

FIGURE 9.2. Estimated Number of Years of Remaining Oil Production in the GCC Countries and the United States, as of 2005

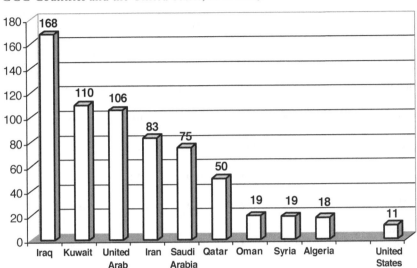

Source: Calculated from US Energy Information Administration (EIA), "World Proved Crude Oil Reserves" data, 2007, and EIA, "World Crude Oil Production" data, 2006, at http://www.eia.doe .gov/.

investments in infrastructure, education, and industry, Gaddafi's great man-made river, Saddam's large investments in social services and infrastructure before the Iran-Iraq War, and the big industrial pushes in Algeria and in Iran under the shah. For various reasons, these efforts largely failed in the RRLA countries (see Chapter 8). In the past decade, public investment took the brunt of the adjustment, and private investment did not rise. Moreover, the lack of pro-business reforms, whether in Syria, Iran, or Algeria, has kept the profitability of these investments low.

In the GCC countries, investment levels, whether from public or private sources, dipped in the 1980s and 1990s, but they have risen again during the second oil boom of the 2000s. Although investment ratios stood at only about 22 percent of GDP in the past few years (about the global average), the more revealing figure— since these ratios do not include investment in the oil sector—is investment as a share of non-oil GDP, which stood at much higher levels, rising from 33 percent in the 1980–2000 period to 40–50 percent after 2000. But where did all this investment go, and by how much will it fall if oil prices and revenue fall.

The twin challenge has been to diversify the economy and create new industries that can create productive jobs. There are essentially two ways to meet these challenges: the state can invest funds directly, or it can channel some funds to the private sector. As we saw in Chapter 8, most often the political winds of the 1970s encouraged the state to focus mostly on the first solution by creating public enterprises, hiring civil servants, expanding social services, and investing in infrastructure.[16] We have documented the ills of this approach. In many cases, the state became a drain on resources. Not only did the state's interventions often generate

TABLE 9.2. Oil Rents, Oil Exports and Revenues, Government Revenues, and Public-Private Investment in Selected Middle Eastern Countries, 2010

Country	Oil Rent (in billions of 2010 US dollars)	Oil Rent per Capita (in 2010 US dollars)	Oil Rent (percentage of GDP)	Oil Exported (percentage of exports)	Oil Revenue (percentage of government revenue)	Government Revenue (percentage of GDP)	2010 Public to Private Investment Ratio
Bahrain	$4.4	$3,490.0	19%	76.8%	79.6%	24.6%	39%
Kuwait	59.9	21,858.4	48.3	93.5	76.0	54.6	60
Oman	20.9	7,505.7	36.1	76.4	83.6	36.2	59
Qatar	18.5	10,535.2	14.6	89.0	60.2	41.1	37
Saudi Arabia	248.6	9,074.8	47.2	88.2	88.1	48.8	42
United Arab Emirates	54.8	7,301.2	18.4	42.7	75.3	38.2	21
Libya	31.6	4,974.9	42.3	na	na	na	470
Algeria	27.4	732.0	16.9	72.2	92.0	37.5	97
Iraq	105.1	3,118.7	73.6	98.0	85.0	na	na
Islamic Republic of Iran	99.3	1,259.2	23.5	73.0	80.7	29.1	54
Syrian Arab Republic	9.6	427.6	16.3	46.2	69.0	23.8	103

Sources: World Bank, World Bank Institute (WBI) data; Hodson (2013); and Espinoza, Fayad, and Prasad (2013).

misleading price signals for private actors (for example, when the state spent a lot on various subsidies, or when it subsidized inefficient public enterprises that competed against the private sector), but its bloated bureaucracies and inefficient state-owned enterprises devoured resources with little gain in return. For various reasons, these efforts have failed more spectacularly in the RRLA countries.

The Algerian case, already discussed in Chapters 7 and 8, demonstrates clearly the risks posed by state-led industrializing strategies. In 1969 Algeria launched a "big-push" strategy of heavy industrialization—oil revenues were used to finance massive industrial investments based on imported technology, capital goods, and turnkey industries. Large petrochemical and basic metals industries were developed to support the production of a wide range of intermediate and finished goods: fertilizers, butane gas, plastic sheeting and sacking, irrigation pipes, tractors, motors, and consumer durables. It was assumed that with the importation of state-of-the-art technology (for instance, gas liquefaction plants), many of these industries would be able to compete in international markets. But the new industries (except for some petroleum products) remained infant industries and did not manage to become internationally competitive, owing to management problems and the sophistication of the imported technology. In the 1980s, Algeria's earnings from petroleum exports fell from US$11 billion to US$4 billion. Not only was any further push of development out of the question, but Algeria started borrowing abroad to keep its industries afloat. That strategy ultimately led to a bigger fallout in the 1990s, which contributed in no small way to the tumultuous political events that have unfolded since.

Other extravagant examples, in the area of agriculture, come from Saudi Arabia and Libya (see also Chapter 4). To counteract growing dependence on food imports from the United States and Europe, Saudi Arabia entered into successive agricultural development plans in 1970 aimed at "self-sufficiency," a spirit that still guides its policy. Between 1970 and 1997, subsidies to agriculture made up about 55 percent of total government subsidies. These subsidy efforts generated successes: by 1984 Saudi Arabia claimed to be self-sufficient in wheat production, and by 1992 wheat exports peaked at 2.4 million tons. However, this was a case of massive negative value added: it has been estimated that the unit cost of wheat produced during this period in Saudi Arabia was four times the world price (Rivlin 2009). By now, nearly all support for growing wheat domestically has been stopped, and the government seeks instead to oversee investment opportunities in partnership with the private sector to advance the cause of food security. Libya's large investment in the "man-made great river" is equally if not more expensive and unsustainable.

But there have also been happier stories connected to public investments. Dubai famously has carved out a niche in state-owned transport, logistics, and real estate services, all of which are exported across the Middle East and beyond and are globally competitive. The Dubai model was born out of necessity—its oil reserves are modest, making it no match for the pressure posed by its rival emirate, oil-rich Abu Dhabi (Davidson 2007)—and it has been exported across the region. The other emirates have also been quite successful in developing service economies through state-owned enterprises. In addition, the GCC countries, especially Saudi Arabia, Bahrain, and Abu Dhabi, have made large investments in the highly capital- and energy-intensive area of petrochemical complexes, fertilizer plants, aluminum smelting, and steel production. Many of these countries have been able, in spite of the overall clientelistic structure of society, to insulate some "islands of quality" from rent-seeking pressures and develop efficient and competitive corporations (Hertog 2010a).

The second avenue, channeling part of the oil revenues to the private sector, has become much more commonly used in recent years in the GCC, especially after Saudi Arabia decided in the mid-1990s to undertake structural adjustments (joining the WTO, privatizing various utilities, and opening up for FDI). The risk, as always, is that support to the private sector, while necessary for growth, can create its own problems if not managed properly with a view to performance—often, rent seekers will take advantage of the support without delivering on performance.

As summarized by Giacomo Luciani (2013), there are five ways in which oil revenues have been transformed, historically, into private wealth: (1) local representation of foreign companies; (2) land distribution and real estate activities; (3) government procurement; (4) government's support for industry; and (5) the promotion of extensive agriculture. Another indirect channel is the demand by public servants for goods and services. In recent years, a two-legged strategy seems to have emerged in the GCC countries to support private-sector growth: countries have adopted economic reforms favorable to the private sector, while also promoting more directly several sectors such as education, tourism, heavy industry, and finance (Hodson 2013).

Saudi Arabia did not come to reforms until the late 1990s, and then only as a result of a growing conviction among ruling circles, including the king, that hiring Saudis in the public sector was not sustainable and a dynamic private sector was needed. Private manufacturing has been developed in Saudi Arabia mostly through government policies and a large local market. Reforms have involved lowering tariffs (including joining the WTO), some privatization, and a relatively favorable environment for foreign direct investment. This has exposed local businessmen to global competition and reduced the potential for cronyism and rent-seeking.

The other GCC countries had been divided over the need to open up space for the private sector. The United Arab Emirates, and especially Dubai, has been the most open to investment, though it tends to benefit the elite; private-sector investment works more easily in the Emirates partly because it is easier for them to hire all their small local populations for the public sector. (But interestingly, the UAE corporate landscape remains dominated by state-owned enterprises.) On the other side of this debate, Kuwait is less in favor of the private sector because policy there has been constrained by a divided parliament, which tends to view private investment with some suspicion because it does not benefit the middle class (Herb 1999). Bahrain and Oman, like Saudi Arabia, have opted for a pro–private sector policy regime because their reserves of oil and gas are diminishing.

In addition to creating a favorable investment climate, direct support for the business sector has also been rising in the GCC. Besides energy subsidies (discussed later), about 20 percent of the budgets of Qatar, Bahrain, and Kuwait is now spent on supporting this sector (Espinoza, Fayad, and Prasad 2013). Efforts have also been made to encourage the development of financial markets to channel funds, including oil revenues, to the private sector in ways to ensure profitability and thus control efficiency. The banking sector and the financial markets have rapidly matured and expanded since the 1980s. In Saudi Arabia, SAMA's emphasis on customer service and adherence to a universal banking model has fostered competition between it and regional and foreign banks. The emphasis on banking has led to the expansion of foreign banks' involvement (but not in Saudi Arabia), especially after a 2001 GCC decision to allow foreign banks to make reciprocal entries into the market (Al-Suhaimi 2001). And governments in Oman, Qatar, and Saudi Arabia have initiated privatization programs—mainly in telecom, utilities, gas companies, and petrochemicals—with the state divesting parts of its share on the local exchanges.

FIGURE 9.3. Public and Private Investment in the GCC, 1974–2010

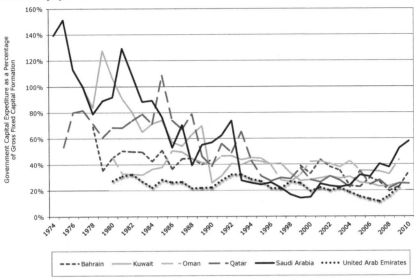

Source: Hodson (2013).

Unlike the 1980s, when they were completely dependent on the government, private businesses in the GCC are becoming more autonomous as they serve a growing internal demand and increase their exports. Currently, private investment is larger than public investment in all the GCC countries except Saudi Arabia, where public investment picked up after 2006 (see Figure 9.3). Much of this private investment has been made in real estate, heavy industry, health and education, and utilities. There has also been a rise in the number of public-private partnerships in petrochemicals between governments and large business groups. The manufacturing sectors in Saudi Arabia, Bahrain, and the United Arab Emirates in particular have become increasingly diversified and populated by strong private-sector groups that cater to fairly competitive markets. Reserving certain privileges for its local citizens, the UAE has still been able to foster significant direct foreign investment since the 1980s, mostly in special free zones. The share of the private sector in its non-oil GDP increased from 15 percent in 1970s to over 50 percent in 2012. Thus, even in times of flagging oil revenues—for instance, when oil prices dropped to $50 a barrel in 2008—the UAE has continued to sustain economic growth (Almezaini 2013).

All of the GCC countries have sought to give a comparative advantage to their industries by heavily subsidizing energy costs. This strategy has elicited a strong supply response. Manufacturing activities have expanded rapidly, and so have exports, helping the economies of the GCC diversify somewhat. A large proportion of this expansion has occurred in the petrochemical and highly energy-intensive sectors. In 2011 manufacturing as a share of non-oil GDP stood at 22 percent in

Saudi Arabia and Qatar, 19 percent in Bahrain, and 13 percent in the United Arab Emirates—in all cases, well above these shares in the 1990s.[17] And while most exports are dominated by oil and gas (over 90 percent of exports in Saudi Arabia, Qatar, and Kuwait and 75 percent in Bahrain and Oman), non-oil exports have been growing, too. But here, too, 50 to 60 percent of non-oil exports are petrochemical and high-energy-intensive products. These are heavily subsidized sectors, and so performance is artificially boosted.[18] There are clearly some benefits to this strategy: it has encouraged technologically advanced sectors to develop and grow, and there should be positive externality in terms of technological transfers and skill formation. Moreover, it attracts foreign direct investment, which typically boosts technological transfers and the acquisition of skills.

To evaluate whether energy subsidies are a good thing, then, we should look at the drawbacks of the strategy. Energy is sold above its extraction cost, so at least on paper the government is making a profit. But one should be considering opportunity cost, as this energy could be sold internationally. By this measure, the cost of these subsidies is huge: in 2011 they were estimated by the IMF, at international prices, to stand at $44 billion in Saudi Arabia, $8 billion in Kuwait, $18 billion in the United Arab Emirates, and $4 billion in Qatar (see Espinoza, Fayad, and Prasad 2013).[19] But the real opportunity cost could actually be lower than this, on two accounts: first, much of the energy sold is gas, a by-product of oil extraction, which is hard to export and would be burned if there was no local demand (as in Saudi Arabia); and second, these countries are bound by export quotas, so the oil and gas would have to stay underground if not used locally. Although these arguments seem to make sense and suggest that the costs of the subsidies are less than suggested by the IMF, three trends remain worrisome. First, the energy used by unit of output is very large, with large environmental costs. Second, domestic demand for energy, boosted by low prices, has been growing so fast as to threaten to reduce these countries' ability to export oil, given current capacity, particularly in high-population countries (essentially Saudi Arabia and Iran). Third, and perhaps most important, these sectors tend to be heavily energy- and thus capital-intensive, so they create few jobs, and some of the jobs they do create require skills that are not available in these countries, so they tend to be occupied by foreign workers.

This last point embodies the main problem with private-sector development in the GCC countries. The incentives private firms face—cheap labor imports and cheap energy—push them to develop dualistic industrial structures that are either very capital-intensive (in sectors that depend on cheap energy) or very labor-intensive (in sectors that depend on cheap labor imports). Thus, these industries do not create the types of high-paying private-sector jobs that are attractive to educated and high-wage GCC nationals.[20] Private-sector development has mostly benefited entrepreneurs, who have become richer, but it has so far not had a positive effect on the GCC's budding middle class (with the exception of the middlemen noted above).

In the RRLA countries, support for the private sector is minimal to nonexistent. No private sector, beyond informal operations, can develop in the shadow of insecurity and repression. With such high levels of political risk, the private sector tends to shy away. Moreover, it is not welcomed by regimes bent on exerting tight controls on society. In Syria, laws that started to gradually open up the economy to private investment mainly served to produce a huge rise in car imports (under the guise of establishing tourism companies) because the country had not allowed the importation of cars for several decades. In Algeria, the top ten companies are all state-owned, and entrepreneurs are still not allowed to take more than $200 with them when they travel outside the country. In both countries, the only firms that are allowed to grow are those owned by friends of the regime. And although the Iranian economy is larger and more complex, it is not very different in the essential ways (as we have seen in Chapter 8).

The Pervasive Effects of Revenue Volatility

Besides the difficulties of diversifying the economy and encouraging the private sector, another major challenge of oil is its volatility. The boom-bust cycle—the boom of the late 1970s, followed by an eighteen-year bust, and then by a fourteen-year boom—is one aspect of this volatility that has led to the enormous challenges that Chaudhry (1997) has called the "discontinuous construction" of economic (and political) institutions. A second challenge—related to the shorter-term price volatility—has made government income hard to predict from year to year. For example, oil prices collapsed to around $20 a barrel during the global crisis of 2008 before coming back to the $80 to $100 level. At the time of writing in 2014, they had precipitously fallen to $60 to $70 per barrel.

The long oil cycle had created all types of difficulties for oil countries. They were all unprepared for the initial gush of revenues, and while expenditures increased relatively fast, it was much harder to adjust for the downside. Government also increased the size of their bureaucracies and their social programs. When the bust came, investment projects were sharply curtailed, but it was much harder to cut subsidies, social programs, and state employment.

Saudi Arabia's outsized responsibility to OPEC—in its role as "swing producer"—has made stabilizing expenditures around a highly volatile income stream more challenging for it than for most of the other oil economies. In the early 1980s, when revenues collapsed, investments were deeply cut, but King Abdallah refused to touch social programs. Indeed, state employment kept growing, since this was by then perceived by educated Saudis as an entitlement. The state also declined to turn to taxation as a means to offset the large government welfare costs (Auty 2001). As a result, Saudi Arabia reduced its expenditures by only half the amount of the revenue fall in the early 1980s. A second adjustment was undertaken in the 1990s, at the end of the First Gulf War. Saudi Arabia thus had large fiscal deficits for eighteen years in a row, resulting in a ballooning debt (mostly domestic). It was only in the late 1990s, when state debts reached dangerously high levels (over $100 billion) that the Saudi ruling elite decided to move beyond the model of public-sector jobs for all. That was just a few years before the second oil boom. With the extra support of high oil prices, Saudi Arabia has been able to run a surplus since. But since the Arab uprisings, the irresistible push to respond by returning to the old policies of patronage quickly reversed the hard gains achieved, and oil surpluses started to shrink. They will shrink further if oil prices remain depressed in the future, a distinct possibility given the fast-rising energy supply in the United States.

During the second oil boom, most GCC governments expanded expenditures, but unlike their response to the first boom, infrastructure spending was more subdued. Instead, it was spending on social programs and salaries that rose the most. As a result, government spending, especially in Saudi Arabia, has become concentrated in wages as well as in education and health, while public investment in infrastructure has decreased in relative terms. As a result, the budget has become more inflexible than in the past. In most GCC countries, the share of the budget going to recurrent expenditures (as opposed to investment) has risen to 60 to 80 percent, with Saudi Arabia at the lower end of the spectrum because of a recent boost in public investment (Hodson 2013, 113).

Nevertheless, the good years have allowed all GCC countries to set funds aside for rainy days. Assets accumulated by the sovereign wealth funds (SWFs) of GCC countries as a whole amount to more than $1.8 trillion, equivalent to 34 percent of the assets accumulated by SWFs worldwide (see Figure 9.4). The United Arab Emirates has the highest proportion of these funds at about $820 billion. Moreover, GCC ownership of public enterprises, which can be privatized over time, is also very large—Saudi Arabia alone is said to have domestic assets valued at over $1 trillion. Together with its sovereign fund, its reserves could sustain the same level of spending as today, on a price of $50 a barrel, for the next ten years before being forced into adjusting its expenditures. But this would be a high-risk strategy.

The costs of macro-instability, both short and long cycles, are also high for the private sector. Decisions about investment become harder when risk rises, and in the presence of irreversibilities, investment falls. Espinoza and his colleagues (2013) estimate that a 1 percent increase in volatility in the GCC reduces growth by 0.3 percent. To get a sense of the magnitude, it can be estimated that the standard deviation (SD) of growth in the GCC is very high—it was about 7 percent in the period 1976–1990, then fell to 4 percent during 1990–2010. In comparison, it is only 2 percent in the OECD. This represents an important cost for businesses, especially if they are liquidity-constrained—that is, unable to smooth out their income flows. The development of financial markets did help businesses smooth their flows to some extent. But it also led to the growth of asset bubbles (real estate, local stock markets), which were followed by crashes in some countries, thus exacerbating the oil cycle—the main examples include the Souq Al-Manakh stock market crash in Kuwait in 1982 and, more recently, the real estate market collapse in Dubai after the 2008 global depression.

There is no role for monetary policy in the GCC because the exchange rate is pegged to the dollar. But fiscal policy is powerful in the GCC because the private sector is so connected to government spending—investment projects become procurement and wages become demand. Espinoza and his colleagues (2013) estimate fiscal multipliers of 0.3 percent for recurrent expenditures, and as much as 0.6 percent for investment expenditures, which are high figures by international standards. These multipliers have been falling slowly over time as the private sector gradually becomes less dependent on government expenditures. They also show that Saudi Arabia and Oman have been quite successful at countercyclical fiscal policies, while

FIGURE 9.4. Sovereign Wealth Funds Around the World (in billions of US dollars)

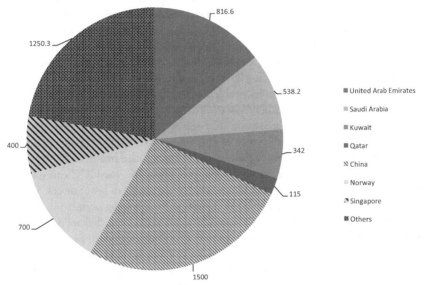

Source: Sovereign Wealth Fund Institute (2014).

the other countries have not. Saudi Arabia not only ran a fiscal deficit for eighteen years in a row when oil prices were low, but more recently it has run a budget surplus during most years since 2003 when oil prices rose. This is exactly what a stabilizing countercyclical fiscal policy is supposed to look like.

Budgetary constraints tend to be much tighter in RRLA countries because per capita oil wealth is a constraining factor and thus governments are under greater pressure to deliver, since typically repression can only go so far. As a result, these countries do not accumulate reserves in good time and tend to live "hand to mouth"—Algeria is a partial exception, having accumulated about $200 billion of reserves before the Arab uprisings. The pressure to spend has been unrelenting after oil prices rose in the mid-2000s. A major subsidy reform took place in Iran in the mid-1990s, but it was soon reversed, and subsidies again consume a large share of the budget (Chapter 8). Another example is the massive buildup of the civil service that occurred in Iraq after oil revenues rose in the past few years.

CONCLUSION: THE FUTURE OF THE GCC

Is the growth model that has taken off in the Gulf and started to achieve notable successes on the economic front in the past ten years sustainable? The arguments developed in this chapter suggest that the answer is a resounding no. From a purely economic perspective, the problem facing the GCC states is a good problem—a problem of riches. In the GCC, the development strategy has been to first import labor while at the same time subsidizing industry. In parallel, there has been a big push to educate national labor and employ it at high wages in government. As education and infrastructure have improved over time, the next step has been to initiate nationalization programs, that is, to replace foreign labor with domestic labor. The policy issues that arise on the technical front—issues of timing and sequencing—have occupied policymakers and consulting firms in the past decade all around the GCC. But the more challenging issues are on the political front: how can governments ensure that social contracts will evolve to allow for such economic transformations?

As discussed, the sustainability problem of the Gulf states is not (yet) how to live in a world without oil, but rather, how to effectively employ a fast-growing national labor force. The current strategy of public-sector employment will reach its limits sooner or later, given the high rate of population growth (now at 2 percent) and especially growth in the labor force (now at about 4 percent). Already 40 to 60 percent of budgets are going into wages and social programs. But the GCC can only sell so much oil given global demand, as oversupply only leads to lower prices. So economically speaking, the real constraint is that, with a growing population, current patronage practices are increasingly unsustainable. What is needed are new ways to lower transfers per capita and new ways to reduce inefficiencies in how energy and labor inputs are used in the economy in order to create a larger pie.

The essential problem is that the tools for gradually achieving such a vision have not yet been found. By the 1990s, growth in Saudi Arabia's native labor force had overwhelmed the government's capacity to employ nationals in a bureaucratic system already plagued by overemployment. The higher wages that government jobs afford discourage many Saudis from pursuing private-sector employment; for the same reasons, the local workforce is not attractive to private employers. The only way to effectively bring native workers into the private labor force is to reduce the wage gap between them and migrant workers. National quota systems and occupation bans for foreigners—not to mention the mass deportation of foreign workers in recent years in Saudi Arabia—have not succeeded and have led instead to widespread avoidance efforts. The dynamic of reforms seems broken. New and more creative ideas—such as cash transfers to the population and income taxation—need to be part of the policy tool box as incentives to businesses and Saudi labor alike to create wealth in a private sector–led development model.

The political problem with this transition is that it pits the interests of labor against those of the elite in the private sector, which explains why the policies to constrain foreign labor migration, which have been implemented since the early 2000s, have not yet started to work. To create jobs in the private sector, the "rents" that accrue to that sector—in part in the form of cheap labor—must be reduced. Sooner or later, the system will have to move to less conditional (and smaller) transfers and to taxation. The question then becomes: how will this shift affect the "legitimacy" of a political system that has remained staunchly autocratic? The question is all the more important given the population's rising income and education levels, which have made Saudis more demanding of freedoms and autonomy. Presumably the private sector, as a class, would want to have a greater voice.

The GCC regimes, and especially Saudi Arabia, have reacted to the Arab uprisings with a dramatic rise in patronage commitments. In Saudi Arabia, the cost of the package announced in February and March 2011 to mollify popular grievances included employment, housing, and welfare measures estimated at $130 billion. In 2012 nearly 300,000 young Saudis were hired in the public sector—as many as during the previous decade.[21] Similarly, public-sector salaries were raised by 70 percent in the United Arab Emirates. At the same time, in an attempt to please the private sector, policies of open migration have not been questioned and so it remains difficult to employ Saudis in this sector. The return to the practices of the 1970s—but on a much grander scale—seems to mark, for now, a rollback of the reforms of the last decade intended to confer more autonomy on Saudi businesses and citizens. At the same time, the Saudi government has overreached financially— it now has quadrupled its expenditure relative to the early 2000s—and needs oil prices to remain around $90 a barrel to keep its fiscal accounts balanced. The state is far from broke. But the current policies are not sustainable. The day of reckoning simply depends on the price of oil, and sooner or later the economic system will have to change. The only question, then, is how smooth or chaotic this adjustment will be, and whether it will preserve the gains of the past and build toward greater prosperity in the future. Unlike the RRLA countries, the RRLP countries hold an enormous amount of wealth in the private sector, and they are also investing a great deal in developing the skills of the population. Thus, these countries are more likely to find win-win solutions between princes, elite entrepreneurs, and the growing domestic middle class.

NOTES

1. Or perhaps it is more correct to say that their emergence coincided with a broad phase of rapid global industrialization that created great demand for new energy sources. In other words, we do not take the waning of colonial empires and the discovery of oil as a coincidence per se, but we do see the increasing demand for energy as a legacy of the vast twentieth-century colonial projects of industrialization and development worldwide.

2. This independence is an important difference from other countries, such as Jordan and Egypt, that received large external rents, not from oil, but from foreign donors; the dependence of these countries on donors restricted the extent of the repression they could use.

3. Moreover, for some states the characteristics that make them susceptible to violence are exactly what led colonials to construct them as they are: Iran, Iraq, Syria, Yemen, and Sudan are all examples of states where a divide-and-rule strategy carved out states that included unhappy minorities and disputed borders.

4. The last attempt by the Ottoman Empire to reform, during the Tanzimat of the 1840s to 1880s, was indeed focused on making society more autonomous and dynamic.

5. For instance, as religious leaders took lead roles in the government's Ministry of Education, an increasing proportion of the state budget was drawn toward primary and secondary education development in the 1970s and 1980s. In part, Abdulaziz and his successors impressed conservative religious factions by cultivating personal images as men of religious piety. Incorporating religious leadership into the structure of the government further ensured their quiescence.

6. On the costs of the Iran-Iraq war, see Alnasrawi (1994).

7. In addition to patronage, the emphasis on military development reflected some unique geographical challenges for Saudi Arabia, such as a widely dispersed population and infrastructure, long coastlines, and close proximity to highly militarized regional

rivals such as Iraq and Iran. Moreover, the military buildup relied heavily on the purchase of US military technology. Saudi Arabia reciprocated such deals in the late 1970s and 1980s with promises to keep oil prices low.

8. States that base their legitimacy on Arab nationalism (such as Iraq) or on Islam (such as Saudi Arabia) face contradictions when they deny other Arabs or Muslims the same treatment as natives.

9. The Grand Mosque seizure occurred during November and December 1979 when Islamist insurgents calling for the overthrow of the House of Saud took over Al-Masjid al-Haram in Mecca during the annual Hajj pilgrimage. The siege resulted in the death of hundreds of militants, security forces, and hostages caught in crossfire.

10. In more recent years, there has been less reliance on this, except in Bahrain, where they get citizenship after a while.

11. After the second oil boom, the government sold foreign currency at even lower prices than the already low market equilibrium in order to ration foreign currency among its favored "clients."

12. Even in Iraq, up to 14 percent of workers were foreign in 1980, when the war with Iran was stretching its national labor force (Sherbiny 1984).

13. This is in contrast to the relatively low public-sector wages in the poorer MENA countries after the rollback of the state of the 1980s to 1990s.

14. In 2010 the GCC supplied 21 percent of global crude oil production (and roughly 15 million barrels per day for export) and had about 36 percent of oil reserves. The GCC has also become a big player in the growing gas market.

15. Most of the rest of exports in the UAE are re-exports, which generate very little value added.

16. Another area in which states spent large amounts of resources was the maintenance of large, lethal arsenals and standing armies, partly to protect their now more valuable oil resources from possible predation by foreign neighbors (Iraq, Iran, Kuwait) or by possible secessionists at home (Sudan, Yemen, Iraq; see Chapter 13).

17. Saudi Arabia today is the largest exporter of industrial products in the region—$20 billion compared to Egypt's $5 billion.

18. Other exports include agro industries, base metals, electrical machinery, and services, especially transport and tourism.

19. These amounts represent the quantity sold to the private sector times the difference between international prices and the price at which energy was sold at to local producers.

20. One can imagine, for example, that if the labor market was protected, the wages paid in the services sector would be bid up, which would encourage entrepreneurs to invest in these sectors in ways that would increase labor productivity.

21. This still was not sufficient to absorb the 400,000 Saudis who reach working age *every year.*

10

WAR, CONFLICT, AND THE MILITARY IN THE MIDDLE EAST

The security forces are key actors in the political settlements of many MENA countries, shaping whether and how uprisings have unfolded across the region. Middle Eastern societies have experienced prolonged periods of rule by the military. Even when, de jure, regimes are headed by civilians, the power wielders may be military officers who have left their uniforms in the closet. Atatürk himself was the first general to follow this path and to insist that those of his officer colleagues who wished to pursue political careers do likewise. Still, it is hard to see Atatürk's regime as other than quasi-military. Next door to Turkey, Reza Shah, commander of the Iranian Cossacks, founded a monarchy, but throughout his rule his regime was reliant upon the military. His son, Mohammad Reza Pahlavi, continued to depend on his military establishment.

As the Arab countries gained their independence, several fell under nearly uninterrupted military rule. Since 1949, Syria has known only brief periods of civilian rule. Today Bashar al-Assad may wear a suit to work, but he and his fellow Alawite officers constitute the power elite of the government and of the Ba'ath Party. Iraq since the toppling of the monarchy in July 1958 had constant military rule, although Saddam Hussein came out of the police rather than the military. Several of his closest associates from his home area of Tikrit were strategically placed in the military and in the Iraqi Ba'ath Party. Saddam Hussein gradually transformed Iraq into a police state of unparalleled proportions in the Arab world. As much as one-quarter of the Iraqi workforce may have been associated with spying and intelligence gathering for the regime, atomizing and destroying civil society (al-Khalil 1989). Although Iraq acquired an elected government in 2006, the presence of over 140,000 US troops perpetuated military rule after the fall of Saddam Hussein, and it arguably continues to this day in a different form, as political leaders maintain close links with the regular and irregular security forces. In many other Middle

Eastern countries, such as Algeria, Egypt, and Yemen, the military and security forces continue to be central actors in ruling coalitions.

Across the region, even when they did not emerge from the army or police themselves, rulers have secured their power in part by maintaining close personal ties—and often blood ties—with the military and security forces. In turn, military and security officials and their corporate organizations have played key roles in the political settlements established since independence in the MENA countries. The fact that the MENA is among the most geostrategically important regions for the West and the site of many ongoing wars and conflicts has contributed to the predominance of the military and security forces in MENA political systems.

In this chapter, we address the role of coercive institutions in the political economies of the Middle East, outlining the ways in which military rule affects development trajectories, contributes to authoritarian durability, and arguably shaped the trajectories of political transitions during and after the Arab uprisings. First, we trace military spending across country groups in the region, situating them in cross-national perspective and highlighting debates about the relationship between military and development spending. Second, we describe the historical record of war and conflict in the region and its implications for development and governance. Third, we show how the military and security forces feature in diverse political settlements in the region, detailing the often central positions they occupy in authoritarian coalitions in diverse Middle Eastern political regimes. We then probe more deeply to show how shared ethnic ties and the vested economic interests of the military and security forces cement their positions in underlying political settlements. Finally, we address ongoing debates about the role of the military in shaping the nature and outcomes of the recent wave of popular uprisings across the Middle East.

MILITARY SPENDING AND DEVELOPMENT

As Rudolf Goldscheid (1917, cited in Schumpeter 1918, 100) famously stated, "The budget is the skeleton of the state stripped of all misleading ideologies." If government budgets reveal the priorities of the state, then the share devoted to spending on defense and security reveals the disproportionate importance of the military and security forces in Middle Eastern political economies. Figure 10.1 shows the importance of the military in government budgets across time.

Military spending as a percentage of GDP has been consistently higher for all three MENA country subgroups than for the average of all middle-income countries. (In Table 10.1, we benchmark the Middle East against other developing regions.) In the early 1990s, military spending hit an all-time high in the RRLP countries, some of which were the most affected by the First Gulf War, and it has been consistently highest in these relatively wealthy countries. Since the mid-1990s, the RRLA countries have had the second-highest levels of military spending. Furthermore, the estimates for these countries are biased downward because data for Iraq, which has been involved in virtually nonstop war and armed conflict since 1980, are missing until 2004, one year after the US occupation began.

The collapse of oil prices in the late 1980s and 1990s and its ripple effect on the region's economies had a substantial impact on the military establishments of

FIGURE 10.1. Military Expenditures (as a percentage of GDP) in the MENA Countries and Middle-Income Countries, by Political Economy Subgroup, 1988–2012

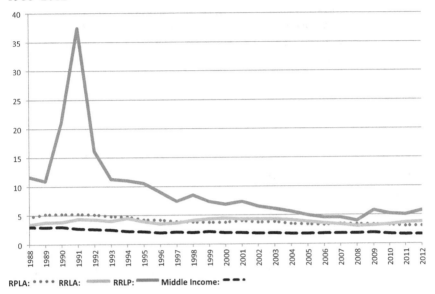

RPLA: • • • •   RRLA: ▬▬▬   RRLP: ▬▬▬   Middle Income: ▬ ▬ •

Source: World Bank, World Development Indicators (WDI).

Note: Oil rent is oil production, valued at market prices, minus cost of production.

the Middle East. From an average of 17 percent of GDP in 1983, military expenditures for the countries of the region fell to 4.2 percent in 1993. Nonetheless, relative to the other major regions of the world, the Middle East remained the most generous in military spending (see Table 10.1). Note, however, that three countries—Israel, Saudi Arabia, and Turkey—account for more than half of all military expenditures in the region (see Figure 10.2). Moreover, reductions in military expenditures were not uniform across the region; they crept up over time in Tunisia and surged in Sudan in the 2000s as the government in Khartoum stepped up the military campaign against the southern insurrectionary forces (see Table 10.1).

Guns vs. Butter?

Conventional wisdom has long posited that heavy outlays on defense and warfare divert scarce resources away from directly productive investment and human capital formation. A counterargument with respect to the LDCs is that defense expenditures may act as an economic stimulus. They finance heavy industry (armaments), the acquisition of advanced technologies, the formation of skilled personnel (from truck drivers to radar operators), and the provision of employment. Defense expenditures or a large military establishment may attract foreign aid and investment

TABLE 10.1. Average Military, Education, and Public Health Spending (as a percentage of GDP) Across the MENA Region and in Other Regions of the World, 2000–2012

	Average Military Expenditure		Average Public Spending on Education		Average Public Health Expenditure	
	2000–2005	2006–2012	2000–2005	2006–2012	2000–2005	2006–2012
RPLA	**3.7%**	**3.3%**	**4.9%**	**3.9%**	**2.9%**	**3.2%**
Egypt	3.2	2.2	4.8	3.8	2.2	2.0
Jordan	5.6	5.3			4.7	5.6
Lebanon	4.8	4.2	2.5	2.1	3.4	2.9
Morocco	3.4	3.4	5.7	5.5	1.4	2.0
Tunisia	1.5	1.4	6.4	6.3	2.9	3.5
RRLA	**4.2**	**3.4**	**5.6**	**4.6**	**1.9**	**2.3**
Algeria	3.4	3.6		4.3	2.7	3.3
Iran	3.4	2.8	4.7	4.5	2.2	2.7
Iraq	2.0	2.5			1.5	2.4
Sudan	3.9	4.4			1.1	2.0
Syria	5.4	4.0	5.3	5.0	2.2	1.7
Yemen	5.7	4.2	9.5	5.2	2.0	1.4
RRLP	**6.2**	**5.0**	**5.3**		**2.4**	**2.2**
Bahrain	4.3	3.2		3.0	2.5	2.8
Kuwait	6.5	3.5	6.0	3.8	2.4	2.1
Libya	2.4	1.1			2.3	2.2
Oman	11.9	8.8	3.8	4.1	2.5	2.0
Qatar	2.9	1.8	2.1	2.5	2.4	1.8
Saudi Arabia	9.4	8.2	6.7	5.5	2.9	2.5
United Arab Emirates	4.8	4.5			1.6	1.9
Israel	8.7	6.6	6.6	5.8	4.8	4.7
Turkey	3.3	2.4	2.8	2.9	3.6	4.5
MENA	**5.0**	**4.0**	**5.2**	**4.3**	**2.6**	**2.7**
East Asia	**1.5**	**1.7**	**3.8**	**4.2**	**4.7**	**4.6**
Latin America	**1.3**	**1.3**	**4.0**	**4.6**	**3.1**	**3.7**
South Asia	**2.9**	**2.6**	**2.9**	**2.6**	**1.0**	**1.1**
Africa	**1.8**	**1.5**	**3.6**	**4.0**	**2.5**	**2.8**
World	**2.4**	**2.5**	**4.2**	**4.7**	**5.7**	**6.1**

Source: WDI (2013), adapted from Economic and Social Commission for Western Asia (ESCWA) (2013), 16.

FIGURE 10.2. Average Military Expenditures (as a percentage of GDP) in the MENA Countries, 2000–2012

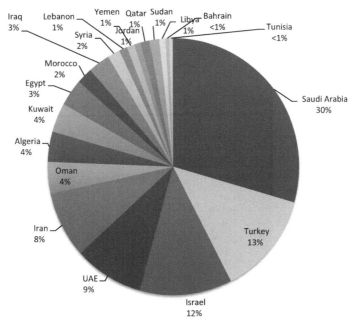

Iraq 3%
Lebanon 1%
Yemen 1%
Qatar 1%
Sudan 1%
Libya 1%
Bahrain <1%
Jordan 1%
Syria 2%
Tunisia <1%
Morocco 2%
Egypt 3%
Kuwait 4%
Algeria 4%
Oman 4%
Iran 8%
UAE 9%
Israel 12%
Turkey 13%
Saudi Arabia 30%

Source: Stockholm International Peace Research Institute (SIPRI) (2012), military expenditure database.

and thus enhance a country's foreign exchange position. Several decades ago, the argument provoked a great deal of debate (summarized in Deger 1992), and many studies have found that defense outlays bear a high opportunity cost because they shift resources from "high-growth development projects" and reduce public outlays as well as the private outlays that depend on them. Only countries flush with foreign exchange (such as Saudi Arabia before 1986) show any positive correlation between defense outlays and economic growth; generally, the two areas compete with each other. More recent literature, including some that focuses on the Middle East, is similarly inconclusive (Abu-Bader and Abu-Qarn 2003; Ali 2011; Al-Yousif 2002; Aslam 2007; Chang, Huang, and Yang 2011; Lebovic and Ishaq 1987; Lin, Ali, and Lu 2013; Yildirim and Sezgin 2002; Yildirim, Sezgin, and Öcal 2005).

What can the Middle East tell us about this argument? Unfortunately, nothing very conclusive. When defense expenditures in all regional groupings in the developing world are compared, those in the Middle East come out the highest (see Table 10.1). When oil prices were at their twentieth-century peak, Middle Eastern countries were spending US$40 billion a year on defense, with Iran and Saudi Arabia leading the way. Petroleum revenues allowed some countries to indulge in this luxury—outlays in Egypt were about US$3 billion, and those in Syria and Morocco

FIGURE 10.3. The Relationship Between Military Spending and Economic Growth in the Middle East, 1993–2010

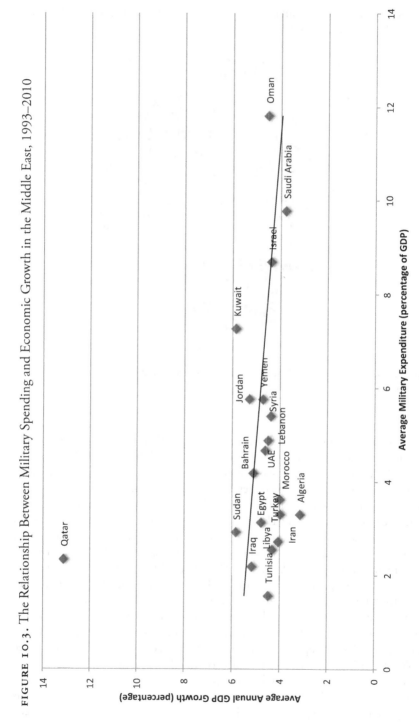

Source: WDI.

about US$2 billion. One might suppose that such defense burdens would cripple most economies, at least those without significant petroleum earnings. But there is only a weak, albeit negative, correlation in the Middle East between defense expenditure as a proportion of GDP and rates of growth (see Figure 10.3).

Thus, we cannot conclude that defense expenditures contribute more than direct public or private investment to economic growth, nor can we assume a causal relation between high defense outlays and growth. We can estimate, counterfactually, the returns on alternative uses of the monies devoted to defense, but practically nowhere in the world is there any evidence that reducing defense budgets results in increased outlays for, say, social welfare or infrastructure. Ultimately, the distribution of government budgets is the product of political struggles and decisions. That resources could be better spent on human welfare is undeniable, but it is doubtful that most governments would even be willing to make such shifts.

Furthermore, an accounting exercise on the effects of military spending on growth is fraught with conceptual and methodological complications. For example, the indirect benefits of military expenditures, when they exist, are difficult to measure. It is also conceivable that, in some MENA countries, reducing military spending could lead to insurrections and regime change that might or might not result in greater freedom but at the same time might lead to economic downturns. And yet a period of institutional destruction could be followed by higher economic growth once the violence and turmoil subside. Calculating the costs and benefits of military spending for development as a whole therefore is challenging at best.

Yet, a comparison of budgetary outlays in the MENA and other global regions lends some credence to the "guns versus butter" argument, or the claim that military expenditures crowd out investment in social sectors. Middle Eastern governments have devoted a disproportionate amount of their resources to the military rather than to social investment. Table 10.1 depicts the average expenditures on the military, education, and health care for the MENA countries, the subregional groupings, and other global regions. These data show that spending on the military in the Middle East as a whole and in all three country subgroupings exceeds that of all other global regions by a significant margin. This is just as true for the RPLA countries—though they lack the wealth from oil to buy expensive weapons systems and pay for large armies and security forces—as it is for the richer RRLA and RRLP countries. Even South Asia, a region that has witnessed its fair share of conflict and interstate tensions, falls well below Middle Eastern levels of military spending. On the other hand, spending on education is relatively high in the MENA as a whole, even when benchmarked against other parts of the world. Yet a more disaggregated perspective reveals that, in the poorer, labor-abundant countries of the Middle East, public expenditures on education lag behind other regions. The picture is even worse for public health spending: on average, MENA governments spend less on health than those in East Asia and Latin America and are roughly on par with sub-Saharan African governments in this regard. In this case, the oil exporters—both labor-abundant and labor-poor countries—spend less on health than their poorer cousins, the RPLA countries.

Resources are but one factor affecting the delivery of social services, and money is no guarantee that schooling and health care will meet quality standards. Nonetheless, these comparative data indicate that Middle Eastern governments have favored defense and security over social development, particularly given their resource levels. A recent UN report notes:

> Such heavy investment in the security sector is indicative: security is a priority. By propping up a massive security apparatus, Arab states have created funding shortages or inefficiencies in social spending and public infrastructure, where investment is needed most. Given that many of these states face dire economic straits, the overwhelming focus on the security sector has arguably done less, not more, for human security in the Arab region. Governments have focused almost exclusively on their own survival instead of the well-being of their own populations. (ESCWA 2013, 16)

Indeed, this report contends that the mismatch between military and social spending in the Middle East provides evidence for a potential "crowding-out effect that military expenditure can have on social expenditure, particularly in countries with limited budgets" (ESCWA 2013, 17).

The beginning of peace negotiations in 1991 between Israel and its Arab adversaries raised hopes that the region might one day benefit from a large "peace dividend" (see el-Naggar and el-Erian 1993). Unfortunately, such hopes have been dashed. First, of course, the Israeli-Palestinian conflict dramatically escalated with the Al-Aqsa (Second) *intifada,* beginning in late 2000. Second, developments in Iraq and more recently Syria have greatly exacerbated regional tensions. Third, there have always been a number of other conflicts in the region unrelated to these three: Saudi Arabia versus Yemen, Turkey versus Greece, Egypt versus Sudan, and Algeria versus Morocco. These unresolved conflicts—which are used by the warring parties to justify continued high levels of military expenditure and arms acquisition—do not even include ongoing or unresolved civil wars, such as those in Iraq, Sudan, Turkey, and Lebanon. Since 2001, the American "war on terrorism" has greatly strengthened the political voice of Middle Eastern military, and other security, officers.

As some MENA countries experience greater popular participation in the political arena, it is worth asking whether a (more) democratic order entails more or less spending on the military. In a recent paper, Ibrahim Elbadawi and Philip Keefer (2014) offer a nuanced answer to this question. Democratization entails enhanced accountability of governments to citizens, but the effects of increased accountability on military spending are not clear-cut and thus cannot be reduced to a dichotomous distinction between democratic versus authoritarian rule. Rather, the relationship between government accountability and spending depends on the level of national security risks and legacies of military spending. When countries face higher national security risks and have historically spent more on the military, current military spending should increase by less when governments are more accountable to their citizens. Given that democratic deepening, in which a mobilized

TABLE 10.2. Types of Wars by Global Region, 1816–2007

Region	Nonstate	Intrastate	Interstate	Extrastate	Total
Middle East	19	45	47	13	124
Africa	6	104	12	6	128
Asia	18	60	58	11	147
Europe	0	19	17	0	36
Oceania	0	0	0	0	0
Western Hemisphere	0	18	6	0	24

Source: Correlates of War (COW) database.

and organized citizenry can effectively hold their government accountable, remains on a distant horizon in virtually all MENA countries, by this logic a decline in military spending is not in the cards in the Middle East for the foreseeable future, particularly in light of ongoing regional instability. Whether the emergence of more accountable governments produces shifts in military spending in the region remains to be seen and, in any case, is contingent on a more stable regional environment, which sadly seems to be a long way off.

War and Geostrategic Rents in the MENA Region

If regional conflict is a key predictor of military spending, then it may not be surprising that MENA governments devote so much of their budgets to defense. The Middle East has a reputation for being a region plagued by violence. As Table 10.2 shows, however, other regions have experienced similar and even higher numbers of armed conflicts, yet they do not devote as much of their budgets to defense spending (see also Table 10.1).[1] Although the Middle East has indeed experienced many armed conflicts over the past two centuries, Africa has experienced a comparable number of wars, and Asia even more than the Middle East, yet both continents spend less on their defense budgets as a percentage of GDP.

Where the Middle East distinguishes itself is in the global attention that its wars attract and its use of repression in the domestic arena (see Chapter 3). The region's geostrategic importance for the West has translated into a high volume of military aid and arms flowing into the region, some of which is used to bolster the coercive apparatus of the state (Bellin 2004). Figure 10.4 depicts US military aid to all global regions from 1948 to 2011. Until the early 1970s, East Asia, the site of large US war efforts in Korea and Vietnam, was the recipient of the largest share of American military assistance. US military aid to the Middle East gradually rose after World

FIGURE 10.4. US Military Aid by Global Region, 1948–2011

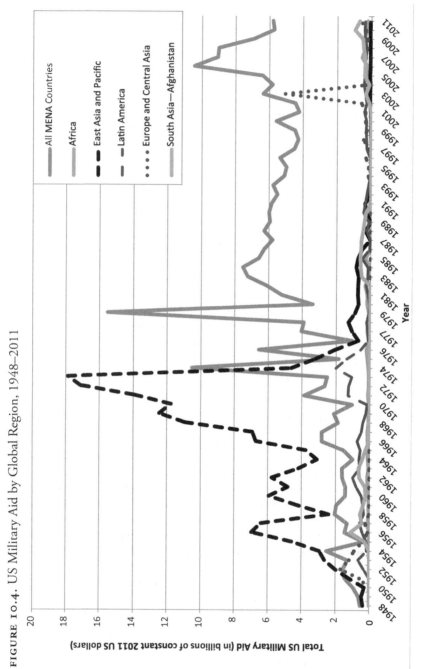

Source: US Agency for International Development (USAID), "US Overseas Loans and Grants [Greenbook]."

FIGURE 10.5. US Military Aid to the Middle East, 2010

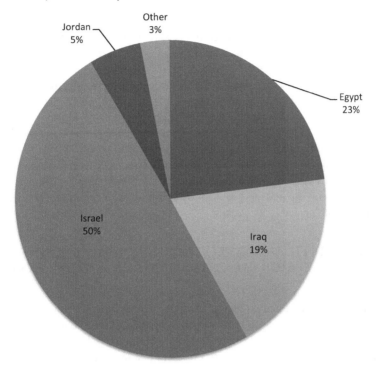

Source: USAID, Greenbook.

War II, then spiked in the early 1970s; it has been maintained at high levels since then. For the past four decades, the Middle East has exceeded all other regions by a wide margin as the largest recipient of US military aid. Within the Middle East, US military aid disproportionately flows to a few select countries: in 2010 Israel received 50 percent of American military aid to the MENA region, followed by 23 percent to Egypt, 19 percent to Iraq, and 5 percent to Jordan (see Figure 10.5). The remaining countries in the region collectively received 3 percent of all US military aid to the Middle East.

Big defense establishments attract flows of foreign resources because they represent important markets for arms exporters and because they are located in geo-politically strategic regions. Through the supply of arms and military expertise, great and lesser powers can buy political and strategic leverage that no other sphere of economic activity offers. In the same vein, there is often a large concessional component in the pricing and financing of the arms deliveries; in the Middle East, arms worth billions of dollars have been given away annually. As is the case with domestic military expenditures, it is unlikely that these grants would have ever materialized—at least not on the same scale—for nonmilitary development purposes.

The data on arms sales to Middle Eastern countries after the end of Operation Desert Storm are indicative. Over the 1991–1993 period, some US$20 billion in arms were transferred to Saudi Arabia and Kuwait alone. Between 2009 and 2013, the United Arab Emirates and Saudi Arabia were the fourth- and fifth-largest arms importers in the world, each accounting for about 4 percent of the world's total arms imports. The ongoing blockages on imports of most weapons stemming from the UN sanctions restricted Iran to only 1 percent of the region's arms imports in 2009–2013 (SIPRI 2014, 7). Iran and Syria, however, acquired missiles from North Korea and the People's Republic of China (Kerr, Nikitin, and Hildreth 2014; Pollack 2011), and Iran has also made major gains in missile production over the past two decades, although its true capabilities are debated (Rubin 2012). The simple fact is that major arms suppliers such as the United States, Russia, Germany, China, and France will not forgo the opportunity to profit from lucrative contracts and to mitigate balance-of-payments problems by selling arms to countries already replete with them and located in war zones.

THE POLITICAL AND ECONOMIC CONSEQUENCES OF WAR AND MILITARIZATION IN THE MIDDLE EAST

The militarization of Middle Eastern polities and societies has important political and economic consequences. First and foremost, the strong coercive apparatuses of most MENA countries buttress authoritarian rule (Bellin 2004; Elbadawi and Makdisi 2007). The presence of robust military and security forces helps to explain the persistence of the diverse varieties of dictatorships in the region (although it does not provide a satisfactory explanation for the *origins* of authoritarian rule). The army and police are constituent components of the institutional landscape of authoritarian rule throughout the Middle East.

Both international and domestic actors have vested interests in the maintenance of Middle Eastern authoritarian rulers. For Western powers like the United States, Britain, France, and Russia, the Middle East is of vital geostrategic importance. Checking Soviet influence during the Cold War, exploiting the region's high oil and gas endowments, and, most recently, combating Islamic extremism have all been reasons for the West to forge and maintain close alliances with friendly authoritarian rulers in order to maintain regional stability. International support in the form of financial and technical assistance plays a key role in maintaining strong defense and security forces. Conversely, the loss of international backing leads to "an existential and financial crisis for the regime that often devastates both its will and capacity to carry on" (Bellin 2004, 144). Domestic actors, particularly the military, are also motivated to maintain their backing for incumbent authoritarian rulers by their desire to maintain good relations with Western powers (Cook 2007). International support for cooperative authoritarian rulers is a compelling explanation for the durability, if not the origins, of authoritarianism in the Middle East.

Domestic actors also develop vested interests in the maintenance of authoritarian rule, further cementing the hold on power of incumbent dictators. Selected local elites—usually some combination of family members, personal friends, and business associates—are core members of authoritarian coalitions. Rulers employ selective incentives, such as access to power and lucrative economic opportunities, to ensure the loyalty of these elites. In the 1980s, these kinds of crony capitalist arrangements expanded with the introduction of markets that had no true competition in many sectors (see Chapter 8). On a mass scale, certain social groups, particularly the new middle classes that emerged after independence, were also important components of political settlements across the region. With shrinking public investment and the decline in the public sector, the fortunes of the middle classes began to decline.

The military and security forces are critical allies for authoritarian rulers. Indeed, as noted earlier, in some MENA countries the army directly controls the state, while in others it controls governing institutions from the sidelines. In virtually all countries in the region, rulers maintain close ties with the senior officers' corps and provide relatively generous perks to members of the armed forces. The authoritarian kings and presidents of the Middle East face strong incentives to keep their military and security forces content: the will and ability of the coercive apparatus to suppress opposition can enable rulers to ward off threats from elites and non-elites alike (Bellin 2004, 143).

The high levels of defense expenditures across the region generate rents for the military, thus helping most governments in the region secure the loyalty of the military while also serving as a large source of patronage. In some countries, the military is among the largest employers, and globally the Middle East stands out as the region with the highest percentage of its labor force employed in the military. Approximately 3 percent of workers were employed in the armed forces in the MENA region as a whole in 2012, as compared to an average of 0.8 percent in middle-income countries (World Bank, World Development Indicators [WDI]). Half of the ten countries in the world with the largest share of their workforce employed in the military are located in the Middle East. In Iraq almost 10 percent of the labor force is enlisted in the army, and in Jordan the share is 7 percent. These figures probably understate the full extent of the military's role as an employer and, in any case, do not include the security forces, which account for a large share of the workforce in these and most other MENA countries. In some regions of Jordan, for example, virtually the entire population benefits from military welfare programs. In Lebanon, many Sunni young men still aspire to positions in the army as their ticket to financial security, even as they increasingly believe that their ideological opponents, notably Hezbollah, effectively control this national institution (Malas and Abi-Habib 2014).

The fact that military expenditures rise and fall with the size of government expenditures and that they decline even when military risks are rising suggests that the armed forces are a vital institutional vehicle for patronage. Table 10.3 shows the rise and fall of military expenditures at the peak and low points of government expenditures.[2] The data indicate that expenditures on the military were cut substantially during the period of economic adjustment, particularly in the RPLA and

TABLE 10.3. Peak, Low, and Recent Peak Expenditures on Security and Defense (as percentages of GDP) in the MENA Countries

	Peak Security	Low Security	Recent Peak Security	Peak Defense	Low Defense	Recent Peak Defense
RRLP	**6.1%**	**2.5%**	**2.0%**	**10.4%**	**6.2%**	**5.7%**
Bahrain	na	3.2	3.3	5.6	4.0	4.7
Kuwait	6.1	2.4	2.5	7.3	3.7	3.0
Libya	na	na	na	na	6.7	0.0
Oman	na	1.8	0.4	23.8	11.0	9.6
Qatar	na	na	1.7	4.6	3.3	2.0
Saudi Arabia				18.1	10.1	15
United Arab Emirates	na	na	na	3.0	4.3	5.3
RRLA	**0.0**	**0.7**	**1.2**	**14.5**	**3.2**	**4.6**
Algeria	na	na	1.8	2.0	1.5	3.8
Iran	0.0	0.9	1.8	5.7	1.7	3.7
Syria	0.0	0.6	0.0	35.9	6.4	6.2
RPLA	**1.6**	**1.8**	**2.4**	**6.4**	**3.7**	**2.8**
Egypt	1.7	1.4	1.7	7.1	2.8	2.6
Jordan	na	2.0	4.1	10.7	6.6	5.9
Lebanon	na	1.4	1.3	4.1	3.6	3.6
Morocco	na	na	na	7.2	3.9	3.4
Tunisia	1.5	2.4	2.5	3.0	1.7	1.5

Source: International Monetary Fund (IMF), World Financial Statistics.

Note: See Table 2.2 for the peak, low, and recent peak years for each country.

RRLA countries. The fact that reductions in military budgets were less extreme in the RRLP countries accords with the less draconian adjustment measures adopted by these countries, especially in spending for patronage. In all MENA countries, however, spending on the military and security forces was also likely to be off budget; thus, the cuts to these sectors may have been less extreme than the data in Table 10.3 indicate. Furthermore, as we discuss in more detail later, many Middle Eastern armies generate revenue through their own enterprises, and so military officers have an incentive to support stable and friendly rulers when they do not control the organs of the state themselves.

As the recent experiences of some MENA countries such as Tunisia and Egypt show, armies may defect from the authoritarian coalition under certain conditions. For example, Eva Bellin argues that "the robustness of the coercive apparatus, or . . .

its will to repress reform initiatives, is inversely related to its level of institutionalization. The more institutionalized the security establishment is, the more willing it will be to disengage from power and allow political reform to proceed." An institutionalized coercive apparatus is one that is

> rule-governed, predictable, and meritocratic . . . with established paths of career advancement and recruitment; promotion . . . based on performance, not politics; . . . a clear delineation between the public and private that forbids predatory behavior vis-à-vis society; and discipline . . . maintained through the inculcation of a service ethic and strict enforcement of a merit-based hierarchy. (Bellin 2004, 145; see also Keefer 2012)

The responses of Middle Eastern armies to mass mobilization during the Arab uprisings also indicate that militaries will not defend unpopular rulers at all costs, particularly if senior officers perceive that their interests are better served under different political arrangements (Bellin 2004, 146; Brooks 2013). In general, however, the military and security forces are a strong local constituency for authoritarian rule across the Middle East.

In addition, war has important implications for economic growth and development in the Middle East, although the effects are not clear-cut and depend on the nature and geographic scope of the conflict in any given country. On the one hand, war has devastating effects on populations by directly and indirectly causing death, disease, and disability. It leads to economic breakdown by destroying physical and human capital, wiping out basic infrastructure such as roads and sanitation networks and disrupting the social and political institutions that enable markets to function (Levy and Sidel 2008). On the other hand, the historical record shows that war can stimulate economies by spurring technological progress and institutional innovations that promote economic development. In debates about the sources of East Asian economic growth, one interpretation holds that war and security threats have been a key factor driving development in the region (Doner, Ritchie, and Slater 2005; see also Weinstein 2005 on East Africa). Another line of scholarship maintains that war—and particularly interstate wars and wars of territorial conquest—have facilitated the development of strong and capable government institutions in Europe (for example, Acemoglu and Robinson 2006; Ferguson 2002; Tilly 1975, 1992). In the post-independence Middle East, war and conflict have undoubtedly contributed to the construction and strengthening of coercive institutions and may have had secondary effects on bureaucratic capacity more generally. This remains a relatively unexplored area of research in scholarship on the region, however, and its destructive effects on the economic and social fabric are readily apparent.[3]

POLITICAL SETTLEMENTS AND THE
MILITARY IN THE MIDDLE EAST

Across the Middle East, the military is an important actor in virtually all regimes, in both formally democratic systems and authoritarian systems, but it plays a more direct role in the political settlements of some countries than in others and exhibits varying degrees of professionalization from country to country. In this section, we highlight the distinct ways in which the coercive institutions—the army and police as well as irregular forces and militias—operate in the political systems of diverse MENA countries. The impact of ethno-religious ties and economic holdings on the position of the military and security forces in the domestic political economies of the Middle East also deserves special attention.

In some countries, such as Algeria, Egypt, and Turkey, the military was a founding member of the post-independence regime and is relatively professionalized. As a result, the army has been a major corporate actor in politics, and often the economy, for decades. The military is also central to the national narrative and views itself, particularly in Turkey, as the guardian of the secular, nationalist project. In Egypt, history seems to have come full circle: under the rule of Gamal Abdel Nasser (1956–1970), the role of the military as the vanguard of development and social progress reached its apogee. After deposing Mohammed Morsi, the democratically elected president of Egypt, in July 2013, General Abdel Fattah Al-Sisi effectively took power and was formally elected president in June 2014. During his presidential campaign, al-Sisi presented himself as the successor to Nasser while promoting himself as the savior of Egypt.

The era when Middle Eastern militaries focused on interstate warfare had largely come to an end by the late 1970s. Since then, the role of the army has evolved. In many cases, the army has retired to the barracks while benefiting from regime patronage and the opportunity to profit from economic ventures. Armies in some MENA countries also play an increasingly active role in cementing authoritarian rule by involving themselves in domestic security.

Egypt is a quintessential example of a country in which the military has played, and continues to play (though to a far lesser degree since the 1970s), a central role in the national political settlement. The overt importance of the army in politics was most pronounced under Nasser's rule, but it remained a key corporate actor under Sadat and Mubarak. And, as noted, it experienced a resurgence, first after Mubarak was overthrown in January 2011 and again after the Muslim Brotherhood was deposed from power in July 2013. Until recently, the Turkish military was central to that country's political system, with constitutional arrangements guaranteeing its preeminent role as the self-appointed guardian of secularism in Turkey. As noted previously, Turkey oscillated between civilian and military rule from 1950 until the 1990s (see Chapter 3). The government's continued use of the military in its efforts to eradicate the Kurdistan Workers' Party (PKK) gave the armed forces leverage in Turkish politics. One of the major stumbling blocks to Turkey's accession to the European Union (EU) has been doubt about whether its civilian institutions are firmly and irrevocably anchored. In other countries, notably Algeria, the military has historically played an important role in domestic politics, but increasingly from behind the scenes.

For more than forty years, since it gained independence from Britain and Egypt in 1956, Sudan has been in a state of civil war. In that time, the country's government has seen eight successful coups, all but one of which were military-led (Cline

Center for Democracy 2013). As a result of decades of war and near-continuous military rule, Sudan's government and the Sudanese Armed Forces (SAF) have become inextricably intertwined, with the SAF exerting considerable influence on national politics.

Military rule has proved to be the norm throughout Sudan's post-independence history, up to and including the tenure of President Omar al-Bashir, who came to power as an army general in yet another bloodless coup in 1989. As the head of the Revolutionary Command Council (RCC), Bashir ruled Sudan in a form of military dictatorship until 1993, at which point the RCC voluntarily dissolved, appointing Bashir as the civilian head of state. Though Sudan remains largely militarized under the civilian government—with continued armed conflict, particularly in Darfur and the disputed border region of Abyei—Bashir no longer draws his power from the military but only consolidates power through the military.

One should not, however, underestimate the possible significance of the "civilianization" of military regimes. Over time, moves that initially may be largely symbolic, such as dropping military titles and substituting mufti for uniforms, can lead to a real transfer of power and control to civilian hands. That transfer took place in dramatic fashion in Turkey in 1950, although the military would later intervene in politics in 1960, 1971, 1980, and 1997. In Egypt and Algeria over the past several decades, nonmilitary technocrats have played increasingly prominent roles in economic and social policymaking, although President Hosni Mubarak of Egypt, a former professional military officer, maintained close links to the senior officers' corps. Key positions in internal security and administration, national defense, and foreign affairs are still reserved for senior officers. The confrontation between the military and the Islamic Salvation Front (FIS) in Algeria in many respects led to the remilitarization of the regime, making it the most praetorian of any regime in the Middle East, although the current president, Abdelaziz Bouteflika, came from a diplomatic, rather than a military, background and the army's role in politics has been somewhat diminished under his tenure.

A handful of regimes have had a reputation for civilian predominance. Tunisia enjoyed uninterrupted civilian government from 1956 to 1988 under Habib Bourguiba. Although the military was relatively institutionalized and professional, it was not part of the founding coalition of the state and has never been a central actor in the evolving political settlement. The size of the military was contained, few military men played any role in the civilian administration, and there were no serious attempts at military intervention. Bourguiba single-mindedly built his coalitions among civilian forces and insulated his regime from military influence. In recent years, however, Tunisia's military has been growing substantially in both size and cost. Moreover, it was the minister of defense, General Zine El Abidine Ben Ali, who deposed Bourguiba in 1988. Nonetheless, the army has not been a dominant actor in Tunisian politics recently. Some attribute this to the apparent decision of its top brass, notably General Rachid Ammar, not to back Ben Ali during the Tunisian revolution (Barany 2011; Bellin 2012; Brooks 2013; Droz-Vincent 2011), although this narrative is contested for lack of evidence (Pachon 2014).

In many MENA countries, the military is less professionalized yet holds a key place in national political settlements through patrimonial ties to the ruler. This is true in diverse regimes types, from the authoritarian republics such as Iraq and Syria to the oil-rich monarchies of the Gulf and the resource-poor monarchies like Jordan and Morocco (Bellin 2004, 149). In all the major monarchies—Jordan, Morocco, and Iran from 1923 until 1979 and Saudi Arabia—the king is intimately linked to the military. Members of the royal family, if not the king himself, direct the ministry of defense, command key units in the armed forces, and review all promotions in the officers' corps. Before becoming king, Hassan of Morocco was put in command of the royal armed forces, and King Hussein, whose throne was dependent upon the support of the largely Bedouin Jordan Legion, was always a king in uniform.

In the oil-rich Gulf countries, the ruling monarchs appoint military officials as a form of familial cronyism, and members of the ruling family fill top military posts in order to ensure the regime's continued dynastic stability. Such dynastic regimes necessitate a great deal of intrafamily bargaining to gain the support of the entire ruling family for whichever member is chosen for power. Vast state bureaucracies, often created as a result of oil wealth, offer an outlet for these bargaining sessions: order within the family is maintained when key members are given influential and lucrative positions. As one arm of the state's bureaucracy—one rife with opportunities for appointments—the military becomes an important locus for regime longevity (Herb 1999). The result of this familial cronyism is a military that is led and controlled by members of the royal family (Rubin 2001, 54). Of course, having family members in top military positions does not entirely guard against the possibility of opposition arising from within the armed forces. Like other rulers, however, the Gulf monarchies use a number of other techniques, such as access to economic opportunities (discussed in more detail later), to ensure the loyalty of the military and security forces and to decrease the risk of military coups.

Recent Turkish history provides a rare example of the marginalization of the military from the core political settlement in a context where it was previously a dominant actor. The influence of the European Union is one piece of the story. In 2003 reforms introduced as part of the EU accession process attenuated the formal mechanisms by which the Turkish military operated in the political system (Cook 2007), and its role was diminished even further in the 2007 presidential elections. Although the military opposed the election of a member of the Justice and Development Party (AKP) as president of the republic and even threatened to intervene in civilian politics to prevent this outcome, the party successfully called for early elections and won 47 percent of the vote, an increase of 13 percent from the previous elections in 2002. As a result, Abdullah Gül, a senior AKP leader, became the next president, signaling the fallibility of the powerful army and bureaucratic elite of the country.

The Ergenekon scandal, in which hundreds of suspects were rounded up on charges of plotting to overthrow the AKP government, also represented an important shift in civil-military relations in Turkish politics. The legal indictment holds that a wide network of individuals from the Turkish "deep state," including the army, intelligence services, executive branch, academia, media, and civil society, were involved in the plot and were behind a variety of acts of political violence over the past thirty years. In 2007, following a police raid that initiated the "Ergenekon process," eighty-six suspects were indicted, including high-profile figures such as a commander of the Turkish Air Force, a commander of the gendarmerie, a retired army brigadier general, and others from academia and journalism. More were detained following subsequent indictments. The timing of the charges overlapped with the closure of a case against the AKP for carrying out "anti-secular activities," raising suspicions that the ruling party was using the scandal as retribution against its opponents (Ünver 2009, 9–10). As of the spring of 2014, more than 1,200 people have been charged and over 500 defendants have been convicted, including many former military commanders, although some have subsequently been released. Critics claim that many of the charges were trumped up. The politics behind the scandal appears even more complex with the eruption of open tensions between two erstwhile Islamist allies, the AKP and the Gülenist movement, a popular transnational religious and social movement led by a Turkish Islamic scholar, Fethullah Gülen, who is based in the United States. Some maintain that the Ergenekon prosecutions were spearheaded by the members of the Gülenist movement in the Turkish judiciary in order to stifle anti-Gülenist activity. To marginalize its former ally, the AKP leadership has allegedly facilitated the release of some detainees held as part of the Ergenekon process and moved to cut off key recruitment channels for the Gülenist movement (Jenkins 2014; *Today's Zaman* 2013).

There was a time when Lebanon appeared to be a solid civilian republic, but appearances were deceiving. Civil war broke out in Lebanon in the summer of 1958, at the time of the overthrow of the Iraqi monarchy. The violence provoked US military intervention. President Camille Chamoun, a civilian, was judged to have mishandled the situation and was replaced by General Fuad Chehab, who, like Chamoun, was a Christian. For six years under Chehab, Lebanon was under lightly veiled military rule. Between 1964 and 1976, Lebanese presidents were civilian, but their presence did not head off the civil war that after 1975 devoured civilian institutions, the Lebanese armed forces, and the country itself. Today, however, a (fractured) civilian parliamentary system once again uneasily governs Lebanon. Where there is no effective central government, armed bands and militias are found. In Lebanon from 1976 to 1990 and, to varying degrees, in Palestine and Iraq today, armed militias have constituted an "alternative security force." That they often act precipitously, violently, and with contempt for human rights is hardly surprising. Even when a political agreement is forged, disarming, demobilizing, and integrating such forces into the civilian economy and society is a difficult task, as the case of Lebanon since 1990 clearly illustrates.

Israel has apparently escaped military rule, but soon after independence, Prime Minister David Ben-Gurion feared a coup d'état engineered by the leaders of the outlawed Jewish terrorist organizations (principally the Irgun, led by Menachem Begin). It is an irony of sorts that Begin went on to become prime minister himself some thirty years later through the ballot box. More important, however, is the thorough intermingling of the civilian and military spheres in Israeli politics and in the economy. Israel is a nation-in-arms—it has fought six major wars and has faced threats of various kinds. It maintains a large defense industrial base, and many public activities are regulated by national security concerns. The military does not have to seize power in Israel because on most issues it is already positioned to get what it wants. Moreover, many of Israel's most visible politicians have come out of the military: Yitzhak Rabin, Ezer Weizman, Shaul Mofaz, Ehud Barak, and Ariel Sharon, to name but the most illustrious (for a contrasting view, see Gutmann and Landau 1985, 191). Current Prime Minister Benjamin Netanyahu, for his part, is officially billed as a military hero, having taken part in the famous "Flight 571" hostage rescue operation, as well as having fought in the 1973 war.

Despite sharing similar backgrounds, this does not mean that the views of the prime minister and those of military officials are always in line. In fact, recent events reveal a divergence in the level of hawkishness between the two branches. In 2012, responding to Iran's perceived nuclear capabilities, Israel's top policymakers fell largely into one of two camps: Netanyahu and Defense Minister Ehud Barak supported a preemptive military strike on Iranian nuclear facilities, while everyone else supported a less militaristic approach. According to one report, "not one *high-ranking official in the Israeli establishment*—not in the Israel Defense Forces' (IDF) top echelons, nor in the defense establishment and not even the President of Israel—currently supports an Israeli attack" (Barnea and Shiffer 2012). The fact that even the civilian rulers making such decisions have a strong military background is telling of the militarism of Israeli politics, but the level of dissent that remains even then demonstrates that a military background is not necessarily the sole determinant of their politics.

Sole determinant or not, the military culture in Israel runs deep, and what may be one of the most comfortable coexistences between the professional military and armed civilians can be found in its government. The Israeli defense forces were born in the kibbutz movement and the irregular Haganah before independence in 1948. Although the Haganah was rapidly professionalized after 1948, its civilian origins have never been forgotten. Israel's near-universal policy of mandatory service, recently extended to include the previously exempt ultra-orthodox community, blurs most boundaries between soldiers and civilians. Israelis ride buses and sit on park benches with their weapons with the same nonchalance as a businesswoman with her attaché case. Because the military is so closely integrated into Israeli society, the nation's leaders do not fear an armed citizenry. (Palestinians, on the other hand, have much to fear from armed Israeli settlers in cities like Hebron and elsewhere.) More likely, mandatory service instills a sense of allegiance in a country where identity has been forged in the threat of violence.

In Iran, the shah's enormous repressive apparatus, built on the armed forces and the secret police (the Iranian Security and Intelligence Organization, or SAVAK), was neutralized by persistent street demonstrations and strikes orchestrated by both Iranian Muslim organizations and radical leftist groups. It would be hard to describe the Islamic Republic of Iran as civilian, but it is equally hard to describe it as a military dictatorship. Rather, Iran offers an example of irregular forces cohabiting uneasily with the regular military. The regular military has been contained by a dominant coalition of the clergy (the mullahs) and the irregular Pasdaran, also known as the Islamic Revolutionary Guard Corps (IRGC); the IRGC became a nationwide militia, initially at the service of the now-disbanded Islamic Republican Party. Many of the Pasdaran's leaders came out of the radical secular leftist Mojahedin-e-Khalq (MEK) before 1979, were introduced to radical Shi'ite Islam through the teachings of Ali Shariati, and were drawn to Ayatollah Khomeini because of his fiercely anti-imperialist and antidespotic stance. After Khomeini came to power, these militants turned on their erstwhile leftist allies. They organized the revolutionary tribunals that meted out arbitrary justice to a host of presumed enemies of the republic, waged war against the Kurds, and were instrumental in the seizure of the US embassy in Tehran. With time, they took on the role of a security force–cum–vigilante group in the countryside.

The Pasdaran have become a very powerful force in Iranian politics. The regular armed forces were unable to oppose the ascendancy of the Pasdaran because the senior officers' corps had been so badly compromised in its loyalty to the shah, although they partially refurbished their image in the war with Iraq. Perhaps numbering around 125,000, the Pasdaran are armed, control substantial financial resources through institutions such as the Bonyad e-Mostazafan (the Foundation of the Oppressed), and espouse a common militant brand of Shi'ism. They have powerful allies among the mullahs and numerous allies in the *majlis,* or parliament.

The Pasdaran, along with the Basij, a decentralized volunteer militia under their command, played a critical role in suppressing the mass protests known as the Green Movement (see Chapter 11). When some Basij forces refused the orders to violently quash these protests following the 2009 presidential elections, other volunteers were recruited from outside of Tehran to put a stop to the protests. These irregular forces first gained prominence during the Iran-Iraq War when hundreds of thousands of them were deployed as "cannon fodder." Although the Basij is a highly ideological force, some claim that its members are often compelled to enlist in order to gain access to membership benefits, including low-interest loans and scholarships (Martonosi 2012).

Ethno-Religious Politics and the Military

In some countries, a common ethnic or religious identity helps to sustain alliances between rulers and the military and security forces. Communal bonds alone do not fully explain such relationships, which are invariably cemented by economic interests, but they can enhance trust among rulers and security officials, particularly when perceived threats to the common ethnic or sectarian group are on the rise.

The Syrian and Iraqi experiences illustrate the ways in which identity politics can shape the position of the coercive institutions in political settlements. For decades, the Syrian regime has been controlled by the Assad family, which comes from the minority Alawite community (Barany 2011; Quinlivan 1999). The Syrian officers' corps is also dominated by Alawis, which helps to cement their loyalty to the regime. That said, the Assad regime's elite social coalition, including members of the top brass, spans all religious communities, despite popular depictions of the present war in Syria in sectarian terms. Elite networks cross sectarian lines and are first and foremost held together by personal ties and economic interests (Haddad 2012). In Iraq, sectarian politics has increasingly characterized the composition of the security forces. After 2008, Prime Minister Nouri al-Maliki progressively alienated the non-Shi'a, while ensuring that military officers and even the rank and file were overwhelmingly composed of Shi'a Iraqis. Indeed, al-Maliki's alienation of Sunnis has been widely credited with explaining the rising appeal of Sunni extremist organizations such as the Islamic State of Iraq and the Levant (ISIL) (also known as the Islamic State of Iraq and Syria [ISIS]) (Rubin and Nordland 2014). Al-Maliki's moves were not unprecedented; indeed, the prime minister took a page out of an older playbook used in the opposite direction by his predecessor, Saddam Hussein—to the detriment of the Shi'a and in favor of the Sunni and, especially, his tribesmen from Tikrit.

To view Sudan's civil wars and ongoing conflicts through the lens of ethnic or religious divisions alone would be an oversimplification; competition for limited resources, regional differences, changing migratory patterns, and colonial legacies have all played a role. Nevertheless, ethnic and religious differences illuminate the relationship between the central state and various regions of the country. Prior to the establishment of independent South Sudan in 2011, the ethno-religious landscape of Sudan was largely divided between the North and South, with Arab Muslims constituting the vast majority of the population in the North and dominating the Khartoum government. The exclusion and repression of the South's largely black practitioners of Christianity and indigenous religions were root causes of the conflict between these regions, although it is unclear that these social cleavages were institutionalized in the armed forces. Ethnic and religious divisions in Sudan's military forces also characterize the region's war in Darfur. In 2003, echoing the grievances of the South and in the face of an uptick in land-related disputes with the region's nomadic Arab tribes, non-Arab groups in the Darfur region took up arms against the government in Khartoum. In response, the government recruited local Arab militias known as the Janjaweed to crush the rebellion. The International Criminal Court (ICC) ultimately declared the violence that ensued to be genocide and indicted President Bashir on this and other charges.

Ethno-religious differences ostensibly contribute to conflict in Sudan, and as in other MENA regimes such as Syria or Iraq, the Sudanese government manipulates identity-based ties to reinforce its rule. In Sudan's case, however, the role of ethnicity and religion takes on a more regional bent: confrontations continue to this day between the Arab Muslims who control the central government and the non-Arab populations in the South.

Identity politics also helps to maintain tight alliances between the military and ruling families in the Gulf countries. As noted earlier, the Gulf monarchies often appoint members of the royal family to top military positions, yielding the double benefit of ensuring familial solidarity and military loyalty. Nevertheless, in some countries in the subregion, sectarian and tribal identities shape the composition of the military and security forces.

Perhaps the most overt links between sectarianism and military forces in the Gulf are found in Bahrain. Like the ruling regimes of Saudi Arabia and Kuwait, Bahrain's al-Khalifa is a Sunni monarchy reigning over a significant Shi'a population. Unlike Saudi Arabia and Kuwait, however, Bahrain's Shi'a are a clear majority, representing about two-thirds of the native population, yet the Sunni minority occupies the vast majority of top positions in the state and economy. (The use of the term "native" here is key given that about 60 percent of the population is composed of immigrants.) Fearing the potential social repercussions of these inequalities, the al-Khalifa regime maintains a Sunni-only military, even importing Sunnis from neighboring countries such as Pakistan to staff its armed forces (Barany 2011, 31–32; Mashal 2011). This strategy for maintaining regime stability became particularly apparent in 2011. Although protests in Bahrain were initially carried out by a cross-sectarian movement, with both Sunnis and Shi'a calling for government reform, the al-Khalifa regime proved adept at manipulating fears, claiming the protests were an Iranian-bred Shi'a uprising. Reinforcing this sectarian narrative, the regime bolstered its military by importing Sunni mercenaries, most notably from Pakistan, and it also benefited from Saudi Arabia's direct intervention to suppress the uprisings (Mashal 2011; McMurray and Ufheil-Somers 2013).

Identity politics helps to maintain military loyalty in other Gulf regimes, albeit not to the same extent as in Bahrain. One tool used by Gulf countries to secure the allegiance of the military is the recruitment of Bedouin populations (Herb 1999, 245–246). Particularly in the mid twentieth century, as Arab nationalism was at its peak, Bedouin were seen as a safe bet for staffing the armed forces. As Arab nationalists dominated the opposition to ruling monarchies, any attempted coup would surely result in a government controlled by the nationalists and the marginalization of the Bedouin. Thus, the Gulf monarchies selectively recruited the Bedouin populations to fill the ranks of the military and security forces with those who had less incentive to defect. In recent years, this strategy has declined as Islamists, who tend to win support among now-settled Bedouin populations, have replaced Arab nationalists as the primary opponents to the monarchies.

A final note on the composition of Gulf state militaries relates to the availability of labor. As labor-poor but resource-rich economies, the Gulf countries often have difficulty finding enough enlistees to maintain their militaries. Wealth exacerbates this problem, as the indigenous populations have little incentive to join the military when lucrative positions are readily available in the public sector and, to a lesser degree, in local private firms. Several solutions to this problem have been proposed. The Gulf Cooperation Council (GCC), composed of Bahrain, Kuwait, Oman, Qatar, Saudi Arabia, and the United Arab Emirates, aims to pool manpower within the region. With divided national interests, the regional organization has failed to meet many of its goals, but maintaining joint security operations remains an option, as Bahrain witnessed with an official GCC intervention in March 2011 (BBC News 2011; Rubin 2001, 49). With a limited base of citizens for enlistment in the armed forces, the Gulf monarchies, including Bahrain as previously noted, have also tried another solution: hiring foreign mercenaries. These forces now play a major role in the Gulf militaries, and they bring the added benefit of "depoliticizing" the militaries (Rubin 2001, 49, 54). A final response to insufficient manpower—and one that has recently gained traction in a few Gulf states—is conscription. As part of its recent military buildup, Qatar announced mandatory, albeit short, military service for males between the ages of eighteen and thirty-five. The United Arab Emirates established a similar conscription law soon thereafter, in June 2014, and Kuwait, with a draft of a similar law supposedly in preparation, is expected to follow suit as well (*Al Jazeera* 2014; Kovessy 2014).

Communal bonds alone, however, are insufficient to explain the allegiance of the military to authoritarian rulers. Even where minorities keep a firm grip on power by stacking the top brass with in-group members, they need to sweeten the pot with economic incentives. In the next section, we turn to the economic role of the military in the MENA region.

The Economic Weight of the Military

Keeping the officers' corps happy is a crucial step that rulers take to "coup-proof" their regimes. Access to lucrative economic opportunities is a key component of this strategy across the MENA region. The importance of the military in political settlements is also captured by its economic interests, which can be embodied by the size of what President Dwight Eisenhower termed the "military-industrial complex"—the constellation of industries involved in the production of arms and related matériel—or by the more general business holdings of the military in the domestic economy, whether owned by corporate units or by individual officers.

Israel, Egypt, Turkey, and, most notably, Iran have developed extensive armaments industries that occupy a particularly important niche in their economies. For one thing, the military-industrial sector includes some of these economies' most advanced technological undertakings—research into and direct use or manufacture of strategic technologies, including supercomputers, nuclear fission, lasers, advanced telecommunications and remote sensing, telemetry, and missiles. For another, these enterprises are almost exclusively within the public sector. Except for some contracting out of component manufacture in Israel and Turkey, the military establishments of these countries monopolize the transfer and adaptation of high technology with obvious civilian applications, and anyone who has the expertise and desire to work with such technologies becomes a servant of that monopoly. The military-industrial complex tends to invade the civilian sector of the economy, competing directly with private producers and providers of services. Finally, these growing economic domains have become important sources of foreign exchange through sales of arms. Arms exports have been crucial to Israel's balance of payments for many years, but Egypt, too, partially as a result of Iraq's need for arms, saw the value of its military exports rise from about US$1 billion in 1986 (Springborg 1987) to an estimated US$4 billion in 1988–1989, according to the US Arms Control and Disarmament Agency (1995).

Turkey's military industries employ more than 40,000 people. Many of the country's military contracts have been coproduction deals, with foreign investments in local companies averaging $300 million annually (CAAT 2002). These factories and facilities are involved in overhauling M-48 tanks, manufacturing optical equipment, and manufacturing and assembling Huey helicopters and F-1 jet fighters, submarines, patrol boats, tank guns, and missiles. Significantly, some of Turkey's large private industrial conglomerates are licensed to manufacture ground-to-air missiles, Black Hawk helicopters, heavy trucks, and armored vehicles (see Karasapan 1987; *Middle East Economic Digest,* September 7, 1985). In 1996 the military began a large-scale technological modernization program, with nearly $30 billion allocated over ten years (Hen-Tov 2004). Many of the Turkish army's holdings in defense-related companies are held through the Foundation for Strengthening the Turkish Armed Forces (TSKGV), a corporation established in 1987 that employs about 20,000 people (Demir 2005, 681).

Egypt's defense industry is several decades old. Under Nasser, it expanded from manufacture of munitions and light arms into aeronautics and even took an ill-fated leap into ballistic missiles. But real expansion occurred under Sadat, especially after 1975, when Saudi Arabia and some other Gulf states agreed to finance the Arab Military Industrialization Organization (AMIO) to produce a range of advanced weapons for the Arab countries. Egypt became the home for the AMIO, and when the Arab financiers pulled out of the project as a result of the Camp David Accords, it became an entirely Egyptian undertaking. In 1986, between the AMIO and the original defense industries, the complex included some twenty-four factories, with a workforce of 70,000 to 100,000 and production worth about US$350 million per year (Stork 1987). It manufactured components for MiG aircraft and assembled French Alpha jets, helicopters, and, at Benha Electronics, radar systems. Today at least fifteen Egyptian production plants make everything from small arms to tanks and rocket launchers.

During the 1970s, the shah of Iran sought to make the Iranian military the dominant force in the Gulf and a rival to India in the Indian Ocean. The purchase of arms and military technology ran at more than US$4 billion per annum and led to contracts and licensing arrangements with a host of multinational suppliers: Northrop, Lockheed, Bell Helicopter, Leyland, and Daimler-Benz, among others. The Islamic republic inherited this complex, but had to look to other sources of supply: the People's Republic of China, the Soviet Union, Sweden, Turkey, and the international arms market. From 1995 to 2005, Russia supplied over 70 percent of Iranian arms imports (SIPRI). By 2004, the country was making its own intermediate-range ballistic missile, the Shihab-3, using components that were nearly all manufactured in Iran.

Likewise, Saudi Arabia, on the strength of its petroleum revenues in the 1970s, bought entire military technologies and industries. For instance, Saudi Arabia's Peace Shield air defense system has brought in billions of dollars in radar equipment and computers. In the two years following the end of Operation Desert Storm, Saudi Arabia imported about US$19 billion in arms and defense-related matériel, and from 1990 to 1999 the United States delivered nearly $40 billion worth of armaments to Saudi Arabia (FAS 2005).

Israel has gone the furthest in the development and sophistication of its military industries. Israel's technical expertise is without equal in the region, and its research-and-development facilities put it on an equal footing with the most advanced nations of the world. Israel is one of the world's major arms suppliers. Its scientists have provided the country with all the requisites to assemble and deliver nuclear bombs and warheads, and the country has the necessary expertise to design and manufacture a jet fighter, the Lavi, possessing all the capabilities of the US F-16C. Israel wants to be self-sufficient militarily and in all technological domains, but its own armed forces could never generate sufficient demand to sustain economically the range of military industries that national security would require. In 1990 its two largest armaments industries had a combined turnover of US$2.3 billion. For such industries to be viable, Israel must seek markets abroad. The search has been successful: in 2004, according to General Amos Yaron, director of the Israeli Defense Ministry, Israel exported between $2 billion and $3 billion worth of armaments, and more than 80 percent of Israeli defense production was destined for export (*Israel High Tech and Investment Report* 2004).

Beyond the military-industrial complexes, the militaries and security forces of the Middle East have tended to develop their own powerful economic enclaves, and because of their strategic nature, they are not fully accountable to parliaments or auditors. Owning property, productive assets, and financial institutions and being able to negotiate foreign and domestic loans and put out contracts, they are in a position to harness important private-sector clients and invade civilian markets. It is frequently alleged that the officers' corps uses these assets and points of leverage to line their own pockets and those of their clients.

In building a military-economic enclave, Turkey may have been a pioneer. The economic holdings of the Turkish military are unique in that they are not owned by individual officers but rather through corporate institutions, notably the military pension fund. After the military coup of 1961, the Armed Forces Mutual Assistance Fund (ÖYAK) was set up to provide pensions to officers upon their retirement. Its financial resources come from a 10 percent levy on the salaries of all commissioned and noncommissioned officers, and it enjoys tax-free status. ÖYAK has about 17,000 employees and, as of 2005, was among the top three conglomerates in the country (Demir 2005, 678). ÖYAK has shares in about sixty companies—of which it solely owns twenty-nine—in diverse industrial, agricultural, and financial sectors such as automotives, cement, iron and steel production, chemicals, food, construction, transportation logistics, import-export services, private security, technology, and tourism. In some of these areas, ÖYAK enjoys monopoly or oligopolistic power, although its relative weight in the domestic economy has declined somewhat in recent years. Many of the firms in which it has an interest are either affiliated with or co-owned by the major domestic private conglomerates, such as Sabanci and Koc, and with multinational companies, such as Mobile, DuPont, and Shell. While ÖYAK benefited substantially under Turkey's ISI trade regime, it also profited during the privatization wave of the 1980s by buying up public firms at attractive prices. It maintains an important role in the economy even with democratic deepening in the past decade (Akça 2010, 10, 12; Demir 2005, 678–679; Göktepe and Satyanath 2013).

ÖYAK has bridged a gap between the military establishment and the private sector. Since Ottoman times and even under Atatürk, the military has seen itself as the guardian of the nation's interests and, to some extent, a watchdog against private greed. Over time, ÖYAK and other special funds became dependent on direct investments in the national economy and in joint ventures with foreign and domestic corporations. As a result, the economic interests of the officers' corps have become firmly wedded to the performance of the Turkish economy and to that of its private sector (Çetin 2010, 26–27; Springborg 2011).

In Egypt, the military also has major stakes in diverse sectors, but unlike Turkey, the military's economic interests are more personalized. Egyptian army officers and former officers profit from their political connections to gain control of privatized companies or to form new companies with government contracts. This form of cronyism establishes a vested interest in authoritarianism, restricts government accountability, and creates inefficiencies (Springborg 2011).

The development of the military's involvement in the economy has undergone several phases. After Egypt signed the Camp David Accords in 1979, the army's role in international warfare declined and it shifted its focus toward profit-making enterprises. In this period, the Egyptian Ministry of Defense created an economic body, the National Service Products Organization (NSPO), which focused on public infrastructure projects and the manufacturing of inexpensive consumer goods (Abul-Magd 2013). Since the early 1980s, military industries in Egypt have claimed a growing portion of civilian markets for products, including truck motors, telephone equipment, optical lenses, fans, and air conditioners, and have expanded to encompass other sectors such as construction and telecommunications. Most spectacular was the armed forces' direct entry into food production, allegedly so that in times of hostilities they could ensure their own supply of food. What transpired was a capital-intensive plunge into desert reclamation, hothouse cultivation of vegetables, and commercial production of eggs and poultry. Private producers have cautiously complained—particularly after military production drove down the price of eggs—that by using conscripts as free labor the military has an unfair advantage. These protests may be outweighed by the military's ability to let lucrative contracts to private firms, ensure delivery of supplies or produce to designated wholesalers, and, through a network of retired officers in private and joint-venture firms, maintain a far-flung system of clients and cronies.

In the 1990s, when Mubarak embarked on economic liberalization with the backing of international financial institutions, the army expanded its production of consumer goods and services with the creation of new companies and private-sector initiatives benefiting from tax-free status. In the 2000s, current and retired army officers were increasingly appointed to high-level public-sector positions while at the same time they were expanding their business holdings. In addition to the NSPO, two other bodies, the Ministry of Military Production (MOMP) and the Arab Organization for Industrialization (AOI), were created to manage the economic holdings of the military in diverse consumer and service sectors. The holdings of the army continued to grow even after Mubarak was overthrown, and especially during the period of Supreme Council of the Armed Forces (SCAF) rule before Morsi was elected (Abul-Magd 2013; Morsy 2014).

The Arab uprisings and their aftermath brought international media attention to the economic assets of the Egyptian military, or "Military, Inc.," with estimates of their value ranging from 5 to 40 percent of the economy, although reports on its holdings have been wildly exaggerated.[4] Indeed, the army's willingness to support the overthrow of Mubarak may have stemmed in part from a desire to marginalize economic rivals who were close to the former president and his sons. At the same time, the powerful military unwillingness to tolerate any threat to its interests or public scrutiny of its holdings set limits on the possibilities for true social and political change (Marshall and Stacher 2012).

In Iran, the Pasdaran (or Islamic Revolutionary Guard Corps) also oversees a vast economic empire with major holdings in oil services, construction, port operations, and the media and telecommunications sectors (Springborg 2011). The role of the IRGC in the Iranian economy increased sharply in the 1990s as part of the reconstruction effort after the Iran-Iraq War. When Mohammad Khatami was elected in 1997, the Ayatollah Khamenei, who had become the supreme leader after the death of the Ayatollah Khomeini in 1989, increasingly supported the IRGC as a counterbalance to the new president (Springborg 2011, 52). Members of the Pasdaran have profited from its political connections to win public tenders and large contracts for their firms, gain access to hard currency and subsidized exchange rates in order to accumulate capital, and operate a network of "shadow ports" through which they can smuggle goods into the domestic market (Hen-Tov and Gonzalez 2011, 52).

At the same time, the military's economic interests are not centralized into one or even a handful of organizations. Rather, many competing networks linked to various branches of the military, government foundations, and parastatal organizations have economic holdings. A recent statement by Mohsen Safaei Farahani, the former deputy economic minister and head of the national football organization, indicates that there are about 120 different funds, foundations, and quasi-governmental institutions that control about 50 percent of GDP. Although the portion of the national economy controlled by these interests may be exaggerated, his statement attests to the degree of fragmentation in the economic holdings of military and security institutions and elites in Iran.[5] The IRGC plays an important role in the economy, and various former IRGC officers control companies, holding funds, and shadow banks, but these institutions compete with others linked to other segments of the political elite and different bureaucratic agencies. Thus, unlike the Egyptian military-industrial complex, which is dominated by the army and its top officers, in Iran analogous groups and ex-military men compete with others to carve out their own portions of Iran's "subcontractor state" (Harris 2013).

If the role of the military in Sudan's politics has waned in recent years, its involvement in the country's economy certainly has not. In fact, on a continuum of the most to the least economically involved militaries in the Middle East, Robert Springborg (2011) places the Sudanese Armed Forces (SAF) second only to the militaries of Egypt and Iran. For a brief period in the early 1980s, the Nimeiri regime encouraged the proliferation of "military corporations," which developed private-sector holdings to supplement their state-provided income (Bienen and Moore 1987, 496). While official military corporations went the way of that regime itself in 1985, the influence of the military in the private sector did not. Top officers in the Sudanese military use their political clout and networks to secure themselves lucrative positions in the private sector, particularly in sectors with some military application. As with other forms of cronyism, the regime tolerates, if not actively encourages, this behavior to ensure the loyalty of military officers. For all of its current involvement in the domestic economy, the Sudanese military would probably have far more extensive economic holdings if the economy had a stronger and more developed private sector (Springborg 2011, 397).

In Algeria, the role of the military and security forces in the economy takes on yet another form, which differs from both of the variants we have seen thus far. Although the military has also been an important actor in Algerian politics, its involvement in the economy is far less institutionalized. Rather than building up a large military-industrial complex, Algerian army officers have opted to make their own deals and benefited from side payments on economic transactions (Springborg 2011). The fact that hydrocarbons dominate Algeria's rentier economy partly explains the army's relatively minimal role in the economy. The Algerian military has always had a number of its own enterprises, but these constitute a small share of GDP. Individual generals allegedly control parts of the domestic market, particularly in imported commodities, but virtually no research provides documented evidence for an "officers' economy" on the scale of Egypt or, to some degree, Iran.[6]

In Syria, top officers of the military and the *mukhabarat* (intelligence service) are an organic component of the regime and are thus able to gain disproportionate access to economic opportunities, which further cements their loyalty. These officials have acquired increasingly important holdings in the private sector, particularly after Assad opened up the economy to private investment in the 1990s, and they have used their influence to obtain kickbacks for licenses and access to lucrative contracts. For years, the largest military corporation was the Military Housing Organization (Longuenesse 1985, 18). Initially, the military-industrial complex was more concentrated in industries connected to the military itself, such as armaments, construction, public works, and food processing, and less involved, unlike Egypt, in consumer goods and services (Springborg 2011). By now, its holdings have evolved to include interests in free-trade zones, telecommunications, automobiles, tourism, services, and other sectors. Large military and security networks have become a social stratum in their own right that exists in part outside of government institutions but remains vehemently loyal to the regime. Rami Makhlouf, Assad's cousin and a relative of high-ranking members of the security forces, is a quintessential example. By some estimates, Makhlouf's holdings control almost 60 percent of the Syrian economy, and he allegedly uses his connections as well as intimidation of potential rivals to ensure exclusive access to lucrative business ventures. For the regime's critics, Makhlouf has become the symbol of corruption (Haddad 2011, chs. 4 and 5; Peel 2011).[7]

Outside of the domestic economy, the Lebanese civil war opened up a variety of lucrative economic opportunities for Syrian military and security officers. After Syria was drawn into the Lebanese civil war in 1976, it came to control much of eastern and northeastern Lebanon as well as access to Beirut. Then quasi-socialist Syria thus met relatively freewheeling Lebanon, where entrepreneurs still managed to thrive in the midst of the fighting. Lebanon imported a range of consumer goods that Syrians craved, and the Syrian armed forces found themselves in a position to control the movement of such goods. The result was predictable: a sprawling black market in everything from tape decks to automobiles, operated by Syrian officers, with astronomic profits distributed through several subnetworks. Thus, a wartime economy based on profiteering in neighboring Lebanon supplemented the economic interests of the Syrian army and its officers within its own national borders.

The militaries of the Gulf countries, with the possible exception of Oman, do not control significant portions of their economies compared to the rest of the region, in large part because the loyalty of military officials in Gulf countries is ensured, not through providing them with economic benefits per se, but through familial ties, which of course are themselves associated with access to lucrative economic opportunities. Furthermore, the relative wealth of these countries tends to make military salaries higher than those in the surrounding region, limiting incentives for corruption (Springborg 2011, 398). Among the Gulf monarchies, Oman is a partial exception to this pattern. Akin to the practices of Jordan and Morocco, the Al Said regime uses "intermittent, discretionary patronage doled out to officers by kings anxious to retain their loyalty" (Springborg 2011, 398).

If measured by the magnitude of government expenditures on defense, however, the Gulf militaries maintain considerable weight in their economies. Our earlier discussion of military expenditures as a percentage of GDP showed that the RRLP political economies—by and large the Gulf states—exhibit markedly higher rates of military expenditure by percentage of GDP than the rest of the region (see Figure 10.1). This is particularly the case for Saudi Arabia and the United Arab Emirates, which are far and away the highest spenders in the subregion (see Figure 10.2). As mentioned earlier, Saudi Arabia has bought entire military technologies and industries, including billions of dollars' worth of radar equipment and computers for its Peace Shield air defense as well as arms, armaments, and military matériel (FAS 2005). The other Gulf countries display similar trends. Qatar, for example, showed signs of an extensive military buildup by going on a military "shopping spree" in March 2014 and signing defense contracts worth about $24 billion (Kovessy 2014).

The possible reasons for these buildups are diverse. In most cases, the Iranian threat is the major impetus for military expenditures. Saudi Arabia, a regional superpower and longtime rival to Iran, believes that it must spend on its military capabilities in order to sustain its might. The protection of valuable economic resources is another possible motivation. According to a spokesperson for a defense contractor that benefited from Qatar's recent spending spree, "Every country that wants to have a booming economy must have a strong defense capability . . . [a nation without a powerful military] is like a building made entirely out of sand. There's no strong foundation" (Kovessy 2014). A final incentive for large-scale arms purchases is generally left unstated. As Barry Rubin (2001, 50) argues, "another motive for huge arms purchases from the United States is to create additional links to make certain that country will play the role of a protector for the regimes." Nonetheless, spending huge sums does not necessarily create a more effective military establishment. For example, the United Arab Emirates purchases advanced aircraft from the United States but lacks appropriately trained pilots and even suitable runways (Rubin 2001, 50).

Like many countries in the Middle East, Israel has a great deal of overlap between its top brass and the major players in its economy. The reasons for this military influence and its effects differ, however, from the situation in the surrounding region. Israel's military economy is not one of detrimental cronyism—economic benefits are not given out in exchange for political loyalty. Rather, Israel is a prime example of a military-industrial complex. With military expenditures comprising about 5.6 percent of the nation's GDP in 2013 (World Bank), the Israeli defense industry—which, as previously discussed, is very technologically sophisticated for the region—is a major driver of economic growth. Besides all the military capabilities mentioned earlier, Israel continues to produce its own precision-guided munitions, is second only to the United States in drone production (Moriarty et al. 2013; Wan and Finn 2011), and sustains its range of military industries by selling to markets abroad.

A defining feature of a military-industrial complex is its tendency to bleed into the civilian sphere. Among other sectors, the security industry has moved into the spheres of medicine (where military physicians work with and provide training to civilians), education (with "soldier-teachers" teaching Hebrew and "pre-IDF" courses), and even the media, where the industry controls major publishing houses and radio stations (Mintz 1985, 634). Even those industries that are not directly controlled by the defense establishment are often affected by military influences; retired military officials play prominent roles in a variety of industries and are often sought after for their connections and expertise (Barak and Sheffer 2006, 242).

The extent to which this military-industrial complex affects Israeli policy is unclear. The old adage goes that, when all you have is a hammer—and Israel certainly has no shortage of hammers—everything starts to look like a nail. Although this observation would appear relevant, there is scant evidence either for or against the argument that a military-industrial complex like Israel's will drive a nation toward greater hawkishness. However, it is of little doubt that the complex's influence and importance to the greater Israeli economy pressure the state toward a greater defense budget (Mintz 1985, 635). In addition to budgetary effects, the security orientation of the civilian sector, according to Oren Barak and Gabriel Sheffer (2006, 239–240), "considerably influences Israel's foreign policy and global orientation; thus, it has established close relationships with countries such as Singapore, South Africa, Turkey, Slovenia, and, more recently, with China and India, all of which have purchased Israeli weapons, obtained training by Israeli experts, and in certain cases conducted joint research projects with Israel's [defense establishment]." With top military officials in positions of power, a military-trained citizenry, a culture of security, a vast defense industry, and a budget and foreign policy directed by military concerns, it is difficult to see any demilitarization in Israel's near future.

CONCLUSIONS

The role of the military in the politics of Middle Eastern countries has important implications for economic development and for political change (and stasis). On the whole, the prominent and long-lasting role played by the military in Middle Eastern politics has not been beneficial for the economies of the region. Military regimes do not achieve the kind of structural transformation of their economies or the industrial deepening that they invariably announce as their goals. However, the heavy outlays on the military and on war preparedness that their incumbency entails appear to have done little to impede economic growth. The real questions are whether this growth could have been more rapid in the absence of such heavy spending and whether social outcomes could have continued to advance with more resources devoted to sectors such as health and education. It has certainly been the case that direct rule by the military has not enhanced the military performance of the region's armed forces.

The military has been the catalyst, or at least the conduit, for the introduction of advanced technologies into the region. Military industries and research-and-development facilities are often the most advanced industries of their nations, and they have a wide range of civilian applications. It is less clear, however, to what extent these technologies are merely imported or are absorbed into the scientific community. At a more mundane level, and with the major exception of Israel, the armed forces of the Middle East have not been extensively used to teach literacy skills and provide vocational training to their recruits. Because most countries maintain some form of universal conscription and many recruits may come from rural backgrounds, nations have a real opportunity to build their human resources during the years in which their youth are in the ranks, but that opportunity has not been widely seized.

International involvement in the Middle East's regional conflicts and military rule is one of the most salient characteristics setting the Middle East apart from other regions of the world. This involvement has directly contributed to the durability of authoritarian rule and has been a major obstacle to the emergence of more liberal political practices. At the same time, the Arab uprisings proved that harsh repression ultimately cannot deter people from mobilizing, even at great risk to themselves and their families.

The role of the military in the Arab uprisings has shaped political trajectories in tangible ways in countries that experienced mass mobilization during the uprisings. Arguably, military support—or at least tolerance—for anti-incumbent opposition explains why some rulers were toppled while others maintained power. In Tunisia, Egypt, and, to some degree, Yemen, military and security forces abandoned the incumbent and sided with or did not block the protesters, and long-standing dictators were compelled to step down. Where the army and security forces stuck with the incumbent—for example, in Syria and Bahrain—the regime has persisted, at least thus far. The military also shapes the political transition process in important ways. In Tunisia, where the military did not play a key role in politics, opposing political factions of liberals and Islamists negotiated directly with each other, albeit with much difficulty at times. In Egypt, however, these factions largely interfaced with the military, which retained significant power in the system after Mubarak's departure, and therefore the factions were not forced to compromise with each other.

These points raise further questions about why military officers opt to maintain their support for dictators, even in the face of mass protests. Family and personal ties are one part of the explanation. In many MENA countries, rulers stock the top brass positions with close personal associates and often with their own family members. When military and security officials are so closely associated with authoritarian rulers, it is all the more difficult for them to defect—and to be taken seriously as credible political opponents to incumbent rulers. In addition, shared ethnic and religious identities cement ties between dictators and military officers, particularly when one ethnic or sectarian group dominates the state to the exclusion of other groups, as in Syria and Iraq. Yet such ties, whether based on blood, personal connections, or ethno-religious bonds, are rarely sufficient to secure the loyalty of the army and security forces. Access to lucrative economic opportunities is a major inducement for gaining and maintaining the allegiance of military officers and security officials, and that access binds them all the more to corrupt rulers in the eyes of the population.

The Arab uprisings have shown that even brute force cannot deter people from rising up when they feel that their rights and dignity have been violated. Any stereotypes of Arabs or Muslims as the passive and willing subjects of authoritarian rule by now should be discredited. Even in countries with strong military and security forces that are core components of the political settlement, the people have stood up in the face of harsh repression. In the next chapter, we turn to the rise of the "street" in Middle Eastern politics.

NOTES

1. The armed conflict database compiled by the Uppsala Conflict Data Program (UCDP) and the Peace Research Institute Oslo (PRIO) defines conflict as "a contested incompatibility that concerns government and/or territory where the use of armed force between two parties, of which at least one is the government of a state, results in at least 25 battle-related deaths." The Correlates of War ©) database, which covers the period from 1816 to the present, also shows that the MENA has had fewer conflicts than other regions.

2. The lack of data for Iraq biases the estimates for the RRLA group downward.

3. Heydemann (2000) is an exception. See also Blaydes and Chaney (2013), who argue that the nature of military conscription and, more generally, state-society relations under centuries of Ottoman rule actually retarded the development of effective public institutions in what is now much of the Middle East.

4. For a careful and skeptical discussion of the extent of the military's holdings, see Kandil (2012, 182–185).

5. Email communication with Kevan Harris, Associate Director, Mossavar-Rahmani Center for Iran and Persian Gulf Studies, Princeton University, June 26, 2014.

6. Personal communication with Hugh Roberts, Department of History, Tufts University, June 23, 2014.

7. Email communication with Bassam Haddad, Director, Middle East Studies Program, and Associate Professor, Public and International Affairs, George Mason University, July 23, 2014.

11

SOLIDARISM AND ITS ENEMIES: CIVIL SOCIETY AND SOCIAL MOVEMENTS IN THE MIDDLE EAST

Before the Arab uprisings, the Middle East was widely viewed as a bastion of authoritarianism in which populations were too passive—whether for cultural or political reasons—to express their preferences. Some even contended that Arabs and Muslims did not aspire to democratic rule and were not concerned about making their voices heard in the political system (see, inter alia, Huntington 2002; Kedourie 1992, ch. 1).

The uprisings should put these ideas to bed once and for all. Yet even before 2011, this picture of politically quiescent Middle Easterners was misleading. A closer look at the historical record reveals that people in the region had engaged in diverse forms of opposition for years and expressed demands for greater political freedoms and economic security, in both overt and more subtle ways. In the decade before the uprisings, protests had been steadily on the rise. With scholarly attention largely focused on the roots of persistent authoritarianism in the region, however, even specialists largely overlooked or downplayed the public's expressions of discontent.

This lapse is understandable given the robustness of coercive institutions, the formidable tool kit of carrots and sticks available to dictators throughout the region, and international support for Middle Eastern authoritarian rulers. To the extent that the MENA citizenry was relatively passive in the face of the abuses of governing elites, this was likely due in large part to the reality and constant looming threat of repression. In some countries where per capita oil wealth has enabled rulers to distribute generous benefits to citizens, resources are also an important part of the story.

Our framework for understanding the political economies of the Middle East emphasizes the interplay between the state, the economy, and society. In this

FIGURE 11.1. Antigovernment Demonstrations in the MENA Political Economies, 1950–2012

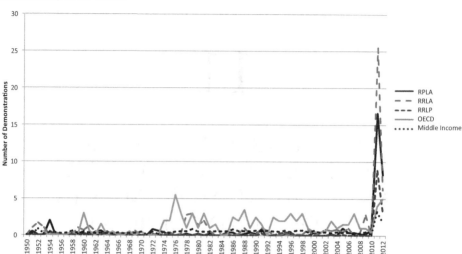

Source: Banks and Wilson (2014).

chapter, we focus on the last leg of this tripartite analytical lens. We first review the record of social mobilization in the region before, during, and after the Arab uprisings. Next, we identify cross-national patterns of social mobilization during the uprisings and offer some tentative and preliminary explanations for them. We then describe the diverse forms of social mobilization within the region, both informal and formal, featuring an array of social actors, both established and relatively new. With the return of the "street" in Middle Eastern politics, these actors have more influence in the political arena—albeit often outside the halls of power.

THE HISTORICAL RECORD:
SOCIAL MOBILIZATION IN THE MIDDLE EAST

The day when Mohamed Bouazizi set himself on fire in December 2010, inadvertently touching off a wave of mass mobilization across the Arab world, did not mark a binary shift in regional politics. Rather, the regional wave of protests that ensued reflected a groundswell of discontent that had increasingly been erupting in antigovernment mobilization throughout the previous decade. Figure 11.1 confirms that while a steep rise in protests began in late 2010, the region was not entirely devoid of political opposition before then, especially since the early 2000s.

The MENA political economy subgroups experienced varied levels of protest that have sometimes exceeded the average for middle-income countries globally. Not surprisingly, the OECD countries, Israel and Turkey, which had more established formal democratic institutions, consistently had the highest levels of social

FIGURE 11.2. Strikes and Other Forms of Protest in Egypt, 1998–2011

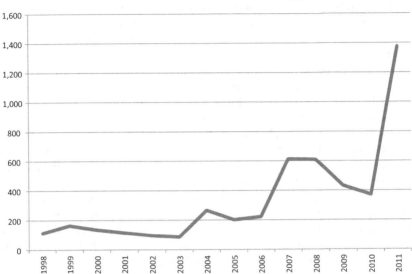

Source: Adapted from Beinin and Duboc (2013), 213–215.

protest before 2010. The RRLA countries, too, experienced notable periods of increased antigovernment mobilization, including the anticolonial struggles of the 1950s, the 1979 Iranian Revolution, the "bread riots" in the late 1970s, early 1980s, and, more recently, the late 2000s. The RPLA countries also exhibited some periods of unrest, most recently from the mid-2000s onward, with growing labor unrest in Egypt and Tunisia. The RRLP countries, many of which did not even exist as independent countries until the late 1960s and early 1970s, consistently had the lowest levels of antigovernment demonstrations.

In all countries, including the relatively quiescent RRLP group, protests increased exponentially in 2010 and 2011. The spike in unrest was most dramatic in the more populous RPLA and RRLA countries, where the uprisings were concentrated, but was also noticeable in the RRLP countries. In all of these country groupings, the levels of protest since 2011 have exceeded the protest levels in the region's two OECD economies and the middle-income average. The case of Egypt illustrates the fallacy of characterizing the region as politically quiescent prior to 2010.[1] Despite heavy state repression and the marginalization of the working classes through market-oriented economic reforms, strikes and other forms of protests were alive and well in Egypt (see Figure 11.2). In the decade prior to the outbreak of mass protests in January 2011, protests were on a steady rise, with a particularly steep upswing from 2007 to 2008 owing to the general strike at the El-Mahalla El-Kubra textile facility (Beinin and Duboc 2013).

In the 2000s, then, mobilization was steadily increasing in Egypt and elsewhere in the region—well before the Arab uprisings. In Egypt, protests broke out in 2004 to call for the end of single-party rule, sparked in part by the upcoming 2005 pres-idential elections and the increasing likelihood that Hosni Mubarak was aiming to transfer power to his son Gamal. These protests were noteworthy not just because of their intensity but also because they marked the first time in over fifty years that political grievances were the sole or primary motivation for mobilization. Of course, these protests, spearheaded by the opposition group Kifaya (or "Enough" in Arabic, the slogan for the Egyptian Movement for Change), reached their targeted scale, with only about 2,500 protesters (El-Mahdi 2009, 1012–1014).

In Tunisia, protests erupted in the southern region of Gafsa in January 2008 after the state-owned phosphate company announced the results of a recruitment competition, which were widely viewed as fraudulent. Job candidates who failed to secure employment at the factory as well as representatives from the national labor union, the General Confederation of Tunisian Workers (UGTT), claimed that the firm's selection process was opaque and nepotistic. The demonstrations rapidly spread to include local residents—who protested against unemployment, poverty, increased living costs, and corruption—and relatives of miners injured or killed while working at the company (Amnesty International 2009). Note that in the two countries where the Arab uprisings began, protests were already growing and gathering strength in the preceding decade.

MASS MOBILIZATION DURING THE ARAB UPRISINGS

As many of the chapters in this volume have shown, people in the Middle East have plenty of causes for their grievances, which were an important background condition for the Arab uprisings and for earlier episodes of social mobilization in these countries. Economic conditions were a key driver of the protests. Rising food prices, long-term unemployment (especially among youth), low wages, high infla-tion, inequality, and the lack of opportunities for social mobility were major factors contributing to discontent. Political grievances, such as routine police brutality and torture, corruption, and repression, were also important. However, with the partial exception of the 2008 global recession, which spread to the region, and a global spike in food prices, these economic and political factors have been present for a long time, and it has long been established that grievances are an insufficient explanation for mass mobilization (McAdam 1982). Economic and political factors do not in and of themselves explain why people rise up, especially at great risk to themselves and their families.

Understanding Mass Mobilization

If macroeconomic and political grievances can offer only limited explanations for the outbreak of large-scale demonstrations across the Arab region, then what can more fully explain these mass protests? The literature on social movements offers some insights into the dynamics of mass mobilization, although often these expla-nations are so all-encompassing that they stop short of a testable theory. Given the complexity of mass mobilization and the impossibility of pinpointing a single factor to explain why people rose up after years of discontent in Tunisia, Egypt, and across the Arab world, however, this generates useful insights.

Classic approaches to understanding social movements emphasize three factors: political opportunities, movement resources, and framing, or how people perceive the issues at stake (McAdam, Tarrow, and Tilly 2001). Political opportunities are openings in the political environment that shake up the status quo. These may come in the form of wars, international political agreements, prolonged unemployment, widespread demographic changes, or other factors that can lead to a realignment of existing power relations. In the case of the Arab uprisings, we might view the declining standards of living, rising real and perceived inequality and corruption, and other macroeconomic and political factors as providing a political opportunity for mass mobilization. True to their name, political opportunities only provide the opportunity for the emergence of mass collective action; they do not actually spur action. In fact, they very often come and go without any effect. Critics rightfully maintain that the concept of political opportunities is vague. More recent approaches emphasize "perceived collective threats"—instances when groups of people believe that they face common risks or dangers and have the capacity to confront them together—rather than objective opportunities per se (Beinin and Vairel 2013, 9).

Compared with political opportunities, it is easier to see how movement resources facilitate large-scale collective action. Without resources, people cannot act—even when they want to or have the opportunity to do so. Resources that facilitate mobilization come in diverse forms. They include leadership and members—who tend to be recruited from established social networks—as well as money and means of communication. Much has been made of the importance of social media and satellite television in the Arab uprisings, as many of the central activists in the Tunisian and Egyptian uprisings were active on Facebook and Twitter. These new forms of media facilitated the spread of ideas, helped to coordinate collective action among disparate individuals, and may have provided a mechanism, or at least a catalyst, for the diffusion of protest throughout the Arab world. Although the role of social media in spurring the uprisings has been exaggerated, Facebook and Twitter certainly helped some activists mobilize others and coordinate their actions. When asked how he learned about the demonstrations at Kasbah Square in Tunis, where tens of thousands of protesters had gathered, a taxi driver told one of us, "Facebook, of course!" To sustain a mass movement, however, requires real—not virtual—resources. This is all the more true when many people lack access to the Internet and are illiterate.

Whether people decide to take to the streets depends to a large degree on how the issues at the center of their grievances are "framed," or presented. In social movement theory parlance, "frames" are "shared understandings of the world . . . that legitimate and motivate collective action," and they are often the product of conscious strategic action by organizers or individuals (McAdam, McCarthy, and Zald 1996, 6). When frames resonate, they are more likely to motivate people to join protests and other forms of collective action. Furthermore, as some argue, people are more likely to join social movements when they experience "cognitive liberation," that is, a shift in their perceptions of the situation such that they come to *believe* in the potential efficacy of the movement. Simply put, people need to believe that they can bring about change. Arguably, this is an important piece of the puzzle in explaining both the emergence of mass mobilization and the ways in which politics in Middle Eastern countries has changed. Thanks to the social mobilization spurred by Mohamed Bouazizi's self-immolation in Sidi Bouzid, a barrier has been broken: people are no longer fearful of their governments—or, at least, they are less fearful. Neuroscience may also explain why Middle Easterners risked their lives en masse to oppose their dictators: emotions, ranging from anger to joy and pride, may have helped people overcome concerns about their personal safety to engage in resistance (Pearlman 2013).

Whether or not one subscribes to the complex framework undergirding social movement theory, it is clear that mass mobilization involves the interplay of multiple factors at the individual, community, and societal levels. Yet economic and political grievances are a crucial backdrop to the complicated processes that ultimately compel individuals to join together in opposition to their governments at great risk to themselves.

Patterns of Protest in the Arab Uprisings

Mass social mobilization in the Arab uprisings ultimately led to the overthrow of dictators in Tunisia, Egypt, and, with the help of international intervention, Libya. Elsewhere, large-scale social protests became the foundations of sustained opposition or pro-reform movements and have altered the nature of politics in enduring ways, even if incumbent rulers remain in place. In still other countries, demonstrations and similar forms of opposition did not occur on a mass scale.

Figure 11.3 depicts occurrences of antigovernment demonstrations across the MENA countries in 2011, the first year of the uprisings. The highest levels of protest occurred in Syria, Yemen, Egypt, and Bahrain. Although Tunisia, the birthplace of the uprisings, experienced significantly lower levels of unrest, its path toward political reform has had its ups and downs, and the country has seen dangerous levels of political polarization and the assassinations of two prominent critics of Islamist groups. Nevertheless, Tunisia ultimately benefited from the decisions of leaders across the political and ideological spectra to set up a relatively institutionalized process to guide the political transition.

A clear pattern emerges from Figure 11.3: on average, the RRLP countries witnessed far lower levels of protest than the RPLA and RRLA countries.[2] Clearly, per capita oil wealth is an important part of this story. Economic benefits facilitated by natural resource wealth help to ensure that citizens have less incentive to oppose their rulers in the first place, and these benefits also undercut emerging opposition movements once they start to take root. Oil is not the whole story, however, as seen in Libya and Bahrain and as attested by rising dissent in Saudi Arabia, the United Arab Emirates, and other wealthy oil exporters.

Of course, social mobilization cannot simply be reduced to the economic factors that constitute the focus of part of this. For instance, differences in underlying

FIGURE 11.3. Antigovernment Demonstrations in the MENA Region, 2011

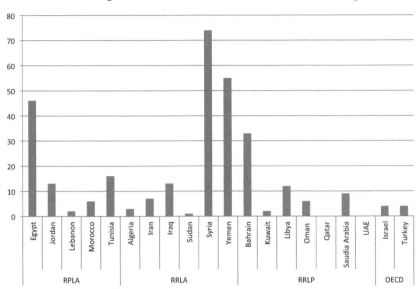

Source: Banks and Wilson (2014).

political settlements have played a significant role. In some countries, rulers have, at least to a limited extent, forged broader social coalitions that help to protect them from full-scale insurrection. This partially explains why Jordan and Morocco witnessed more limited protests (Yom and Gause 2012).

The uprisings have been far more intense in single-party republics than in monarchies, suggesting that regime type may have been a factor in the strength of the uprisings. The heads of state in republics are generally more concerned with engineering hereditary succession because, unlike monarchies, the formal rules of the system do not officially permit them to hand over power to their sons. (Thus far, no Middle Eastern ruler has signaled that he will pass the mantle to a daughter.) Such blatant manipulations of the formal rules can incite dissent, especially when regimes do not deliver and are ideologically bankrupt, compelling republican rulers to crack down. Given their comparatively secure positions, the Jordanian and Moroccan kings have tolerated more political dissent than the single-party republics, as long as it does not question the legitimacy of the monarchy itself.

But regime type does not satisfactorily explain the variation in the extent and nature of the uprisings in the Arab countries (Yom and Gause 2012). After all, like many single-party republics, the Gulf monarchs maintain far more closed political systems than their Jordanian and Moroccan counterparts. That the protest movements in Jordan and Morocco did not reach the same scale as in the republics can, in part, be explained by the political lessons learned by the kings of these two countries. After watching the uprisings play out in Tunisia, Egypt, and other countries, they learned quickly that brute force could backfire. As a result, they adopted a more conciliatory approach by granting at least superficial concessions to take the wind out of the sails of potential mass mobilization. Finally, the Gulf monarchies have faced less opposition than the poorer monarchies of Jordan and Morocco thanks to their more extensive per capita natural resource rents, which help them to both preempt and repress potential dissenters. A glaring exception is Bahrain (discussed later).

As we discuss in the next section, the distinct political contexts of the MENA countries can also help explain why the uprisings played out in such varied ways. In the countries where mass demonstrations erupted, different patterns of protest developed, and even the substance of demands has varied from one country to the next.

The Specifics and the Time Line of the Arab Uprisings

The Arab uprisings began in Tunisia in December 2010, spread to Egypt in January 2011, and subsequently erupted in Morocco, Jordan, and across much of the region, including Saudi Arabia. In total, nineteen countries were affected by the wave of protests, albeit to varying degrees (Holmes 2012, 391). In Bahrain, Yemen, Libya, and Syria, authorities responded with particularly intense violence against peaceful demonstrations, and in the latter two countries armed groups became increasingly dominant in the opposition, overshadowing peaceful resistance movements. Anti-government protests also broke out in Iraq, Lebanon, and Palestine, though their dynamics were distinct partly because the governing authorities of these countries are highly fragmented, complicating efforts by activists to focus their demands.

In Tunisia, antigovernment demonstrations were initiated in the South and quickly spread to the capital and elsewhere, with protesters calling for the overthrow of Zine El Abidine Ben Ali. After Mohamed Bouazizi lit himself on fire on December 17, 2010, family members and friends led initial protests that soon spread throughout rural areas toward the coast. By the end of December, protests had spread to Tunis, supported by networks of unemployed graduates, activists, and local branches of the national trade union. Neither Ben Ali's appeals for calm and offers of reform nor repeated police crackdowns managed to quell the protests. On January 14, 2011, senior army officers stepped in, informing Ben Ali and his wife that they had a three-hour window to depart the country. While an initial government was formed under former prime minister Mohamed Ghannouchi, repeated protests targeted his ties to the previous regime and the continued presence of key officials from the ruling Democratic Constitutional Rally (RCD). When Ghannouchi ultimately stepped down on February 27, 2011, an interim government was formed under former lawyer Béji Caid Essebsi.

On January 25, 2011, just ten days after Ben Ali fled Tunisia, thousands of protesters gathered in Cairo's Tahrir Square to demonstrate against poverty and political repression in Egypt, demanding higher minimum wages, reform of the country's security and political institutions, and term limits for the Egyptian presidency. Initial protests were promoted by online activists and political organizations such as the April 6th Youth Movement and the Egyptian Movement for Change (*Kifya*), as well as by more established opposition parties such as the El-Ghad and

Al-Karama Parties. Although other key groups and figures—such as the Muslim Brotherhood and Nobel Laureate Mohamed ElBaradei—kept their distance from the initial protests, the initial success of the demonstrations secured their backing for a much larger rally three days later.

Protests quickly spread throughout Egypt, with mass demonstrations in Alexandria, Suez, Aswan, and various cities and towns of the Nile Delta. As Egyptian security forces employed increasingly harsh tactics—shutting off access to phone and Internet traffic, firing on protesters, encouraging gangs of armed thugs to attack crowds—demonstrators dug in, transforming major open areas like Tahrir Square into tent cities of prolonged sit-in demonstrations. Throughout these events, Egypt's army remained neutral, with commanding officers claiming that they would not fire on protesters despite wide deployment of tanks and soldiers. Mubarak repeatedly refused to step down, even in the face of protests estimated in the millions and appeals to do so from the United States, Germany, France, and the United Nations. Instead, Mubarak reshuffled the cabinet (now under Mubarak loyalist and former general Ahmed Shafik), offered some political reforms, and promised to step down the following September—even as he cautioned that Egypt was "not yet ready for democracy." After a final, defiant speech on February 10, Mubarak resigned the following day, heading for Sharm el-Sheikh with his family as the Supreme Council of the Armed Forces (SCAF) assumed power.

By the middle of January 2011, protests had begun in parts of Yemen.[3] Demands focused on economic stagnation, government corruption, and the consolidation of regime power that ran counter to promised reforms. Early protests adopted the styles, slogans, and rhetoric used in other protests across the Arab countries. Demonstrators shouted, "The people want the overthrow of the regime!" (*al-sha'ab yurid isqat al-nizam!*) and established a tent city in which solidarity and egalitarianism prevailed—secular socialists shared space with conservative Islamists, women and men chewed *qat* together, and tribal rivals shared tents (Vom Bruk, Alwazir, and Wiaceck 2013, 290). But Yemen's movement took a violent turn on March 18, when rooftop snipers, assumed to be government forces, shot and killed fifty-two demonstrators (Fattah 2011). Though President Ali Abdullah Saleh denied his involvement, major regime defections soon occurred—most notably, the powerful General Ali Mohsen. With these defections, what started as a peaceful popular movement was soon hijacked by elite infighting, factionalism, and violence.

Yemen faced deepened fissures as the uprising continued. The Islamist Al-Islah, the dominant party of the formal opposition coalition known as the Joint Meeting Parties (JMP), gradually gained control over the protest movement, while powerful tribal elites sought to benefit politically from Saleh's vulnerability. Power struggles between the president and elite factions made parts of the capital, Sana'a, a war zone (Fattah 2011). In the North and the South, secessionist rebels expanded their military campaigns. Meanwhile, taking advantage of the chaos, Al-Qaeda in the Arabian Peninsula (AQAP) and its affiliates increased their presence, particularly in the South. Ultimately, with the country facing further chaos, the Gulf Cooperation Council (GCC), and later the United Nations, persuaded Saleh to sign an agreement, accepting resignation in exchange for immunity (Vom Bruk, Alwazir, and Wiaceck 2013). Although power was successfully transferred in early 2012 to the consensus candidate, Vice President Abd Rabbuh Mansur Hadi, Yemen remains divided, with large portions controlled by tribal alliances, if not by outright opponents of the state. Significant barriers remain for the establishment of democratic institutions, while the 2014 National Dialogue Conference, which successfully integrated the diverse opposition groups into a singular discussion and took steps toward addressing key problems facing the country, has not yet forged a way out of the political impasse (Gaston 2014).

In early 2011, the wave of protests spread to Bahrain, a country with a longer history of activism than most other Gulf monarchies. Against a backdrop of youth unemployment, government corruption, inequality largely structured along sectarian lines, and stagnant political reform, the initial protests were relatively small. However, the violent suppression by government forces, which resulted in the deaths of two protesters, ignited a broader wave of mass mobilization, escalating the cycle of demonstrations and violent repression. On February 25, in an unprecedented level of societal mobilization, about one-third of all Bahraini citizens marched to the Pearl Roundabout in Manama in solidarity with the protest movement (Ulrichsen 2014, 337).

Though initial demonstrations largely transcended sectarian divisions, government fearmongering about Iranian conspiracies fomenting Shiite uprisings began to divide the movement. On March 14, the GCC, led by Saudi Arabia, sent armed forces across the King Fahd Causeway into Bahrain to assist the monarchy and crush the protests. The following day, a state of national emergency was declared. With a Sunni-only military, heavily reinforced by recruits from other countries, the violent clampdown continued. For a brief time, the state's tactics achieved their objective. By the summer of 2011, the protests had subsided, and a national dialogue was held in July to address grievances; many felt, however, that the gesture and the resultant reforms were empty. The situation is far from resolved, and the grievances that motivated the initial protests remain. In February 2012, renewed protests were followed by yet another crackdown. Two months later, more protests began, this time against the decision to host the Formula One Grand Prix in Bahrain.

Even the most repressive authoritarian regimes have proved not to be immune to protest in the wave of Arab uprisings. On March 13, 2011, teenagers in the rural town of Daraa in Syria spray-painted the slogan of the uprisings, *al-sha'ab yurid isqat al-nizam* ("The people want the overthrow of the regime!"), on a number of walls. In response, the young men were arrested and tortured by Assad's powerful security apparatus. Several days later, four people were killed when security forces opened fire on family members peacefully demonstrating for the boys' release. The events of March 18 launched a cycle of demonstrations, harsh regime responses, and further demonstrations in Syria. The demonstrations began in the economically neglected and drought-ridden rural areas.[4] They then spread to include urban areas such as Homs and Hama. The demands of protesters quickly evolved from grievances related to local issues to more far-reaching and sensitive political demands such as calls for the ouster of an unpopular governor, an end to emergency law, and, ultimately, Assad's removal (Noueihed and Warren 2012, 227). The regime refused to address these demands, dismissing them as the product of foreign conspiracies.

In response to repeated violent crackdowns on the peaceful opposition movements that had sprung up across the country, some opposition groups took up arms and the spiral of violence intensified. Although sectarian divisions are not the root cause of the conflict, they have become increasingly salient as the conflict has progressed. Sunni members of the armed forces, including officers, began to defect, while Alawi officers typically remained loyal (Noueihed and Warren 2012, 231–232). In July 2011, a group of army defectors formed the Free Syrian Army, which became a major player in the resultant civil war, although it has since been eclipsed by other actors, particularly Islamist extremist groups such as the al-Nusra Front and the Islamic State of Iraq and the Levant (ISIL, or the "Islamic State," as it now refers to itself). In August, the Syrian National Council was established as an opposition coalition based in Istanbul; however, it has been plagued from internal divisions and has failed thus far to unify the opposition as its supporters had hoped. As the cycle of demonstrations, repressions, and clashes escalated, Syria descended into a destructive civil war with a humanitarian crisis of enormous proportions.

In February 2011, protests erupted in Libya in response to the arrest of Fathi Terbil, a lawyer representing the families of the more than 1,000 people killed in the 1996 Abu Salim Prison massacre. The demonstrations were quickly, and violently, quashed. But this did not stop others in marginalized parts of the country from rising up to call for an end to Muammar Gaddafi's repressive regime. As the demonstrations continued and violence by both regime and opposition forces escalated, major military officials soon began to defect from a regime that had sidelined them and often marginalized their regions of origin in the distribution of resources. With mounting defections and the formation of the rebel National Transitional Council (NTC), the country was quickly plunged into a chaotic civil war. Organized rebel forces and militias, some Islamist, as well as organized government forces and loyalist militias battled over the control of territory across the country, with rebel forces holding greater sway in the previously marginalized East (McQuinn 2012).

On March 17, the UN Security Council responded to the ongoing violence with Resolution 1973, establishing a no-fly zone and an operation for intervention. Officially under NATO control, the international intervention shifted the balance of power, ultimately enabling the disparate rebel factions to defeat the regime.[5] On September 16, the UN recognized the NTC as the legitimate government of Libya, despite the fact that it remained unable to exert control over all of the rebel groups. On October 20, a NATO bombing of a train facilitated the capture and subsequent murder of Gaddafi by rebel forces (Gazzini 2011). Much of the country remains controlled by militias of varying allegiances, as groups that fought in the civil war, opportunistic militias that emerged post-Gaddafi, and former Gaddafi loyalists all continue to vie for influence.

Morocco and Jordan have also experienced protest movements, although not as widespread and long-lived as elsewhere, especially in Morocco. In both countries, protesters' demands were more focused on reforming the system than on overthrowing the monarchy. In Morocco, the protests were organized by the February 20 Movement, which was named after the date in 2011 when thousands of Moroccans marched on the capital to demand constitutional reform and greater attention to economic and social problems. Demonstrations were held in Casablanca, Marrakesh, and Tangiers, while many other smaller cities also experienced unrest. Protests continued through 2012, although the number of participants declined over time. In response to the initial wave of demonstrations, King Mohammed VI announced the formation of a commission to work on constitutional reforms, which were approved by a referendum in July 2011. The reforms placed some formal constraints on the king's power and stipulated that the prime minister be appointed by the party with the plurality of seats in parliament, among other changes. In practice, however, the monarchy remains the most powerful actor in the system (Benchemsi 2012). The state's proactive response to the demonstrations as well as the heterogeneous nature of the February 20 Movement help to explain why the protests fizzled (Desrues 2013).

In January 2011, demonstrations erupted in Amman and other cities in Jordan, and they have continued sporadically since then. Among those participating in the protests were the Muslim Brotherhood, leftist groups, trade unionists, and student groups. As in Morocco, protesters' demands generally focused on social and economic issues and called for constitutional reform but not the overthrow of the monarchy. In response, the Jordanian king, like his Moroccan counterpart, defused the protests by offering concessions. Repeated cabinet reshufflings and the sacking of multiple prime ministers have elicited jokes about the "revolving door" nature of ministerial positions in Jordan. Other Arab countries have experienced protests and online activism as part of the wave of uprisings sweeping across the region, albeit on a smaller scale.

Protests also took place in the non-Arab countries of the Middle East. In mid-2011, mass demonstrations erupted in Israel, touching off the largest protest movement in the country's history (Gordon 2012, 1). The Israeli social justice protests can be seen as one manifestation of global social protests and a precursor to the "Occupy" protests in the United States and elsewhere. Although the dynamics of Israel's protests were quite different from the uprisings in nearby Arab countries, owing to its distinct political and social context, protesters shared the common concerns about social justice being heard throughout the Middle East. The protests began in July 2011 when a young woman was evicted from her apartment in Tel Aviv. Outraged over Israel's rising housing prices, she erected a tent in Tel Aviv's Rothschild Boulevard and created a Facebook group as a site for cyber-mobilization on the issue. Others encampments soon sprang up in major towns and cities across Israel. Although the social justice concerns of protesters varied—from the rising cost of living to general income inequality—their demands came under the banner of the common chant: "the people demand social justice."

Composed mostly of young, educated adults from middle-class backgrounds (Rosenhek and Shalev 2013), the protesters insisted on greater government intervention to address social justice, but they shied away from overtly political or anti-neoliberal sentiments. Rather, in a political culture dominated by the

Israeli-Palestinian conflict and fear of the Arab world, the protesters embedded their rhetoric in appeals to Zionism and national unity (Gordon 2012). Despite broad support for the movement—by some estimates amounting to 90 percent of the general public (Gordon 2012, 1)—its demands failed to elicit concrete results, and after sporadic protests, it largely died down after a few months. The protests did not produce immediate economic and social reforms, but their demands for social justice may have laid the groundwork for further mobilization.

In 2013, Turkey witnessed a mass protest movement of its own. The Gezi Park protests, Turkey's own brand of uprising, started in late May when a small demonstration against the demolition of a park to make way for a shopping mall was met with excessive police force. Other people, largely educated youth from middle- and working-class backgrounds, soon joined the demonstrations, united in their opposition to the growing heavy-handedness of Prime Minister Recep Tayyip Erdogan and the AKP government. Occupying the park and nearby Taksim Square, the çapulcu—a term for looters used derogatorily by Prime Minister Erdogan and later appropriated by the protesters—often clashed with police forces trying to clear the area. Within the park, a sense of utopianism abounded, with solidarity between activist groups of all sorts—feminists, LGBT activists, students, Kurdish, and Alevi, to name a few (Holmes 2013; Yörük 2014).

The Gezi Park protest came on the heels of a year that had been marked by a sharp increase in activism among these groups and represented a uniquely broad coalition of demonstrators, many of whom felt disillusioned with the AKP, which they had hoped would represent a break from the authoritarianism of its predecessors (Yörük 2014). By the end of the summer of 2013, however, the protests had begun to die out, though sporadic demonstrations continue to this day. Ultimately, major demonstrations took place in all but two of the country's eighty-one provinces, with participation from over 12 percent of the entire country's population (Yörük 2014, 424). The intensity of the protests marked a major challenge to Erdogan and the AKP and created a lasting legacy in the country's history of social mobilization.

Two years before the Arab uprisings, Iran witnessed its own mass opposition movement. The Iranian Green Movement was one of many revolutionary movements, including the color revolutions of Eastern Europe and the former Soviet Union, that influenced Tunisians, Egyptians, and other Arabs in the 2011 uprisings (Kurzman 2012, 162). In 2009 social mobilization filled the streets of Iran at a level that had not been seen since the revolution thirty years before. The 2009 election pitted the reformist Mir-Hossein Mousavi, who espoused the rhetoric of rule of law, democratic reform, and civil and political freedoms, against the hard-line incumbent Mahmoud Ahmadinejad. Despite Mousavi's recently found popularity, which seemed to predict a close election, the results of the June 12 election were announced as a landslide in Ahmadinejad's favor: 64 percent to Mousavi's 34 percent (Ehsani, Keshavarzian, and Moruzzi 2009).

Protesters' cries of "Where is my vote?" soon filled the streets. From fairer elections, the demands soon turned, more generally, toward greater civil and political liberties, government reform, and an end to authoritarian rule (Harris 2012, 442). Educated youth from middle-class backgrounds appear to have played a prominent role in the protests that ensued, but neither class definitions nor the urban-rural divide accurately depict the Green Movement's participants, particularly in its early days (Bayat 2009; Harris 2012, 436). Demonstrations stayed strong through the end of June, despite the regime's harsh repression tactics, including beatings, sniper fire, and the arrest and torture of movement leaders (Harris 2012, 437). As time wore on, however, the crackdown took its toll. Ultimately, the Green Movement retreated from the streets for the most part, evolving into the Green Path of Hope Coalition. Despite its abatement, the Green Movement remains a watershed moment in Iran's recent history, as a popular movement for democratic reform that demanded change from an increasingly divided regime.

FORMAL AND INFORMAL MODES OF COLLECTIVE ACTION IN THE MIDDLE EAST

The protesters who rose up against repressive, authoritarian rule in the Arab countries in 2010 and 2011 and in Iran in 2009 took great risks in the face of the formidable coercive apparatuses in place across the Middle East states. Yet civil society was never entirely absent in the region, despite the state's co-optation of associations, political parties, and other types of organizations. True, in most MENA countries formal groups were often suppressed, manipulated by rulers, or forced to function as little more than empty shells. But the mass mobilizations during and after the uprisings, whether as individuals or under the banner of established and new civic associations, belie this image of societal docility under authoritarian rule. For example, in Tunisia, one of the most restrictive political environments in the region, activists from civil society groups quickly mobilized during the uprisings to call for the overthrow of Ben Ali. Similarly, in contemporary Syria and in Iraq after the fall of Saddam Hussein, the rapid emergence of local committees, parties, and other formal and informal associations shows that the social fabric was alive and well even under highly repressive dictatorships.

The picture of a quiescent civil society in the Middle East derives in part from defining civil society in a way that privileges formal, secular associations and in part from overlooking the myriad ways in which people across the region have organized collectively. For decades, the people of the Middle East have engaged in diverse forms of solidarism, both formal and informal. Here we review some of the key forms of social mobilization and the civil society associations that operated before, during, and after the uprisings.

Religion and Ethnicity

Common stereotypes of the Middle East hold that religion and ethnicity are the primary forms of social and political organization. Some of the obstacles to new forms of social organization, such as parties, unions, and other such civic associations, have lain in the older forms of social and political insurance—clans, ethnic groups, tribes, religious sects—whose purposes include protecting their members from the vagaries of powerful states and markets (Clark and Salloukh 2013; Kingston 2013;

Migdal 1987). To see these forms as atavistic is to lose sight of their redefined roles and the political interests they embody in the new state systems of the contemporary Middle East.

One trap we must avoid is that of seeing older forms of political organization and action as direct reenactments of their forebears. Tribes and tribal loyalty in the twenty-first-century Middle East are qualitatively different from their seventeenth- or eighteenth-century antecedents. So, too, are sects, ethnic groups, families, and coteries. The degree of state and market penetration into all sectors of Middle Eastern society has changed momentously—economic subsistence is a thing of the past, as is political isolation. Central authorities are now able to make effective claims on ever-growing proportions of societies' wealth, but they tend to do so in arbitrary and sometimes punitive ways. Markets, having captured large producing populations, do not behave predictably. And for those who play the national political game, the stakes are high, with death, torture, imprisonment, exile, or, at best, forced retirement as probable outcomes.

Parties and formal associations have not yet provided effective means to protect members from the new order, and so people retreat into, or invent, "security groups" to protect themselves and promote their interests. One may find in a small band of friends or members of one's tribe, ethnic group, home region, or religious sect a framework for mutual support, accountability, shared obligations, or plain psychological reassurance that no formal organization can offer. Robert Putnam (1993) has termed these small-group resources "social capital." The more people adhere to these unrecognized, loosely organized forms of political and social action, the more the formal associations and political parties lose their cohesion and viability. Leaders have so far reacted in one or both of two ways: beating the political fragments into submission, and abandoning solidarism and trying to manipulate them through state patronage.

One form of social organization in Middle East politics is the congeries of small and non-exclusive units that have varying degrees of cohesion and durability (Bill and Springborg 1994, 84–135). Throughout the area we find political and economic actors associating with small clusters of cronies of similar status. The members of these groups help each other along in their careers, for it is likely that at any given time some will be doing better than others and will be in a position to promote the interests of the less fortunate. People from the same village or region, or perhaps from the same university class, or people who are of common descent or related through marriage may come together in such groups. Whether it takes the form of Iran's *dawrehs* (circles) or Egypt's *shillas,* cronyism is an important form of political and economic insurance.

We often hear of clans in Middle Eastern politics. Sometimes we find fairly persistent coteries at the elite level, such as the Oujda Group in Algeria, but these groupings are fragile and power struggles within them can be brutal. Several members of Egypt's Revolutionary Command Council (RCC), which seized power in 1952, were classmates in the staff college in the late 1930s and served together in various postings and in the 1948 war with Israel. Over the years after 1952, members dropped away in disgrace, exile, or early retirement.

The Tikriti clan in Saddam Hussein's Iraq and the Alawi clan in Syria are also cited as the true power centers in the politics of these countries at certain periods. Unlike the Algerian and Egyptian examples, these clans combine cronyism with common regional and sectarian loyalties. Moreover, both Saddam Hussein and Hafiz al-Assad to some extent surrounded themselves with confidants from their own lineages. When violent change in governing elites occurred in Iraq in 2003, the new incumbents—first the Americans, and then the Shi'ite- and Kurdish-dominated Iraqi government—sought to ferret out all real or suspected members of the Tikriti clan. President Nouri al-Maliki's increasing marginalization of Sunnis in his government is credited with spurring rebellion and facilitating the rise of Islamist groups such as the ISIL in sections of Iraq. The Syrian Alawis have drawn the logical conclusion that they would certainly lose their privileged status and probably meet a bloody fate should regime change come to Syria. This realization makes them cling to power all the more tenaciously.

Ethnic and sectarian identity and conflict have vexed Middle Eastern leaders as much as they have fascinated outside observers (Cammett 2014; Esman and Rabinovich 1988; Haddad 2011; Khoury and Kostiner 1990; Makdisi 2000; Weiss 2010). Communalism and sectarianism have been viewed in the modernization literature as anachronisms that will slowly erode in the face of economic development, literacy, and nation building (see, for example, Lerner 1959). As any observer of the persistence of racial discrimination in the United States knows, however, issues of blood, skin color, and creed do not always respond to treatment through public policy.

The major corporatist experiments, which aimed to organize citizens as workers or peasants rather than as members of different "primordial" communities, have to some extent foundered on the rocks of ethnic and sectarian loyalties. As early as 1926, Atatürk confronted a Kurdish rebellion with Islamic overtones in eastern Anatolia that represented the first major challenge to the new secular, republican regime. In Egypt, Nasser was challenged by the Muslim Brotherhood in 1954 and 1965. Coptic Christian and Muslim confrontations became commonplace in Egypt during the Sadat era, and eventually Muslim extremists assassinated him. Bourguiba had to back away from his own secularizing proclivities early on, and despite Ben Ali's harsh crackdown, Tunisia still has active and well-organized Islamist movements today. Lebanon was nearly destroyed as a nation, ostensibly by sectarian strife, although a deeper look at the issues at stake shows that the war and the ongoing tensions should not be reduced to religious motivations. Today Iraqi Shi'as, Sunnis, and Kurds engage in mutual massacres, kidnappings, torture, and assassinations, and the Syrian conflict has taken on increasingly sectarian overtones as it has intensified. Ethnic strife has plagued Sudan throughout its history as an independent state.

The issues become murky when sects or ethnic groups overlap with relative wealth or deprivation. Lebanese Shi'a were the underclass in Lebanon's economy until the post–civil war period, while Maronites formed the core of the business elite (Nasr 1985). Oriental Jews in Israel were in a situation similar to that of the Shi'as in Lebanon. In North Yemen in the early 1960s, Shi'a tribesmen fought

Sunni townsmen, and in 1986 South Yemeni Marxists fought among themselves along clan lines. At least since Ottoman times until 2003, Iraqi Shi'as were economically deprived and politically marginalized. A multidimensional overlap of ethnic origin, distinctive language, shared sect, geographic location, and common economic way of life makes the ethno-sectarian issue particularly intractable and difficult to reduce to identity-based motivations alone.

More often than not, the stakes of ostensibly ethnic or religious conflict are not clear-cut. Ethnic and sectarian groups may not be geographically fixed or separate, there may be considerable degrees of inequality among their members, and they may share important characteristics with majority populations, such as language (Shi'ite Arabs in Iraq) or religion (Muslim Berbers in North Africa). The result is a multidimensional set of actors. It is hard to know at any point which factor is driving the actors—ethnicity, region, religion, or class status. Even the Israeli-Palestinian conflict, which is depicted in popular accounts as the product of religious animosities, is at its core a struggle over land and resources.

Ethnicity and sectarianism should be seen as resources that can be drawn upon when they best suit the needs of an individual or a group, and they are often manipulated by political leaders to consolidate or increase their power. The political salience of these social identities is not constant. When communal tensions run high, when clans are settling scores, or when sectarian or ethnic witch hunts are under way, individuals cannot shed the ethnic or sectarian labels with which they were born, and so the political importance of these identities may be greater. In calmer times, however, individuals may as easily act in accordance with their occupations or their material interests. "Identity politics" is a political strategy, not an immutable force.

The Kurds and the non-Muslim populations of southern Sudan have long sought regional autonomy, at a minimum; ultimately, they would prefer to opt out of existing systems as sovereign states. Although the goal of independence was not shared by all Kurds or by all southern Sudanese, these communities and their leadership have gained little from the Iraqi and Sudanese regimes. Since the overthrow of Saddam Hussein—and to some degree before then—the Kurds have set up their own de facto separate state in northern Iraq, which is the most stable part of that country at present, while in 2011 South Sudan opted for independence.

In contrast, most ethnic dissidence arises from efforts to opt *into* existing political systems—violence or its threat are used to extract more resources (roads, schools, clinics, industrial projects, and so forth) from the central authorities. Even though the Turkish authorities give no recognition to their Kurdish minority, they have nonetheless invested heavily in dams, hydropower projects, and agricultural schemes in the Kurdish heartland. The Kurds of the Islamic Republic of Iran have also tried to fight for a more favored position in the newly established republic. Similarly, the Berbers of Algeria and Morocco have confronted the central authorities to enhance their position in the political establishment and to draw more resources to their home regions. At the same time, in both Algeria and Morocco, many Berbers enjoy elite status and have prominent roles in the state technocracy, party leadership, and officers' corps. The interests of North African Berbers are not homogeneous, and for that very reason there has never been a unified Berber front, much less a movement, to opt out of existing political systems (see Gellner and Micaud 1972; Roberts 1982, 1983).

When religious identity is invoked, it tends to take two forms. First, religious minorities generally adopt a defensive posture as they seek guarantees of some degree of legitimacy and freedom of practice within the majority society. Some minorities have not fared well, notably the Baha'is in Iran. Historically in the Middle East, the most violent repression of a religious minority was that of the Armenians in Turkey at the beginning of the twentieth century, and since 1948, when the state of Israel was founded, Jewish minorities in the Arab countries have experienced varying degrees of repression, even though the right to practice their religion has never been questioned. The second form of religious identity is that taken by religious movements within the dominant Islamic majority. Here the objective is to transform existing political systems and force them, either from without or from within, to adhere to the Sharia and Islamic principles (see Chapter 12).

In summary, no sectarian or ethnic group can be analyzed or understood within its own terms of reference. At stake in every instance are conundrums such as how to distribute scarce resources, or avoid making concessions that might jeopardize national unity, or respond to minority demands without calling the regime's legitimacy into question. Just as sectarian and ethnic groups are the enemies of corporatist solidarity, so, too, are they often the enemies of class formation and consciousness. Sectarianism and ethnicity more often than not cut across class lines. No corporatist or class-based organization has succeeded in fully co-opting or defanging ethnic and sectarian groups. Until national political systems can provide institutions and rules of political conduct that are reliable and respected, such groups will continue to act as buffers against the arbitrary use of state power.

Finally, minorities have the pesky habit of living on strategic real estate: Iraq's Kurds live in an important oil-bearing region of their country, while Saudi Arabia's Shi'a live predominantly in the oil-rich Eastern Province; so, too, South Sudan sits on important oil reserves and controls the headwaters of the White Nile. Central authorities almost always suspect strategically located minorities of colluding with hostile foreign powers to destroy the nation, and sometimes those authorities are right.

Patronage and Clientelism

Yet another manifestation of the small group is the pervasive patron-client network. Unlike clusters of cronies, clientelistic groupings bring together people of very different status and power. The patron is the power wielder, and his clients need his protection. In turn, the clients render the patron a number of services that enhance his power and hence his ability to act as their protector. The classic example in the Middle East and elsewhere was the large landowner, who monopolizes and controls access to land—the most precious fixed asset. The landowner's clients are his tenants, laborers, and sharecroppers. He protects them physically, supplies them with agricultural inputs and monetary credit, assists them if they fall ill, and helps them pay for extraordinary events such as marriages and funerals. The clients in turn produce for him, supply free labor for a host of menial tasks, vote for him if elections are an issue, and fight for him if he is attacked by outsiders. In this classic example, the patron controls what are called "first-order resources"—land and money. As long as he maintains his local monopoly, his clients will have little choice but to seek his protection. Migration may be an option, but in some countries, such as Iraq in the interwar years, peasants with outstanding debts could not legally migrate. However, agrarian reform has eroded the power of the classic rural patron around the world.

Today, with the growth of large bureaucratic states that invade and regulate all aspects of life, the patron is more likely to be a broker. Although he may continue to control first-order resources, his real services to his clients are provided through his ability to obtain state resources, deliver public goods, or protect his clients against various forms of state action. He may help procure a birth certificate, a work permit, a commercial license, a passport, or any of the other vital pieces of paper that the modern state routinely requires but does not routinely deliver. He may help place a son in secondary school or the university, find a migrant a job in a public agency or factory, get the courts to drop charges for a misdemeanor, or swing a loan through the agricultural credit bank. What the broker receives in return is somewhat amorphous. In the few systems where votes count, he will surely receive them, but his relative weight in the political system may well hinge on his ability to demonstrate the size and cohesion of his group of clients. If he is perceived as being able to "deliver" his clients—even in elections where official candidates receive 99.9 percent of the votes—or to keep them out of street demonstrations, strikes, or land seizures, the higher authorities will make sure that public resources sufficient to maintain his clientele are put at his disposal.

As the socialist and solidarist élan of several of the radical republics began to wane, the large, all-encompassing parties that they set up became simple conduits for the distribution of state patronage. Party cadres, rather than educating, indoctrinating, and mobilizing the populations with which they dealt, adopted the broker role, establishing their reputations on their ability to deliver state resources to their clients. Intended to be members of the vanguard, they became ward heelers. The party thus became an instrument in the slow drift of the leadership into divide-and-rule politics; the cadres were there not to be encouraged to do something but rather to be rewarded for doing nothing.

Clientelism inhibits the appointment or election of qualified candidates on meritocratic grounds and forces the poor and needy to seek benefits not as the entitlements of citizenship but through participation in unequal power relationships. Wealthier citizens must also participate in clientelist exchanges, although they enjoy higher levels of social capital—in this case, *wasta*—and in any case, their independent means enable them to opt out of the system more frequently. Clientelism therefore creates inefficiencies through excessive red tape and transaction costs and makes life all the more difficult, especially for the poor.

Nevertheless, clientelism does not necessarily imply the absence of competition. In Mubarak's Egypt, Lisa Blaydes (2010) argues, electoral clientelism entailed competition among elites who vied to buy off sufficient numbers of voters to win seats in the national parliament. This was a far cry from democratic competition; rather, these arrangements bolstered authoritarianism by shifting the costs of redistribution away from the state toward elites, whose struggle to win seats through vote buying further bound them to the system. Across the Middle East, "competitive clientelism" entails contests over state resources among parliamentarians who use their positions to distribute resources to their network. In this way, elections under authoritarian rule are not mere empty charades to affirm incumbent dictators: they also set up competition over limited state resources (Lust 2009, 122).

In countries with politicized ethnic and sectarian cleavages, clientelism has additional layers and tends to operate on identity-based lines. Where power-sharing arrangements enshrine identity in political institutions, dominance in the political representation of the in-group community is of paramount importance and drives intense competition among in-group parties. Only then can parties afford to reach out across communal lines to woo voters from other ethnicities or sects (Cammett 2014; Corstange 2012; Horowitz 2000). Two caveats are important: First, electoral competition is but one arena for clientelist exchange. In countries with contested political institutions, an array of non-electoral goals—such as encouraging participation in demonstrations, riots, sit-ins, or even armed militias—may compel patrons to expand their client base (Cammett 2014). Second, not all citizens support ethnic or sectarian parties for the purposes of material exchange. Rather, they may genuinely support the ideas and positions of the party or appreciate the sense of meaning and communal belonging that it provides (Cammett 2014, ch. 1; Hermez 2011, 532).

Political Parties

Political parties in the postcolonial Middle East are generally weak in terms of their ability to act as political opposition, aggragate interests, and create meaningful change. In many countries, political parties outside of the ruling regime are not allowed to exist, while in countries with greater political pluralism, parties are often played against one another by the ruling regime in order to reduce their efficacy. Consequently, for decades, few meaningful political parties have existed in the Middle East, and those who run for office in the region are those who either already possess close ties with the government or can foresee developing them (Lust 2009, 129). After the Arab uprisings, the number of parties greatly increased, but thus far most have failed to create cohesive platforms and their constituencies are limited.

People across the Middle East have little confidence in political parties (see Figure 11.4). In Turkey, respondents expressed the highest levels of trust in parties, coming closest to the average for middle-income countries, and in Lebanon and Morocco about 25 percent of their populations expressed some level of trust in parties. Yet the overall picture shows very little confidence in political parties, which have not proven to be effective representatives of popular interests across the region. It is particularly striking that Tunisians express such low levels of trust in parties (about 3 percent) given that their country is considered a relative success case among

FIGURE 11.4. Confidence in Political Parties in the Middle East, 2010–2014

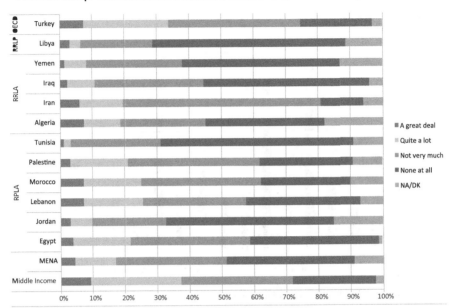

Source: World Values Survey Association, World Values Survey (WVS), wave 6 (2010–2014).

Note: Iran data are from 2005 (wave 5 of the WVS).

the transitional Arab countries. At the time of the 2013 survey, however, Tunisia was in a state of political paralysis, with assassinations of major political figures and mounting acts of violence. It is no wonder, then, that Tunisians had become disillusioned with political institutions such as parties.

Party membership levels in the Middle East are also low, although a few countries in the region exceed the average level for middle-income countries (see Figure 11.5). In Lebanon, where sectarian parties dominate the political scene and broker access to services and favors, partisanship is significantly higher than both the MENA and middle-income averages. The same is true for Palestine and Yemen. In both Egypt and Tunisia, where the uprisings were initiated, party membership is conspicuously low. Even in Turkey, where respondents in the same survey expressed higher levels of trust in parties than did those in the Arab countries sampled, reported party membership levels are low.

It is not hard to see why Middle Easterners are not enthralled with their political parties. Driven to divide and rule rather than to unite, to contain rather than to mobilize, to repress rather than to inspire, leaders have emasculated the very political organizations they created to mobilize and integrate the masses. For years the common pattern was the dissolution and legal abolition of all political parties and the establishment of monopoly fronts to represent "all the people," although whether they ever intended to be truly representative is questionable at best. Egypt from 1953 on, Algeria since independence in 1962, and Sudan between 1969 and

FIGURE 11.5. Party Membership in the Middle East, 2010–2014

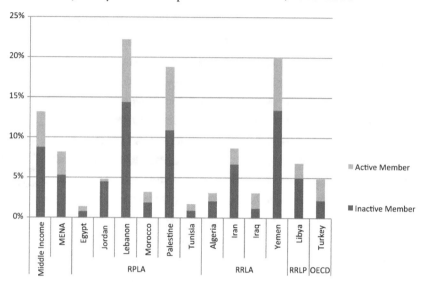

Source: World Values Survey Association, WVS, wave 6 (2010–2014).

Note: Iran data are from 2005 (wave 5 of the WVS).

1985 established corporatist monopolies in the Arab Socialist Union (ASU), the National Liberation Front (FLN), and the Sudanese Socialist Union (SSU), respectively. The Ba'ath regimes of Iraq and Syria and the Socialist Destour Party of Tunisia allowed for coalitions of the dominant party with small marginal groupings such as Communists, Nasserists, and liberals, but there was never any question of these groupings being allowed to organize freely or to play anything but a subordinate role. Those enjoying legal monopolies on "representing" citizens, such as Egypt's ASU or Algeria's FLN, rejected the "party" label—having no rivals, they needed no partisans. Through some mysterious process from which freedom of speech, open debate, and freedom of choice were notably absent, the front or union would distill the essence of "popular" will and transmit it to the regime's leaders for policy action. It did not take long for the citizens to recognize this for what it was.

Liberal experiments in the region were also shams in their own way. The monarchical regimes of Iran, Morocco, and Jordan have carefully policed multiparty systems, and Sadat's Egypt boasted party-competitive systems. But like several of their socialist counterparts (and in Egypt's case, like its predecessor), most of the parties competing for power were created from above and the outcome of elections was more or less known in advance (al-Ansari 1986, 203). Iran's shah habitually dabbled in the fabrication of parties. In the 1950s, he established a loyal opposition party, Mardom, and a loyalist party, the Melliyun, which came to be known as the "Yes" party and the "Yes Sir!" party. After 1963, the shah replaced his two creations with the Modern Iran Party, run by the young technocrats who engineered the

White Revolution. Then, in 1975, he founded the Renaissance Party and made Iran a one-party state.

We should not overlook the ground-up parties, organized during nationalist struggles or in defense of specific interests and classes. The Neo-Destour Party of Tunisia, which Ben Ali later renamed the Democratic Constitutional Rally (RCD), and the Wafd Party of Egypt, which was resuscitated under Sadat after Nasser had dissolved it, were the standard-bearers of the two countries' nationalist movements. Morocco's nationalist Independence Party hangs on in the king's carefully controlled political arena. In some countries, communist and socialist parties, often of illegal origins and the objects of constant repression, developed strong organizations and toughened cadres that compensated for their small membership, but most have been dismantled and are barely operational. Instead, since the 1970s, Islamist groups have captured more and more grassroots support. Parties allied with the Muslim Brotherhood, established in Egypt in 1928, are significant players in Egypt, Jordan, Palestine, and elsewhere.

Against the few examples of successful party organization, a pervasive gloom envelops partisan activity in the Middle East, for four main reasons. The first, discussed earlier, is that parties have been created from the top down and seldom strike roots in the population in whose name they claim to speak. With a stroke of a pen, Sadat dissolved Egypt's ASU in 1975 without the slightest murmur from the "masses" or the party's cadres. When the same fate befell Sudan's SSU in 1985, the "masses" were positively jubilant.

The second reason is the hesitancy of leaders to use the parties they have created to mobilize the people and motivate them to participate in national politics and share responsibility. Parties have repeatedly been used to control and *de*mobilize the populace. Infiltrated by police informers, parties have become associated with the repressive apparatus of the state—as in Saddam Hussein's Iraq, Ben Ali's Tunisia, Mubarak's Egypt, and Assad's Syria. Cadres are all too often bureaucrats who have been seconded to the party from the civil service and whose careers are ultimately based in their ministries or citizens who become party members to gain access to services or economic favors. Thus, parties have evolved into instruments for social control and for dispensing favors to the connected and to those who claim allegiance to the state.

The third reason for the region's desultory participation in electoral activities is that, for a time, many Middle Eastern states pursued economic strategies that brought forth a technocratic elite of planners, financial experts, managers, and engineers whose quest for orderly and disciplined change reinforced the party's mission as an instrument of control, especially in the workplace. Boumediene's Algeria is a forceful example of this concept of party organization and technocratic supremacy.

And finally, in countries with thriving parties prior to independence, there was a tendency post-independence to siphon off the best cadres from these parties to staff government agencies in an ever-expanding state apparatus. Thus, these parties were left with no mission and very few experienced organizers. The Neo-Destour, the Ba'ath in Syria and Iraq, and Algeria's FLN have all fallen victim to this form of "brain drain" and lack of purpose.

The Arab uprisings have changed the landscape of political parties in striking ways, particularly in Tunisia and Egypt. The sheer number of parties has increased almost exponentially in these countries. Yet newly created parties face many challenges. For one, many have little experience as formal organizations and thus do not have practical political skills. This partly explains the relative success of the region's Islamist parties, many of which have existed, formally or informally, for decades. New parties also must confront the challenge of dealing with the remaining power and influence of the old regimes—the SCAF in Egypt being a prime example. Finally, groups that were especially marginalized from political participation within the old regimes (for example, women and minorities) have found it difficult to increase their political capacity after the uprisings.

Tunisia is a prime example of the proliferation of political parties during and after the uprisings. Before the revolution, Tunisia was a single-party state: the RCD was the dominant party, and a handful of other parties that did not seriously challenge the regime were permitted to win seats in the national assembly. After the revolution, the RCD was dissolved and over seventy new parties were established. Initially the Hizb ut-Tahrir, an Islamist party that aims to establish a Muslim caliphate, was banned, but the government legalized the party in July 2012. After the October 2011 elections for the Constituent Assembly, postrevolutionary Tunisian politics was largely controlled by a coalition of three major parties, the Islamist Ennahda and two center-left secular parties, the Congress for the Republic (CPR) and the Democratic Forum for Labor and Liberties (Ettakatol). These parties split the major positions in the government, with Moncef Marzouki as president; Ennahda's Hamadi Jebali as prime minister; and Mustapha Ben Jafar from Ettakatol as speaker of the Constituent Assembly. As a result of the slow pace of reform, contentions that the coalition was not sufficiently inclusive, and allegations that Ennahda maintained ties to violent Islamist groups, Jebali agreed to resign, and a government of technocrats took over.

Ennahda's most serious competitor is now Nidaa Tounes (Call for Tunisia Party), formed in the spring of 2012 under the leadership of the octogenarian Béji Caid Essebsi, a former official under Bourguiba and the interim prime minister after Ben Ali's ouster. Nidaa Tounes appeals in part to Tunisians who are concerned about the secular heritage of the country, and it attracted some controversy because it includes some former members of the RCD. Meanwhile, the CPR and Ettakatol, which benefited in 2011 from their perceived openness to working with Ennahda, lost some ground because of their association with the Islamist party (Dworkin 2013, 7–8).

Egypt's party system has opened gradually, oscillating between more and less tolerance of opposition parties. After the 1952 revolution, parties were abolished, setting up a single-party state until 1976, when Sadat at least initially promoted the Muslim Brotherhood as a counterbalance to leftists. Under Mubarak, political life opened more during the 1980s, with the return of the Wafd Party and the Brotherhood's participation in elections, but it stagnated once again in the 1990s with the suppression of Islamist groups, some of which had employed violence. Although elections held in the 2000s were more competitive than in the previous decade, the state intimidated the opposition and employed increasingly repressive tactics over the course of the decade. As in many other countries in the region, Islamists (in this case, the Muslim Brotherhood) were better organized and made greater inroads into the population than leftist and liberal parties (Hamzawy and Dunne 2008).

The Egyptian experience of party politics after the uprisings resembles that of Tunisia with the proliferation of new parties and movements across the ideological spectrum, including youth movements, leftists, liberals, secularists, Islamists, and Salafists. Under the period of SCAF rule, multiple parties were approved, including Islamist parties such as the Brotherhood's Freedom and Justice Party (FJP), the Al-Wasat Party (a moderate offshoot of the Muslim Brotherhood that was established prior to the uprisings), the Salafist Al-Nour Party, and several parties that split off from the Brotherhood. In the run-up to the national elections, various liberal parties formed a coalition, the Egyptian Bloc, to counter the apparent popularity of Islamist parties. Ultimately, liberal parties were eclipsed by the Islamists, who won a large share of the seats in parliament as well as the subsequent presidential election (Sharp 2011, 4). Since the overthrow of Mohammed Morsi in July 2013, Islamist parties, especially the FJP, have been suppressed, and the new constitution, passed in January 2014, officially bans parties based on religion.

Egypt's liberal parties, like many of their counterparts across the region, remain relatively weak and organizationally deficient, with little outreach beyond urban areas, limited fund-raising possibilities, and underdeveloped policy platforms. The Wafd Party, the oldest among them, is in the best position, but it fails to capture the support of many youth and faces internal dissension (Sabry 2013). Under the rule of President Al-Sisi, the political space has once again contracted and critics from diverse ideological orientations have been brutally repressed, leaving little room for the formation of independent parties.

Although political parties in Jordan were officially legalized in 1992 and about thirty parties are officially registered as of this writing, Jordan lacks major organized political parties. The one exception is the Islamic Action Front (IAF), the party of the Jordanian branch of the Muslim Brotherhood, which is relatively well structured and enjoys some mass appeal. Apart from the IAF, parties in Jordan are formed and dissolved with regularity, often enduring for only one electoral cycle, and the vast majority of members of Jordan's legislature run as independents.

The Jordanian monarchy, the real seat of power in the country, is particularly adept at designing electoral rules to its advantage. Until recently, Jordan was one of a handful of countries with a single nontransferable vote system: each elector had one vote, but multiple candidates were elected in each district. In general, this system inhibited the formation of strong parties because it incentivized voters to back the candidates who were most likely to deliver patronage goods rather than those with appealing ideological positions. As such, the system was widely interpreted as a way to undercut support for the IAF. For the most recent elections, held in January 2013, the system was amended slightly, with each voter receiving two votes, one for a candidate in his or her district and the other for a closed proportional list. The reform aimed to address the criticism of the previous system, but opposition parties were not satisfied with the new law on the grounds that it did not substantially alter the prospects for their representation in parliament. The Jordanian regime also has a history of gerrymandering by setting up districts in which regime supporters, mainly in rural areas with lower populations, are overrepresented (*Jordan Times* 2012).

As in Jordan, political contestation is tolerated in Morocco more than in the MENA authoritarian republics and oil-rich monarchies. Since 1993, when the number of parties represented in parliament increased significantly, Moroccan politics has been relatively pluralistic, although of course the makhzen remains the most powerful actor in the country and has a long history of manipulating the political scene by creating new parties and fostering splits within them. Until recently, elections were often characterized by vote buying, fraud, and manipulation, while about six major parties have dominated the parliament. At best, they play a marginal role in aggregating and representing societal interests (Storm 2014, 38–41).

In response to the protests of the February 20 Movement, the monarchy held elections in November 2011. Designed to take the wind out of the sails of the opposition, the elections were fairer than previous rounds had been, permitting greater participation for the Islamists and fewer incidents of fraud. For the first time, the prime minister was named by the party with the greatest vote share rather than by royal appointment, enabling Abdelilah Benkirane of the Islamist PJD to take over the premiership. In addition, in September 2011 a new constitution was approved, decreasing the formal power of the monarchy in the political system, although few concessions were actually made. Thus, while Morocco experienced a tangible political opening after its version of the uprisings and parties became more institutionalized, in practice the makhzen is still firmly in control and the opposition remains circumscribed (Benchemsi 2012; Buehler 2013).

Prior to the Yemeni revolution, formal political opposition to President Saleh's party, the General People's Congress (GPC), was dominated by the Joint Meeting Parties (JMP), a coalition that included Islah, the leading Islamist party, the Yemeni Socialist Party (YSP), and three other small parties. During the uprisings, the bulk of the protesters were supporters of the JMP or of other regionally based groups and prominent clans. After President Saleh stepped down in a GCC-brokered deal, Vice President Abd Rabbuh Mansur Hadi assumed the presidency of the interim government, composed of a cabinet equally divided between the GPC and the opposition (JMP), with the premiership held by an opposition figure. In February 2012, Hadi easily won the presidential election, and one year later the National Dialogue Conference (NDC) was launched, convening delegates from across the country to debate the future of the country and guide the ongoing process of writing and approving the new constitution (Alley 2013, 74). Its entrenched patronage network enables the GPC to retain significant influence in Yemen. Yet other parties and actors, especially Islah, are gaining power in the new political context. With the country's dwindling economic assets, and especially with declining oil production, control over valuable patronage networks will undoubtedly intensify interparty tensions and political conflict (Wolff 2013).

Organized Labor

Labor unions, unlike political parties, have a long history of activism in the region, and in some countries they have been meaningful sites of mobilization for workers. In organizing strategic sectors of the working population, post-independence governments created real occupational associations that have since gained organizational and political skills and substantial bargaining power. Concomitantly, the disbursement of large state-investment budgets and the very real economic growth that has occurred in some Middle Eastern societies has transferred resources to white-collar workers, skilled trade unionists, capitalist farmers, and a few entrepreneurial groups that have even contested, cautiously, certain state policies. Endowed with resources and accumulated experience, these groups can bargain directly with the state and its agents, and especially in Tunisia, they were key actors in the Arab uprisings.

Given the distinctive population and natural resource endowments of Middle Eastern countries, as well as their histories of institutional development, patterns of labor organization naturally differ across the RRLP monarchies, on the one hand, and the more populous RRLA and RPLA countries, on the other.[6] Until the past decade, when several GCC countries signed international trade agreements stipulating greater respect for labor rights, all of the Gulf oil monarchies had banned unions and strikes altogether (except for Kuwait, which did not ban unions, thanks in large part to its history of relative political pluralism) (Crystal 2007). Given the nature of their workforces, which include a large share of low-skilled foreign workers, the Gulf monarchies have dualistic labor regimes: citizens enjoy extensive job security, but there are few formal protections for low-wage foreign workers, who are subject to widespread abuses, as international human rights organizations have documented extensively (see Amnesty International 2009; Human Rights Watch 2007, 2009).

In the countries with larger citizen populations, labor representation evolved in distinct ways, with consequences for labor mobilization. In the non-oil monarchies, Jordan and, especially, Morocco, greater tolerance for pluralism permitted more scope for independent labor organizations and competitive unions. By positioning themselves above the fray of political competition while maintaining ultimate authority over key decisions and policies, monarchs could permit the emergence of livelier civil society organizations, including unions (Lust-Okar 2005; Zartman 1997). Unlike Jordan, which has a single labor confederation, Morocco permitted competitive unionism, affording Moroccan workers the greatest freedom in the region. Direct ties between Moroccan and French trade unions also helped establish a tradition of labor activism dating back to the colonial era (Ayache 1993).

In the single-party republics, both oil-rich and oil-poor, labor unions have tended to be heavily controlled by authoritarian rulers through state corporatism, that is, institutional arrangements in which "non-competing groups are officially sanctioned, and supervised by the state" and are effectively instruments for social control (Collier and Collier 1979, 967). Although the word "corporatism," to the best of our knowledge, does not exist in any of the languages spoken in the Middle

East, its logic certainly is not alien to the region. The corporatist imagery, especially its statist variant, comes out of European Fascism, which allowed no place for class conflict or any organization along class lines. Likewise, open competition among a myriad of opposed interests and parties could not be accepted. Corporatist systems structure organization and representation around the major functional or occupational groups in society—agricultural producers, industrial producers, entrepreneurs, white-collar workers, the armed forces—cutting vertically through horizontal strata of wealth and poverty. There is no question that everywhere in the world it has prevailed corporatism has been aimed at containing Marxists and any attempt to incite class conflict, but while European corporatism was aimed directly at containing the radicalization of the industrial proletariat, that class has not acquired much weight in the Middle East.

Corporatism becomes an arm of the struggle to regiment large segments of the population that are officially entitled to a fair share of the national pie but in fact are denied that share as resources are channeled away from consumption and toward investment and speculation. It is rare that the relatively disenfranchised masses—peasants, workers, low-income white-collar workers—feel that they are adequately represented through corporatist structures, and they are quite literally bought off by consumer subsidies, guaranteed employment schemes, and a blind eye to moonlighting, speculation, and low productivity. Almost never does corporatism seek to give proportionate and effective weight to the poor majority of the adult populations of the Middle East. Nasser's distribution of 50 percent or more of elected seats in the ASU and the National Assembly to peasants and workers was window-dressing.

Corporatist regimes pursue dual strategies vis-à-vis labor. One is to encourage organization and unionization. Strategically placed labor, mainly in public-sector enterprises and the transportation sector, may receive favorable wage and social benefits packages. Such workers are co-opted by the corporatist state; their leaders are given significant roles in the "party" organization, in legislative assemblies, and sometimes in the government itself. In exchange for favorable unionwide wage and benefit packages, union leadership is expected to keep the rank and file in line. The second strategy is to segment the labor force, relying on the organized labor elite to keep the economic wheels turning while looking over its shoulder at the majority of unorganized labor in the urban informal sector, in the private sector, and in the countryside—workers who would clearly love the jobs of the labor elite.

In Algeria, Boumediene purged the unions of militant leadership in 1967, including the national-level General Confederation of Algerian Workers (UGTA), and subordinated them to his statist industrialization drive. After a 1971 reform, every major workplace would have an elected assembly of workers, but it included management as well. The clear goal of socialist management was to increase production, not promote proletarian democracy (DERSA 1981, 132; Nellis 1977, 549).

Labor leaders co-opted into the corporatist power structure must walk a fine line between serving the state leaders and maintaining some semblance of credibility among the rank and file. Sometimes the balancing act is impossible to maintain. In 1966 the dominant Türk-I4 labor confederation in Turkey condemned a strike in a glassworks. This led to the hiving-off of a faction of Türk-I4 and the founding of the radical Confederation of Progressive Trade Unions (DISK). By 1970, DISK had 40,000 members and Türk-I4 had 700,000, but DISK would become an active element in the agitation of the 1970s. When the military took over in 1980, DISK was disbanded and many of its leaders were arrested. A similar process unfolded in Tunisia.

The General Confederation of Tunisian Workers (UGTT) had been a pillar of the Destourian coalition before and after independence. Whenever labor leaders appeared ready to use its organizational strength in any way that conflicted with regime goals, Bourguiba had them removed. In 1978 cost-of-living riots broke out in several Tunisian cities. The UGTT rank and file was hit hard, yet the regime wanted the leadership to condemn the violence. In order not to lose support among his following, Habib Achour, the UGTT head, had to distance himself from the regime. As a consequence, he was jailed, but the relative autonomy of the UGTT had been asserted.

Sometimes the regime will tolerate strikes and labor agitation in the private sector but forbid them in the public sector, as public enterprise is the motor of national development and, in any case, is owned by "the people." Such double standards have seldom precluded public enterprise strikes. In 1977 there were 129 strikes, involving 31,000 workers, in the Algerian public sector (DERSA 1981). Egypt experienced major strikes twice in 1968, and dockworkers in Alexandria sparked three days of cost-of-living riots in 1977 that spread throughout most Egyptian cities. The prospect of privatization in 1995 triggered strikes in public-sector textile firms, especially in Kafr el-Dawwar.

Over time corporatist arrangements can fray. In Tunisia, cost-of-living riots erupted once again in January 1984, when the regime sought to reduce consumer subsidies. Calling for a "social dialogue," the regime could no longer rely on the relatively pampered members of the UGTT to remain aloof from the agitation (Baduel 1983). Corporatist discipline appeared to have broken down: after Achour was jailed again, the UGTT called for a boycott of local elections in May 1984 and even threatened to run its own list of candidates in the 1986 legislative elections.

An unexpected result of corporatist experiments is to inculcate organizational skills and eventually some sort of autonomy from the state in the very functional groups the experiment was designed to control. The evolution of the Confederation of Egyptian Labor is instructive. Its autonomy was limited in the Nasserist-socialist era, when rhetoric in favor of the workingman was at a high pitch. During the Sadatist era of economic liberalization, the confederation's leadership was co-opted into prominent official positions, and the confederation became the "largest, wealthiest and most representative association in Egyptian society" (Bianchi 1986, 438). Under Mubarak it became an effective veto group, notably in preventing any further joint ventures between public-sector companies and foreign investors. Corporatism thus gave the union leadership the capacity to check the autonomy of the regime in key issues (Bianchi 1984, 434). Yet increased autonomy need not entail greater radicalism. Unions and other professional associations can evolve into important economic enterprises in their own right and thereby develop a stake in the overall smooth functioning of the economic system.

Several Middle Eastern labor organizations gradually distanced themselves from close corporatist control. In Egypt, the Egyptian Trade Union Federation (ETUF) had enjoyed a legal monopoly over labor representation for decades and largely served as a channel for defusing labor demands. But wildcat strikes and labor activism by breakaway unions that split from ETUF several years before Mubarak's ouster were increasing. In 2009 real estate tax collectors formed the first "independent" union, followed by teachers and health technicians.[7] The new teachers' union broke off from the teachers' syndicate but was not able to capture a large number of followers, thus creating two camps—one belonging to the new union and the other belonging to the old syndicate. The tax collectors, on the other hand, succeeded in eventually recruiting the majority of real estate tax collectors into their independent union.[8]

On January 30, 2011, while the uprisings were under way, a new labor union umbrella group, the Egyptian Federation of Independent Trade Unions (EFITU), was founded; by late 2013, it encompassed about 300 unions. Later in 2011, the Egyptian Democratic Labor Congress (EDLC) was formed, and new parties claiming to represent labor interests were later established. The new unions face serious constraints, in no small part owing to the fact that as long as EFITU remains the only legally recognized union federation, its competitors cannot collect membership dues. Furthermore, the leaders of the new unions lack organizational capacity and experience. While EFITU and EDLC have a relatively strong presence in government institutions, they have not organized in blue-collar sectors, which remain under the EFITU umbrella (Abdalla 2014; Bishara 2014; see also Beinin and Duboc 2013, 222).

In Tunisia, new labor federations also emerged in the postrevolutionary landscape, but their status is quite different than in Egypt. The Tunisian constitution never explicitly prohibited the formation of multiple unions, even under Ben Ali's rule, although in practice no alternatives to the national-level union were established. In the aftermath of the Tunisian revolution, several unions emerged as legal alternatives to the UGTT. However, given the UGTT's history, its legitimacy as a key component of the anticolonial struggle, and its relative autonomy under Ben Ali's rule, as well as its superior resource base, these new labor organizations have struggled to gain a foothold among Tunisian workers (Bishara 2014, 1–3).

By the 2000s, the region was seeing an increasing number of strikes, often organized without the authorization of the union leadership. In Egypt, labor unrest increased dramatically in the middle of the decade: the rise in the number of strikes from 222 in 2006 to over 700 in 2009 reflected the deterioration of labor rights with accelerated liberalization and privation under the Nazif government (Land Center for Human Rights 2011, cited in Sallam 2011, 2, 4; see also Figure 11.3). In December 2006, the biggest strike yet broke out in Egypt at the Misr Spinning and Weaving Company in El-Mahalla El-Kubra, where about 25 percent of all workers in public-sector textile and apparel factories were employed. When promises to the workers were not fulfilled, additional strikes were held in 2007 and 2008 at El-Mahalla El-Kubra and elsewhere. Increasingly, the organizers explicitly framed their demands as a "challenge to the regime" and called for a new system of labor representation. ETUF lost further credibility among workers when it effectively sided with the regime and failed to support the workers' demands (Beinin and Duboc 2013, 218–220). Although ETUF discouraged its members from participating in the uprisings against the regime in January 2011, individual workers took part en masse and a decade of mounting labor unrest arguably set the stage for mass mobilization (Bishara 2014, 1). The irony, as Hesham Sallam (2011, 3) points out, is that labor protests were not demonized under Mubarak's Egypt, but after his downfall, they were increasingly viewed as parochial expressions of special interests (*ihtijajat fi'awiyya*) that threatened the national order.

Tunisia, too, experienced a marked uptick in strikes in the decade prior to the uprisings. Increasingly, workers staged wildcat strikes throughout the country. The best-known episode of labor unrest—also not supported by the UGTT—occurred in 2008 in the mining region of Gafsa, as discussed at the beginning of this chapter. Yet the UGTT ultimately played a far more central role in the uprisings than its Egyptian counterpart, ETUF. Although it did not initially support the uprisings, the Tunisian national-level union eventually lent its support to the protests and managed to enhance its credibility as an opponent of authoritarianism, even though its top leadership had been viewed as complicit with the Ben Ali regime during his rule. The UGTT has been crucial to the political scene since Ben Ali's departure. In particular, the agreement it brokered between Nidaa Tounes and Ennahda led to the appointment of the new technocratic caretaker government in December 2013, thereby easing Tunisia out of political deadlock. As a sign of its national legitimacy, the UGTT's membership has nearly doubled since Ben Ali's ouster (Bishara 2014, 6–7).

Women's Movements

Like organized labor, women's movements became increasingly active during and after the uprisings in some Middle Eastern countries. Yet the MENA region is renowned for the underrepresentation of women in public life as well as its patriarchal values. Of all global regions, the Middle East has the smallest percentage of female parliamentarians, by a significant margin (see Figure 11.6). Some countries in the region, including Iraq, Jordan, Morocco, Tunisia, and Algeria, have adopted quotas to increase female representation in national parliaments (Moghadam 2013). Within the region, this institutional reform appears to lead to an increased number of women in political life. In Algeria, for example, the proportion of women in parliament jumped from 8 percent in 2010 to over 32 percent in 2011 after quotas were adopted (World Bank, WDI, 2013). Some research suggests that greater female representation spurs increased political engagement among women: Pippa Norris and Mona Krook (2009, 12) find that the "inclusion of women in elected office provides visible role models and social cues about the responsiveness and openness of the political system that encourages more women to become interested and active in grassroots politics."

FIGURE 11.6. Women in Parliament by Global Region, 2013

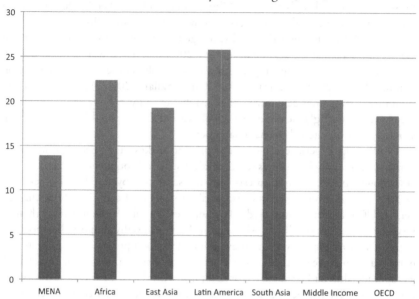

Source: World Bank, World Development Indicators (WDI).

A spate of research also links persistent authoritarianism and underdevelopment with low female participation in political institutions and in the workforce (Fish 2002; Inglehart and Norris 2003; Ross 2008). One thing is clear: democracy in any context is not fully developed and is of poor quality if women lack parity in public life, an issue that has been neglected in the mainstream literature on democratization (Baldez 2010). Although the MENA region has greater female representation in government and high-level managerial positions, gender parity in these spheres is a long way off in all global regions.

The Middle East, and predominantly Muslim countries more generally, also stand out for their conservative attitudes toward gender equality. In exploring the differences in values in societies around the world, Pippa Norris and Ronald Inglehart (2002, 237) conclude that what distinguishes the region from other regions is "Eros and not Demos." Patriarchal values are especially pronounced in Muslim societies and even among Muslims in predominantly non-Muslim societies. In a variety of subgroup comparisons of values related to gender, age, religiosity, and education between Muslim and non-Muslim societies, between democratic and authoritarian countries, and between oil-rich and oil-poor economies, Muslims expressed more support for patriarchal values (Alexander and Welzel 2011). Data from the latest round of the World Values Survey support this claim. As can be seen in Figure 11.7, the Middle East had the highest percentage of respondents expressing agreement with the statement "Men make better political leaders." At the same time, reduced support for patriarchal values among younger and more educated people as well as

FIGURE 11.7. Acceptance of Women as Political Leaders by Global Region, 2010–2014

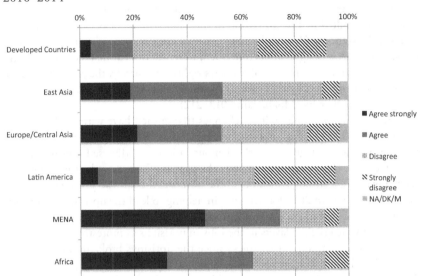

Source: WVS, wave 6, 2010–2014.

Note: Based on responses to the statement "Men make better political leaders."

among Muslims living in non-Muslim societies indicates that these attitudes can be changed and are subject to "emancipative forces" (Alexander and Welzel 2011, 272).

Women in the Middle East have not been passive in response to what many perceive to be their second-class status in the region. Well before the uprisings, a wide array of women's groups had emerged in MENA countries. Valentine Moghadam (2013, 213) lists a few of the formal organizations that have emerged in countries such as Egypt, Iran, Morocco, Palestine, and Tunisia, but every country in the region boasts organizations agitating for women's advancement. The major goals of these groups tend to be family law reform, the criminalization of violence again women (including "honor" killings, sexual harassment in public and in the workplace, and domestic violence), equality of citizenship rights for women married to foreigners and their children, and increased participation of women in political institutions and the workforce. Some women activists focus on issues unique to their national contexts, such as the campaigns in Saudi Arabia to legalize driving by women.

In a few countries, such as Tunisia and Turkey, women's rights were relatively well secured thanks to the vision of their founding leaders and legislation pushed through soon after independence. Of course, these gains, such as the banning of polygamy and more equitable divorce and child custody laws, occurred in the context of "state feminism" promoted by authoritarian rulers and as such did not entail a fundamental reordering of power relations (Khalil 2014, 131). In countries with

422   11. SOLIDARISM AND ITS ENEMIES

less progressive family codes, major mobilization by women or related to women's issues in the region enjoyed some tangible achievements prior to the uprisings. In Morocco, women's groups mobilized for over a decade to push for a reform of family law, which resulted in a major reform of the Moudawana, or personal status code, in 2004. In Iran, the One Million Signatures Campaign, spearheaded by women's groups in 2007, was a grassroots movement to repeal discriminatory laws and urge constitutional reforms in favor of women's rights. Ultimately, the government suppressed the campaign, but its success in simply raising these issues in the public sphere was noteworthy (Moghadam 2013, 212).

The uprisings and the political changes that ensued have witnessed enhanced and new forms of political mobilization by women. Women and women's groups have been major protagonists in the demonstrations and diverse forms of activism that emerged before, during, and after the protests. For example, the Yemeni activist Tawakkol Karman, a member of the Islamist Al-Islah Party, was awarded the Nobel Peace Prize in 2012 for her work in helping to lead the uprisings against the government of ousted president Ali Abdullah Saleh (CARE International 2013, 8). Women were crucial players in the Libyan uprisings as protesters, activists, and medical workers, among other roles. Since the uprisings broke out, hundreds of new civil society organizations have emerged, many of which incorporate women. Thus far, however, they have not been able to push through legislation, and women remain relatively marginal in formal political institutions (Langhi 2014). Of course, prior to the uprisings, women were also important participants in social mobilization. In Egypt, Israa Abdel Fattah, a female activist, was the first person to be detained for her work in supporting the 2008 workers' strikes in El-Mahalla El-Kubra.

In Tunisia, women's participation in the uprisings and in political processes has been significant, in large part because of that country's history of relatively progressive policies on women's rights and family law. Unlike in Egypt, women's organizations, notably the Tunisian Association of Democratic Women (ATFD) and the Association of Tunisian Women for Research and Development (AFTURD), were actively involved in drafting the law regulating the October 2011 elections for the Constituent Assembly. After the elections, women enjoyed comparatively high representation in the body, including in the Islamist Al-Nahda Party. In particular, the electoral law stipulated that one-half of all candidates on party slates must be women, although the effects of this requirement were somewhat diluted by the fact that few women were placed at the heads of district lists and, given the proportional representation system, few parties had more than one candidate elected in any given district. For this reason, women's groups unsuccessfully pushed for the further requirement that parties name women as the top candidates on at least one-half their slates.

Women's political participation during and after the uprisings has included a broader array of participants, with younger, poorer, and more marginalized women engaging in protests and less institutionalized forms of engagement. Some of the newer participants in women's activism find themselves in tension with older feminist groups, which operated under authoritarian governments and are often seen as collaborators with antidemocratic rulers (CARE International 2013, 8).

Not all forms of women's activism in the Middle East conform to liberal, Western notions of a feminist agenda. Women are key actors in many Islamist movements and parties in the region. Indeed, in some countries, women are more active in Islamist parties than in non-Islamist parties. Furthermore, some women, such as the Yemeni Tawakkol Karman, have opted to work within Islamist parties rather than in opposition to them in order to challenge their stances on women's rights. These women express a wide array of views on gender and society. On the one hand, more conservative activists support distinct but "complementary" roles for men and women and aim for "equity" rather than equality between the sexes, emphasizing women's responsibilities toward their families. On the other hand, some women's groups call for a reinterpretation of gender roles with reference to Islamic law. For example, Musawah ("equality" in Arabic) is an international group that promotes a faith-based reading of equality in Islamic family law by drawing on Qur'anic scripture and teaching (CARE International 2013, 11). More generally, "Islamic feminism" (Coleman 2006) promotes women's rights but within the context of Islamic law. Many Islamic feminists maintain that there is nothing inherently inimical to women's rights in Islam, and that the religion is open to multiple interpretations on these questions. Some point out that what Islamist women view as beneficial to their advancement often does not conform to Western, liberal ideas of equality; however, this difference does not necessarily make their perspectives less "feminist" (Krause 2012, 17).

Islamist parties do not adopt uniform positions on women's rights and family law. To a great degree, their policies on these issues reflect and respond to country-specific political dynamics. In Tunisia, the Al-Nahda Party has a history of relatively progressive positions on a number of issues, and its comparatively liberal statements on women's rights are at least partly a response to both the prevailing societal preferences and the strength of women's groups in the country. International politics also affects the stances of Islamist parties on women's issues. Both domestic and international pressure may have compelled President Morsi to launch an initiative on women's rights in March 2013. The Moroccan monarchy's support for some policies promoted by Islamist groups, along with the positioning of the king as the "Commander of the Faithful," may have enabled the state to undercut potential religious opposition while enabling the government to push through the Moudawana reform (CARE International 2013, 11).

Even within the same country, however, Islamists may adopt divergent perspectives. In Egypt, the Muslim Brotherhood has supported the right of women to work, while the Salafist Al-Nour Party has opposed this. Competitive dynamics between Islamist parties may ratchet up their public support for conservative policies. The Egyptian Al-Nour Party may have been signaling its superior commitment to alleged religious principles in its efforts to repeal the ban on female genital mutilation or cutting (FGM/C). So-called secular parties also often adopt positions that seem to conform more with the views of Islamists. In Libya, the National Forces Alliance (NFA) party, which prevailed in the 2012 elections, is not an Islamist party but has articulated its support for the implementation of Sharia law (CARE International 2013, 10–11).

Despite enhancing opportunities for women's civic and political participation, the uprisings also brought up cause for concern about women and women's groups across the region. In Egypt, for example, the adoption of a quota system for female representation in the national parliament increased women's share of seats from 2 percent to 12.7 percent in 2010. Ironically, the institutionalization of a more democratic system after Mubarak's overthrow resulted in regression on this front. After the uprisings, when the quota system was dismantled, the female share of parliamentary seats declined (Moghadam 2013, 223). More generally, some Islamist parties that have gained power in the aftermath of the uprisings—notably the Muslim Brotherhood and its coalitional partner in Egypt, the Islamist Al-Nour Party—have advocated policies that are less favorable to women's rights and espouse patriarchal interpretations of Islamic law. Even in Tunisia, where women had gained more legal rights after independence than in other Arab countries and had higher rates of labor force participation, the revolution brought challenges. When the governing Islamist Al-Nahda Party proposed to change the term "equality between the sexes" to "complementarity between the sexes" in the new constitution, women's groups and others mobilized successfully to oppose this amendment (Charrad and Zarrugh 2014). In Egypt, women were conspicuously absent from the committee that drew up the new constitution in March 2011, and the Muslim Brotherhood and its allies opposed legislation to promote gender equality when it was in power. At the same time, the Islamist parties instituted new measures to funnel economic assistance to female-headed households (Morsy 2014). Andrea Khalil (2014, 134) succinctly summarizes the "gender paradoxes" of the uprisings: "While women's voices are heard at a new level across the revolutionary geography there are intense levels of public violence against women being committed under the eyes of the governments and society."

Sexual harassment of women received increasing (and overdue) attention during and after the uprisings. The growing public attention to incidents of sexual harassment, some of which went viral on social media and in the international press, has contributed to growing awareness of this issue. The "blue bra incident," which is but one of hundreds of documented cases of harassment since the uprisings broke out, became a symbol of the abuses of military power in Egypt. In December 2011, a female activist was stripped of her *abaya* (a robe-like outer garment), exposing her blue bra, then beaten and dragged through the streets by army officers. The incident received global attention and sparked massive demonstrations against sexual harassment. Beyond everyday harassment in public places, protests and demonstrations have been prime sites of assaults against both men and women, before, during, and after the uprisings. A growing body of evidence suggests that these assaults are not spontaneous acts: security officials may be hiring thugs to attack protesters in order to intimidate them. In response, male and female activists have established groups to protect demonstrators in public places (Langohr 2013, 2014). Women (and men) have also mobilized in opposition to the "virginity tests," which have been administered by Egyptian security officials in order to humiliate and harass female detainees, both under Mubarak's rule and after his overthrow (Morsy 2014).

Youth Movements and Cyber-Activism

The "rise of the youth" has garnered significant attention in the wake of the Arab uprisings, which are sometimes referred to as "youth uprisings" or as a "youth quake" (Al-Momani 2011), owing to the predominance of young people in the recent mass demonstrations across the Arab world. To some extent, this is to be expected, since young people, considering their place in the life cycle, are the most common protagonists in street politics everywhere. However, as some youth activists themselves argue, the characterization of the uprisings as a youth phenomenon masks the broad array of participants, which cut across class and age lines (Shehata 2012, 106). Yet there is truth to the notion that these are youth revolutions, not merely because younger cohorts were well represented on the streets but also because of the common concerns that youth articulated during the uprisings. Across the region, young people face similar constraints on their life prospects, aspirations, and living conditions. The Middle East boasts a large share of young people in its population who are more educated and plugged into social media than ever but lack the economic opportunities and possibilities for social mobility that older generations enjoyed (Dhillon and Yousef 2009).

For years, youth as a social category in the Middle East received limited attention. Most young activists participated in the youth wings of formal associations such as political parties and trade unions, which were largely co-opted by authoritarian rulers. At the same time, some of the most vocal and active opponents of authoritarian regimes were found on campuses in student associations. Yet, as Linda Herrera and Asef Bayat (2010, 8) argue, youth movements and student groups have distinct orientations and goals and should be not be conflated.

The spread of the Internet and communications technologies (ICT) has altered the nature of youth civic and political engagement and fundamentally changed the nature of social mobilization in the Middle East. During and after the uprisings, the use of new technologies and social media by young people to galvanize protests—the so-called Twitter or Facebook Revolution—garnered widespread attention. However, the narrative that Internet activism and, with it, the tools for revolution suddenly emerged from previously passive societies both overstates the role of new technologies in driving the uprisings and undervalues the very real and risky forms of collective action that workers and others had undertaken well before 2010. At the same time, under repressive governments, cyber-activism was a valuable and often more feasible tool for expressing dissent and coordinating opposition actions, and it changed social mobilization in important ways. Young people and relatively new youth movements and associations were at the forefront of using these tools to oppose their regimes.

Since the early 2000s, the Internet was an outlet in Tunisia for criticizing the regime, and it spurred a cat-and-mouse game between regime opponents and government censors. (In the predigital era, such criticism was distributed through anonymous pamphlets with titles like *Les Sept familles qui pillent la Tunisie,* or "The "Seven Families Who Are Pillaging Tunisia.") One of the earliest examples of cyber-activism in Tunisia was TUNeZine, which was created in 2001 and regularly published human rights–focused articles until the arrest, and subsequent death, of its creator in 2005 (Chomiak 2014). In the face of harsh government crackdowns, many Tunisians devised strategies, such as the use of code words, to avoid detection; for instance, the color mauve, an official color of the state, was used to represent Ben Ali in the many blogs and forums where online dissent took place (Kuebler 2011, 5). Internet censorship in Tunisia had become so significant under Ben Ali's rule that it became a cause of its own. In 2005, in response to Tunisia's hosting of the World Summit on the Information Society, the Tunisian Association for the Promotion of the Defense of Cyberspace established the site YezziFock Ben Ali! and organized an alternative summit to promote Internet freedom. The Internet freedom movement reached its peak with the "Tunisie en Blanc" Facebook event on May 22, 2010. Organized and spread via Facebook, the protest called on those who favored greater Internet freedom to meet at cafés along Tunis's main thoroughfare, Avenue Habib Bourguiba, dressed in all white. Though the event was quickly shut down and its organizers detained, this form of cyber-activism paved the way for Internet-based organized actions later in the year (Chomiak 2014).

With the onset of the protests of December 2011, Internet activism took on re-newed importance in Tunisia. A video of Bouazizi's self-immolation was posted on-line by a relative and picked up by satellite television stations, which broadcast the story far and wide; Facebook events spread information on upcoming protests. The Tunisian rap artist El Général published an anti-regime anthem on his Facebook page, for which he would later be detained. Perhaps most significantly, Nawaat.org, a blog site that had been a center for cyber-activism since 2004 (its publishing of Wikileaks cables had contributed to anti-regime sentiments), covered the protests with a dedication unmatched by formal media. As a source of information and a form of organizing that could, at least temporarily, evade regime censorship, cyber-activism proved to be a useful tool in the Tunisian revolution.

As Tunisia has embarked on post–Ben Ali institution building, cyber-activism has adapted to the new political context. The watchdog NGO Al Bawsala tweets the presence or absence, and vote, of every member of the Constituent Assembly (Malmvig and Markus Lassen 2013). Now, rather than expressing anti-regime sen-timents, cyber-movements, often led by lawyers, have turned to supporting the enforcement of rule of law.[9] While Tunisian politics and society have changed, the forms of Internet activism, present for at least a decade before the uprising, have evolved as well.

In Egypt, youth movements also became increasingly active after the early 2000s, and Internet technologies played an important role in their activities. As Dina Shehata (2012, 109) notes, Egyptian youth mobilization evolved through sev-eral different phases in the decade leading up to the uprisings. In the initial phase, it focused largely on external issues, such as solidarity with the Palestinian intifada or opposition to the war in Iraq. By 2004, youth activists had expanded their focus to domestic political and constitutional reform and organized themselves separately from older regime opponents by establishing the Youth for Change, a group under the umbrella of the Kifaya movement. Among the first major cyber-movements in

Egypt, Kifaya, a coalition of Marxist, Nasserite, and Islamist opposition groups, gained prominence in 2005 with its successful rallies and demonstrations, opening the door for future political dissent in Egypt (El-Mahdi 2014, 55–56). The mid-2000s brought some intergenerational splits between activists and a slight drop in Internet activism (Kuebler 2011, 11), but by 2008 new youth-led movements with strong online profiles emerged in the form of the April 6 Movement and Tadamon. The April 6 Movement, founded by a member of Youth for Change, was created in solidarity with striking textile workers in the town of El-Mahalla El-Kubra. Mobilizing through Facebook, the April 6 Movement gained 70,000 supporters within two weeks—which is especially impressive given that there were only 800,000 active Facebook users in Egypt at the time—and many participated in demonstrations to show their solidarity with the striking textile workers (Kuebler 2011, 11). Over time, the April 6 Movement expanded its mission, strongly backing the 2011 protests and demonstrating sporadically until its banning by the Al-Sisi government in April 2014 (Ahram Online 2014). Tadamon, too, links economic and political demands; its mission is to build ties with labor activists and engage in other forms of grassroots mobilization.

Egyptian cyber-activism remained strong throughout the late 2000s, largely as a source of news on topics avoided by the state-sanctioned mainstream media, such as videos of police violence or torture. The creation of the Facebook page "We Are All Khaled Said" by Wael Ghonim, a Google executive, is a case in point. On June 6, 2010, a young man named Khaled Said was dragged out of an Internet café by plainclothes police officers and, allegedly, beaten to death. As postmortem pictures of Said's beaten body were circulated on the Internet, the Facebook page gained prominence, and protests organized by the administrators of the "We Are All Khaled Said" Facebook page are seen as predecessors to the 2011 revolution (El-Mahdi 2014).

In the run-up to the January 25 protests, cyber-activism once again played a major role. In addition to general organizing and planning, notably by the April 6 Movement, the Internet was used as a rallying point for the upcoming demonstrations. On January 18, one week before the National Police Day protests, April 6 Movement cofounder Asmaa Mahfouz posted a video online pleading for the Egyptian people to join in demonstrations for change. The video, which quickly went viral, came to be seen as a spark for the 2011 uprisings.

As in Tunisia, cyber-activism in Egypt remains a key form of youth civic and political engagement and has intensified since the overthrow of Mubarak. New forms of Internet-based activism, for example, were a key factor leading to the ouster of President Morsi. A simple but effective form of online activism during his administration was the "Morsi Meter," a website that tracked the extent to which Morsi fulfilled his campaign promises (Malmvig and Markus Lassen 2013). Similarly, Tamarod, or the "revolt" movement, used grassroots mobilization—on the Internet, in formal media, and in the streets—to collect signatures demanding Morsi's resignation. Though total numbers are disputed, the Tamarod movement, which was itself created by members of Kifaya, reports that it collected at least 22 million signatures in a matter of weeks. The publicity and public pressure surrounding the campaign was a catalyst for the 2013 protests that resulted in Morsi's ouster by a military coup.

In virtually all countries in the Middle East, cyber-activism has become a crucial form of political expression, particularly among the youth, and it played a key role in mobilizing opposition during the wave of uprisings in the Arab region. For example, in Morocco a wide array of Facebook activist groups preceded the February 20 Movement. The anti-nepotism and anti-corruption campaigns "All Against Bequeathing Public Positions" and "All for Justice: The Minister's Son Should Stand Trial" were created in response to specific notable incidents. When a Moroccan man, Fodil Aberkan, was tortured to death by police officers in 2010, a Facebook group named "All for Disclosing the Truth on the Aberkan Affair" received wide publicity. Another Facebook group, "Moroccans Converse with the King," asked users to publicly list their principal demands for change. When the group's name was later changed to "Freedom and Democracy Now," the list of demands was consolidated and a video was posted calling for action. The February 20 Movement would later emerge out of this group. Drawing on the tactics of the Tunisian Nawaat.org, a group of Moroccans, mostly expatriates, helped to organize the protests by creating the website Mamfakinch, or "We Won't Give Up." This website, which was first used largely for blog posts and sharing information about protests, later took a more technologically advanced approach by mapping protests across the country (Benchemsi 2014).

In the Syrian uprising, protesters, particularly youth, have used cyber-activism to publicize the demonstrations that the formal media could not otherwise capture. Through the *tanseeqiat,* or local coordination committees, youth activists and groups emerged to collect and disseminate images and videos taken with cell-phone cameras. Activists have used Skype and YouTube to widen their audience, further support for their cause, and increase turnout at their demonstrations (Achcar 2013, 130; Sawah and Kawakibi 2014). In a country long cut off from communication with the outside world, the introduction of the Internet to Libya in 1998 provided an invaluable medium for expressing dissent. Though often censored by government authorities, or self-censored, blogs and forums became important tools for spreading information that the regime would otherwise have disallowed and for connecting Libyans in Libya with those abroad (Rajabany and Ben Shitrit 2014, 85). During the 2011 uprisings, YouTube videos posted by cyber-activists publicized protests and particularly the violent repression of antigovernment mobilization. Facebook was instrumental for organizing mass demonstrations, most notably for publicizing the February 17 Day of Rage (Rajabany and Ben Shitrit 2014, 92). The Internet also plays a vital role in mobilizing opposition and facilitating the expression of dissent, even in the countries where mass mobilization has been far more muted or virtually nonexistent, such as in some of the Gulf oil monarchies.

Social media made up, however, but one piece of the puzzle—and in some places a small piece—in explaining mass mobilization during the uprisings (Lynch 2011). Figure 11.8 shows that in some countries in the region only a small percentage of

FIGURE 11.8. Internet Usage in the MENA Region, 2000, 2010, and 2012

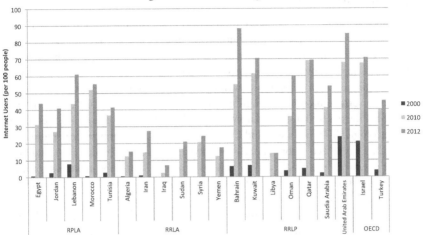

Source: World Bank, WDI.

Note: Data for Iraq for 2000 are from 2001 and data for Libya for 2012 are from 2011.

the population had access to the Internet on the eve of the uprisings. For example, Yemen, Syria, and Libya had comparatively few Internet users, and yet they had some of the most widespread protests. Even in more developed Tunisia and Egypt, only about 37 percent and 31 percent of the population had access to the Internet in 2010, respectively. Figure 11.8 also suggests cross-group variation in Internet usage, which was especially low among the RRLA countries. While low levels of development and disrupted infrastructure due to protracted conflict undoubtedly explain this pattern in some countries (Sudan, Yemen, Iraq), in others repression and censorship restrict access to the Internet (Iran, Syria) (Achcar 2013, 130). Even in countries where access to social media is relatively high, cyber-activism obviously provides an insufficient explanation for the occurrence of mass mobilization. Building grassroots support to sustain a mass uprising necessitates linkages with local social networks, and the young organizers of Tadamon and the April 6 Movement seemed to understand that when they reached out to striking textile workers. As access to the Internet and mobile technology rises, cyber-movements and other forms of online activism will only rise in importance.

Social media tools such as Facebook and Twitter can help to mobilize turnout at protests but are less useful for building long-term institutional change. The youth groups that helped to spark the uprisings in Egypt, as well as liberal parties and organizations started by older generations, found themselves marginalized in the post-Mubarak political scene owing to their limited capacity to build broader support and their lack of mass appeal. As a result, Islamist organizations and parties, which have long maintained social networks at the local level, were far more successful in winning elections and building mass support in the new political context.

Social Non-Movements

Like cyber-activism, another predominant form of social organization in the Middle East also occurs below the radar—but in this case offline. Across the region, much collective action occurs informally and does not engage directly with the state. These include the "myriad silent refusals, bypassing of authority, day-to-day forms of resistance, evasion of power practices, or other behavior" (Beinin and Vairel 2013, 11). Aptly termed "social non-movements" by Asef Bayat (2010, 14–15), these forms of collective action take place within ordinary life, are action-oriented rather than ideologically motivated, and are practiced by large numbers of fragmented rather than organized actors directly rather than as claims aimed at governments.

The everyday, seemingly minor actions of social non-movements can oppose governing authority, even inadvertently, and thus ultimately become subversive. Examples of these forms of everyday encroachment include the de facto claiming of public spaces through unlawful land holding (slums), illegal building or siphoning off of electricity or water infrastructure, cross-border and rural-to-urban migration, and unlicensed street vendors, who are a backbone of the large and growing informal economies throughout the Middle East. Women's participation in education, sports, arts, music, or work outside the home is another form of social non-movement, one that challenges patriarchal authority in everyday life without organized action or ideology. The choices of youth with respect to dress, music, and entertainment are another example of Bayat's non-movements. In an authoritarian context—in which formal modes of opposition are suppressed—non-movements have become a key form of collective action throughout the Middle East, particularly among those who are marginalized and excluded from decision-making processes.

Some informal modes of expressing opposition overtly address the state. Graffiti, which sparked the uprising in Daraa, Syria, and was ubiquitous in the Tunisian, Egyptian, and Gezi Park protests, among others, is a popular medium of dissent. Even everyday jokes are a subtle form of resistance (Wedeen 2000). One such joke, popular in Tunisia, lamented the nepotism and corruption that ran rampant in the family of Ben Ali's wife, Leila Trabelsi. Out for a drive by himself, the joke goes, President Ben Ali is stopped by a traffic cop. "Ben Ali explains he is the President, Zine el Abidine Ben Ali, but the cop says 'Never heard of you,' and takes Ben Ali to the police station. The station chief looks at Ben Ali's identification card and says, 'It's okay. He's related to the Trabelsis'" (Parvaz 2011). Nonparticipation is also used to implicitly oppose elections perceived to be a sham; when the choice is between voting for a repressive regime and an opposition that will never win, abstaining may be the only available form of resistance (Rajabany and Ben Shitrit 2014, 79).

Although non-movements lack formal organizational networks, their "passive networks" can forge solidarity among those who engage in forms of "quiet encroachment."[10] For example, as Bayat notes, informal street vendors who work in the same area develop a kind of solidarity simply through their daily presence together. Similarly, women who openly practice sports in the same park may not have formal or established social ties, but their regular shared company over time can constitute a tacit form of feminist non-movement.

The forms of everyday solidarity that emerge mainly in poor, urban neighborhoods across the Middle East provide social networks that help people meet their daily needs under difficult conditions. Yet the de facto claiming of space and infrastructure means that the state loses its authority in certain realms. Because the state aims to keep streets orderly and under its control, the use of the streets for nonsanctioned purposes is effectively subversive. Furthermore, social non-movements can evolve into more overtly politicized movement. This is most likely to occur, Bayat presciently argues (writing in 2010), when an action that has become routinized, such as peddling goods in the street, is suddenly blocked or opposed by authorities. An example of this is Mohamed Bouazizi's self-immolation in response to harassment by a police officer who confronted him for his lack of a license for his fruit stand and abused him. Although Bouazizi indeed operated his cart without a license, informal work like his, which is widespread across Tunisia and the Middle East, becomes so normalized through daily repetition that regime action against it is perceived as an infringement of rights. The "ordinary" so encroaches on the power of the regime that it gains the status of rights and autonomy. When he was challenged, Bouazizi felt that his rights had been infringed upon, and through the solidarity of passive networks, the non-movement became politicized.

In some respects, Bayat's social non-movements resemble the networks that Diane Singerman (1995, esp. ch. 3) describes in her study of the urban neighborhoods of Cairo. However, people operating in the networks she describes may interact with local elites and government bureaucrats to obtain publicly subsidized goods and services. Other forms of exchange in these informal modes of participation— such as seeking marriage partners or employment opportunities, migrating to seek better jobs, or exchanging gifts—do not entail engagement with the authorities but rather play out among neighbors and community members (Singerman 1995, 138).

The actions of participants in these networks are not simply efforts to obtain goods or improve living conditions, but contain an ideological component grounded in particular notions about the rules and morality of the community. Furthermore, like non-movements, these actions "fill a political need in the community by representing and furthering the interests of the *sha'b* [people], which have little access to, or influence over, the formal political system" (Singerman 1995, 133), and therefore they can indirectly serve as a form of political subversion. Informal networks create a mentality of solidarity among the urban poor, carving out a sphere that is somewhat autonomous from the control of authoritarian regimes. In this way, networks "provide a critical avenue of participation for men and women among *sha'abi* [popular] communities. . . . If extensive networks coordinate masses of people to achieve particular goals, they clearly serve as a political institution for this particular constituency" (Singerman 1995, 172).

If we merely focus on formal political institutions and state-centered forms of political engagement, we miss these important, less visible forms of civic engagement and collective action in the Middle East. Furthermore, although difficult to trace, these types of informal networks clearly played a role in facilitating mobilization against incumbent dictators during the Arab uprisings and in earlier instances of opposition to state policies. Indeed, as we noted earlier, social mobilization emphasizes the importance of informal networks as a key "resource" for mass collective action.

At the same time, these forms of everyday exchange are not uniformly empowering and can actually inhibit political participation by reinforcing unequal, clientelist relationships. By maintaining autonomy from the state, the informal networks arguably reinforce the status quo by preventing political accountability or demand for change. In effect, networks substitute for effective state institutions (Jamal and Khatib 2014).

THE FAILURE OF IDEOLOGY

Had Middle Eastern leaders been able to nurture some sort of broad ideological and programmatic consensus, it might have been possible to keep all these old and new actors within the political game. But ideologies fabricated by house ideologues or, worse yet, bureaucrats in ministries of culture, information, and "national guidance" have failed to penetrate strategically placed elites, let alone the people as a whole. For over three decades after most countries gained independence in the region, the official ideologies spawned in the Middle East, especially in the republican regimes, shared several common themes, all similar to, if not derived from, Atatürk and the Turkish republic's six principles: (1) developing national strength—meaning freedom from imperial control coupled with a strong economy and strong armed forces—as both a goal and a promise; (2) building a new citizen and a new sense of citizenship with the end of foreign control and the elimination of domestic oppressor classes such as large landowners and compradors; taking care of the physical and work needs of the population, giving each adult a new sense of dignity and self-worth, through (3) mass literacy, (4) public health, and (5) a booming planned economy; and (6) satisfying the psychic needs of the populace through the mass party, which would educate new generations in nationalist and civic duties.

Every regime, including the less populist monarchies, espoused the equitable distribution of the benefits of economic growth. The shah of Iran, King Hassan of Morocco, King Hussein of Jordan, and, indeed, the Saudi monarchy were as concerned with modernization and national strength as the more obvious "socialist" republican leaders. An examination of the rhetoric of the White Revolution launched by the shah in 1963 reveals familiar themes of destroying the feudal landowners through agrarian reform, redistributing national wealth through the sale of shares to workers in private and public industry, bringing literacy to all the people, and liberating women. Ten years later, the shah added the national-military dimension, proclaiming that within a decade or so Iran would become a world military power.

Had the planned, state-dominated economies worked up to expectations, had the expansion and increasing quality of education and social services kept pace with unchecked population growth, and had Middle Eastern nations built measurably powerful military establishments (only Turkey, the Middle East's sole member of

NATO, and Israel can be said to have done so), then perhaps the accompanying ideologies might have had some impact on broad strata of Middle Eastern society. But the many performance failures—from unprofitable public enterprise and the failure to achieve sustained and equitable growth to the repeated military setbacks for some Arab armed forces—rendered the rhetoric hollow and ultimately a target of derision and anger. Philip Khoury (1983) has rightly written of regime "exhaustion," the collective playing out of a set of policy and ideological options by an entire generation of Middle Eastern leaders. The statist, socialist, and implicitly secularizing experiments of the past four or five decades have resolved few of the problems they promised to tackle. Other than in Iran, Sudan, and perhaps Saudi Arabia, the one option that has not been tried is Islamic government—at least not until Islamist parties were elected in Tunisia and Egypt after 2011.[11] Still, nearly twenty-five years after Khoury wrote his article, the same "exhausted" regimes cling to power.

For decades, then, there has been a kind of organizational and ideological vacuum in the Middle East—a lack of a national project—that several different actors are trying to fill. Incumbent elites with the economic and coercive might of the state at their disposal still have the upper hand, but they may lack the conviction or confidence to use it. Secular liberals are a tiny minority, and very often they suffer from "guilt by association" with incumbent and former authoritarian rulers and with a West widely seen in the region as an aggressive imperialist power and intolerant of Islam. Islamists have enthusiasm and popular symbols, which in part explains their grassroots appeal, yet they offer few answers to questions of governance and economic management and have lost credibility as Islamist parties have failed to bring more stability and equity during their short-lived experiences holding office in Egypt and Tunisia (see Chapter 12).

In the current historical juncture, it is not clear what ideology will take hold in the region. The importance of private sector–led development and greater redistribution are policy priorities in many countries; however, no clear blueprint for building effective and fair capitalist systems has emerged. Furthermore, polarization on social and cultural issues inhibits broad societal consensus on how to achieve greater political and economic inclusion.

CONCLUSIONS

The landscape of civil society in the Middle East has evolved. Older forms of interest group aggregation and associationalism have been discredited. Well before the uprisings broke out in late 2010, workers were staging wildcat strikes and new labor unions were forming as alternatives to the national-level federations that largely worked in the interests of authoritarian regimes. Women and youth were becoming increasingly active, albeit not often through traditional organizations, and online activism and opposition groups were on the rise throughout the 2000s.

Some of these new or revitalized actors took part in and even helped to organize the uprisings in Tunisia, Egypt, and across the region. For example, young people who took part in cyber-activism against their governments played an important role in mobilizing participation in demonstrations. But so, too, did more established groups, such as unions. Everyday networks, which help poor and marginalized communities meet their needs, were probably the most important organizational resource at the local level, even if they are difficult to measure.

Different kinds of collective actors have varied abilities to affect macro-level politics in distinct political moments. Networks and cyber-movements may help to mobilize participation in demonstrations. As youth activists found, however, in the aftermath of Mubarak's and Ben Ali's ousters, when they were increasingly sidelined from the halls of power, loose networks and groups are often less effective at influencing public policy, lobbying, and taking part in the formal political process. For these tasks, the classic features of strong party organizations, such as established structures, human resource capacities, and an extensive grassroots presence, are critical. While we should not fetishize formal organizations—parties and other associations have long been weak and co-opted in the MENA region—they remain important vehicles for aggregating and transmitting interests and effecting concrete political change.

Contests over the relationships between ruler and ruled are ongoing throughout the Middle East, but one thing is clear: the status quo is over. A revolution has occurred across the region—at a minimum, in the form of "cognitive liberation." People across the Middle East have experienced the exhilaration of demonstrating and standing up for their rights, they have gained experience organizing in both the formal and informal arenas, and many are no longer as fearful of their governments, even in the face of harsh crackdowns. People have had a taste of dignity and acquired valuable collective action skills, both online and offline, that will undoubtedly be deployed again and again in efforts to hold their leaders accountable. Sometimes they will succeed; many times they will not. In the short term, mass mobilization against incumbent rulers may be checked in some countries, such as Egypt, because many of the constituencies that militated for a more democratic order have been scared by street protest, protracted instability, and government crackdowns in the wake of the uprisings. As a result, some who had opposed authoritarian governments and militated for more just and inclusive political and economic institutions have retreated and now seem to support a strong ruler. But other elements of society have been emboldened by the uprisings and will not be as easily repressed in the future. The monopolization of economic opportunities and wealth by corrupt leaders and their entourages is now under more scrutiny, and it will be harder for rulers to get away with such massive and overt pillaging of their countries.

NOTES

1. On this point, see Beinin and Vairel (2013).

2. The OECD countries, Israel and Turkey, also experienced fewer protests than the RRLA and RPLA countries, although opposition movements developed there, too, with the rise of the Israeli "social justice" protests beginning in the summer of 2011 and, later, the Gezi Park protests in Turkey.

3. On the historical precursors of the uprisings in Yemen, see Philbrick Yadav (2011).

4. The fact that the protests began in drought-affected areas prompted some to consider the Syrian conflict partly a product of climate change; see Friedman (2013) and Brown and Crawford (2009). For a dissenting position, see Sowers, Waterbury, and Woertz (2013).

5. For a discussion of the legitimacy of the UN-sanctioned operation and the motivations of the major international players, see Gazzini (2011). Hugh Roberts (2011) provides a trenchant critique of the NATO intervention.

6. Parts of the following discussion draw on Cammett and Posusney (2010).

7. A real estate tax collectors' union had never existed under the ETUF, but rather was incorporated into a broader union for employees in banks and financial administration.

8. Email communication with Dina Bishara, Jarvis Doctorow Research Fellow in the Politics and International Relations of the Middle East, University of Oxford, July 24, 2014.

9. Email communication with Laryssa Chomiak, Director, Centre d'Études Maghrébines à Tunis, July 25, 2014.

10. According to Bayat (2010, 45), "Quiet encroachment refers to noncollective but prolonged direct actions of dispersed individuals and families to acquire the basic necessities of their lives (land for shelter, urban collective consumption or urban services, informal work, business opportunities, and public space) in a quiet and unassuming illegal fashion."

11. Islamists also govern in Turkey and, in coalition with non-Islamist Kurdish parties, in Iraq.

12

IS ISLAM THE SOLUTION?

"Islam is the solution!"—the rallying cry of Islamist political parties—has appeared on walls in virtually every popular quarter in the Middle East and North Africa. Since at least the 1970s, a wide range of thinkers and political activists throughout the Muslim world have increasingly framed their approaches to politics, economics, and social issues in self-consciously Islamic terms. In this chapter, we investigate the role and effects of Islamism on the political economy of the region.

TERMINOLOGY AND TYPOLOGY

Problems of definition and terminology immediately confront us. Many accounts in the popular Western press refer to "Muslim fundamentalism." We find the term, and the perspective it implies, deeply misleading, since it assumes, among other things, that Islamists do not engage in interpretation (*ijtihad*), a position that is untenable.[1] Furthermore, all Muslims believe that the Qur'an is the literal "dictation" from God to the Prophet Muhammad. However, exactly *how* to apply the whole of God's message to modern life is much debated among Muslims, though the sacredness of the message itself is not.

The phrase "political Islam" is often used to describe the social phenomena covered in this chapter. This expression gained currency in Western discourse in the aftermath of the Iranian revolution. Although more apposite than "fundamentalism," the term is both too broad and too narrow for our purposes. It is too broad because if "political" means "having religious views on social organization and governance," then Islam is inherently political. From its very inception, Islam has been a religion that stresses people's involvement in community, society, and the polity. And by some interpretations, even forms of everyday life that do not deal with the realm of government are political (Bayat 2009; Mahmoud 2004). Islam appeared nonpolitical to Americans only during the 1950s and 1960s, when Arab politics was dominated by the supporters and opponents of Arab nationalism and socialism (for example, Nasserism and Ba'athism). Even during that era, the opponents of Arab nationalism, whether the Muslim Brotherhood or the Kingdom of Saudi Arabia, deployed an Islamic political discourse. Such opposition was often supported by other opponents of Arab nationalism, whether the United States or Israel. The term is likewise too narrow because if "political" means "making the current acquisition of state power one's primary goal and activity," then many Islamists are not political, since they focus on spreading the faith (*da'wa*), shaping popular culture and mores, and molding popular discourse. Even within Islamist groups focused on *da'wa*, however, ultimate goals may vary, with some viewing proselytism as a bottom-up form of gradual political change while others aim to make people more pious for the sake of piety itself.

We choose instead to use the term "Islamism," defining it as activism carried out by Islamists or Islamist groups (see, for example, ICG 2005). In this definition, Islamists seek to bring all elements of social, economic, and political life into harmony with *what its adherents believe* is "true Islam." Islamists criticize current social conditions as tyrannical and unjust, oppose authoritarian ruling elites, and couch their appeals and policies in religious terms (Hamzawy 2005). Minimally, they call for the application of Sharia (Islamic law), but they differ hugely in their interpretation of what exactly that means in the concrete circumstances of today's world.

Their tactics also diverge widely. At one end of the spectrum are Islamists who recognize the existence of current states and boundaries and participate in democratic political processes (for example, the Turkish Justice and Development Party [AKP]). At the other extreme are those who seek to seize power violently and who denounce both formal democracy and nation-states as illegitimate (for example, the followers of Osama bin Laden) or the Islamic State of Iraq (ISIL) or simply the Islamic State, as it now calls itself. Still others are undecided as to the specific mix of coercion and persuasion that is appropriate to the pursuit of their goals, and there are many intermediate cases. Such differences are reminiscent of the diversity of views among European socialists in the twentieth century, when, for example, social democrats and Bolsheviks hurled anathemas at one another. As was true of socialism during that earlier time, today's Islamist tent is wide indeed.[2]

A possible typology of Islamism would first distinguish between Sunni and Shi'a Islamism.[3] Its organized, semi-hierarchical clergy makes Shi'a Islam less fissiparous than Sunni Islam, which lacks any such formal organization. Nevertheless, there are significant disagreements among Shi'a Islamists concerning (1) whether they accept or reject Ayatollah Khomeini's concept of the *wilayat al faqih* ("rule by the jurisprudent"), and, if they accept it, (2) *which* ayatollah they think should occupy this post.[4] These differences are typically less severe, however, than those found among Sunni Islamists.

Within Sunni Islamism, we can distinguish three broad approaches: (1) political Islamism (in a restricted sense), (2) missionary or *da'wa* activity, and (3) violent jihadism. We use the phrase "political Islamism" to refer to all those who (a) pursue political power in order to (b) bring society more into alignment with its adherents' understanding of Islam through (c) nonviolent means. Two prominent examples of political Islamists, as we have defined the term, are the Justice and Development Party of Turkey and the Muslim Brotherhood of Egypt. They are distinguished with respect to their goals from the second group, whose focus is on diffusing their interpretation of Islam through preaching, personal example, and charitable activities. This second group includes the "New Islamists," or the *waseteyya* ("middle path") intellectuals of Egypt (Baker 2003), who resemble the so-called Islamic modernists—like Muhammad Abduh of a century ago—in their creative use of *ijtihad* to develop what they view as an "Islamic" approach to social, economic, and political problems. It also includes the very different *salafiyya* movement, which stresses imitation of (what adherents think was) the behavior of the Prophet Muhammad and his companions. *Salafis* are very concerned about the details of living, such as how to dress, eat, sleep, and even brush one's teeth. They also have rather vague, but strongly held, views on the requirements of a true "Islamic state," which they typically find to exist nowhere.[5]

Finally, there are the violent militants. The most notorious of these, the followers of al-Qaeda and its offshoots, emerged as the product of two currents in militant thought: First, *as-salafiyya al-jihadiyya* or *salafis* who have been radicalized and have abandoned pacific missionary work to engage in political violence. Second, other jihadists consider themselves "Qutbists," or followers of the thinking of Sayyid Qutb, the Egyptian who was executed in 1966 and who applied the notion of *takfir,* or "pronouncement of unbelief," to the polities in the region at that time.[6] Qutbists believe that those who disagree with their interpretation of Islam are infidels—rather than Muslims who understand Islam differently—and that these infidels can, and should, be violently resisted and killed. Such militants often categorize Shi'a Muslims as unbelievers and denounce those Muslims who participate in elections, like the Muslim Brotherhood. Non-jihadists have also been inspired by Qutb's ideas, even if they do not accept the use of violence against so-called nonbelievers.

Nearly all other Islamists sharply distinguish between the violence of *jihadi salafis* such as Osama bin Laden and the violence of the Palestinian and Lebanese Islamic resistance movements. They argue that the violence of the former is unjustified and immoral, whereas the violence of the latter is legitimate resistance to the humiliation and oppression of occupation. Some Islamists, such as Hezbollah (the Shi'a "Party of God") of Lebanon, differentiate between al-Qaeda's attacks on the civilian target of the World Trade Center—which they denounced—and the attack on the military target of the Pentagon—which they did not criticize. A broad spectrum of Islamist factions is visible in Iraq, where there is now something approaching an "Islamist civil war" pitting Shi'a Islamists (themselves divided) against jihadi salafis (who are allied with Ba'athists). Beyond these controversies, there is a fierce debate over the meaning of *jihad,* which means "struggle" and is often interpreted as the struggle to remain an observant, pious Muslim, without reference to the use of violence.

It is important to note that our definition and typology have inherent weaknesses. The boundary between "Muslim" and "Islamist" remains rather vague. (Is *any* Muslim trying to propagate the faith an "Islamist"?) Further, the elements of our typology are not mutually exclusive. For example, many explicitly nonviolent political movements (or political Islamists, in our usage) also engage in missionary activity. Indeed, it is precisely this overlap in activity that provided the official rationale of the Mubarak regime in Egypt for not legalizing the Muslim Brotherhood: the government claimed that they could not be both a political party and an organization devoted to the spread of religion. Now, under President Al-Sisi, the Muslim Brotherhood is once again illegal in Egypt, although this time the government justifies the ban on the basis that it is a "terrorist" organization.

Circumstances also may lead political Islamists, who are nonviolent by our definition, to engage in violence—such as when they are faced with the violence of others. And as noted earlier, political Islamists, in our sense, do not necessarily renounce violence if peaceful means are blocked. In contrast to the official US government position, we think that it is more useful to categorize Hamas in Palestine and Hezbollah in Lebanon as political Islamists, as we have defined it, to distinguish them from the jihadi salafis, with whom they are often at odds. Certainly Hamas and Hezbollah deploy physical force; however, they both participate in elections and aim to hold political offices. These Palestinian and Lebanese movements more closely resemble the Irish Nationalists of Sinn Fein/IRA than the followers of al-Qaeda. Placing them in the same category as jihadi salafis clouds the picture more than it illuminates it.

The rest of this chapter is organized using the analytical axes of Figure 1.1: social actors, economic growth and structural transformation, state policy and governance, and social actors. From the "social actors" perspective, we examine Islamism as a social movement, investigating its social bases and the coalitions of actors it represents. We then turn to three modes of social activism: social welfare, electoral contestation, and political violence. From the perspective of economic growth and structural transformation, we investigate Islamists' ideas about how to cope with the many problems presented by their political economies. Like adherents of the Post–Washington Consensus, Islamists agree that the key issues facing their societies are governance questions, so we turn lastly to a review of the behavior of Islamists when they have actually wielded state power—in Iran, Turkey, and Sudan and, more recently, in Tunisia, Egypt, and Morocco.

ISLAMISM AS A SOCIAL MOVEMENT: SOCIAL SUPPORT BASES

Islamism is a social movement, that is, a group challenge to established authority by people sharing common purposes (Tarrow 1994). Such movements engage in campaigns, demonstrations, public meetings, electoral contestation, public announcements, pamphleteering, and any other activities that demonstrate the group's "worthiness, unity, numbers, and commitments" (Tilly 2002, 120). As Charles Tilly (2002) argues, such movements—very much including Islamism—are *modern* phenomena. There is nothing "backward" about Islamist movements. One may deplore the goals and methods of some Islamists (for example, jihadi salafis). From such disapproval, however, it hardly follows that they should be understood as "primitive" or "backward," any more than disagreement with Leninist goals and methods implied that Communists were "backward."

Both international and national forces forged the context within which Islamism grew. At the global level, Islamism first appeared as a form of resistance to Western colonialism in all its forms—political, cultural, economic, and military. The classic case is the oldest Sunni Islamist movement, the Muslim Brotherhood, which arose under the leadership of Hassan al-Banna in Egypt in the 1930s (Mitchell 1969). Such opposition has always included rejection of the Zionist project, which the large majority of Islamists view as a variety of Western colonialism.

Islamists were hardly the only opponents of Western colonialism or of Zionism. Part of the strength of Islamist movements derives from the defeat of their competitors, particularly those of the secular left (Arab nationalists, Communists, Ba'athists) and liberals, whose anticolonial and Arab nationalist discourse was adapted by Islamists for their own purposes. To some extent, the defeats of these forces were self-inflicted wounds deriving from their failures in power and their inability to create viable mass political movements. They were also undermined by external forces. The United States has long had a strategic alliance with the Kingdom of Saudi Arabia, whose state ideology is a form of *salafi* Islam known to its detractors as "Wahhabism." A core element of the relationship throughout the twentieth century was joint US-Saudi opposition to Nasserism, Ba'athism, and communism. Consequently, both governments supported Islamist movements; Saudi Arabia favored salafi tendencies and others allied with or friendly to its own distinctive interpretation of Islam. Cooperation between the two governments peaked during the war of the Afghan and international *mujahedin* ("holy warriors") against the Soviet occupation of Afghanistan during the 1980s and was renewed in their joint effort to eject Saddam Hussein from Kuwait in 1990–1991. The role of Saudi wealth and American diplomacy, military and otherwise, in strengthening Islamism should not be underestimated (Abu Khalil 2002, 2004; Mamdani 2004).

Globalization provides a second international context for recent Islamist success. The technological revolution in computation and communication has greatly facilitated the interaction of everyone in the world—which very much includes Islamists—through blogs, websites, and social media accounts that facilitate group communications as well as engagement with other communities, both online and in the real world (Bohn 2011; Lynch 2007). At the same time, the ideological hegemony of Western "neoliberal" ideas, such as the Washington Consensus (see Chapter 8), and America's increasingly muscular Wilsonianism have prompted countermovements everywhere—as the recent upsurge of populism in Latin America attests. In the MENA region, Islamism has provided the main resistance to Western hegemony, and globalization provided Islamists with important tools for this opposition (Lubeck 1999). Furthermore, in the context of popular reactions against crony capitalism and corruption, Islamists have often claimed the moral high ground, expanding their support.

At the national level, the rise of Islamic movements was partially a function of the hesitancy of incumbent elites to continue to repress and harass militant groups. Although relatively few might welcome Islamic governments, a far broader swath of the population shared the militants' moral indignation. Aware of this popular state of mind, elites hesitated to confront the militants for fear of isolating themselves further. Nearly all political leaders could feel the repressed heat of Muslim militants; Nasser, Atatürk, the shah of Iran, and Ben Ali, among others, broke up their organizations and put the leaders in jail. Significantly, however, nearly all republican constitutions in the Middle East state that the president must be a Muslim, and several declare that Islam is the state religion and that all law must conform to the Sharia. Leaders from Nasser to Saddam Hussein have frequently invoked Muslim themes in an attempt to legitimize their rule, and few have failed to make the pilgrimage, ostentatiously, to Mecca. And we should not forget that several "secularizing" leaders, including Nasser and Boumediene, were in fact pious Muslims who performed their religious duties regularly.

Understanding the national dimension of Islamist social movements requires an examination of the social groups supporting such movements. What social coalitions undergird Islamism? As a rough generalization, we can say that Islamist movements often loosely join three social actors: a counter-elite composed of businessmen and professionals, a second stratum of frustrated intellectuals and unemployed or underemployed university or secondary school graduates, and a mass base of the young, semi-educated unemployed. And increasingly, the Islamists are able to recruit from the ranks of the urban lumpen proletariat.

The relative weight of these elements in any specific Islamist coalition varies widely. Some organizations, such as the Iraqi Shi'a movement of Muqtada al-Sadr, draw most of their support from poor slum dwellers, especially in Baghdad (ICG 2006). Others, such as the Egyptian New Islamists of the Al-Wasat Al-Gadeed Party, find most of their supporters among professionals and other members of the urban middle classes (Baker 2003). Some evidence suggests that the Egyptian Salafi Al-Nour Party, which was officially established after Mubarak's overthrow, built support among those who had been ill served by the prior regime's economic liberalization policies (Ahmed 2012), whereas the Muslim Brotherhood was seen as supportive of the reforms and as relatively "disconnected from the street" in lower-class neighborhoods (Lacroix 2012, 7). Al-Islah, a Yemeni Islamist political party, relies heavily on the power of various Zaydi tribes of the North, particularly the Hashid confederation (ICG 2003b). In Iraq, more prosperous Shi'a tribes from around Najaf and Karbala tend to support Islamist parties such as the Supreme Council for Islamic Revolution in Iraq (SCIRI) and the Islamic Dawa Party, while those from poorer, less favored areas, such as Maysan Governorate in the South, tend to support the Sadrists (ICG 2006).[7] As with all political movements and parties, these coalitions shift, break apart, and reconfigure. To assess the social bases of Islamism is to track a moving target.

Appeals to the "counter-elite" of business often arise from those in the entrepreneurial classes who have been excluded (or feel themselves to have been excluded) from the favors bestowed by the state under import substitution industrialization (ISI) and, later, under liberalization characterized by cronyism. Such groups have emerged in Egypt, Morocco, Turkey, and elsewhere (see Chapter 8 on economic liberalization across the MENA region). In Palestine, the Muslim Brotherhood and its offshoot, Hamas, have "always enjoyed the support of landowners, merchants, and shopkeepers" (Abu-Amr 1994, 20). Islam explicitly sanctions a very broad range of profit-making activities, and wealth, when used for social benefit, is fully sanctioned. Where the state has been both exclusionary and aggressively secular, religiously pious businessmen form a natural component of many Islamist coalitions.

The appeal of Islamism to the youth is not hard to understand. We have seen in Chapters 4 and 5 that education and exposure to the wider world have broadened their horizons, but the grim realities of the job and housing markets have dashed their hopes. Too often they cannot find jobs, especially jobs that match their expectations, and rarely can they locate suitable housing. Many must postpone marriage, often for a long time. Because young people everywhere are trying to establish their identity, they care greatly about their relationships with others. They also care about questions of justice and fairness and find that such ethical norms are routinely violated by their own government, by Israel, and by the United States and "the West" more generally.

Increasingly, Islamism has become the region's mass movement opposing humiliation, both at home and abroad, although the Arab uprisings show that perceived violations of dignity and justice by rulers also mobilize non-Islamist youth and their elders in the Middle East. The youth of today are as attracted to nationalism as were their fathers and grandfathers. Many view the wider community of Muslims as attacked and abused, and they identify with those who resist these attacks. The "Afghans," or those who fought the Soviets in Afghanistan, were hugely popular during the 1990s. After the summer of 2006, when Hezbollah fought the Israelis to a standoff in South Lebanon, pictures of its leader, Hassan Nasrallah, were widely displayed throughout the Arab world.

The failures of the old order have stimulated Islamist movements. The grandiose promises and disappointing performances of national development strategies in the region since independence have left many searching for alternatives. Here we review three phases: the ISI phase, the oil-boom era, and the era of the Washington Consensus. We have discussed throughout this text how ISI policies increased industrial production and opened educational systems, particularly for secondary and university education. However, these policies also fostered excessive capital-intensity, which retarded job creation, generated severe balance-of-payments constraints, which slowed growth, and fostered rural-to-urban migration by discriminating against agriculture.

The oil boom of the 1970s further blunted incentives for the production of tradables and stimulated rural-to-urban migration even more. It also stimulated large-scale labor emigration from poor countries to the Gulf states, the rise of new, often Islamist financial intermediaries channeling the flow of remittances back home, and the acceleration of state largesse. States trying to pursue the partial, halting liberalization known as *infitah* encouraged Islamist militants as counterweights to the socialist left. The counter-elite of Islamist businessmen and professionals was also greatly strengthened in this period.

The oil bust of the 1980s and 1990s witnessed declining resources, governmental retrenchment, and tentative economic reform efforts (see Chapter 8). The economic downturn and government budgetary austerity coincided with the acceleration of new entrants to the labor force, coming on top of a legacy of economic failure. Government spending cutbacks and administrative deficiencies further weakened an already tattered social safety net, and this created opportunities for Islamist movements, which moved to provide their own services. As we saw in Chapter 8, the Washington Consensus policies in other economic areas failed to reduce unemployment or raise real wages by any significant measure and led to the rise of the very rich and a sense of unfairness and immorality in society. It seems clear that neither state-led ISI nor the Washington Consensus were able to provide economic and social development or defend vital national interests. Unsurprisingly, Arabs, Turks, and Iranians have been examining their own traditions for the potential building material of alternative models.

In short, government policies during the past three decades have fostered a counter-elite of Islamist businessmen, dissatisfied intellectuals, frustrated educated youth, and elements of the urban poor who may sympathize with the Islamist message, even if their shared sympathies do not result in cross-class identities and explicit coordination. State economic, political, and cultural weaknesses have promoted Islamist movements by stimulating grievances and evacuating critical spaces in the political economy. Islamist movements cannot be understood without a grasp of the uneven and sometimes stalled developmental processes that we have chronicled throughout this book.

However, the phenomenon of Islamism cannot be *reduced* to these developmental problems. Blocked careers, unemployment, rampant corruption, and unavailable housing all set the context for Islamism, but they are poor predictors of exactly who will participate in such movements. Unemployed and frustrated young men throughout the region can turn to Islamism, to drugs and crime, or to indifference, and they can use any number of other personal coping strategies, from muddling through to hard work and determination. As social scientists, we have a tendency to explain a given phenomenon in terms of others. In this instance, we see the strengthening of militant, and sometimes violent, Islamic groups in terms of unemployment among the educated and semi-educated, bleak career prospects, and resentment of those who have done well—often expressed via illegal means or as a quest for justice. This understanding is surely "true" to some degree, but it assumes that if economic and employment conditions could be improved, militant Islam would lose its constituency. It diminishes the place in Islamic identity of piety and faith. One of Morocco's best-known Islamic leaders, Abdessalam Yassine, chided a French social scientist, François Burgat, precisely for falling into this analytic error: "I find this explanation a little too easy and that it does not take into account the subjective factor. People do not come to Islam as an alternative for their social misfortunes. People come to Islam in response to a call, a call which goes very far and deep in the human soul" (Burgat 1993, 75).

Ultimately, the decision to join a social movement is a deeply personal, idiosyncratic one. Socioeconomic contexts are important for understanding these movements, but they by no means fully explain them. However, such trends, when combined with the continuing failure of Palestinians to obtain a state enjoying mass legitimacy, along with the increasing reliance by both the United States and Israel on naked military force, do much to explain the surging popularity and legitimacy of Islamism. Meanwhile, nearly any Arab or Muslim can see daily images of violence in Lebanon, Iraq, and Palestine on the Al Jazeera network, while websites, email, and smartphones bring Islamists of all types and from all regions into close contact. The largest generation of young Muslims in history is increasingly

FIGURE 12.1. Support for Religion in Politics by Age in Selected MENA Countries, 2010–2014

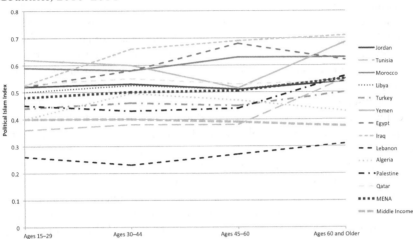

Source: WVS, wave 6, 2010–2014.

Note: The vertical axis measures the percentage of respondents who exceed or fall below the middle-income average.

educated, informed, and frustrated. Furthermore, the failure of the state in places such as Iraq, Libya, Syria, and parts of Yemen has created a hospitable breeding ground for extremist Islamic movements, such as the Islamic State of Iraq (ISIL). The current historical conjuncture has favored Islamist social movements.

That said, the appeal of Islamism has its limits, and in many countries it appears to be less compelling to younger citizens than to their elders. Figure 12.1 depicts support for Political Islam in twelve MENA countries as well as the regional average and the average for all middle-income countries based on the sixth wave of the World Values Survey (WVS), which was carried out between 2010 and 2014. Because respondents were asked whether religious authorities should ultimately interpret the laws, the question provides a measure of support for religion in politics rather than for political Islam per se. The horizontal axis of Figure 12.1 divides the sample into four different age groups, arrayed from youngest to oldest, and the vertical axis measures the percentage of respondents who rated above or below the average for all middle-income countries. In general, support for religion in politics, which taps into attitudes toward political Islam in the Muslim-majority countries, was higher in MENA countries than in middle-income countries and increased with age. Furthermore, this trend was somewhat reversed in middle-income countries, where support for religion in politics revealed a slight decrease with age.

The endorsement of political Islam in MENA populations is characterized by considerable cross-national variation, suggesting that context matters greatly for interpreting the role of religion in politics in each country. In both Lebanon and Tunisia, people generally reported less support for political Islam than was reported by the middle-income average. In both countries, and especially in Tunisia, older people were more favorable toward the role of religion in politics. The remaining countries in the sample all backed political Islam at above-average levels when benchmarked against middle-income countries, with levels that exceeded the MENA average in Yemen, Egypt, Morocco, Iraq, Qatar, Jordan, and Libya (in roughly descending order). Each of these countries shows interesting patterns in its own right. For example, in Yemen the forty-five- to fifty-nine age group revealed a sharp dip in its favorability toward Islamism, whereas in Egypt the same cohort was especially supportive of religion in politics. In Jordan, Libya, and Qatar, however, the thirty- to forty-four-year-old group exhibited a similar trend, albeit to a lesser degree. In Morocco and, especially, Iraq, older cohorts were increasingly supportive of political Islam. In Iraq, high levels of support may also have been fueled by state failure. Algerians bucked the general trend: support for political Islam declined there after a peak in the thirty- to– forty-four age group.

The relationship between educational attainment and support for political Islam among Middle Eastern populations also points to considerable variation in attitudes toward religion in politics, both within and across different MENA countries. Figure 12.2 depicts education levels (horizontal axis) and favorability toward the role of religious authorities in politics vis-à-vis the average for middle-income countries (vertical axis) among the same respondents in twelve Arab countries. In general, support for Islamism declines with increased education, and again, the average for the MENA region exceeds that of middle-income countries globally.

Lebanon and Tunisia, once again, are outliers owing to their below-average scores vis-à-vis both middle-income countries and the rest of the Middle East. In Lebanon, what is particularly striking—although perhaps not surprising given that country's history of conflict in the name of religion—is that low levels of support for religion in politics were relatively constant across all levels of education. Palestine, Turkey, and Algeria showed lower levels of support for political Islam than the MENA average, with a particularly marked drop in Turkey among those with university degrees. In Iraq, Qatar, Egypt, Yemen, Morocco, Jordan, and Libya, people reported relatively high levels of support for political Islam, albeit with interesting cross-national variation. Yemenis with only a primary education were the most supportive of Islamism, but Yemenis' support dropped dramatically with education. Libya, Morocco, and, again, Algeria bucked the trend, with increased support for political Islam among the most educated in the first two countries and among those with a secondary degree in the latter country. In Morocco, this result may have reflected favorability toward the king, who adopted the mantle of Islam as "commander of the faithful."

Thus, while the MENA region as a whole is more supportive of the role of religion in politics than comparable countries in other regions, variation across countries indicates that attitudes toward religion in politics differ from place to place. Furthermore, it is important to distinguish religiosity from support for political Islam. While Middle Easterners report higher levels of piety than the global average, religiosity and favorability toward the involvement of religious authorities in politics are distinct; indeed, they are not correlated (Tessler 2011).

FIGURE 12.2. Support for Political Islam by Education Level in Selected MENA Countries, 2010–2014

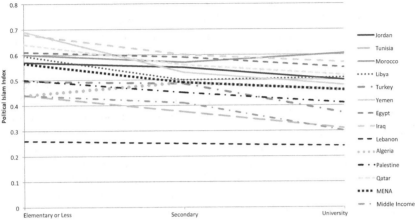

Source: WVS, wave 6, 2010–2014.

ISLAMISM AS A SOCIAL MOVEMENT: COLLECTIVE ACTION

Islamist collective action takes many forms, including, most prominently, providing social welfare, contesting elections, and engaging in armed struggle. The mix of these three activities varies widely: some Islamists engage in only one of these activities, others engage in all three, and still others carry out only two. Some of the da'wa Islamists limit themselves to preaching and social welfare provision. Al-Qaeda's refusal to embrace social welfare and health initiatives in Iraq allegedly contributed to the group's lack of a popular support base there during the early 2000s—and ultimately the weakening of the organization's presence in that country (RAND 2008). Recently, however, there is evidence that al-Qaeda and its various affiliates and offshoots have moved toward establishing social welfare networks for the communities where they are based. Reports note the employment of "hearts and minds" tactics in the Syrian conflict by extremist groups such as the al-Nusra Front, Ahrar al-Sham, and ISIL, which purportedly offer subsidized food and services, repair infrastructure, and supply humanitarian assistance in areas under their control (Garterstein-Ross and Smyth 2013; IHS 2013). The Palestinian Islamic Resistance Movement (Hamas) and Lebanese Hezbollah engage in all three activities, while the Egyptian Muslim Brotherhood confines itself to social welfare and electoral contestation.

Social Welfare Provision

Social welfare provision is extremely common among all political Islamists. Islamist student *jama'at* in Egypt in the 1970s and 1980s provided their members with low-cost lecture notes and textbooks, minibus transportation for (veiled) women, and access to the study groups and tutoring services necessary to pass examinations. Islamic organizations provide day care centers, private medical clinics and even hospitals, and schools. Consider the case of Hamas, which emerged shortly after the beginning of the first intifada in Palestine in December 1987. The progenitor of the movement, the Palestinian branch of the Muslim Brotherhood, had been particularly active in promoting charity associations, religious schools, kindergartens, libraries, and sports clubs after 1967. As with most Islamist movements, these activities were funded by *zakat* (alms), *waqf* income, and contributions from abroad.[8] With such funds, the Muslim Brotherhood also built 350 mosques in the West Bank and 400 in Gaza from 1967 to 1987 (when the first intifada began). Hamas has developed an extensive, highly respected network of charitable and service organizations. Over a quarter-million (278,000 in 2000) low-income people in the occupied territories receive income supplements, while in Gaza alone nearly two-thirds of all primary and pre-primary schools are funded and staffed by Hamas. Foreign observers agree that the organization does not demand any quid pro quo of political support from beneficiaries of such largesse. However, they do not need to do so: the probity, dignity, and efficiency of their staffs (widely recognized by external aid agencies in the European Union, for example) create a reservoir of respect and admiration among many Palestinians (ICG 2003a). Since 2000, a cycle of rising poverty (due to conflict with Israel), increasing social need, intensified Islamist social outreach, and a wider and deeper Islamist social constituency has emerged.

The performance of Hezbollah in Lebanon is even more extensive, owing in part to the group's financial strength and greater freedom of action.[9] Hezbollah runs a large array of social programs focused on health, education, and material assistance as well as agricultural extension, infrastructure and construction, microcredit, sports and youth clubs, media outlets, and religious institutions. Distributed through the Mu'assasat al-Shahid (Martyrs' Institution), its most extensive benefits are reserved for the families of fighters, or "martyrs" who died fighting for the Resistance, Hezbollah's armed wing, which is focused on armed struggle against Israel (and, more recently, in Syria). The agency provides housing, education, clothing, health services, and other social services for these families as well as job placement services for the children of martyrs. Similarly, Mu'assasat al-Jarha (Institution of the Wounded) caters to fighters and civilians injured during wars or as a result of land-mine accidents. Benefits include monthly cash allowances, medical care, and rehabilitation services. The Lajnat Emdad al-Imam al-Khomeini (Islamic Emdad Charitable Committee) serves orphans and families in severe poverty, providing a monthly income to buy food, medical services, education for school-age children, and job placement services for graduates, and it runs its own network of schools. The Jihad al-Bina' (Struggle for Construction Institution) was established in 1985 to restore buildings damaged by Israeli bombings. Later, the agency initiated larger-scale infrastructure projects across parts of Lebanon, including the repair of homes damaged by Israeli attacks, and opened several schools that are linked to the Al-Mahdi schools network. To this day, the agency continues to remove waste from the southern suburbs of Beirut and other regions in Lebanon and provide potable water to residents, activities that it initiated during the civil war (Qāsim 2005, 83–84).

Hezbollah's Al-Haya' al-Suhiyya al-Islamiyya (Islamic Health Unit) operates a network of hospitals, clinics, dispensaries, dental offices, and mobile clinics and runs various vaccination and health education campaigns.[10] In 2008 the organization had over sixteen clinics in its network in addition to several mobile clinics. The Islamic Health Unit is recognized as a major health care provider in Lebanon and has cooperated regularly with Lebanese government bodies, including the ministries of public health and education, as well as international organizations, such as the World Health Organization (WHO) and United Nations International Children's Emergency Fund (UNICEF), in sponsoring vaccination and health education campaigns, school health programs, and other initiatives. In addition to outpatient health centers, Hezbollah runs six hospitals in Lebanon. Other institutions under the umbrella of the Hezbollah social affairs wing or affiliated with the party, such as the Islamic Scout Organization and the Hezbollah Civil Defense, run their own parallel health institutions or arrange subsidized or free access to the centers of the Islamic Health Unit.

The Hezbollah Education Unit runs schools, provides educational scholarships, and supervises pedagogical training for the party's educational institutions. Several groups of schools are associated with Hezbollah. The two major private school networks are the Al-Mahdi and Al-Mustapha schools, which include both private subsidized and nonsubsidized schools, complemented by schools officially linked to other Hezbollah institutions, including the Islamic Emdad Charitable Committee, the Martyrs' Institution, and the Struggle for Construction Institution. (The Al-Mustapha schools, run by the Islamic Religious Teaching Association, are not official Hezbollah institutions but are closely linked to the party because they are run by an important party leader, Na'īm Qāsim.)

Hamas and Hezbollah are examples of the absence of state services providing such social movements with opportunities. In Palestine, Hamas's efficiency and probity contrast sharply with the venality and sluggishness of the Palestinian Authority (ICG 2003a; Abu-Amr 1994). The Lebanese case is more striking still: Hamzeh (2004, 53) notes that the Lebanese government "has almost ceased to offer social welfare services." The government effectively abandoned health care in the south of the country, leaving the field to Hezbollah and, to a lesser degree, the Amal Movement, another Shi'a political party that, unlike Hezbollah, largely subsists on state patronage. In the health sector, the Lebanese state provides minimal services and exerts little regulatory capacity, although private and nonstate providers benefit from and often claim credit for the public financing of health services. The parlous state of public education in the country likewise opens important social space for collective action by the party and many other political, religious, and for-profit providers. The destruction of the Iraqi state by the American invasion has had similar effects in that country.

Less dramatic than state collapse, but trending in a similar direction, have been the austerity programs and social welfare spending cutbacks of structural adjustment programs in Egypt, the Maghreb, and Turkey. In Yemen, religious schools of considerable antiquity—and often allied with Islamists—educated approximately 20 percent of Yemeni high school students during the 1990s (ICG 2003b). Egyptian

Islamist NGOs responded quickly to provide assistance after the Cairo earthquake of 1992; their performance contrasted favorably with the sluggish response of the government (Kepel 2002).

Elections

Islamist collective action increasingly includes participation in elections. At the national level, we may observe four patterns. First, Islamist parties may contest elections, win, and then be denied the reins of government, whether by physical force or financial strangulation. The FIS in Algeria provides one example of such a phenomenon; the Palestinian election of 2006 offers another. The FIS won the first round in the Algerian election of 1990 and was poised to sweep the field. The ruling elite (le pouvoir) refused to allow this outcome, driving the Islamists underground and provoking the civil war. Nearly three-quarters of Palestinians voted in the parliamentary elections of January 2006. Hamas won an absolute majority of parliamentary seats (74 of 132) in an election closely monitored by external (largely EU) observers.[11] The Israeli government refused to negotiate with the party, and it withheld the customs taxes that it has collected for the Palestinian Authority since the 1992 Palestinian-Israeli agreement. The United States and the European Union likewise cut off all financial aid. As in Algeria, violence escalated, and a split between the Western-backed Fatah and Hamas ensued, with the former maintaining control over the West Bank and the latter dominating Gaza.

A second pattern has been seen in Egypt under Mubarak and elsewhere. Egyptian elections were widely derided as unfair. The government controlled access to media, vetoed (and sometimes arrests) candidates, stuffed ballot boxes, and forcibly broke up opposition demonstrations. Until Mubarak's overthrow—and now again, since December 2013—the Muslim Brotherhood was not allowed to exist legally as a political party. Many observers believed that it would win at least a plurality of seats if allowed to openly participate in a free and fair election—a prediction that was upheld after the 2011 parliamentary elections. Despite a sharply tilted playing field, Muslim Brotherhood–affiliated candidates managed to win an upset 88 seats in Egypt's 2005 elections out of 451 seats in play (Meital 2006, 275). Prior to the subsequent 2010 elections, however, the Mubarak regime moved to prevent a repeat performance, arresting hundreds of Brotherhood activists. As a result, the Brotherhood's representation in parliament dropped from nearly 20 percent to none (HRW 2010). The Moroccan PJD (Justice and Development Party) won 46 of 325 parliament seats in 2007, a respectable showing, yet, contrary to predictions, short of the number required to form a government; at the same time, Morocco's largest Islamist opposition party, al-'Adl wa'l Ihsan (Justice and Charity), was banned and its leader, Abdessalam Yassine, placed under house arrest (Wegner 2011, 116–119). Election irregularities also reduced the representation of Jordanians in parliament, from twenty seats in 2003 to just six following the 2007 elections. In 2010 the Islamic Action Front, the Jordanian branch of the Muslim Brotherhood, boycotted the elections altogether (Abu Rumman 2012).

Two more hopeful patterns, however, are increasingly apparent. In Lebanon, Kuwait, and Yemen, relatively fair elections have been conducted (and, of course, in Egypt and Tunisia, which we discuss later). Islamist parties have vied for seats, gained representation, and then participated in parliamentary politics. Until 2011, they had usually acted as part of the parliamentary opposition; in one case before then, however, in Lebanon in 2005–2006, Islamist parties joined the coalition government. Such a pattern was also observable in Turkey in the 1990s, when the Welfare Party governed in coalition with others. That Islamist party reverted to the first role, however, when the Turkish state forced it from power in 1997, though without violence. In Kuwait, Islamists in coalition with other reformers won a parliamentary majority in the 2006 elections; that parliament's power relative to the emir, however, is limited.

Until 2011, there was only one case of the fourth and final pattern: an Islamist party participating in an election, winning a parliamentary majority, and then forming a government and governing the country. In 2002 the Turkish Justice and Development Party won the national election, and it has governed since then. In Bahrain, Islamist parties have generally performed well in a constrained political arena. Various Sunni and Shi'ite Islamist parties garnered nineteen out of forty seats in 2002 and increased this number to twenty-nine in 2006, though not in alliance (NDI 2002, 14; Gause 2007, 170). While the Shi'ite party, the Al-Wefaq National Islamic Society, retained all of its seats in the Kingdom's 2010 elections, amid a crackdown on Shi'ite activists, Sunni Islamist groups lost five seats between them (*Daily News Egypt* 2010). To the extent that political inclusion breeds moderation and, provided that, Islamists opt to participate in the first place, then it makes sense to encourage or enable Islamists to take part in formal, institutionalized politics (Schwedler 2011).

In 2011, Egyptian and Tunisian Islamists won a majority and a plurality of parliamentary seats, respectively, while Mohammed Morsi of the Muslim Brotherhood's Freedom and Justice Party won the 2012 Egyptian presidential elections. In Egypt, the results of both national elections were effectively reversed with the military overthrow of President Morsi in July 2014; in Tunisia, the ruling Al-Nahda Party stepped down in January 2014 in favor of a neutral government charged with drafting the new constitution and accepted the results when it failed to win elections in fall 2014. Moroccan Islamists also fared well in the elections held in 2011, winning more than 27 percent of seats in parliament. To signal the new mood of political openness in that country, the king permitted the Justice and Development Party to hold the premiership and form a government.

Several arguments are commonly advanced for the electoral successes of Islamist parties, whether in elections rigged against them under authoritarian rule or in the cleaner, founding elections after the Arab uprisings.[12] Two major explanations center on the embeddedness of these parties in the social fabric. Islamists and Islamic organizations have long been important actors in civil society and social movements in the MENA region. First, their provision of social welfare, particularly when public services are lacking and other providers do not match their quality or price, is often credited with winning them support (Alterman 2000; Bayat 2002; Flanigan 2008;

Hamzeh 2001; Harik 1994; Ismail 2001; Malka 2007; Öniş 2006; Walsh 2006).
Nonetheless, little empirical evidence supports these claims, and furthermore, this
account does not explain why they have mass appeal given their relatively minimal
role in welfare regimes in many MENA countries.[13] A second explanation holds that
Islamists have an organizational advantage that enables them to mobilize support
more effectively than their competitors. Access to diverse and extensive funding
sources through Islamic charities, influence within formal and informal mosques
and affiliated institutions, and networks of committed followers and local leaders
and followers enable Islamists to develop superior organizational capacity, which
has obvious benefits for mobilizing voter turnout. Yet organizational resources cannot by themselves account for the apparent electoral strength of Islamist parties, in
part because these resources are likely to be exaggerated in many contexts and also
because they cannot account for the resonance of the Islamist message. This points
to a third possible reason for the electoral appeal of Islamists—ideological hegemony. The domination of the public ideological space by Islamists since the 1970s
across most MENA countries enables Islamist parties to provide a "credible slogan"
to voters (Tessler 2011, 46). The resonance of their ideas and propositions enables
them to generate mass appeal, which then pays off at the ballot box. Although
ideological hegemony offers a motivation for MENA citizens to support Islamists,
it applies mainly to core supporters, who probably constitute only a small portion
of their vote share, and cannot explain why some Islamists gain more votes than
others in the same electoral contests.

Although each of these accounts undoubtedly contains some grains of truth,
a reputational advantage, or a reputation for good governance, provides a more
proximate explanation for the popularity of Islamist parties. Indeed, each of the
aforementioned factors—the provision of social services, organizational capacity,
and ideological appeal—helps to boost the reputation of Islamists, even among
those who have little or no contact with them. To the extent that they are perceived
as more trustworthy, competent, and pure than their competitors, they have an
advantage that translates into electoral gains.

When Islamists dominated elections in Egypt and Tunisia in the first free elections held after the uprisings, many observers spoke of an Islamist tide taking over
the region, yet these claims should be subjected to closer scrutiny. A closer look at
recent electoral returns in the Middle East suggests that these claims are overblown
(see Table 12.1). In Egypt and, especially, Turkey, Islamist parties did relatively
well, although turnout rates were far lower in Egypt, where almost half of registered
voters did not even participate in the elections. In Tunisia, the Ennahda Party won
a significantly lower percentage of the popular vote, and its performance is further
qualified by the fact that half of eligible voters did not participate. In other countries, such as Morocco and, especially, Libya and Algeria, Islamist parties won far
fewer votes and seats in national elections.

The experiences of Islamist political parties across the MENA region show that
the forms and patterns of collective action by social movements to a large degree depend on state policy, not just on their own behavior. Neither "moderation" nor violence is inevitable or "inherent" in Islamist social movements.[14] Everything depends

TABLE 12.1. The Performance of Islamist Parties in MENA Elections After the 2011 Arab Uprisings

Year	Country	Election	Party/Parties	Votes Won (percentage)	Seats Won (percentage)	Turnout Rate (percentage)
2011	Tunisia	Constituent Assembly	Ennahda	37.0	41.0	51.7
2011	Turkey	National Assembly	Justice and Development (AKP)	48.9	59.5	83.2
2011	Morocco	Parliament	Justice and Development	22.8	27.1	45.0
2011–2012	Egypt	People's Assembly	Freedom and Justice (FJP) Al-Nour Building and Development Authenticity Al-Wasat Al-Gadeed	68.9	69.7	54.0
2012	Egypt	Shura Council	Freedom and Justice (FJP) Al-Nour Al-Wasat Al-Gadeed	75.8	85.0	26.0
2012	Egypt	Presidential election (first round)	Freedom and Justice (FJP) (Mohammed Morsi)	42.6	na	46.4
2012	Libya	General National Congress	Justice and Construction Homeland	16.2	8.5	62.0
2012	Algeria	National Assembly	Green Alliance (Movement of Social Progress, Islah, Ennahda) Front of Socialist Forces Justice and Development	9.3	12.3	43.0 (18% of ballots ruled invalid)
2013	Jordan	Parliamentary elections	Muslim Centre Party (and affiliated independents) Islamic Action Front (boycotted)	na	11.3	56.7

Sources: Gamha (2011); Çarkoğlu (2011); NDI (2011); El Amrani (2012); *Al Jazeera* (2012); Sanhoori (2012); Carter Center (2012a); BBC News Africa (2012); Carter Center (2012b); NDI (2012); European Union Election Observation Mission (2013).

on the local context, which is profoundly shaped not only by Islamists in opposition but by non-Islamists in power—as well as by the behavior of powerful extraregional actors, such as the United States.

"Armed Struggle"

The old Marxist term "armed struggle" is highly apposite to many Islamist movements, suggesting the organization of violence for revolutionary political ends by a social movement. Under conditions of occupation (Palestine, Lebanon), Islamist violence is best understood as part of the long history of anticolonial violence, a history as old as colonialism itself. Furthermore, when a party wins an election, as in Algeria, and then is denied the fruits of its victory, violence will always be an option supported by many adherents to the frustrated social movement.

Resorting to violence is a political decision, however—there is nothing inevitable about it, as can be seen in the behavior of the Egyptian Muslim Brotherhood since the late 1960s. The Brotherhood has a violent past—first against the British colonialists and then against the Arab nationalist regime of Nasser, which violently suppressed them. However, the Brotherhood made a strategic decision to eschew violence, regardless of regime provocations, in the early 1970s. Indeed, it was precisely this decision that prompted various young militants to split off from the Muslim Brotherhood, engage in political violence—first in the late 1970s, episodically in the 1980s—and then launch a mini-insurrection from 1992 to 1997. The insurrection was crushed by the Egyptian state, and the Muslim Brotherhood repeatedly denounced the violence of groups such as Islamic Jihad and Al-Gama'a al-Islamiyya. The latter responded with vitriol; among salafi jihadis, the term *ikhwani* ("Muslim Brother") has become a term of abuse (ICG 2005). The defeated remnants of this Egyptian insurrection joined with Osama bin Laden's forces to become al-Qaeda, while the Muslim Brothers continued to vie for seats in elections, participate in parliament, engage in public debate, and support social welfare activities.

Even Islamist groups that have espoused and carried out acts of violence have evolved. Al-Gama'a al-Islamiyya officially renounced bloodshed in 2003 after a series of terrorist attacks in the mid-1990s; the Egyptian government responded by freeing thousands of imprisoned members. In the aftermath of the Arab uprisings, its members formed the Building and Development Party, winning thirteen seats in Parliament. The party's founder, Tareq al Zumour, was once a member of Islamic Jihad and was imprisoned for involvement in the assassination of Anwar Sadat. President Morsi's attempt to nominate a member of the group, Adel Asaad al-Khayyat, to be governor of Luxor backfired, given that Luxor's ancient temples were the scene of infamous attacks carried out in 1997 by the group (Beach 2013). Former members of Islamic Jihad created a minor Islamist party, called the Islamic Party, which failed to win any parliamentary seats but stood with the Muslim Brotherhood as part of the anti-coup alliance.

This is hardly to suggest that political Islamists (in our terminology) are committed democrats. (Many of their more secular opponents also do not have strong track records as champions of democracy.) Islamists primarily view themselves as the defenders of cultural authenticity, tradition, patriarchy, and the tenets of their religion as they understand them. Many informed Westerners would describe their gender policies as misogynistic (Cavdar 2010, 344–345, 349; Rouleau 2001). Most are emphatically *not* ideological liberals. The same, of course, may be said of other, non-Muslim social movements rooted in religion, including the Christian right in the United States or Christian democracy in Europe before World War II. All such cases strongly suggest that social and historical conditions may either favor or discourage the political choice to substitute nonviolent political competition for armed struggle. Such comparative experiences also indicate that it is not only Islamists' actions but also the actions of their opponents that determine that choice.

ISLAMIST ECONOMIC THOUGHT AND PRACTICE

Islamism may be usefully understood as a broad, diverse movement demanding "cultural authenticity." It seeks to change society as well as governance at all levels of society to conform more directly with its adherents' understanding of Islam. Since these understandings diverge, the theories and applications likewise differ. Most transnational social movements have theories, and these theories are typically diverse and varied, displaying quite different emphases, concepts, and specific ideas and notions—all within a broadly agreed-upon framework. Such was the case for socialism and liberalism, for example. This is certainly true for Islamism, which displays very different characteristics in, for example, Turkey, Morocco, Tunisia, Yemen, Iran, and Sudan.

Theories

There is much diversity in Islamist thinking and practice concerning economic policymaking. We consider here only two of the many strands of thinking: a general "angle of vision" exemplified by Egyptian "New Islamists," and the more specific movements to develop "Islamic finance," both private (Islamic banking) and public (*zakat,* or alms). One perspective on the differences between these two broad approaches can be found in their understanding of Qur'anic injunctions. The New Islamists tend to interpret the message of the Qur'an as something that must be "taken as a whole" and understood primarily in its ethical dimension; others interpret the Qur'anic message more literally, on a sentence-by-sentence basis. Economic thinking of the latter sort originated in the Deobandi movement of India, a defensive, literalist movement akin to the *salafiyya* (Kuran 2004). By contrast, New Islamism derives from ex-Muslim Brothers, who are largely middle-class professionals and religious scholars who take a broader, less defensive view of Islam. Although the more literal approach may be more visible, the broader perspective may prove to be more durable.

All Islamist economic thinking stresses the social and collective nature of human action. The myth of Robinson Crusoe, so beloved in neoclassical economics, gets short shrift in this tradition. Thinkers such as the very influential Egyptian religious scholar Yusuf al-Qaradawi (based in Qatar) reject such atomistic individualism, arguing that humans are restricted by belief and ethics (Baker 2003). Islamists note that all five pillars of Islam have an inherently social dimension. While Islamists are hardly collectivists—since Islam explicitly recognizes individual moral responsibility and approves of private property—they place much greater stress on ethics, particularly on a concept of justice, than is typically found in orthodox economics. Although some scholars have criticized this ethical perspective (for example, Kuran 2004), rejection of individualism as a basis for studying society is hardly limited to Islamists. Indeed, even within the economics profession, giants such as Nobel

Prize–winner Amartya Sen have long been at pains to go beyond notions of simple utilitarianism.

Islamist thinkers typically view humans as "regents"—that is, as beings endowed by God with the power to make decisions over the allocation of the earth's resources. Regency confers power, but also responsibility. This ethical burden falls particularly upon the rich, who have moral obligations toward the poor. Unlike orthodox Marxism, with its dichotomy between the "bourgeoisie" (owners) and the "proletariat" (workers), Islamist thinkers typically contrast the "arrogant" (*mustakbariin*) with the "deprived" (*mustadha'fiin*). Islamists, in other words, do not oppose wealth as such. They oppose excess, display, and neglect of the underprivileged. They judge economic policies by their outcomes and argue that meeting the basic needs of the poor should take precedence over other interests. They refrain from offering views on every specific policy but rather tend to stress this general ethical dimension of thinking about questions of political economy.[15] They tend to be gradualists and pragmatists (Baker 2003).

However, a danger lurks here. Ethical critiques of existing policy and mobilization of political forces to act on such critiques may well be essential for protecting the poor. Exhortations to the rest of us to "do the right thing" can be very powerful. But if institutions are based on the notion that humans *will* act ethically, trouble is likely to follow. The Islamist position often seems to argue that harmony and social order will be achieved by the promotion of individual virtue—by individuals altering their behavior to conform with Divine Revelation.

However laudable such a goal may be, it is a problematic basis for public policy formation. First, as Timur Kuran argues (2010), Islamic institutions may have contributed to underdevelopment in the Middle East, although this argument is contested (see Blaydes and Chaney 2013; Goldstone 2012). Second, since the seventeenth century, Western political thinkers have abandoned the notion that religious exhortation can be relied upon to restrain destructive human behavior. The alternative advocated by Saint Augustine and Calvin—repression—merely displaces the problem to the level of the sovereign. Beginning with Machiavelli and Vico and culminating in the Scottish Enlightenment and Adam Smith, we try—whenever possible—to "make private vices into public virtues." Most notably in economics, society seeks to control the social consequences of greed by pitting greed against greed. Every businessperson would love to be a monopolist; therefore, we create rules that make this very difficult. Human viciousness is taken as a given, and so we try to design institutions—to create "rules of the game"—that assume that many of us (most of the time) and all of us (some of the time) will behave selfishly, perhaps even callously. Our debates then turn on when such behavior can produce socially desirable outcomes.[16]

Such, at least, is the classical liberal theory. And yet, in a world of ever more dangerous environmental externalities (for example, carbon emissions), an increasingly monopolized mass media, and a political system often dominated by political action committees, the harmony of the "invisible hand" can easily seem like a utopian fantasy (Gray 1998). Many contemporary Western thinkers stress the importance of community, solidarity, "law-abiding as a public good," and so on. Our own perspective would be that the danger typically lies in thinking of *any* set of social arrangements as "perfect," "ideal," or "final," whether such utopianism be Islamist, Marxist, or neoliberal. And when Islamist, Marxist, or neoliberal thinkers recognize such limitations, they may then free themselves to make valuable contributions to the complex, contradictory, constantly evolving institutional framework within which we human beings pursue our disparate goals.[17]

The history of capitalism strongly suggests that the capitalism of England or of the United States does not offer a blueprint that other countries must follow. For example, Japanese capitalism, Korean capitalism, and Chinese capitalism have each evolved under very different institutional frameworks. Little "convergence" is visible. Much the same is likely to be the case for Islamic capitalism. Just as Christianity and Christian democracy played an important role in the evolution of German and Italian capitalism, so is it likely that Islam and Islamism (broadly conceived) will shape the evolution of capitalism in the MENA region. Islam is likely to mold standards of public and private conduct that could strengthen both economic performance and political order and liberty.

As we have seen throughout this book, however, such standards of conduct seem often observed more in the breach than in the observance throughout the region.[18] This becomes quite clear when we examine two specific experiments with self-consciously Islamic economic institutions, *zakat* and Islamic banking. In both cases, the concept is that wealth confers social responsibility; in both cases, the hope is that institutions grounded in (an interpretation of) Islamic law will channel private funds toward socially desirable purposes, whether to provide for basic needs and a social safety net (zakat) or to make job-creating investments in agriculture and industry (Islamic banking). In both cases, when judged by these criteria, the results have been decidedly mixed.

Islamic Charity

Zakat, or giving alms, is one of the five pillars of Islam. The Qur'an, however, provides only a very broad set of guidelines. Unsurprisingly, it deals with the main sources of wealth in seventh-century Arabia—farm output, livestock, precious metals, and other minerals. Prescribed rates of giving vary (from 2.5 percent to 20 percent), and there are several exemptions and special provisions. Today, zakat is more widely used in Muslim countries outside the MENA region than in the MENA countries themselves, though many Islamist groups seek to recentralize zakat and make it compulsory (Kuran 2004). Several states in the region began collecting and administering zakat as a tax in the twentieth century, including Saudi Arabia (1951), Yemen (1975), Libya (1971), and Sudan (1984) (Singer 2008, 202). In other cases, such as Jordan, Kuwait, and the United Arab Emirates, the government oversees a central zakat fund—usually administered by the country's ministry of *Awqaf*, or Islamic affairs—where citizens can make voluntary contributions (Powell 2009, 61–64). In each case, the collecting body supervises the disbursement of funds as well. Local governments in the former Yemen Arab Republic used the notion of zakat in taxing migrant remittances, spending the proceeds locally on badly needed physical infrastructure.

Although many studies have highlighted the potential for zakat to confront income inequality in the Muslim world (Ahmed 2004; Shirazi and Amin 2009), the system has fallen far short of making any critical contribution to meeting basic needs in the region. Whether required by law or voluntary, official donations represent only a small portion of countries' GDP (Powell 2009, 59). Kuran (2004) notes that even the highest zakat tax rate, 20 percent, is well below the typical marginal tax rate for upper-income brackets in most OECD countries, and therefore it seems unlikely that zakat, even if rigorously enforced, would have a very equalizing effect. Where zakat is voluntary, many people simply do not pay—in 2013 the head of Qatar's zakat fund claimed that the countries' businesses were contributing only 2 to 3 percent of the actual zakat due (*Qatar Tribune* 2013). Additionally, there are concerns that existing disbursal mechanisms for zakat funds focus more on short-term handouts than on development goals (IRIN 2012). One study in Sudan found that investments in adult literacy and education from 1990 to 2009 had a proportionally larger effect on alleviating poverty than zakat contributions (Abdelmawla 2011).

Islamic Banking

Perhaps the most visible attempt to forge modern Islamic economic institutions is the phenomenon of "Islamic finance." The Qur'an forbids a practice known historically as *riba'*. Although a minority position among Islamic scholars is that this injunction prohibits only usury, the majority of scholars interpret it as forbidding fixed-interest payments. The interpretation is somewhat subtle, since all agree that Islam allows time to be priced—which is what "interest" is in orthodox economic theory.[19] Islamic scholars also assert that all financial transactions should be based on real economic activity, and certain investments—such as investments in alcohol, gambling, and armaments—are prohibited (El Qorchi 2005; Kuran 2004).

The majority view has led to the rise of a large and diverse set of Islamic financial institutions and practices. Starting essentially from zero in the early 1970s, the number of Islamic financial institutions in the world has risen to more than seven hundred, spread out over more than sixty-one countries. In 2014 the auditing firm Ernst & Young estimated that the system's total assets amounted to $1.7 trillion, and that amount is expected to double by 2018 (Karam and El Baltaji 2014). During the 1970s, oil prices exploded, and conservative actors in the Gulf sought channels for their greatly increased wealth. The Organization of the Islamic Conference established the Islamic Development Bank in 1973. The first modern private Islamic bank, the Dubai Islamic Bank, was founded in 1975. At about the same time, in the late 1970s, a series of Islamic banks was founded by Prince Mohammed al-Faisal (son of King Faisal, who had died in 1975), through a holding company, beginning with the Faisal Islamic Bank of Egypt. The bank, operating under the aegis of al-Faisal's Dar al-Maal al-Islami (DMI) Trust since 1981, has now expanded its operations across the world. Over time, Islamic finance has established a global reach, including East Asia.

Islamic banking meets a strong demand arising from those pious depositors who wish to ensure that their money is used in a manner congruent with their understanding of their faith. International Western banks such as BNP Paribas, Citibank, HSBC, Credit Suisse, and UBS have opened "Islamic windows" to gain access to the funds of such depositors—in all, about 104 conventional banks offer Sharia-compliant products—and some banks, such as CitiIslamic, have established their own Islamic banks. Once considered a niche product, Islamic banking has gained an increasingly high international profile and become a "permanent feature of the global financial system" (Warde 2010, 247). In 2013, for example, the World Islamic Economic Forum was held not in a Muslim country but in London, where Sharia-compliant investments have helped to finance the construction and operation of many landmark buildings, such as The Shard, an 87-storey skyscraper completed in 2012 (El Qorchi 2005, 46; Henry and Wilson 2004; World Islamic Economic Forum 2014).

The intellectual origins of modern Islamic banking can be traced to India, with the early twentieth-century Deobandi thinker Sayyid Abul A'la Maududi. Other major contributions were made by the father of Egyptian jihadi salifiyya, Sayyid Qutb, and the Iraqi Ayatollah Muhammad Baqir al-Sadr (the father-in-law of Muqtada al-Sadr), who was tortured and murdered by the regime of Saddam Hussein. The underlying perspective seems to be that interest payments foster inequality and injustice. Advocates of Islamic finance argue that ideally all contracts between lender and borrower should be of the profit-and-loss-sharing type or asset-backed securities; that is, equity contracts are permitted, but debt contracts are prohibited. It is legitimate to invest money in a venture in which the investor bears part of the risk of the failure of the investment, but it is not acceptable for a lender to insist on his right to a return, regardless of the outcome of the investment. One hope of Islamist economic thinkers has been that the promotion of such profit-and-loss-sharing contracts would stimulate investment in the real economy, in a manner mimicking that of venture capital. They have hoped that Islamic banking would thereby contribute to economic growth and structural transformation in their societies.

Proponents further claim that Islamic banking helped to minimize the ill effects of the 2008 financial crisis in countries where it constitutes a significant share of transactions. As a system of economics, they argue, Islamic finance provides greater stability than traditional finance, with a greater emphasis on risk-sharing and closer ties between financial instruments and real assets (Mohieldin 2012, 1–2). However, while Islamic banks did prove to be more resilient in the initial stages of the financial crisis, they later faced reduced profitability as their underlying assets (in many cases, real estate) declined in value (Hasan and Dridi 2010, 15, 33–34). The countries that host the region's largest Islamic banks—the six countries of the GCC—still experienced fallout from the crisis similar to the impact in Western countries, with aggregate GDP growth falling from 7.2 percent in 2008 to just 0.8 percent in 2009, as well as a sharp decline in housing prices in Qatar, Dubai, and Kuwait (Salah 2011, 100).

Actual practice has been rather different. Most transactions of Islamic banks are *murabaha* contracts (over 75 percent overall, and as high as 90 percent), an arrangement very similar to "debt" contracts (Kettell 2011, 60; Khan 2010, 812). The contract is a purchase and resale contract: a tangible asset is bought by the bank at the request of the borrower and then resold to the customer at a previously agreed-upon, marked-up price. The similarities with interest payments are striking; some *ulema* have ruled that a *murabaha* contract, to be Islamically legitimate (*halal*), must include the actual, physical delivery of the commodity to the bank. In practice, this seldom happens, and the ensuing contract is simply a form of disguised interest. Because these contracts are far more common than "equity" contracts, called *musharika*—under which the bank and the customer co-finance a project and share the profits (or the losses) of the venture—critics have been led to point to the existence of a "murabaha syndrome," the idea that much of Islamic banking merely mimics conventional banking practices (El-Gamal 2006; El Qorchi 2005; Khan 2010; Kuran 2004; Stiansen 2004). In reality, many Sharia scholars may be more concerned with the implementation of Islamic law than with shifting the underlying nature of the economic practice, partly because they recognize that middle-class borrowers need these instruments and would not be able to support a very risk-heavy investment portfolio.[20]

Both Tarek Yousef (2004) and Timur Kuran (2004) explain why debt contracts are so much more prevalent than equity contracts, even for Islamic banks, in the political-economic environment of the MENA region. First, debt dominates equity as a contract form everywhere in the world. A study carried out a decade ago showed that the debt-to-equity ratio in MENA countries (5.0) exceeded that in the OECD (3.7) countries, but was lower than in South Asia (7.2) or Latin America (7.6) (Yousef 2004). Second, debt contracts are far less information-intensive than equity contracts. Under a debt contract, the bank need only be convinced that the debtor has collateral; in fact, under most debt contracts, the bank retains ownership of the asset and can seize it if the borrower defaults. This is not what happens under equity contracts, which stipulate that the risk is jointly shared. Such considerations underlie much of the Islamist critique of interest. Finally, the "principal-agent" problem is severe with equity contracts, especially in countries with fragmented markets, poor information, and highly uncertain, seriously backlogged, and sometimes arbitrary litigation systems. The prevalence of "double bookkeeping"—one set for the owner, one set for the authorities—in many places compounds the difficulties that bankers face in obtaining reliable knowledge about their borrowers' activities (Kuran 2004). Both Kuran (2004) and Yousef (2004) plausibly argue that these and other institutional weaknesses in the MENA countries impede the spread of the ideal Islamic investment contracts—the profit-and-loss-sharing contracts.

Even murabaha contracts have incentive problems. What happens if the borrower fails to meet the previously agreed-upon payment schedule? In principle, this should not be a problem, since the bank has taken physical possession of the commodity being financed. In practice, however, physical possession rarely takes place and the loan is secured by a financial asset. If the borrower defaults, the bank must take the borrower to court, where the bank would be likely to prevail—but because of the prohibition of interest, it would simply receive the original price of the good (that is, not the marked-up price). This moral hazard problem plagued Islamic banking in Sudan, for example (Stiansen 2004).

As with any other set of contractual forms, Islamic contracts depend for their success on a highly developed institutional environment, one characterized by transparency, probity, and relatively swift, predictable justice systems (Yousef 2004). The weakness of these institutional features in the region helps to explain the prevalence of contracts that mimic interest payments. In the past decade, the importance of establishing a global framework for regulating Islamic finance has gained traction. For example, in 2002 the Islamic Financial Services Board was established in Malaysia with the support of the IMF to issue principles and standards for the banking, insurance, and capital market sectors within the Islamic financial services industry. The worldwide regulation of Islamic finance remains a work in progress (Archer and Karim 2007; Vizcaino 2014). In short, the evidence thus far suggests that Islamic banking has not been able to become the "venture capital" system that its proponents had hoped. There is also little evidence that Islamic banking has actually increased the flow of funds to agricultural or industrial activities.

The political consequences of Islamic banking may well be more important than the immediate economic impacts. Throughout the modern Islamic financial world, a social, economic, and (sometimes) political alliance has emerged between Sharia scholars and bankers. Most Islamic banks have a "Sharia board"—an advisory committee of ulema who rule on the legitimacy of various practices (Kahf 2004). As with all such alliances, it is founded on mutual benefits. The board helps bankers reach potential depositors who may be persuaded by the ulema's rulings that placing money in these banks is religiously sanctioned; thus, such committees provide a "competitive edge" for attracting the funds of these depositors. In turn, the scholars gain considerably enhanced income, social respectability, and a sense of achievement—they are helping to make society "more Islamic." Based on this analysis, Islamic banks, by creating an alliance of businessmen, middle-class lawyers, depositors, and small entrepreneurs, have helped to consolidate part of the Islamist social coalition (Henry and Wilson 2004; Kuran 2004). By some accounts, they have had a moderating influence upon it as well (Henry 2004).

ISLAMISTS IN POWER

Policymaking rarely conforms to any theory. The requirements of coalition formation and maintenance typically far outweigh ideological stakes in economic policy implementation, especially when the economic policies in question cause significant hardship to many people. The key determinants of economic policymaking under Islamism are the same as anywhere else: the balance of interests, the structure of institutions, and the timing of events.

So far, there are only a relatively small number of cases of governing Islamism, some of them with long experience in power and others short-lived: Iran, Sudan, Turkey, and, more recently, Tunisia, Egypt, and Morocco. (Here we exclude the cases of Lebanon, where Hezbollah has governed as part of a power-sharing government, and Palestine, where Hamas won the 2006 national elections but was denied its victory and has since taken control of Gaza only, while subject to the limitations imposed by international sanctions and Israeli blockades.) The economic, political, social, and cultural contexts in which Islamists attained power were radically different in each case, and their international alignments and the international and regional conjunctures when they acceded to power were likewise fundamentally asymmetric. Arguably, these circumstances are far more important in explaining outcomes than any putatively shared "Islamist" ideology.

Since the onset of the Arab uprisings, Islamist parties in Egypt, Morocco, and Tunisia have led the governments of their countries in a time of deteriorating economic conditions, bringing a renewed focus to their proposed economic policies. Although Islamist parties (as well as many of their competitors) called for reductions in poverty and unemployment, little about their approach to economic issues while in power was notably "Islamist," aside from their attempts to issue government debt in the form of *sukuk* or Islamic bonds, which represent an important strategy for diversifying the array of Islamically acceptable investment vehicles (*The Economist* 2013).[21] Tunisia's Ennahda and Egypt's Freedom and Justice Party, recognizing the importance of continuing to attract tourist dollars, initially sought to dispel fears that they might impose blanket bans on the consumption of alcohol out of commitment to Islamic principles (Saif and Abu Rumman 2012). Far from rejecting previous neoliberal economic policies, both the FJP and Ennahda courted international financial institutions, such as the IMF, in an attempt to secure multibillion-dollar loans. Unlike their stances on economic policy, Islamist positions on women's issues distinguish them more from other parties, although cross-national variation even in this policy area shows that politics and social context, more than doctrine, shape their approaches on this question as well. Brief synopses of the experiences of Islamists in power reveal the diversity of their positions on these and other issues.

Tunisia

In preparing for the elections to the Constitutional Assembly held in October 2011, Ennahda was forced to move beyond articulating demands for civil freedoms and government transparency, and its resounding election victory (37 percent of the votes cast) only accelerated this process (see Table 12.1). Its ambitious economic platform sought to achieve economic growth rates of 7 percent while reducing unemployment to 8 percent by undertaking a range of policies, including reform of the banking sector, training and education support for the unemployed, the establishment of a commission for combating corruption, and greater trade integration with Europe and North Africa (Saif and Abu Rumman 2012, 8). Once in power, Ennahda sought to boost the economy by increasing government spending by as much as 20 percent, mainly via development funding and higher government wages (Achy 2012). Although these measures undoubtedly helped the country achieve 3.6 percent GDP growth in 2012, Tunisia struggled to attract foreign investment as deficit levels rose to over 6 percent of GDP, raising questions about the long-term sustainability of the party's expansionist strategy. The party also faced accusations that its economic policies were scarcely different from those of Ben Ali: securing loans from international financial institutions, boosting tourism, and attracting foreign investment, all while relying on government employment as a social palliative.

Political gridlock, including disagreement on other Ennahda proposals, soon contributed to a mounting economic crisis. Throughout 2012 and 2013, Tunisia witnessed growing political tensions, ostensibly arrayed along secularist and Islamist lines. With regard to the new Tunisian constitution, the party's representatives first proposed, then compromised on, Islamist-themed articles that would have incorporated Sharia into the document and criminalized blasphemy (Marks 2014). Prior to the October 2011 elections, Ennahda officials had stressed their commitment to equality between men and women and emphasized that they were not out to dictate a dress code for society, stances that were in line with Tunisia's long history of progressive policies on women's rights, which had been instituted under Bourguiba and were continued under Ben Ali. Yet the party representatives involved in drafting the new constitution proposed an article that would have defined men and women as having "complementary roles" within the family, reflecting the party's traditional views on gender roles. Amid a sharp backlash from liberal parties—including protests in downtown Tunis—the party agreed to language invoking full equality (*musawa*) instead (Marks 2014). At the same time, Ennahda's critics accused the party of catering to Tunisia's hard-line Salafi Islamists, some of whom were associated with attacks on foreign institutions and linked to the assassinations of two prominent leftist politicians in 2013. Political instability led the IMF to delay payments of $1.78 billion in loans, while the African Development Bank canceled a $300 million loan outright.

Egypt

Like most of Egypt's established opposition forces, the Muslim Brotherhood was caught off guard by the uprising of January 25, 2011. Though many of its youth members took part in the protests from the start, the Islamist organization's leadership took several days to officially commit to demonstrations. After eighteen days of mass protests led President Hosni Mubarak to step down, the Muslim Brotherhood announced the formation of the Freedom and Justice Party (FJP), but emphasized electoral restraint, claiming that it would not seek a parliamentary majority or the Egyptian presidency (Hamid 2014, 145–155).

The unified opposition front present at the outset of the revolution began to crack during the army-proposed March 2011 referendum, when the Muslim Brotherhood and nascent Salafi groups successfully campaigned in favor of prioritizing parliamentary elections over the drafting of a new constitution. Various liberal opposition groups, at a clear electoral disadvantage against the well-organized Brotherhood, opposed the measure, arguing for delayed elections.

Islamists dominated the first post-Mubarak elections, spread out in three stages between the end of 2011 and the start of 2012. The Muslim Brotherhood–led

Democratic Alliance won 37.5 percent of the votes and almost 45 percent of the seats, and the Salafist Al-Nour Party gained almost 28 percent of the votes, or 25 percent of the seats. Offshoots of the former ruling National Democratic Party (NDP) were permitted to participate in the elections, but won only 6.4 percent of the votes, or 3.5 percent of the seats, while parties headed by the liberals who had been key organizers of the protests fared poorly as well. The FJP and the Al-Nour Party then won a combined 85 percent of the seats in the legislature's upper house, the Shura Council. The Muslim Brotherhood also reversed its position on running for the Egyptian presidency, particularly after onetime Brotherhood member Abdel Moneim Aboul Fotouh resigned from the party in order to run for the position. In June 2012, the Muslim Brotherhood candidate, Mohammed Morsi, narrowly won the presidency in a runoff election, defeating Ahmed Shafik, who was seen as close to the former regime. Morsi soon appeared to gain the upper hand over the previously dominant Supreme Council of the Armed Forces (SCAF) by forcing its leader, Mohamed Hussein Tantawi, to step down and appointing General Abdel Fattah Al-Sisi, who initially appeared to defer to civilian rule.

Leading into the 2011–2012 parliamentary elections, the Freedom and Justice Party's platform contained several provisions to tackle the corruption and abuses of the previous regime as well as to provide for greater social justice, political freedoms, and economic opportunity in the "New Egypt" (Freedom and Justice Party 2011). Its proposed economic policies were a collection of "commonsense" measures advocated by many parties—fighting corruption, opposing monopolies, and supporting small businesses. In a nod to the party's Islamist character, the platform also looked to "activating charitable work" as an economic strategy, encouraging compliance with the payment of zakat and reforming the country's system of charitable trusts (*awqaf*). With regard to redistribution, the party set out to rein in inflation through a combination of price controls and increased domestic production; address poverty by adopting a progressive tax code, setting minimum and maximum wages, and optimizing charitable giving via zakat, awqaf, and other Islamic institutions; and combat unemployment through training programs, a national unemployment fund, and the expansion of economic opportunities by attracting foreign and domestic investments.

During its political campaigns and while in power, the FJP articulated and attempted to push through even more conservative positions on women's issues than its Tunisian counterpart. The official party platform largely avoided discussion of women, beyond noting that their rights should be subject to the principles of Sharia law. During his presidential campaign, Mohammed Morsi's "Renaissance Project" emphasized women's "authentic role as wife, mother and purveyor of generations," which was echoed in the party's official platform. Although the party issued no new policies on family law while in power, the Muslim Brotherhood provoked controversy in March 2013 when it denounced a proposed UN declaration on women's rights for contradicting the principles of Islam (Nichols 2013). Ultimately the FJP's positions on the role of women in politics and society were contradictory: the party vowed to "ensure women's access to all of their rights," yet only insofar as this was "consistent with the values of Islamic law"—a stipulation that opposed earlier declarations that all citizens were equal before the law.

Once in office, the Muslim Brotherhood was unable to enact policies and take measures to create tangible improvements in the lives of ordinary Egyptians. President Morsi initially touted his party's "Renaissance Plan" for economic recovery, which sought to achieve economic growth of up to 7 percent within five years while reducing unemployment by 5 percent per year. Instead, growth fell to around 2 percent during Morsi's year in office, while unemployment rose from 9 percent in early 2011 to over 13 percent in 2013 (Halime 2013b). Macroeconomic policy under Morsi largely amounted to repeated attempts to secure a $4.8 billion IMF loan and other lines of credit from regional countries ($5 billion from Qatar, $2 billion each from Turkey and Libya, and $1 billion from Saudi Arabia) (Halime 2013a).

President Morsi also marginalized the government's opponents, preventing them from taking part in decision-making processes and pushing through its own reforms with little attempt to gain broader consensus over sensitive issues (see Chapter 3). In July 2013, Morsi was deposed in a coup by General Al-Sisi, who has ushered in a return to military rule in Egypt.

Morocco

Although Morocco's Justice and Development Party (PJD) did not participate in the country's protests on February 20, 2011, it leveraged public discontent with the regime and the monarchy-backed Authenticity and Modernity Party (PAM) to secure victory in the following November elections. PJD members were forbidden in advance by PJD secretary general Abdelilah Benkirane to take part in the protests, yet several youth members and party leaders spoke out in favor of the planned demonstrations. Over the following months, the party successfully used the threat of exit from the political process to secure significant concessions from the regime regarding the power of the monarchy and the Islamic character of Morocco in a newly drafted constitution and, critically, to prevent changes to the electoral law that would have undermined the PJD's prospects in the November elections (Buehler 2013). The party ultimately won 107 of 395 seats (27 percent) in Morocco's Constituent Assembly with 27 percent of the valid votes cast (see Table 12.1). Benkirane was named Morocco's first Islamist prime minister and formed a coalition government with the pro-palace Istiqlal Party.

Though the monarchy and its associates retain the upper hand in determining key policy decisions (leading to accusations that it will tolerate the PJD only so long as it acts as a buffer against economic discontent), the PJD has managed to enact a number of economic reforms. Looking to the private sector to spur economic growth, the party's platform offered to reduce corporate tax rates from 30 percent to 25 percent, but it has struggled in its attempts to increase funding for social programs (Al-Sharqi 2013; Saif and Abu Rumman 2012). The party has sought to expand the social safety net—in 2012 it launched a new medical assistance program aimed at expanding health care to 8.5 million citizens—but slashed subsidies on fuel and basic foodstuffs (Boukhars 2014). Under pressure to reduce government spending after securing a conditional $6.2 billion IMF loan in 2012, the government reduced overall spending on subsidies from 53 billion dirhams in 2012 to 42 billion dirhams in 2013 and just 30 billion dirhams in 2014 (Reuters 2014).

The focus on subsidy reform without adequate provisions for social welfare prompted the Istiqlal Party to withdraw from the government, sparking a government crisis in the summer of 2013 until a new coalition partner could be found. The PJD government has thus far taken great pains to placate the monarchy while maintaining party coherence in the face of a weak opposition, and by one measure it held an approval rating of about 58 percent in early 2014 (Boukhars 2014, 4). Though affected by the economic downturn in the EU—Morocco's largest trading partner—the PJD-led government has achieved relative macroeconomic stability, with the economy growing at a rate of 4.5 percent in 2013.

Compared to other Islamist parties in the Middle East, the Moroccan PJD has been more accepting of legislation in favor of women's rights, at least in some areas. In 2003, King Mohammed VI proposed a set of reforms to the country's family laws, following over a decade of demonstrations and petitions by the country's women's rights groups. The proposed reforms would strictly regulate polygamy, equalize divorce proceedings, raise the minimum marriage age, and remove a requirement that women obey their husbands. Though the Moroccan PJD had previously helped organize counterdemonstrations against reform efforts, its representatives in the Moroccan parliament ultimately voted in favor of reform in 2004. The only recently legalized party was willing to compromise owing to the pressures from competing leftist parties and the willingness of the monarchy to couch the reformed family code in Islamic—rather than Western—legal language (Clark and Young 2008, 341–342, 345). The other main Islamist movement in Morocco, the Justice and Charity Organization—banned from participating in parliament—opposed the new family code with mass demonstrations prior to reforms, and it has repeatedly criticized aspects of the code (mainly the regulation of polygamy and the age of marriage) as against Islam and Moroccan identity (Williams 2008; see also Harrak 2009, 6–7).

Prior to the electoral victory of the PJD in November 2011, the new Moroccan constitution raised civil society hopes for further reform by explicitly stating the equality of men and women, while acknowledging the authority of international conventions on the subject, such as the Convention on the Elimination of Discrimination Against Women (CEDAW) (Article 19). Yet the Benkirane government attracted criticism when it named just one female minister—PJD member Bassima Hakkouioui—as head of the relatively marginal Ministry of Solidarity, Women, Family, and Social Development, compared with seven female ministers in the previous government. (A cabinet reshuffle in 2013 would lead to the addition of five additional female ministers. [Hajji 2013]). Although obstacles to the enforcement of the 2004 family code predate the PJD's victory (Eisenberg 2011), the Islamist-led government now bears the brunt of criticism for failing to advance reform, with several laws mandated by the 2011 constitution yet to be passed by parliament and existing laws often unenforced by local and regional courts. In 2014 the government finally responded to protests by changing a controversial law (Article 475 of the penal code) that offered amnesty to accused rapists if they married their alleged victim, following a high-profile case of a sixteen-year-old girl's suicide after such a marriage (*Al Jazeera English* 2014; Hanafi and Alaoui 2014).

Turkey

Turkey has a longer history of Islamists in power than the other countries we have covered thus far. In Turkey, the 2002 national election brought to power a party representing Anatolian business and pro-Islamist middle and lower classes in an environment of deep financial crisis and widespread public disgust with the governing elite. During its electoral campaign, the Justice and Development Party (AKP) presented no independent economic policy, choosing instead to abide by the terms of a three-year IMF plan negotiated by the outgoing administration, though it promised to address poverty and unemployment. Nonetheless, the party devoted little attention to these issues during its early years in office, focusing instead on satisfying the IMF by raising taxes on consumer goods and cutting agricultural subsidies, prioritizing the reduction of inflation and government debt in the run-up to a sought-after EU membership (Patton 2006). AKP policies helped to reduce chronically high rates of inflation to single digits while achieving impressive growth rates, averaging almost 7 percent from 2002 to 2007 (Karagol 2013, 117, 119). With a favorable global liquidity environment helping to attract foreign investment funds and low inflation aiding the trickle-down effects of economic growth, the rate of poverty decreased from 27 to 18 percent between 2002 and 2009 (Öniş 2013, 139–140). The country's strong economic growth under the AKP has won it supporters at home (its vote share has increased in every set of national elections since 2002) as well as numerous admirers abroad.

Many argue that the AKP has sought to reduce state responsibility for the provision of welfare even as its pro-market economic policies have reduced the number of its citizens with access to corporate sources of welfare via state employment. For example, although state spending on health care rose from 3.7 percent of GDP in 2002 to over 5 percent in 2009, much of this increase has been attributed to the rising costs of health care associated with government privatization efforts, while the cost of medicine consumption alone in the country rose 100 percent from 2002 to 2007 (Eder 2009, 171; Öniş 2013, 135). The party has emphasized the importance of private charities and NGOs in providing welfare, whether in a private or semi-official capacity, while devolving the administration of welfare groups to local governments. This has prompted concerns that the high number of actors in this welfare mix increases the likelihood that social welfare provision in Turkey will be subject to political patronage or clientelism, undermining faith in state institutions (Eder 2009, 184).

Like their counterparts in Tunisia, Turkey's Islamists operate in a context in which the establishment of an independent state brought significant advances in women's rights. Thus, the AKP has tread carefully in its positions in this area, yet has pushed for some policies that have alarmed its opponents. Since the party's rise to power in 2002, it has placed rhetorical and policy emphasis on the idea of a "strong Turkish family," at times using the importance of family ties as justification for shifting the burden of social welfare provision from the state to the family and equating "social policy" with "family policy" (Yazc 2012). While the AKP has passed key legislation in support of women—for example, it signed a Council of Europe declaration on violence against women and domestic violence and expanded social security provisions to women in the workplace—dismissive rhetoric from Prime Minister Recep Tayyip Erdogan and other AKP officials has often undermined the party's official commitment to women's rights (Sussman 2011). According to official statistics, women make up the vast majority of the approximately 3.8 million illiterate citizens in Turkey, while in 2012 women's employment in the country was still below 30 percent (Hatipoglu 2014). In 2011, Erdogan instituted changes to the Ministry for Women and Family, renaming it the Ministry of Family and Social Policies and restricting its focus on women's issues. Furthermore, the AKP-led government has rejected the idea of a quota for the Turkish parliament to improve women's representation (Ayata and Tutuncu 2008, 375; HRW 2011).

Iran

Of all the cases discussed thus far, Iran has had the longest experience of Islamists in power. In Iran, a violent revolution, followed by a brutal eight-year war, consolidated statist economic institutions in one of the world's major oil exporters. Initially, the Iranian economy declined rapidly following the establishment of the Islamic Republic. Per capita incomes fell by 50 percent over the course of the Iran-Iraq War, owing to a combination of revolutionary upheaval, war, and falling oil prices, and they did not regain their pre-revolution peak until 2004 (Salehi-Isfahani 2006). At the same time, public investment in potable water, schools, health clinics, and food subsidies helped drive notable improvements in human development indicators (Salehi-Isfahani 2006). By 2001, the poverty rate was one-third of pre-revolution levels (15.5 percent versus 47 percent), development gaps between rural and urban areas had narrowed, and infant and child mortality rates had plummeted (World Bank 2001). After a wave of nationalizations in the wake of the revolution, public enterprises accounted for 72 percent of employment and 65 percent of investments by 1991 (Amuzegar 1993).

With the regime resting on an alliance of populist lower- and middle-class supporters and prosperous mullahs (as well as their business contacts), the regime's economic policies have had a tendency to oscillate between market-oriented liberalization measures, designed to increase trade and private-sector opportunities, and populist measures of subsidies on energy and food and price controls. Under President Mahmoud Ahmadinejad, for example, about $80 billion in state assets were privatized between 2006 and 2010, yet many of the shares in these newly "private" holdings went to various military firms and other state-connected companies, and reduced-price "justice shares" were mainly made available to lower-income members of Ahmadinejad's populist support base and regime supporters such as members of the Basij militia (Habibi 2013; Harris 2013).

The Iranian Revolution brought some setbacks for women's rights. Once Aya-tollah Khomeini and clerical forces consolidated power in the wake of the 1979 revolution, they abolished the existing 1975 Family Protection Law, reduced the minimum age for marriage for women, discouraged women from taking up governmental or professional positions, and banned them outright from serving in the judiciary (Gheissari 2009, 132). Although initial protests forced the new regime to back down on compulsory veiling, a law requiring all women to wear the *hijab* eventually came into effect in 1983. Nonetheless, women's political participation had greatly expanded in the lead-up to the shah's overthrow, and women's continued activism in the 1980s and 1990s helped force concessions on the part of the state: improved grounds for women to request divorce or seek redress if divorced against their will (through provisions in marriage contracts by 1985 and a reformed divorce law in 1989), custody of children for widows rather than the deceased husband's family, and legal loopholes for women to continue working in the judiciary as legal "advisers" to courts and companies (Keddie 2000, 416–418). At the same time, less explicitly family-focused policies helped to expand opportunities for women in rural and poor areas, mainly through provisions of health and education services—women's literacy rates, for example, doubled in rural areas from 1976 to 1986 (Higgins and Shoar-Ghaffari 1994, 26–27).

Though there are relatively few women in Iran's parliament (only 3.1 percent of its members in 2012), they are an increasingly vocal minority, with women MPs helping push through the ratification of the UN Convention on the Elimination of Discrimination Against Women (CEDAW) in 2002 to encourage reform of Iran's laws regarding women (Gheissari 2009, 137). Iran's governing regime puts clear limits, however, on the impact of these efforts; for instance, the adoption of the CEDAW was ultimately rejected by the country's unelected Guardian Council.

Sudan

The case of Sudan, which like Iran has had a relatively long experience of rule by Islamists, confirms the point that the behavior and policy positions of Islamists are best explained by the national and international contexts in which they came to power and by the social forces that they represent. The Islamist regime in Sudan has, at best, engaged in crisis management since its accession to power in 1989. At worst, it has engaged in mass murder and other grotesque violations of human dignity.

For nearly two hundred years, Sudan has been dominated by a Nile Riverain elite of traders and merchants, Arabic-speaking Muslims who define themselves as "Arabs." The vast western and eastern regions of the country, although overwhelmingly Muslim, have only occasionally participated directly in power. Conflict between the Muslim elite in the North and the non-Muslim Southern Sudanese has been endemic. Before the 1970s, however, the country boasted one of the best universities in Africa, a sophisticated intellectual elite, strong trade unions, and a reasonably competent civil service. The dictatorship of Jaafar al-Nimeiri (1969–1985), together with other regional developments, changed all of this. As was done in so many MENA countries during the period, Nimeiri nationalized banks and factories upon taking power, and then, with rising oil prices, trade and budgetary deficits ballooned and the economy deteriorated. Nimeiri turned increasingly toward the Sudanese Muslim Brotherhood for support and imposed Sharia on the country in 1983. The Southern rebellion immediately reignited and widespread human rights abuses ensued (de Waal and Abdel Salam 2004). After an interregnum of ineffectual democratic rule, a military coup in 1989 brought the Islamist forces of the National Islamic Front (NIF), led by the charismatic intellectual Hassan al-Turabi, to power.

In sharp contrast to other Islamist movements, the 1989 coup in Sudan represented almost exclusively members of the elite; there was no popular mobilization, as in Iran, Iraq, Algeria, and Lebanon (de Waal and Abdel Salam 2004; Kepel 2002). The Islamist coalition contained three elements: Islamist intellectuals, a "new middle class," and army officers (de Waal and Abdel Salam 2004; Kepel 2002). With the defeat of alternatives such as the Communists or the Nasserists, Islamism increasingly appealed to young, educated (or semi-educated) Muslim Sudanese in the cities. Turabi, a brilliant thinker, strategist, and tactician, ensured that a network of these young people gained positions of influence in the government bureaucracy. Under his leadership, they were then ready to implement the Islamist program once the military had seized power.

The second element of the coalition was the "new middle class." These people were distinguished both by social origins and by economic activities from the older, rural power holders, who were largely allied with the traditional Sufi Brotherhood political parties. The new men prospered in the export-import trade, utilizing contracts in Saudi Arabia, where huge numbers of Sudanese professionals sought employment during the oil boom. Islamic financial houses, especially the Faisal Islamic Bank of the Sudan, were Islamist strongholds, employing the movement's adherents and advancing them loans (Kepel 2002; Stiansen 2004). Such patronage helped recruit still more members from the devout lower-middle classes.

The final component of the coalition was a group of army officers, led by General Omar al-Bashir. The army officers, already embarked on a vicious colonial counterinsurgency campaign in the South, were offered the ideological justification of jihad, which they embraced enthusiastically. This elite coalition, brought to power through a coup d'état, ruled through intimidation and violence.

The government's economic policies were in many ways the reverse of the norm during the reform era elsewhere in the MENA region. We saw in Chapter 8 that, in general, macroeconomic management improved, while microeconomic changes proceeded more slowly. In Sudan, however, the latter moved fairly swiftly, as Sudan decontrolled prices, privatized some fifty-seven companies by 2000, and slashed jobs in the public sector (Musa 2000). The economy also became increasingly open to trade as import and export licensing was ended and the exchange rate was devalued. All of this was implemented under a "homegrown" structural adjustment program, without any assistance or advice from the international financial institutions. (Sudan had been declared in a state of "noncooperation" with the IMF since 1990, and the country's voting rights in the IMF were suspended in 1993 owing to its failure to service the national debt.) Until the mid-1990s, macroeconomic management was dismal. Large budgetary and balance-of-payments deficits, driven by war spending, declining terms of trade, poor rainfall, dreadful transportation networks, and increasing international isolation, were covered by printing money. The result was triple-digit inflation. The privatization program was of the *nomen-klatura* variety: formerly public enterprises became the private property of regime adherents and supporters. Islamic banks (the only kind allowed) strengthened the position of their officers and clients (de Waal and Young 2005, 3).

Beginning in the mid-1990s, this newly entrenched elite began to shift their policies. It had been known since the early 1970s that the South contained substantial oil deposits, and many viewed the war there as an "oil war" (Rone 2003). It slowly became apparent that outright military victory over the Sudan People's Liberation Army (SPLA) was impossible. At the same time, the international isolation of the country under Turabi's leadership had become intense. A number of elements in the ruling coalition, particularly some of those in the army and the wealthier Islamist business interests, began to think that a rapprochement with the West, the Saudis, and the international community would be in their interest.

An early step in this direction was the turn toward the IMF in 1996. (Another step, taken in the same year, was the expulsion of Osama bin Laden.) Although Sudan remained banned from funding, the IMF did advise the government on the formulation of a macroeconomic stabilization plan, beginning in 1996. The plan was largely successful in bringing down inflation, which had fallen to single digits by 2002. A key to balancing the budget was the beginning of significant oil exports in 1999, when, for the first time, Sudan had a balance-of-trade surplus. Political changes helped open the oil tap. Beginning in 1997, the government reached peace agreements with some rebel factions, and after 2000 it began to feel its way toward a deal with the SPLA, resulting in the Naivasha Comprehensive Peace Agreement, signed in January 2005. The agreement strengthened the security of the oil fields and pipelines and moderated some of the worst human rights abuses in the South.

Part of this transition involved a power shift at the core of the regime. Turabi was removed from power in a bloodless coup in 1999. He did not go quietly, and he retains a political presence. His attempt at mobilizing support in the West, including Darfur, against Bashir and the generals is one of the complex forces that contributed to the destruction of Darfur. The peace in Sudan is very fragile, and in Darfur it does not exist. Elsewhere in the country, a new elite of Islamist businessmen and military officers now benefit from oil contracts, real estate investment, and joint ventures in fields such as telecommunications (de Waal and Young 2005). By 2014, the country had a debt of nearly $41 billion, which has been exacerbated by the loss of three-quarters of its oil production when South Sudan seceded in 2011 (CIA 2014).

Islamist rule has imposed significant constraints on women in Sudan. In the wake of the 1989 coup by Sudan's National Islamic Front, Islamist officials sought to encourage women to follow "Islamic" roles in society by dressing in conservative black clothing, staying home rather than working, and remaining separate from men in public spaces (Gruenbaum 1992, 29–30). These expectations were increasingly backed up by various decrees and laws: Article 152 of the 1991 Criminal Act, for example, criminalized acts "contrary to public morality," which have been interpreted broadly to justify the prosecution of women deemed to have been wearing inappropriate dress. The 1991 act is part of a larger set of "public order" laws that require, among other provisions, gender segregation at public festivities, in hair salons, and on mass transportation (Nageeb 2004, 21). Although the government's 1998 constitution does not discriminate between men and women in terms of freedoms, rights, and responsibilities, the public order laws are still in effect; in one notable 2009 case, a female Sudanese journalist working for the UN was convicted of public indecency solely for wearing trousers in public.

To say the very least, the recent history of Sudan presents an unedifying picture of Islamists in power. The notion that Islamist rule should foster greater reliance on ethical behavior seems, in the Sudanese context, something of a sick joke. Ethnic cleansing, famine, "ghost houses," pronouncements of *takfir*, and the systematic use of rape and murder as instruments of state policy square poorly indeed with pious pronouncements. Nor has corruption, that very justifiable target of Islamists in opposition, markedly decreased: in Transparency International's 2005 ranking, Sudan ranks *last* of all MENA countries (number 174 of 177 countries worldwide). One can only hope that the violence in Darfur ends, that conflict with the South subsides, and that the benefits of the oil will be more widely shared.

The Islamist tent is clearly one of some breadth, housing both the neoliberal, pro-EU Turks and the (at times) statist, go-it-alone Iranians, with many permutations in between. Islamists in power have articulated and pursued a diverse array of economic policies, and even on the sensitive question of the role of women in economic and political life, Islamists in power have not exhibited uniform policy preferences. The different political contexts in which Islamist parties have operated when in power, as well as their distinct interpretations of Islamic doctrine, have produced quite a variety of positions on economic and social questions.

CONCLUSIONS

Is Islam the solution? Perhaps before answering, we should ask two other questions: Was import substitution industrialization (ISI) the solution? Was the Washington Consensus the solution? We argued in Chapters 5, 7, and 8 that the latter two questions may best be answered: well, yes—and no! The answer is yes when we consider that, under the policies adopted everywhere in the region during the import-substituting period, basic infrastructure was constructed, a manufacturing base was built, higher education systems (for all their faults) emerged, and historically high rates of economic growth were achieved. But the answer is also no, ISI was not the solution, for all of the reasons outlined in Chapter 7. The same is true for the Washington Consensus policies. The answer is yes in light of the many cases in which the macroeconomy was stabilized, exports were increased, and greater integration into the global economy was achieved. But as we saw in Chapters 5 and 8, the answer is also no, since in no country have Washington Consensus policies managed to create enough jobs to significantly reduce unemployment, much less dramatically raise real wages and living standards.

History may render a similar verdict on the Islamist experiment. This diverse social movement may make important contributions to some of the many development problems facing the region. Suitably anchored to peaceful politics, as it was for at least a decade in Turkey, Islamism could strengthen civil society, the rule of law, and human rights. It could provide a mechanism for the upward mobility of newly educated groups, consolidate greater reliance on market mechanisms, and promote greater integration into the global community, where, after all, one of five human beings is Muslim. It may also succeed where other movements have failed—in protecting a genuine national independence.

However, Islamism seems unlikely to fulfill these promises without major political and, in some cases, ideological changes. The problems of how to relate to non-Muslim minorities have not been adequately theorized or put into political practice, and there is no evidence that the movement offers distinctive, workable solutions to the very serious economic and social problems plaguing the region. That said, if Islamists continue to find themselves in increasingly sharp conflict with Israel and the United States, which has lost much popularity in the Middle East in the wake of the War on Terror, they may be bolstered as the perception deepens that they are the only forces willing to stand up to the West and to the Israeli occupation of Palestine.

Islamism, like statism and neoliberalism, is a response to concrete, complex historical conditions. It is likely to ameliorate some problems and exacerbate others. But whatever the answer to the question that forms the title of this chapter, it seems likely that those who continue to answer yes—who believe Islam is the solution—will remain central actors in the region's immediate future.

NOTES

1. *Ijtihad* is a term from Islamic law referring to independent interpretation of the Qur'an and *hadith* (sayings of the Prophet Muhammad).

2. The literature on Islamism is huge. Key works surveying Islamism across the MENA region include Ayubi (1991), Bayat (2007), Ismail (2006), Kepel (2002), Mandaville (2007), Roy (1994, 2002), and Ruthven (2000). For reviews, see Cammett and Luong (2014) and Sadowski (2006), as well as a useful overview of diverse types of Islamists by the International Crisis Group (ICG 2005).

3. Our typology is drawn from the work of Baker (2003), Hamzawy (2005), and ICG (2005).

4. The followers of Muqtada al-Sadr in Iraq, for example, accept the concept of *wilayat al faqih*, but unlike the Islamists of the Iranian government, they do not think that Ayatollah Khamenei should fill that post (ICG 2006).

5. *Salafi jihadis* in Afghanistan thought that the "Islamic Emirate of Afghanistan" under the Taliban from 1996 to 2001 was the sole legitimate and authentic Islamic government in existence at the time.

6. Many scholars trace the origins of the concept of *takfir* to the medieval theologian Ibn Taymiyyah (d. 1328) (Ruthven 2000).

7. "Porters in the *shurja* (Baghdad) souk are all Sadrists, while merchants are all Sistanists (supporters of Ayatollah Sistani)," said a Baghdad merchant cited in ICG (2006, 19n136).

8. *Waqf* income refers to the income flows derived from a piece of property that has been inalienably granted to charity.

9. The information on Hezbollah's social welfare institutions is based on Cammett (2014, ch. 6).

10. Hamzeh (2004, 54–55) provides information on the number of beneficiaries of the services provided by these institutions through 2000.

11. Hamas won 44 percent of the popular vote; as in Turkey, the electoral system, combined with disarray among non-Islamist political parties, produced the overrepresentation of Islamists in the parliament. Such overrepresentation of minorities is a commonplace of US politics as well, owing to constitutional structures such as the electoral college and the US Senate (Dahl 2003).

12. This section draws on Cammett and Luong (2014).

13. On this point, see Masoud (2014).

14. For an assessment of the argument that the inclusion of Islamists in the political process leads to their "moderation" and a critique of the concept of "moderation" itself, see Schwedler (2011).

15. Some modern utilitarians would agree. Peter Singer (1999), for example, forcefully argues that the failure of most Americans to give at least 30 percent of their income to the world's poor is morally indefensible.

16. Kuran (2004) forcefully makes this classical liberal critique of Islamist economic thought.

17. As Ruthven (2000, 400–401) concludes in his study of contemporary Islam: "Freed from the rigidity which makes so much Islamist activity seem culturally sterile . . . there is a message (in Islam) addressed to the whole of humanity . . . it is a message which calls on men and women to show gratitude for the world's bounty, to use it wisely and distribute it equitably. It is a message phrased in the language and imagery of a pastoral people who understood that survival depended upon submission to the natural laws governing their environment and upon rules of hospitality demanding an even sharing of limited resources. In a world increasingly riven by the gap between rich and poor nations, and in growing danger of environmental catastrophe, this message has an urgent relevance. It is one we ignore at our peril."

18. The same, of course, may be said of Western values and conduct.

19. That is, the interest rate represents the marginal rate of substitution between present and future consumption.

20. Email communication with Kristin Diwan, Assistant Professor, School of International Service, American University, and Nonresident Senior Fellow, Rafik Hariri Center for the Middle East, Atlantic Council, July 22, 2014.

21. Ibid.

13

REGIONAL AND GLOBAL
ECONOMIC INTEGRATION

Arab populations have long dreamed of unity, aspiring to be part of a large and powerful regional entity that would allow for a more effective defense of Arab interests. When asked whether they saw themselves as part of one Arab nation divided by artificial borders, or as part of one nation with various people with distinguishable characteristics, a remarkable 42 percent picked the first option in an opinion survey conducted in 2012–2013 by the Arab Center for Research and Policy Studies (ESCWA 2013). This yearning for unity is rooted historically in the golden age of the Islamic empires. The Arab revolt of the early twentieth century failed to establish a unified dominion over the territories lost by the Ottomans. Instead, the region was fragmented into multiple nation-states by the colonial powers. Before the rise of secular nationalism, Muslims cherished a vision of one polity under one ruler—the Dar al-Islam, ruled by the caliph, the Prophet's successor. Secular Arab nationalism, spearheaded by Gamal Abdel Nasser, became a hugely popular pan-Arab ideology in the 1960s. In recent years, Arab nationalism has given way to the rising tide of political Islam. There have been several attempts to realize these visions politically. The best-known attempt was the formation of the United Arab Republic when Egypt and Syria merged for three years (1958–1961). The most recent has been the creation of the so-called Islamic caliphate in Syria and Iraq by ISIL, an al-Qaeda–inspired movement.

At a more pedestrian level are the many attempts at economic integration in the region, the focus of this chapter. Deliberate efforts to integrate the region's trade, labor, capital, or investment at the state level have shown only modest success. There have long been dreams of integrating the Middle East into the world economy, but they have all ended in failure. In the nineteenth century, Muhammad Ali's big industrialization push, and later the Tanzimat reforms of the Ottoman era, saw global integration as a means to strengthen the empire. In more recent times, there have been countless agreements between Arab countries meant to increase inter-Arab trade in goods and services, but results have been modest, largely because MENA countries tend to produce very similar goods. The Euro-Mediterranean Partnership (EUROMED), an initiative meant to connect the Middle East to European markets, was essentially superseded by EU enlargement, which brought poorer European countries that compete with MENA exports into the heart of Europe. The short-lived vision of a "New Middle East," promoted by US and Israeli interests after the Oslo Accords, tried to foster Israel's regional insertion as a quid pro quo for the integration of the region at more favorable terms in the global economy.

The unplanned, market-driven integration, achieved thanks to the efforts of uncoordinated individuals—migrants, investors, and traders—has been far more successful than these official efforts. Labor migration on a historically unprecedented scale has been a fundamental force in transforming national political economies, as it has integrated the most remote areas of the most backward countries into a rising regional economy, fueled by record levels of oil revenues. But as we shall see, the boom years of labor migration have passed and are unlikely to return. On the other hand, capital flows to and investments in the poorer parts of the region, stemming in large part from the rich Gulf, have accelerated in recent years and are bound to rise further if the second oil boom of the 2000s lasts for a prolonged period, which seems likely. Trade in goods and service has been the orphan so far, for various reasons that we explore later in this chapter.

The glue in the emergence of this new form of regional integration is increasing cultural integration among Arab societies, which has expanded over time with the rise in educational levels, the take-off of a dynamic regional media, and the spread in global communications technology. The fast spread of the revolutionary contagion in the wake of the 2011 uprisings was a testimony to the spontaneous appearance of a large cultural space that shared not only a similar culture (food, music, literature) but also, increasingly, similar political aspirations. Nevertheless, the rising sectarian and ethnic feuds that divide the region continue to pose a profound threat to this newfound cohesion.

On the global front, thirteen Arab countries now belong to the WTO and, officially at least, seek integration into the global free system of trade in goods and services, though with only modest success so far. In contrast, the ISI era was more insular, favoring state-driven economic exchanges within the region over engagement with the wider world. But while ISI strategies can be blamed for integration failures in the distant past, the more recent culprits have to be found in the low dynamism of the private sector that emerged in the era of crony capitalism and the region's new political divisions. Although Turkey managed by the 2000s to break through and become an export powerhouse, attracting large-scale FDI, principally in manufacturing activities, and thus creating millions of jobs, Egypt faltered—until recently, workers' remittances were still larger than manufactured exports as a source of foreign revenue. The various Arab countries' experiences fall somewhere between those of Turkey and Egypt.

Meanwhile, the GCC remains dominant in global petroleum markets. Indeed, large oil revenues have colored the evolution of regional economic relations, with a predominance of labor movement over regional trade. As we explore in this chapter, fragmented regional markets in goods and services have not only made the vision of a more politically unified MENA region more difficult to achieve but also hurt its global integration. In the rest of this chapter, we assess in more detail the extent of regional and global integration that has been achieved by the region in terms of trade in goods and services, look at how oil markets operate, and examine the role of capital and labor movements in integration.

TRADE IN GOODS AND SERVICES

Exporting can be a good way to grow an economy that cannot rely on natural resources. Ideally, an export-led strategy allows for the gradual accumulation of knowledge and skills in ways that are not possible in closed economies, especially small ones. Instead of being stuck with meeting only their own internal demand for goods and services, workers and firms can concentrate on what they do best by producing for the very large global markets, and they can also go up the technology ladder over time as their skills improve by shifting to the production of more sophisticated products. The one requirement that cannot be avoided is global competitiveness, which requires, as we noted in Chapter 8, effective state institutions. East Asia, the paragon of export-led growth, has taken advantage of the growing global demand that started in the 1960s to achieve remarkable economic growth.

In the 1960s and 1970s, however, as discussed in Chapter 7, the Arab region focused on producing for its own markets and would not shift to private-sector growth until the 1980s and 1990s. The transition was not wholly successful, principally because institutions and policies were not adequate to the task. As a result, the Arab world has not seen its export revenues driving its economic growth, in spite of good endowments of labor (in the labor-rich countries), capital (in the oil exporters), and energy and its closeness to the European markets.

The region now represents about 4 percent of the world economy (up from 3 percent in the 1990s). Its share of global exports of goods and services was about 5 percent in 2010, but over 80 percent of this is accounted for by oil. The region's share of non-oil global exports of goods and services was only about 1.2 percent, up from 1 percent in the 1990s, with much of the improvement coming from services exports, including tourism (Chauffour 2013). Although these outcomes imply that the MENA region is not as poorly integrated into the global economy as some observers suggest when one takes account of its oil exports, when one looks at the export of manufactured goods it is also clear that the region has not been able to take advantage of global markets to grow as East Asia has done. Here we look in some detail at the region's export performance in non-oil products first, before taking a closer look at the way global oil markets operate.

Performance in Non-Oil Trade

Exports have increased in most of the MENA countries over time, but overall performance has been uneven at best. Petroleum exports still dominate trade and, indeed, the economy of much of the region. Compared to East Asia, which exported 40.1 percent of its GDP during the 2000s, the RPLA subregion compares rather favorably: it exported 33.3 percent of its GDP in goods and services in the 2000s (see Table 13.1). However, there are two reasons why, for many countries, this is not considered a good performance. First, the share of manufacturing goods in total exports remains considerably smaller than in East Asia, with 22.7 percent of GDP in manufactures exports, against 31.8 percent of GDP in East Asia. Second, and equally as important, most of the regional economies are small, and as such, they would be expected to trade more with the outside world. Taking into consideration population size, GDP per capita, and distance to market, Alberto Behar and Caroline Freund (2011) estimate that the oil-importing countries of the region export about 30 percent less than their potential. By their measure, only Morocco, Tunisia, and Jordan overperform. Indeed, these countries, along with Lebanon and Syria, increased their manufacturing exports the most in the last decade (see Table 13.1). However, other countries, and especially Egypt, did not increase their manufacturing exports. Turkey and Israel remain way ahead of the Arab countries on this score. As to be expected, among the oil-exporting countries, manufacturing goods make up only a small share of total exports. While Saudi Arabia, Bahrain, and the UAE have all had remarkable success in their respective expansions of manufacturing export, this growth was largely dependent on the enormous energy subsidies provided to the industrial sector.

A more detailed analysis reveals that the main constraint on Arab countries' exports performance has not been any difficulty in finding new products to export—what the international trade literature calls the "extensive margin." Indeed, the region seems no less capable than other regions in discovering new market niches where it might have comparative advantages (Chauffour 2011). Instead, and in contrast to East Asian exporters, the main constraint has been the problem of *expanding* the production of these market niches, or exploiting the "intensive margin." Indeed, even the more successful exporters, such as Morocco and Tunisia, have not been able to penetrate large shares of their export markets. For example, their share of the EU's garment sector has not risen above 3 to 4 percent of the market, and it has even gone down under pressure from other more competitive exporters in recent years. As a result, exports from the MENA region have been largely made up of traditional products such as processed foods, raw materials, and oil products, with services accounting for most of the growth. The evidence, using various measures of the technological sophistication of exported products, suggests that the skills and knowledge that go into Arab products for export have increased slowly and only moderately since 1990 (Chauffour 2011).

Trade in Services

Access to efficient services—banking, insurance, telecommunications, transport, retailing—is crucial for productivity and global competiveness. Services represent a large share of the value of industrial production—an average of 20 percent—and much more for the more sophisticated products that combine inputs from many

TABLE 13.1. MENA Export Performance, 1971–2010

	Exports of Goods and Services (% of GDP)			Manufactures Exports (% of GDP)		
	1971–1990	*1991–2000*	*2001–2010*	*1971–1990*	*1991–2000*	*2001–2010*
RRLP	**65.5%**	**48.3%**	**63.3%**	**17.3%**	**7.7%**	**4.7%**
Bahrain	107.3	81.6	89.8	39.8	22.7	8.5
Kuwait	64.5	46.0	58.4	14.7	4.3	2.5
Libya	39.7	28.3	59.6		1.3	2.2
Oman	57.3	46.8	54.6	2.6	6.9	4.2
Qatar		51.4	59.8		7.3	4.6
Saudi Arabia	51.4	37.2	54.8	1.1	3.2	4.8
United Arab Emirates			65.8			2.2
RRLA	**18.7**	**22.0**	**31.9**	**1.4**	**1.0**	**2.5**
Algeria	25.9	27.6	39.9	0.4	0.9	0.7
Iran	21.5	20.5	28.7	0.8	1.6	2.6
Sudan	9.4	6.6	17.9	0.0	0.3	0.1
Syria	18.2	30.5	36.7	3.1	3.1	7.3
Yemen	12.2	24.6	36.0		0.1	0.5
RPLA	**27.6**	**28.4**	**33.3**	**9.7**	**18.8**	**22.7**
Egypt	21.0	21.4	25.6	4.6	7.8	7.9
Jordan	39.9	49.2	50.0	16.4	25.4	35.6
Lebanon	18.2	12.2	20.1		9.8	13.9
Morocco	21.2	26.1	31.9	6.6	14.8	21.2
Tunisia	34.2	40.7	46.0	14.2	31.3	34.8
Israel	**38.3**	**31.3**	**38.5**	**30.8**	**28.1**	**32.8**
Turkey	**9.6**	**19.0**	**23.5**	**4.6**	**14.2**	**19.2**
Overall MENA	**34.7**	**32.5**	**42.6**	**10.0**	**10.2**	**10.8**

Source: World Bank, World Bank Indicators (WBI)

Note: Averages over decades.

destinations and thus include large research and development and travel inputs. The services sector offers other advantages as well: it can grow fast through rapid technological development, employ skilled youth and more women than traditional sectors, and offer a comparative advantage to Arab speakers given the need to conduct much of the work in Arabic.

As in the rest of the world, the region has seen a rapid rise in the export of services, most of which has gone into regional trade—the sector doubled in size between 1990 and 2010, though its share in the global service trade remained flat at 2.8 percent. Some countries of the region did better than this: today 20 percent of Lebanon's exports and 50 percent of Jordan's are services; the figure is also high, at more than 25 percent, for Egypt, Tunisia, and Morocco.[1]

There is a large underexploited potential in many of the service industries, which are notorious for depending heavily on effective regulatory regimes (anti-monopoly laws, banking supervision, telecom rules) in order to balance their growth with their social value. Regulatory agencies have considerable discretion, however, and services have been a main area for cronyism in the past (Malik and Awadallah 2013). Thus, compared to other exporting regions, the MENA region ranks relatively low in terms of the openness of its services sector on the Overall Trade Restrictiveness Index (OTRI) (Mattoo, Rathindran, and Subramanian 2006).

Intraregional Trade

Many countries in the MENA region have also not been able to increase exports within the region, despite the comparative advantage provided by cultural and individual connections. There are several factors underlying this relative failure, besides a general lack of competiveness on the home front. The costs associated with administrative red tape and weaknesses in regional transport-related infrastructure are two of the most important constraints on intraregional trade (Hoekman and Zarrouk 2009). In addition, because the MENA countries tend to produce similar products, the added pressure from fellow MENA producers tends to impede intraregional trade. And of course, the various conflicts between the countries of the region have not helped.

Using intraregional exports as a share of total exports as a measure of trade integration, we calculate that MENA trade integration has not improved since the 1970s. The share of intraregional exports was 6.0 percent of total exports in 1970, 10.8 percent in 1990, and 5.2 percent in 2010. These fluctuations largely represent changes in the value of oil export, though intraregional trade is mainly in non-oil goods and services. A more precise estimate of regional trade would thus exclude oil. In 2010 exports of non-oil goods within the region were 18 percent of the MENA region's total non-oil exports (ESCWA 2013). By way of comparison, 25 percent of Association of Southeast Asian Nations (ASEAN) trade, 49 percent of North American Free Trade Agreement (NAFTA) trade, and 65 percent of European trade is intraregional.

Is 18 percent too little or too much? After all, if trade destination was completely random, the MENA region should sell only 4 percent of its exports within the region, since it represents only 4 percent of the world economy. To properly evaluate performance we need to factor into this calculation the drivers that normally foster regional trade. Studies that use the standard "gravity model" of international trade theory to ask whether MENA's intraregional trade flows are lower than what could be expected given levels of GDP, geography, culture, and trade agreements yield ambiguous answers. Although earlier studies were somewhat negative (Hoekman and Sekkat 2010), more recent studies suggest that the MENA region's intraregional trade is now greater than what standard gravity models would predict (Abedini and Péridy 2008). Still, much more progress could be made if goods and services flowed more easily within the region, and many have argued that the creation of an effective regional free-trade association or custom union could raise intraregional trade significantly, perhaps even doubling it (ESCWA 2013).

With intraregional exports at only 4.3 percent of their total exports, the Maghreb countries, whose economies are more turned toward Europe, have the lowest share of intraregional trade. GCC trade is just a bit more integrated into the region: though only 5 percent of exports from these countries stay within the MENA region, this represents 20 percent of the GCC's relatively small non-oil export revenues. Some Mashriq countries, building on historical ties with neighboring countries and with the GCC (for a history, see Owen 1998), have expanded their intraregional exports significantly. On average, 19.1 percent of the Mashriq's exports went to the MENA region in 2010, and regional markets represented more than 50 percent of (the small) exports from Syria and Yemen, 35 to 40 percent of exports from Lebanon, Bahrain, and Oman, and 25 percent of exports from Jordan and Egypt.

The Mashriq, Maghreb, and GCC subregions are at different stages of economic convergence. The GCC countries have already moved to a customs union (meaning that they have free trade among themselves and similar tariffs for the rest of the world), with a possible monetary union on the horizon.[2] The level of intraregional trade in the GCC has not changed significantly over recent years, however, and indeed, it probably reached its full potential during the first decade of the GCC's existence (Boughanmi 2008), as there has been little change since then in production structure, except possibly in the United Arab Emirates (Insel and Tekce 2011). In both the Maghreb and Mashriq subregions, there is not enough diversity in endowments to allow for large volumes of trade (Miniesy, Nugent, and Yousef 2003). Moreover, these two subregions have been internally divided by long-standing political disputes and conflicts.

An important, but not very appreciated, implication of this fragmentation of the regional market is that it impedes global integration. Indeed, in other parts of the world, regional economic integration and global economic integration have been complementary, with regional integration supporting global integration, and vice versa. The quintessential example is the "flying geese" phenomenon in East Asia: investment and trade opportunities that originated in Japan eventually moved down the peninsula to expand the "Asia Factory." Europe, too, became more competitive globally by expanding its own market and unleashing capital and labor movement, inter-industry trade, and the forces of innovation and competition. The main reason why regional and global integration are connected is that regionally integrated economies have a much better chance at attracting FDI. For foreign companies to move their production to a region, they must be able to lower the costs of serving the region by doing so. Such FDI flows fit neatly with the vision of the "Arab factory," which would grow initially by selling to the large Arab market before expanding to integrate globally into profitable global supply chains (Chauffour 2011; ESCWA 2013). In a fragmented regional market, however, the development of free trade with Europe or the United States can actually *hurt* the region further by encouraging investment (and especially FDI) to move out of the region and locate instead in the EU (or Eastern Europe) or in the United States (or rather, in Mexico, which NAFTA has made essentially part of the US market). This phenomenon, termed the "hub-and-spoke" problem in the international trade literature, arises when a foreign investor established in Europe or the United States can better serve all the MENA markets from that location, while a MENA producer remains handicapped by the fragmented MENA market.

The Effects of Trade Agreements

The most significant trade treaties are those negotiated with the World Trade Organization, the European Union,[3] and, to a lesser extent, the United States,[4] rather than within the region. As we mentioned earlier, thirteen MENA countries have joined the WTO, and eight others are in various stages of application.[5] The association agreements with the European Union are highly significant for Algeria, Morocco, and Tunisia, while the national project to join the European Union seems to be receding in importance in the political economy of Turkey. The same is true for investment agreements: the MENA countries have signed nearly twice as many of these agreements with OECD countries as with each other (142 compared with 75) (MENA-OECD Investment Programme 2005).

The main attempt at opening up a regionwide unified market was the 1997 agreement to establish the Greater Arab Free Trade Area (GAFTA), which focuses on gradually reducing tariffs between Arab countries. GAFTA was initiated by the Arab League as early as 1953, and it has now been ratified by eighteen countries. Studies have found that the effect of the agreement has so far been modest, increasing regional trade by about 20 percent (Abedini and Péridy 2008). There are two reasons for this modest effect of the agreement. First, it applies only to goods deemed to be sufficiently Arab in origin—at least 40 percent of a product's value needs to be produced by the exporting country if it is to benefit from the lower protection afforded by the agreement. However, there are very few goods, besides food and natural resources, that satisfy this requirement—for example, garments typically use imported textile, and the labor content tends to be only about 10 percent of the value of the final goods. Second, importing countries were allowed to develop a list of goods that would be excluded from free trade. This list grew to be quite long, as local producers feared competition from similar producers in neighboring countries and lobbied for protection (World Bank 2013). Negotiations on free trade in services were initiated in 2003 but have not been completed, owing again to differences in interests. More recently, a decision was taken to establish an Arab custom union by 2020.[6]

Were these various trade agreements useful? When a country opens up its trade regime, it faces costs and benefits. The main cost is the greater competition faced by its producers in their domestic market. Imports become cheaper, which is good for consumers and allows local producers to use cheaper, foreign inputs. However, the pressure of foreign competition also squeezes domestic producers, who now have to compete with the most efficient global producers. Inefficient producers have to close down, and workers have to move to new, more competitive sectors. For this to work, new investments are needed in the more promising sectors. Thus, the investment climate and the availability of investments are key parts of a successful trade liberalization. As we have noted previously, however, the region has not been successful at improving its investment climate—partly because of the crony capitalism that took hold post-liberalization, and partly because of the climate of high political risk in many of the countries. As a result, while MENA countries lost domestic jobs in the face of increased foreign competition, the supposed gains from trade liberalization have not materialized as hoped (except in the more attractive GCC market).

Let us compare the challenges that Tunisia and Egypt faced when they entered the WTO. Part of their commitment was to open up their local textile markets. The influx of cheap Asian textiles into local markets hurt domestic manufacturers; these were public-sector enterprises (in both countries) that lost out to Asian manufacturers in local markets and could not compete in the global market (Henry and Springborg 2010, 48). The high tax and regulatory barriers affecting trade in services, such as in the heavily regulated airline, transportation, and communication industries, impeded competiveness in both countries. Still, Tunisia's supply response was more dynamic than Egypt's—many Tunisian firms, especially those in the offshore sector, took advantage of new market opportunities abroad to expand production in new sectors such as electrical goods and food processing. Overall, some studies have calculated that trade liberation resulted in a small net gain of jobs in Tunisia, while Egypt, which was more "structurally impeded" from expanding new exports, ended up with a net loss of jobs (Konan and Kim 2004).

The second reason for the MENA countries' lack of supply response was that even with the reductions in tariffs everywhere, over time other types of impediments arose. Known as non-tariff barriers (NTBs), these included slow clearance and inspection processes, complex signatures needed to process trade, license and registration requirements for importers, packaging requirements, regulations on production and distribution processes, traceability, sanitary restrictions, and product quality requirements. Such regulations can be useful when their goal is to protect the national interest, but they can also be pushed by local producers to defend their individual interests, as often happens in Europe—for example, in the case of agricultural imports. Recent studies of cronyism in Tunisia and Egypt (Diwan, Keefer, and Schiffbauer 2014) show that NTB restrictions were driven by the lobbying activities of politically connected large firms trying to defend their domestic market interests in the face of rising global competition. For example, tariff rates were reduced in Egypt by the end of the 2000s (from an average rate of 16.5 percent in 1995 to 8.7 percent in 2009), but Egypt responded by increasing the use of non-tariff technical import barriers. By 2009, there were fifty-three types of regulations that could be construed as instruments of protection. Of all the NTBs in place in Egypt in 2009, almost half (twenty-four) were introduced or amended around 2000. Ishac Diwan and his colleagues (2014) found that politically connected firms were much more likely than other firms to be located in sectors protected by NTBs. More specifically, 71 percent of politically connected firms were in sectors that had at least three types of NTBs, but only 4 percent of all firms were in such sectors.

In the larger picture, it remains unclear how the MENA region could fit in the evolving global division of labor, and this must have colored the incentives of its policymakers to attempt to make their economies more competitive. Indeed, the MENA region does not have an obvious trade bloc that it can latch on to in order to increase its growth through trade and investment—a role that Japan played for Asia, the United States for Mexico, and Europe for the Eastern European countries after they moved away from communism. Europe would have been the perfect partner, with the Mediterranean acting as the *mare nostra* ("the sea that connects"), a role going back to the history of the Phoenician and Greek traders in the region (Braudel 1966, 514–516). The EUROMED agreements were built to achieve the dream of an "Arab factory," but they failed to produce the kind of gains hoped for in the grand vision. At the political level, this failure must be largely attributable to the declining appetite in Europe for a zone of low-cost production in the MENA after the Eastern European countries started to join the EU bloc in the 1990s.

Operationally, those agreements have done little to attract new investments in manufacturing exports or to increase intraregional MENA trade because they were unable to resolve the hub-and-spoke problem discussed earlier (Ülgen 2011). As a result, while MENA imports from the European Union have increased rapidly since the EUROMED agreements began, exports from the MENA region to the EU have stagnated. Those involved in the negotiations were aware of the hub-and-spoke problem, and some efforts were made to avoid it. The agreements forecasted the creation of a regional market at the same time as the region opened up to the EU market; the stated hope was that the region's association with Europe would foster positive dynamics in the MENA regional economy.[7] But unsurprisingly, negotiating separate agreements between the EU and each MENA nation, while at the same time each MENA country had to negotiate free trade agreements (FTAs) with all other MENA countries, turned out to be an unmanageable logistical nightmare. Still, a few new regional FTAs were signed, which only further complicated the "spaghetti bowl" of overlapping trade agreements in effect in the region. Here, too, an important impediment to regional trade was the "rules of origin" issue. Each small country alone could not produce a large share of the value of exported products, but the "accumulation" of a product's origin among countries was not allowed.[8]

In sum, trade policy has been an active area for reforms, in both its regional and global aspects, but there remains a lot of unfinished business, much of it related to "behind-the-border" trade facilitation. In the broader picture, investment risk, cronyism, and an unfavorable global environment have continued to tax the economies of the region up to the present. As a result, it is difficult to expect regional and global exports to become an effective vehicle for economic growth until there are serious national reforms that can support a move to a more innovative, competitive, and dynamic private sector.

THE FORMATION OF OIL PRICES

We now take a small detour to focus on the one global market that has shaped MENA's economic history most—oil. Given the region's overwhelming, and indeed increasing, dependence on oil exports, how oil prices are determined and why they vary so much, and whether high levels of oil revenues can be sustained in the future, are obviously crucial issues for the region.

As with all tradable commodities, oil prices are determined by the international market and by the interplay of supply and demand, but oil prices have been more variable than other commodities. Oil prices are affected by long-term trends in both production and consumption, as well as by short-term shocks and imbalances that can have large effects on prices. Both global oil supply and oil demand are highly price-inelastic in the short to medium term, because an increase in price does not necessarily prompt an immediate increase in supply, given that new capacity typically needs to be developed and this takes time. Oil's scarcity, its control by governments, and the high (and rising) costs of extraction of new oil function to stymie the investment cycle and the development of new resources. Producers of marginal reserves in difficult geological conditions cannot be competitive with low-cost producers unless prices rise to create the economic incentives to produce the high-cost reserves. Even low-cost producers are slow to increase supply to keep pace with price increases—either because they do not have spare capacity and it takes time to increase capacity, or because it is not in their interest to do so. While the international companies (the "majors") are constantly struggling to find projects with the scale and profitability required to make their investment profitable, the national oil companies (NOCs) which dominate in the MENA region the corporate landscape often struggle to muster the financial, political, or commercial ability to develop reserves.

Similarly, demand is also relatively inelastic in the short to medium term. When oil prices increased threefold in the early 1980s, it took about ten years for most of the OECD countries to reduce their consumption of oil and to develop and install substitute technologies for cheaper energy sources. It is particularly because oil consumption is concentrated in the transportation sector, that, there is no easy substitute for oil. But in the last ten years, high oil prices have encouraged the development of both substitute energy sources like biofuels, gas, and solar and conservation technologies that improve engine and turbine efficiencies.

Given oil's relative inelasticity of both demand and supply to shocks, oil prices are likely to remain volatile. Any shock to demand or supply will require a large price change if equilibrium is to be regained in the short term—essentially, when a negative supply shock occurs, it takes a large price increase in the short term to convince some demanders to exit the market and some new suppliers to engage in additional production.

Various "cartels" have, over the course of history, tried to control oil prices and to set them at levels that ensure monopoly profits. This can be done by restricting supply just enough to allow for price increases that maximize monopolist profits. In this case, opportunity cost functions as an upper limit to maximum price setting (that is, the cost of producing the best alternative technology). A significant part of the history of oil price fluctuations can be explained by cartel dynamics. Smaller members of a cartel have an incentive to free-ride and increase supply, in order to reap larger profits, but if they are allowed to do so unchecked, the result can be an oil glut and lower prices. At times, the larger cartel members may decide to discipline the "cheaters" by lowering prices and increasing their market share, especially when its production costs are lower. Saudi Arabia has found itself in this situation at various points in time.

On the other hand, an overly successful cartel that sets supply too low and prices too high will provoke the emergence of new producers outside the cartel as well as investment in conservation technologies and alternative energy sources by oil users, both of which will weaken the cartel over time. The Organization of the Petroleum-Exporting Countries (OPEC) seemed to discover this the hard way in 1980 after it attempted to raise its price to a then-record high $40 per barrel. The result was a sharp decrease in demand owing to a shift toward conservation and alternative forms of energy consumption, particularly as oil was pushed out as an energy source in the OECD countries. OPEC was forced to retreat to lower prices. After the economic crisis in emerging markets slowed demand in 1998, Saudi Arabia led a more successful price-setting effort in 1999 by loosely organizing oil states worldwide in an agreement to constrict supply, thereby inaugurating a steady climb in oil prices that peaked in 2008. Since the global economic downturn in the late 2000s, prices have fluctuated in a high-price range until late 2014, mostly owing to higher marginal costs to incentivizing new production and the large supply disruptions of oil flows from Libya, Iran, Syria, Yemen, and Sudan since 2012. The collapse of oil prices at the end of 2014 is connected to the fast rise in US production, low global demand, and on unwillingness of Saudi Arabia to cut its own production.

The geographical concentration of petroleum deposits in the Middle East is an indisputable geological fact. Four countries alone—Saudi Arabia, Iraq, Iran, and Kuwait—have about 75 percent of the region's oil reserves and about 55 percent of known conventional oil reserves in the world. This excludes shales and oil sands—though they are very abundant, extraction of oil from these sources is expensive and requires complex technologies. Considering the size of the MENA region's reserves, as well as the amount of exports coming from the Persian/Arabian Gulf, events in the MENA region will always be critical to the international oil markets—and any loss of production will have an impact on global prices.

It is common to point out how long countries' reserves will last at current production rates. For Iraq, Kuwait, and Saudi Arabia, the figures vary between 75 and 150 years. Knowing the sizes of various countries' reserves is important for understanding differences over pricing strategies within OPEC. Other things being equal, countries whose oil will last a long time have little interest in large price increases, which would induce more conservation and the discovery of new sources of supply. The differences among countries are dramatic: Kuwait and the United Arab Emirates can go on producing oil at current rates for a few decades with the right level of investments, whereas Algeria's and Syria's official reserves will last for only about a generation at the 2010 rate of production.

More important from an economic point of view, Gulf oil is the cheapest oil in the world to produce. The estimated 2010 cost of production of a barrel of Saudi, Kuwaiti, Iraqi, or Iranian Gulf oil is about US$5 per barrel for fields already in production. New greenfield development now varies between $10 and $20 per barrel. This must be compared with new developments outside the region—in particular, new production costs in technically challenging deepwater fields, where most new production is coming from, are somewhere between $60 and $70 per barrel. Gulf oil's low production costs are the key to the massive transfer of economic rents to the oil states—rents that have fueled economic expansion and change throughout the region since the 1970s. The figures for oil rents (which are, as defined earlier, the value of oil production, valued at world prices, minus total costs of production) over the past four decades are shown for all the countries of the region in Table 13.2.

The First Oil Boom

The history of the oil business has been a cycle of attempts to create a cartel followed by the erosion and demise of that cartel. From the discovery of oil in 1908 in southwestern Iran until the early 1970s, eight major international oil companies managed to control much of global oil supply.[9] By 1953, the "Seven Sisters" oil companies controlled 95 percent of non-US, non-Communist reserves, 90 percent of production, 75 percent of refining capacity, and 74 percent of product sales (Blair 1976). The extensive and deep-seated relationships among these companies took the form of long-term supply contracts (such as twenty-year contracts) and, most prominently, joint ventures. The height of control of world oil by this oil company cartel may have been 1953, when the Seven Sisters countered Mohammad Mosaddegh's nationalization of British Petroleum's Iranian oil facilities by simply refusing to refine or market Iranian oil. When Mosaddegh was overthrown and the Pahlavi Shah reinstated, another joint venture was established in which nearly all of the major oil companies were represented. The Seven Sisters kept prices relatively low, but they also reaped enormous profits and paid low royalties to the oil-producing countries, which had no other choice given the extensive control of the vertically integrated cartel over the shipping, refining, and marketing of oil.

The Seven Sisters cartel gradually disappeared with the entry of smaller independent oil companies into the industry, starting in the 1950s. Then the Arab-Israeli War in 1967 set the stage for the explosion of oil prices that triggered the flood of rent into the region. When the war closed the Suez Canal, Gulf crude had to be transported around the Cape of Good Hope, a journey that was more expensive and provoked a tanker shortage. Western European nations increased their reliance on cheaper oil from west of Suez and from Libya in particular. The new government of Muammar Gaddafi (who took power in 1969) immediately demanded an increase in the royalties it was receiving from the companies working in Libya. Although the larger oil companies refused, the independent oil companies were more vulnerable to pressure. Libya prevailed through a classic divide-and-rule policy. Its success prompted the Gulf producers to follow suit, and nominal oil prices began to rise. But on the whole, oil prices remained stable.

The next large price shock took place in 1973, initiated by the Arab-Israeli October War, which prompted a temporary Saudi embargo. By then, two additional factors had come into play that opened a historical window allowing for the formation of OPEC. First, in 1972 the large oil companies had been nationalized—in Libya by Gaddafi and in Iraq by Saddam Hussein. And second, the rise in the demand for oil in the late 1960s and early 1970s had started to strain supply, slowly

488

TABLE 13.2. Oil Rents in the MENA Region (share of GDP), by Country, 1970–2010

Country	1961–1970	1971–1980	1981–1990	1991–2000	2001–2010
RRLP	**41.9**	**62.4**	**35.3**	**26.5**	**35.1**
Bahrain		76.6	34.8	17.5	20.4
Kuwait	42.5	67.4	41.3	36.5	49.2
Libya			32.4	24.7	50.2
Oman	47.4	60.9	40.3	31.0	37.2
Qatar	46.2	66.4	38.1	26.0	23.5
Saudi Arabia	31.3	59.9	37.7	32.7	46.7
United Arab Emirates		43.3	22.3	17.1	18.7
RRLA	**10.1**	**27.7**	**14.5**	**28.0**	**34.1**
Algeria	7.7	20.4	10.0	8.9	17.7
Iran	14.3	32.2	13.9	24.2	30.4
Iraq	17.0	48.6	27.4	83.2	86.8
Sudan			0.0	1.7	18.0
Syria	1.5	9.7	12.8	22.2	20.9
Yemen			23.0	27.6	30.9
RPLA	**1.3**	**6.8**	**7.0**	**2.7**	**2.8**
Egypt	1.7	12.3	18.9	7.8	7.8
Jordan			0.0	0.0	0.0
Lebanon					
Morocco	0.0	0.0	0.0	0.0	0.0
Palestine					
Tunisia	2.2	8.0	9.0	2.8	3.5
Israel	**0.7**	**1.0**	**0.0**	**0.0**	**0.0**
Turkey	**0.2**	**0.5**	**0.5**	**0.2**	**0.2**

Source: World Bank, World Bank Indication (WBI).

Note: Average over decades. Oil rents are the value of crude oil produced, at international prices, minus production costs.

eroding the excess capacity that the Seven Sisters had created in earlier times; by the early 1970s, the United States had become a net oil importer. As a result, the Saudi embargo created an atmosphere of panic buying on the spot, or open, market. The shah of Iran in particular took the opportunity to hold an auction in order to see what price his oil might fetch—the answer was between US$9.00 and US$17.34 per barrel, while the Rotterdam spot price hit US$26.00 per barrel (Danielson 1982, 172). The final price that OPEC agreed to charge customers was US$11.65, a price negotiated between the "price doves," led by Saudi Arabia, and the "price hawks," led by Iran. With nearly all the excess capacity inside the OPEC countries, and with few short-run alternatives, consuming countries had little choice in the short run but to pay whatever price OPEC demanded.[10]

Political events again opened the next act in the oil-price drama. The 1979 Iranian Revolution removed about 2 million barrels a day from production; although the Saudis at first tried to make up the shortfall, they had already been producing close to capacity in an attempt to restrain further price increases, which they (reasonably) believed were not in their medium- and long-term economic interest. However, the Camp David Accords, in neglecting to address the Palestinian issue, angered the Saudis considerably. In response, they reduced production in the immediate aftermath of Camp David, setting the stage for another round of panic buying on the spot market (Quandt 1981). The resulting record-breaking market price helped the OPEC hawks to carry the day: the OPEC reference price leapt to US$17.26 in 1979 and then to US$28.67 in 1980. This price hike was lower in proportional terms than the 1973–1974 hike but considerably greater in absolute dollar value.[11] The increase in revenues for OPEC countries was prodigious. Governments launched development projects that were even more massive than before. Never had so much been paid by so many to so few; never before in human history had such an enormous amount of wealth been transferred in such a short amount of time to governments with such (typically) small populations.[12]

But booms do not last forever. Although it was not immediately apparent, OPEC overreached itself from 1979 to 1981, as we explained earlier. Conserving energy became an economic necessity, especially once the United States decontrolled petroleum prices. OPEC soon fell victim to both the "external" and "internal" cartel problem. The external problem is the simple fact that very high prices give consumers and producers incentive to change their behavior. The demand for oil is a derived demand—we want oil not for its own sake but because we want to move around, heat our homes, light our lamps, and so forth. And so, with high oil prices, consuming countries shifted to lower-cost energy sources to fuel their economies and initiated policies to improve oil efficiency, especially in transport, heating, and electricity. In short, conservation was greatly stimulated across the world, and by the late 1980s the industrial countries were using less than 70 percent as much oil per unit of output as they had been in 1973. Oil demand fell globally as oil became relegated largely to use as a transportation fuel only and was increasingly removed from industrial production and electricity generation. Non-OPEC producers compounded the external cartel problem: high oil prices provided incentives for countries to open their territory to new exploration, and the oil industry provided the necessary investments and resources after being shut out of most OPEC countries following the nationalization of the international oil companies. Alaskan, North Sea, and Mexican oil became especially important new sources of oil supply. When lower demand combined with higher non-OPEC supply, OPEC's market share of world oil production fell from 48.8 percent in 1979 to 28.7 percent in 1985 (OPEC 1993).

These developments aggravated the internal cartel problem—the temptation for cartel members to cheat on production quotas and oversupply oil markets. In fact, OPEC lacked formal production quotas until 1982, and quotas have often been openly ignored (by Kuwait, Iraq, and Iran). In practice, just as OPEC was the "residual supplier" to the world market, Saudi Arabia was the "residual supplier" within OPEC. Only Saudi Arabia could play this "swing producer" role: it could vary its production from a low of 2.2 million barrels per day (in August 1985) to a high of nearly 10 million barrels per day (in 1980). Saudi Arabia had long demanded that other oil producers agree to production quotas in order to control supply in a disciplined way. They remonstrated vainly in OPEC councils: quota agreements, first established in March 1982, were violated almost as soon as they were drafted. Saudi Arabia became the enforcer of production discipline to stabilize prices, but acting largely alone, it saw its own production and exports decline dramatically in 1985. With the decline in the Saudi exports market share, from 21 percent of the market in the 1980s to 8.5 percent in 1985, Saudi government revenues declined, too, even as the government had made extensive commitments to development expenditures and projects. Saudi spending began to exceed revenues in 1983.

The Saudis' patience was finally exhausted. In July and August 1986, Saudi Arabia opened the taps, producing about 7 million barrels per day.[13] Prices collapsed, falling to under US$10 in the late summer of 1986. By this action, the Saudis sent messages to fellow OPEC members ("Quit cheating! We can take losses better than you can!"), to non-OPEC producers ("Let's make a deal—your production costs are much higher than ours"), and to investors in conservation technology ("We can push the price down and drive you out of business!"). Only the last message seems to have been heard. Although OPEC tried to fix production quotas, enforcement mechanisms were weak and cheating remained rife. Britain refused to cooperate with OPEC, and prices rebounded to around US$18 per barrel and hovered there until the end of the 1980s. From this episode, Saudi Arabia learned that it cannot act alone, and that a workable strategy within OPEC that allows for shared sacrifices in order to successfully control supply is needed, even if Saudi Arabia has to bear the lion's share of the sacrifice. The lessons learned in the 1980s influenced the Saudi stance within OPEC during the economic crises of 1998 and 2008 and in 2014, when collective action was required to restrict supply and stabilize prices.

The Second Oil Boom

The Iraqi invasion of Kuwait in 1990 further weakened OPEC and strengthened the positions of both OECD consumers and Saudi producers. Although there was sufficient excess capacity to replace the lost production from occupied Kuwait and embargoed Iraq, prices doubled in two months as fear gripped oil markets. The rapid defeat of Iraqi forces in Operation Desert Storm and the increase in production elsewhere, especially in Saudi Arabia, swiftly brought prices back to their prewar levels. In the early 1990s, prices continued to hover around US$18 per barrel in nominal terms. Producing close to capacity kept prices at around $20 and helped to avoid further demand "destruction." (There was also an alleged secret promise by Saudi Arabia to the United States to keep oil prices relatively low.)

Oil prices reached their post-1973 nadir during the Asian financial crisis of 1998 (US$10.81 per barrel in December); prices have shot up since then (see Figure 9.1). These changes can be explained by forces on both the demand side and the supply side. On the demand side, the apparently insatiable thirst for oil from the developing countries of Asia has steadily shifted the demand function for oil. As the Chinese and Indian economies have boomed, oil consumption has grown in tandem. Chinese oil consumption rose from some 2 million barrels per day in 1990 to more than 7 million in 2006. Indian consumption roughly doubled during the same period. These rates of growth have since proved to be unsustainable, and China has adopted the OECD policies of restricting oil demand to the transportation sector, thus reducing the growth of its demand for oil since 2010. As for the United States, low oil prices combined with the lack of government policies supporting conservation spurred demand for ever larger, more fuel-intensive cars, particularly the notorious gas-guzzling sport utility vehicles (SUVs). And because US energy production stagnated during the 1990s, imports supplied a steadily growing percentage of consumption.

On the supply side, the extremely low prices of the late 1990s prompted the two largest Gulf producers, Saudi Arabia and Iran, to settle their differences and coordinate their oil policies. OPEC cut production by 1.5 million barrels per day, or by about 5.4 percent, from 1998 to 1999. OPEC discipline continued through 2002. Such coordination was naturally greatly assisted by the steadily growing demand from Asia after 2002. In reality, quota discipline was not needed, as OPEC could barely keep up with rising demand. Oil prices collapsed for a short period during the global crisis of 2008, driven more by speculation than by a real reduction in demand, but they quickly bounced back and have hovered between $100 and $120 per barrel until the end of 2014.

Looking forward, prices will be determined, as always, by the forces of supply and demand and by the marginal cost of extracting an extra barrel of oil. On the demand side, much will depend on the health of the global economy. With a global economy growing at 2 to 3 percent a year, the global demand for energy will grow at about 3 percent a year, though oil will take up only a fraction of that growth. While population growth is expected to slow down, the global middle class will continue to grow. Over the next twenty years, the waves of growth unleashed in India and China may extend to most other developing countries. By 2030, the world's population will exceed the year 2000 population levels by 2 billion—and 95 percent of that increase will come in the developing world, nearly all of it concentrated in urban areas. The increased urban population will strain current supply levels and require massive new investments to increase energy production and build new distribution infrastructure (Wolfram, Shelef, and Gertler 2012). On the other hand, the 2008–2011 global market crash and recession confounded the demand outlook for the near future. If low economic growth becomes the "new normal," as it is now alleged in some quarters, then global demand will grow at a slower pace. Moreover, increased conservation efforts will have a similar impact. Between 2010 and 2012, for instance, energy use decreased 5 percent per capita in the United States, 1.5 percent in Canada, 4.5 percent in France, 6 percent in Britain, and 7 percent in Germany. The demand for oil is likely to continue to increase in this environment, but at a slower rate than total energy consumption. Both developing and developed economies are increasingly providing economic incentives to switch to cheaper and cleaner sources of energy.

As global demand for oil rose in the 2000s, the preponderance of unconventional, deepwater, and frontier supply markets also rose in relation to more traditional, developed, and easily accessible conventional sources that have been exploited and are facing depletion and exhaustion to varying degrees. Indeed, the high price of conventional oil has stimulated the development of unconventional production sites that in the pre-boom climate of lower prices had been ruled out as too expensive to develop. New ongoing expansions include deepwater and ultra-deepwater sites in the Gulf of Mexico and off West Africa and Brazil, as well as rapidly increasing shale exploitation in the United States. The development of the new oil frontier provinces (both geological and technological) and the potentially large but uncertain growth of production in Iran and Iraq eventually pose a threat to high oil prices and to Saudi Arabia's ability to keep its market share stable as witnessed by the larger drop in price at the end of 2014 (Maken and Hume 2013).

It is also important to note that the consequences of the world's increasing use of fossil fuels, with its attendant impacts on global climate change, are likely to affect the demand for—and therefore the price of—oil in the near future. Such changes will occur only if the policies of major oil-consuming countries change to accommodate these serious climatological realities. At this writing, there is little evidence that such changes are under way. For good or ill, oil from the Middle East will continue to be central to the world's energy economy for several decades to come.

Have we, then, gone "back to the future"? No one knows. The answer will depend in important ways on the rate of growth of the global economy, on the politics of global warming, and on technological change. All that can be said is that the political crises driven by the social and economic forces described in this book are likely to persist for some time, both pushing oil prices up and increasing the GCC's need for oil revenues. Production decisions by Middle Eastern producers, and especially by Saudi Arabia, will continue to play a major role in determining the future path of oil prices. As we saw in Chapter 9, GCC states have responded to the Arab uprisings with a mix of increased domestic spending and patronage. In 2012 a Saudi official expressed the desire to maintain a price of $100 per barrel in perpetuity, up from the $75 per barrel that King Abdullah had suggested as a fair price in 2008—a reflection of the Saudis' new spending obligations after the Arab uprisings (Blas and Chazan 2012). But high oil prices contain the seeds of their own destruction: in just a short four years, US oil shale production has increased by over 3 million barrels per day, putting the United States on the verge of self-sufficiency.

The recent price decline will test whether the rise in the production of US shale production can continue in the new environment.

CAPITAL MOVEMENT

Regional and global integration have multiple dimensions, and focusing on the trade dimension alone paints an incomplete picture. Indeed, given the predominance of the oil sector, the more important areas for potential MENA regional integration are the flow of capital from the Gulf, the flow of labor to the Gulf, and the integration of services (Hoekman and Zarrouk 2009). Although both analysts and policymakers have focused excessively on trade in goods, the prospects for—and returns on—efforts to deepen the integration of other markets (services, labor, capital) are likely to be higher (Hoekman and Sekkat 2010). The big story here is the relatively recent rise in capital flows from the Gulf. Although the bulk of GCC investments were channeled to the United States, Europe, and the rising economies of China and India, a growing proportion of GCC investments have started to stay in the region. Indeed, over the past few years, partly because of the geopolitical ramifications of the events of September 11, 2001, GCC investments have started to pour into the MENA region, and increasingly in the form of FDI (Baabood 2009; Hertog 2007).

To set the stage for an analysis of recent FDI flows, it is useful to start by looking at the broader context of financial external flows. The Middle East, as we noted in Chapter 8, relied heavily on external debt to delay the day of reckoning in the 1980s, when import substitution strategies had run their course. Since then, debt-creating capital flows, from both public and private sources, have dwindled, and they stopped being important sources of funds in most countries of the region in the 1990s and especially in the 2000s (see Table 7.3).

Although the region continued to receive more than its fair share of external official development assistance (ODA)—GCC, EU, and US bilateral aid, as well as regional and multilateral support from international financial institutions (IFIs)—these flows became more concentrated over time. Countries undergoing postwar reconstruction received the largest share. During the 2000s, official development assistance went mainly to Palestine (30.2 percent of its GDP per year on average during the decade), to Iraq (16 percent of GDP per year), and to a lesser extent to Sudan (4 percent of GDP per year, mostly to South Sudan). Among the other countries of the region, and until the Arab uprisings in 2011, ODA levels remained relatively large only in Jordan, at 5.5 percent of GDP per year during the 2000s, still largely below what the country received in the 1970s (22.7 percent of GDP per year) and the 1980s (13.4 percent of GDP). ODA has remained low and flat in Morocco, Tunisia, and Lebanon (1 to 2 percent of GDP per year) in the last decade. And it went down dramatically in Syria, where it stood at 0.6 percent of GDP in the 2000s (compared to 9.9 percent in the 1970s and 4.9 percent in the 1980s), and in Yemen, which has received 1.5 percent of GDP in recent years (down from 6.9 percent in the 1980s). So on the eve of the 2011 uprisings, the MENA region was largely being weaned off official assistance, after being the most assisted region historically (Malik and Awadallah 2013), a reflection of the fall in strategic rents in the region between the Second Gulf War and the Arab uprisings.

Turning to the international capital markets, the region did not take advantage of the huge expansion of the international credit markets that took off in the 1990s and 2000s until the 2008 global crisis (see Table 7.3). Net borrowing was actually negative in the RRLP and RPLA countries, which took advantage of being flush with petrodollars to repay old debts and start heavily investing some of their surpluses abroad. Among the RPLA countries, Lebanon continued borrowing heavily (6.8 percent of GDP per year in the 2000s, after 5.4 percent a year in the 1990s and 9.2 percent per year in the 1980s). It now has one of the largest external debt ratios in the world. Most other countries, however, now have comfortably low external debts, after the large deleveraging of the 1990s (see Table 7.3). Except for Lebanon and Jordan, all the other countries in the RPLA group have external debt-to-GDP ratios below the 50 percent danger limit, with only Tunisia approaching the red zone. Jordan and Tunisia borrowed moderately, at about 2 to 3 percent of GDP per year, during the 2000s—for Jordan this was a very large change compared to its heavy borrowing in the past (11 percent of GDP per year in the 1980s and 6 percent of GDP per year in the 1990s). Egypt and Morocco, on the other hand, did not borrow any substantial amounts and relied instead on domestic debt to finance government deficits.

The Rise of Gulf Capital

The major oil-exporting countries spent most of their increased incomes between 1974 and 1984 on their own internal investment projects. Most of the surplus was held in short-term liquid assets in the OECD countries, but some money was channeled toward their poorer neighbors as economic aid—both direct and bilateral and as contributions to regional and multilateral agencies. However, increased spending on domestic programs and (by the mid-1980s) plummeting real oil prices slashed such aid, which was further reduced by the Gulf War and the ensuing massive deficits in Saudi Arabia. But even in 1993 the Saudi government was giving away proportionally 80 percent more of its national income than the most generous OECD donor, Norway.[14] Such aid made up a large proportion of total investment in recipient countries between 1973 and 1987.[15] Saudi largesse continued even during the long period of low oil prices. In 2003 the Saudis gave away $2.4 billion, about 1 percent of their GNI—compared with a developed-country average of only 0.25 percent.

Perhaps the most notable attempts to use capital as an instrument of economic integration have been the region's various development funds. The earliest of these, the Kuwait Fund for Arab Economic Development, was founded in 1961, followed by the Arab Fund for Economic and Social Development, established by the Arab League in 1968. Run along the lines of the World Bank, these funds extend loans for development projects ranging from railroads and fertilizer plants to sewage and water supply systems to livestock and crop production schemes.

Of these, the Arab Fund, with its focus on expanding regional infrastructure in ways that enhance regional cooperation, has had the most self-consciously political agenda. In addition to making development loans to specific countries, it has sought to promote the main regional infrastructure grids. It invested in the Arab electrical interconnection projects in the Mashriq (between Egypt, Iraq, Jordan, Lebanon, Libya, Syria, and Turkey) and the Maghreb (Algeria, Egypt, Libya, Morocco, Tunisia, and Spain, thus connecting these countries to the European grid) and in the GCC interconnection project. The Arab Fund also financed the interconnection of Arab communication networks, the Arabsat satellite network, and a marine cable network, as well as the interconnection of gas networks between Egypt, Jordan, Lebanon, and Syria. Other important regional projects financed by the Arab Fund include investments in major shared water resources, joint agricultural productions, especially in Sudan, the preservation of historical sites, and the digitalization of the Arabic language. These activities have laid the groundwork for regional economic integration in important ways.

As the economies of countries that experienced political upheaval after the 2011 uprisings have weakened, GCC countries (except Bahrain) have mobilized to provide financing. Egypt, Jordan, Morocco, Tunisia, and Yemen have been so far the principal beneficiaries of this increased support. Given the reduced access of these countries to capital markets and the relatively low level of support from the West under the umbrella of the Deauville agreements, such support has allowed transition countries to continue providing economic stimulus longer than they could have otherwise. By the end of 2013, total pledges by GCC countries came to around $40 billion—mainly in the form of soft loans and commodity aid (see Table 13.3). Saudi Arabia alone contributed 43 percent of the pledges. Much of the financing is for budget and balance-of-payments support. Approximately 55 percent of these pledges were designated for Egypt, with much of the pledges made after Morsi's removal from office. By the end of 2012, the GCC countries had disbursed about $7 billion, which amounted to 40 percent of the global support for the transition countries over this period (World Bank 2013).

At the same time, surging oil prices have transformed the countries of the GCC into major players on the world financial stage and large investors in the MENA countries (see next section on FDI). Even if oil prices stay at moderate levels in the next decade, the coming oil windfall will dwarf anything we have seen so far. At $70 per barrel, the McKinsey Global Institute (2007) projects that Gulf oil export revenues will add up to $6.2 trillion over the next fourteen years—more than triple what they earned over the past fourteen years. At $100 per barrel, this would rise to almost $9 trillion. Decisions by Gulf leaders on how to use this wealth will have global as well as regional repercussions for decades to come. Their foreign investment choices will affect global interest rates and the evolution of various asset markets around the world. Their domestic investments will determine which local industries and cities thrive, and their regional involvement will affect the ways in which the region's economies diversify and whether they will manage to generate enough jobs to employ their young people (De Boer et al. 2008).

TABLE 13.3. Pledges (in billions of US dollars) by the GCC Countries During 2011–2013 to Support Countries in Transition

	Kuwait	Qatar	Saudi Arabia	United Arab Emirates	Total
Egypt	4,000	3,000	9,000	6,000	22,000
Jordan	1,250	1,250	2,700	1,250	6,450
Tunisia	0	1,000	750	200	1,950
Yemen	500	500	3,250	136	4,386
Morocco	1,250	1,250	1,250	1,250	5,000
Total	7,000	7,000	16,950	7,658	39,786

Source: World Bank (2013).

Foreign Direct Investment

Foreign direct investment (FDI) inflows can supplement domestic investment by bringing in much-needed finance to the struggling private sectors in the region. But more important, it has the potential to expand manufacturing sectors, which can be a major source of new jobs, by bringing in much-needed transfers of technology and management know-how to boost productivity and allow countries to catch up with the technology frontier. Foreign manufacturing multinational corporations (MNCs) tend to have better access to external markets than domestic firms, and so, by developing linkages with domestic firms as producers of intermediary products and services, they can create benefits that spill over to the whole economy.

FDI flows to developing countries rose substantially in the 2000s, more than quadrupling relative to their level during the 1990s. By 2012, FDI flows to developing countries, at about $800 billion, were as large as those going to developed countries—a historical first—owing to rising commodity prices, increased global liquidity, and excess production capacity in much of the developed world. This wave of rising FDI flows did not bypass the Middle East. Starting from a relatively low base in the 1990s at less than 0.5 percent of total FDI flows, FDI flows to the MENA region rose to nearly 5 percent of total flows by 2010 (see Figure 13.1). Given that Arab economies oscillate between 3 and 4 percent of global GDP, the region seems to be getting more than its share of global FDI. In some countries, FDI supplemented domestic private investment in important ways, especially in the smaller economies of Lebanon, Jordan, and Bahrain. Indeed, FDI flows became a major source of foreign exchange in many countries, competing with remittances and exports.

Between 2001 and 2010, most of the FDI flows went to the GCC countries, and especially to Saudi Arabia and the United Arab Emirates. In contrast to the earlier period, when most of the funds went to the RPLA countries, Saudi Arabia and the UAE each received more than 20 percent of total FDI flows to the region during this period because high oil prices had made oil exploration more attractive. The GCC received on average about 3.4 percent of its GDP in FDI flows, with the

FIGURE 13.1. Foreign Direct Investment (as a share of GDP) in the MENA Region, 1991–2012

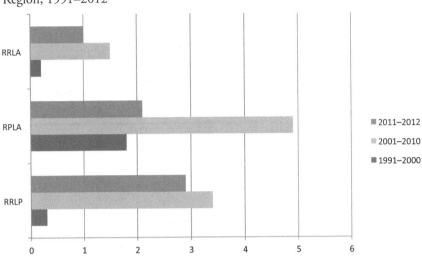

Source: UN Conference on Trade and Development (UNCTAD) data, aggregated from data presented in World Bank (2013).

smaller economy of Bahrain continuing to lead at 6 percent of GDP (after having received 8 percent of GDP during the previous decade), followed by Saudi Arabia, Qatar, and the UAE at about 4 percent of GDP each. The RPLA countries received about 30 percent of total FDI flowing to the region, constituting on average 4.9 percent of their GDP. Flows to Lebanon and Jordan were especially large, at 12 and 10.1 percent of GDP, respectively, followed by Tunisia and Palestine (5 percent of GDP), Egypt (4 percent of GDP), and Morocco (about 2.5 percent of GDP). The RRLA countries started the decade with low flows, but by the end of the decade they were receiving more than the RPLA countries. For the decade as a whole, they received on average 1.5 percent of GDP annually, with FDI flows going predominantly to the natural resource sectors of Algeria, Iraq, and Syria.

FDI global flows collapsed during the worldwide financial crisis in 2008, but quickly recovered by the early 2010s. However, FDI flows continued to retreat in the MENA region, with the most marked retreat in the RPLA countries, many of which were most affected by political instability during the Arab uprisings.

Using a unique data set for new greenfield investment from the FDI Markets database, compiled by the World Bank (2013), we note several important characteristics of these investments (see Table 13.4).[16] First, FDI inflows were concentrated in nontradables (mostly real estate) and mining, each receiving about one-third of total FDI. Services (mainly transport and tourism) received a bit less, but manufacturing got much less (16 percent of total FDI). In the GCC, real estate, mining, and manufacturing each attracted about one-fourth of total FDI. In the RRLA countries,

TABLE 13.4. Characteristics of Cumulative Foreign Direct Investment (in billions of US dollars) in the MENA Region, 2003–2012

FDI Suppliers

FDI recipients	Developed Countries	MENA	Less Developed Countries	Total
RRLP	293	89	64	446
RPLA	100	128	12	240
RRLA	109	99	41	249
Total	502	316	117	937

Sector Destination of FDI

FDI recipients	Oil	Manufacturing	Services	Nontradables	Jobs Created (thousands)
RRLP	137	87	115	106	582
RPLA	50	31	74	88	482
RRLA	97	35	52	66	278

Sector Destination of FDI

FDI suppliers	Oil	Manufacturing	Services	Nontradables	Jobs Created (thousands)
Developed countries	200	90	102	109	716
MENA	23	29	125	139	452
Less developed countries	59	33	13	12	136
Total	283	153	241	260	1,340
Percentage of total FDI in sector	30%	16%	26%	28%	
Percentage of total jobs created in sector	7%	55%	19%	19%	

Source: Computed from data in World Bank (2013).

more than half of total FDI went to mining, and the rest went mainly to real estate. In the RPLA countries, nontradables and services each received about one-third of total FDI, but manufacturing received only 13 percent.

Second, the largest share of these investments, more than 50 percent, came from MNCs in developed countries (see top panel of Table 13.4). MNCs tend to have high research-and-development capacity and could have done much to support the development of manufacturing in MENA countries; however, more than 60 percent of their investments went into the oil sector and the nontradable sectors such as real estate and construction (see bottom panel of Table 13.4). Thus, there was a huge missed opportunity to grow the type of sectors that can create a large number of skilled jobs.

Third, the share of FDI provided by the GCC was large, and more than one-third of it was directed at the RPLA countries. Indeed, in these countries the largest source of FDI was the GCC. But here, too, the main sectors that benefited did not include manufacturing—instead, real estate and tourism projects and investments in services came first. In many Arab capitals, from Cairo to Beirut, Amman, and Casablanca, the high-end real estate market is now dominated by GCC companies and buyers. This pattern has ushered in a new and unprecedented phase of regional integration in which businesses are playing a more important role than governments (Hertog 2008). The GCC countries have also been not just a major investor but also the largest destination of FDI to the region, principally by western MNCs seeking to develop oil reserves.

Fourth, because of their concentration in mining and construction, FDI inflows have not generated many jobs—close to $1 trillion of investment has generated "only" about 1.3 million jobs, which implies that it took nearly $1 million to generate one job! In contrast, the smaller FDI in manufacturing (16 percent of total FDI) created 55 percent of total jobs. The manufacturing sectors that benefited include food processing, consumer products, textile industries, and petrochemicals. The countries that gained most of the jobs were Saudi Arabia and the United Arab Emirates, countries that rely largely on migrant workers. Among the investors, Arab investment was highest in terms of labor intensity, as most of it went into construction activity.

The recent FDI surge is surprising given the high degree of political instability, cronyism, and corruption that has characterized the region and impeded the growth of its private sectors. What, then, explains the high level of (pre-2011) FDI to the region? Researchers pondering the FDI figures have come up with two explanations. First, from a profitability and diversification perspective, GCC investors seem to be "overinvesting" in the region, but perhaps their cultural affinity gives them special incentives to work in the region and also helps them remain less affected by corruption and political instability, as their inside knowledge allows them to navigate the regional waters better than Western MNCs (Sekkat 2014; World Bank 2013). Second, political instability and high levels of corruption mainly affect investment in manufacturing sectors, but not investment in the oil sector, which tends to operate as an enclave. In effect, manufacturing MNCs have a choice of location and tend to select sites with stability and high levels of skills, while MNCs in oil tend to have less choice (World Bank 2013). These explanations suggest that the high levels of cronyism and corruption and the high political risk driven by the recent political instability have severely cost the region in terms of job loss. These factors have negatively affected the composition of FDI, pushing it toward sectors that may be safer but that have the least capacity to spread knowledge externalities and create the skilled jobs that are needed in the region.

LABOR MIGRATION

Regional labor migration has transformed the political economy of the region more—at least so far—than trade in goods or capital flows. Labor markets have become much more integrated across national boundaries. Huge numbers of urban and rural citizens of the poorer countries of the region have left their homes, often for the first time, for extended stays abroad. Their departures, their remittances, and their subsequent returns have altered family structures, village customs, neighborhood layouts, and national economies. The interaction of people from different parts of the region in the Gulf has renewed the sense of a regional culture and fostered its dynamism, with the spread of satellite TV and a host of new corporate, intellectual, and political regional endeavors. Equally, the large influx of Maghrebis in Europe has also had profound effects on society in the Maghreb.

Severe issues with the accuracy of data plague all estimates of the magnitude of migration. For labor migration, the data typically count inflows, not outflows. They usually enumerate work permits rather than persons, making no allowance for multiple entries. They also suffer from a variety of other difficulties, including the underreporting of unauthorized migration, which all analysts agree is substantial. Moreover, different countries use different definitions for "visitor," "short-term migrant," and "long-term resident foreigner." The distinction between "temporary" and "permanent" migrants is contentious, as is that between "economic migrant" and "refugee." Although some of these problems bedevil EU statistics on MENA immigrant labor, they are especially severe in the data on labor migration to the major oil-exporting countries of the Persian Gulf. In that area, where some of the problems are due to imprecise definitions, labor force numbers are lower than total migrant population numbers.

Unsurprisingly, then, estimates of the magnitude of migration and refugees vary widely. Broadly speaking, somewhere between 18 million and 20 million Arabs were working outside their country of origin in 2010 (World Bank 2010), as were about 3 million Turks. The number of economic migrants—the overwhelming majority of all migrants—in GCC states in 2010 has been estimated at about 12.5 million, compared to 4.2 million national workers. While workers in the Gulf were predominantly from Arab countries in the 1970s, the share of Arabs had fallen to less than 50 percent by 2001. All in all, about half of the Arab migrants worked in Arab countries in 2010, mostly in the GCC—significantly, at least one-third of all Arab migrants are now in Saudi Arabia. Most of the rest, and especially Maghrebis,

TABLE 13.5. Refugees in and from Various Middle
East Countries, 2012

	Country of Origin	*Country of Asylum*
Algeria	3,621	94,122
Egypt	12,784	230,055
Iraq	401,362	246,294
Jordan	1,602	641,894
Lebanon	3,805	856,529
Mauritania	34,225	92,752
Somalia	1,121,692	2,416
Sudan	649,285	159,838
Syria	2,468,341	149,266
Yemen	2,383	241,276
Total	4,708,147	2,764,502

Source: UN Refugee Agency (UNHCR) (2014).

Note: The total includes countries of the region that are not listed
here and whose figures are below 1,000.

work in the EU countries—more than 3 million Maghrebis, and about the same
number of Turks, live in the countries of the European Union.

Refugee populations in the region are also considerable, and they have risen
dramatically in the recent past, especially among Syrians and Iraqis. The largest in
terms of both numbers and political impact is the Palestinian refugee population—
some 5 million were registered by the United Nations Relief and Works Agency
(UNRWA) in 2013. Several million Sudanese refugees live in Egypt, mainly in and
near Cairo; estimated numbers vary from a low of 15,000 (CIA 2006) to a high of
5 million (Baldwin-Edwards 2005). There are nearly 100,000 Sahrawis in Algeria
and just under 1 million (down from over 2 million) Afghan refugees in Iran.[17]
Internally displaced Somalis number over 1 million (see Table 13.5).

Recent events in Iraq and Syria have led to huge population movement in the
past three years—and to what amounts to a humanitarian disaster. There were
nearly 800,000 refugees from Iraq in the region in 2012, a figure that, officially,
declined to 401,000 in 2013. But the events of 2014 have sent hundreds of thousands of minorities and Shi'a populations fleeing the areas occupied by ISIL for the
relative security of the Kurdish-controlled areas and Baghdad. Syria has witnessed
the highest number of conflict-driven displaced persons, with a total of nearly 10
million as of September 2014—more than 3 million are refugees in neighboring
countries, and 7 million are internally displaced persons (IDPs) residing in Aleppo,
rural Damascus, Homs, and Idleb (SNAP 2014). According to the UN Refugee
Agency (UNHCR 2014), Syrian refugees are spread out across the region and

are mainly in Lebanon (1.2 million), Jordan (620,000), Turkey (850,000), Iraq (215,000), and Egypt (140,000). In Jordan and Turkey, most refugees live in camps, whereas in Lebanon, Iraq, and Egypt they live with local host families or in public spaces such as schools and parks.

Labor migration in the MENA region can be roughly divided into two "streams" and three "tiers" that delineate the direction of regional migration. The first stream is the migration flow to the European Union; the second stream is the flow to the GCC states. The three tiers apply to the various countries receiving or sending migrant laborers. Tier 1 is made up of the major receiving countries of the European Union and the GCC states. Tier 2 consists of countries that both send and receive migrants—they send workers to Tier 1 countries and receive migrants from poorer countries. Tier 2 countries that send workers to the GCC include Egypt, Jordan, Lebanon, and Yemen; those that send workers to the EU include Algeria, Morocco, Tunisia, and Turkey. Tier 3 consists of those poor, sub-Saharan African countries (for example, Sudan, Mali, and Somalia) that send workers to Tier 2 countries. Jordan and Lebanon increasingly send skilled workers to the Gulf and attract unskilled workers from Egypt and Syria.

Regional migration has become increasingly complex over time. For example, Yemen, which sends approximately 400,000 to 500,000 workers to GCC countries, now hosts a large number of Somali refugees. In North Africa, 80,000 to 100,000 African migrants pass through the Maghreb seeking entry to the European Union every year.

The First Stream: Flows to the European Union

The older of the two streams is the migration of Maghrebis and Turks to Western Europe. Migration from Morocco and Algeria dates back at least to World War I. However, the real boom in such migration dates to the 1960s and early 1970s, when rapid economic growth attracted large numbers of Algerians, Moroccans, and Tunisians to France and Holland (for Moroccans), as well as Turks to Germany. The Maghrebi population of France increased by about 60,000 people every year from 1968 to 1975. The flows subsequently decelerated but nevertheless remained positive. Huge wage gaps between sending and receiving countries remain the fundamental drivers of migration. Maghreb migrants are predominantly low-skill workers, with more than 70 percent having a primary education or less. Nevertheless, there are among them still a high number of skilled workers. Today about 75 percent of the migrants from the Maghreb are in the EU.

The first generation of guest worker programs from the 1950s to the 1980s, principally in France and Germany, did not succeed in their goal of avoiding overstay by low-skill workers. In many cases, temporary migration turned into permanent stay followed by family reunification. Immigration into the European Union countries has since become more restrictive, and as a result, they now have a larger share of unauthorized migrants. The difficulty in integrating second- and third-generation migrant populations has led to increased levels of unrest as well as a rise in xenophobia in many parts of Europe.

During the 1990s, the flow of North African workers to Belgium, France, and Holland—the earlier receiving countries—declined. However, large increases in migration to other European countries, mainly of Moroccans to Italy and Spain, more than compensated for the decline in numbers in the more traditional receiving countries. Between 1985 and 1999, the number of North Africans in Spain rose from 6,000 to 214,000, of which 90 percent were Moroccan. Although economic slowdown combined with increasingly anti-immigrant political pressures to slow and then marginally reverse immigration to Europe, geographical proximity and extremely long and difficult-to-police coastlines stimulated migration, especially into Italy and Spain. The combination of high unemployment among Spanish nationals (between 15 and 25 percent in the 1990s) and continued Moroccan immigration suggests considerable labor market segmentation—migrants filling jobs that nationals are unwilling to perform. (We discuss later a similar pattern in the Gulf countries.)

The phenomenon of migration boom followed by deceleration, or "maturing," of migration flows from sending to receiving countries also occurred in Germany. The growth in the number of Turkish guest workers (*Gaestarbeiter*) surged along with the economic boom in what was then West Germany during the 1960s, but then subsequently decelerated. In 1972 there were about 2.6 million Turks in the European Union; today there are perhaps 3.2 million. Of these, some 2.7 million live in Germany, where they face significant problems of integration. The Turkish government has estimated that in 2001 emigration had slowed to about 10,000 emigrants per year (Aslan 2005). Turkey itself has attracted migrants, particularly Iraqis, Syrians, Iranians, and Afghans seeking to obtain entry, whether authorized or unauthorized, into the European Union. Every year the Turkish authorities apprehend some 90,000 unauthorized immigrants (Baldwin-Edwards 2005). With low growth in Europe, the difficulty of the integration of Arab migrants into European societies, and rising xenophobia, it is increasingly unauthorized worker flows that are on the rise. The prospects for further growth of labor flows in the future are not promising.

The closing of legal migration channels to Europe has put more pressure on illegal migration. Limited opportunities for safe and regular migration push desperate would-be migrants into the hands of unscrupulous smugglers. Illegal migration into Spain and Italy, often by boat, is not without risk: since 2000, it is estimated, 22,000 people drowned while trying to cross the Mediterranean, and the numbers seem to have risen dramatically in the recent past. More than 3,000 migrants died trying to cross the Mediterranean between January and August 2014, more than double the previous peak in 2011, the year of the Arab uprisings, according to the International Organization for Migration, and nearly five times the prior peak of 630 in 2007 (IOM 2014). More than 112,000 "irregular migrants" were detected by Italian authorities during the first eight months of 2014—nearly three times as many as in all of 2013. One of the deadliest wrecks on record took place in August 2014, when a ship carrying an estimated 500 migrants, including Syrians, Palestinians, and Egyptians, sank. That catastrophe came less than a year after two shipwrecks near the Italian island of Lampedusa left more than 400 migrants dead.

The rising toll reflects the increased pressure in the Middle East and Africa to flee conflict, persecution, and poverty.

The Second Stream: Flows to the Gulf

As with the first stream, migration to the Gulf is driven by the huge gap in wages between sending and receiving countries. During the late 1970s, an unskilled rural Egyptian could earn *thirty times* more money working at a Saudi construction site than he could on an Egyptian farm. Jordanian engineers could double or triple their incomes by going to Kuwait. Migration remains an excellent investment for workers from poorer countries. The cause of the upward spiral of wages in the oil countries was equally straightforward: the demand for labor shot up, while domestic labor supply was limited by economic, social, and political factors. Today wage differentials have been reduced by the entry of Asian labor into the Gulf, and new migration by Arabs is mostly among skilled workers.

The modern history of migration in the region can be divided into four phases. During the first phase, prior to 1974, more than 80 percent of immigrating workers were Arabs—mainly Egyptians, Syrians, Yemenis, and Palestinians—and most of the migrants were skilled workers. The second phase began with the oil price increase of 1974. The number of Arab immigrant workers rose dramatically, with immigration from poorer countries such as Egypt, Sudan, and the two Yemens being especially prominent. The number of expatriates working in the Gulf states rose from 1.1 million in 1975 to some 5.2 million in the late 1980s, and the share of Asian workers—Indians, Pakistanis, Sri Lankans—started to rise. The third phase began with the Iraqi invasion of Kuwait in August 1990, when some 2.8 million Arab workers (principally from Yemen, Palestine, Jordan, Egypt, and Sudan) were expelled from the Gulf and Iraq. After 1995, net Arab immigration into the Gulf resumed, especially from Egypt and Yemen, and the "Asianization" of the labor force continued. The fourth phase has been the past fifteen years or so, during which time migration flows to the Gulf "matured": inflows decelerated and the decline in the proportion of Arabs continued.[18] In 2010, of the estimated 12.5 million migrants in the GCC, more than 7 million were Asians, mainly from India (3.2 million), Pakistan (1.7 million), Bangladesh (820,000), the Philippines (730,000), and Sri Lanka (705,000). Asians have been preferred not only because of their greater political docility but also because they are willing to accept lower wages and poorer working conditions than Arab workers.

The influx of Asians has not, however, precluded the employment of large numbers of nonnational Arabs in the Gulf. Over 3 million Egyptians, 481,000 Sudanese, 564,000 Jordanians, 614,000 Syrians, 2.7 million Palestinians, and perhaps 1 million Yemenis worked in other Arab countries in 2010, most of them in the GCC (see Table 13.6). Migrants bring a whole range of skills to their employment in the GCC, but in general, unskilled work and domestic service in the Gulf today is largely performed by Asians, while Arabs tend to be found more in the semiskilled and skilled tasks. For example, roughly 40 percent of Egyptians employed in Saudi

TABLE 13.6. The Arab Migrant Labor Force in Arab Countries, 2010

Labor-Exporting Country	Number of Migrant Workers Exported to Arab Receiving Countries	Share of Total Migrants from Country
Egypt	3,068,000	82.0%
Iraq	364,000	23.5
Jordan	564,000	76.9
Lebanon	95,000	14.3
Morocco	38,000	1.3
Palestine	2,683,000	88.9
Sudan	481,000	49.7
Syria	614,000	65.0
Tunisia	106,000	16.3
Yemen	992,000	87.5
Total	8,747,000	47.8

Source: World Bank (2010).

Note: The total includes countries of the region that are not listed here and whose figures are below 1,000.

Arabia today are scientific and technical workers; unskilled Egyptians tend to migrate to Jordan and Lebanon (Baldwin-Edwards 2005).

All data cited thus far refer to the workers in a country at any one time. The total number of workers who have *ever* participated in work abroad is obviously much larger than the stock in any one year. Data on the turnover of workers do not exist. However, given that the average length of stay abroad is two to three years, the total number of workers who have ever emigrated for employment must be many times larger than the stock of migrants at any moment in time. A majority of the males of some countries, such as Yemen, have worked in Saudi Arabia at least once. Various estimates place the number of Egyptians who migrated at any time between 1973 and 1985 at roughly one-third of the labor force (Adams 1991; Fergany 1988). The socioeconomic consequences of migration are much larger and the benefits probably much more widely shared than the numbers in the tables suggest.

THE IMPACT OF LABOR MIGRATION ON SENDING COUNTRIES

The economic benefits of migrant workers in the receiving countries are clearly great. Major oil exporters simply could not have undertaken their large-scale development projects without foreign workers, who made possible the rapid physical capital formation and infrastructure construction of the oil boom period. The immigration of teachers also enabled the oil countries to embark on the rapid expansion of their educational systems. Over time, nationalist rhetoric notwithstanding, this dependence on migrant workers has only grown—the reliance of the Gulf states on foreigners for labor has no parallel in modern economic history.

The impact of labor migration on sending countries is more debatable. The *private* benefits of emigration are evident. Presumably, if the benefits were not extensive, people would not go. As we have noted before, the fundamental force driving the private decision to migrate is the huge gap between local and foreign wages, which is large even for skilled and technical workers and especially large for unskilled, rural workers. Although immigrant workers often have to finance their travel abroad, these costs are reduced by labor contractors and by various informal information systems that typically involve whole villages and urban neighborhoods. Some analysts of labor migration stress that the appropriate unit of analysis is not the individual but the household: one or two members may be selected to seek work abroad while others remain behind to tend the store or the farm, to retain government jobs, and so forth (Stark 1983). This household strategy enables migrant workers to undertake extended job searches, thus reducing the riskiness of unemployment and increasing the incentive to migrate. It seems undeniable that this strategy, employed by millions of Middle Eastern families, has usually improved the private welfare of emigrants' families.

Assessing the *social* costs and benefits of labor migration, however, is much more contentious. This debate can be decomposed into a dispute about the net social benefits of three aspects of the migration process: "people out" (emigration), "money back" (remittances), and "people back" (return migration).

"People Out": Emigration

Perhaps the central question in debates over emigration is its impact on employment and its role in creating labor shortages. Those who applaud the migration phenomenon argue that emigration has acted as a safety valve for the sending countries' labor markets by providing jobs for the unemployed. The critics counter that most migrants were already employed and maintain that emigration fosters labor shortages that have impeded development.

In assessing these arguments, it is important to distinguish between different types of labor. Although the emigration of adult males from rural areas of the region during the oil boom era may have created certain short- to medium-term adjustment problems, there is little evidence that it produced labor shortages sufficient to constrain the growth of agricultural production. The same point holds for the exit of unskilled urban workers; there is no evidence that unskilled-labor shortages have retarded industrial growth. The emigration of unskilled labor has created far more benefits than costs for the sending countries. The fall of unskilled wages and the upsurge in poverty in Egypt after 1986 and in Jordan and Yemen after 1990 dramatically illustrate the importance of emigration in a context of rapid growth of labor supply and sluggish increases in domestic demand. Emigration, combined with remittances, lifted 1.2 million Moroccans out of poverty in 2002 (Sorensen 2004).

Assessing the balance of social costs and benefits for the emigration of skilled manpower is somewhat more complicated, at least for the 1970s oil boom era. Although emigration may also have helped to alleviate the chronic unemployment of university graduates, the "brain drain" made it more difficult for the public sector in poorer countries to find qualified, skilled personnel and for the private sector to expand. By definition, skills cannot be reproduced overnight, and so the supply of skilled workers is relatively inelastic. As a general rule, the greater the skill, the longer the period of necessary training and therefore the greater the interval of shortages induced by emigration. However, these shortages seem to have been fairly brief, as the ever-increasing number of new labor force entrants replaced the departed migrants. Many teachers, engineers, computer programmers, and high-level managers went to work in the Gulf states. Labor costs rose in the sending countries' domestic private sectors for managers, engineers, and architects and their public educational systems witnessed massive outflows of teachers. By the mid-1990s, however, all such effects had been swamped by the rising tide of job seekers, as skilled unemployment started to rise. In fact, in some countries such as Lebanon and Jordan, skills are produced for export. Graduates from these countries, which cannot hope to employ the large number of highly educated workers who come out of their school systems, probably would not invest in their educations in the absence of the Gulf markets.

In summary, emigration on balance has had a beneficial impact on the economies of the sending countries. Millions of unskilled workers and their families improved their living standards; there is little reason to believe that economic growth would have been more rapid in these countries had these workers remained at home; and with the exception of the emigration of the most skilled professionals, especially from the poorest countries such as Sudan, the so-called labor shortages have been largely seasonal, short-run disequilibria. Emigration has lowered unemployment, raised wages, and reduced poverty in the sending countries of the MENA region.

"Money Back": Remittances

Workers go abroad to earn and save money, which they then usually save and bring home. Some official estimates of the magnitude of remittances are shown in Table 13.7. Even after the economically devastating Gulf War started in 1990, remittances remained a crucial source of foreign exchange in the region. Indeed, remittances—estimated at some $13 billion in 2010 just from the GCC and up to $20 billion from all sources—still dwarf both FDI and ODA for the region (Kapur 2003). For Yemen and Egypt, the value of remittances exceeded that of any commodity exports. Remittances often paid for a substantial fraction of imports, especially in Egypt, Jordan, Morocco, and Yemen. On the eve of the Gulf War of 1990–1991, remittances to Egypt were the equivalent of 10 percent of its GDP, and in Yemen remittances were at nearly one-third of GDP. Lebanese remaining in their country at the end of the civil war subsisted primarily on remittances, which were the equivalent of two-thirds of Lebanon's GDP.

Official figures for remittances represent only the tip of the iceberg. Much money enters labor-exporting countries through unofficial channels, especially when the

TABLE 13.7. Personal Remittances Received from Migrant Workers (as a percentage of GDP), by Country, 1961–2010

Country	1961–1970	1971–1980	1981–1990	1991–2000	2001–2010
RRLA	**4.34%**	**3.14%**	**7.99%**	**5.54%**	**2.91%**
Algeria	4.34	2.07	0.72	2.33	0.92
Iran				1.09	0.54
Iraq					0.61
Sudan		1.59	1.96	3.00	4.88
Syria		5.77	2.78	2.52	2.45
Yemen			26.50	18.78	8.05
RPLA		**8.63**	**9.96**	**11.62**	**13.65**
Egypt		10.56	9.89	6.99	4.53
Jordan		14.71	18.75	19.76	19.21
Lebanon					21.88
Morocco		5.72	6.94	6.14	7.71
Palestine				21.62	24.10
Tunisia		3.54	4.27	3.57	4.47
Israel	**1.34**	**1.55**	**1.39**	**1.04**	**0.34**
Turkey		**2.42**	**2.63**	**1.90**	**0.38**
Overall MENA	**2.84**	**4.88**	**6.94**	**6.36**	**5.90**

Source: World Bank Indicators, WBI.

banking sector is weak and/or the exchange rate is overvalued (Choucri 1986). For example, only about 13 percent of remittances to Sudan from Saudi Arabia and Kuwait in the early 1980s came through national banks; between one-half and three-fourths of the total value of remittances was simply carried by hand (Berar-Awad 1984). Similar phenomena have been observed in other countries, including Turkey, Yemen, Jordan, Syria, and Egypt, particularly when their national currencies were seriously overvalued. By contrast, sound macroeconomic and financial management in Morocco ensured that most remittances moved through the banking system (de Haas 2005).

Critics of the effects of remittances at the macroeconomic level point out that the combination of labor migration and remittances undermines the potential for an export-led growth strategy—much like the effects of the Dutch Disease, as discussed throughout the book. The reduced labor supply leads to an increase in domestic wages. Moreover, a portion of workers' remittances is spent on nontradables such as housing and land. These forces tend to cause an appreciation of the real exchange rate and thus contribute to making labor-exporting countries less competitive than they would otherwise be if they were exporting labor-intensive products.

Some critics of emigration have argued that the export of labor turns out to be an alternative to the export of labor-intensive manufactured goods (Katanani 1981). However, this has not really been a choice for most countries. The political policies, institutions, and entrepreneurial skills needed for successful export of manufactured goods were nowhere in sight in the region in 1973; even today they are often absent (see Chapter 8).

Another area of debate on the microeconomic effect of remittances concerns the division of the funds between consumption and investment, and the types of investments that are selected. Some detailed surveys tend to contradict the conventional wisdom that remittances are largely consumed. For example, Richard Adams (1991) shows that in the Minya Governorate in Egypt, one of the poorest areas of the country, migrants in the 1980s invested much of their earnings, particularly in housing and land. It does seem that remittances have often been spent on housing—various surveys in Egypt, Sudan, Turkey, Tunisia, and Morocco have found that more than one-fifth of remittances were so used (Berar-Awad 1984; el-Dib, Ismail, and Gad 1984). Moreover, some remittances have found their way into productive investments, such as irrigation equipment, small workshops and factories, and transportation equipment (trucks and cars). However, when these investments constitute a small proportion of the total spending of remittances, national policies are to blame for reducing the profitability of investments in productivity-enhancing technologies.

"People Back": Return Migration

The vast majority of migrants want to return home. Neither they nor the receiving countries view labor migration as permanent resettlement. Most migrants do return home eventually, and before then, the large majority come back temporarily for major holidays and for important family events such as weddings. The impact of returning migrants ranges from labor market impacts to cultural, political, and even demographic consequences.

There are two important consequences of return migration. First, migration to the GCC produced a social, cultural, and even political phenomenon known in Egypt as *golfeyya*, or "Gulfization." That is, migrants to the Gulf, particularly those from poorer, less skilled, and/or more rural backgrounds, tended to return from the Gulf having absorbed the more conservative social mores of that region. The diffusion of *salafi* ideas and behaviors may also have been greatly stimulated by migration to Saudi Arabia. One field study in northern Sudan found that migrants returning from Saudi Arabia had "embraced a new orthodoxy, representing a move away from local, parochial identities toward perceived conformity with a universalistic set of beliefs and practices" (Bernal 1999).

A congruent impact might be found in fertility behavior. Philippe Fargues (2005) contrasts the fertility behavior of the Maghreb with that of Asian Arab countries. Fertility in the latter is typically considerably above that in the former. Fargues suggests that lower fertility in the Maghreb may be in part explained by the impact of Western lifestyles, carried home by migrants returning from work in the European Union. Moreover, he found that in Egypt the number of returnees from the Gulf as a percentage of the total population is inversely correlated with fertility across Egyptian governorates (Fargues 2005, 15). Fargues is careful not to read too much into such evidence, but it is suggestive that returned migrants shape the political economies of their countries of origin in a wide range of diverse ways.

However, forced return, can exacerbate problems that already exist from the return flow of migrant workers. Consider the question of how well (or ill) national labor markets absorbed the return flow of workers in the wake of the Gulf War. At first, returnees actually provided some economic stimulus by spending money on housing—this effect was particularly noticeable in Jordan. But returnees tended to settle in urban areas (with the exception of Yemen, where perhaps 50 percent returned to villages), and there they constituted an additional drag on already over-burdened labor markets, driving the unemployment rate up to 25 percent in Yemen and 19 percent in Jordan. Jordan's economic crisis was also compounded by the loss of its major export markets in Iraq and the Gulf. Recently, the massive outflow of Syrian refuges to Lebanon, Jordan, and Turkey in particular has complicated economic difficulties in these countries, from pressures on labor and housing markets to heightened fiscal pressure emanating from the low levels of international support to defray the financial costs of meeting humanitarian needs.

CONCLUSIONS

In retrospect, labor migration can be seen as the main way in which oil revenues from the oil-exporting countries have been redistributed to the oil-importing countries, to the great benefit of millions of households. Whether this redistribution strategy reduced the incentives of regimes to reform their own economic structures earlier remains a matter for debate. What is clear, however, is that the dynamism of labor migration as a force for raising wages and living standards in the poorer rural areas of the region, so prominent during the oil boom years, is a thing of the past. Migration will almost certainly never again boom as it did in the late 1970s or even the 1980s. The evidence for this prediction comes not only from the 1990s, when oil prices were low, but also from the past decade of much higher oil prices. The post-2000 second oil wave has not led to any boom in immigration. Governments in the oil-exporting countries of the GCC have been far more prudent in their spending patterns, seeking to avoid the Dutch Disease of the 1970s and 1980s. Most major infrastructural projects have long since been completed; locals are increasingly educated and skilled—though also unemployed. Asians now dominate unskilled jobs, while locals compete ever more insistently with more-skilled Arab migrant workers. Although migration and remittances continue to help alleviate poverty in sending countries, these countries can no longer hope to relieve their own labor market pressures through the "safety valve" of immigration. The boom years of migration are fading into history.

For the labor-abundant countries, focusing on trade and FDI as the main vehicles for growth and job creation does not seem to be a realistic short-term goal. Political and economic stabilization will have to come first. But both trade and FDI may become central parts of a more realistic medium-term vision for these countries if they manage to combine the varying strengths of the region in ways that can take advantage of the opportunities offered by the global economy.

Over time, the main growth opportunity in the region lies in the melding of the labor and capital present in the region into a successful partnership. Both capital (in the Gulf) and skilled labor (in the labor-abundant countries) are in excess supply in the region. The second oil boom is transforming the GCC into the main growth center of the region. Although this will not lead to new growth in migration, there has been a steep rise in capital flows from the GCC into the labor-intensive countries, in the form of both direct investments and aid to transition governments. So far, most of these investments have gone to real estate and tourism projects, with few going into manufacturing, and the financing of governments has gone into supporting consumption rather than investments. It remains to be seen whether these massive flows of funds could be shifted in the future toward sectors that create good jobs in more sustainable ways.

The challenge, then, is to improve the effectiveness of the emerging partnership between Arab capital and labor. For the first time, the GCC and the transition countries are sitting at the same table, with little interference by other global players, to discuss macro plans for the future. This will encourage the discovery of win-win arrangements. As during the structural adjustment period of the 1980s and 1990s, the two players—the creditor and the debtor—have different goals to achieve. The financier, the GCC, hopes to make a good return on its loan by convincing the borrower (say Egypt) to shift financing from consumption, which may be needed in the short term for political stability, into investment, which is needed in the medium term for sustainability. To boost his credibility with his main financiers, one of President Al-Sisi's first actions in government was to reduce the level of energy subsidies, a sensitive area of reform in Egypt. Recent donors meetings in Tunisia and Egypt have stressed not just state-led reforms but, instead, public-private partnerships to open up new growth opportunities.

In the past, other borrowers, like Morocco, have been more reluctant to institute reforms that were pushed by the IFIs. For example, it took three different structural adjustment loans to get Morocco to initiate serious reforms in its trade sector. But Morocco's bargain with the GCC can more easily shift into win-win opportunities. The GCC could encourage its own firms to invest in and trade with Morocco, thus not only helping itself as a creditor but also widening the growth opportunities of its own firms. Indeed, the GCC has recently invited Morocco to join its own trade sphere. (Jordan was also invited to join.) Back in the Washington Consensus days, the IFIs did not have the same opportunities to strike good deals. They might have advocated for the opening of Western markets, but they did not have the power to dictate the terms of the opening of these markets. On the other hand, financing arrangements with the GCC can include preferential treatment for regional FDI or partnerships with Western MNCs to invest in more skill-intensive sectors or the granting of special favors to regional exports in the GCC.

In the end, an important question confronting the region remains: how will it participate in the emerging global division of labor? So far, the effects of the Dutch Disease, private sectors that lack dynamism, and poor policies have prevented the region from becoming the big "Arab factory" that it could have become. The time for manufacturing export-led growth may have passed as the world is now witnessing excess capacity in these sectors and a slackening of demand. There is thus no tested model that could be used as a blueprint for the region's future. But it is now also clear that the future of the MENA region will have to involve tighter regional linkages and win-win arrangements within the region.

NOTES

1. In Egypt, Jordan, Morocco, and Tunisia, however, up to 50 percent of services exports are revenues from transport and travel by tourists.

2. The GCC is facing critical challenges, however, as the free trade agreements signed by Bahrain and Oman with the United States contradict the common tariff.

3. The members of the Euro-Mediterranean Partnership are, as of 2014, Algeria, Egypt, Israel, Jordan, Lebanon, Morocco, Palestine, and Tunisia.

4. Bahrain, Jordan, Israel, Lebanon, Morocco, and Oman have signed various free trade agreements with the United States.

5. Turkey is a charter member of the WTO. Other MENA members (and their date of accession) are Bahrain (1995), Egypt (1995), Israel (1995), Jordan (2000), Kuwait (1995), Morocco (1995), Oman (2000), Qatar (1996), Saudi Arabia (2005), Tunisia (1995), the United Arab Emirates (1995), and Yemen (2014). Countries with applications pending are Algeria, Iran, Iraq, Lebanon, Libya, Sudan, Syria, and Yemen.

6. But given that many Arab countries have their own free trade agreements (FTAs) with non-Arab countries, this project will have difficulty progressing. Establishing a custom union between the Arab countries would require that either all FTAs with non-Arab countries are abolished or that all Arab countries join those agreements.

7. In addition, in most countries these agreements included support for industrial upgrading to help domestic firms improve their competitiveness and withstand competition by European firms.

8. Only the "deeper" integration of the Agadir Agreement, signed between Egypt, Jordan, Morocco, and Tunisia and implemented in 2007, has started to allow these countries to "accumulate" a product's origin. It is too early to tell if this new agreement will advance the cause of intraregional trade more than its predecessors (Cieślik and Hagemejer 2009). It should be noted that the US rules for FTAs do not allow accumulation and that this has hampered a US-MENA trade agreement just as it has hampered the EUROMED agreements.

9. The so-called Seven Sisters—British Petroleum (BP), Texaco, Exxon, Royal Dutch Shell, Mobil, Standard Oil of California (Chevron), and Gulf Oil—plus the state-owned Compagnie Française de Petrole (CFP).

10. The combined oil import bill of the United States, Germany, France, Japan, and Italy rose from $23.8 billion to $67.6 billion from 1973 to 1974.

11. OPEC revenues increased by over $82 billion from 1978 to 1981.

12. The only comparable transfer of wealth would be the Spanish plundering of the Americas of precious metals in the sixteenth century.

13. Political considerations also influenced the Saudi decision to open the taps. The Saudis sought to deny revenue to the Iranians, who were advancing in the Fao Peninsula of Iraq at that time. Some reports assert that William Casey, the director of the CIA, asked

the Saudis to slash prices to deny revenue to the Soviets. When economic and political interests coincide, it is impossible to determine their relative weights.

14. In 1993 Saudi Arabian aid was 0.70 percent of GNP, while Norwegian aid was 0.038 percent. US aid was 0.04 percent of GNP in that year (World Bank 1995, 197).

15. Specifically, such aid made up 58.2 percent of investment in Jordan, 27.1 percent in Yemen, 237.8 percent in Syria, and 36.2 percent in Sudan (van den Boogaerde 1990).

16. The data are built on the base of formal announcements and represent 79 percent of global FDI. The data cover FDI in seventeen Arab countries between January 2003 and December 2012 and represent, overall, 7,426 projects by over 4,500 multinational corporations.

17. Although not considered "international migrants," the number of internally displaced persons (IDPs) in some countries is also substantial: 3 million–5 million in Sudan; 400,000–600,000 in Algeria; 350,000–1 million in Turkey; and (before 2006) 300,000 in Lebanon (CIA 2006). By January 2007, the United Nations estimated that some 1.7 million Iraqis were internally displaced and about 2 million had fled the country. Most Iraqi migration occurred after 2003.

18. This shift was most marked in Kuwait, where Arab migrants made up 59 percent of the foreign population in 1989 but only 45 percent by 2001. By contrast, Asians constituted 67 percent of the total Kuwaiti labor force in 2000, up from 54 percent in 1989.

14

CONCLUSION

In the conclusion of the previous edition of this book, Richards and Waterbury observed that the most important development in the Middle East "lies in the powerful countercurrent embodied by the spread of education, the growth of the middle classes, the shift of populations to urban centers, and the entry of women into the formal economy. These forces, and above all, the rise of the largest, best-educated, most-urbanized generation of young people in the region's history constitute profoundly destabilizing forces, which are hard to contain within authoritarian constraints." Needless to say, we concur that the dramatic improvements in economic and social development after independence have proved to be "destabilizing," to put it mildly, the least, particularly in the absence of inclusive growth and with rising repression. Although this combination of factors does not explain the immediate processes that compel people to join mass protests at great risk to themselves and their families, they are certainly a central part of the story.

MENA governments have long been either incapable of responding to the demands of their populations or unwilling to do so. Middle Eastern states have been "fierce," particularly in their coercive control over society, but as Nazih Ayubi (1996, 449) points out, such states are neither strong nor capable when it comes to delivering shared growth and development. And now, in the aftermath of the massive street protests of 2011–2012, the situation in much of the region has become more unsettled and chaotic. So far, the Arab uprisings have not ushered in a more inclusive polity or more effective state institutions. At this juncture, many countries in the region face the serious risk of falling into deep violence traps (Cox, North, and Weingast 2013).

From the mid-1980s to about the year 2000, profound socioeconomic changes in the region were coupled with hard economic times: the collapse of the oil boom, the drying up of strategic rents, and the consequent necessity for profound structural shifts in the economy at a time when public resources were limited. A momentous side effect has been the exacerbation of unemployment and underemployment among the educated. Furthermore, while the region made enormous gains in health, literacy, and other social outcomes in the first few decades after independence, fiscal constraints coupled with the challenges of deepening human development after initial advances have stalled progress on these fronts.

Although oil prices and thus state revenues revived over the course of the 2000s, the lack of jobs persists to this day, and additional destabilizers have emerged: renewed rounds of all-out war between Palestinians and Israelis; the nearly universal regional perception of American bias toward Israel; the invasion, occupation, and descent into civil war in Iraq; the violence in Lebanon in the summer of 2006; and the Green Movement in Iran. The wave of mass uprisings across the Arab world since 2011 has led to the breakdown of political order in Libya and Yemen and a protracted and very violent war in Syria, which is sparking humanitarian crises across the region. The acute crises of legitimacy of many Middle Eastern regimes have only intensified, and although strategic rents have surged as a consequence of the attacks of September 11, 2001, utilizing them only further undermines people's already low trust in their leaders.

The economic crises of the 1980s compelled some Middle Eastern rulers to make attempts at economic reform and, less frequently, at political liberalization. The turn toward the private sector has been partial, and virtually nowhere has it been premised on the construction of truly competitive markets. Even where embraced enthusiastically, private sector–led development has not reduced unemployment; it has largely enriched the close associates of rulers and their entourages. Although there are exceptions, so far states cannot—and private investors will not—provide the resources needed to address problems such as lowering unemployment, ensuring water supply and food security, improving health, providing broad access to high quality health care and education, and managing labor markets.

In the years leading up to the 2011 uprisings, the region's growth rate was already faltering compared to a sustained boom in the global economy. Macro-instability had started to reappear, and the private sector was not showing the kind of dynamism that would have allowed the region to take off. Exports, for example, were stagnant. The 2007–2008 global crises did hurt the region, although growth (per capita) was back to the 2 to 3 percent level by 2010. The oil producers were doing well, growing at about 4 percent from 2003 to 2012 on the back of rising oil prices, but still below the rates achieved globally by the middle-income countries in the favorable 2000s.

The uprisings resulted in a negative economic shock in the transition countries. Tourism took a hit, capital flight accelerated, exports declined, and investment collapsed in Tunisia, Egypt, and Yemen. As a result, economic growth declined sharply in 2011, and unemployment increased (see Figure 14.1). Initially, governments in transition countries reacted with expansionary policies to smooth out the downturn, especially in the face of rising social demands and the high expectations generated by the uprisings. Public-sector wages, subsidies, and government investment were increased in many countries around the region. In the Gulf countries, budgets expanded massively; for example, expenditure increased by over one-third in Saudi Arabia. In the oil-importing countries, both external accounts and budget balances deteriorated. By 2012, fiscal deficits in Morocco, Jordan, Tunisia, and Lebanon had

FIGURE 14.1. GDP Growth in the Transition Countries of the Middle East in Recent Years

Source: World Development Indicators

shot up to between 6 and 7 percent of GDP. In Egypt, the fiscal deficit ballooned at 12 percent of GDP and international reserves plummeted.

These developments meant that by 2013 governments in oil-importing countries had no fiscal space to continue with stimulus programs, and therefore growth remained low (about 2 to 3 percent). Expansionary policies were supported mainly by domestic debt levels, as aid did not rise despite repeated promises.[1] Unlike other regions that have undergone economic and political transitions simultaneously, notably Eastern Europe, no external actor was available to ease the transition with large-scale aid and promises of a future economic and political union. Indeed, the uprisings occurred during a global economic downturn and the Eurozone crisis, a context that restricted the availability of foreign support. More recently, however, the GCC has increased its financial support for countries in transition, ushering in a new era of regional cooperation that could evolve into a growth pact over time.

As of this writing in mid-2014, economic indicators are still flashing yellow in most of the transition countries as the macroeconomic situation remains unstable and the outlook poor. The political transition has not produced broad coalitions that can afford to implement major reforms. Notwithstanding the initiation of reforms in Tunisia, Egypt, Morocco, and Jordan in 2014, the heightened fear of the "street" and its reactions and protests on the part of regional governments is preventing determined efforts to contain deficits and to shift resources into investment. Economic recovery will not proceed until the political crises are resolved. Indeed, a downward spiral may ensue in some countries: polarized politics may exacerbate economic difficulties, which in turn will lead to more fractious politics.

The shift in economic strategy since the 1980s, however problematic in its implementation and outcomes, has not been accompanied by parallel political reforms in the Middle East. In the 1980s, fiscal crises compelled dictators in many developing countries around the world to initiate some political reform programs, but steps toward political liberalization in the Middle East were minimal. In Egypt, Tunisia, and Yemen before the uprisings, political reform was halfhearted at best, and since their authoritarian presidents were overthrown, it has stalled or even regressed in some of these countries. In Algeria political liberalization was aborted, in Sudan it was subverted, and in Jordan and Morocco it was carefully orchestrated. With the major exception of Kuwait and, to some degree, Bahrain before 2011, the Gulf monarchies have largely evaded, or made only minor concessions to, the internal and external pressures they face to open up the political space.

Until authoritarian rulers were overthrown in Tunisia and Egypt, aggressive moves toward electoral democracy had been stymied by the fear that the majority would vote for Islamic parties, as Algeria's ill-fated experiment revealed in 1991. Morsi's ouster from his position as the elected president of Egypt shows that antipathy toward Islamist rule remains high among elites as well as large segments of the population. When Palestinian elections were won by Islamists, they were effectively prevented from governing. Turkey shows that democracy and political Islam can be compatible, but that country's distinct political context and prospect of EU integration (albeit less of a policy priority at present) make the Turkish model less relevant to the Arab countries. Recent political crises also reveal deep polarization in Turkey, both between competing Islamist groups and between Islamists and liberals. Incumbent dictators in the Middle East have hardly been concerned that elected Islamic parties will snuff out democracy; instead, they fear that Islamists will use elections to drive them from power. For their part, many liberal critics of authoritarian rulers tend to opt for secular dictators rather than rule by Islamists.

As we have tried to show throughout this book, there is no single story about how politics, economics, and society interact to produce economic and political change in the region. Patterns of economic and political development vary across all of the countries of the Middle East. Yet some common trends can be seen within the distinct political economy subtypes that we identify in the book. The RPLA group of countries includes the most diverse array of political regimes. Until the uprisings, Egypt, Tunisia, and the two Yemens (before the unified Yemen began to exploit oil in the 1990s) were authoritarian republics; Egypt is now returning to this status several years after its dictator was overthrown. Jordan and Morocco are resource-poor monarchies, while Lebanon has a long history of democratic rule, albeit highly imperfect.

Despite the diversity of regime types and informal political settlements underlying their formal political institutions, the countries in the RPLA group share some important commonalities that partly help explain why many have witnessed the most extensive and persistent levels of social mobilization in the region since the Arab uprisings broke out. First, all of these countries implemented statist economic policies in the first decades after independence, but when they were forced to cut back public investment sharply in the 1980s, they saw a decline in the prospects for social mobility for their key constituents in the middle class, especially those in public-sector positions. In addition, in all RPLA countries, structural adjustment narrowed social coalitions and led to rising cronyism as a small group of elites profited the most from lucrative economic opportunities. Second, their low oil endowments give them fewer resources than their neighbors have to use for investing in co-optation and repression. Finally, it is perhaps no accident that protests have been less pervasive in the monarchies, where hereditary succession and more diverse social coalitions have muted calls for total regime change. Lebanon has witnessed the lowest levels of social mobilization, in part because the highly fragmented structure of power in its consociational system inhibits opponents of the system from focusing their protests on a single political office or leader, and also because both power and social organization are largely divided along sectarian lines.

The RRLA countries are all authoritarian republics, with Algeria, Iraq, Syria, and Yemen classified as the secular variants and Iran (post-1979) and Sudan (post-1989) as Islamic republics. Despite their distinct types of political institutions and underlying political settlements, some common patterns have emerged among these countries. Post-independence, most embarked on a statist development project, leading to the expansion of public employment and heavy investment in state-owned enterprises. Yet given their high populations, their substantial resource endowments have not cushioned them from the economic crises that began in the 1980s. In response to the failure of their development strategies, none of the RRLA countries has been able to launch a new ideological project that could mobilize the masses. Substantial oil revenues have instead largely been spent on the development of a formidable repressive apparatus and, in some cases, on risky regional adventures. Economic liberalization has been characterized by forms of cronyism that are narrower than is found in their oil-poor republican cousins, and their exclusion of the poor and middle classes from the social contract has been more extreme as well. Since the 1980s, rulers in some of these countries, such as Syria, Iran, and Iraq, have increased repression and come to rely on a more restricted coalition of forces to stay in power. They have taken advantage of the second oil shock to dole out resources to their supporters and consolidate power. These regimes have fiercely resisted change and have reacted to contestation violently. Algeria spent the 1990s in a state of civil war. Syria, Iraq, Libya, and, to a lesser extent, Yemen have been devastated by civil strife since 2011. The human toll in death and suffering is staggering. Millions have been made refugees, in their own countries as well as in neighboring countries. Economic production has taken a big hit, and the destruction of assets is immense. The economies of Lebanon, Jordan, and Tunisia have also been negatively affected by regional instability and the influx of refugees. In these countries, reforms will have to start on the political front, with some broadening of ruling coalitions to allow for a modicum of stability. As of this writing, the contours of such broader coalitions are just starting to appear in countries as diverse as Iraq, Yemen, Libya, and Iran. In others, notably Algeria, popular protests have increased while state elites remain indifferent to societal demands.

Finally, the RRLP countries, which include the Gulf monarchies and Libya, have exhibited the most continuity since their establishment or independence from colonial rule. In part, their relative stability arises from their high per capita resource wealth, which enables rulers to maintain a modicum of support among their citizen populations. With its revolution in 2011, Libya is a glaring exception, but Gaddafi's neglect of key groups and growing repression, as well as the NATO bombing campaign, set this country apart from the Gulf monarchies. Opposition mobilization has also been intense in Bahrain, where the Sunni royal family rules over a Shi'a majority population in an exclusionary fashion. But the second oil boom has been managed better than the first. Fueled by strong government support and by free labor mobility, the private sector has grown and become a central driver of economic growth, and it has also started investing in the broader region. Since oil wealth has cushioned RRLP countries from making major changes in their founding political settlements, those settlements continue to pit the interests of the local business class against those of non-national labor. With youth unemployment on the rise, opposition has risen, even where indigenous populations benefit disproportionately from the spoils of oil wealth, although this opposition remains limited and is expressed largely through social media rather than in the streets.

In all countries in the Middle East—both where millions have protested and managed to oust long-standing dictators and where opposition is muted and regime critics present limited demands for reform—politics has changed significantly since the last edition of this book was published, and particularly in the last three years. New political actors have taken the reins of state power. Islamists have won free and fair elections in Tunisia, Egypt, and Morocco, even if their time in office has been relatively short-lived and their actual strength in society is less extensive than many long assumed. New political movements and parties are forming and may bolster their organizational capacity and gain support in the years to come. Perhaps most important, with the resurgence of the "street" as a force to be reckoned with in Middle Eastern societies, the public is now more overtly engaged in politics.

The Middle East faces major challenges to economic, political, and social development. The engagement of a broader segment of populations beyond a narrow, well-connected elite may facilitate more inclusive policymaking, which should be a goal in and of itself, and may generate valuable approaches for addressing the region's deep problems. Can the region's political leaders and decision-makers provide the inclusive growth needed to promote social mobility and create good jobs for the cohorts of educated youth? A lot will depend on the evolution of politics (which has been the main inhibitor of inclusive growth), the reaction of the private sector, and the outcome of efforts to "fix" the state, since functional public services are a key determinant of social mobility. Prospects vary with regional differences in both polities and economic structures and opportunities.

The political and economic challenges facing the Arab transitioning countries are compounded by high popular expectations and problematic legacies from the past. How political challenges are addressed will largely determine the course of economic policies. Unless new surprises arise, the contours of the emerging political settlement will include fewer favors for elite capital. Yet new rulers should attempt to make peace with large capital-holders and convince them to invest in the future, as is already happening in Egypt, rather than withdraw, as happened with the socialist revolutions of the 1960s. At the same time, the interests of the poorer segments of the population should be balanced with those of the better-off, who benefit disproportionately under authoritarian bargains.

The main economic challenges will be difficult to resolve, even if politics becomes less polarized. The first and most immediate challenge is economic stabilization in order to avoid an economic and financial meltdown, which would further complicate the political process. Building a package of measures that reduce expenditures, raise revenues, and command some minimum level of popular support is a tricky endeavor in the best of circumstances, and it will be very challenging in the current hyperpoliticized environment. A more stable political environment, however, also offers the possibility of initiating other important reforms.

The second area of focus should be the modernization of the state and the rehabilitation of public services, especially health, education, and social protection. New governments with broader popular support should be able to redirect expenditures toward social services and away from subsidies that benefit the better-off and to make tax systems more progressive while enlarging the tax base. Improving service delivery and fighting petty corruption will require increased public-sector wages, which will be complicated by the large size of the civil service.

The third item on the agenda is the business environment and job creation. Past experiences, and especially the failures of both socialism and state capitalism, now limit policy choices for the Arab region. For example, developing an effective industrial policy that supports rising sectors of the economy with targeted subsidies, as was done in East Asia, would be an unreasonable goal in the next three to five years given institutional weaknesses and the risks of capture by powerful interest groups. Priority issues such as improving competition, democratizing credit, and reducing the constraints faced by the informal sector do not have easy solutions.

These are complicated challenges, technically, politically, and administratively. In the end, what will make a difference in the transition countries is the process by which solutions adapted to the particular environments of each country are found and implemented. The greatest contribution of the "revolutions" to these challenges should be in fostering greater popular participation in the policymaking process. The real revolution—but one that remains in the making—is the sense of empowerment of new actors such as labor unions, employers' associations, student groups, women's organizations, and other civil society organizations that can cross ideological lines to represent social interests and hold their representatives accountable.

Three years after the spark of the Arab uprisings, the Arab region faces unprecedented challenges. Political turmoil, violence, and unresolved governance challenges underlie the deep social polarization of the region along identity and sectarian lines, which threatens political progress, economic recovery, and regional peace. The extent of intolerance for differences of opinion, the necessity in some cases to rebuild founding political settlements, and the conflicts over basic issues of identity in many of these countries are threatening the very fabric of societies. Syria and Iraq are now at risk of becoming failed states, while the Islamic State and other groups pose violent challenges to governments, to the integrity of the nation-state model, and to regional stability. The sharp politicization of the so-called Sunni-Shi'a divide has fueled widespread political violence, leading to mounting fear among populations and great human suffering, and it threatens reconciliation within and across countries. Rebuilding national coalitions that can preserve a modicum of stability is now a priority in much of the region, and a prerequisite to building new political solutions and pursuing policy solutions for the challenges facing the Middle East.

To end on a positive note, we ought to point out that opportunities for progress exist. In particular, the second oil boom, which was in full swing until the end of 2014, flooded the region with resources that, if well used and managed, could transform it even more profoundly than the first oil boom did. Oil revenues have turned the GCC into a vibrant growth center. Although this growth will not lead to new growth in migration, there has been a steep rise in capital flows from the GCC into the labor-intensive countries, in the form of both direct investments and aid to transition governments. So far, Arab FDI has not gone into the type of activities that could generate large numbers of new jobs, and the financing of governments has gone into supporting consumption rather than investment. But combining Gulf capital with Arab labor and skills to build a globally successful "Arab factory"—perhaps starting with niche products in information technologies and agro-business for regional markets, and then moving up the ladder with consumer durables and automotives for the global market—is more than ever a viable medium-term vision provided that the wealthy Gulf countries can ride our fluctuations in oil prices. It remains to be seen whether the chaotic political landscape and the apparent predominance of forces that divide will allow for progress on this more hopeful agenda.

NOTE

1. In particular, the Deauville Partnership, an international effort launched by the G8 countries in May 2011, aimed to provide assistance for economic stabilization, job creation, good governance, and regional integration in the Arab transitioning countries.

REFERENCES

CHAPTER 1: INTRODUCTION AND FRAMEWORK OF THE STUDY

Acemoglu, Daron, Johnson, Simon, and Robinson, James A. (2001), "Reversal of Fortune: Geography and Institutions in the Making of the Modern World Income Distribution," National Bureau of Economic Research (NBER), Working Paper 8460.

Acemoglu, Daron, and Robinson, James A. (2012), *Why Nations Fail: The Origins of Power, Prosperity, and Poverty,* New York, Crown Publishers.

Ali, Omer, and Elbadawi, Ibrahim (2012), "The Political Economy of Public Sector Employment in the Resource Dependent Countries," Economic Research Forum (ERF), Working Paper 673.

ASDA'A/Burson-Marsteller (2010), "Arab Youth Survey," Dubai, ASDA'A/Burson-Marsteller.

Axelrod, Robert (1984), *The Evolution of Cooperation,* New York, Basic Books.

Beblawi, Hazem (1990), "The Rentier State in the Arab World," in Luciani, Giacomo, ed., *The Arab State,* London, Routledge, 85–98.

Beinin, Joel, and Vairel, Frédéric (2013), *Social Movements, Mobilization, and Contestation in the Middle East and North Africa,* 2nd ed., Stanford, CA, Stanford University Press.

Belhaj, Nadia, and Wissa, Christian (2011), "Inequality Trends and Determinants in the Arab Region," paper presented at the Economic Research Forum (ERF) conference on "Inequality in the Arab Region," Cairo, December 10.

Bellin, Eva (2002), *Stalled Democracy: Capital, Labor, and the Paradox of State-Sponsored Development,* Ithaca, NY, Cornell University Press.

Bellin, Eva (2004), "The Robustness of Authoritarianism in the Middle East: Exceptionalism in Comparative Perspective," *Comparative Politics* 36, 2, 139.

Benchemsi, Ahmed (2012), "Morocco: Outfoxing the Opposition," *Journal of Democracy* 23, 1, 57–69.

Besley, Timothy, and Kudamatsu, Masayuki (2008), "Making Autocracy Work," in Helpman, Elhanan, ed., *Institutions and Economic Performance,* Cambridge, MA, Harvard University Press.

Bibi, Sami, and Nabli, Mustapha K. (2010), "Equity and Inequality in the Arab Region," Cairo, Egypt, Economic Research Forum (ERF) Policy Research Report.

Browers, Michaelle L. (2009), *Political Ideology in the Arab World: Accommodation and Transformation,* Cambridge, Cambridge University Press.

Brubaker, Rogers (2006), *Ethnicity Without Groups,* Cambridge, MA, Harvard University Press.

Burgat, François (2003), *Face to Face with Political Islam,* London, I. B. Tauris.

Cammett, Melani (2007), *Globalization and Business Politics in Arab North Africa: A Comparative Perspective,* New York, Cambridge University Press.

Cammett, Melani (2014), *Compassionate Communalism: Welfare and Sectarianism in Lebanon,* Ithaca, NY, Cornell University Press.

Cammett, Melani, and Luong, Pauline Jones (2014), "Is There an Islamist Political Advantage?" *Annual Review of Political Science* 17, 187–206.

Catusse, Myriam (2008), *Le Temps des entrepreneurs? Politique et transformations du capitalisme au Maroc,* Paris, Maisonneuve et Larose.

Chandra, Kanchan, ed. (2012), *Constructivist Theories of Ethnic Politics,* Oxford, Oxford University Press.

Chaudhry, Kiren Aziz (1993), "The Myths of the Market and the Common History of Late Developers," *Politics and Society* 21, 3, 245–274.

Chaudhry, Kiren Aziz (1997), *The Price of Wealth: Economies and Institutions in the Middle East,* Ithaca, NY, Cornell University Press.

Demiralp, Seda (2009), "The Rise of Islamic Capital and the Decline of Islamic Radicalism in Turkey," *Comparative Politics* 41, 3, 315–335.

Dhillon, Navtej, and Yousef, Tarik (2009), "Generation in Waiting: The Unfulfilled Promise of Young People in the Middle East," Washington, DC, Brookings Institution Press.

Diamond, Jared M. (1997), *Guns, Germs, and Steel: The Fate of Human Societies,* New York, W. W. Norton & Co.

Esposito, John L. (1997), *Political Islam: Revolution, Radicalism, or Reform?* Boulder, CO, Lynne Rienner Publishers.

Evans, Peter B. (1995), *Embedded Autonomy: States and Industrial Transformation,* Princeton, NJ, Princeton University Press.

Fearon, James D., and Laitin, David D. (1996), "Explaining Interethnic Cooperation," *American Political Science Review* 90, 4, 715–735.

Fuller, Graham (2004), *The Future of Political Islam,* New York, Palgrave Macmillan.

Gumuscu, Sebnem, and Sert, Deniz (2009), "The Power of the Devout Bourgeoisie: The Case of the Justice and Development Party in Turkey," *Middle Eastern Studies* 45, 6, 953–968.

Haddad, Bassam (2012), "Syria's State Bourgeoisie: An Organic Backbone for the Regime," *Middle East Critique* 21, 3, 231–257.

Haggard, Stephan, Kang, David, and Moon, Chung-In (1997), "Japanese Colonialism and Korean Development: A Critique," *World Development* 25, 6, 867–881.

Hanieh, Adam (2012), "Finance, Oil, and the Arab Uprisings: The Global Crisis and the Gulf States," *Socialist Register* 48.

Henry, Clement M. (1996), *The Mediterranean Debt Crescent: Money and Power in Algeria, Egypt, Morocco, Tunisia, and Turkey,* Gainesville, University Press of Florida.

Henry, Clement M., and Springborg, Robert (2010), *Globalization and the Politics of Development in the Middle East,* 2nd ed., Cambridge, Cambridge University Press.

Hertog, Steffen (2010), *Princes, Brokers, and Bureaucrats: Oil and the State in Saudi Arabia,* Ithaca, NY, Cornell University Press.

Heydemann, Steven, ed. (2004), *Networks of Privilege in the Middle East: The Politics of Economic Reform Revisited,* New York, Palgrave Macmillan.

Hibou, Beatrice (2006), *La Force de l'obéissance: Économic politique de la répression en Tunisie,* Paris, Éditions de la Découverte.

International Monetary Fund (IMF), *World Economic Outlook (WEO)* database (various years), Washington, DC, at http://www.imf.org/external/ns/cs.aspx?id=28.

Iqbal, Farrukh (2006), *Sustaining Gains in Poverty Reduction and Human Development in the Middle East and North Africa,* Washington, DC, World Bank.

Jabar, Faleh (2003), *The Shiite Movement in Iraq,* London, Saqi Books.

Kaboub, Fadhel (2013), "The Making of the Tunisian Revolution," *Middle East Development Journal* 5, 1, 1–21.

Karshenas, Massoud, and Moghadam, Valentine M., eds. (2006), *Social Policy in the Middle East: Economic, Political, and Gender Dynamics,* New York, United Nations Research Institute for Social Development and Palgrave Macmillan.

Kazemi, Farhad, and Norton, Augustus Richard, eds. (1995), *Civil Society in the Middle East,* Leiden and New York, Brill.

Khan, Mushtaq (2009), "Governance Capabilities and the Property Rights Transition in Developing Countries," Research Paper Series on Governance for Growth, School of Oriental and African Studies (SOAS), London, University of London, at http://eprints.soas.ac.uk/9966/1/Property-Transitions.pdf.

Khan, Mushtaq H. (2010), *Political Settlements and the Governance of Growth Enhancing Institutions,* London, SOAS.

Kienle, Eberhard (2001), *A Grand Delusion: Democracy and Economic Reform in Egypt,* London, I. B. Tauris.

Kienle, Eberhard (2002), *Contemporary Syria: Liberalization Between Cold War and Cold Peace,* London, University of London, Centre of Near and Middle Eastern Studies.

Kohli, Atul (2004), *State-Directed Development: Political Power and Industrialization in the Global Periphery,* Cambridge, Cambridge University Press.

Lasswell, Harold D. (1936), *Politics: Who Gets What, When, How,* New York, Whittlesey House.

Levy, Brian, and Fukuyama, Francis (2010), "Development Strategies: Integrating Governance and Growth," World Bank, World Bank Policy Research, Working Paper 5196.

Lieberman, Evan S., and Singh, Prerna (2012), "Conceptualizing and Measuring Ethnic Politics: An Institutional Complement to Demographic, Behavioral, and Cognitive Approaches," *Studies in Comparative International Development* 47, 3, 255–286.

Lust, Ellen (2011), "Missing the Third Wave: Islam, Institutions, and Democracy in the Middle East," *Studies in Comparative International Development* 46, 2, 163–190.

Makdisi, Ussama (2000), *The Culture of Sectarianism: Community, History, and Violence in Nineteenth-Century Ottoman Lebanon,* Berkeley, University of California Press.

Marshall, Shana, and Stacher, Joshua (2012), "Egypt's Generals and Transnational Capital," *Middle East Research and Information Project (MERIP) Reports* 262, 12–18.

Masoud, Tarek E. (2014), *Counting Islam: Religion, Class, and Elections in Egypt,* New York, Cambridge University Press.

Massad, Joseph (2001), *Colonial Effects: The Making of National Identity in Jordan,* New York, Columbia University Press.

McAdam, Doug (1982), *Political Processes and the Development of the Black Insurgency, 1930–1970,* Chicago, University of Chicago Press.

Mecham, R. Quinn (2004), "From the Ashes of Virtue, a Promise of Light: The Transformation of Political Islam in Turkey," *Third World Quarterly,* 25, 2, 339–358.

Moore, Pete (2004), *Doing Business in the Middle East: Politics and Economic Crisis in Jordan and Kuwait,* Cambridge, Cambridge University Press.

Nasr, Seyyed Vali Reza (2009), *Forces of Fortune: The Rise of the New Muslim Middle Class and What It Will Mean for Our World,* New York, Simon & Schuster.

North, Douglass (1990), *Institutions, Institutional Change, and Economic Performance,* Cambridge, Cambridge University Press.

North, Douglass C., Wallis, John Joseph, Webb, Steven B., and Weingast, Barry R., eds. (2013), *In the Shadow of Violence: Politics, Economics, and the Problems of Development,* New York, Cambridge University Press.

Olson, Mancur (1965), *The Logic of Collective Action: Public Goods and the Theory of Groups,* Cambridge, MA, Harvard University Press.

Organization of the Oil-Exporting Countries (OPEC) (various years), *Annual Statistical Bulletin,* online edition, at http://www.opec.org/opec_web/en/publications/337.htm.

Osman, Tarek (2010), *Egypt on the Brink: From Nasser to Mubarak,* New Haven, CT, Yale University Press.

Ostrom, Elinor (1990), *Governing the Commons: The Evolution of Institutions for Collective Action,* Cambridge, Cambridge University Press.

Parks, Thomas, and Cole, William (2010), "Political Settlements: Implications for International Development Policy and Practice," Asia Foundation, Occasional Paper 2.

Pepinsky, Thomas B. (2009), *Economic Crises and the Breakdown of Authoritarian Regimes: Indonesia and Malaysia in Comparative Perspective,* Cambridge, Cambridge University Press.

Pew Research Center (2011), "Arab Spring Fails to Improve US Image," Washington, DC, Pew Research, Global Attitudes Project.

Rodrik, Dani (2013), "Roepke Lecture in Economic Geography: Who Needs the Nation State?" *Economic Geography* 89, 1, 1–19.

Roll, Steven (2010), "Finance Matters! The Influence of Financial Sector Reforms on the Development of the Entrepreneurial Elite in Egypt," *Mediterranean Politics* 15, 349–370.

Ross, Michael L. (1999), "The Political Economy of the Resource Curse," *World Politics* 51, 297–322.

Sachs, Jeffrey D. (2001), "Tropical Underdevelopment," National Bureau of Economic Research (NBER), Working Paper 8119.

Salamé, Ghassan, ed. (1994), *Democracy Without Democrats? The Renewal of Politics in the Muslim World,* London, I. B. Tauris.

Schlumberger, Oliver, ed. (2007), *Debating Arab Authoritarianism: Dynamics and Durability in Nondemocratic Regimes,* Stanford, CA, Stanford University Press.

Schultz, T. W. (1981), *Investing in People: The Economics of Population Quality,* Berkeley, University of California Press.

Schwedler, Jillian (2007), *Faith in Moderation: Islamist Parties in Jordan and Yemen,* Cambridge, Cambridge University Press.

Sen, Kunal (2013), "The Political Dynamics of Economic Growth," *World Development* 47, 71–86.

Sfakianakis, John (2004), "The Whales of the Nile: Networks, Businessmen, and Bureaucrats During the Era of Privatization in Egypt," in Heydemann, Steven, ed., *Networks of Privilege in the Middle East: The Politics of Economic Reform Revisited,* New York, Palgrave Macmillan.

Shahin, Emad El-Din (2005), "Political Islam: Ready for Engagement?" Working Paper, Madrid, Spain, Fundación para las Relaciones Internacionales y el Diálgo Exterior (FRIDE).

Slater, Dan (2010), *Ordering Power: Contentious Politics and Authoritarian Leviathans in Southeast Asia,* Cambridge, Cambridge University Press.

Smith, Benjamin B. (2007), *Hard Times in the Lands of Plenty: Oil Politics in Iran and Indonesia,* Ithaca, NY, Cornell University Press.

Tamimi, Azzam S. (2001), *Rachid Ghannouchi: A Democrat Within Islamism,* Oxford, Oxford University Press.

Vitalis, Robert (2006), *America's Kingdom: Mythmaking and the Saudi Oil Frontier,* Stanford, CA, Stanford University Press.

Weiss, Max (2010), *In the Shadow of Sectarianism: Law, Shi'ism, and the Making of Modern Lebanon,* Cambridge, MA, Harvard University Press.

Wickham, Carrie Rosefsky (2002), *Mobilizing Islam: Religion, Activism, and Political Change in Egypt,* New York, Columbia University Press.

Wickham, Carrie Rosefsky (2013), *The Muslim Brotherhood: Evolution of an Islamist Movement,* Princeton, NJ, Princeton University Press.

World Bank (various years), World Development Indicators (WDI), at http://publications.worldbank .org/ecommerce/catalog/product?item_id=631625.

Yom, Sean L., and Gause, F. Gregory, III (2012), "Resilient Royals: How Arab Monarchies Hang On," *Journal of Democracy* 23, 4, 74–88.

Yousef, Tarik M. (2004), "Development, Growth, and Policy Reform in the Middle East and North Africa Since 1950," *Journal of Economic Perspectives* 18, 3, 91–116.

Zogby International (2005), "Attitudes of Arabs: An In-Depth Look at Social and Political Concerns of Arabs," Zogby International, Young Arab Leaders, Arab American Institute.

CHAPTER 2: ECONOMIC GROWTH AND STRUCTURAL CHANGE

Abouleinem, Soheir, Al-Tathy, Heba, and Kheir-el-Din, Hanaa (2009), "The Impact of Phasing Out the Petroleum Subsidies in Egypt," Cairo, Egyptian Center for Economic Studies, Working Paper 145.

Adelman, Irma (1984), "Beyond Export-Led Growth," *World Development* 12, 9 (September), 937–950.

Alvaredo, Facundo, and Piketty, Thomas (2014), "Measuring Top Incomes and Inequality in the Middle East: Data Limitations and Illustration with the Case of Egypt," *May,* Economic Research Forum, Working Paper 832.

Assaad, Ragui, Krafft, Caroline, Hassine, Nadia Belhaj, and Salehi-Isfahani, Djavad (2012), "Inequality of Opportunity in Child Health in the Arab World and Turkey," *Middle East Development Journal,* 4, 2, 1–37.

Assaad, Ragui, Krafft, Caroline, and Salehi-Isfahani, Djavad (2013), "Does the Type of Higher Education Affect Labor Market Outcomes? A Comparison of Egypt and Jordan," Economic Research Forum (ERF), Working Paper 826.

Assaad, Ragui, and Saleh, Mohamed (2013), "Does Improved Local Supply of Schooling Enhance Intergenerational Mobility in Education? Evidence from Jordan," Economic Research Forum (ERF), Working Paper 788.

Assaad, Ragui, Salehi-Isfahani, Djavad, and Hendy, Rana (2013), "Inequality of Opportunity in Educational Attainment in Middle East and North Africa: Evidence from Household Surveys," Economic Research Forum (ERF), Working Paper 834.

Bibi, Sami, and Nabli, Mustapha K. (2010), "Equity and Inequality in the Arab Region," Cairo, Egypt, Economic Research Forum (ERF) Policy Research Report.

Bibi, Sami, El-Lahga, Abdel-Rahmen, and Duclos, Jean-Yves (2012), "Inequality and Polarization in the Arab World," Economic Research Forum, *Policy Perspective* 6 (December 15), at http://www.erf .org.eg/CMS/uploads/pdf/PP6_.pdf.

Chaudhry, Kiren Aziz (2005), "New and Recurring Forms of Poverty and Inequality in the Arab World," unpublished paper, Berkeley, University of California.

Chemingui, Mohamed Abdelbasset (2005), "Harnessing Public Spending for Poverty Reduction in Yemen," Kuwait, Arab Planning Institute, at http://www.arab-api.org/w_cairo5.pdf.

Davis, Eric (1983), *Challenging Colonialism: Bank Misr and Egyptian Industrialization, 1920–1941,* Princeton, NJ, Princeton University Press.

Diwan, Ishac (2013), "Understanding Revolution in the Middle East: The Central Role of the Middle Class," *Middle East Development Journal* 5, 1 (March).

Diwan, Ishac, and Akin, Tarik (2014), "Fifty Years of Fiscal Policy in MENA," Economic Research Forum, Working Paper.

Diwan, Ishac, Keefer, Philip, and Schiffbauer, Mark (2014), "On Top of the Pyramids: Cronyism and Private Sector Growth in Egypt," Center for International Development, Working Paper.

Easterlin, Richard (1995), "Will Raising the Incomes of All Increase the Happiness of All?" *Journal of Economic Behavior and Organization* 27, 1, 25–38.

Economic and Social Commission for Western Asia (ESCWA) (2013), *Arab Middle Class Report,* United Nations.

El Badawi, Ibrahim Ahmed, and Keefer, Philip (2014), "Democracy, Democratic Consolidation, and Military Spending," Economic Research Forum, Working Paper 848.

El Laithy, Heba, Lokshin, Michael, and Banerji, Arup (2003), "Poverty and Economic Growth in Egypt, 1995–2000," World Bank, Development Research Group, Policy Research Working Paper 3068 (June).

Haggard, Stephan (1990), *Pathways from the Periphery: The Politics of Growth in the Newly Industrializing Countries,* Ithaca, NY, Cornell University Press.

Heydemann, Steven, ed. (2004), *Networks of Privilege in the Middle East: The Politics of Economic Reform Revisited,* New York, Palgrave Macmillan.

Imam, Patrick A., and Jacobs, Davina F. (2007), "Effect of Corruption on Tax Revenues in the Middle East," Washington, DC, International Monetary Fund (IMF), IMF Working Paper.

International Labor Organization (ILO) (2013a), *Global Wage Report 2012–2013: Wages and Equitable Growth,* Geneva.

International Labor Organization (ILO) (2013b), *Rethinking Economic Growth: Towards Productive and Inclusive Arab Societies,* Geneva.

International Monetary Fund (IMF) (2013), *World Economic Outlook (WEO)* database (various years), Washington, DC, at http://www.imf.org/external/ns/cs.aspx?id=28.

Iqbal, Farrukh (2006), *Sustaining Gains in Poverty Reduction and Human Development in the Middle East and North Africa,* Washington, DC, World Bank.

IRIN Humanitarian News and Analysis (2012), "Yemen: Time Running Out for Solution to Water Crisis," August 13, at http://www.irinnews.org/report/96093/yemen-time-running-out-for-solution-to-water-crisis (accessed June 16, 2014).

Kravis, Irving, Heston, Alan, and Summers, Robert (1978), *International Comparisons of Real Product and Purchasing Power,* Baltimore, Johns Hopkins University Press.

Layard, Richard (2005), *Happiness: Lessons from a New Science,* New York, Penguin Press.

Lewis, W. Arthur (1954), "Economic Development with Unlimited Supplies of Labour," *Manchester School of Economic and Social Studies* 22, 139–191.

Malik, Adeel, and Awadallah, Bassem (2013), "The Economics of the Arab Spring," *World Development* 45, 296–313.

Mellor, John (1976), *The New Economics of Growth: A Strategy for India and the Developing World,* Ithaca, NY, Cornell University Press.

Noland, Marcus, and Pack, Howard (2005), "The East Asian Industrial Policy Experience: Implications for the Middle East," Washington, DC, Peter G. Peterson Institute for International Economics, Working Paper 05-14.

Noland, Marcus, and Pack, Howard (2007), *The Arab Economies in a Changing World,* Washington, DC, Peter G. Peterson Institute for International Economics.

Piketty, Thomas (2014), *Capital in the Twenty-First Century,* Cambridge, MA, Belknap Press of Harvard University Press.

Polanyi, Karl (2001), *The Great Transformation: The Political and Economic Origins of Our Time,* 2nd ed., Boston, Beacon Press.

Rijkers, Bob, Freund, Caroline, and Nucifora, Antonio (2014), "The Perils of Industrial Policy: Evidence from Tunisia," World Bank.

Roemer, John E. (1998), *Equality of Opportunity,* Cambridge, MA, Harvard University Press.

Sadowski, Yahya M. (1991), *Political Vegetables? Businessman and Bureaucrat in the Development of Egyptian Agriculture,* Washington, DC, Brookings Institution.

Salehi-Isfahani, Djavad (2003), "Mobility and the Dynamics of Poverty in Iran: What Can We Learn from the 1992–1995 Panel Data?" Cairo, World Bank, Economic Research Forum.

Salehi-Isfahani, Djavad (2013), "Rethinking Human Development in the Middle East and North Africa: The Missing Dimensions," *Journal of Human Development and Capabilities* 14, 3, 341–370.

Salehi-Isfahani, Djavad, Hassine, Nadia Belhaj, and Assaad, Ragui (2014), "Equality of Opportunity in Educational Achievement in the Middle East and North Africa," *Journal of Economic Inequality* (December), 489–515.

Stallings, Barbara (1990), "The Role of Foreign Capital in Economic Development: A Comparison of Latin America and East Asia," in Gary Gereffi and Don Wyman, eds., *Manufacturing Miracles: Patterns of Development in Latin America and East Asia,* Princeton, NJ, Princeton University Press.

Tignor, Robert L. (1984), *State, Private Enterprise, and Economic Change in Egypt, 1918–1952,* Princeton, NJ, Princeton University Press.

United National Development Program (UNDP) and International Labour Organization (ILO) (2011), "Arab Development Challenges Report: Towards Developmental States in the Arab Region," Cairo, UNDP.

World Bank (2003), Middle East and North Africa Region Strategy Paper, Washington, DC.

World Bank (2009), *From Privilege to Competition: Unlocking Private-Led Growth in the Middle East and North Africa,* MENA Development Report, Washington, DC.

World Bank (2013), *Jobs for Shared Prosperity: Time for Action in the Middle East and North Africa,* vol. 4, Washington, DC.

World Bank (various years), World Bank Institute (WBI) data, World Bank, Washington, DC, at http://wbi.worldbank.org/wbi/.

World Bank (various years), World Development Indicators (WDI), at http://data.worldbank.org/data-catalog/world-development-indicators.

CHAPTER 3: POLITICAL REGIMES IN THE MIDDLE EAST

Acemoglu, Daron, and Robinson, James A. (2012), *Why Nations Fail: The Origins of Power, Prosperity, and Poverty,* New York, Crown Publishers.

Al-Anani, Khalil (2013), "The Salafi-Brotherhood Feud in Egypt," *Al-Monitor,* February 21, at http://www.al-monitor.com/pulse/originals/2013/02/muslim-brotherhood-salafist-feud-in-egypt.html#.

Alesina, Alberto, Baqir, Reza, and Easterly, William (1999), "Public Goods and Ethnic Divisions," *Quarterly Journal of Economics* 119, 2, 565–611.

Anderson, Lisa (1986), *The State and Social Transformation in Tunisia and Libya, 1930–1980,* Princeton, NJ, Princeton University Press.

Anderson, Lisa (1991), "Absolutism and the Resilience of Monarchy in the Middle East," *Political Science Quarterly* 106, 2, 1–15.

Atallah, Sami (2010), "The Gulf Region: Beyond Oil and Wars—The Role of History and Geopolitics in Explaining Autocracy," in Ibrahim Elbadawi and Samir Makdisi, eds., *Democracy in the Arab World: Explaining the Deficit,* London, Routledge, 166–195.

Barkey, Karen (1994), *Bandits and Bureaucrats: The Ottoman Route to State Centralization,* Ithaca, NY, Cornell University Press.

Beblawi, Hazem, and Luciani, Giacomo, eds. (1987), *The Rentier State: Nation, State, and Integration in the Arab World,* vol. 2, London, New York, Croom Helm.

Bellin, Eva (2004), "The Robustness of Authoritarianism in the Middle East: Exceptionalism in Comparative Perspective," *Comparative Politics* 36, 2, 139.

Benchemsi, Ahmed (2012), "Morocco: Outfoxing the Opposition," *Journal of Democracy* 23, 1, 57–69.

Binder, Leonard (1957), "Prolegomena to the Comparative Study of Middle East Governments," *American Political Science Review* 51, 3, 651–668.

Brownlee, Jason (2007), "Hereditary Succession in Modern Autocracies," *World Politics* 59, 4, 595–628.

Cammett, Melani (2014), *Compassionate Communalism: Welfare and Sectarianism in Lebanon,* Ithaca, NY, Cornell University Press.

Chaudhry, Kiren Aziz (1993), "The Myths of the Market and the Common History of Late Developers," *Politics and Society* 21, 3, 245–274.

Chaudhry, Kiren Aziz (1997), *The Price of Wealth: Economies and Institutions in the Middle East,* Ithaca, NY, Cornell University Press.

Cingranelli, David L., and Richards, David L. (various years), Cingranelli-Richards (CIRI) Human Rights Database, at http://www.gaportal.org/global-indicators/cingranelli-richards-ciri-human -rights-database.

Cingranelli, David L., and Richards, David L. (1999), "Measuring the Level, Pattern, and Sequence of Government Respect for Physical Integrity Rights," *International Studies Quarterly* 43, 2, 407–417.

Cingranelli, David L., and Richards, David L. (2010), "The Cingranelli and Richards (CIRI) Human Rights Data Project," *Human Rights Quarterly* 32, 2, 401–424.Cingranelli, David L., Richards, David L., and Clay, K. Chad (2014), "The CIRI Human Rights Dataset," at http://www .humanrightsdata.com, version 2014.04.14.

Crystal, Jill (1990), *Oil and Politics in the Gulf: Rulers and Merchants in Kuwait and Qatar,* New York, Cambridge University Press.

Crystal, Jill (1995), *Oil and Politics in the Gulf: Rulers and Merchants in Kuwait and Qatar,* updated edition, Cambridge Middle East Library, Cambridge, Cambridge University Press.

Dagne, Ted (2011), "The Republic of South Sudan: Opportunities and Challenges for Africa's Newest Country," Congressional Research Service, Congressional Research Report R41900.

Diwan, Ishac (2013), "Understanding Revolution in the Middle East: The Central Role of the Middle Class," *Middle East Development Journal* 5, 1, 29–56.

Dunning, Thad (2006), *Does Oil Promote Democracy? Regime Change in Rentier States,* Berkeley, University of California, Berkeley.

Easterly, William, and Levine, Ross (1997), "Africa's Growth Tragedy: Policies and Ethnic Divisions," *Quarterly Journal of Economics* 112, 4, 1203–1250.

El Badawi, Ibrahim, Makdisi, Samir, and Milante, Gary (2009), "Explaining the Arab Democracy Deficit: The Role of Oil and Conflicts," unpublished paper, Washington, DC, World Bank.

Evans, Peter (1995), *Embedded Autonomy: States and Industrial Transformation,* Princeton, NJ, Princeton University Press.

Freedom House (2014), "Freedom in the World 2014," Washington, DC, at http://freedomhouse.org/ report/freedom-world/freedom-world-2014?gclid=CLf2tKWl978CFQto7AodD0gABA #.UuF9cmOo6Uk.

Gall, Carlota (2014), "Tunisia's Premier Resigns, Formally Ending His Role," *New York Times,* January 9, at http://www.nytimes.com/2014/01/10/world/middleeast/tunisias-leader-resigns.html.

Gause, Gregory (1994), *Oil Monarchies: Domestic and Security Challenges in the Arab Gulf States,* New York, Council on Foreign Relations.

Greenblatt, Alan (2011), "In Arab States, It's Good to Be the King," National Public Radio, November 10, at http://www.npr.org/2011/11/10/142218146/in-arab-states-its-good-to-be-the-king.

Greif, Avner (1994), "Cultural Beliefs and the Organization of Society: A Historical and Theoretical Reflection on Collectivist and Individualist Societies," *Journal of Political Economy* 102, 5 (October), 912–950.

Habyarimana, James, Humphreys, Macartan, Posner, Daniel N., and Weinstein, Jeremy M. (2009), *Coethnicity: Diversity and the Dilemmas of Collective Action,* New York, Russell Sage Foundation.

Haddad, Bassam (2012), "Syria's State Bourgeoisie: An Organic Backbone for the Regime," *Middle East Critique* 21, 3, 231–257.

Halpern, Manfred (1963), *The Politics of Social Change in the Middle East and North Africa,* RAND Report, RAND Corporation.

Helms, Christina (1984), *Iraq: Eastern Flank of the Arab World,* Washington, DC, Brookings Institution.

Henry, Clement M., and Springborg, Robert (2010), *Globalization and the Politics of Development in the Middle East,* 2nd ed., Cambridge, Cambridge University Press.

Herbst, Jeffrey (2000), *States and Power in Africa: Comparative Lessons in Authority and Control,* Princeton, NJ, Princeton University Press.

Heydemann, Steven (1992), "The Political Logic of Economic Rationality: Selective Stabilization in Syria," in Barkey, Henri, ed., *The Politics of Economic Reform in the Middle East,* New York, St. Martin's Press, 11–39.

Heydemann, Steven (2002), "La Question de la démocratie dans les travaux sur le monde arabe," *Critique Internationale* 17, 54–62.

Heydemann, Steven (2004), *Networks of Privilege in the Middle East: The Politics of Economic Reform Revisited,* New York, Palgrave Macmillan.

Hibou, Beatrice (2006), *La Force de l'obéissance: Economie politique de la répression en Tunisie.* Paris: Éditions de la Découverte.

Hinnebusch, Raymond (1979), "Party and Peasant in Syria," *Cairo Papers in Social Science* 3, 1 (November).

Hudson, Michael (1968), *The Precarious Republic: Modernization in Lebanon,* New York, Random House.

Hudson, Michael (1977), *Arab Politics,* New Haven, CT, Yale University Press.

Issawi, Charles (1982), *An Economic History of the Middle East and North Africa,* New York, Columbia University Press.

Itzkowitz, Norman (1972), *The Ottoman Empire and Islamic Tradition,* Chicago, University of Chicago Press.

Kafadar, Cemal (1995), *Between Two Worlds: The Construction of the Ottoman State,* Berkeley, University of California Press.

Karpat, Kemal (1982), "*Millets* and Nationality: The Roots of the Incongruity of Nation and State in the Post-Ottoman Era," in Braude, Benjamin, and Lewis, Bernard, eds., *Christians and Jews in the Ottoman Empire,* New York, Holmes & Meir Publishers.

Katouzian, Homa (1981), *The Political Economy of Modern Iran: Despotism and Pseudo-Modernism, 1926–1979,* New York, New York University Press.

Kaufmann, Daniel, Kraay, Aart, and Mastruzzi, Massimo (2010), "The Worldwide Governance Indicators: Methodology and Analytical Issues," Washington, DC, World Bank, Policy Research Working Paper 5430.

Khan, Mushtaq H. (2010), *Political Settlements and the Governance of Growth Enhancing Institutions,* London, School of Oriental and African Studies (SOAS).

Kirby, Owen (2000), "Want Democracy? Get a King," *Middle East Quarterly* (December), 3–12.

Kohli, Atul (2004), *State-Directed Development: Political Power and Industrialization in the Global Periphery,* New York, Cambridge University Press.

Kuran, Timur (2012), *The Long Divergence: How Islamic Law Held Back the Middle East,* Princeton, NJ, Princeton University Press, 2012.

Leca, Jean (1975), "Algerian Socialism: Nationalism, Industrialization, and State-Building," in Helen Desfosses and Jacques Levesque, eds., *Socialism in the Third World,* New York, Praeger.

Loveluck, Louisa (2014), "Sisi Says Muslim Brotherhood Will Not Exist Under His Reign," *The Guardian,* May 6, at http://www.theguardian.com/world/2014/may/06/abdel-fatah-al-sisi-muslim -brotherhood-egypt.

Lucas, Russell (2004), "Monarchical Authoritarianism: Survival and Political Liberalization in a Middle Eastern Regime Type," *International Journal of Middle East Studies* 36, 1, 103–119.

Lust, Ellen, ed. (2013), *The Middle East,* 13th ed., Thousand Oaks, CA, CQ Press.

Mahoney, James (2010), *Colonialism and Postcolonial Development: Spanish America in Comparative Perspective,* Cambridge, Cambridge University Press.

Mikhail, Alan (2011), *Nature and Empire in Ottoman Egypt: An Environmental History,* New York, Cambridge University Press.

Ottaway, Marina, and Muasher, Marwan (2011), *Arab Monarchies: Chance for Reform, Yet Unmet,* Washington, DC, Carnegie Endowment for International Peace.

Owen, Roger (1981), *The Middle East in the World Economy, 1800–1914,* London and New York, Methuen.

Parks, Robert P. (2013), "Algeria and the Arab Uprisings," in Clement Henry and Jang Ji-Hyang, eds., *The Arab Spring: Will It Lead to Democratic Transitions?* New York, Palgrave, 101–125.

Penner Angrist, Michele, ed. (2013), *Politics and Society in the Contemporary Middle East,* 2nd ed., Boulder, CO, Lynne Rienner Publishers.

Posusney, Marsha Pripstein, and Angrist, Michele Penner (2004), *Authoritarianism in the Middle East: Regimes and Resistance,* Boulder, CO, Lynne Rienner Publishers.

Project on Middle East Democracy (2014), "Obama Pledges $500 Million in Loans to Tunisia," April 4, at http://pomed.org/blog-post/uncategorized/obama-pledges-500-million-in-loans-to-tunisia/.

Quandt, William (1998), *Between Bullets and Ballots: Algeria's Transition from Authoritarianism,* Washington, DC, Brookings Institution Press.

Reuters (2013), "Tunisia Expects $750 Million in World Bank, IMF Loans Soon, Plans Sukuk Issue," Reuters, October 28, at http://uk.reuters.com/article/2013/10/28/uk-tunisia-economy-idUKBRE99 R0I220131028

Rivlin, Paul (2010), *The Israeli Economy from the Foundation of the State Through the 21st Century,* New York, Cambridge University Press.

Roberts, Hugh (1984), "The Politics of Algerian Socialism," in Richard Lawless and Allan Findlay, eds., *North Africa: Contemporary Politics and Economic Development,* London, Croom Helm.

Roberts, Hugh (2013), "The Revolution That Wasn't," *London Review of Books* 35, 17 (September), 3–9.

Roeder, Philip G., and Rothchild, Donald, eds. (2005), *Sustainable Peace: Power and Democracy After Civil Wars,* Ithaca, NY, Cornell University Press.

Ross, Michael (2012), *The Oil Curse: How Petroleum Wealth Shapes the Development of Nations,* Princeton, NJ, Princeton University Press.

Roy, Sara (1987), "The Gaza Strip: A Case of Economic De-Development," *Journal of Palestine Studies* 17, 1.

Roy, Sara (2001), "Palestinian Society and Economy: The Continued Denial of Possibility," *Journal of Palestine Studies* 30, 4, 5–20.

Saleh, Heba (2014), "IMF Releases $500 Million Loan to Tunisia as New Cabinet Is Sworn In," *Financial Times,* January 30, at http://www.ft.com/intl/cms/s/0/0d4647f2-89cc-11e3-8829 -00144feab7de.html#axzz37uD07pHd.

Schlumberger, Oliver (2008), "Structural Reform, Economic Order, and Development: Patrimonial Capitalism," *Review of International Political Economy* 15, 4, 622–649.

Smith, Benjamin B. (2007), *Hard Times in the Lands of Plenty: Oil Politics in Iran and Indonesia,* Ithaca, NY, Cornell University Press.

Soifer, Hillel (2008), "State Infrastructural Power: Conceptualization and Measurement in Empirical Analysis," *Studies in Comparative International Development* 43, 3–4 (November), 231–251.

Thomas, M. A. (2010), "What Do the Worldwide Governance Indicators Measure?" *European Journal of Development Research* 22, 31–54.

Thompson, Elizabeth (2013), *Justice Interrupted: The Struggle for Constitutional Government in the Middle East,* Cambridge, MA, Harvard University Press.

Transparency International (various years), Corruption Perceptions Index (CPI) data, at http://www .transparency.org/research/cpi/overview.

Transparency International (various years), Corruptions Perceptions Index, at http://cpi.transparency .org/cpi2013/in_detail.

Trimberger, Ellen Kay (1978), *Revolution from Above: Military Bureaucrats and Development in Japan, Turkey, Egypt, and Peru,* New Brunswick, NJ, Transaction Books.

Vandewalle, Dirk (2012), *A History of Modern Libya,* 2nd ed., New York, Cambridge University Press.

Vitalis, Robert (2006), *America's Kingdom: Mythmaking and the Saudi Oil Frontier,* Stanford, CA, Stanford University Press.

Wilson Center (2014), "Tunisia: Islamist-Led Government Steps Down," The Islamists Are Coming, January 9, at http://www.wilsoncenter.org/islamists/article/tunisia-islamist-led-government-steps-down.

World Bank (various years), Worldwide Governance Indicators (WGI), produced by Kaufmann, Daniel, Kraay, Aart, and Mastruzzi, Massimo, Washington, DC, at http://info.worldbank.org/ governance/wgi/index.aspx#home.

Yom, Sean L., and Gause, F. Gregory, III (2012), "Resilient Royals: How Arab Monarchies Hang On," *Journal of Democracy* 23, 4, 74–88.

Zahar, Marie-Joëlle (2005), "Power Sharing in Lebanon: Foreign Protectors, Domestic Peace, and Democratic Failure," in Philip G. Roeder and Donald Rothchild, eds., *Sustainable Peace: Power and Democracy After Civil Wars,* Ithaca, NY, Cornell University Press.

CHAPTER 4: THE IMPACT OF DEMOGRAPHIC CHANGE

Abbasi-Shavazi, Mohammad Jalal (2001), "The Fertility Revolution in Iran," *Population et Sociétés* 373 (November), 1–4.

Abdel-Fadil (1983), "Informal Sector Employment in Egypt," in Lobban, Richard A., Jr., ed., *Urban Research Strategies for Egypt,* Cairo Papers in Social Science, American University in Cairo, 6, 2 (June), 16–40.

Al-Momani, Mohammad (2011), "The Arab Youth Quake: Implications on Democracy and Stability," *Middle East Law and Governance* 3, 1–2, 159–170.

Al-Nashif, Nada and Tzannatos, Zafiris (2013), "Only Fair." *Finance & Development.* 50, 1.

Amin, Magdi et al. (2012), *After the Spring: Economic Transitions in the Arab World,* New York, Oxford University Press.

Barakat, Bilal, and Urdal, Henrik (2009), "Breaking the Waves? Does Education Mediate the Relationship Between Youth Bulges and Political Violence?" Washington, DC, World Bank Policy Research, Working Paper 5114.

Bennoune, Mahfoud (1988), *The Making of Contemporary Algeria, 1830–1987,* Cambridge: Cambridge University Press

Bourdarbat, Brahim (2005), "Job-Search Strategies and the Unemployment of University Graduates in Morocco," paper presented at the International Conference on Labor Market Dynamics, Italy, University of Bologna, May 5–8, at http://www.iza.org/conference_files/iza_ebrd_2005/boudarbat_b1612.pdf.

Bricker, Noah Q., and Foley, Mark C. (2013), "The Effect of Youth Demographics on Violence: The Importance of the Labor Market," *International Journal of Conflict and Violence* 7, 1, 179–194.

Campante, Filipe R., and Chor, Davin (2012), "Why Was the Arab World Poised for Revolution? Schooling, Economic Opportunities, and the Arab Spring," *Journal of Economic Perspectives* 26, 2, 167–187.

Courbage, Youssef (1999), "New Demographic Scenarios in the Mediterranean Region," Paris, National Institute of Demographic Studies.

Dhillon, Navtej, and Yousef, Tarik (2009), "Generation in Waiting: The Unfulfilled Promise of Young People in the Middle East," Washington, DC, Brookings Institution Press.

Diwan, Ishac (2012), "A Rational Framework for the Understanding of the Arab Revolutions," Cambridge, MA, Harvard University, Center for International Development, Working Paper 237.

Donno, Daniela, and Russet, Bruce (2004), "Islam, Authoritarianism, and Female Empowerment: What Are the Linkages?" *World Politics* 56, 4, 582–607.

Dyer, Paul, and Yousef, Tarik M. (2003), "The Fertility Transition in MENA: Causes and Consequences, 1950–2000," Washington, DC, World Bank Unpublished Paper.

El-Kogali, Safaa (2002), "For Better or Worse? The Status of Women in the Labor Market in Egypt, 1988–1998," Washington, DC, World Bank, and Cairo, Economic Research Forum, at http://www.iceg.org/NE/projects/labor/woman.pdf.

Fargues, Philippe (1997), "State Policies and the Birth Rate in Egypt: From Socialism to Liberalism," *Population and Development Review* 23, 1, 115–138.

Fish, M. Steven (2002), "Islam and Authoritarianism," *World Politics* 55, 1, 4–37.

Gilbar, Gad (1992), "Population Growth and Family Planning in Egypt, 1985–92," *Middle East Contemporary Survey* 16, 335–348.

Halpern, Manfred (1963), *The Politics of Social Change in the Middle East and North Africa,* Princeton, NJ, Princeton University Press.

Ibrahim, Saad Eddin (1994), "Sociological Profile of Muslim Militants in Egypt," paper presented at the Workshop on Egypt's Domestic Stability, Washington, DC, US Department of Defense, National Defense University, Fort McNair, April 28–29.

International Labor Organization (ILO) (2012), *Rethinking Economic Growth: Towards Productive and Inclusive Arab Societies,* Beirut, International Labor Organization.

International Monetary Fund (IMF) (2012), "Costly Mideast Subsidies Need Better Targeting," IMF Survey Online, Middle East and North Africa, at http://www.imf.org/external/pubs/ft/survey/so/2012/car051412b.htm.

Kaplan, Robert (1994), "The Coming Anarchy," *Atlantic Monthly* 273.

Kepel, Gilles (2002), *Jihad: The Trail of Political Islam,* Cambridge, MA, Belknap Press of Harvard University Press.

LaGraffe, Daniel (2012), "The Youth Bulge in Egypt: An Intersection of Demographics, Security, and the Arab Spring," *Journal of Strategic Security* 5, 2, 65–79.

Lapham, R. J. (1983), "Background Notes and Illustrative Tables on Populations in the Middle East," paper prepared for the Conference on Population and Political Stability in the Near East and South Asia Region, Washington, DC, March.

Marcus, George (1998), *Ethnography Through Thick and Thin,* Princeton, NJ, Princeton University Press.

Meillassoux, Claude (1981), *Maidens, Meal, and Money,* Cambridge, Cambridge University Press.

Mirkin, Barry (2013), "Arab Spring: Demographics in a Region in Transition," Arab Human Development Report, Research Paper Series.

Mishra, Vinod (2004), "Muslim/Non-Muslim Differentials in Fertility and Family Planning," Honolulu, East-West Center, Population and Health Series, 112 (January).

Moghadam, Valentine, and Karshenas, Massoud (2006), *Social Policy in the Middle East: Political, Economics and Gender Dynamics,* Basingstoke, Palgrave Macmillan.

Mosk, Carl (1983), *Patriarchy and Fertility: Japan and Sweden 1880–1960,* New York, Academic Press.

Nabli, Mustapha K., and Keller, Jennifer (2002), "The Macroeconomics of Labor Market Outcomes in MENA over the 1990s: How Growth Has Failed to Keep Pace with a Burgeoning Labor Market," World Bank, Washington, DC, World Bank Unpublished Paper.

National Research Council (1986), *Population Growth and Economic Development: Policy Questions,* Washington, DC, National Academy Press.

Norris, Pippa, and Inglehart, Ronald (2002), "Gender Equality and Democracy," *Comparative Sociology* 1, 3–4, 321–346.

Organization for Economic Cooperation and Development (OECD) (2009), "Is it Normal? Towards More and Better Jobs in Developing Countries," OECD.

Ouadah-Bedidi, Zahia, and Vallin, Jacques (2013), "Fertility and Population Policy in Algeria: The Ironies of Planning," *Population and Development Review* 38 (February).

Ouadah-Bedidi, Zahia, Vallin, Jacques, and Bouchoucha, Ibtihel (2012), "Unexpected Developments in Maghrebian Fertility," *Population and Societies* 486 (February).

Pew Research (2011), "The Future of the Global Muslim Population," January 27.

Rashad, Hoda, and Khadr, Zeinab (2002), "The Demography of the Arab Region: New Challenges and Opportunities," in Abdel-Hamid Sirageldin, Ismail, ed., *Human Capital: Population Economics in the Middle East,* Cairo, American University in Cairo Press.

Ross, Michael (2012), *The Oil Curse: How Petroleum Wealth Shapes the Development of Nations,* Princeton, NJ, Princeton University Press.

Roudi-Fahimi, Farzaneh (2002), "Iran's Family Planning Program: Responding to a Nation's Needs," Population Reference Bureau.

Roudi, Farzaneh (2012), "Iran Reverses Family Planning, Calls for More Children," August 29, United States Institute of Peace, The Iran Primer.

Roudi-Fahimi, Farzaneh, and Kent, Mary Mederios (2007), "Challenges and Opportunities: The Population of the Middle East and North Africa," Population Reference Bureau.

Roy, Olivier (1994), *The Failure of Political Islam,* Cambridge, MA, Harvard University Press.

Schultz, T. W. (1981), *Investing in People: The Economics of Population Quality,* Berkeley, University of California Press.

Soffer, Arnon (1986), "Lebanon—Where Demography Is the Core of Politics and Life," *Middle Eastern Studies* 22, 2 (April), 192–205.

Tzannatos, Zafiris (2014), "The Youth and the Arab Spring," *Executive Magazine,* (December 12, 2013), 50–51.

UNICEF (2005), *Monitoring the Situation of Women and Children: Fertility and Contraceptive Use,* UNICEF World Summit for Children.

UNICEF (2013), *Towards an AIDS-Free Generation: Children and AIDS Sixth Stocktaking Report, 2013,* New York, UNICEF.

UNICEF and United Nations Population Fund (UNFPA) (2008), *Egypt Demographic and Health Survey 2008,* UNICEF and UNFPA.

UNICEF Yemen (2014), "Humanitarian Action for Children: Yemen," UNICEF, at http://www.unicef.org/appeals/yemen.html.

United Nations (2003), *United Nations Common Country Assessment for the Islamic Republic of Iran,* Tehran, United Nations (August 11).

United Nations (UN) (2013), *World Population Prospects,* UN Population Division, at http://esa.un.org/wpp/documentation/pdf/WPP2012_Volume-II-Demographic-Profiles.pdf.

United Nations Population Fund (UNFPA) (2012a), *By Choice, Not by Chance: Family Planning, Human Rights, and* Development, UNFPA, State of World Population 2012, at http://www.unfpa.org/public/home/publications/pid/12511.

United Nations Population Fund (UNFPA) (2012b), "Women's Need for Family Planning in Arab Countries," UNFPA, July.

UN Women Watch (2011), Convention on the Elimination of All Forms of Discrimination Against Women, "Country Reports: Bahrain."

Urdal, Henrik (2004), "The Devil in the Demographics: The Effect of Youth Bulges on Domestic Armed Conflict, 1950–2000," *Social Development Papers: Conflict Prevention and Reconstruction.*

USAID (US Agency for International Development) (1992), "Country Program Strategy, FY 1992–1996: Population," Cairo, May, Unpublished Report.

US Census Bureau (various years), international database, at http://www.census.gov/population/international/data/idb/informationGateway.php

US Census Bureau (2012), "The 2012 Statistical Abstract," US Census Bureau, at http://www.census.gov/compendia/statab/.

Wahba, Jackline (2009), "The impact of Labor Market Reforms on Informality in Egypt," Gender and Work in the MENA Region Working Paper Series no. 3, The Population Council, Cairo.

Waterbury, John (1973), *Land, Man, and Development in Algeria,* pt. 2, *Population, Employment, and Emigration,* American University Field Services Reports, North Africa Series, 17, 2.

Williamson, Jeffrey, and Yousef, Tarik (2002), "Demographic Transitions and Economic Performance in the Middle East and North Africa," in Abdel-Hamid Sirageldin, Ismail, ed., *Human Capital: Population Economics in the Middle East,* London, I. B. Tauris, 16–36.

World Bank (1984), *World Development Report,* New York, Oxford University Press.

World Bank (2004), *Unlocking the Employment Potential in the Middle East and North Africa: Toward a New Social Contract,* Washington, DC.

World Bank (various years), World Development Indicators (WDI), at http://publications.worldbank.org/ecommerce/catalog/product?item_id=631625.

Wrigley, Edward, and Schofield, Roger (1981), *The Population History of England, 1541–1871: A Reconstruction,* London, Edward Arnold.

CHAPTER 5: HUMAN CAPITAL: HEALTH AND EDUCATION

Abdel-Fadil (1983), "Informal Sector Employment in Egypt," in Lobban, Richard A., Jr., ed., *Urban Research Strategies for Egypt,* Cairo Papers in Social Science, American University in Cairo, 6, 2 (June), 16–40.

Adams, Richard (1986), *Development and Social Change in Rural Egypt,* Syracuse, NY, Syracuse University Press.

Al-Amri, Arwa, Annuzaili, Khekra, and al-Deram, Arwa (2003), *Overview of the Situation of Children, Women, and ECD in Yemen,* World Bank, Early Childhood Development Virtual University, at http://www.ecdvu.org/mena/downloads/yemenreport/yemenreport.pdf.

Alayan, Samira, Rohde, Achim, and Dhouib, Sarhan, eds. (2012), *The Politics of Education Reform in the Middle East,* New York, Berghahn Books.

Aoyama, Atsuko (2001), "Reproductive Health in the Middle East and North Africa: Well-Being for All," World Bank.

Aran, Meltem A., and Ersado, Lire (2013), "Inequality of Opportunity in Access to Basic Services Among Egyptian Children," Development Analytics Research Paper Series 1304, July 8, at http://ssrn.com/abstract=2292461 or http://dx.doi.org/10.2139/ssrn.2292461.

Bennoune, Mahfoud (1988), *The Making of Contemporary Algeria 1830–1987: Colonial Upheavals and Post-Independence Development,* Cambridge, Cambridge University Press.

Bourdarbat, Brahim (2005), "Job-Search Strategies and the Unemployment of University Graduates in Morocco," paper presented at International Conference on Labor Market Dynamics, University of Bologna, Italy, May 5–8, at http://www.iza.org/conference_files/iza_ebrd_2005/boudarbat_b1612.pdf.

Burnham, Gilbert, et al. (2006), "Mortality After the 2003 Invasion of Iraq: A CrossSectional Cluster Sample Survey," *The Lancet,* October 11.

Caldwell, John C. (1986), "Routes to Low Mortality in Poor Countries," *Population and Development Review* 12, 2 (June), 171–220.

Colclough, Christopher (1982), "The Impact of Primary Schooling on Economic Development: A Review of the Evidence," *World Development* 10, 3, 167–185.

Cornia, Giovanni Andrea, and Menchini, Leonardo (2001), "The Pace and Distribution of Gains in Child Well-Being over 1980–2000: Some Preliminary Results," in Cornia, Giovanni Andrea, ed., *Harnessing Globalization for Children,* Florence, Italy, Innocenti Research Center, ch. 2.

Crawford, Neta C. (2013), "Civilian Death and Injury in the Iraq War, 2003–2013," Costs of War, Boston University.

Dewachi, Omar (2013), "War and the Costs of Medical Travel for Iraqis in Lebanon," http://costsofwar .org/sites/default/files/Medicaltraveliraq.pdf.

El-Kogali, Safaa (2002), "Women and Work in Egypt: A Decade of Change in the Egyptian Labor Market in an Era of Reform," in Assaad, Ragui, ed., *The Egyptian Labor Market in an Era of Reform*, Cairo, American University in Cairo Press, 161–177.

El-Saharty, Sameh, (2010), "Human Resources for Health: Policies for Thought . . . ," South Asia Regional High Level Forum on Health Financing, June 2–4.

Eltayib, Galal Eldin (2003), "The Case of Khartoum, Sudan," in *Understanding Slums: Case Studies for the 2003 Report*, UN Habitat, at http://www.ucl.ac.uk/dpu-projects/Global_Report/pdfs/ khartoum.pdf.

El-Zanaty, Fatma, and Way, Ann (2001), "Egypt Demographic and Health Survey 2000," January, Calverton, MD, National Population Council, Ministry of Health and Population (Egypt), and ORC Macro.

El-Zanaty, Fatma, and Way, Ann (2006), "Egypt Demographic and Health Survey 2005," Cairo, Egypt, Ministry of Health and Population, National Population Council, El-Zanaty and Associates, and ORC Macro.

Farmer, Paul (2003), *Pathologies of Power: Health, Human Rights, and the New War on the Poor*, Berkeley, University of California Press.

Garfield, Richard (1999), "Morbidity and Mortality Among Iraqi Children from 1990 Through 1998: Assessing the Impact of the Gulf War and Economic Sanctions," Columbia University, July, at http: //www.casi.org.uk/info/garfield/dr-garfield.html.

Garfield, Richard (2005), "On the Efficiency and Effectiveness of the Development Fund for Iraq in the Health Sector," testimony before the House Subcommittee on National Security, Emerging Threats, and International Relations, June 20.

Global Policy Forum (2002), "Iraq Sanctions: Humanitarian Implications and Options for the Future," at http://www.globalpolicy.org/security/sanction/iraq1/2002/paper.htm.

Halliday, Fred (1974), *Arabia Without Sultans*, New York, Penguin.

Harik, Iliya (1974), "Political Mobilization of Peasants: A Study of an Egyptian Community," *Studies in Development* 8.

Hinnebusch, Raymond (1979), "Party and Peasant in Syria," *Cairo Papers in Social Science* 3, 1 (November).

Hoffman, Michael, and Jamal, Amaney (2012), "The Youth and the Arab Spring: Cohort Differences and Similarities," *Middle East Law and Governance* 4, 168–188.

Ibrahim, Saad Eddin (1994), "Sociological Profile of Muslim Militants in Egypt," paper presented at Workshop on Egypt's Domestic Stability, National Defense University, US Department of Defense, Fort McNair, Washington, DC, April 28–29.

International Monetary Fund (IMF) (various years), World Financial Statistics.

International Monetary Fund (IMF) (2012), "Costly Mideast Subsidies Need Better Targeting," IMF Survey Online, Middle East and North Africa, at http://www.imf.org/external/pubs/ft/survey/so /2012/car051412b.htm.

Kepel, Gilles (2002), *Jihad: The Trail of Political Islam*, Cambridge, Belknap Press of Harvard University Press.

Lara, George, and Pullum, Thomas (2005), "Infant Mortality in Egypt: Exploring the Role of Prenatal Care, and Implications for Public Policy," paper presented to the annual meeting of the Population Association of America, Philadelphia, Pennsylvania, March 31–April 2.

Leca, Jean (1975), "Algerian Socialism: Nationalism, Industrialization, and State Building," in Desfosses, Helen, and Levesque, Jacques, eds., *Socialism in the Third World*, New York, Praeger.

Levine, Ruth (2007), *Case Studies in Global Heath: Millions Saved*, Sudbury, MA, Jones and Bartlett Publishers, at http://www.jblearning.com/samples/0763746207/46207_fmxx_levine.pdf.

Lewis, Bernard (2002), "What Went Wrong?" *Atlantic Monthly* (January), 43–45.

Lopez, George, and Cortright, David (2004), "Containing Iraq: Sanctions Worked," *Foreign Affairs* (July/August).

Loveluck, Louisa (2013), "Education in Egypt: Key Challenges," background paper for the Middle East and North Africa Programme, Chatham House, at http://www.erf.org.eg/grp/GRP_Sep03/Algeria -Growth.pdf.

Marmot, Michael, and Wilkinson, Richard G. (2005), *Social Determinants of Health*, New York, Oxford University Press.

Minujin, Alberto, and Delamonica, Enrique (2003), "Mind the Gap! Widening Child Mortality Disparities," *Journal of Human Development* 4, 3, 397–418.

Moghadam, Valentine (2000), "Enhancing Women's Participation in the Middle East and North Africa," in Heba Handoussa and Zafiris Tzannatos, eds., *Employment Creation and Social Protection*, Cairo, American University in Cairo Press, 237–279.

Nabli, Mustapha K., and Keller, Jennifer (2002), "The Macroeconomics of Labor Market Outcomes in MENA over the 1990s: How Growth Has Failed to Keep Pace with a Burgeoning Labor Market," Washington, DC, World Bank Unpublished Paper.

Ng, S. W., Zaghloul, S., Ali, H. I., Harrison, G., and Popkin, B. M. (2011), "The Prevalence and Trends of Overweight, Obesity, and Nutrition-Related Non-Communicable Diseases in the Arabian Gulf States," *Obesity Reviews* 12, 1–13.

Nyrop, Richard F., ed. (1983), *Egypt: A Country Study*, American University Foreign Area Studies, Washington, DC, US Government Printing Office.

Özgediz, Selcuk (1980), "Education and Income Distribution in Turkey," in Özbudun, Ergun, and Ulusan, Aydin, eds., *The Political Economy of Income Distribution in Turkey*, New York, Holmes and Meier.

Psacharopoulos, George, and Patrinos, Anthony (2002), "Returns to Investment in Education: A Further Update," World Bank.

Roberts, Les, Lifta, Riyadh, Garfield, Richard, Khudhairi, Jamal, and Burnham, Gilbert (2004), "Mortality Before and After the 2003 Invasion of Iraq: Cluster Sample Survey," *The Lancet* 364 (November 20), 1857–1864.

Roudi-Fahimi, Farzaneh, and Moghadam, Valentine (2003), "Empowering Women, Developing Society: Female Education in the Middle East and North Africa," Population Reference Bureau.

Rowat, Colin (2000), "UN Agency Reports on the Humanitarian Situation in Iraq," Campaign Against Sanctions on Iraq, University of Cambridge, June 9, at http://www.casi.org.uk/briefing /000707versailles.pdf.

Salehi-Isfahani, Djavad, Hassine, Nadia Belhaj, and Assaad, Ragui (2014), "Equality of Opportunity in Educational Achievement in the Middle East and North Africa," *Journal of Economic Inequality* (December), 489–515.

Schiavo-Campo, Salvatore, at al. (2003), "An International Statistical Survey of Government Employment and Wages," World Bank.

Semba, Richard D., et al. (2008), "Effect of Parental Formal Education on Risk of Child Stunting in Indonesia and Bangladesh: A Cross-Sectional Study," *The Lancet* 371, 322–328.

Sen, Amartya (1981), *Poverty and Famines: An Essay on Entitlement and Deprivation*, Oxford, Oxford University Press.

Trends in International Mathematics and Science Study (TIMSS) (2007).

Tripp, Charles (2000), *A History of Iraq*, Cambridge, Cambridge University Press.

UNESCO (2011), "Education Counts Towards the Millennium Development Goals," Paris, UNESCO, at http://unesdoc.unesco.org/images/0019/001902/190214e.pdf.

UNESCO (various years), "The Official Source of Literacy Data," UNESCO Institute for Statistics, at http://www.uis.unesco.org/literacy/pages.

UNESCO (various years), "The Official Source of Literacy Data," UNESCO Institute for Statistics, at http://www.uis.unesco.org/literacy/pages.

UNICEF (1999), *Child and Maternal Mortality Survey, 1999: Preliminary Report*, New York, at http:// www.fas.org/news/iraq/1999/08/990812-unicef.htm.

UNICEF (2001), *Progress Since the World Summit for Children: A Statistical Review*, at http://www .unicef.org/publications/files/pub_wethechildren_stats_en.pdf.

UNICEF (2005), *Monitoring the Situation of Women and Children: Fertility and Contraceptive Use*, UNICEF World Summit for Children, at http://www.childinfo.org/eddb/fertility/index.htm #progress.

UNICEF (2006), *Global Database on Breastfeeding Indicators*, at http://www.childinfo.org/areas/ breastfeeding/countrydata.php.

UNICEF (2007), *Monitoring the Situation of Women and Children*, UNICEF, at http://www.data .unicef.org/child-health.

UNICEF (2012), *Levels and Trends in Child Mortality*, New York, United Nations Children's Fund.

United Nations (2002), *Millennium Development Goals: Report on the Kingdom of Saudi Arabia*, Riyadh, United Nations.

United Nations (2003), *United Nations Common Country Assessment for the Islamic Republic of Iran,* Tehran, United Nations, August 11.

United Nations Development Program (UNDP) (2002), *Reporting on Millennium Development Goals at the Country Level: Egypt,* Cairo, UNDP, at http://www.undp.org.eg/rc/mdg.pdf.

United Nations Development Program (UNDP) (2005), *Iraq Living Conditions Survey,* Baghdad, UNDP.

United Nations Development Program (UNDP) (2011), "Arab Development Challenges Report: Towards Developmental States in the Arab Region," UNDP.

United Nations Development Program (UNDP) and Arab Fund for Economic and Social Development (AFESD) (2002), *Arab Human Development Report, 2002,* New York, UNDP.

United Nations Development Program (UNDP) and Institute of National Planning, Egypt (INP) (2003), *Egypt Human Development Report, 2002–2003,* Cairo, UNDP and INP.

United Nations Development Program (UNDP) and Institute of National Planning, Egypt (INP) (2005), *Egypt Human Development Report, 2004,* Cairo, UNDP and INP.

United Nations Development Program (UNDP) and Iraq Ministry of Planning and Development Cooperation (2005), *Iraq Living Conditions Survey, 2004,* vol. 3, *Socioeconomic Atlas of Iraq,* Baghdad, Ministry of Planning and Development Cooperation.

UN Refugee Agency (UNHCR) (2014), "Syria Regional Refugee Response," at http://data.unhcr.org /syrianrefugees/regional.php.

US Agency for International Development (USAID) (2003), *Interim Strategic Plan for Assistance to the Republic of Yemen, 4/2003–4/2006,* San'a, US Embassy.

US Institute of Medicine (1979), "Health in Egypt: Recommendations for US Assistance," prepared for USAID, Washington, DC (January).

Vick, Karl (2004), "Children Pay Cost of Iraq's Chaos: Malnutrition Nearly Double What It Was Before Invasion," *Washington Post,* November 21, A1.

Waterbury, John (1983), *The Egypt of Nasser and Sadat: The Political Economy of Two Regimes,* Princeton, NJ, Princeton University Press.

Watkins, Kevin (2000), *The Oxfam Education Report,* London, Oxfam GB.

World Bank (1986), *Poverty and Hunger,* Washington, DC.

World Bank (1999), "Education in the Middle East and North Africa: A Strategy Towards Learning for Development," at http://www.worldbank.org/education/strategy/MENA-E.pdf.

World Bank (2002), *Reducing Vulnerability and Increasing Opportunity: Social Protection in the Middle East and North Africa,* Washington, DC.

World Bank (2008), *The Road Not Traveled: Education Reform in the Middle East and North Africa,* Washington, DC, World Bank.

World Bank (2013), *World Development, 2013,* Washington DC, World Bank, at http://databank .worldbank.org/data/download/WDI-2013-ebook.pdf.

World Bank (2014), "Poor Women in Urban and Rural Areas in Yemen Will Have Access to Safe Motherhood Services," World Bank, Press Release, March 31.

World Bank (various years), World Development Indicators (WDI), at http://publications.worldbank .org/ecommerce/catalog/product?item_id=631625.

World Health Organization (WHO) and UNICEF (2011), *Joint Malnutrition Dataset from UNICEF, World Bank, and WHO,* UNICEF Data, at http://data.unicef.org/nutrition/malnutrition.

Yuki, Takako, and Kameyama, Yuriko (2013), "Improving the Quality of Basic Education for the Future Youth of Yemen Post Arab Spring," in *Global Economy and Development,* Working Paper 59.

Zaidi, Sarah, and Smith-Fawzi, Mary (1995), "Health of Baghdad's Children," *The Lancet* 346, 8988, 1485.

CHAPTER 6: WATER AND FOOD SECURITY

Ababsa, Myriam (2010), "Agrarian Counter-Reform in Syria (2000–2010)," in Hinnebusch, Raymond, El Hindi, Atieh, Khaddam, Mounzer, and Ababsa, Myriam, eds., *Agriculture and Reform in Syria,* Fife, University of St. Andrew's Center for Syrian Studies, 83–108.

Abaza, Deya (2013), "Let Them Eat Vegetables: Egypt's Wheat Farmers Hit Hard by Diesel Price Hikes," AhramOnline, April 16, at http://english.ahram.org.eg/NewsContent/3/12/69016/ Business/Economy/Let-them-eat-vegetables-Egypts-wheat-farmers-hit-h.aspx (accessed September 2, 2013).

Abdel-Dayem, Safwat, Taha, Faisal, Choukr-Allah, Redouane, Kfouri, Claire A., Chung, Christophe C., and Al Saiid, Dalia (2012), "Water Reuse in the Arab World: From Principle to

Practice—Voices from the Field," Washington, DC, World Bank, at http://documents.worldbank .org/curated/en/2012/01/16588132/water-reuse-arab-world-principle-practice-voices-field.

Abderrahman, Walid A. (2001), "Water Demand Management in Saudi Arabia," in Faruqui, Naser I., Biswas, Asit K., and Bino, Murad J., eds., *Water Management in Islam,* Ottawa, IDRC/UNU Press.

Abun-Nasr, Jamil M. (1971), *A History of the Magrib,* Cambridge, Cambridge University Press.

Adams, Richard H., Jr. (1986), *Development and Social Change in Rural Egypt,* Syracuse, NY, Syracuse University Press.

Adelman, Irma (1984), "Beyond Export-Led Growth," *World Development* 12, 9 (September), 937–950.

Alderman, Harold, and von Braun, J. (1984), *The Effects of the Egyptian Food Ration and Subsidy System on Income Distribution and Consumption,* Washington, DC, International Food Policy Research Institute (IFPRI) Research Report 45.

Al-Khafaji, 'Issam (1983), *The State and the Evolution of Capitalism in Iraq: 1968–1978* (in Arabic), Cairo, Dar al-Mustaqbal al-Arabi.

Allan, Tony (2001), *The Middle East Water Question: Hydropolitics and the Global Economy,* London, GBR.

Allan, J. A., and Karshenas, M. (1996), "Managing Environmental Capital: The Case of Water in Israel, Jordan, the West Bank and Gaza, 1947 to 1995," in Allan, J. A., and Court, J. H., eds., *Water, Peace, and the Middle East: Negotiating Resources in the Jordan Basin,* London, I. B. Taurus.

Al-Qa'id, Yusuf (1978), *War in the Land of Egypt,* Gloucestershire, UK, Arris Books.

AWWA Research Foundation (1999), "Residential End Uses of Water," American Water Works Association (AWWA), Denver, CO, at http://www.waterrf.org/PublicReportLibrary/RFR90781_1999 _241A.pdf (accessed September 2, 2013).

Baer, Gabriel (1962), *A History of Landownership in Modern Egypt, 1800–1950,* London, Oxford University Press.

Batatu, Hanna (1978), *The Old Social Classes and the Revolutionary Movements of Iraq,* Princeton, NJ, Princeton University Press.

Belloumi, Mounir, and Matoussi, Mohamed (2007), "Water Demand Management in Tunisia," Technological Transformation and Competitiveness in the Middle East, Inderscience Enterprises Ltd., at http://www.academia.edu/3515343/Water_Scarcity_Management_in_the_MENA_Region_ from_a_Globalization_Perspective (accessed September 2, 2013).

Ben-Gal, Alon (2010), "Sustainable Water Policy for Agriculture in Israel," in Rabbo, Alfred Abed, and Tal, Alon, eds., *Water Wisdom,* Piscataway, NJ, Rutgers University Press, 211–223.

Binswanger, Hans (1989), "The Policy Response of Agriculture," *Proceedings of the World Bank Annual Conference on Development Economics,* 231–258.

Braverman, Avishay (1989), "Comment," *Proceedings of the World Bank Annual Conference on Development Economics,* 259–262.

Breisinger, Clemens, Ecker, Olivier, and Al-Riffai, Perrihan (2011), "Economics of the Arab Awakening: From Revolutions to Transformation and Food Security," Washington, DC, International Food Policy Research Institute (IFPRI), Policy Brief 18.

Bush, Ray, ed. (2002), *Counter-Revolution in Egypt's Countryside: Land and Farmers in the Era of Economic Reform,* London, Zed Books.

Bush, Ray (2010), "Food Riots: Power, Poverty, and Protest," *Journal of Agrarian Change* 10, 1 (January), 119–129.

Central Intelligence Agency (CIA) (2000), *World Factbook,* Washington, D.C., at https://www.cia.gov /library/publications/download/download-2000/index.html.

Chemingui, Mohamed Abdelbasset, and Thaber, Chokri (2001), "Internal and External Reforms in Agricultural Policy in Tunisia and Poverty in Rural Areas," Global Development Project on Explaining Growth in Developing Countries, at http://www.gdnet.org/pdf/chemingui.pdf.

Christensen, J. H., et al. (2007), "Regional Climate Projections," in Solomon, S., et al., eds., *Climate Change 2007: The Physical Science Basis: Contribution of Working Group I to the Fourth Assessment Report of the Intergovernmental Panel on Climate Change,* Cambridge and New York, Cambridge University Press.

Dann, Uriel (1969), *Iraq Under Qassem: A Political History, 1958–1963,* Jerusalem, Israel Universities Press.

Davis, Eric (1983), *Challenging Colonialism: Bank Misr and Egyptian Industrialization, 1920–1941,* Princeton, NJ, Princeton University Press.

Davis, Diana K. (2006), "Neoliberalism, Environmentalism, and Agricultural Restructuring in Morocco," *Geographic Journal* 172, 2 (June), 88–105.

Dethier, Jean-Jacques (1989), *Trade, Exchange Rate, and Agricultural Pricing Policies in Egypt,* Washington, DC, World Bank.

Dethier, Jean-Jacques (1991), "Egypt," in Krueger, Anne O., Schiff, Maurice, and Valdes, Alberto, eds., *The Political Economy of Agricultural Pricing Policy,* vol. 3, *Africa and the Mediterranean,* Baltimore, Johns Hopkins University Press for the World Bank, 15–78.

Devereux, Stephen (1993), *Theories of Famine,* New York, Harvester-Wheatsheaf.

Devlin, Julia (2003), "From Citrus to Cellphones? Agriculture as Source of New Comparative Advantage in the Middle East and North Africa," in Lofgren, H., ed., *Food, Agriculture, and Economy in the Middle East and North Africa,* Research in Middle East Economics 5, 33–52.

De Waal, Alexander (1989), *Famine That Kills: Darfur, Sudan, 1984–85,* Oxford, Clarendon Press.

De Waal, Alexander (2004), "Tragedy in Darfur," *Boston Review* (October/November), at http://www.bostonreview.net/BR29.5/dewaal.html.

Elhadj, Elie (2008), "Saudi Arabia's Agricultural Project: From Dust to Dust," *Middle East Review of International Affairs* 12, 2 (June), 29–37.

Erian, Wadid, Katlan, Bassem, and Babah, Ouldbdey (2010), "Drought Vulnerability in the Arab Region: Special Case Study: Syria," UN Office for Disaster Risk Reduction, at http://www.preventionweb.net/english/hyogo/gar/2011/en/bgdocs/Erian_Katlan_&_Babah_2010.pdf (accessed September 4, 2013).

Falkenmark, Malin (1989), *Natural Resource Limits to Population Growth: The Water Perspective,* Gland, Switzerland, International Union for the Conservation of Nature.

Food and Agriculture Organization (FAO) (2003), *Sustainable Water Resources Management for Food Security in the Near East Region,* Jeddah, High-Level Technical Workshop, FAO and Islamic Development Bank, October 8–9, at www.fao.org/docrep/meeting/007/ad387e/ad387e00.htm.

Food and Agriculture Organisation (FAO) (2013), AQUASTAT databases, at http://www.fao.org/nr/water/aquastat/dbases/index.stm.

Food and Agriculture Organisation (FAO) (2013), FAOSTAT, *FAO Statistical Yearbook 2013,* Rome, FAO, 2013.

Food and Agriculture Organisation (FAO) (various years), FAOSTAT, "Food and Agricultural Commodities Production," FAO, at http://faostat.fao.org/site/339/default.aspx.

Femia, Francesco, and Werrell, Caitlin (2013), "Climate Change Before and After the Arab Awakening: The Cases of Syria and Libya," in Werrell, Caitlin, and Femia, Francesco, eds., *The Arab Spring and Climate Change: A Climate and Security Correlations Series,* Washington, DC, Center for American Progress.

FEWS NET (2012), "East Africa Food Security Brief," USAID Famine Early Warning Systems Network (FEWS NET), February.

Haddad, Bassam (2011), "The Political Economy of Syria: Realities and Challenges," *Middle East Policy* 18, 2 (Summer), 46–61.

Hansen, Bent (1991), "A Macro-Economic Framework for Economic Planning in Egypt," in Handoussa, H., and Porter, Gilian, eds., *Labour Absorption and Structural Adjustment: Egypt in the 1990s,* Geneva, ILO, 189–218.

Hansen, Bent (1992), *The Political Economy of Poverty, Equity, and Growth: Egypt and Turkey,* New York, Oxford University Press.

Harrigan, Jane, et al. (2012), "The Political Economy of Food Security in North Africa," African Development Bank Economic Brief.

Hatuqa, Delia (2012), "Palestinian Farmers Thirsty for Exports," *Al Jazeera English,* April 10, at http://www.aljazeera.com/indepth/features/2013/04/20134312648559299.html (accessed June 12, 2014).

Hazell, Peter (2007), "Managing Drought Risks in the Low-Rainfall Areas of the Middle East and North Africa," case study 7–5 of the program "Food Policy for Developing Countries: The Role of Government in the Global Food System," eds. Per Pinstrup-Anderson and Fuzhi Cheng, Ithaca, NY, Cornell University.

Hazell, Peter, Oram, Peter, and Chaherli, Nabil (2003), "Managing Livestock in Drought-Prone Areas of the Middle East and North Africa: Policy Issues," in Lofgren, H., ed., *Food, Agriculture, and Economy in the Middle East and North Africa, Research in Middle East Economics* 5, 79–104.

Hooglund, Eric (1982), *Land and Revolution in Iran: 1960–1980,* Austin, University of Texas Press.

Hung, Ming-Feng, and Chie, Bin-Tzong Chie (2013), "Residential Water Use: Efficiency, Affordability, and Price Elasticity," *Water Resources Management* 27, 275–291.

International Crisis Group (ICG) (2004a), *Darfur Rising: Sudan's New Crisis,* Africa Report 76, March 25, Nairobi/Brussels.

International Fund for Agricultural Development (IFAD) (2001), *The Syrian Arab Republic: Country Programme Evaluation Report,* Rome, IFAD Report 1178-SY, August.

International Monetary Fund (IMF) (2013), "Case Studies on Energy Subsidy Reform: Lessons and Implications," IMF, January 28, at http://www.imf.org/external/np/pp/eng/2013/012813a.pdf (accessed June 13, 2014).

IRIN (2012), "Yemen: Time Running Out for Solution to Water Crisis," IRIN: Humanitarian News and Analysis, August 13, at http://www.irinnews.org/report/96093/yemen-time-running-out-for-solution-to-water-crisis.

Ismail, Abdel-Mawla (2008), "Drinking Water Protests in Egypt and the Role of Civil Society," in *Reclaiming Public Water,* Transnational Institute, April 9, at http://www.tni.org/sites/www.tni.org/files/drinking_water_protest_in_egypt_by_abdel_mawla.pdf (accessed June 16, 2014).

Jayousi, Anan (2010), "The Oslo II Accords in Retrospective: Implementation of the Water Provisions in the Israeli and Palestinian Interim Peace Agreements," in Rabbo, Alfred Abed, and Tal, Alon, eds., *Water Wisdom,* Piscataway, NJ, Rutgers University Press, 43–48.

Johnson, D. Gale (1950), "The Nature of the Supply Function for Agricultural Products," *Journal of Farm Economics* 42, 2, 539–564.

Johnston, Bruce, and Kilby, Peter (1975), *Agriculture and Structural Transformation: Economic Strategies in Late-Developing Countries,* New York, Oxford University Press.

Johnstone, Sarah, and Mazo, Jeffrey (2011), "Global Warming and the Arab Spring," *Survival: Global Politics and Strategy* 53, 2, 11–17.

Katouzian, Homa (1981), *The Political Economy of Modern Iran: Despotism and Pseudo-Modernism, 1926–1979,* New York, New York University Press.

Khashman, Khaldon (2011), "Best Practices in Decentralizing the Management of the Water Sector in the Arab States," United Nations Development Program, World Governance Program for Arab States, at http://www.wgpas-undp.org/Reports/Final%20Report%20Decentralization.pdf (accessed September 1, 2013).

Kherallah, Mylene, Minot, Nicholas, and Gruhn, Peter (2003), "Adjustment of Wheat Production to Market Reform in Egypt," in Lofgren, H., ed., *Food, Agriculture, and Economy in the Middle East and North Africa, Research in Middle East Economics* 5, 133–160.

Land Center for Human Rights (LCHR) (1999), "Violence in the Egyptian Countryside: 1998–1999," at www.derechos.org/human-rights/mena/lchr/violence.html.

Leveau, Rémy (1985), *Le Fellah marocain: Defenseur du trone,* Paris, Presses de la FNSP.

Lichtenhaler, Gerhard (2010), "Water Conflict and Cooperation in Yemen," *Middle East Report* 254 (Spring), at http://www.merip.org/mer/mer254/water-conflict-cooperation-yemen (accessed September 2, 2013).

Lichtenthaler, G., and Turton, A. R. (1999), "Water Demand Management, Natural Resource Reconstruction, and Traditional Value Systems: A Case Study from Yemen," London, Water Issues Study Group, School of Oriental and African Studies, University of London, Occasional Paper 14.

Little, I. M. D., Scitovsky, Tibor, and Scott, Maurice (1970), *Industry and Trade in Some Developing Countries,* London, Oxford University Press.

Lofgren, Hans, and Richards, Alan (2003), "Food Security, Poverty and Economic Policy in the Middle East and North Africa," in Lofgren, H., ed., *Food, Agriculture, and Economy in the Middle East and North Africa, Research in Middle East Economics* 5, 1–32.

McFarlane, Sarah (2013), "Egypt's Wheat Problem: How Mursi Jeopardized the Bread Supply," Reuters, July 25, at http://www.reuters.com/article/2013/07/25/us-egypt-mistakes-wheat-idUSBRE96O07N20130725.

McFerron, Whitney (2013), "Saudi Arabia Wheat Output Seen Dropping 10% by UN on Phase Out," *Bloomberg Businessweek,* May 20, at http://www.businessweek.com/news/2013-05-20/saudi-arabia-wheat-output-seen-dropping-10-percent-by-un-on-phase-out (accessed September 2, 2013).

Mellor, John (1976), *The New Economics of Growth: A Strategy for India and the Developing World,* Ithaca, NY, Cornell University Press.

Mitchell, Timothy (2002), *Rule of Experts: Egypt, Techno-Politics, Modernity,* Berkeley, University of California Press.

Moghadem, Fatemah Etemad (1982), "Farm Size, Management, and Productivity: A Study of Four Iranian Villages," *Oxford Bulletin of Economics and Statistics* 44, 4 (November), 357–379.

Nasser, Rabie, Mehchy, Zaki, and Ismail, Khaled Abu (2013), "Socioeconomic Roots and Impact of the Syrian Crisis," Syrian Center for Policy Research, at http://scpr-syria.org/en/S34/%E2%80%9CSocioeconomic-Roots-and-Impact-of-the-Syrian-Crisis%E2%80%9D-2013.

Nouschi, Andre (1970), "North Africa in the Period of Colonization," in *Cambridge History of Islam,* vol. 1, *The Further Islamic Lands: Islamic Society and Civilization,* Cambridge, Cambridge University Press, 299–326.

Olmsted, Jennifer (2003), "Reexamining the Fertility Puzzle in MENA," in Doumato, Eleanor Abdella, and Posusney, Marsha Pripstein, eds., *Women and Globalization in the Arab Middle East: Gender, Economy, and Society,* Boulder, CO, Lynne Rienner Publishers, 73–92.

Owen, Roger (1986), "Large Landowners, Agricultural Progress, and the State in Egypt, 1800–1970: An Overview," in Richards, Alan, ed., *Food, States, and Peasants: Analyses of the Agrarian Question in the Middle East,* Boulder, CO, Westview Press, 69–96.

Paulino, Leonardo (1986), *Food in the Third World: Past Trends and Projections to 2000,* International Food Policy Research Institute (IFPRI) Research Report 52 (June).

Pfeiffer, Tom (2012), "Morocco to Lease 30,000 Hectares of Farms per Year," Reuters, April 30, at http://www.reuters.com/article/2010/04/30/ozatp-food-morocco-grain-idAFJOE63T00X20100430 (accessed September 3, 2013).

Post, Alison (2014), "The Politics of 'Contracting Out' to the Private Sector: The Case of Water and Sanitation in Argentina," in *Foreign and Domestic Investment in Argentina: The Politics of Privatized Infrastructure,* Cambridge, Cambridge University Press.

Prunier, Gerard (2005), *Darfur: The Ambiguous Genocide,* Ithaca, NY, Cornell University Press.

Qadir, Manzoor, Bahri, Akissa, Sato, Toshio, Al-Karadsheh, Esmat (2010), "Wastewater Production, Treatment, and Irrigation in Middle East and North Africa." *Irrigation Drainage Systems* 24, 37–51.

Reuters (2013), "Egypt Sees Wheat Self-Sufficiency for Subsidy Program by 2019," *Egypt Independent,* November 19, at http://www.egyptindependent.com/news/egypt-sees-wheat-self-sufficiency-subsidy-program-2019.

Richards, Alan (1982), *Egypt's Agricultural Development, 1800–1980: Technical and Social Change,* Boulder, CO, Westview Press.

Richards, Alan (2002), "Coping with Water Scarcity: The Governance Challenge," University of California, Institute for Global Cooperation and Conflict (IGCC) Policy Paper 54, at http://repositories.cdlib.org/cgi/viewcontent.cgi?article=1050&context=igcc.

Rosegrant, Mark W., and Binswanger, Hans (1994), "Markets in Tradable Water Rights: Potential for Efficiency Gains in Developing Country Water Resource Allocation," *World Development* 22, 11, 1613–1625.

Salman, M., and Mualla, W. (2008), "Water Demand Management in Syria: Centralized and Decentralized Views," *Water Policy* 10, 6, 549–562.

Selby, Jan (2003), *Water, Power, and Politics in the Middle East,* London, I. B. Tauris.

Sen, Amartya (1981), *Poverty and Famines: An Essay on Entitlement and Deprivation,* Oxford, Oxford University Press.

Shah, Tushaar, Molden, David, Sahthivadivel, R., and Seckler, David (2000), *The Global Groundwater Situation: Overview of Opportunities and Challenges,* Colombo, Sri Lanka, International Water Management Institute.

Shaheed, Ahmed, Orgill, Jennifer, Montgomery, Maggie A., Jeuland, Marc A., and Brown, Joe (2014), "Why 'Improved' Water Sources Are Not Always Safe," *Bull World Health Organ* 92, 283–289, at http://dx.doi.org/10.2471/BLT.13.119594 (accessed June 26, 2014).

Sheffield, Justin, and Wood, Eric F. (2008), "Projected Changes in Drought Occurrence Under Future Global Warming from Multi-Model, Multi-Scenario, IPCC AR4 Simulations," *Climate Dynamics* 31, 79–105.

Small Arms Survey (2010), "Under Pressure: Social Violence over Land and Water in Yemen," Yemen Armed Violence Assessment Issue Brief 2 (October), at http://www.yemenviolence.org/pdfs/Yemen-Armed-Violence-IB2-Social-violence-over-land-and-water-in-Yemen.pdf.

Smith, Tony (1975), "The Political and Economic Ambitions of Algerian Land Reform, 1962–1974," *Middle East Journal* 29, 3 (Summer), 259–278.

Sowers, Jeannie, Vengosh, Avner, and Weinthal, Erika (2011), "Climate Change, Water Resources, and the Politics of Adaptation in the Middle East and North Africa," *Climatic Change* 104, 3–4, 599–627, at doi:http://dx.doi.org/10.1007/s10584-010-9835-4.

Springborg, Robert (1981), "Baathism in Practice: Agriculture, Politics, and Political Culture in Syria and Iraq," *Middle Eastern Studies* 17, 2 (April), 191–209.

Swearingen, Will D. (1987), *Moroccan Mirages: Agrarian Dreams and Deceptions, 1912–1986,* Princeton, NJ, Princeton University Press.

Tignor, Robert L. (1984), *State, Private Enterprise, and Economic Change in Egypt, 1918–1952,* Princeton, NJ, Princeton University Press.

Timmer, C. Peter, Falcon, Walter P., and Pearson, Scott (1983), *Food Policy Analysis,* Baltimore, Johns Hopkins University Press.

Tuluy, A. Hassan, and Salinger, B. Lynn (1991), "Morocco," in Anne O. Krueger, Maurice Schiff, and Alberto Valdes, eds., *The Political Economy of Agricultural Pricing Policy,* vol. 3, *Africa and the Mediterranean,* Baltimore, Johns Hopkins University Press for the World Bank, 122–170.

Tuma, Elias (1978), "Bottlenecks and Constraints in Agrarian Reform in the Near East," Rome, FAO, World Conference on Agrarian Reform and Rural Institutions Background Paper.

Tyner, Wallace (1993), "Agricultural Sector Analysis and Adjustment: Recent Experiences in North Africa and the Baltics," lecture at USAID, sponsored by Agricultural Policy Analysis Project-II, Washington, DC, May 19.

UNICEF and World Health Organization (WHO) (2011), UNICEF/WHO Joint Monitoring Programme, at http://www.wssinfo.org/documents/?tx_displaycontroller%5Btype%5D=reference_documents.

United Nations Human Rights Council (2014), "Genocide in Darfur," November 19, at http://www.unitedhumanrights.org/genocide/genocide-in-sudan.htm.

US Department of Agriculture (USDA) (1987), *Middle East and North Africa: Situation and Outlook Report,* Washington, DC, Economic Research Service.

US Department of Agriculture (USDA) Foreign Agricultural Service (FAS) (2012a), *Morocco Grain and Feed Annual, March 2012,* Rabat, US Embassy, GAIN Report 1203, March 12, at http://gain.fas.usda.gov/Recent%20GAIN%20Publications/Grain%20and%20Feed%20Annual_Rabat_Morocco_3-12-2012.pdf.

US Department of Agriculture (USDA) Foreign Agricultural Service (FAS) (2012b), *Morocco Grain and Feed Update, July 2012,* Rabat, US Embassy, GAIN Report 1209, July 25, at http://www.thefarmsite.com/reports/contents/morgupau12.pdf.

US Department of Agriculture (USDA), Foreign Agricultural Service (FAS) (2013a), "Morocco Grain and Feed Annual," 2012 GAIN Report 1203, March 12, Rabat, US Embassy, at http://gain.fas.usda.gov/Recent%20GAIN%20Publications/Grain%20and%20Feed%20Annual_Rabat_Morocco_3-12-2012.pdf (accessed September 4, 2013).

US Department of Agriculture (USDA), Foreign Agricultural Service (FAS) (2013b), "Morocco Grain and Feed Update," 2012 GAIN Report 1209, July 25, Rabat, US Embassy, at http://www.thefarmsite.com/reports/contents/morgupau12.pdf (accessed September 4, 2013).

Valdes, Alberton (1989), "Comment on 'The Policy Response of Agriculture' by Binswanger," *Proceedings of the World Bank Annual Conference on Development Economics,* 263–268.

Van der Kloet, Hendrik (1975), *Inégalités dans les milieux ruraux: Possibilités et problèmes de la modernisation agricole au Maroc,* Geneva, United Nations Research on International Social Development (UNRISD).

Viney, Steven (2012), "Abandoned by the System, Egypt's Farmers Suffer Discrimination, Violence, and Poverty," *Egypt Independent,* September 16, at http://www.egyptindependent.com/news/abandoned-system-egypt-s-farmers-suffer-discrimination-violence-and-poverty (accessed September 3, 2013).

Ward, Christopher (2000), "The Political Economy of Irrigation Water Pricing in Yemen," in Dinar, Ariel, ed., *The Political Economy of Water Pricing Reform,* Washington, DC, World Bank.

Ward, Christopher (2007), "Practical Responses to Extreme Groundwater Overdraft in Yemen," in Mahdi, Kamil A., Würth, Anna, and Lackner, Helen, eds., *Yemen into the Twenty-First Century: Continuity and Change,* Reading, UK, Ithaca Press, 155–181.

Waterbury, John (1979), *Hydropolitics of the Nile Valley,* Syracuse, NY, Syracuse University Press.

White, Chris (2012), "Understanding Water Scarcity: Definitions and Measurements," Global Water Forum, May 7, at http://www.globalwaterforum.org/2012/05/07/understanding-water-scarcity-definitions-and-measurements/ (accessed June 16, 2014).

Wilson, Peter W., and Graham, Douglas F. (1994), *Saudi Arabia: The Coming Storm,* New York, M. E. Sharpe.

World Bank (1985), *Sudan: Prospects for Rehabilitation of the Sudanese Economy,* Report 5496-SU, October 7.

World Bank (1986), *Poverty and Hunger,* Washington, DC.

World Bank (1987), *World Development Report,* New York, Oxford University Press.

World Bank (2001), *Syrian Arab Republic: Irrigation Sector Report,* report no. 22602-SYR, Washington, D.C.

World Bank (2003), *Middle East and North Africa Region Strategy Paper,* Washington, DC.

World Bank (2006), "Tunisia Agricultural Policy Review," Washington, DC, Report 35239-TN, July 20, at http://www-wds.worldbank.org/external/default/WDSContentServer/WDSP/IB/2006/11 /14/000011823_20061114112932/Rendered/PDF/352390TN.pdf (accessed September 3, 2013).

World Bank (2007a), "Distortions to Agricultural Incentives in Egypt," Washington, DC, Agricultural Distortions Working Paper 36, at http://siteresources.worldbank.org/INTTRADERESEARCH/ Resources/544824-1146153362267/Egypt_0708.pdf (accessed September 3, 2013).

World Bank (2007b), "Making the Most of Scarcity: Accountability for Better Water Management Results in the Middle East and North Africa," Washington, DC, MENA Development Report, at http://siteresources.worldbank.org/INTMENA/Resources/Water_Scarcity_Full.pdf (accessed September 1, 2013).

World Bank (2009a), "Assessment of Restrictions on Palestinian Water Sector Development," Washington, DC, at http://siteresources.worldbank.org/INTWESTBANKGAZA/Resources/ WaterRestrictionsReport18Apr2009.pdf (accessed September 1, 2013).

World Bank (2009b), *Improving Food Security in Arab Countries,* Washington, DC, World Bank.

World Bank (various years), World Development Indicators (WDI), at http://publications.worldbank .org/ecommerce/catalog/product?item_id=631625.

Yohannes, Okbazghi, and Yohannes, Keren (2013), "Turmoil on the Nile River: Back to the Future?" *Journal of Asian and African Studies* 48, 195–208.

Zghal, Abdelkader (1977), "Pourquoi la réforme agraire ne mobilise-t-elle pas les paysans, Maghrebins?" in Etiènne, Bruno, ed., *Problèmes agraires au Maghreb,* Paris, Éditions du CNRS, 295–312.

CHAPTER 7: THE RISE AND FALL OF STATE-LED DEVELOPMENT

Ahmad, Feroz (1981), "The Political Economy of Kemalism," in Kazancigil, Ali, and Özbudun, Ergun, eds., *Ataturk: Founder of a Modern State,* Hamden, CT, Archon Books, 145–164.

Al-Khafaji, 'Issam (1983), *The State and the Evolution of Capitalism in Iraq: 1968–1978* (in Arabic), Cairo, Dar al-Mustaqbal al-Arabi.

Al-Khalil, Samir (1989), *Republic of Fear,* New York, Pantheon Books.

Alnasrawi, Abbas (1986), "Economic Consequences of the Iraq-Iran War," *Third World Quarterly* 8, 3, 869–895.

Alnasrawi, Abbas (1992), "Iraq: Economic Consequences of the 1991 Gulf War and Future Outlook," *Third World Quarterly* 13, 2, 335–352.

Anderson, Lisa (1986), *The State and Social Transformation in Tunisia and Libya, 1930–1980,* Princeton, NJ, Princeton University Press.

Arian, Asher (1985), *Politics in Israel: The Second Generation,* Chatham, NJ, Chatham House.

Ayubi, Nazih (1985), "Arab Bureaucracies: Expanding Size, Changing Roles," master's thesis, Politics Department, University of Exeter.

Bakhash, Shaul (1984), *The Reign of the Ayatollahs,* New York, Basic Books.

Batatu, Hanna (1978), *The Old Social Classes and the Revolutionary Movements of Iraq,* Princeton, NJ, Princeton University Press.

Beblawi, Hazem (1984), *The Arab Gulf Economy in a Turbulent Age,* London, Croom Helm.

Ben-Dor, Gabriel (1983), *State and Conflict in the Middle East,* New York, Praeger.

Bienen, Henry S., and Gersovitz, M. (1985), "Economic Stabilization, Conditionality, and Political Stability," *International Organization* 39, 4 (Autumn), 729–754.

Boratav, Korkut (1981), "Kemalist Economic Policies and Etatism," in Kazancigil, Ali, and Özbudun, Ergun, eds., *Ataturk: Founder of a Modern State,* Hamden, CT, Archon Books, 165–190.

Celasun, Merih (1983), *Sources of Industrial Growth and Structural Change: The Case of Turkey,* Washington, DC, World Bank, Staff Working Paper 641.

Central Intelligence Agency (CIA) (various years), World Factbook Online, at http://www.cia.gov/cia /publications/factbook/index.html.

Chatelus, Michel (1982), "De la rente pétrolière au développement économique: Perspectives et contradictions de l'évolution économique dans la péninsule," in Bonnenfant, Paul, ed., *La Peninsule arabique d'aujourd'hui,* vol. 1, Paris, Éditions du CNRS, 75–154.

Destanne de Bernis, G. (1971), "Industries industrialisantes et options algériennes," *Tiers Monde* 47, 545–563.

Drysdale, Alasdair (1982), "The Asad Regime and Its Troubles," *Middle East Research and Information Project (MERIP) Reports* 110 (November-December), 3–11.

Economic Research Forum (ERF) and Institut de la Méditerranée (IM) (2005), *Turkey Country Profile: The Road Ahead for Turkey,* Cairo, Economic Research Forum and Institut de la Méditerranée.

El-Malki, Habib (1982), *L'Économie Marocaine: Bilan d'une décennie, 1970–1980,* Paris, Éditions du CNRS.

El-Midaoui, Ahmed (1981), *Les Entreprises publiques au Maroc et leur participation au développement,* Casablanca, Éditions Afrique-Orient.

Esfanani, Hadi, and Gurakar, Esra (2014), "Social Order, Rents, and Economic Development in Iran Since the Early 20th Century," in Diwan, Ishac, ed., *Understanding the Political Economy of the Arab Uprisings,* Singapore, World Scientific, 219–262.

Fathaly, Omar, and Palmer, Monte (1980), *Political Development and Social Change in Libya,* Lexington, MA, Lexington Books.

Floyd, Robert H. (1984), "Some Topical Issues Concerning Public Enterprises," in Floyd, Robert, Gray, Clive S., and Short, R. P., *Public Enterprise in Mixed Economies: Some Macroeconomic Aspects,* Washington, DC, IMF, 1–35.

Hale, William (1981), *The Political and Economic Development of Modern Turkey,* London, Croom Helm.

Hannoyer, Jean, and Seurat, Michel (1979), *État et secteur public industriel en Syrie,* Lyon, Centre des Études et des Recherches sur le Moyen Orient Contemporain (CERMOC), Presses Universitaires de Lyon.

Harris, Kevan (2013), "Vectors of Iranian Capitalism: Privatization Politics in the Islamic Republic," in Hertog, Steffan, Luciani, Giacomo, and Valeri, Mark, eds., *Business Politics in the Middle East,* London, Hurst Publishers, 211–244.

Hershlag, Z. Y. (1968), *Turkey: The Challenge of Growth,* Leiden, E. J. Brill.

Hertog, Steffen, Luciani, Giacomo, and Valeri, Marc, eds. (2013), *Business Politics in the Middle East,* London, Hurst Publishers.

Horton, Brendan (1990), *Morocco: Analysis and Reform of Economic Policy,* Washington, DC, World Bank.

Islami, A. Reza, and Kavoussi, R. M. (1984), *The Political Economy of Saudi Arabia,* Near Eastern Studies no. 1, Seattle, University of Washington Press.

Issawi, Charles (1978), "The Iranian Economy 1925–1975: Fifty Years of Economic Development," in Lenczowski, George, ed., *Iran Under the Pahlevis,* Stanford, CA, Hoover Institution, 129–166.

Karpat, Kemal (1959), *Turkey's Politics,* Princeton, NJ, Princeton University Press.

Katouzian, Homa (1981), *The Political Economy of Modern Iran: Despotism and Pseudo-Modernism, 1926–1979,* New York, New York University Press.

Khoury, Philip (1983), *Urban Notables and Arab Nationalism: The Politics of Damascus, 1860–1920,* New York, Columbia University Press.

Kimmerling, Baruch (1983), *Zionism and Economy,* Cambridge, Schenkman.

Kubursi, Afif (1984), *Oil, Industrialization, and Development in the Arab Gulf States,* London, Croom Helm.

Leca, Jean (1975), "Algerian Socialism: Nationalism, Industrialization, and State Building," in Desfosses, Helen, and Levesque, Jacques, eds., *Socialism in the Third World,* New York, Praeger.

Lewis, Bernard (1961), *The Emergence of Modern Turkey,* Oxford, Oxford University Press.

Longuenesse, Elisabeth (1979), "The Class Nature of the State in Syria," *Middle East Research and Information Project (MERIP) Reports* 9, 4 (May), 3–11.

Longuenesse, Elisabeth (1985), "Syrie, secteur public industriel," *Maghreb-Machrek* 109 (July–September), 5–24.

Morrison, Christian (1991), *Adjustment and Equity in Morocco,* Paris, OECD Development Centre.

Nelson, Harold D., ed. (1985), *Algeria: A Country Study,* Washington, DC, Area Handbook Series, American University Press.

Öniç, Ziya, and Webb, Steven (1994), "Turkey: Democratization and Adjustment from Above," in Haggard, Stephan, and Webb, Steven B., eds., *Voting for Reform: Democracy, Political Liberalization, and Economic Adjustment,* Washington, DC, World Bank.

Penrose, Edith, and Penrose, E. F. (1978), *Iraq: International Relations and National Development,* Boulder, CO, Ernest Benn/Westview Press.

Razavi, Hossein, and Vakil, Firouz (1984), *The Political Environment of Economic Planning in Iran, 1971–1983,* Boulder, CO, Westview Press.

Rivier, François (1980), *Croissance industrielle dans une économie assistée: Le Cas Jordanien,* Lyon, CER-MOC, Presses Universitaires de Lyon.

Rivlin, Paul (2009), *Arab Economies in the Twenty-First Century,* Cambridge, Cambridge University Press.

Roos, Leslie, and Roos, Noralou (1971), *Managers of Modernization: Organization and Elites in Turkey (1950–1969),* Cambridge, MA, Harvard University Press.

Rosenfeld, H., and Carmi, S. (1976), "The Privatization of Public Means, the State-Made Middle Class, and the Realization of Family Value in Israel," in Peristiany, J. G., ed., *Kinship and Modernization in Mediterranean Society,* Rome, American Universities Field Staff, 131–153.

Schwedler, Jillian (2013), "Islamists in Power? Inclusion, Moderation, and the Arab Uprisings," *Middle East Development Journal* 5, 1, March.

Stork, Joe (1982), "State Power and Economic Structure: Class Determination and State Formation in Contemporary Iraq," in Niblock, Tim, ed., *Iraq: The Contemporary State,* London, Croom Helm 27–46.

Walstedt, Bertil (1980), *State Manufacturing Enterprise in a Mixed Economy: The Turkish Case,* Baltimore and London, World Bank and Johns Hopkins University Press.

Waterbury, John (1983), *The Egypt of Nasser and Sadat: The Political Economy of Two Regimes,* Princeton, NJ, Princeton University Press.

Waterbury, John (1992), "Export-Led Growth and the Center-Right Coalition in Turkey," *Comparative Politics* 24, 2.

World Bank (1995), *Bureaucrats in Business: The Economics and Politics of Government Ownership,* New York, Oxford University Press.

CHAPTER 8: STRUCTURAL ADJUSTMENT
AND THE RISE OF CRONY CAPITALISM

Achy, Lahcen (2010), "Morocco's Experience with Poverty Reduction: Lessons for the Arab World," December, Carnegie Middle East Center, Paper 25.

African Economic Outlook (2014), Algeria 2014, AfDB, OECD, and UNDP.

Alley, April Longley (2010), "The Rules of the Game: Unpacking Patronage Politics in Yemen," *Middle East Journal* 64, 3, 385–409.

Al-Mashat, Rania A., and Grigorian, David A. (1998), "Economic Reforms in Egypt: Emerging Patterns and Their Possible Implications," World Bank, Policy Research Working Paper 1977.

Amsden, Alice H. (1992), *Asia's Next Giant: South Korea and Late Industrialization,* New York and London, Oxford University Press.

Amsden, Alice H. (2001), *The Rise of "The Rest": Challenges to the West from Late-Industrializing Countries,* New York and London, Oxford University Press.

Amuzegar, Jahangir (1983), *Oil Exporters' Economic Development in an Interdependent World,* IMF Occasional Paper 18.

Aran, Meltem, Demir, Sırma, Sarıca, Özlem, and Yazıcı, Hakan (2010), "Poverty and Inequality Changes in Turkey (2003–2006)," Ankara, State Planning Organization of the Republic of Turkey and the World Bank, Welfare and Social Policy Analytical Work Program, Working Paper 1, March.

Atiyas, Izak (2012), "Regulatory Innovations in Turkey," in Diwan, Ishac, ed., *Understanding the Political Economy of the Arab Uprisings,* London and Hackensack, NJ, World Scientific, 2014.

Atiyas, Izak (2014), "Enhancing Competition in a Post-Revolutionary Arab Context: Does the Turkish Experience Provide Any Lessons?" in Ishac Diwan, ed., *Understanding the Political Economy of the Arab Uprisings,* London and Hackensack, NJ, World Scientific.

Atiyas, Izak, Bakis, Ozan, Dutz, Mark, Rowe, Francis, and O'Connell, Stephen (forthcoming), "Enterprise Growth in Turkey in the 2000s: A Story of Structural Change and Regional Convergence?" Washington, DC, World Bank, Staff Working Paper.

Beaugé, Florence (2011), "Orange Tunisie passe sous la tutelle de l'état Tunisien," *Le Monde,* March 30, 18.

Bechri, Mohamed Z., and Naccache, Sonia (2003), "The Political Economy of Development Policy in Tunisia," Cairo, Economic Research Forum, www.erf.org.eg/grp/GRP_Sep03/Tunisia-Pol_Econ.pdf.

Beinin, Joel, and Vairel, Frédéric, eds. (2011), *Social Movements, Mobilization, and Contestation in the Middle East and North Africa,* Stanford, CA, Stanford University Press.

Bellin, Eva (2002), *Stalled Democracy: Capital, Labor, and the Paradox of State-Sponsored Development,* Ithaca, NY, Cornell University Press.

Bennoune, Mahfoud (1988), *The Making of Contemporary Algeria, 1830–1987,* Cambridge, Cambridge University Press.

Bergh, Sylvia (2005), "Explaining Slow Economic Growth and Poor Social Development Indicators: The Case of Morocco," Oxford, Oxford Council on Good Governance, *Economy Analysis* 7 (October).

Boubekeur, Amel (2013), "Rolling Either Way? Algerian Entrepreneurs as Both Agents of Change and Means of Preservation of the System," *Journal of North African Studies* 18, 3, 469–481.

BSB (2005), "Turkey in 2005 and Beyond: Macroeconomic Policy, Patterns of Growth, and Persistent Fragilities," *Bagimsiz Sosyal Bilimciler* (Independent Social Scientists Alliance), posted to Global Policy Network, June 9, at http://www.gpn.org/data/turkey/turkey-analysis.pdf.

Cammett, Melanie (2004), "Challenges to Networks of Privilege in Morocco: Implications for Network Analysis," in Heydemann, Steven, ed., *Networks of Privilege in the Middle East: The Politics of Economic Reform Revisited,* New York, Palgrave Macmillan, 245–280.

Cammett, Melani Claire (2007), "Business-Government Relations and Industrial Change: The Politics of Upgrading in Morocco and Tunisia," *World Development* 35, 11, 1889–1903.

Chang, Ha-Joon (2002), *Kicking Away the Ladder: Development Strategy in Historical Perspective,* London, Anthem Press.

Chaudhry, Kiren Aziz (1993), "The Myths of the Market and the Common History of Late Developers," *Politics and Society* 21, 3, September.

Chekir, Hamouda, and Diwan, Ishac (2013), "Distressed Whales on the Nile: Egypt Capitalists in the Wake of the 2010 Revolution," April, Economic Research Forum, Working Paper 747.

Chekir, Hamouda, and Menard, Claude (2012), "Barriers to Private Firm Dynamism in Tunisia: A Qualitative Approach," Washington, DC, World Bank.

Chemingui, Mohamed Abdelbasset, and Ayadi, Nassima (2003), "Understanding the Poor Human Capital Contribution to Economic Growth in Algeria," Global Development Project on Explaining Growth in Developing Countries: The Case of Algeria, at http://www.gdnet.org/pdf2/gdn_library/global_research_projects/explaining_growth/Algeria_human_capital_final.pdf.

Denoeux, Guilain (2001), "Morocco's Economic Prospects: Daunting Challenges Ahead," *Middle East Policy* 8, 2 (June), 66–87.

Devaux, Pascal (2003), "Iran: The Future of the Rentier System in Question," *Conjuncture,* London, BNP Paribas (October).

Diwan, Ishac, Keefer, Philip, and Schiffbauer, Mark (2014), "On Top of the Pyramids: Cronyism and Private-Sector Growth in Egypt," Economic Research Forum Working Paper.

Diwan, Ishac, and Nabli, Mustapha (2013), "How Does the Arab Street View the Private Sector? An Analysis of the Gallup Polls 2009–2012 in 18 Arab Countries," Geneva, Switzerland, World Economic Forum.

Easterly, William (2011), "The Lost Decades: Developing Countries' Stagnation in Spite of Policy Reform, 1980–1998," *Journal of Economic Growth* 6, 1, 135–157.

Economic Research Forum (ERF) and Institut de la Méditerranée (IM) (2005), *Turkey Country Profile: The Road Ahead for Turkey,* Cairo, Economic Research Forum and Institut de la Méditerranée.

Elster, Jon (1979), *Ulysses and the Sirens: Studies in Rationality and Irrationality,* Cambridge, Cambridge University Press.

Ersel, Hassan (2013), "Politico-Economic Developments in Turkey and the Transformation of Political Islam," *Middle East Development Journal,* 5, 1, March.

Fishlow, Albert, et al. (1994), *Miracle or Design? Lessons from the East Asia Experience,* Washington, DC, Overseas Development Council.

Gray, John (1998), *False Dawn: The Delusions of Global Capitalism,* New York, New Press.

Habibi, Nader (2013), "The Economic Legacy of Mahmoud Ahmadinejad," Waltham, MA, Brandeis University, Crown Center for Middle East Studies, MEB74.

Haddad, Bassam (2012), *Business Networks in Syria: The Political Economy of Authoritarian Resilience,* Stanford, CA, Stanford University Press.

Harris, Kevan (2013), "Vectors of Iranian Capitalism: Privatization Politics in the Islamic Republic," in Hertog, Steffen, Luciani, Giacomo, and Valeri, Marc, eds., *Business Politics in the Middle East,* London, Hurst Publishers.

Hegasy, Sonja (2007), "Young Authority: Quantitative and Qualitative Insights into Youth, Youth Culture, and State Power in Contemporary Morocco," *Journal of North African Studies* 12, 1, 19–36.

Henry, Clement (1996), *The Mediterranean Debt Crescent: Money and Power in Algeria, Egypt, Morocco, Tunisia, and Turkey,* Gainesville, University Press of Florida.

Henry, Clement M. (2003), "The Clash of Globalizations in the Middle East," *Review of Middle East Economics and Finances,* 1, 1, 3–16.

Henry, Clement Moore, and Springborg, Robert (2006), *Globalization and the Politics of Development in the Middle East,* vol. 1, Cambridge, Cambridge University Press.

Henry, Clement M., and Springborg, Robert (2010), *Globalization and the Politics of Development in the Middle East,* vol. 1, 2nd ed., Cambridge, Cambridge University Press.

Hertog, Steffen (2013), "Introduction," in Hertog, Steffen, Luciani, Giacomo, and Valeri, Marc, eds., *Business Politics in the Middle East,* London, Hurst Publishers.

Heydemann, Steven, ed. (2004), *Networks of Privilege in the Middle East: The Politics of Economic Reform Revisited,* New York, Palgrave Macmillan.

Hibou, Beatrice (2004), "Fiscal Trajectories in Morocco and Tunisia," in Heydemann, Steven, ed., *Networks of Privilege in the Middle East: The Politics of Economic Reform Revisited,* New York, Palgrave Macmillan, 201–222.

International Crisis Group (ICG) (2001), *Algeria's Economy: The Vicious Circle of Oil and Violence,* Africa Report 36 (October 26), Brussels.

International Monetary Fund (IMF) (2012), "Tunisia: Financial System Stability Assessment," August, IMF Country Report 12/241.

International Monetary Fund (IMF) (2013), Algeria 2012 article IV consultation, IMF Country Report 13/47 (February).

Kaboub, Fadel (2014), "The Making of the Tunisian Revolution," in Diwan, Ishac, ed., *Understanding the Political Economy of the Arab Uprisings,* London and Hackensack, NJ, World Scientific.

Keyder, Caglar (2004), "The Turkish Bell Jar," *New Left Review* 28 (July-August), 65–84.

Khan, Mohsin, and Mezran, Karim (2014), "No Arab Spring for Algeria" (May 29), Atlantic Council, Issue Brief.

Kienle, Eberhard (2002), *Contemporary Syria: Liberalization Between Cold War and Cold Peace,* London, University of London, Centre of Near and Middle Eastern Studies.

King, Stephen (2009), *The New Authoritarianism in the Middle East and North Africa,* Bloomington, Indiana University Press.

Layachi, Azzedine (1999), "Economic Reform and Elusive Political Change in Morocco," in Zoubir, Yahia H., ed., *North Africa in Transition: State, Society, and Economic Transformation in the 1990s,* Gainesville, University Press of Florida, 43–60.

Lowi, Miriam R. (2005), "War-Torn or Systematically Distorted: Rebuilding the Algerian Economy," paper presented at the workshop "Rebuilding War-Torn Economies in the Middle East and North Africa," University of California, Los Angeles, Center for Near Eastern Studies, February 4–5.

Malik, Adeel, and Awadallah, Bassem (2013), "The Economics of the Arab Spring," *World Development* 45, 296–313.

Mansouri, Brahim, et al. (2004), "The Role of Political and Institutional Factors in the Moroccan Reform Process," 11th Economic Reform Forum Conference, Beirut, December, at http://www.erf.org.eg/11conf_Lebanon/Macro/Mansouri&Riger&Ziky.pdf.

Martinez, Luis (1998), *The Algerian Civil War, 1990–1998,* trans. Jonathan Derrick, New York, Columbia University Press.

Mojaverhosseini, Farshid (2003), "An Inquiry into the Sources of Growth and Stagnation in the Iranian Economy," International Center for Economic Research, Working Paper 12/203 (March).

Noland, Marcus, and Pack, Howard (2007), *The Arab Economies in a Changing World,* Washington, DC, Peterson Institute for International Economics.

Öniç, Ziya (2004), "The Political Economy of Turkey's Justice and Development Party," November 4, at http://papers.ssrn.com/sol3/papers.cfm?abstract_id=659463.

Öniç, Ziya, and Senses, Fikret (2003), "Rethinking the Emerging Post–Washington Consensus: A Critical Appraisal," Ankara, Middle East Technical University, Economics Research Center, Working Paper in Economics 03/09.

Osman, Tarek (2010), *Egypt on the Brink: From Nasser to Mubarak,* New Haven, CT, Yale University Press.

Owen, Roger (2004), *State, Power and Politics in the Making of the Modern Middle East,* 3rd ed., London, Routledge.

Pew Research Center (2011), "Arab Spring Fails to Improve US Image," Washington, DC, Pew Research, Global Attitudes Project.

Posusney, Marsha Pripstein, and Angrist, Michele Penner (2005), *Authoritarianism in the Middle East: Regimes and Resistance,* Boulder, CO, Lynne Rienner Publishers.

Richards, Alan (1991), "The Political Economy of Dilatory Reform: Egypt in the 1990s," *World Development* 19, 12, 1721–1730.

Rijkers, Bob, Freund, Caroline, and Nucifora, Antonio (2013), "The Perils of Industrial Policy: Evidence from Tunisia," Washington, DC, World Bank, at http://siteresources.worldbank.org/FINANCIALSECTOR/Resources/PerilsofIndustrialPolicy_Tunisia.pdf.

Rivlin, Paul (2009), *Arab Economies in the Twenty-First Century,* Cambridge, Cambridge University Press.

Rodrik, Dani (2004), "Rethinking Growth Policies in the Developing World," Luca d'Angliano Lecture in Development Economics, Turin, Italy, October 8.

Rodrik, Dani (2012), *Who Needs the Nation State?* London, Centre for Economic Policy Research (CEPR), CEPR Discussion Paper 9040.

Sadowski, Yahya M. (1991), *Political Vegetables? Businessman and Bureaucrat in the Development of Egyptian Agriculture,* Washington, DC, Brookings Institution Press.

Salehi-Isfahani, Djavad (2009), "Poverty, Inequality, and Populist Politics in Iran," *Journal of Economic Inequality* 7, 1, March, 5–24.

Salehi-Isfahani, Djavad (2013), "The Future of the Iranian Labor Market: Demography and Education," London, Legatum Institute, at http://www.li.com/docs/default-source/future-of-iran/the-future-of-iran-economy-the-future-of-the-iranian-labour-market-demography-and-education-pdf-.pdf?sfvrsn=4.

Salehi-Isfahani, Djavad (2014), "Iran's Subsidy Reform: From Promise to Disappointment," Economic Research Forum (ERF), Policy Perspective 13.

Schlumberger, Oliver, ed. (2007), *Debating Arab Authoritarianism: Dynamics and Durability in Nondemocratic Regimes,* Stanford, CA, Stanford University Press.

Scott, James (1998), *Seeing Like a State: How Certain Schemes to Improve the Human Condition Have Failed,* New Haven, CT, Yale University Press.

Sekkat, Khalid, and Achy, Lahcen (2007), "Competition, Efficiency, and Competition Policy in Morocco," in Sekkat, Khalid, ed., *Competition and Efficiency in the Arab World,* New York, Palgrave Macmillan, 123–158.

Sfakianakis, John (2004), "The Whales of the Nile: Networks, Businessmen, and Bureaucrats During the Era of Privatization in Egypt," in Steven Heydemann, ed., *Networks of Privilege: Rethinking the Politics of Economic Reform in the Middle East,* New York, Palgrave Macmillan.

Stiglitz, Joseph E. (2003), *Globalization and Its Discontents,* New York and London, W. W. Norton.

Stiglitz, Joseph (2004), "The Post Washington Consensus Consensus," Columbia University, Institute for Policy Dialogue, Working Paper, November 4, at http://www0.gsb.columbia.edu/ipd/pub/Stiglitz_PWCC_English1.pdf.

Tlemcani, Rachid (1999), "État, bazar, et globalisation: L'Aventure de l'Infitah en Algérie," Algiers, Les Éditions El-Hikma.

US Department of State (USDS) (2005), "Investment Climate Statement: Tunisia," at http://www.state.gov/e/eb/ifd/2005/43042.htm.

Wade, Robert (1990), *Governing the Market: Economic Theory and the Role of Government in East Asian Industrialization,* Princeton, NJ, Princeton University Press.

Waterbury (1973), *Land, Man, and Development in Algeria,* pt. 2, *Population, Employment, and Emigration,* American University Field Services Reports, North Africa Series, 17, 2.

Williamson, John, ed. (1990), *Latin American Adjustment: How Much Has Happened?* Washington, DC, Institute for International Economics.

World Bank (2001), "Memorandum of the President of the IBRD to the Executive Directors on an Interim Assistance Strategy for the Islamic Republic of Iran," Washington, DC, World Bank, Report 22050-IRN.

World Bank (2006a), *Kingdom of Morocco: Country Economic Memorandum: Fostering Higher Growth and Employment with Productive Diversification and Competitiveness,* Washington, DC, World Bank, Social and Economic Development Group, Middle East and North Africa Region, Report 32948-MOR.

World Bank (2006b), *Middle East and North Africa: Economic Developments and Prospects 2006,* Washington, DC, World Bank, Middle East and North Africa Region, Office of the Chief Economist.

World Bank (2009), *From Privilege to Competition: Unlocking Private-Led Growth in the Middle East and North Africa,* Washington, DC, World Bank.

World Bank (2013), *Jobs for Shared Prosperity: Time for Action in the Middle East and North Africa,* vol. 4, Washington, DC, World Bank.

World Bank (2014), *Jobs or Privileges: Releasing Prosperity in the Middle East and North Africa,* Washington, DC, World Bank.

CHAPTER 9: THE EFFECTS OF OIL ON DEVELOPMENT
AND THE RISE OF THE GULF COOPERATION COUNCIL

Acemoglu, Daron, Johnson, Simon, and Robinson, James A. (2000), "The Colonial Origins of Comparative Development: An Empirical Investigation," Cambridge, MA, National Bureau of Economic Research, Working Paper 7771.

Ali, Omar, and Elbadawi, Ibrahim (2012), "The Political Economy of Public Sector Employment in the Resource Dependent Countries," Economic Research Forum (ERF), Working Paper 673.

Almezaini, Khaled (2013), "Private Sector Actors in the UAE and Their Role in the Process of Economic and Political Reform," in Hertog, Steffen, Luciani, Giacomo, and Valeri, Marc, eds., *Business Politics in the Middle East,* London, Hurst Publishers, 43–66.

Alnasrawi, Abbas (1994), *The Economy of Iraq: Oil, Wars, Destruction of Development, and Prospects, 1950–2010,* Westport, CT, Greenwood Press.

Al-Suhaimi, Jammaz (2001), "Consolidation, Competition, Foreign Presence, and Systemic Stability in the Saudi Banking Industry," Basel, Switzerland, Bank for International Settlements (BIS), Background Paper 128.

Auty, Richard M. (2001), "The Political State and the Management of Mineral Rents in Capital-Surplus Economies: Botswana and Saudi Arabia," *Resources Policy* 27, 2, 77–86.

Baldwin-Edwards, Martin (2005), *Migration in the Middle East and the Mediterranean,* Geneva, Switzerland, Global Commission on International Migration.

Beblawi, Hazem (1987), "The Rentier State in the Arab World," in Luciani, Giacomo, ed., *The Arab State,* Berkeley, University of California Press, 85–219.

Bellin, Eva (2004), "The Robustness of Authoritarianism in the Middle East: Exceptionalism in Comparative Perspective," *Comparative Politics* 36, 2, 139–157.

Besley, Timothy, and Kudamatsu, Masayuki (2008), "Making Autocracy Work," in Helpman, Elhanan, ed., *Institutions and Economic Performance,* Cambridge, MA, Harvard University Press.

Chaudhry, Kiren Aziz (1997), *The Price of Wealth: Economies and Institutions in the Middle East,* Ithaca, NY, Cornell University Press.

Cordesman, Anthony H. (2003), *Saudi Arabia Enters the Twenty-First Century: The Political, Foreign Policy, Economic, and Energy Dimensions,* vol. 2, Westport, CT, Greenwood Publishing Group.

Crystal, Jill (1990), *Oil and Politics in the Gulf: Rulers and Merchants in Kuwait and Qatar,* Cambridge Middle East Library 24, Cambridge and New York, Cambridge University Press.

Davidson, Christopher (2012), *After the Sheikhs: The Coming Collapse of the Gulf Monarchies,* London, Hurst & Co.

Espinoza, Raphael, Fayad, Ghada, and Prasad, Ananthakrishnan (2013), *The Macroeconomics of the Arab States of the Gulf,* Oxford, Oxford University Press.

Gardner, Andrew (2010), *City of Strangers: Gulf Migration and the Indian Community in Bahrain,* Ithaca, NY, Cornell University Press.

Girgis, Maurice (2002), "National Versus Migrant Workers in the GCC: Coping with Change," in Handoussa, Heba, and Tzannatos, Zafiris, eds., *Employment Creation and Social Protection in the Middle East and North Africa,* Cairo, American University in Cairo Press.

Gray, Matthew (2011), "A Theory of 'Late Rentierism' in the Arab States of the Gulf," Georgetown University, School of Foreign Service in Qatar, Center for International and Regional Studies.

Henry, Clement Moore, and Springborg, Robert (2010), *Globalization and the Politics of Development in the Middle East,* vol. 1, Cambridge, Cambridge University Press.

Herb, Michael (1999), *All in the Family: Absolutism, Revolution, and Democracy in Middle Eastern Monarchies,* Albany, State University of New York Press.

Hertog, Steffen (2010a), *Princes, Brokers, and Bureaucrats: Oil and the State in Saudi Arabia,* Ithaca, NY, Cornell University Press.

Hertog, Steffen (2010b), "Defying the Resource Curse: Explaining Successful State-Owned Enterprises in Rentier States," *World Politics* 62, 2, 261–301.

Hertog, Steffen (2013a), "State and Private Sector in the GCC After the Arab Uprisings," *Journal of Arabian Studies* 3, 2, 174–195.Hertog, Steffen (2013b), "Introduction," in *The Role of MENA Business in Policy-Making and Political Transitions*, London, Hurst Publishers.

Hodson, Nathan (2013), "Breaking Loose: Reduced Private Sector Dependence on Governments in GCC Economies," in Hertog, Steffen, Luciani, Giacomo, and Valeri, Marc, eds., *Business Politics in the Middle East*, London, Hurst Publishers, 101–132.

Kapiszewski, Andrzej (2004), "Arab Labour Migration to the GCC States," in *Arab Migration in a Globalized World*, Geneva, International Organization for Migration and League of Arab States, 115–133.

Levy, Brian, and Fukuyama, Francis (2010), "Development Strategies: Integrating Governance and Growth," January 1, World Bank, Policy Research Working Paper 5196.

Lofgren, Hans, and Richards, Alan (2003), "Food Security, Poverty, and Economic Policy in the Middle East and North Africa," in Lofgren, Hans, ed., *Food, Agriculture, and Economic Policy in the Middle East and North Africa*, Amsterdam, Elsevier, 1–32.

Luciani, Giacomo (1995), "Resources, Revenue, and Authoritarianism in the Arab World: Beyond the Rentier State," *Political Liberalization and Democratization in the Arab World* 1, 211–227.

Luciani, Giacomo, Hertog, Steffen, Woertz, Eckart, and Youngs, Richard, eds. (2012), *The Gulf Region: Economic Development and Diversification*, vol. 2, *Resources Blessed: Diversification and the Gulf Development Model*, Berlin, Gerlach Press.

Malik, Adeel, and Auty, Richard (2013), "From Resource Curse to Rent Curse: Toward a New Political Economy of the Middle East," Oxford, University of Oxford University.

Marx, Karl (2012), *Economic and Philosophic Manuscripts of 1844*, Mineola, NY, Dover, originally published in 1932.

Mitchell, Timothy (2011), *Carbon Democracy: Political Power in the Age of Oil*, London and New York, Verso.

Moghadam, Valentine M. (1999), "Gender and Globalization: Female Labor and Women's Mobilization," *Journal of World-Systems Research* 5, 301–314.

North, Douglass Cecil, Wallis, John Joseph, and Weingast, Barry R. (2009), *Violence and Social Orders: A Conceptual Framework for Interpreting Recorded Human History*, Cambridge, Cambridge University Press.

Owen, E. Roger (2008), "One Hundred Years of Middle Eastern Oil," *Middle East Brief* 24, 1–6.

Posusney, Marsha Pripstein, and Angrist, Michele Penner (2005), *Authoritarianism in the Middle East: Regimes and Resistance*, Boulder, CO, Lynne Rienner Publishers.

Rivlin, Paul (2009), *Arab Economies in the Twenty-First Century*, Cambridge, Cambridge University Press.

Ross, Michael (2006), "A Closer Look at Oil, Diamonds, and Civil War," *Annual Review of Political Science* 9, 265–300.

Ross, Michael (2012), *The Oil Curse: How Petroleum Wealth Shapes the Development of Nations*, Princeton, NJ, Princeton University Press.

Rosser, Andrew (2006), "Escaping the Resource Curse," *New Political Economy* 11, 4, 557–570.

Sachs, Jeffrey D., and Warner, Andrew M. (1995), "Natural Resource Abundance and Economic Growth," Cambridge, MA, National Bureau of Economic Research, Working Paper 5398, at http://www.nber.org/papers/w5398.

Sala-i-Martin, Xavier, and Subramanian, Arvind (2003), "Addressing the Natural Resource Curse: An Illustration from Nigeria," Cambridge, MA, National Bureau of Economic Research.

Salehi-Isfahani, Djavad (2013), "Iran's Economy Under Sanctions," Virginia Tech.

Schlumberger, Oliver (2008), "Structural Reform, Economic Order, and Development: Patrimonial Capitalism," *Review of International Political Economy* 15, 4, 622–649.

Shah, Nasra M. (2008), "Recent Labor Immigration Policies in the Oil-Rich Gulf: How Effective Are They Likely to Be?" Cornell University ILR School, at http://digitalcommons.ilr.cornell.edu/cgi/viewcontent.cgi?article=1055&context=intl.

Sherbiny, Naiem A. (1984), "Expatriate Labor Flows to the Arab Oil Countries in the 1980s," *Middle East Journal* 38, 4, 643–667.

Sovereign Wealth Fund Institute (2014), general website, at http://www.swfinstitute.org/.

Tétreault, Mary Ann (1993), "Civil Society in Kuwait: Protected Spaces and Women's Rights," *Middle East Journal* 47, 2, 275–291.

Waterbury, John (1997), "From Social Contracts to Extraction Contracts," in Entelis, John P., ed., *Islam, Democracy, and the State in North Africa,* Bloomington, Indiana University Press, 141–176.

Wittfogel, Karl August (1957), *Oriental Despotism: A Comparative Study of Total Power,* New Haven, CT, Yale University Press.

Yousef, Tarek M. (2005), "The Changing Role of Labor Migration in Arab Economic Integration," paper for the policy seminar "Arab Economic Integration: Challenges and Prospects," Abu Dhabi, UAE, February 23–24.

CHAPTER 10: WAR, CONFLICT, AND THE
MILITARY IN THE MIDDLE EAST

Abu-Bader, Suleiman, and Abu-Qarn, Aamer S. (2003), "Government Expenditures, Military Spending, and Economic Growth: Causality Evidence from Egypt, Israel, and Syria," *Journal of Policy Modeling* 25, 6–7, 567–583.

Abul-Magd, Zeinab (2013), "The Egyptian Military in Politics and the Economy: Recent History and Current Transition Status," *CMI Insight,* October, 2.

Acemoglu, Daron, and Robinson, James A. (2006), *Economic Origins of Dictatorship and Democracy,* New York, Cambridge University Press.

Akça, İsmet (2010), "Military-Economic Structure in Turkey: Present Situation, Problems, and Solutions," TESEV Democratization Policy Report, Security Sector 2.

Ali, Hamid E. (2011), "Military Expenditures and Human Development: Guns and Butter Arguments Revisited: A Case Study from Egypt," *Peace Economics: Peace Science and Public Policy* 17, 1, 8.

Al Jazeera (2014), "UAE Introduces Compulsory Military Service," June 8, at http://www.aljazeera .com /news /middleeast /2014 /06 /united-arab-emirates-issues-conscription-law -20146872230517860.html.

Al-Khalil, Samir (1989), *Republic of Fear,* New York, Pantheon Books.

Al-Yousif, Yousif Khalifa (2002), "Defense Spending and Economic Growth: Some Empirical Evidence from the Arab Gulf Region," *Defence and Peace Economics* 13, 3, 187–197.

Aslam, Rabia (2007), "Measuring the Peace Dividend: Evidence from Developing Economies," *Defence and Peace Economics* 18, 1, 39–52.

Barak, Oren, and Sheffer, Gabriel (2006), "Israel's 'Security Network' and Its Impact: An Exploration of a New Approach," *International Journal of Middle East Studies* 38, 2, 235–261.

Barany, Zoltan (2011), "The Role of the Military," *Journal of Democracy* 22, 4, 24–35.

Barnea, Nahum, and Shiffer, Shimon (2012), "Israel's Top Brass Torn over Possible Iran Attack," *Al-Monitor,* August 13, at http://www.al-monitor.com/pulse/tr/politics/2012/08/for-and-against -an-attack-the.pr.html.

BBC News (2011), "Gulf States Send Force to Bahrain," July 11, at http://www.bbc.com/news/world -middle-east-12729786.

Bellin, Eva (2004), "The Robustness of Authoritarianism in the Middle East: Exceptionalism in Comparative Perspective," *Comparative Politics* 36, 2, 139.

Bellin, Eva (2012), "Reconsidering the Robustness of Authoritarianism in the Middle East: Lessons from the Arab Spring," *Comparative Politics* 44, 2, 127–149.

Bienen, Henry, and Moore, Jonathan (1987), "The Sudan: Military Economic Corporations," *Armed Forces and Society* 13, 4, 489–516.

Blaydes, Lisa, and Chaney, Eric (2013), "The Feudal Revolution and Europe's Rise: Political Divergence of the Christian West and the Muslim World Before 1500 CE," *American Political Science Review* (American Political Science Association) 107, 1, 16–34.

Brooks, Risa (2013), "Abandoned at the Palace: Why the Tunisian Military Defected from the Ben Ali Regime in January 2011," *Journal of Strategic Studies* 36, 2, 205–220.

Campaign Against the Arms Trade (CAAT) (2002), "Turkey Submission January 2002," at http:// www.caat.org.uk/resources/countries/turkey/fac-submission-2002-01.php.

Çetin, Tamer (2010), "The Role of Institutions over Economic Change in Turkey," in Çetin, Tamer, and Yilmaz, Feridun, eds., *Understanding the Process of Economic Change in Turkey: An Institutional Approach,* NY, Nova Science Publishers, 21–39.

Chang, Hsin-Chen, Huang, Bwo-Nung, and Yang, Chin Wei (2011), "Military Expenditure and Economic Growth Across Different Groups: A Dynamic Panel Granger-Causality Approach," *Economic Modelling* 28, 6, 2416–2423.

Cline Center for Democracy (various years), Coup D'état Project (CDP) data set, Champaign, University of Illinois, at http://www.clinecenter.illinois.edu/research/speed-coupdata.html.

Cook, Steven A. (2007), *Ruling but Not Governing: The Military and Political Development in Egypt, Algeria, and Turkey,* Baltimore, Johns Hopkins University Press.

Correlates of War (COW) (various years), COW data sets, at http://www.correlatesofwar.org/datasets .htm.

Deger, Saadet (1992), "Military Expenditure and Economic Development: Issues and Debates," in Lamb, Geoffrey, and Kallab, Valeriana, eds., *Military Expenditure and Economic Development,* Washington, DC, World Bank, 35–52.

Demir, Firat (2005), "Militarization of the Market and Rent-Seeking Coalitions in Turkey," *Development and Change* 36, 4, 667–690.

Doner, Richard F., Ritchie, Bryan K., and Slater, Dan (2005), "Systemic Vulnerability and the Origins of Developmental States: Northeast and Southeast Asia in Comparative Perspective," *International Organization* 59, 2, 327–361.

Droz-Vincent, Philippe (2011), "A Return of Armies to the Forefront of Arab Politics?" Rome, Istituto Affari Internazionali, Working Paper 1121.

Economic and Social Commission for Western Asia (ESCWA) (2013), "An Overview of the Arab Security Sector Amidst Political Transition: A Reflection on Legacies, Functions and Perceptions," New York, ESCWA (July 31), at http://www.escwa.un.org/information/publications/edit/upload /E_ESCWA_ECRI_13_2_E.pdf.

Elbadawi, Ibrahim Ahmed, and Keefer, Philip (2014), "Democracy, Democratic Consolidation, and Military Spending," Economic Research Forum, Working Paper 848.

Elbadawi, Ibrahim, and Makdisi, Samir (2007), "Explaining the Democracy Deficit in the Arab World," *Quarterly Review of Economics and Finance* 46, 5, 813–831.

El-Naggar, Said, and el-Erian, Mohamed (1993), "The Economic Implications of a Comprehensive Peace in the Middle East," in Fischer, Stanley, et al., eds., *The Economics of Middle East Peace,* Cambridge, MA, MIT Press, 205–226.

Federation of American Scientists (FAS) (2005), "Arms Sales, Saudi Arabia," at http://fas.org/programs /ssp/man/militarysumsfolder/saudiarabia.html.

Ferguson, Niall (2002), *Empire: The Rise and Demise of the British World Order,* London, Allen Lane.

Göktepe, Gökçe, and Satyanath, Shanker (2013), "The Economic Value of Military Connections in Turkey," *Public Choice* 155, 3–4, 531–552.

Goldscheid, Rudolf (1917), *Staatssozialismus oder Staatskapitalismus,* Leipzig, Anzengruber-Verlag, Brüder Suschitzky.

Gutmann, Emanuel, and Landau, Jacob (1985), "The Political Elite and National Leadership in Israel," in Lenczowski, George, ed., *Political Elites in the Middle East,* Washington, DC, American Enterprise Institute (AEI), 163–200.

Haddad, Bassam (2011), *Business Networks in Syria: The Political Economy of Authoritarian Resilience,* Stanford, CA, Stanford University Press.

Haddad, Bassam (2012), "Syria's State Bourgeoisie: An Organic Backbone for the Regime," *Middle East Critique* 21, 3, 231–257.

Harris, Kevan (2013), "The Rise of the Subcontractor State: Politics of Pseudo-Privatization in the Islamic Republic of Iran," *International Journal of Middle East Studies* 45, 1, 45–70.

Hen-Tov, Elliot (2004), "The Political Economy of Turkish Military Modernization," *Middle East* 8, 4, 50.

Hen-Tov, Elliot, and Gonzalez, Nathan (2011), "The Militarization of Post-Khomeini Iran: Praetorianism 2.0," *Washington Quarterly* 34, 1, 45–59.

Herb, Michael (1999), *All in the Family: Absolutism, Revolution, and Democracy in the Middle Eastern Monarchies,* Albany, State University of New York Press.

Heydemann, Steven, ed. (2000), *War and Social Change in the Middle East,* Berkeley, University of California Press.

International Monetary Fund (IMF) (various years), IMF World Financial Statistics, at http://www .imf.org/external/data.htm#financial.

Israel High Tech and Investment Report (2004), "Israel Accounts for 12% of World's Military Exports," September, at http://www.ishitech.co.il/0904ar2.htm.

Jenkins, Gareth (2014), "The Ergenekon Releases and Prospects for the Rule of Law in Turkey," *The Turkey Analyst* 7, 5.

Kandil, Hazem (2012), *Soldiers, Spies, and Statesmen: Egypt's Road to Revolt,* London, Verso.

Karasapan, Omer (1987), "Turkey's Armaments Industries," *MERIP Reports* 144 (January-February), 27–31.

Keefer, Philip (2012), "Why Follow the Leader? Collective Action, Credible Commitment and Conflict," in Garfinkel, Michelle, and Skaperdas, Stergios, eds., *Oxford Handbook of the Economics of Peace and Conflict,* Oxford, Oxford University Press, 816–839.

Kerr, Paul K., Nikitin, Mary Beth D., and Hildreth, Steven A. (2014), "Iran–North Korea–Syria Ballistic Missile and Nuclear Cooperation," Washington, DC, Congressional Research Service Report R43480.

Kovessy, Peter (2014), "Qatar's Military Build-up Continues with $24bn in New Arms Deals," *Doha News,* March 28, at http://dohanews.co/qatars-military-build-continues-24bn-new-arms-deals/.

Lebovic, James H., and Ishaq, Ashfaq (1987), "Military Burden, Security Needs, and Economic Growth in the Middle East," *Journal of Conflict Resolution* 31, 1, 106–138.

Levy, Barry S., and Sidel, Victor W., eds. (2008), *War and Public Health,* Oxford, Oxford University Press.

Lin, Eric S., Ali, Hamid E., and Lu, Yu-Lung (2013), "Does Military Spending Crowd Out Social Welfare Expenditures? Evidence from a Panel of OECD Countries," *Defence and Peace Economics,* 1–16.

Longuenesse, Elisabeth (1979), "The Class Nature of the State in Syria," *MERIP Reports* 77 (May), 3–11.

Malas, Nour, and Abi-Habib, Maria (2014), "Lebanese Army Strained by Spillover from Syria Conflict," *Wall Street Journal,* May 27.

Marshall, Shana, and Stacher, Joshua (2012), "Egypt's Generals and Transnational Capital," *MERIP Reports* 262, 12–18, at http://www.merip.org/mer/mer262/egypts-generals-transnational-capital.

Martonosi, Péter (2012), "The Basij: A Major Factor in Iranian Security," *Academic and Applied Research in Military Science* 11, 1, 27–38.

Mashal, Mujib (2011), "Pakistani Troops Aid Bahrain's Crackdown," *Al Jazeera,* July 30, at http://www.aljazeera.com/indepth/features/2011/07/2011725145048574888.html.

McMurray, David, and Ufheil-Somers, Amanda, eds. (2013), *The Arab Revolts: Dispatches on Militant Democracy in the Middle East,* Bloomington, Indiana University Press.

Mintz, Alex (1985), "The Military-Industrial Complex: American Concepts and Israeli Realities," *Journal of Conflict Resolution* 29, 4, 623–639.

Moriarty, J. Thomas, Katz, Daniel, Korb, Lawrence J., Caverley, Jonathan, and Kapstein, Ethan B. (2013), "Outgunned? A Debate over the Shifting Global Arms Market," *Foreign Affairs* 92, 2.

Morsy, Ahmed (2014), "The Military Crowds Out Civilian Business in Egypt," Washington, DC, Carnegie Endowment for International Peace (June 24).

Pachon, Alejandro (2014), "Loyalty and Defection: Misunderstanding Civil-Military Relations in Tunisia During the 'Arab Spring,'" *Journal of Strategic Studies,* 1–24.

Peel, Michael (2011), "Assad's Family Picked Up by the West's Radar," *Financial Times,* April 27.

Pollack, Joshua (2011), "Ballistic Trajectory," *Nonproliferation Review* 18, 2, 411–429.

Quinlivan, James T. (1999), "Coup-Proofing: Its Practice and Consequences in the Middle East," *International Security* 24, 2, 131–165.

Rubin, Alissa J., and Nordland, Rod (2014), "Sunnis and Kurds on Sidelines of Iraqi Leader's Military Plans," *New York Times,* June 16.

Rubin, Barry (2001), "The Military in Contemporary Middle East Politics," *Middle East Review of International Affairs Journal* 5, 1, 47–63.

Rubin, Uzi (2012), "Showcase of Missile Proliferation: Iran's Missile and Space Program," *Arms Control Today* (January-February).

Schumpeter, Joseph A. (1918), "The Crisis of the Tax State," in Swedberg, Richard, ed., *The Economics and Sociology of Capitalism,* Princeton, NJ: Princeton University Press, 99–140.

Springborg, Robert (1987), "The President and the Field Marshall," *MERIP Reports* 147 (July-August), 4, at http://www.merip.org/mer/mer147/president-field-marshall.

Springborg, Robert (2011), "Economic Involvements of Militaries," *International Journal of Middle East Studies* 43, 3, 397–399.

Stockholm International Peace Research Institute (SIPRI) (various years), data sets, at http://www.sipri.org/databases.

Stork, Joe (1987), "Arms Industries of the Middle East," *MERIP Reports* 144, 17, at http://www.merip.org/mer/mer144/arms-industries-middle-east.

Tilly, Charles, ed. (1975), *The Formation of National States in Western Europe,* Princeton, NJ, Princeton University Press.

Tilly, Charles (1992), *Coercion, Capital, and European States, AD 990–1992,* Cambridge, MA, Blackwell.

Today's Zaman (2013), "Long Sentences for Ergenekon Suspects, Life for Ex-Army Chief," July 15, at http://www.todayszaman.com/news-322781-long-sentences-for-ergenekon-suspects-life-for-ex-army-chief.html.

Ünver, H. Akin (2009), "Turkey's 'Deep-State' and the Ergenekon Conundrum," Washington, DC, Middle East Institute, Policy Brief 23.

Uppsala Conflict Data Program (UCDP) and Peace Research Institute Oslo (PRIO) (various years), "UCDP/PRIO Armed Conflict Dataset," at http://www.prio.org/Data/Armed-Conflict/UCDP-PRIO/.

US Arms Control and Disarmament Agency (1995), World Military Expenditures and Arms Transfers (WMEAT), Washington, DC.

US Agency for International Development (USAID) (various years), "US Overseas Loans and Grants [Greenbook]," data sets, at http://gbk.eads.usaidallnet.gov/.

Wan, William, and Finn, Peter (2011), "Global Race On to Match US Drone Capabilities," *Washington Post*, July 4.

Weinstein, Jeremy M. (2005), "Autonomous Recovery and International Intervention in Comparative Perspective," Center for Global Development, Working Paper 57.

World Bank (various years), World Development Indicators (WDI), at http://publications.worldbank.org/ecommerce/catalog/product?item_id=631625.

Yildirim, Jülide, and Sezgin, Selami (2002), "Defence, Education, and Health Expenditures in Turkey, 1924–1996," *Journal of Peace Research* 39, 5, 569–580.

Yildirim, Jülide, Sezgin, Selami, and Öcal, Nadir (2005), "Military Expenditure and Economic Growth in Middle Eastern Countries: A Dynamic Panel Data Analysis," *Defence and Peace Economics* 16, 4, 283–295.

CHAPTER 11: SOLIDARISM AND ITS ENEMIES: CIVIL SOCIETY AND SOCIAL MOVEMENTS IN THE MIDDLE EAST

Abdalla, Nadine (2014), "Egyptian Labor and the State," Washington, DC, Middle East Institute (July 1).

Achcar, Gilbert (2013), *The People Want: A Radical Exploration of the Arab Uprising*, Berkeley, University of California Press.

Ahram Online (2014), "We Will Not Be Silenced: April 6, After Court Order Banning Group," April 28, at http://english.ahram.org.eg/NewsContent/1/64/100015/Egypt/Politics-/We-will-not-be-silenced-April-,-after-court-order-.aspx.

Al-Ansari, Hamied (1986), *Egypt: The Stalled Society*, Albany, State University of New York Press.

Al-Momani, Mohammad (2011), "The Arab 'Youth Quake': Implications on Democratization and Stability," *Middle East Law and Governance* 3, 159–170.

Alexander, Amy C., and Welzel, Christian (2011), "Islam and Patriarchy: How Robust Is Muslim Support for Patriarchy?" *International Sociological Review* 21, 2, 249–276.

Alley, April Longley (2013), "Yemen Changes Everything . . . and Nothing," *Journal of Democracy* 24, 4, 74–85.

Amnesty International (2009), "Behind the Economic Miracle: Inequality and Criminalization of Protest," New York, Amnesty International.

Ayache, Albert (1993), *Le Mouvement syndical au Maroc*, 3rd ed., Paris, l'Harmattan.

Baduel, Pierre-Robert (1983), "Le VIe plan tunisien: 1982–86," *Grand Maghreb* (March 21), 54–57.

Baldez, Lisa (2010), "The Gender Lacuna in Comparative Politics," *Perspectives on Politics* 8, 1, 199–205.

Banks, Arthur S., and Wilson, Kenneth A. (2014), "Cross-National Time-Series Data Archive," Jerusalem, Databanks International, at http://www.databanksinternational.com/32.html.

Bayat, Asef (2009), "Iran: A Green Wave for Life and Liberty," openDemocracy, July 7, at https://www.opendemocracy.net/article/iran-a-green-wave-for-life-and-liberty.

Bayat, Asef (2010), *Life as Politics: How Ordinary People Change the Middle East*, Stanford, CA, Stanford University Press.

Beinin, Joel, and Duboc, Marie (2013), "A Worker's Social Movement on the Margin of the Global Neoliberal Order, Egypt, 2004–2012," in Beinin, Joel, and Vairel, Frédéric, eds., *Social Movements, Mobilization, and Contestation in the Middle East and North Africa*, 2nd ed., Stanford, CA, Stanford University Press, 205–227.

Beinin, Joel, and Vairel, Frédéric (2013), *Social Movements, Mobilization, and Contestation in the Middle East and North Africa*, 2nd ed., Stanford, CA, Stanford University Press.

Benchemsi, Ahmed (2012), "Morocco: Outfoxing the Opposition," *Journal of Democracy* 23, 1, 57–69.

Benchemsi, Ahmed (2014), "Morocco's Makhzen and the Haphazard Activists," in Khatib, Lina, and Lust, Ellen, eds., *Taking to the Streets: The Transformation of Arab Activism,* Baltimore, Johns Hopkins University Press, 199–235.

Bianchi, Robert (1984), *Interest Groups and Political Development in Turkey,* Princeton, NJ, Princeton University Press.

Bill, James A., and Springborg, Robert (1994), *Politics in the Middle East,* 4th ed., New York, Harper-Collins.

Bishara, Dina (2014), "Labor Movements in Tunisia and Egypt," *SWP Comments,* January, Berlin, Stiftung Wissenschaft und Politik (SWP).

Blaydes, Lisa (2010), *Elections and Distributive Politics in Mubarak's Egypt,* New York, Cambridge University Press.

Brown, Oli, and Crawford, Alec (2009), "Rising Temperatures, Rising Tensions: Climate Change and the Risk of Violent Conflict in the Middle East," Winnipeg, Canada, International Institute for Sustainable Development (IISD).

Buehler, Matthew (2013), "Safety-Valve Elections and the Arab Spring: The Weakening (and Resurgence) of Morocco's Islamist Opposition Party," *Terrorism and Political Violence* 25, 1, 137–156.

Cammett, Melani (2014), *Compassionate Communalism: Welfare and Sectarianism in Lebanon,* Ithaca, NY, Cornell University Press.

Cammett, Melani, and Posusney, Marsha Pripstein (2010), "Labor Standards and Labor Flexibility in the Middle East: Freer Markets, Freer Unions?" *Studies in Comparative International Development* 45, 2, 250–279.

CARE International (2013), "Arab Spring or Arab Autumn? Women's Political Participation in the Uprisings and Beyond: Implications for International Donor Policy," September, London, CARE International.

Charrad, Mounira, and Zarrugh, Amina (2014), "Equal or Complementary? Women in the New Tunisian Constitution After the Arab Spring," *Journal of North African Studies* 19, 2, 230–243.

Chomiak, Laryssa (2014), "Architecture of Resistance in Tunisia," in Khatib, Lina, and Lust, Ellen, eds., *Taking to the Streets: The Transformation of Arab Activism,* Baltimore, Johns Hopkins University Press, 22–51.

Clark, Janine, and Salloukh, Bassel (2013), "Elite Strategies, Civil Society, and Sectarian Identities in Postwar Lebanon," *International Journal of Middle East Studies* 45, 4, 731–749.

Coleman, Isobel (2006), "Women, Islam, and the New Iraq," *Foreign Affairs* 85, 1, 24–38.

Collier, Ruth Berins, and Collier, David (1979), "Inducements Versus Constraints: Disaggregating 'Corporatism,'" *American Political Science Review* 73, 4, 967–986.

Corstange, Daniel (2012), "Vote Trafficking in Lebanon," *International Journal of Middle East Studies* 44, 3, 483–505.

Crystal, Jill (2007), "Eastern Arabian States: Kuwait, Bahrain, Qatar, United Arab Emirates, and Oman," in Gasiorowski, Mark, Long, David E., and Reich, Bernard, eds., *The Government and Politics of the Middle East and North Africa,* 5th ed., Boulder, CO, Westview, 153–196.

DERSA (1981), *L'Algérie en débat,* Paris, Maspero.

Desrues, Thierry (2013), "Mobilizations in a Hybrid Regime: The 20th February Movement and the Moroccan Regime," *Current Sociology* 61, 4, 409–423.

Dhillon, Navtej, and Yousef, Tarik, eds. (2009), *Generation in Waiting: The Unfulfilled Promise of Young People in the Middle East,* Washington, DC, Brookings Institution Press.

Dworkin, Anthony (2013), "A Delicate Balance: Consolidating Tunisia's Success," *World Politics Review* (July 23), at http://www.worldpoliticsreview.com/articles/13108/a-delicate-balance-consolidating-tunisias-successes.

Ehsani, Kaveh, Keshavarzian, Arang, and Moruzzi, Norma Claire (2009), "Tehran, June 2009," *MERIP Reports* (June 28), at http://www.merip.org/mero/mero062809.

El-Mahdi, Rabab (2009), "Enough! Egypt's Quest for Democracy," *Comparative Political Studies* 42, 8, 1011–1039.

El-Mahdi, Rabab (2014), "Egypt: A Decade of Ruptures," in Khatib, Lina, and Lust, Ellen, eds., *Taking to the Streets: The Transformation of Arab Activism,* Baltimore, Johns Hopkins University Press, 52–75.

Esman, Milton, and Rabinovich, Itamar, eds. (1988), *Ethnicity, Pluralism, and the State in the Middle East,* Ithaca, NY, Cornell University Press.

Fattah, Khaled (2011), "Yemen: A Social Intifada in a Republic of Sheikhs," *Middle East Policy* 18, 3.

Fish, Steve (2002), "Islam and Authoritarianism," *World Politics* 55, 4–37.

Friedman, Thomas L. (2013), "Without Water, Revolution," *New York Times,* May 18.

Gaston, Erica (2014), "Process Lessons Learned in Yemen's National Dialogue," Washington, DC, United States Institute of Peace, Special Report 342.

Gazzini, Claudia (2011), "Was the Libya Intervention Necessary?" *MERIP Reports* 261, at http://www.merip.org/mer/mer261/was-libya-intervention-necessary.

Gellner, Ernest, and Micaud, Charles, eds. (1972), *Arabs and Berbers,* London, Duckworth.

Gordon, Uri (2012), "Israel's 'Tent Protests': The Chilling Effect of Nationalism," *Social Movement Studies: Journal of Social, Cultural, and Political Protest* 11, 3–4.

Haddad, Fanar (2011), *Sectarianism in Iraq: Antagonistic Visions of Unity,* London, Hurst Publishers.

Hamzawy, Amr, and Dunne, Michele (2010), "Brotherhood Enters Elections in a Weakened State," Washington, DC, Carnegie Endowment for International Peace (November 15), at http://carnegieendowment.org/2010/11/15/brotherhood-enters-elections-in-weakened-state/b1j.

Harris, Kevan (2012), "The Brokered Exuberance of the Middle Class: An Ethnographic Analysis of Iran's 2009 Green Movement," *Mobilization: An International Journal* 17, 4, 435–455.

Hermez, Sami (2011), "On Dignity and Clientelism: Lebanon in the Context of the 2011 Arab Revolutions," *Studies in Ethnicity and Nationalism* 11, 3, 527–537.

Herrera, Linda, and Bayat, Asef, eds. (2010), *Being Young and Muslim: New Cultural Politics in the Global South and North,* New York, Oxford University Press.

Holmes, Amy Austin (2012), "There Are Weeks When Decades Happen: Structure and Strategy in the Egyptian Revolution," *Mobilization* 17, 4, 391–410.

Holmes, Amy Austin (2013), "Everywhere Is Taksim: The Crackdown on the Commons," *Counterpunch* (June 26), at http://www.counterpunch.org/2013/06/26/everywhere-is-taksim/.

Horowitz, Donald (2000), *Ethnic Groups in Conflict,* Berkeley, University of California Press.

Human Rights Watch (2007), *Exported and Exposed: Abuses Against Sri Lankan Domestic Workers in Saudi Arabia, Kuwait, Lebanon, and the United Arab Emirates,* New York, Human Rights Watch (November 14), at http://www.hrw.org/en/reports/2007/11/13/exported-and-exposed-1.

Human Rights Watch (2009), "The Island of Happiness: Exploitation of Migrant Workers on Saadiyat Island, Abu Dhabi," New York, Human Rights Watch (May 19), Report 1–56432–481–8, at http://www.hrw.org/en/reports/2009/05/18/island-happiness.

Huntington, Samuel (2002), *The Clash of Civilizations and the Remaking of World Order,* New York, Simon & Schuster.

Inglehart, Ronald, and Norris, Pippa (2003), "The True Clash of Civilizations," *Foreign Policy* 135, 62–70.

Jamal, Amaney, and Khatib, Lina (2014), "Actors, Public Opinions, and Participation," in Lust, Ellen, ed., *The Middle East,* 13th ed., Thousand Oaks, CA, CQ Press.

Jordan Times (2012), "King Approves Amended Elections Law," *Jordan Times,* July 23, at http://jordantimes.com/king-approves-amended-elections-law.

Kedourie, Elie (1992), *Democracy and Arab Political Culture,* Washington, DC, Washington Institute for Near East Policy.

Khalil, Andrea (2014), "Gender Paradoxes of the Arab Spring," *Journal of North African Studies* 19, 2, 131–136.

Khoury, Philip (1983), "Islamic Revivalism and the Crisis of the Secular State in the Arab World: An Historical Appraisal," in Ibrahim, Ibrahim, ed., *Arab Resources,* London, Croom Helm, for the Center for Contemporary Arab Studies, 213–236.

Khoury, Philip, and Kostiner, Joseph, eds. (1990), *Tribes and State Formation in the Middle East,* Berkeley, University of California Press.

Kingston, Paul W. T. (2013), *Reproducing Sectarianism: Advocacy Networks and the Politics of Civil Society in Postwar Lebanon,* Albany, State University of New York Press.

Krause, Wanda (2012), *Civil Society and Women Activists in the Middle East: Islamic and Secular Organizations in Egypt,* London, I. B. Tauris.

Kuebler, Johanne (2011), "Les Révolutions arabes et le web 2.0: Tunisie et Égypte," *Revue Averroès* 4–5.

Kurzman, Charles (2012), "The Arab Spring: Ideals of the Iranian Green Movement, Methods of the Iranian Revolution," *International Journal of Middle East Studies* 44, 162–165.

Langhi, Zahra (2014), "Gender and State-Building in Libya: Towards a Politics of Inclusion," *Journal of North African Studies* 19, 2, 200–210.

Langohr, Vickie (2013), "'This Is Our Square': Fighting Sexual Assault at Cairo Protests," *MERIP Reports* 268, at http://www.merip.org/mer/mer268/our-square.

Langohr, Vickie (2014), "New President, Old Pattern of Sexual Violence in Egypt," *MERIP Reports* (July 7), at http://www.merip.org/mero/mero070714.

Lerner, Daniel (1959), *The Passing of Traditional Society*, Glencoe, IL, Free Press.

Lust-Okar, Ellen (2005), *Structuring Conflict in the Arab World: Incumbents, Opponents, and Institutions*, New York, Cambridge University Press.

Lust, Ellen (2009), "Competitive Clientelism in the Middle East," *Journal of Democracy* 20, 3, 122–135.

Lynch, Marc (2011), "After Egypt: The Limits and Promise of Online Challenges to the Authoritarian Arab State," *Perspectives on Politics* 9, 2, 301–310.

Makdisi, Ussama (2000), *The Culture of Sectarianism: Community, History, and Violence in Nineteenth-Century Ottoman Lebanon*, Berkeley, University of California Press.

Malmvig, Helle, and Markus Lassen, Christina (2013), "The Arab Uprisings: Regional Implications and International Responses," Institut Europeu de la Mediterrania (IEMED), *Mediterranean Yearbook: Transitions in the Arab World*, 41–46, at http://www.iemed.org/observatori-en/arees-danalisi/arxius-adjunts/anuari/iemed-2013/Malmvig%20Lassen%20Arab%20Uprisings%20Regional%20Implications%20EN.pdf.

McAdam, Doug (1982), *Political Processes and the Development of the Black Insurgency, 1930–1970*, Chicago, University of Chicago Press.

McAdam, Doug, McCarthy, John D., and Zald, Mayer N., eds. (1996), *Comparative Perspectives on Social Movements: Political Opportunity, Mobilizing Structures, and Cultural Framings*, New York, Cambridge University Press.

McAdam, Doug, Tarrow, Sidney, and Tilly, Charles, eds. (2001), *Dynamics of Contention*, Cambridge, Cambridge University Press.

McQuinn, Brian (2012), "Armed Groups in Libya: Typologies and Roles," *Small Arms Survey Research Notes* 18.

Migdal, Joel (1987), "Strong States, Weak States: Power and Accommodation," in Weiner, Myron, and Huntington, Samuel P., eds., *Understanding Political Development*, Boston, Little, Brown, 391–436.

Moghadam, Valentine M. (2013), *Modernizing Women: Gender and Social Change in the Middle East*, 3rd ed., Boulder, CO, Lynne Rienner Publishers.

Morsy, Maya (2014), "Egyptian Women and the 25th of January Revolution: Presence and Absence," *Journal of North African Studies* 19, 2, 211–229.

Nasr, Salim (1985), "Roots of the Shi'i Movement," *MERIP Reports* 133 (June), 10–16.

Nellis, John (1977), "Socialist Management in Algeria," *Journal of Modern African Studies* 15, 4, 529–544.

Norris, Pippa, and Inglehart, Ronald (2002), "Islamic Culture and Democracy: Testing the 'Clash of Civilizations' Thesis," *Comparative Sociology* 1, 3–4, 235–263.

Norris, Pippa, and Krook, Mona (2009), "One of Us: Multilevel Models Examining the Impact of Descriptive Representation on Civic Engagement," Cambridge, MA, Harvard University, John F. Kennedy School of Government, HKS Faculty Research Working Paper 09–030.

Noueihed, Lin, and Warren, Alex (2012), *The Battle for the Arab Spring: Revolution, Counter-Revolution, and the Making of a New Era*, New Haven, CT, Yale University Press.

Parvaz, D. (2011), "Cable: US Knew of Corruption," *Al Jazeera*, January 16, at http://www.aljazeera.com/news/africa/2011/01/2011116191654327302.html.

Pearlman, Wendy (2013), "Emotions and the Microfoundations of the Arab Uprisings," *Perspective on Politics* 11, 2, 387–409.

Philbrick Yadav, Stacey (2011), "Antecedents of the Revolution: Intersectoral Networks and Post-Partisanship in Yemen," *Studies in Ethnicity and Nationalism* 11, 3.

Putnam, Robert (1993), *Making Democracy Work: Civic Traditions in Modern Italy*, Princeton, NJ, Princeton University Press.

Rajabany, Intissar K., and Ben Shitrit, Lihi (2014), "Activism and Civil War in Libya," in Khatib, Lina, and Lust, Ellen, eds., *Taking to the Streets: The Transformation of Arab Activism*, Baltimore, Johns Hopkins University Press, 76–108.

Roberts, Hugh (1982), "The Unforeseen Development of the Kabyle Question in Contemporary Algeria," *Government and Opposition* 17, 3, 312–334.

Roberts, Hugh (1983), "The Economics of Berberism: The Kabyle Question in Contemporary Algeria," *Government and Opposition* 18, 2, 218–235.

Roberts, Hugh (2011), "Who Said Qaddafhi Had to Go?" *London Review of Books* 33, 22, 8–18.

Rosenhek, Zeev, and Shalev, Michael (2013), "The Political Economy of Israel's 'Social Justice' Protests: A Class and Generational Analysis," *Contemporary Social Science: Journal of the Academy of Social Sciences* 9, 1.

Ross, Michael (2008), "Oil, Islam, and Women," *American Political Science Review* 102, 1, 107–123.

Sabry, Bassem (2013), "The Uncertain Fate of Egypt's Political Parties," *Al-Monitor,* September 12, at http://www.al-monitor.com/pulse/originals/2013/09/uncertain-fate-egypts-political-parties.html #.

Sallam, Hesham (2011), "Striking Back at Egyptian Workers," *MERIP Reports* 259, 41, at http://www.merip.org/mer/mer259/striking-back-egyptian-workers.

Sawah, Wael, and Kawakibi, Salam (2014), "Activism in Syria: Between Nonviolence and Armed Resistance," in Khatib, Lina, and Lust, Ellen, eds., *Taking to the Streets: The Transformation of Arab Activism,* Baltimore, Johns Hopkins University Press, 136–171.

Sharp, Jeremy M. (2011), "Egypt in Transition," Washington, DC, Congressional Research Service, Report RL33003.

Shehata, Dina (2012), "Youth Movements and the 25 January Revolution," in Korany, Bahgat, and El-Mahdi, Rabab, eds., *The Arab Spring in Egypt,* Cairo, American University in Cairo Press, 105–124.

Singerman, Diane (1995), *Avenues of Participation: Family, Politics, and Networks in Urban Quarters of Cairo,* Princeton, NJ, Princeton University Press.

Sowers, Jeannie, Waterbury, John, and Woertz, Eckart (2013), "Did Drought Trigger the Crisis in Syria?" Footnote no. 1 (September 12), at http://footnote1.com/did-drought-trigger-the-crisis-in-syria/.

Storm, Lise (2014), *Party Politics and Prospects for Democracy in North Africa,* Boulder, CO, Lynne Rienner Publishers.

Ulrichsen, Kristian Coates (2014), "Bahrain's Uprising: Domestic Implications and Regional and International Perspectives," in Gerges, Fawaz A., ed., *The New Middle East: Protest and Revolution in the Arab World,* New York, Cambridge University Press, 330–351.

Vom Bruck, Gabriele, Alwazir, Atiaf, and Wiacek, Benjamin (2013), "Yemen: Revolution Suspended?" in Gerges, Fawaz A., ed., *The New Middle East: Protest and Revolution in the Arab World,* New York, Cambridge University Press.

Wedeen, Lisa (2000), "Ambiguities After Assad," *ISIM Newsletter* 6, 25, at https://openaccess.leidenuniv.nl/handle/1887/17414.

Weiss, Max (2010), *In the Shadow of Sectarianism: Law, Shi'ism, and the Making of Modern Lebanon,* Cambridge, MA, Harvard University Press.

Wolff, Stefan (2013), "Managing Expectations: Yemen's National Dialogue Conference," *World Politics Review* (July 23), at http://www.worldpoliticsreview.com/articles/13104/managing-expectations-yemen-s-national-dialogue-conference.

World Bank (various years), World Development Indicators (WDI), at http://publications.worldbank.org/ecommerce/catalog/product?item_id=631625.

World Values Survey Association (various years), World Values Survey (WVS), at http://www.worldvaluessurvey.org/wvs.jsp.

Yom, Sean L., and Gause, F. Gregory, III (2012), "Resilient Royals: How Arab Monarchies Hang On," *Journal of Democracy* 23, 4, 74–88.

Yörük, Erdem (2014), "The Long Summer of Turkey: The Gezi Uprising and Its Historical Roots," *South Atlantic Quarterly* 113, 2, 419–426.

Zartman, William I. (1997), "Opposition as Support of the State," in Luciani, Giacamo, ed., *The Arab State,* London, Routledge, 220–246.

CHAPTER 12: IS ISLAM THE SOLUTION?

Abdelmawla, Mutasim (2011), "The Impacts of Zakat and Knowledge on Poverty Alleviation in Sudan: An Empirical Investigation (1990–2009)," Eighth International Conference on Islamic Economics and Finance, conference paper, at http://conference.qfis.edu.qa/app/media/239.

Abu-Amr, Ziad (1994), *Islamic Fundamentalism in the West Bank and Gaza: Muslim Brotherhood and Islamic Jihad,* Bloomington, Indiana University Press.

Abu Khalil, As'ad (2002), *Bin Laden, Islam, and America's New "War on Terrorism,"* New York, Seven Stories Press.

Abu Khalil, As'ad (2004), *The Battle for Saudi Arabia: Royalty, Fundamentalism, and Global Power,* New York, Seven Stories Press.

Abu Rumman, Muhammad (2012), "Jordan's Parliamentary Elections and the Islamist Boycott," *Sada* (Carnegie Endowment for International Peace) (October 20), at http://carnegieendowment.org /2010/10/20/jordan-s-parliamentary-elections-and-islamist-boycott/6bho (accessed July 11, 2014).

Achy, Lahcen (2012), "Ennahda Proposes Big Spending to Boost Tunisia's Economy," *Al-Monitor,* February 8, at http://www.al-monitor.com/pulse/ar/business/2012/04/tunisian-economy-weak -performanc.html#.

Ahmed, Habib (2004), "Role of Zakah and Awqaf in Poverty Alleviation," Islamic Research and Training Institute, Occasional Paper 8, at http://www.irtipms.org/PubText/201.pdf (accessed July 20, 2014).

Ahmed, Yasmine Moataz (2012), "Who Do Egypt's Villagers Vote For? And Why?" *Egypt Independent,* April 10, at http://www.egyptindependent.com/opinion/who-do-egypt%E2%80%99s-villagers -vote-and-why (Accessed July 8, 2014).

Al Jazeera (2012), "Muslim Brotherhood Tops Egyptian Poll Result," *Al Jazeera,* January 22, at http:// www.aljazeera.com/news/middleeast/2012/01/2012121125958580264.html.

Al Jazeera English (2014), "Morocco Repeals 'Rape Marriage Law,'" *Al Jazeera English,* January 23, at http:// www.aljazeera.com/news/africa/2014/01/morocco-repeals-rape-marriage-law-2014123254643455.html.

Al-Sharqi, Mohammed (2013), "Political Differences Threaten Moroccan Economy," *Al-Monitor,* June 14, at http://www.al-monitor.com/pulse/politics/2013/06/political-differences-morocco-economy.html#.

Alterman, Jon B. (2000). "Egypt: Stable, but for How Long?" *Washington Quarterly,* 23, 4, 107–118.

Amuzegar, Jahangir (1993), *Iran's Economy Under the Islamic Republic,* London and New York, I. B. Tauris.

Archer, Simon, and Karim, Rifaat Ahmed Abdel, eds. (2007), *Islamic Finance: The Regulatory Challenge,* Singapore, John Wiley & Sons.

Ayata, Ayşe Gunes, and Tutuncu, Fatma (2008), "Party Politics of the AKP (2002–2007) and the Predicaments of Women at the Intersection of the Westernist, Islamist, and Feminist Discourses in Turkey," *British Journal of Middle Eastern Studies* 35, 3, 363–384.

Ayubi, Nazih (1991), *Political Islam: Religion and Politics in the Arab World,* London and New York, Routledge.

Baker, Raymond William (2003), *Islam Without Fear: Egypt and the New Islamists,* Cambridge, MA, Harvard University Press.

Bayat, Asef (2002), "Activism and Social Development in the Middle East," *International Journal of Middle East Studies* 34, 1, 1–28.

Bayat, Asef (2007), *Making Islam Democratic: Social Movements and the Post-Islamist Turn,* Stanford, CA, Stanford University Press.

Bayat, Asef (2009), *Life as Politics: How Ordinary People Change the Middle East,* Stanford, CA, Stanford University Press.

BBC News Africa (2012), "Libya Election Success for Secularist Jibril's Bloc," BBC News Africa, July 18, at http://www.bbc.com/news/world-africa-18880908.

Beach, Alistair (2013), "Luxor Protests Against Morsi's New Governor for the City—Former Islamist Terror Leader Adel el-Khayat," *Independent,* June 18, at http://www.independent.co.uk/news/world /africa/luxor-protests-against-morsis-new-governor-for-the-city-former-islamist-terror-leader-adel -elkhayat-8662675.html (accessed July 20, 2014).

Blaydes, Lisa, and Chaney, Eric (2013), "The Feudal Revolution and Europe's Rise: Political Divergence of the Christian West and the Muslim World Before 1500 CE," *American Political Science Review* 107, 1, 16–34.

Bohn, Lauren E. (2011), "The Muslim Brotherhood Takes Twitter," *Foreign Policy* (November 18), at http://mideastafrica.foreignpolicy.com/posts/2011/11/18/the_muslim_brotherhood_takes_twitter (accessed July 8, 2014).

Boukhars, Anouar (2014), "Morocco's Islamists: Bucking the Trend?" FRIDE (June), Policy Brief 182, at http://www.fride.org/descarga/PB_182_Morocco_Islamists.pdf.

Buehler, Matt (2013), "The Threat to 'Un-Moderate': Moroccan Islamists and the Arab Spring," *Middle East Law and Governance* 5, 1–27.

Burgat, François (1993), *The Islamic Movement in North Africa,* Austin, University of Texas Press.

Cammett Melani (2014), *Compassionate Communalism: Welfare and Sectarianism in Lebanon*, Ithaca, NY: Cornell University Press.

Cammett, Melani, and Luong, Pauline Jones (2014), "Is There an Islamist Political Advantage?" *Annual Review of Political Science* 17 (May-June), 187–206.

Çarkoğlu, Ali (2011), "Turkey's 2011 General Elections: Towards a Dominant Party System?" *Insight Turkey* 13, 3, 43–62, at http://file.insightturkey.com/Files/Pdf/20120903122353_insight-turkey_volume_11_number_3_-ali_carkoglu_towards-a-dominant.pdf (accessed July 26, 2014).

Carter Center (2012a), "Presidential Elections in Egypt: Final Report," May-June, at http://www.cartercenter.org/resources/pdfs/news/peace_publications/election_reports/egypt-final-presidential-elections-2012.pdf.

Carter Center (2012b), "General National Congress Elections in Libya: Final Report," July 7, at http://www.cartercenter.org/resources/pdfs/news/peace_publications/election_reports/libya-070712-final-rpt.pdf.

Cavdar, Gamze (2010), "Islamist Moderation and the Persistence of Gender: Turkey's Persistent Paradox," *Totalitarian Movements and Political Religions* 11, 3–4 (September-December), 341–357.

Clark, Janine A., and Young, Amy E. (2008), "Islamism and Family Law Reform in Morocco and Jordan," *Mediterranean Politics* 13, 3, 333–352.

Dahl, Robert (2003), *How Democratic Is the American Constitution?* 2nd ed., New Haven, CT, Yale University Press.

Daily News Egypt (2010), "Bahrain Sunni Islamists Hit as Woman Makes History in Polls," *Daily News Egypt*, November 1, at http://www.dailynewsegypt.com/2010/11/01/bahrain-sunni-islamists-hit-as-woman-makes-history-in-polls/ (accessed July 20, 2014).

De Waal, Alex, and Abel Salam, A. H. (2004), "Islamism, State Power, and Jihad in Sudan," in de Waal, Alex, ed., *Islamism and Its Enemies in the Horn of Africa,* Bloomington, Indiana University Press, 71–113.

De Waal, Alex, and Young, Helen (2005), *Steps Towards the Stabilization of Governance and Livelihoods in Northern Sudan,* Washington, DC, USAID.

The Economist (2013), "Sukuk It and See It," *The Economist,* April 19, at http://www.economist.com/blogs/pomegranate/2013/04/egypt-finance (accessed July 15, 2014).

Eder, Mine (2009), "Retreating State? Political Economy of Welfare Regime Change in Turkey," *Middle East Law and Governance* 2, 152–184.

Eisenberg, Ann M. (2011), "Under-enforcement of Morocco's Reformed 2004 Family Law, the Moudawana," *Cornell International Law Journal* 44, 693–728.

El Amrani, Issander (2012), "Final Results for Egypt's Parliamentary Elections," Arabist.com (January 22), at http://arabist.net/blog/2012/1/22/final-results-for-egypts-parliamentary-elections.html.

El-Gamal, Mahmoud (2006), *Islamic Finance,* West Nyack, NY, Cambridge University Press.

El Qorchi, Mohammed (2005), "Islamic Finance Gears Up," *Finance and Development* 42, 4 (December), 46–49.

European Union Election Observation Mission (2013), "The Hashemite Kingdom of Jordan Final Report: Parliamentary Elections 2013," January 23, at http://www.eods.eu/library/FR%20JORDAN%2027.03.2013_en.pdf.

Flanigan, Shawn Teresa (2008), "Nonprofit Service Provision by Insurgent Organizations: The Cases of Hizballah and the Tamil Tigers," *Studies in Conflict and Terrorism* 31, 6, 499–519.

Freedom and Justice Party (2011), "Election Program: The Freedom and Justice Party," at http://kurzman.unc.edu/files/2011/06/FJP_2011_English.pdf.

Garterstein-Ross, Daveed, and Smyth, Phillip (2013), "How Syria's Jihadists Win Friends and Influence People," *The Atlantic,* August 22, at http://www.theatlantic.com/international/archive/2013/08/how-syrias-jihadists-win-friends-and-influence-people/278942/ (accessed July 10, 2014).

Gahma, Eymen (2011), "Final Results of Tunisian Elections Announced," *Tunisia Live,* November 14, at http://www.tunisia-live.net/2011/11/14/tunisian-election-final-results-tables/.

Gause, F. Gregory, III (2007), "Bahrain Parliamentary Election Results: 25 November and 2 December 2006," *International Journal of Middle East Studies* 39, 2 (May), 170–171.

Gheissari, Ali (2009), *Contemporary Iran: Economy, Society, Politics,* Oxford, Oxford University Press.

Goldstone, Jack A. (2012), "Is Islam Bad for Business?" *Perspectives on Politics* 10, 1, 97–102.

Gray, John (1998), *False Dawn: The Delusions of Global Capitalism,* New York, New Press.

Gruenbaum, Ellen (1992), "The Islamist State and Sudanese Women," *Middle East Report* 179 (November-December), 29–32.

Habibi, Nader (2013), "The Economic Legacy of Mahmoud Ahmadinejad," Waltham, MA, Brandeis University, Crown Center for Middle East Studies, MEB74.

Hajji, Rim (2013), "Morocco: Women After the Arab Spring," in *Women in Democratic Transitions in the MENA Region,* Wilson Center, Global Women's Leadership Initiative (March), 26–28, at http://www.wilsoncenter.org/sites/default/files/Women_in_democratic_transitions_in_the_MENA_region_compilation.pdf (accessed July 26, 2013).

Halime, Farah (2013a), "Egypt's Islamist Groupies," *Rebel Economy,* March 27, at http://rebeleconomy.com/abu-dhabi/egypts-islamist-groupies/.

Halime, Farah (2013b), "Egypt's Long-Term Economic Recovery Plan Fails," *New York Times,* May 2.

Hamid, Shadi (2014), *Temptations of Power: Islamists and Illiberal Democrats in a New Middle East,* New York, Oxford University Press.

Hamzawy, Amr (2005), *The Key to Arab Reform: Moderate Islamists,* Washington, DC, Carnegie Endowment for International Peace (August), Policy Brief 40.

Hamzeh, A. Nizar (2001), "Clientelism, Lebanon: Roots and Trends," *Middle Eastern Studies* 37, 3, 167–178.

Hamzeh, Ahmad Nizar (2004), *In the Path of Hizbullah,* Syracuse, NY, Syracuse University Press.

Hanafi, Leila, and Alaoui, Sara (2014), "Beyond the Law: Protecting Morocco's Women," *Al Jazeera English,* February 15, at http://www.aljazeera.com/indepth/opinion/2014/02/beyond-law-protecting-morocco-2014212104721165904.html.

Harik, Judith Palmer (1994), *The Public and Social Services of the Lebanese Militias,* Oxford, Oxford University, Center for Lebanese Studies.

Harrak, Fatima (2009), "The History and Significance of the New Moroccan Family Code," Buffet Center (March), Working Paper 09–002, at http://www.cics.northwestern.edu/documents/workingpapers/ISITA_09-002_Harrak.pdf.

Harris, Kevan (2013), "A Martyrs' Welfare State and Its Contradictions: Regime Resilience and Limits Through the Lens of Social Policy in Iran," in Heydemann, Steven, and Leenders, Reinoud, eds., *Middle East Authoritarianisms: Governance, Contestation, and Regime Resilience in Syria and Iran,* Stanford, CA, Stanford University Press.

Hasan, Maher, and Dridi, Jemma (2010), "The Effects of the Global Crisis on Islamic and Conventional Banks: A Comparative Study," International Monetary Fund (IMF) (September), Working Paper, at http://www.imf.org/external/pubs/ft/wp/2010/wp10201.pdf.

Hatipoglu, Esra (2014), "Women's Rights and Social Problems in Turkey," Al Jazeera Center for Studies (February 9), at http://studies.aljazeera.net/en/reports/2014/02/201429104351767777.htm.

Henry, Clement M. (2004), "Financial Performance of Islamic Versus Conventional Banks," in Henry, Clement M., and Wilson, Rodney, eds., *The Politics of Islamic Finance,* Edinburgh, Edinburgh University Press, 104–128.

Henry, Clement M., and Wilson, Rodney, eds. (2004), *The Politics of Islamic Finance,* Edinburgh, Edinburgh University Press.

Higgins, Patricia J., and Shoar-Ghaffari, Piraz (1994), "Women's Education in the Islamic Republic of Iran," in Afkhami, Mahnaz, and Friedl, Erika, eds., *In the Eye of the Storm: Women in Post-Revolutionary Iran,* Syracuse, NY, Syracuse University Press.

Human Rights Watch (HRW) (2010), "Elections in Egypt: State of Permanent Emergency Incompatible with Free and Fair," New York, HRW, at http://www.hrw.org/sites/default/files/reports/egypt1110WebforPosting.pdf (accessed July 11, 2014).

Human Rights Watch (HRW) (2011), "Turkey: Step Backward for Women's Rights," June 10, at http://www.hrw.org/news/2011/06/09/turkey-backward-step-women-s-rights.

IHS Aerospace, Defense, and Security (IHS) (2013), "Analysis: Syria's Insurgent Landscape," Englewood, CO, IHS (September), at http://www.ihs.com/pdfs/Syrias-Insurgent-Landscape-oct-2013.pdf.

International Crisis Group (ICG) (2003a), *Islamic Social Welfare Activism in the Occupied Palestinian Territories: A Legitimate Target?* Middle East Report 13 (April 2), Amman/Brussels.

International Crisis Group (ICG) (2003b), *Yemen: Coping with Terrorism and Violence in a Fragile State,* Middle East Report 8 (January 8), Amman/Brussels.

International Crisis Group (ICG) (2005), *Understanding Islamism,* Middle East/North Africa Report 37 (March 2), Brussels.

International Crisis Group (ICG) (2006), *Iraq's Muqtada Al-Sadr: Spoiler or Stabiliser?* Middle East Report 55 (July 11), Amman/Brussels.

IRIN (2012), "Analysis: A Faith-Based Aid Revolution in the Muslim World?" IRIN: Humanitarian News and Analysis (June 1), at http://www.irinnews.org/report/95564/analysis-a-faith-based-aid-revolution-in-the-muslim-world.

Ismail, Salwa (2001), "The Paradox of Islamist Politics," *Middle East Report* 221, 34–39.

Ismail, Salwa (2006), *Rethinking Islamist Politics: Culture, the State, and Islamism,* London, I. B. Tauris.

Kahf, Monser (2004), "Islamic Banks: The Rise of a New Power Alliance of Wealth and Shari'ah Scholarship," in Henry, Clement M., and Wilson, Rodney, eds., *The Politics of Islamic Finance,* Edinburgh, Edinburgh University Press, 17–36.

Karagol, Erdal Tanas (2013), "The Turkish Economy Under the Justice and Development Decade," *Insight Turkey* 15, 4, 115–129.

Karam, Souhail, and El Baltaji, Dana (2014), "Morocco Weighs Pursuing $1.7 Trillion Industry: Islamic Finance," January 21, at http://www.bloomberg.com/news/2014–01–21/morocco-weighs-pursuing-1-7-trillion-industry-islamic-finance.html.

Keddie, Nikki (2000), "Women in Iran Since 1979," *Social Research* 67, 2 (Summer), 405–438.

Kepel, Gilles (2002), *Jihad: The Trail of Political Islam,* Cambridge, MA, Belknap Press of Harvard University Press.

Kettell, Brian (2011), *Introduction to Islamic Banking,* Hoboken, NJ, John Wiley and Sons.

Khan, Feisal (2010), "How 'Islamic' Is Islamic Banking?" *Journal of Economic Behavior and Organization* 76, 3, 805–820.

Kuran, Timur (2004), *Islam and Mammon,* Princeton, NJ, Princeton University Press.

Kuran, Timur (2010), *The Long Divergence: How Islamic Law Held Back the Middle East,* Princeton, NJ, Princeton University Press.

Lacroix, Stéphane (2012), "Sheikhs and Politicians: Inside the New Egyptian Salafism," Washington, DC, Brookings Doha Center (June), Policy Briefing, at http://www.brookings.edu/~/media/research/files/papers/2012/6/07%20egyptian%20salafism%20lacroix/stephane%20lacroix%20policy%20briefing%20english.pdf (accessed July 8, 2014).

Lubeck, Paul (1999), "Antimonies of Islamic Movements Under Globalization," University of California, Santa Cruz, Center for Global, Regional, and International Studies, Working Paper 99–1.

Lynch, Mark (2007), "Young Brothers in Cyberspace," *MERIP Reports* 245 (Winter), at http://www.merip.org/mer/mer245/young-brothers-cyberspace (Accessed July 8, 2014).

Mahmood, Saba (2004), *Politics of Piety: The Islamic Revival and Feminist Subject,* Princeton, NJ, Princeton University Press.

Malka, Haim (2007), "Hamas: Resistance and Transformation of Palestinian Society," in Alterman, Jon B., and von Hippel, Karin, eds., *Understanding Islamic Charities,* Washington, DC, Center for Strategic and International Studies, 98–113.

Mamdani, Mahmood (2004), *Good Muslim, Bad Muslim: America, the Cold War, and the Roots of Terror,* New York, Pantheon.

Mandaville, Peter (2007), *Global Political Islam,* London, Routledge.

Marks, Monica (2014), "Convince, Coerce, or Compromise?" Brookings Doha Center Analysis Papers 10 (February), at http://www.brookings.edu/~/media/research/files/papers/2014/02/10%20ennahda%20tunisia%20constitution%20marks/ennahda%20approach%20tunisia%20constitution%20english.pdf.

Masoud, Tarek (2014), *Counting Islam: Religion, Class, and Elections in Egypt,* New York, Cambridge University Press.

Meital, Yoram (2006), "The Struggle over Political Order in Egypt: The 2005 Elections," *Middle East Journal* 60, 2 (Spring), 257–279.

Mitchell, Richard P. (1969), *The Society of the Muslim Brothers,* London, Oxford University Press.

Mohieldin, Mahmoud (2012), "Realizing the Potential of Islamic Finance," World Bank, *PREM Network* 77, at http://siteresources.worldbank.org/EXTPREMNET/Resources/EP77.pdf.

Musa, E. A. (2000), *Sudan Structural Adjustment Programme: Some Implications for Labour in the Formal Sector,* Tangier, Morocco, African Training and Research Centre in Administration for Development.

Nageeb, Salma Ahmed (2004), *New Spaces and Old Frontiers: Women, Social Space and Islamization in Sudan,* Lanham, MD, Lexington Books.

National Democratic Institute for International Affairs (NDI) (2002), "Bahrain's October 24 and 31, 2002 Legislative Elections," at https://www.ndi.org/files/2392_bh_electionsreport_engpdf_09252008.pdf (accessed July 11, 2014).

National Democratic Institute for International Affairs (NDI) (2011), "Final Report on the Moroccan Legislative Elections," NDI International Observer Mission: Morocco, November 25, at https://www.ndi.org/files/Morocco-Final-Election-Report-061812-ENG.pdf (accessed July 26, 2014).

National Democratic Institute for International Affairs (NDI) (2012), "Final Report on Algeria's Legislative Elections," May 10, at https://www.ndi.org/files/Algeria-Report-Leg-Elections-ENG.pdf.

Nichols, Michelle (2013), "Egypt's Islamists Warn Giving Women Some Rights Could Destroy Society," Reuters, March 14, at http://www.reuters.com/article/2013/03/15/us-women-un-rights-idUSBRE92E03D20130315.

Öniş, Ziya (2006), "The Political Economy of Turkey's Justice and Development Party," in Yavuz, H., ed., *The Emergence of a New Turkey: Islam, Democracy, and the Emergence of the AK Party*, Salt Lake City, University of Utah Press.

Öniş, Ziya (2013), "The Triumph of Conservative Globalism: The Political Economy of the AKP Era," *Turkish Studies* 13, 2 (June), 135–152.

Patton, Marcie (2006), "The Economic Policies of Turkey's AKP Government: Rabbits from a Hat?" *Middle East Journal* 60, 3 (Summer), 513–536.

Powell, Russell (2009), "Zakat: Drawing Insights for Legal Theory and Economic Policy from Islamic Jurisprudence," *University of Pittsburgh Tax Review* 7, 43, 43–101.

Qāsim, Na'im *(2005), Hizbullah: The Story from Within*, London, Saqi Books, 2005.

Qatar Tribune (2013), "Qatar Firms Fail to Pay Zakat Dues: Kubaisi," *Qatar Tribune*, April 12, at http://qatar-tribune.com/data/20130412/pdf/main.pdf (accessed July 20, 2014).

Reuters (2014), "Morocco Ends Gasoline, Fuel Oil Subsidies," Reuters, January 17, at http://www.reuters.com/article/2014/01/17/morocco-economy-subsidies-idUSL5N0KR2EV20140117.

Rouleau, Eric (2001), "Politics in the Name of the Prophet," *Le Monde Diplomatique* (November).

Roy, Olivier (1994), *The Failure of Political Islam*, Cambridge, MA, Harvard University Press.

Roy, Olivier (2002), *Globalized Islam: The Search for the New Ummah*, New York, Columbia University Press.

Ruthven, Malise (2000), *Islam in the World*, 2nd ed., New York, Oxford University Press.

Sadowski, Yahya (2006), "Political Islam: Asking the Wrong Questions?" *Annual Review of Political Science* 9, 215–240.

Saif, Ibrahim, and Abu Rumman, Muhammad (2012), "The Agenda of Islamist Parties," Carnegie Endowment for International Peace (May 29), at http://carnegieendowment.org/2012/05/29/economic-agenda-of-islamist-parties/b0fh (accessed July 15, 2014).

Salah, Islam (2011), "The Effect of the Economic Crisis on the Middle East," *Global Business Law Review* 1, 99, 99–108, at http://www.globalbusinesslawreview.org/wp-content/uploads/2011/01/gSalah.pdf.

Salehi-Isfahani, Djavad (2006), "Revolution and Redistribution in Iran: Changes in Poverty and Distribution 25 Years Later," at http://siteresources.worldbank.org/INTDECINEQ/Resources/1149208-1147789289867/IIIWB_Conference_Revolution&Redistribution_Iran.pdf.

Sanhoori, Mohammed (2012), "'Al-Masry al-Youm tansharu bil-asma' nata'ig al-intikhabat 'al-shura,'" *Egypt Independent*, February 25, at http://www.almasryalyoum.com/news/details/154502.

Schwedler, Jillian (2011), "Can Islamists Become Moderates? Rethinking the Inclusion-Moderation Hypothesis," *World Politics* 63, 2, 347–376.

Shirazi, Shah Nasim, and Amin, Fouad Bin (2009), "Poverty Elimination Through Potential Zakat Collection in the OIC-Member Countries: Revisited," *Pakistan Development Review* 48, 4, II (Winter) 739–745, at http://pide.org.pk/pdr/index.php/pdr/article/viewFile/2652/2619.

Singer, Amy (2008), "A Mixed Economy of Charity," in *Charity in Islamic Societies*, Cambridge, Cambridge University Press, 176–216.

Singer, Peter (1999), "The Singer Solution to World Poverty," *New York Times Magazine*, September 5.

Stiansen, Endre (2004), "Interest Politics: Islamic Finance in the Sudan, 1977–2001," in Henry, Clement M., and Wilson, Rodney, eds., *The Politics of Islamic Finance*, Edinburgh, Edinburgh University Press, 155–167.

Sussman, Anna Louise (2011), "Why Turkey Is Backsliding on Women's Rights," *The Atlantic*, June 16, at http://www.theatlantic.com/international/archive/2011/06/why-turkey-is-backsliding-on-womens-rights/240547/?single_page=true.

Tarrow, Sidney (1994), *Power in Movement: Collective Action, Social Movements, and Politics*, Cambridge, Cambridge University Press.

Tessler, Mark (2011), "The Origins of Political Support for Islamist Movements: A Political Economy Approach," in Tessler, Mark, ed., *Public Opinion in the Middle East: Survey Research and the Political Orientations of Ordinary Citizens,* Bloomington, Indiana University Press.

Tilly, Charles (2002), *Stories, Identities, and Political Change,* Lanham, MD, Rowman & Littlefield.

Tilly, Charles (2004), *Social Movements, 1768–2004,* Boulder, CO, Paradigm.

Vizcaino, Bernardo (2014), "IMF Launches Consultations on Islamic Finance," Reuters, October 13.

Walsh, John (2006), "Egypt's Muslim Brotherhood: Understanding Centrist Islam," *Harvard International Review* (March 10).

Warde, Ibrahim (2010), *Islamic Finance in the Global Economy,* Edinburgh, Edinburgh University Press.

Wegner, Eva (2011), *Islamist Opposition in Authoritarian Regimes: The Party of Justice and Development in Morocco,* Syracuse, Syracuse University Press.

Williams, Daniel (2008), "2 Activists (and 2 Views) of Women's Rights in Morocco," *New York Times,* June 10.

World Bank (2001), "Memorandum of the President of the IBRD to the Executive Directors on an Interim Assistance Strategy for the Islamic Republic of Iran," Washington, DC, World Bank, Report 22050-IRN.

Yazc, Berna (2012), "The Return to the Family: Welfare, State, and Politics of the Family in Turkey," *Anthropological Quarterly* 85, 1 (Winter), 103–140.

Yousef, Tarek M. (2004), "The *Murabaha* Syndrome in Islamic Finance: Laws, Institutions, and Politics," in Henry, Clement M., and Wilson, Rodney, eds., *The Politics of Islamic Finance,* Edinburgh, Edinburgh University Press, 63–80.

CHAPTER 13: REGIONAL AND GLOBAL ECONOMIC INTEGRATION

Abedini, Javad, and Péridy, Nicolas (2008), "The Greater Arab Free Trade Area (GAFTA): An Estimation of Its Trade Effects," *Journal of Economic Integration* 23, 4, 848–872.

Adams, Richard H., Jr. (1991), *The Effects of International Remittances on Poverty, Inequality, and Development in Rural Egypt,* Washington, DC, International Food Policy Research Institute Research, Report 86.

Aslan, Mehmet (2005), "A Panorama of Turkey's Migration Regime with an Emphasis on the Prospects of Turkish Immigration to the EU on the Eve of the Membership Negotiations," at http://pdf .mutual-learning-employment.net/pdf/05_irland/TR_Aslan.pdf#search=%22Turkish %20migration%20to%20Gulf%20%22.

Baabood, Abdullah (2009), "The Growing Economic Presence of Gulf Countries in the Mediterranean Region," *Mediterranean Politics: Middle East,* 203–209, at http://www.iemed.org/anuari/2009 /aarticles/a203.pdf.

Baldwin-Edwards, Martin (2005), *Migration in the Middle East and Mediterranean: A Regional Study Prepared for the Global Commission on International Migration,* Geneva, Global Commission on International Migration.

Behar, Alberto, and Freund, Caroline (2011), "The Trade Performance of the Middle East and North Africa," Washington, DC, World Bank, Middle East and North Africa Region, Working Paper 53.

Berar-Awad, Azita (1984), *Employment Planning in the Sudan: An Overview of Selected Issues,* Geneva, International Labor Organization.

Bernal, Victoria (1999), "Migration, Modernity, and Islam in Rural Sudan," *Middle East Report* 211 (Summer).

Blair, John M. (1976), *The Control of Oil,* New York, Vintage Books.

Blas, Javier, and Chazan, Guy (2012), "Saudi Arabia Targets $100 Crude Price," *Financial Times,* January 16, at http://www.ft.com/intl/cms/s/0/af13f09c-405f-11e1-9bce-00144feab49a.html (accessed January 19, 2014).

Boughanmi, Houcine (2008), "The Trade Potential of the Arab Gulf Cooperation Countries (GCC): A Gravity Model Approach," *Journal of Economic Integration* 23, 1 (March 1), 42–56.

Braudel, Fernand (1966), *La Méditerranée et le monde méditerranéen à l'époque de Philippe II,* vol. 2, Paris, Armand Colin.

Chauffour, Jean-Pierre (2011), "Trade Integration as a Way Forward for the Arab World: A Regional Agenda," Washington, DC, World Bank (February 1), Policy Research Working Paper 5581, at http://papers.ssrn.com/abstract=1774428.

Chauffour, Jean-Pierre (2013), *From Political to Economic Awakening in the Arab World: The Path of Economic Integration,* Washington, DC, World Bank, at https://openknowledge.worldbank.org/ handle/10986/12221.

Choucri, Nazli (1986), "The Hidden Economy: A New View of Remittances in the Arab World," *World Development* 14, 6, 697–712.

Chauffour, Jean-Pierre (2011), *Trade Integration as a Way Forward for the Arab World: A Regional Agenda,* Rochester, NY, Social Science Research Network, SSRN Scholarly Paper (February 1), at http://papers.ssrn.com/abstract=1774428.

Cieślik, Andrzej, and Hagemejer, Jan (2009), "Assessing the Impact of the EU-Sponsored Trade Liberalization in the MENA Countries," *Journal of Economic Integration* 24, 2, 343–368.

Danielson, Albert L. (1982), *The Evolution of OPEC,* New York, Harcourt Brace Jovanovich.

De Boer, Kito, Farrell, Diana, Figee, Chris, Lund, Susan, Thompson, Fraser, and Turner, John (2008), *The Coming Oil Windfall in the Gulf,* McKinsey Global Institute, at http://www.mckinsey.com/insights/middle_east_and_africa/the_coming_oil_windfall_in_the_gulf.

De Haas, Hein (2005), "Morocco's Migration Transition: Trends, Determinants, and Future Scenarios," *Global Migration Perspectives* 28 (April), Geneva, Global Commission on International Migration.

Diwan, Ishac, Keefer, Philip, and Schiffbauer, Marc (2014), "On Top of the Pyramids: Cronyism and Private-Sector Growth in Egypt," Economic Research Forum, Working Paper.

Economic and Social Commission for Western Asia (ESCWA) (2013), "Arab Integration: A Twenty-First-Century Development Imperative," Beirut, ESCWA.

El-Dib, M. A. M., Ismail, S. M., and Gad, Osman (1984), "Economic Motivations and Impacts of External Migration of Agricultural Workers in an Egyptian Village" (in Arabic), *Population Studies* 11, 68, 27–46.

Fargues, Philippe (2005), "How International Migration May Have Served Global Demographic Security," Annual World Bank Conference on Development Economics, Amsterdam, The Netherlands, May 23–24.

Fergany, Nader (1988), "Some Aspects of Return Migration in Egypt," Cairo (April), unpublished paper.

Henry, Clement Moore, and Springborg, Robert (2010), *Globalization and the Politics of Development in the Middle East,* vol. 1, Cambridge, Cambridge University Press.

Hertog, Steffen (2007), "The GCC and Arab Economic Integration: A New Paradigm." *Middle East Policy* 14, 1, 52–68.

Hertog, Steffen (2008), "The GCC and Arab Economic Integration: A New Paradigm," *Middle East Policy* 14, 1, 52–68.

Hoekman, Bernard, and Sekkat, Khalid (2010), "Arab Economic Integration: Missing Links," *Journal of World Trade* 44, 6 (December), 1273–1308.

Hoekman, Bernard, and Zarrouk, Jamel (2009), "Changes in Cross-Border Trade Costs in the Pan-Arab Free Trade Area, 2001–2008," Washington, DC, World Bank, at https://openknowledge.worldbank.org/handle/10986/4223.

Insel, Aysu, and Tekce, Mahmut (2011), "Bilateral Trade Flows in the Gulf Cooperation Council Countries: What Happened to the Middle East Integration After 2003?" *Journal of Economic Integration* 26, 2 (June 1), 244–275.

International Organization for Migration (IOM) (2014), "Fatal Migrant Fatalities Across Land and Sea," Geneva, IOM.

Kapur, Devesh (2003), "Remittances: The New Development Mantra?" Cambridge, MA, Harvard University, Center for Global Development (August 25).

Katanani, Ahmad K. (1981), "Economic Alternatives to Migration," paper presented to the Conference on International Migration in the Arab World, United Nations Economic Commission for West Africa (UNECWA), Nicosia, Cyprus (May).

Konan, Denise Eby, and Kim, Karl E. (2004), "Beyond Border Barriers: The Liberalization of Services Trade in Tunisia and Egypt," *The World Economy* 27, 9, 1429–1447.

Maken, Ajay, and Hume, Neil (2013), "Iran Threatens to Trigger Oil Price War," *Financial Times,* December 4, at http://www.ft.com/intl/cms/s/0/be2d119e-5cd2-11e3-81bd-00144feabdc0.html (accessed January 19, 2014).

Malik, Adeel, and Awadallah, Bassem (2013), "The Economics of the Arab Spring," *World Development* 45, 296–313.

Mattoo, Aaditya, Rathindran, Randeep, and Subramanian, Arvind (2006), "Measuring Services Trade Liberalization and Its Impact on Economic Growth: An Illustration," *Journal of Economic Integration* 21, 1, 64–98.

MENA-OECD Investment Programme (2005), *Inventory of International Investment Agreements Concluded by MENA Countries,* Paris, OECD.

Miniesy, Rania S., Nugent, Jeffrey B., and Yousef, Tarik M. (2003), "Intra-Regional Trade Integration in the Middle East," in Hakimian, Hassan, and Nugent, Jeffrey B., eds., *Trade Policy and Economic Integration in the Middle East and North Africa: Economic Boundaries in Flux,* London, Curzon-Routledge, 41–65.

Organization of the Petroleum-Exporting Countries (OPEC) (1993), *Annual Statistical Bulletin,* Vienna.

Owen, Roger (1998), "Inter-Arab Integration During the Twentieth Century: World Market vs. Regional Market?" in Hudson, Michael, ed., *Middle East Dilemma: The Politics and Economics of Arab Integration,* New York, Columbia University Press.

Quandt, William B. (1981), *Saudi Arabia in the 1980s: Foreign Policy, Security, and Oil,* Washington, DC, Brookings Institution.

Sekkat, Khalid (2014), "Is There Anything Special with Intra-Arab Foreign Direct Investment?" *Journal of Economic Integration* 29, 1 (March), 139–164, at doi:http://dx.doi.org/10.11130/jei.2014.29 .1.139.

Sorensen, Ninna Nyberg (2004), "Migrant Remittances as a Development Tool: The Case of Morocco," International Organization for Migration, Migration Policy Research, Working Paper 2 (June).

Stark, Oded (1983), "A Note on Labor Migration Functions," *Journal of Development Studies* 19, 4 (July), 539–543.

Syria Needs Analysis Project (SNAP) (2014), "Regional Analysis Syria: Quarterly Report," July 3, Relief Web, at http://reliefweb.int/report/syrian-arab-republic/regional-analysis-syria-quarterly-report -03-july-2014 (accessed July 21, 2014).

Ülgen, Sinan (2011), "A Faster, Better Route of Economic Integration Across the Mediterranean," *Carnegie International Economic Bulletin,* October 13, at http://edam.org.tr/document/carnegie_ discussion%20paper-ingnew.pdf.

UN Refugee Agency (UNHCR) (2014), "Syrian Regional Refugee Response," at http://data.unhcr.org /syrianrefugees/regional.php (accessed July 21, 2014).

Van den Boogaerde, Pierre (1990), *The Composition and Distribution of Financial Assistance from Arab Countries and Arab Regional Institutions,* IMF Middle East Department, Working Paper WP/90/67 (July).

Wolfram, Catherine, Shelef, Orie, and Gertler, Paul J. (2012), "How Will Energy Demand Develop in the Developing World?" Cambridge, MA, National Bureau of Economic Research, Working Paper 17747.

World Bank (2010), "Migration and Remittances Data: Migration and Remittances Factbook 2011" (all countries), November 8, at http://econ.worldbank.org/WBSITE/EXTERNAL/EXTDEC/ EXTDECPROSPECTS/0,,contentMDK:22759429~pagePK:64165401~piPK:64165026 ~theSitePK:476883,00.html.

World Bank (2013), "Investing in Turbulent Times," World Bank: Middle East and North Africa Economic Developments and Prospects (October), at https://openknowledge.worldbank.org/bitstream /handle/10986/16577/EDP2013Oct.pdf?sequence=1.

CHAPTER 14: CONCLUSION

Ayubi, Nazih (1996), *Over-Stating the Arab State: Politics and Society in the Middle East,* London, I. B. Tauris.

Cox, Gary W., North, Douglass C., and Weingast, Barry R. (2013), "The Violence Trap: A Political-Economic Approach to the Problems of Development," Stanford University, Hoover Institution, Working Paper, at http://cddrl.stanford.edu/events/the_violence_trap_a_politicaleconomic _approach_to_the_problems_of_development/.

INDEX

rural, 182–183
secondary, 183, 185–187, 188 (table)
social mobility and, 193–195
support for political Islam influenced by,
447 (fig.)
teacher salaries and, 180
tertiary, 183, 188 (table)
TIMSS measurements for, 179–180
university systems, 187–190
vocational training, 190–191
See also Literacy
EEC. *See* European Economic Community
Egypt
agricultural development in, 17
agricultural pricing strategies in,
213–214, 217
agro-export strategies in, 49
Arab socialism in, 241–242
Bank Misr in, 49
British colonial rule in, 95
class engineering in, 22
constitutional reforms in, 101
crony capitalism in, 283, 286, 293–299
defense industry in, 379
economic growth in, 4, 53
economic inequality in, 68
economic reforms in, 100–101
economic stabilization programs in,
100–101
education spending allocations in, 182,
184–185
educational trajectories in, 69–70
export-led economic strategies in, 19, 49
family planning policies in, 136–137
First Gulf War and, 293–294
Five-Year Plans in, 242
Free Officers in, 99
IMRs in, 165
industrial infrastructure investment in,
260
informal labor markets in, 151, 153
investment rates in, 56
Islamism in, 463–465
in June War of 1967, 120, 242
khedive in, 93
labor force growth in, 142
labor strikes in, 391 (fig.)
land cooperative systems in, 211
land tenure in, 210
Law 96 in, 212
literacy rates in, 175
manufacturing sectors in, 57
military in political settlements, 370

Muslim Brotherhood in, 32, 34n9,
34n11, 99–100, 103–104, 195, 268
Nile Agreement in, 227
Al-Nour Party in, 101
NPSO in, 381
oil rents in, 44
oil subsidies in, 64
political corruption in, 31
political freedom in, 85–86
political parties in, 412–413
political protests in, 1, 391 (fig.)
political settlements in, 99, 101–104, 370
population distribution in, by age and
sex, 139 (fig.)
poverty rates in, 67, 296
private investment in, 294 (fig.)
public investment in, 294 (fig.)
RCC in, 371, 403
regime change in, 73
as RPLA nation, 26
Salafi Nur Party in, 103–104
SCAF in, 31, 101, 381, 397
service economy in, 58
Socialist Decrees in, 236, 246
state-business relations in, 31
state-led economic development in, 235,
241–242
strategic rents in, 287
structural adjustment challenges in,
267–268
in Suez War, 241
taxation strategies in, 17
teacher salaries in, 180–181
in UAR, 246
vocational training in, 190
Wafd Party in, 184, 194, 413
Young Egypt Party in, 194
See also Arab uprisings
Elbaradei, Mohamed, 104, 397
Employment
civil-sector, 149
evolution of, 147–153
for females, 132–133
informal sectors of, 150–151, 153
in MENA region, for various sectors, 152
(table)
private formal sector, 149–150
public-sector, 148–149, 149 (table)
See also Unemployment
Energy subsidies
in GCC nations, 346–348
2008 recession and, 4
Erbakan, Necmettin, 290

CPSIA information can be obtained at www.ICGtesting.com
Printed in the USA
LVOW01s2147050215

425871LV00001B/1/P